HAMMER FILMS

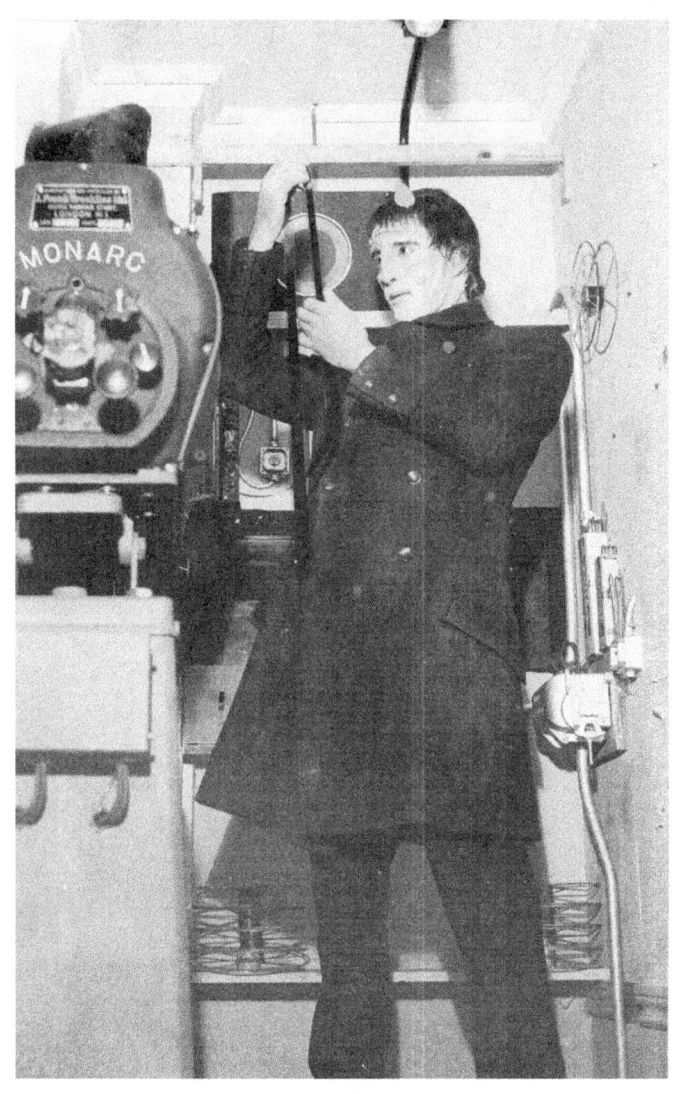

Christopher Lee checks the dailies
during the production of *The Curse of Frankenstein* (1956).

HAMMER FILMS
AN EXHAUSTIVE FILMOGRAPHY

TOM JOHNSON *and*
DEBORAH DEL VECCHIO

with a Foreword by PETER CUSHING, OBE
an Introduction by JIMMY SANGSTER
and an Afterword by JAMES BERNARD

McFarland & Company, Inc., Publishers
Jefferson, North Carolina, and London

Also of interest are the following works from McFarland:
Peter Cushing: The Gentle Man of Horror and His 91 Films, by Deborah Del Vecchio and Tom Johnson (1992; paperback 2009); *Censored Screams: The British Ban on Hollywood Horror in the Thirties* (1997; paperback 2006) by Tom Johnson; *Beverly Garland: Her Life and Career* (2012) by Deborah Del Vecchio; *The Christopher Lee Filmography: All Theatrical Releases, 1948–2003* (2004; paperback 2009) by Tom Johnson; *The Mummy in Fact, Fiction and Film* (2002; paperback 2007) by Susan D. Cowie and Tom Johnson; *The Films of Oliver Reed* (2011) by Susan D. Cowie and Tom Johnson

> *The present work is a reprint of the library bound edition of* Hammer Films: An Exhaustive Filmography, *first published in 1996 by McFarland.*

LIBRARY OF CONGRESS CATALOGUING-IN-PUBLICATION DATA

Johnson, Tom, 1947–
Hammer Films : an exhaustive filmography / by Tom Johnson and Deborah Del Vecchio; with a foreword by Peter Cushing, an introduction by Jimmy Sangster, and an afterword by James Bernard.
p. cm.
Includes bibliographical references and index.

ISBN 978-0-7864-6922-2

softcover : acid free paper

1. Hammer Film Productions—Catalogs.
2. Motion pictures — Great Britain — Catalogs.
I. Del Vecchio, Deborah, 1950–
II. Title.
PN1999.H3J64   2012   016.79143'75'0941— dc20   95-44162

BRITISH LIBRARY CATALOGUING DATA ARE AVAILABLE

© 1996 Tom Johnson and Deborah Del Vecchio. All rights reserved

No part of this book may be reproduced or transmitted in any form or by any means, electronic or mechanical, including photocopying or recording, or by any information storage and retrieval system, without permission in writing from the publisher.

Front cover image: Christopher Lee in *The Curse of Frankenstein,* 1957, directed by Terence Fisher, photographer John Jay (Photofest); cover design by David K. Landis (Shake It Loose Graphics)

Manufactured in the United States of America

McFarland & Company, Inc., Publishers
Box 611, Jefferson, North Carolina 28640
www.mcfarlandpub.com

For Len Harris, who saw most of it and
remembered it all; the Cowies,
who opened many doors (including their own);
and Peter Cushing, OBE
                                    −TJ

For my beloved husband Carl,
for my two mothers − Edna and Antoinette,
my father Raymond,
and James Bernard
                                    − DDV

In Memory of Jon Weaver (1963–1995)

Table of Contents

Preface xi
Foreword by Peter Cushing, OBE 1
Introduction by Jimmy Sangster 3
A History of Hammer Films/Exclusive Films 7

The Films (listed chronologically by year of production)

1935	The Public Life of Henry the Ninth	21		Someone at the Door	48
	The Mystery of the Mary Celeste	22	**1950**	What the Butler Saw .... The Lady Craved Excitement	49 51
	Song of Freedom	25		The Black Widow	53
1936	The Bank Messenger Mystery ..	26		The Rossiter Case	54
	Sporting Love	27		To Have and to Hold	55
1947	Death in High Heels	27		The Dark Light	56
	River Patrol	28	**1951**	Cloudburst	57
	The Dark Road	29		A Case for P.C. 49	59
	Dick Barton, Special Agent	30		Death of an Angel	60
	Who Killed Van Loon?	31		Whispering Smith Hits London	62
1948	Dick Barton at Bay	31		The Last Page	63
	The Jack of Diamonds	34		Wings of Danger	66
	Dick Barton Strikes Back	34		Never Look Back	67
	Dr Morelle—The Case of the Missing Heiress	36		Stolen Face	70
	The Adventures of PC 49	38	**1952**	Lady in the Fog	72
1949	Celia—The Sinister Affair of Poor Aunt Nora	41		The Gambler and the Lady .... Mantrap	74 76
	Meet Simon Cherry	42		The Four Sided Triangle	77
	The Man in Black	43		The Flanagan Boy	79
	Room to Let	45		Spaceways	80

Year	Title	Page
1953	The Saint's Return	83
	Blood Orange	85
	36 Hours	87
	Face the Music	88
	The House Across the Lake	90
	Life with the Lyons	91
	Murder by Proxy	93
	Five Days	95
1954	The Stranger Came Home	96
	Third Party Risk	99
	Mask of Dust	100
	Men of Sherwood Forest	102
	The Lyons in Paris	104
	The Glass Cage	105
	Break in the Circle	106
	The Quatermass Xperiment	108
1955	Women Without Men	111
1956	X—The Unknown	113
	Quatermass 2	116
	The Steel Bayonet	119
	The Curse of Frankenstein	121
1957	The Abominable Snowman	127
	The Camp on Blood Island	130
	The Snorkel	133
	Up the Creek	135
	Dracula	137
1958	The Revenge of Frankenstein	143
	Ten Seconds to Hell	146
	Further Up the Creek	148
	I Only Arsked	150
	The Hound of the Baskervilles	152
	The Man Who Could Cheat Death	156
1959	Yesterday's Enemy	159
	The Mummy	162
	The Ugly Duckling	166
	The Stranglers of Bombay	168
	Don't Panic Chaps!	171
	Never Take Sweets from a Stranger	171
	Hell Is a City	174
	The Two Faces of Dr. Jekyll	176
1960	The Brides of Dracula	180
	The Terror of the Tongs	184
	The Full Treatment	186
	Sword of Sherwood Forest	188
	Visa to Canton	191
	The Curse of the Werewolf	192
	A Weekend with Lulu	197
	Taste of Fear	200
	The Shadow of the Cat	203
1961	Watch It, Sailor!	205
	Cash on Demand	207
	The Damned	209
	The Pirates of Blood River	212
	Captain Clegg	215
	The Phantom of the Opera	218
1962	The Old Dark House	221
	Maniac	224
	Paranoiac	226
	Kiss of the Vampire	229
	Nightmare	232
1963	The Scarlet Blade	234
	Devil-Ship Pirates	235
	The Evil of Frankenstein	238
	The Gorgon	241
1964	Hysteria	243
	The Curse of the Mummy's Tomb	244
	The Secret of Blood Island	246
	She	249
	Fanatic	251
	The Brigand of Kandahar	254
1965	The Nanny	256
	Dracula—Prince of Darkness	258
	Rasputin—The Mad Monk	262
	The Plague of the Zombies	264
	The Reptile	268
	One Million Years B.C.	270
1966	Slave Girls	274
	The Witches	276
	The Viking Queen	277
	Frankenstein Created Woman	280
	The Mummy's Shroud	283
1967	Quatermass and the Pit	285
	A Challenge for Robin Hood	288
	The Anniversary	290
	The Vengeance of She	292
	The Devil Rides Out	295
	The Lost Continent	298

1968	Dracula Has Risen from the Grave 300		Twins of Evil 344
	When Dinosaurs Ruled the Earth 303		Vampire Circus 346
			Demons of the Mind 348
			Dracula A.D. 1972 349
1969	Frankenstein Must Be Destroyed 307		Straight On Till Morning ... 352
			Fear in the Night 353
	Moon Zero Two 311	1972	Mutiny on the Buses 356
	Crescendo 313		Kronos 357
	Taste the Blood of Dracula 315		That's Your Funeral 360
1970	The Vampire Lovers 318		Nearest and Dearest 360
	Horror of Frankenstein 320		Frankenstein and the Monster from Hell 362
	Scars of Dracula 323		
	Creatures the World Forgot 327		The Satanic Rites of Dracula 365
	Lust for a Vampire 329	1973	Love Thy Neighbor 367
	Countess Dracula 332		Man at the Top 368
1971	Blood from the Mummy's Tomb 335		Holiday on the Buses 369
			Legend of the Seven Golden Vampires 370
	Hands of the Ripper 337		
	Dr. Jekyll and Sister Hyde 339		Shatter 372
		1974	Man About the House 375
	On the Buses 342	1975	To the Devil ... A Daughter ... 376

Short Subjects 381

Hammer on Television 389

Afterword by James Bernard 393

Epilogue 395

Selected Bibliography 397

Index 399

PREFACE

Although we, like most fans, were first attracted to Hammer for its Gothic horror movies, our purpose is to present an exhaustive reference work detailing all of their output that will reveal the company as a diversified producer of *entertainment*, rather than as the "House of Horror." While it was certainly pictures like *The Curse of Frankenstein* and *Dracula* that brought Hammer its fame, the company worked in a variety of genres. Saddled with cramped conditions and even tighter budgets, Hammer managed to film war, mystery, science fiction, adventure, comedy, and even musicals in addition to the horrors.

Since Hammer is a British company, the focus of this book is British. The films are referred to by their original British titles and the emphasis is on their release and criticism within the United Kingdom.

We are well aware that not every Hammer film is a masterpiece, and that even many of the company's best pictures are flawed. While we often offer praise, we have tried to criticize each movie at its intended level; we do know the difference between *Ben-Hur* and *The Brides of Dracula*. Conversely, if we are a bit rough on a particular film, it is because of the high standard to which we hold the company.

A book like this requires the help of many people, and we were fortunate in the number of both celebrities and friends who came to our aid. If any big "names" are missing, please be assured that it was *their* decision not to become involved, rather than *our* lack of interest in securing their assistance.

Our special thanks to the late Peter Cushing, and to Jimmy Sangster and James Bernard, who were kind enough to contribute a Foreword, an Introduction, and an Afterword. A book about Hammer could have no better beginning or end. Others in the business who generously gave us their time were Barry Andrews, Samuel Z. Arkoff, Geoffrey Bayldon, George Baxt, Martine Beswicke, Norman Bird, Peter Blythe, Veronica Carlson, Herman Cohen, Hazel Court, Jim Danforth, Robert Day, Richard Gordon, Guy Green, Val Guest, Ken Hughes, Freddie Jones, the late Phil Leakey, Richard Matheson, Kerwin Mathews, Francis Matthews, Ingrid Pitt, Dave Prowse, Michael Ripper, Margaret Robinson, the late Cesar Romero, Don Taylor, and Geoffrey Toone. Without the valuable input of the late Len Harris, we would have been at a loss. Thank you one and all.

We also could not have done without Ann Del Vecchio, Carl Del Vecchio, Linda Greth, Elaine Hahn, Tammy Hahn, Debbie Hart, Fred Humphries, Doug

Kauffman, Dick Klemensen (and *Little Shoppe of Horrors*), Gloria Lillibridge, Jessie Lilley, Greg Mank, Mark Miller, Mike Murphy, Tim Murphy, Joey O'Brien, Ted Okuda, Louis Paul, Ernie Price, Ume Sommerlad, Gary and Sue Svehla (and Fanex), Tony Timpone (and *Fangoria*), Richard Valley, Randy Vest, Carol and Steve Werner, and Brent and Rebecca Worley. Tom Weaver helped rescue this book from overwriting, and Colin and Sue Cowie did far too much to even begin to thank them adequately.

Without the cooperation of Roy Skeggs and Richelle Wilder of Hammer Films, this book could never have been written; and without the British Film Institute and Lincoln Center, we would have had very little to write about. Our sincere thanks to everyone for their kindness.

Tom Johnson
Deborah Del Vecchio
Summer 1995

FOREWORD
by Peter Cushing, OBE

When Tom Johnson and Debbie Del Vecchio told me they were writing a book about Hammer Films I was delighted, and even more so when they asked me if I would contribute a foreword.

It is a lovely feeling for an actor to be associated with success, especially when that success has given—and still gives—such pleasure all over the world. The story of the strides that Hammer made in one of the most competitive markets is remarkable, and perhaps it will inspire others to follow their example.

The narrative incorporates the films I was lucky enough to make with my very dear friend and colleague Christopher Lee, and I thought the following excerpt from my first book of autobiography might provide a fitting ending to this short beginning of what I am sure will be a volume much sought after by all lovers of the cinema:

"Under John's (John Redway & Associates) banner, I started my long and happy association with Hammer Film Productions. During this period of the film industry's turbulent history, a certain animosity existed towards anyone connected with television, because cinema attendance was dwindling, as audiences found that they could get all the entertainment they wanted in their own homes, just by the flick of a switch.

"But one company had other ideas. James (later Sir James) Carreras was the driving force behind that venturesome organisation, and reasoned sagaciously that if someone well-known and popular on the rival medium was starred in a film, that name could lure people back to those empty seats. He had been in constant touch with John, inviting me to work for them, but my commitments elsewhere prevented my accepting until 1957.

"Way back in the thirties, after the tremendous stage success of *Journey's End*, which James Whale had produced in London with Colin Clive as Stanhope, they went to Hollywood to make the film version, which led to their collaborating on *Frankenstein* with Mr. Clive in the name part and Boris Karloff as his creation.

"I had seen that fantasy, and thought it was splendid, so when I heard that Hammer were going into production with a coloured re-make, I asked John if he would suggest me for the part of the Baron. He did and I was chosen.

"Re-entitled *The Curse of Frankenstein*, it caused quite a sensation, and the returns at box offices all over the world were phenomenal. This snowball of success started an avalanche which rolled on to gigantic proportions, making Hammer a multi-million-pound concern, presented with the Queen's Award to Industry in 1968.

"James Carreras and his cohorts launched themselves full tilt into this genre. I appeared as Baron Frankenstein in five more such films, interspersed with five as Professor Van Helsing in their Dracula epics, in which my very dear friend Christopher Lee was quite superb as the sinister Count, chilling to the marrow all those who saw his remarkable performance: and, indeed, his "Monster" in the initial Frankenstein film made the same impact, but he also managed to imbue that part with a certain pathos. The very first time we met he was wearing the grotesque make-up conceived by Phil Leakey, and a story was put about by the Publicity Department that when it was removed at the end of the day's work, he and I came face to face in the corridor, and *then* I screamed! He is a man of so many attributes, among them a most marvellous sense of humour plus the ability to laugh at himself, and uncanny skill as an impersonator, which helped to lighten the darkness hanging over Count Dracula's entombed habitat, when we were not shooting.

"Terence Fisher, another old and delightful companion, directed these pictures, and the professional team spirit was an inspiration to every one of us.

"'The impossible will take a few minutes: miracles a little longer.' This slogan may be heard often within the walls of film studios, when something is needed urgently, usually following the question and answer, 'When do you want it?' 'Yesterday.'"

Now I leave you in the more than capable hands of Mr. Johnson and Mrs. Del Vecchio, and bid you a fond farewell.

May God's blessing be with you always.

Whitstable, Kent. 1992

INTRODUCTION
by Jimmy Sangster

I was having lunch with Michael Carreras the other day. He was my boss when I worked for Hammer. I told him that I'd met these nice Americans who were doing a book about Hammer and how they had asked me to write an introduction.

We started to reminisce, Michael and me. This is something you are inclined to do a great deal of when you reach our time of life. Reminisce and attend horror film festivals.

"What do you remember best about Hammer?" he asked me.

I thought about it. "The end of picture party when we wrapped the second *Frankenstein* ... or maybe it was *The Mummy*. I laughed so much I nearly peed my pants. How about you?"

He gave it a few seconds' thought too. "That time we were in the South of France looking for locations for *Scream of Fear*. That was a great week. All that sun and wine and great food."

(He also said something about girls, but being married at the time, I don't remember that part of the trip at all.)

I only bring this up to show that what we instantly recall when we think of the "old days" of Hammer is the good times.

I suppose there were bad times too, there must have been. I mean, you don't make as many movies as we did without something going wrong somewhere down the line.

If I try very hard I can remember days, when I was assistant director, when actors turned up late (or not at all); days when we were shooting exteriors and it never stopped raining; other location shoots, especially at night, when it was so cold the camera motor would freeze up; airplanes ruining the sound; the sun disappearing in the middle of a shot; going over schedule; worse still, going over budget.

But for memories like that I have to dredge deep. The good times spring easily to mind. Like working as assistant director for Terry Fisher who never asked for anything difficult without apologizing first. "I'm sorry dear people, but could we possibly do this next shot standing on our heads?"

Or delivering a script I had just written and having everybody say, "This is just great we don't need to change a word." *And they didn't!!!*

Names spring to mind too—not the star names, but the nuts and bolts people... Tommy Money (property master), Jack Curtis (chief electrician), Jimmy Needs (editor), Len Harris (camera operator).

On second thought, maybe I shouldn't have started with the names in case those

I haven't mentioned get upset. But let them rest assured, I remember them all. I even married one of them.

It started small: B movies based on characters popularized on the radio. *Dick Barton, PC 49, The Man in Black.* We didn't have a studio of our own. We'd rent a furnished house where we'd shoot the hell out of the place; after the third movie the directors would be hard put to find an angle that had not been featured a dozen times already, so we'd move on to another house, different shaped rooms, different furniture.

We were shooting in our third or maybe fourth house, a venerable old pile called Oakley Court, close to the village of Bray, about twenty miles outside London. We were, as usual, fast running out of fresh camera set ups, when somebody noticed the property next door was empty. Built on the banks of the river Thames and sadly neglected during the war (the 1939 war), it was in imminent danger of collapse. Hammer bought it, christened it Bray Studios, and it became my home away from home for the rest of the days I worked for Hammer.

At first it was just an empty house. We furnished the rooms, shot some film, refurnished them, shot some more. Next we started to actually build sets in a couple of the larger downstairs rooms. Then—the big move—Hammer decided to build a sound stage. One became two which became three. Heaven knows what they've got there now. I don't much care because it isn't Hammer any longer.

I stopped working for Hammer on a

Producer, director, writer Jimmy Sangster on the set of *Horror of Frankenstein* (1970).

regular basis before they actually started to make the horror movies for which they so rightly became famous. The last movie I did for them as a member of the staff (production manager) was also the first movie I wrote, a piece called *X—The Unknown.*

I remember one day after the movie had finished, I was writing a script for somebody else while still being paid by Hammer as a production manager. Michael Carreras came into my office and saw me stuff pen and paper into a drawer like a guilty schoolboy caught cribbing. He asked me what I was doing and I told him. He said I should make up my mind what I wanted for my future, a job as production manager or did I want to be a writer?

I told him I wanted to be a writer. (I think he was vastly relieved because I was not a very good production manager.)

But I was a family man, with all that implied (mortgage, new baby, car payments). It was a cold, hard world out there. I didn't want to give up a regular weekly salary for the perils of the freelance writing market. So Michael, bless him, made me a deal. He'd guarantee to buy one script a year off me for the next three years. I won't tell you how much he was willing to pay me because you wouldn't believe it. But, pittance that it was, it gave me a level of solvency. Not a very high level but one where I wasn't going to starve to death.

So, after ten years I quit the regular payroll. There was a small ceremony presided over by Will Hammer (there actually was a Mr. Hammer), who presented me with a gold cigarette case. (Honestly, he did.) It was inscribed. "Thank you for servicing [sic] ten years with Hammer." And I became a full time writer.

I am eternally grateful to Michael Carreras for this. (The deal, not the cigarette case.) Also to Tony Hinds, who backed him all the way. That's just one more of the good things which spring to mind when I think of Hammer.

Since I became a full-time writer, I've written around fifty film scripts. I remember mentioning this to somebody in Los Angeles once. "Ah," he said, wagging his finger at me. (They do a lot of that in L.A.) "But how many of them have been made into movies?" I didn't know what he was talking about. All of them were made into movies. I mean, that's how it was in those days. Hammer, or some other producer, would come to me and ask if I'd like to write a script on Dracula or a swashbuckler (we used to call them "tits and swords") or could I come up with a "psycho" type idea. I'd say sure. I'd write the script, they'd pay me the money and go make the movie. I mean, what was the point of writing a movie that nobody was going to make.

I've since learned I was lucky. Very lucky indeed. And although some of those fifty movies were written for other people, the majority were Hammer films. It was for Hammer that I produced movies and, bless them, they even allowed me to direct three of them. Anybody tell you directing isn't the best, they're lying. I don't think I was very good at it, but it was the most fun I ever had. I would have paid them if they'd asked.

So, that was Hammer. I don't know what's happened to the old firm. But I'm sure they're doing just fine. I certainly hope so. It would be a pity for all that good groundwork to have gone to waste.

Summer 1994

A History of Hammer Films/Exclusive Films

> In my early teens, I went with groups of friends to go and see certain films. If we saw the logo of Hammer films we knew it was going to be a very special picture ... a surprising experience, usually—and shocking...
>
> Martin Scorsese
> *The Studio That Dripped Blood*

Images associated with Hammer—the world's most unusual independent film producer—are many. From mummies to musicals, Dracula to dinosaurs, outer space to inner London, war to werewolves, Hammer made just about every type of film. The company had low budgets, yet achieved almost impossibly high production standards. In a business associated with huge corporations and overheads, Hammer was family-owned and for most of its history operated out of a tiny country house studio. Despite more negative reviews than positive, the company's films had an almost unbroken success with audiences. Many Hammer films that were once vilified in the British press are now reverently presented as classics at London's National Film Theatre. Although it has been more than fifteen years since the company produced its last film, its best pictures are more popular than ever.

Enrique Carreras (1880–1950) left Spain for England at the turn of the century and, after several failed small business ventures, opened a 2,000 seat cinema in London's Hammersmith in 1913. It was actually two cinemas, each showing a different film—a taste of the future. Its success led to a chain of cinemas called the Blue Halls. Carreras' greatest venture was to hire the Royal Albert Hall to screen the Italian *Quo Vadis*, to which he invited the King and Queen.

Will Hinds (1887–1957), in his youth an expert cyclist, opened a chain of shops, later expanding his interests to include hairdressing salons and jewelry shops. His main interest was the vaudeville stage, and he appeared as half of a comedy act called "Hammer and Smith." Hinds (or Hammer as his name became) bought four theatres and became, as his son Anthony said (*The Studio That Dripped Blood*), "He was a successful businessman and a failed comedian. He failed because he really wasn't very funny."

Carreras and Hammer formed a partnership in 1932. In the late 1920s, Carreras had created Exclusive Films as a distribution company. Together, he and Hammer acquired the rights to *Snowhound* and *Spilt Salt*, and reissued rights to several British Lion pictures. To provide more movies for Exclusive to release, Hammer Films was created to produce low budget features. The first was *The Public Life of Henry the Ninth* (1935), a 60 minute comedy, followed by the prophetic

Left to right: American International Pictures' James H. Nicholson, Irving H. Levin (vice president of National General Corp.), James Carreras, and John F. Wood (president of Cinematograph Exhibitors Assoc.) attend an AIP luncheon at the Cocoanut Grove in Los Angeles on October 28, 1965 (photo courtesy of Tim Murphy).

The Mystery of Mary Celeste (1935), starring Bela Lugosi.

From the beginning, Hammer was a family concern. Enrique's son James (1909–1990) joined the company in 1939, but he left soon afterwards to fight in World War II. He was awarded an MBE in 1944, and rejoined Exclusive in 1946. Producer and friendly "rival" Richard Gordon described Carreras to the authors (June, 1993):

> Jim was a very likeable man—he had enormous charm. He could have sold you London Bridge! He was definitely a "hands off" producer—he set the films up, but had little interest in their day-to-day production. He knew how to get things done—how to negotiate. He was also very sincere—he was no phoney. He took advantage of no person or situation. He enjoyed deal-making but did it on a gentlemanly basis. If you made a handshake deal with James Carreras, you could go home and forget about it. He was *always* willing to help anyone who needed it. It was he who suggested I use Christopher Lee in *Corridors of Blood* (1957). *The Curse of Frankenstein* hadn't been released yet, and Jim tipped me off that Lee would soon be a big horror star—too big for me to afford! This meant a great deal to me. Jim also helped me and others by showing us films to find actors he thought would be good in my films. He was a real gentleman.

Anthony Hinds (born 1922) also briefly joined the company in 1939 and also went off to the war. In 1946, after leaving the Air Force, he returned to supervise Exclusive's release of quota productions. Hammer stopped feature production in the late thirties, but Exclusive continued to distribute films throughout the forties. After the war ended, Hammer was reborn, being officially registered in 1949.

A fifth major player was James' son Michael Carreras (1927–1994), who joined Exclusive in 1943 before being called into military service. He rejoined the company after the war as assistant producer. After his grandfather's death in 1950, Michael replaced him as a company director.

Before settling in at Bray Studios,

Hammer used a variety of country houses in lieu of a conventional studio. The history of Down Place—later Bray Studios—can be traced back to Richard Weston, who granted the estate to Sir Robert Jones in 1518. The house passed through many hands before Hammer arrived on the scene. George Davies and his wife sold the property to Hammer with the understanding that they could remain in residence. Davies, a film fan, was occasionally "put to work" as a clapper boy. Hammer first became interested in the property while filming *The Lady Craved Excitement* in March, 1950, at the adjoining Oakley Court.

The Court was built in 1859 for Sir Richard Hall Say in the style of a French chateau. In 1919, the property was purchased by Ernest Olivier for £27,000, and was used as a headquarters for the French Resistance during World War II. The Court remained in Olivier's possession until his death in 1965 and remained uninhabited—except by film companies—until its conversion to a hotel in 1979. Bray Studios and Oakley Court are located along Windsor Road, about halfway between Maidenhead and Bray Village, and the river Thames flows behind both properties.

Conditions at Bray Studios were initially cramped, with stages built inside the house, minus soundproofing. All offices, dressing rooms, and the like were also located inside Down Place. Makeup man Phil Leakey recalled for the authors (February, 1991) that

A rear view of the magnificent Oakley Court (photo courtesy of Tom Weaver).

The atmosphere was quite unlike any other studio. It was very much a friendly, family affair. Everyone was ready to lend a hand to anyone who needed one, regardless of union lines of demarcation. That attitude continued even after the Horror Era when more money was at stake. I thoroughly enjoyed my years with Hammer, mostly because the crew, artists—everyone—were so pleasant and helpful. It was so unlike the big studios where egos and unions get in the way. It was a sad day when production at Bray came to an end.

In August, 1950, Exclusive announced the first of several important deals with American companies. A five-year contract was signed with Robert Lippert Productions, entitling Exclusive to release all Lippert pictures in the U.K. Richard Gordon recalled (June, 1993), "I was in New York

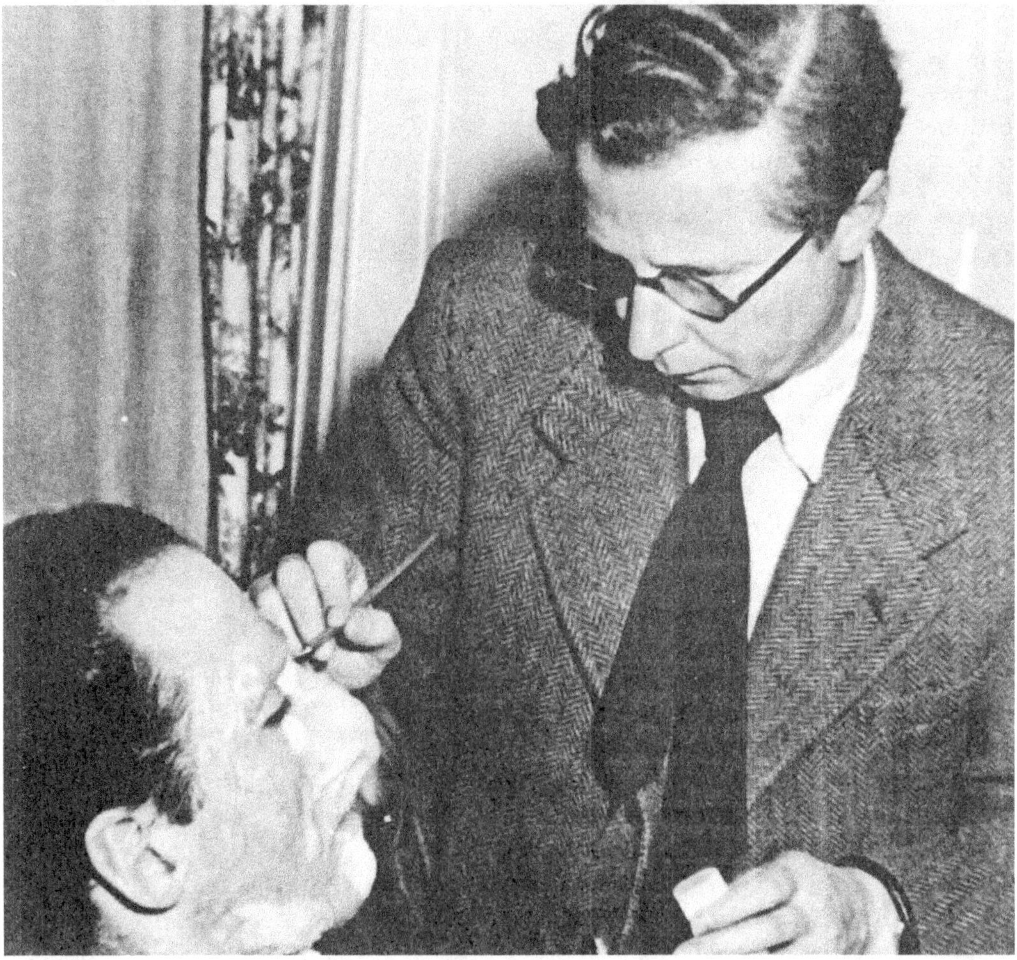

Top: These soundstages from the Hammer days still stand at Bray. *Bottom*: According to Len Harris, "Christopher Lee [left] and Phil Leakey both had fine singing voices and used to sing opera selections in the makeup room."

Hammer's first trade advertisement.

and had dealings with Bill Pizor, who handled Lippert's foreign sales. Pizor was introduced to James Carreras by Walter Bibol of Excelsior Pictures, creating the link." Lippert was producing mostly action films with "good box office titles," Carreras said (*Today's Cinema*, August 25, 1950), "and we have found that they match well with our own product." Hammer's "own product" consisted mostly of adaptations of BBC radio programs, the most successful of which was the *Dick Barton* series. This use of pre-sold titles would become a company staple. The association

Producer Anthony Nelson-Keys and Barbara Shelley on the set of the 1965 *Dracula—Prince of Darkness* (photo courtesy of Ted Okuda).

with Lippert made available fading but still popular American stars. This gave Hammer films an appeal outside Britain, but most of them were routine, grade B productions.

In 1954, the company produced its first color feature—*Men of Sherwood Forest*—and its most important picture to that date—*The Quatermass Xperiment*. Based on a BBC-TV serial, it was Hammer's first attempt at horror; and its success led directly to the groundbreaking film *The*

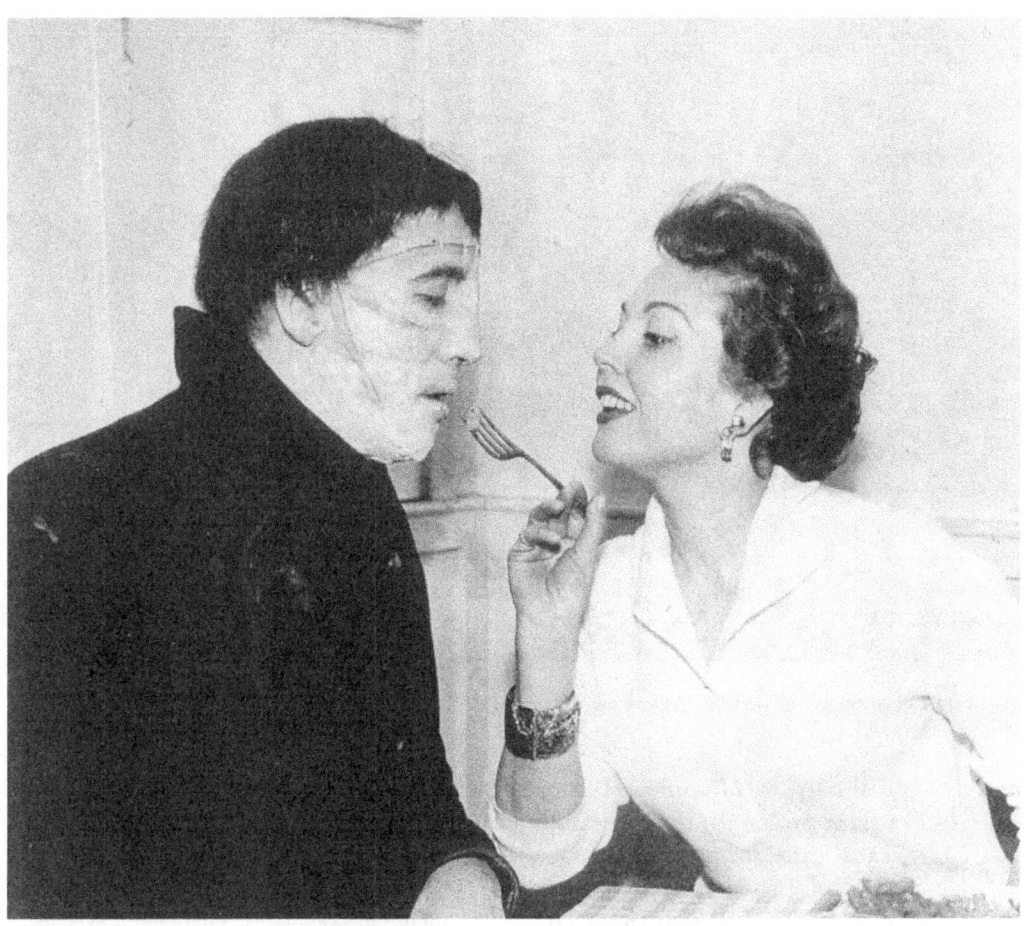

Hazel Court and Christopher Lee share a table for lunch at the Bray Studio canteen in 1956 (photo courtesy of Tim Murphy).

Curse of Frankenstein (1956). This film changed not only Hammer's fortunes, but the direction of horror pictures in general. Following in its wake were remakes of *Dracula* (1957), *The Hound of the Baskervilles* (1958), and *The Mummy* (1959), as well as sequels to their own films—*The Revenge of Frankenstein* (1957) and *The Brides of Dracula* (1960).

These horrors featured either Peter Cushing (1913–1994) or Christopher Lee (born 1922)—or both—and were all directed by Terence Fisher (1904–1980). This trio became indelibly associated with Hammer and were responsible for most of the company's best movies. By 1957, Hammer had become so busy, and profitable, that Exclusive split into a group of companies that included Bray Studios Ltd., Clarion Films Ltd., Concanen Film Productions, Key Films, and Hotspur Films. Richelle Wilder, of the current Hammer company, explained to the authors (March, 1993), "Their directors, offices, and productions were those of Hammer. For accounting ease, each feature was made by a Hammer subsidiary. It allowed production monies to remain distinct from the core expense of running the parent company." The company initially had office space in Imperial House, Regent Street, then moved to 53 Hay-

Although Hammer is gone from Wardour Street, Hammer House remains (photo taken in 1993 by Tom Weaver).

market, and finally, to Hammer House, 113–114 Wardour Street. In the basement was a 128-seat theatre for press showings.

Cameraman Len Harris, who joined Hammer in 1952, told the authors (in December, 1993):

> Many of the Hammer people got their start at Gainsborough Studios—a great training ground for young talent, as was Hammer. Both had their own "rep. companies." Hammer didn't set out to create a stock company, but they got friendly with people and, if they were good, would use them as often as possible. Everyone knew what was wanted of them, and everything usually worked like a well-oiled machine. The top boys seldom came onto the set. I once said "Good morning" to Will Hinds—that was it. I don't think he was much interested in actual production. Enrique Carreras passed away before I joined the company, and his son, the Colonel, was running the show. Working for Hammer was like being part of a family—it really was! We ate lunch at a huge round table. Michael Carreras would carve the meat and serve. Peter Cushing would queue for a place behind an electrician—there were no prima donnas at Hammer. Sometimes we'd lunch at the Queen's Head pub across the street—the locals took us for granted. We were nothing special—just film people. Hammer drifted into horror movies, did them well, and stayed with them. We all enjoyed creating their special atmosphere—it was a real challenge. We never thought of them as "horror pictures," though—that was something the distributors came up with—"Hammer Horror." That's what it's all about—filling the cinemas, making a profit. This is a business, you know! Hammer was as good at this business as anyone. I photographed practically every scene Hammer shot from 1952 to 1962. I won't say that no one ever lost their composure, but I will say that there were absolutely no grudges. We all respected our work and each other.

Despite their popularity, the Hammer horrors took frequent critical bashings for their violence and sexual content. This adverse—and generally unwarranted—criticism often helped the pictures at the box office. "We've never, of course, made films for the critics," said Michael Carreras (*The Horror People*). Although Hammer had moved from obscurity to international prominence, Bray retained its low-key atmosphere. Actor Geoffrey Bayldon told the authors (February, 1991):

> While appearing in *Dracula*—my second film—I was called in quite early, mainly for the makeup man to see how easy or difficult it would be to turn me into an old hall porter. Well—he had a look of despair, for I was only 33! However, he set-to with the curling iron and white greasepaint for my hair. This operation was interrupted when I had to vacate the chair so he could do a rush job on an old lady who had to be made up as a corpse. This done, she was hurried to the set where she promptly had hysterics—no one had told her she had to get into a coffin! Down on the set, I was introduced to Peter Cushing, and we rehearsed our scene. As we had friends in common in the theatre, we got along fine. When it came time for the "take," I still remember standing behind the double doors, quaking. My general memory is of friendliness from everyone—a contrast to the bloodsucking and gore that pervaded the set. I still recall a splendid lunch with Peter and Christopher Lee—two big stars and me!

Michael Carreras takes center stage at the 2nd Annual **Famous Monsters Convention** (November, 1975).

One of the most popular aspects of working at Bray was the food, prepared by Mrs. Thompson. Hammer hero Francis Matthews recalled (February, 1991): "Usually only one picture was in the making at any time, though the *next* one was being busily planned. The entire cast and crew gathered in the small dining room, generating a true family atmosphere. I recall those meals more vividly than the movies!"

When the British film industry slumped in the late fifties, Hammer was immune. James Carreras said (*The London Times*, March 17, 1959), "There's no crisis in our industry which the right kind of films—and plenty of them—can't cure."

Michael Carreras added, "As long as there's a demand for horror entertainment, we shall, of course, provide it. But public taste changes, and our plans are to keep step with such changes." Although not committed to any specific genre, Hammer's interest in horror was cemented by a 1959 deal with Universal-International to remake its library of classic horrors. An even more important pact had been announced on October 22, 1958: Columbia Pictures had acquired a 49 percent interest in Bray. "We shall control our own program as before," said James Carreras (*The Daily Cinema*), "with Columbia sharing the financing." The contrast called for 25 films over a five-year period, with

Peter Cushing meets yet another generation of fans during this photo session at the 1975 Famous Monsters Convention (photo courtesy of Tim Murphy).

Columbia entitled to their worldwide distribution. In addition, Hammer was free to make films for other distributors. During this period, Hammer was a diversified production company, filming comedy, drama, mystery, and war movies as well as horror. Industry insiders truly believed Hammer had the magic touch, but James Carreras (*The Daily Cinema*, May 11, 1959) said, "It's really very simple. We make exploitable pictures. What we have done, others can do. There's no magic involved."

The sixties began promisingly with *Hell Is a City* (1960), *The Brides of Dracula* and *The Curse of the Werewolf* (1960), but ended with nonsense like *The Lost Continent* (1968), *Moon Zero Two* (1968), and *Slave Girls* (1968). One of the first signs that Hammer was slipping was the failure of *The Phantom of the Opera* (1962), which was planned as a major production to attract a mainstream audience. This was closely followed by *The Evil of Frankenstein* (1963), which was, in a word, awful. Christopher Lee, after finally repeating his role in *Dracula—Prince of Darkness* (1965), became disenchanted as the character and "his" films gradually disintegrated. Beginning with *She* (1964), the company became unwisely enamored of "bigger" pictures that could not be produced at Bray, and by 1966, Hammer moved out.

On May 30, 1968, Hammer was presented with the Queen's Award to Industry by Sir Henry Floyd who said (*Kinematograph Weekly*, June 1, 1968), "You are the first British film production company to receive the Queen's Award, and this is a distinction of which you can all be proud." In November, James Carreras signed an agreement with Robert Clark of Elstree Studios to produce five pictures there in 1969. The company had used Elstree 14 times since 1959 and felt it had the potential for "bigger" productions. By then, Hammer's image had changed with the times, with explicit sex and violence gradually replacing imagination. "The image change," said Michael Carreras (*Fangoria* 63), "came about because of the Seven Arts influence. I remember at the time there were more photos of scantily-clad young ladies around the office than we ever had before. Unfortunately, the marketing and distribution were totally out of our hands."

As Hammer began to fade away, James Carreras was knighted in 1970 for his service to youth through the Variety Club. Then, in August, 1972, Michael bought the company from his father.

"I discovered that my father was secretly negotiating to sell Hammer to EMI," he said (*Fangoria* 63). "He didn't tell me about it. I was bloody cross and may have made some rather hasty, regrettable decisions. I knew I didn't want him to do what he was doing, so I set about preventing him and captured Hammer for myself." This unpleasant situation soon grew worse, as *Variety* (July 18, 1973) revealed, "A London film lab was poised to snap up the 'indie' as a subsidiary under a plan that would have dumped Michael Carreras as Hammer's head and restored operation of the company to his father, Sir James." Studio Film Labs had tried to buy Sir James' stock and place him as president of a holding company with Hammer and Sfl as subsidiaries, but Michael "got wind of the plan, finally persuading his father to sell him the shares instead."

Now under Michael Carreras' direction, too many projects were planned but not produced, and the films that actually got made were generally not worth watching. The death blow may have been Hammer's failure to get *Nessie—The Loch Ness Monster* out of the water. Planned as a Hammer/Toho/Paradine production, it saw investors beginning to pull out just after the failure of the *King Kong* (1976) remake. Quite a bit of money was lost by all concerned. The final production under Carreras' control was a 1979 remake of Alfred Hitchcock's 1938 comedy-thriller *The Lady Vanishes*. "Commercially and financially, Hammer was in a huge mess," Carreras lamented (*The Horror People*). "I had been putting my own money into the company and personally kept it going for two years. I finally reached a point where I just couldn't do it any longer. Hammer was taken away from me by the financial people. They don't shoot you—they give you a pistol."

Hammer's artistic slide had been quickened by the death of set designer Bernard Robinson in 1970. In addition to his brilliance at design, he was also a master of economizing. His widow Margaret,

18 *A History of Hammer Films/Exclusive Films*

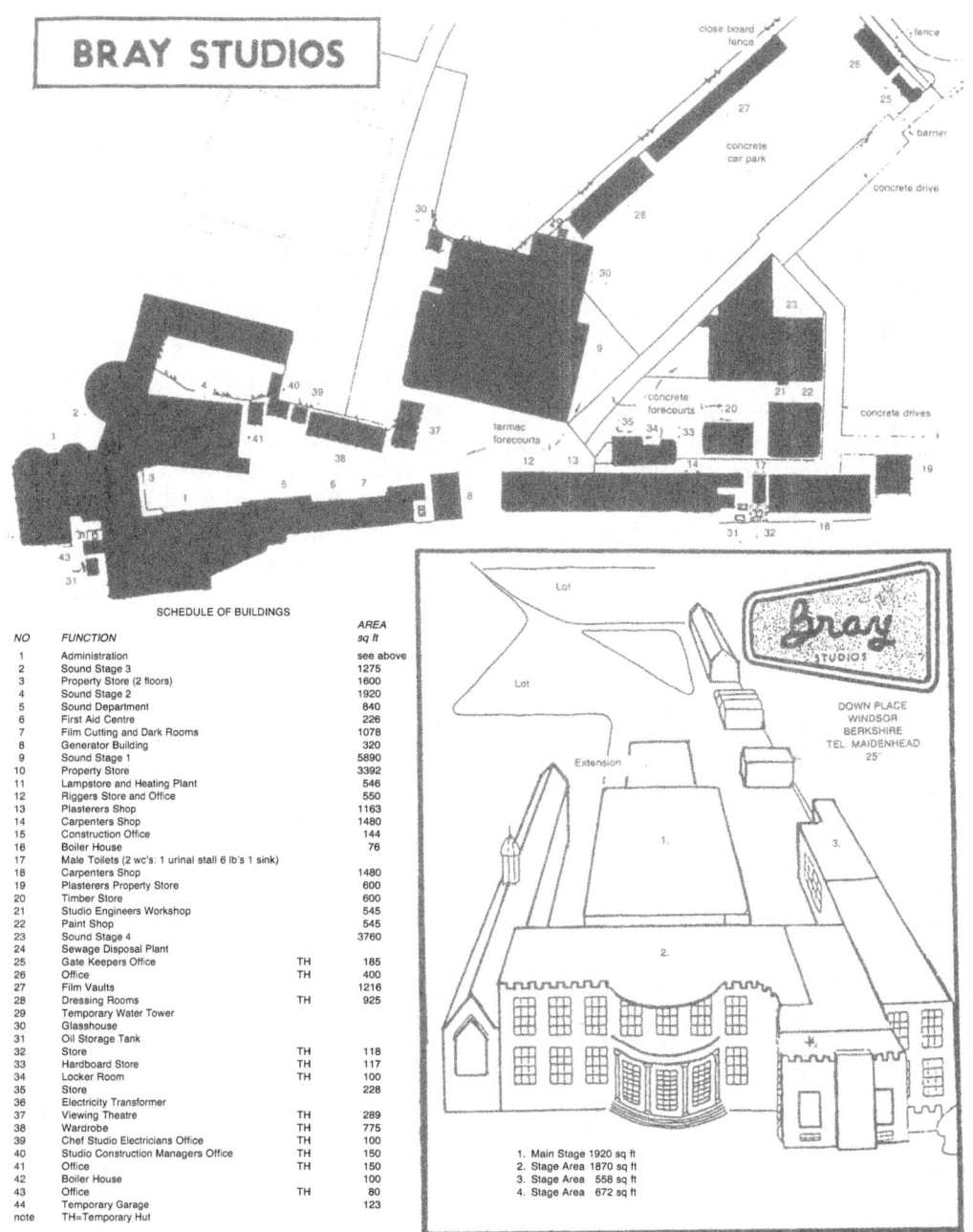

NO	FUNCTION		AREA sq ft
1	Administration		see above
2	Sound Stage 3		1275
3	Property Store (2 floors)		1600
4	Sound Stage 2		1920
5	Sound Department		840
6	First Aid Centre		226
7	Film Cutting and Dark Rooms		1078
8	Generator Building		320
9	Sound Stage 1		5890
10	Property Store		3392
11	Lampstore and Heating Plant		546
12	Riggers Store and Office		550
13	Plasterers Shop		1163
14	Carpenters Shop		1480
15	Construction Office		144
16	Boiler House		76
17	Male Toilets (2 wc's: 1 urinal stall 6 lb's 1 sink)		
18	Carpenters Shop		1480
19	Plasterers Property Store		600
20	Timber Store		600
21	Studio Engineers Workshop		545
22	Paint Shop		545
23	Sound Stage 4		3760
24	Sewage Disposal Plant		
25	Gate Keepers Office	TH	185
26	Office	TH	400
27	Film Vaults		1216
28	Dressing Rooms	TH	925
29	Temporary Water Tower		
30	Glasshouse		
31	Oil Storage Tank		
32	Store	TH	118
33	Hardboard Store		117
34	Locker Room	TH	100
35	Store		228
36	Electricity Transformer		
37	Viewing Theatre	TH	289
38	Wardrobe	TH	775
39	Chef Studio Electricians Office		100
40	Studio Construction Managers Office	TH	150
41	Office	TH	150
42	Boiler House		100
43	Office	TH	80
44	Temporary Garage		123
note	TH=Temporary Hut		

Diagram of Bray Studios in the mid–1960s (courtesy of Mike Murphy).

herself a designer, told the authors (August, 1993):

> Bernard was proud of the fact that he could save the company money without compromising quality. It was a challenge to use bits and pieces over and over again to disguise the fact that the same sets were being used. But, he *did* get a "fan letter" ... "When are you going to design a different set?" He was amused and showed it to management and said, "Isn't it time we spent a bit more?" Bernard appreciated that Hammer did things a bit better than necessary, but felt their themes to be somewhat

repetitious. It never bothered him that he never received awards. Bernard was his own judge and designed to please himself. He actually worried that people talked about his sets—if you noticed them, he thought, there's something wrong with the film! His main concern was that a handrail would wobble or a doorknob fall off. Bernard loved an ornate, opulent look. His sets were influenced by church imagery—stained glass, candelabra. He designed a set to be sturdy because it would be *used*. When he tired of using a particular bit—a door, paneling—he'd offer to buy it and bring it home. Often, they'd just give it to him. The sets were all honeycombed together. He'd place them so several scenes could be shot at once, yet you would not see one set while working on another. Bernard enjoyed working with cameraman Jack Asher—they both had this slightly over-the-top flamboyance. Jack loved rich color and spent ages getting it just right. Bernard often said, "Jack, there must be a fire in the landing!" Too much red light, you see. Bernard was always thinking ahead to the next film, and did a great deal of background reading to be period accurate. He often designed one set per day! He and I recalled with great fondness the kindness of everyone at Bray—it was a real family. Just before Bernard died, he realized that his work was being appreciated—even by the intelligentsia. I think he'd like the readers of this book to know that he took his work very seriously and that he'd certainly be amused by his "cult" status.

Terence Fisher's injuries from two car accidents reduced his output, and after *The Devil Rides Out* (1967), he only directed two more Hammer films. There was no replacement for him, or for Peter Cushing and Christopher Lee, who were both aging (and Lee was tiring of his signature role). In addition to his talent, Cushing brought a measure of respectability to even the worst film, and he refused to accept anything second rate from anyone—including himself. He and Lee, whose presence could not be duplicated, formed an unforgettable team. But, nothing lasts forever, and by the early seventies, the magic was gone. Eroded by internal squabbling, changing audience tastes, and natural attrition, Hammer began to fade.

Who made Hammer the most successful independent of its time? "Jim Carreras discovered the horror market and tailored the product accordingly. He was a real salesman" (Jimmy Sangster, August, 1993). "The reason why Hammer became so successful was that when Anthony Hinds took charge, he realized that if you want to make *good* cheap films, you must hire the best people you can" (Michael Ripper, April, 1993). "Anthony Hinds was the force that made Hammer move. He had his father's sense of showmanship, but was also interested in the day-to-day operations" (Len Harris, August, 1993). "Anthony Hinds knew what audiences wanted and knew how to get the right people to deliver it" (Margaret Robinson, August, 1993). Actually, what made Hammer successful was teamwork—there were no "auteurs" at Bray Studios. Actors Peter Cushing and Christopher Lee, directors Terence Fisher and Val Guest, writer Jimmy Sangster, composer James Bernard, and designer Bernard Robinson gave the company's films their unmistakable atmosphere, sharing in Hammer's success.

The company knew what it was making, and for whom. "I don't have any pretentions about our films," said Michael Carreras (*The Horror People*), "but I think they're good within the areas we lay down. The one thing we never do is make a shoddy film." Francis Matthews (February, 1991) said, "Those films represent one of the clearly defined landmarks in the long history of motion pictures. Like the MGM musicals, the Warner Bros. swashbucklers, the Ealing comedies, and the Hitchcock thrillers, the Hammer Horrors have left their indelible mark."

If the goal is to make a profit, Hammer achieved its goal. Although their films were not embraced by critics, audiences voted at the box office, and the company remains the only film company whose name alone could fill a theatre. Audiences always got what they came for.

THE FILMS

1935

The Public Life of Henry the Ninth

Released June, 1935 (U.K.); 60 minutes; B & W; 5334 feet; a Hammer Film Production; an MGM Release (U.K.); filmed at MGM/ATP Studios, Ealing; Director: Bernard Mainwaring. U.K. Certificate: U.

Leonard Henry (Henry), Betty Frankiss (Maggie), George Mozart (Draughts Player), Wally Patch (Landlord), with Aileen Latham, Mai Bacon.

Henry (Leonard Henry), an unemployed street entertainer, is found a job by a kindly policeman at the local pub, the Henry VIII. He strikes up a friendship with the barmaid, Maggie (Betty Frankiss) and, when business falls off, is allowed by the landlord (George Mozart) to sing. Known as Henry the Ninth, he becomes a minor success along with Maggie, who joins him at the microphone. As their popularity grows, the pub does also, and Henry soon brings in his vaudeville friends. But when they are not given credit for the pub's success, Henry and his friends leave for "the big time" on the London stage.

This is it—the first Hammer Film Production. A full page ad in green, white, and black depicting a blacksmith with hammer and anvil appeared in *The Kinematograph Weekly* on January 13, 1935, announcing the newest entry in the rapidly growing British film industry. The fledgling company's office was at 53 Haymarket with Wardour Street and Bray a long way off. Opposite the ad was Hammer's first headline: "Hammer's First Schedule," informing the industry that "Hammer is preparing an extensive programme for the new year," including *6:30 News* and an untitled costume picture of the Louis XV period to star Huntly Wright, "the well-known comedian." The listed personnel of the new company were Will Hammer (chairman), plus J. Elder Wills, H. Frazer Passmore, George Mozart, and G.A. Gillings. Oddly, Enrique Carreras was unmentioned.

The film's title was obviously a takeoff on the hugely successful *The Private Life of Henry the Eighth* (1933), starring Charles Laughton. The film was released by MGM on June 17, 1935. It is odd that such a large company would bother with such a small picture produced by a new company. It was finished at ATP Studios on January 2, 1935, but its starting date has proved elusive. The trade show was held on January 30, and reviews, although limited, were surprisingly positive. *The Kinematograph Weekly* (June 15, 1935): "Pleasant artless comedy, no serious pretensions, but does fill an hour quite pleasantly. Lighting and photography are up to standard."

Although one hesitates to label any film as "lost," *The Public Life of Henry the Ninth* seems to be. It is unmentioned in *any* film guide, The British Film Institute lacks a copy, and who knows when it was last shown? It is as though the film never existed.

The film that started it all: *The Public Life of Henry the Ninth*.

To put things in perspective, when the film was released, Peter Cushing was 22 and struggling with career decisions, Terence Fisher was 31 and a film editor, and Christopher Lee was 13.

The Mystery of the Mary Celeste

Released April 27, 1936 (U.K.), February, 1937 (U.S.); 80 minutes; B & W; 7261 feet; a Hammer Film Production; a General Film Distributors Release (U.K.), a Guaranteed Pictures Co. Release (U.S.); filmed at Nettlefold Studios and on location at Falmouth, England; Director: Denison Clift; Producer: Henry Fraser Passmore; Screenplay: Charles Larkworthy (based on a story by Denison Clift); Directors of Photography: Geoffrey Faithful, Eric Cross; Music: Eric Ansell; Continuity: Tilly Day; Art Director: J. Elder Wills; Editor: John Seabourne.

Working title: *Secrets of The Mary Celeste*. Title in U.S.: *The Phantom Ship*. U.K. Certificate: A.

Bela Lugosi (Anton Lorenzen/A. Gottlieb), Shirley Grey (Sarah Briggs), Arthur Margetson (Captain Benjamin Briggs), Edmund Willard (Toby Bilson), George Mozart (Tommy Duggan), Ben Welden (Boas Hoffman), Dennis Hoey (Tom Goodschard), Gibson Gowland (Andy Gilling), Clifford McLaglen (Captain Jim Morehouse), Terence de Marney (Charlie Kaye), Herbert Cameron (Volkerk Grot), Ben Souten (Jack Samson), James Carew (James Winchester), Bruce Gordon (Olly Deveau), Johnny Schofield (Peter Tooley), Edgar Pierce (Arian Harbens), J.B. Williams (The Judge), Charles Mortimer (Attorney General), Wilfred Essex (Horatio Sprague), Alec Fraser (Commander Mahon), Gunner Moir (Ponta Katz), Monti de Lyle (Portunato).

On the eve of departing on a long sea voyage (New York to Genoa), Benjamin Briggs (Arthur Margetson), captain of the *Mary Celeste*, proposes to his girlfriend Sarah (Shirley Grey) and asks her to join him on the journey. Sarah accepts, prompting the anger of her other beau, another seafarer, Captain Morehouse (Clifford McLaglen).

"Dracula" stars in an early Hammer production.

Among the men who sign on to sail with the *Mary Celeste* is Anton Lorenzen (Bela Lugosi), a one-armed sailor who seems to have a sinister ulterior motive for wanting to serve under Bilson (Edmund Willard), the ship's first mate. Another recruit is Grot (Herbert Cameron), one of Morehouse's men, who has been promised a promotion by Morehouse if Briggs doesn't reach his destination alive.

As the *Mary Celeste* begins its cross-Atlantic voyage, Sarah witnesses the cruelty of Bilson and the callousness of her own husband toward the men. Grot makes an attempt on Briggs' life, but Tommy (George Mozart), the ship's cook, stabs the attacker and saves the captain's life.

During a storm, Tom Goodschard (Dennis Hoey) enters the captain's cabin and attempts to molest Sarah. Anton appears and kills Goodschard. Anton is deeply affected by the incident, crying out that he has blood on his soul.

A pair of crewmen are mysteriously killed and another attempt is made on Briggs' life. Tommy and the ship's carpenter (Gibson Gowland) are the next to die. The grisly discoveries unhinge one of the sailors (Johnny Schofield) and he jumps overboard to his death.

Briggs has Anton escort Sarah back to her cabin. Anton assures her that he and Death know each other quite well. He notices a painting of a storm-ravaged ship and tells Sarah that, like the ship, he too is a derelict. He tells her that he was once shanghaied and forced to suffer at the hands of a brutal first mate. He was being keelhauled when a shark attacked and tore off his arm.

More murders and disappearances ensue, and accusations begin to fly between the remaining men. Soon only Bilson and Anton are left. Leveling a gun at Bilson, Anton confesses that he murdered the captain and Sarah when he caught them abandoning ship. Anton then reveals his true identity. As recognition dawns on Bilson's face, Anton shoots him in the leg. He then throws Bilson overboard, tied about the waist with a rope as Bilson had done with Anton years before. Laughing maniacally, Anton watches as sharks surround the doomed man.

A swinging spar strikes Anton and the blow clears his befuddled mind. Filled with

Bela Lugosi on a makeup break during filming of *The Mystery of the Mary Celeste* (photo courtesy of Ted Okuda).

remorse over what he has done, Anton throws himself overboard.

Many days later, the *Mary Celeste* is sighted by Capt. Morehouse, who boards the derelict vessel and finds it totally deserted. Only Anton's black cat is found alive. The truth about the *Mary Celeste* would forever be shrouded in mystery.

Hammer's second film, and its first melodrama, dealt with one of the 19th century's most celebrated mysteries. The disappearance of the crew of the *Mary Celeste* is still a matter of speculation with everything from giant squids to UFO's being blamed, so Hammer's solution is as plausible as any. Several major Hollywood studios had plans to film the story, including MGM with Wallace Beery and Robert Taylor considered for the leads. Hammer, however, scooped them all in the summer of 1935 when the company signed Bela Lugosi. By the mid-thirties, Lugosi's career had begun to degenerate after his great success in *Dracula* (1931), and he was looking for an escape from the "B" thrillers in which he was trapped. He may have been aware of the plans to do a big budget version in Hollywood and, eager to associate himself with such a project, signed with Hammer without bothering to read the script. Lugosi's friend and business manager, Richard Gordon, told the authors (June, 1993), "Bela was loath to talk about the film because it was a big disappointment for him. Different companies announced it at one time or another, and Hammer all of a sudden came up and said they were going to do it. Everybody thought they were going to make a big British picture out of it. After all, it *was* a big subject. I think Bela thought the same thing!" Lugosi wasn't alone in his confusion. *The New York Times* (July 7, 1935) reported that Alexander Korda, one of Britain's top producers, was making the picture.

Bela Lugosi poses for this publicity shot during the filming of *The Mystery of The Mary Celeste* (photo courtesy of Tim Murphy).

Bela Lugosi and co-star Shirley Grey both sailed for England on the *Berengaria*, arriving on July 13. A reception was held on the 15th and location shooting on board the schooner *Mary B Mitchell* began the next day. Lugosi attended a trade show of *The Raven*, in which he co-starred with Boris Karloff, at the Prince Edward on July 18. Ironically, *The Raven*'s scenes of torture would soon lead to a ban of horror movies in Britain that would curtail their production in Hollywood. Tilly Day, Hammer's long-time continuity girl, recalled Lugosi for Colin Cowie. "He was very tall, and somehow a rather terrifying man. He was always nice to me, though. He called me 'the English rose' and once made a pass at me!"

Interiors were filmed in August at Nettlefold Studios where a full-sized replica of the *Mary Celeste* was constructed. By mid–August, Lugosi's scenes were completed, and he sailed back to America on the *Majestic* to again co-star with Karloff in *The Invisible Ray*. Producers George Gillings and H. Fraser Passmore were named joint managing directors of the company under Will Hammer just before *The Mystery of the Mary Celeste* was trade shown in October. General Film Distributors premiered the film on November 14 at the Prince Edward, and it went into general release on April 27, 1936. That September, it was released in America by Guaranteed. Several minutes of footage were removed before its release as *The Phantom Ship* on February 15, 1937. Reviews were mostly favorable, especially concerning Lugosi's performance. *Variety* (December 4, 1935): "The illusion of the vessel at sea was excellent"; and *Today's Cinema* (November 16): "It is, in a word, a picture which the popular patron should enjoy—full marks should be awarded this Hammer production." Despite the quality of this film and its successor, *Song of Freedom*, the fledgling company could only produce five pictures during the thirties. Hammer would not produce another thriller on this level for over a decade.

Song of Freedom

Released August, 1936 (U.K.); 80 minutes; B & W; 7244 feet; a Hammer Film Production; a British Lion Release; filmed at Beaconsfield Studios and on location in Africa and London; Director: J. Elder Wills; Producers: Will Hammer, Enrique Carreras; Screenplay: Ingram D'Abbern, Fenn Sherie; Story: Claude Wallace, Dorothy Holloway; Photography: Eric Cross, Harry Rose, Thomas Glower; Sound: Harold King; Editor: Arthur Tavares; Art Director: Norman Arnold; Music: Eric Ansell; Lyrics: Hedrick Ege; Production Supervisor: H. Fraser Passmore; U.K. Certificate: U.

Paul Robeson (John Zinga), Elisabeth Welch (Ruth Zinga), Esme Percy (Gabriel Donozetti), Robert Adams (Monty), Ecce Homo Toto (Mandingo), Ronald Simpson (Blane), George Mozart (Bert Puddick), Jennie Dean (Marian), Joan F. Emney (Nell Pudick), Bernard Ansell (Sir James Pirrie), Arthur Williams (M'Dobo), Cornelia Smith (Queen Zinga), Alf Goddard (Alf), Will Hammer (Potman), and James Solomon, Johnnie Schofield, Ambrose Manning, Arthur Eliot.

Colonial Africa, 1700s. Queen Zinga (Cornelia Smith) orders the execution of her brother, whom she suspects of conspiring with slave traders. Unnoticed in the frenzied crowd, two children steal his royal medallion. Generations pass, and the medallion is now worn in modern London by John Zinga (Paul Robeson), a dockworker. As he works, he sings and dreams about his past. His magnificent voice is heard at a local pub by Donozetti (Esme Percy), a famous impresario, who offers to train him. John and his wife, Ruth (Elisabeth Welch), accept.

After performing the opera *Emperor Jones* at the Covent Garden Theatre, John sings a mysterious song he has known all his life. An audience member tells him that it is an ancient African folk song—and identifies the significance of the medallion. The Zingas travel to John's ancestral home, and find his people in poverty and hoping for the arrival of a legendary king. They embrace John as the man to return them to their former glory. But when he is unable to meet their expectations, the witch doctor (Arthur Williams) orders John's execution. Facing death, he sings the ancient melody, and the tribe, awestruck, accept John and Ruth as their King and Queen.

Despite being a gifted scholar, athlete, vocalist, and actor, Paul Robeson, as a result of racial prejudice had a difficult time making it in America. The son of an escaped slave and a teacher, Robeson questioned the rights supposedly promised to all Americans, and in the 1940s, began extolling the "virtues of Communism." Because of his outspoken beliefs, his career was destroyed, his passport revoked, and he died, forgotten, in 1976.

But, in 1935, Robeson was riding a wave of popularity after starring in *The Emperor Jones* (1933), and was on his way to England to film *Sanders of the River*. After appearing on the London stage in *Toussaint L'Ouverture*, Robeson was signed for *Song of Freedom*. He requested—and received—the right to approve the final cut, which was practically unheard of at the time. Filming began at Beaconsfield in the autumn of 1935, and included a month's shooting in Sierra Leone. Included in the crew were Major R. Wallace and A.T. Glover, explorers and experts in Africa. The film was trade shown in late June, 1936, and was released to great acclaim in August.

During *Song of Freedom*'s extended run at the prestigious Plaza in Piccadilly Circus, *The Kinematograph Weekly* (September 24, 1936) ran an ad summarizing the film's many positive reviews: "It has Paul Robeson acting earnestly and singing magnificently!" (*Daily Mail*); "I would go miles to hear Paul Robeson sing" (*Daily Mirror*); "It gets you as few films do" (*Empire News*); "A picture with artistic value, dignity, and a ring of truth, as well as inspiration" (*Star*).

1936
The Bank Messenger Mystery

Released 1937; 56 minutes; B & W; a Hammer Film Production; a Renown Release (U.K.); Director: Will Hammer; Producer: Lawrence Huntington. U.K. Certificate: U.

George Mozart (George Brown), Francesca Bahrie (Miss Brown), Paul Neville (Harper), with Marilyn Love, Frank Tickle, Kenneth Kove.

Unfortunately, virtually nothing has been unearthed regarding this obscure Hammer film. Apparently, it was a straight drama involving George Mozart's character (George) who finds himself involved with a group of thieves after he is dismissed from his job as a bank teller.

Other than a notice about a December 1936 trade show of the film, it is not known if it ever saw the inside of a theater.

Sporting Love

Released December 6, 1936 (U.K.); 70 minutes; B & W; 6321 feet; a Hammer Film Production; a British Lion Release (U.K.); filmed at Beaconsfield Studios; Director: J. Elder Wills; Screenplay: Fenn Sherie, Ingram D'Abbern, based on Stanley Lupino's play; Director of Photography: Eric Cross; Dance Arranger: Fred Leslie; Music: Eric Ansell; U.K. Certificate: U.

Stanley Lupino (Percy Brace), Laddie Cliff (Peter Brace), Henry Carlisle (Lord Dimsdale), Eda Peel (Maud Dane), Bobby Comber (Gerald Dane), Barry Lupino, Arty Ash.

Percy (Stanley Lupino) and Peter Brace (Laddie Cliff) are broke, but do own Moonbeam, a racehorse which they will soon lose to Mr. Dane (Bobby Comber) to pay a mortgage. Peter is in love with Dane's daughter, Maud (Eda Peel), and the brothers have sold their yacht to two different customers. In another desperate attempt to raise funds, they've told their wealthy aunt that each of them is to be married, hoping she'll send a check. Aunty Fanny arrives to check up on her nephews, and Percy convinces Nellie, an American tourist, to pose as his wife, and Maud to pose as Peter's. This backfires when Mr. Dane and Nellie's fiancé make an unexpected entrance.

Percy next plans to get rid of Nellie's fiancé and, while struggling with him, knocks off his toupee. Nellie, angered at his deception, breaks the engagement; and he makes a play for Aunt Fanny. Adding to their problems, Mr. Dane is planning to withdraw Moonbeam from the Derby, and the boys kidnap her just in time. The race begins, and Percy mistakenly bets on the wrong horse, but the brothers finally get a break. Winterbottom wins 100 to 1.

Stanley Lupino, whose family had a long stage tradition, was one of Britain's biggest musical comedy stars of the thirties. His first stage appearance was in South Africa, when he replaced an ailing actor. Lupino had a Broadway success in 1926 in *The Nightingale*, and was soon a fixture in West End Productions, writing both his scripts and music. *Sporting Love* began as a stage production, opening at the Gaiety in 1934, and was an immediate hit—as were most of his plays. Lupino was quite a catch for a fledging film company like Hammer.

He returned to England on January 15, 1936, after trying to interest his daughter Ida—a rising Hollywood star—in a West End stage production which fell through. Lupino then decided to film *Sporting Love* which began production soon afterward. He and his long-time partner, Laddie Cliff, adapted musical numbers collected from their previous stage productions. Filming ended on June 23 with a location shoot at the Derby, and the trade show was scheduled for August. *Sporting Love* premiered at the Piccadilly on December 3, and was called by the *Kinematograph Weekly* (April 15, 1937) during its general release as "sporting comedy." *Variety* (December 9, 1936) had passed it off as "Good enough to be accepted in America as a programmer."

Hammer's plans for a second Lupino film were cancelled due to *Sporting Love*'s poor performance, and the company itself soon went into a decade-long hibernation.

1947

Death in High Heels

Released July 18, 1947 (U.K.); 48 minutes; B & W; 4300 feet; a Hammer-Marylebone Production; an Exclusive Release (U.K.); filmed at Marylebone Studios; Director: Tommy Tomlinson; Producer: Henry Halstead; Production Supervisor: Anthony Hinds; adapted from the novel by Christianna Brand; Director of Photography: Stanley Clinton; Sound: Charles Hasher, Dick Farge; Makeup: Harry Davo; U.K. Certificate: A.

Don Stannard (Detective Charlesworth), Elsa Tee (Victoria David), Veronica Rose (Agnes Gregory), Denise Anthony (Aileen), Patricia Laffan (Magda Doon), Diana Wong (Miss Almond Blossom), Nora Gordon (Miss Arris), Bill Hodge (Mr. Cecil), Ken Warrington (Frank Bevan), Leslie Spurling (Sergeant Bedd).

Magda (Patricia Laffan) and Agnes (Veronica Rose) are rivals for a French posting in Frank Bevan's (Ken Warrington) dress business. When Aileen (Denise Anthony) uses acetic acid to clean a dirty hat, some crystals fall on the floor. Miss Arris (Nora Gordon) cleans them up, placing the residue on a table as requested by Agnes. At lunch, she and Magda have an argument with Agnes over the new position. Magda takes a plate intended for Agnes and, after eating, falls to the floor. Most of the staff have alibis—as well as motives—to kill Agnes.

Miss Almond (Diane Wong) confesses to Agnes that she put a few poison crystals in the food to make her sick so *she* could take the new position in France. However, Magda ate the food and, inexplicably, died. Almond attempts suicide, but is saved by Detective Charlesworth (Don Stannard). He determines that Magda's body contained more poison than was originally purchased. He reveals Agnes as the murderess. When confronted, she attempts suicide, but is restrained and taken away.

This short film, barely qualifying as a feature, was only recently revealed as a Hammer production, thanks to research by Richelle Wilder, Director of Development. It's another "lost film"—just a post-war "quota quickie"—made and forgotten quickly, and not listed in any major film guides.

Death in High Heels was included, along with ten other pictures, in a January 1, 1947, trade ad for release in 1947. It began production on January 3 as part of a deal between Exclusive and Henry Halstead, head of Marylebone. *The Cinema* (January 8) estimated that the movie would be ready for a March trade show. Anthony Hinds had just been released from active Royal Air Force service and quickly joined the company. This was his first assignment as production supervisor. The production took longer than initially planned, ending on February 5 and trade shown on May 28 at the Hammer Theatre, co-featured with *Paddy's Milestone*, a Hammer short. Release was set for July 28.

A small picture like this is usually not widely reviewed, and those that follow couldn't be more polarized. *Today's Cinema* (May 30, 1947): "The conventional murder mystery in its crudest and most unattractive form, as tedious as it is uninspired. Most of the acting is decidedly amateurish"; and *The Kinematograph Weekly* (June 5): "Ingenious story, exciting denouement, hardy crime featurette."

Considering the film's unavailability, take your pick.

River Patrol

Release date unknown (1948 U.K.); 46 minutes; B & W; 4164 feet; a Hammer-Knightsbridge Production; an Exclusive Release (U.K.); filmed at Marylebone Studios; Director: Ben Hart; Producer: Hal Wilson; Screenplay: no credit; Director of Photography: Brooks-Carrington; Editor: J. Corbett; Music: Paxtons; Sound: Leevers Rich; U.K. Certificate: U.

John Blythe (Robby), Lorna Dean (Jean), Wally Patch (Chief), and Stan Paskin, Wilton West, George Crowther, Fred Collins, Johnny Doherty, Douglas Leigh, Tony Merrett, George Lane, Dolly Gwynne, Audrey Hibbs, George Kane.

The River Patrol and the Water Guard are important but rarely publicized services that protect the London docks. One night, during a smuggling raid, Robby's (John Blythe) partner is shot, and Robby is assigned by the Chief (Wally Patch) to a new case—the smuggling of 20,000 pairs of nylon stockings. He recruits Jean (Lorna Dean) from the women's section to pose as his wife. The couple then trace the contraband to an East End club called "Sure." Robby chats up the bartender and arranges an illegal whiskey delivery, and Jean is offered a waitress position. She learns that the stockings leave the club hidden in laundry baskets, but their identities are discovered, and they are abducted. Hidden in the club warehouse, Robby and Jean await death but are rescued by the Patrol.

The end of World War II in 1945 returned society to many things, including (among the lesser in importance) full time film production. After years of deprivation, Britons were hungry for entertainment and, with no real television industry, for most it meant going to the movies. Quality was no more a prerequisite than it is today for television viewers—entertainment was entertainment. The film industry was dominated by Hollywood, and the U.K. was its top foreign market. Due to the negative effect on the British industry, a 75 percent import tax was placed on American films. To protect Britain against a Hollywood takeover, Parliament had created a quota act in 1927, calling for 30 percent of all films shown in the U.K. to be of British origin. Although it encouraged production, the quota also sanctioned mediocrity. Richard Gordon, long time producer/distributor, shared his memories with the authors (June, 1993):

"*River Patrol* was a small film even for a quota quickie, and its 46 minute running time barely qualified it as a feature. It was shot mostly on location in London, with exteriors filmed at Marylebone." It was trade shown on January 28, 1948, at the Hammer Theatres which was, according to Richard Gordon, "built as a screening room in the basement of Hammer House. It was really state of the art—one of London's largest, seating about 150. Hammer would often rent it out to other companies for cast screenings or for receptions." As for the trade show, the release was "not fixed," and the authors could find no release date, but it was certainly in theatres by spring. *The Kinematograph Weekly* (February 5) was one of the few to review *River Patrol*, calling it a "thumbnail crime melodrama; uneven direction, faulty timing, and cramped staging give its rough-stuff a somewhat phoney ring."

As of this writing, *River Patrol* (and others to be covered later) is a "lost film," and why not? It was nothing special when it was released and was quickly forgotten. It was films like this that caused audiences to shout, "Take it off—it's British!"

The Dark Road

Released October 1, 1948 (U.K.); 72 minutes; B & W; 6668 feet; a Marylebone-Exclusive Production; an Exclusive Release (U.K.); Director: Alfred Goulding; Producer: Henry Halstead; Director of Photography: Stanley Clinton; Camera: Reg Selley; Sound: Charles Hasher, Dick Farge; Makeup: Harry Davo; Art Direction: Jimmy Marchont; Assistant Director: Eric Veendam; U.K. Certificate: U.

Charles Stuart (Sidney Robertson), Joyce Linden (Anne), with Mackenzie Ward, Patrick Hicks, Roddy Hughes, Anthony Holles, Rory McDermott, Joanna Carter, Peter Reynolds, Veronica Rose, Maxine Taylor, Michael Ripper, Sefton Yates, Cyril Chamberlain, Gale Douglas, Sydney Bromley, Gerald Ping, Hay Petrie.

American crime writer Nick Allen is hired to expose the life of petty crook Sidney Robertson (Charles Stuart) who recently came to a bad end. Allen learns that Robertson's problems began when he was a teenager. Having little parental control, he fell in with the wrong people and, after robbing a house, was sent to prison. Released early for good behavior, Robertson found work as Mr. Ashcroft's chauffeur, but he soon weakened and stole from his employer. After being caught for stealing cars, Robertson was arrested and sent to prison for seven years, but soon escaped. He meets Anne (Joyce Linden), an old girlfriend, and they team up to steal jewelry. A policewoman acting as a decoy draws their interest, and Anne is captured. Robertson escapes but, during a rooftop chase, falls to his death.

The Dark Road was the second Exclusive-Marylebone coproduction, the result of a multi-picture pact negotiated by Enrique Carreras, Will Hammer, and Henry Halstead in 1946. Filming began on February 17, 1947, with a story based on the life of Stanley Thurston, a former jewel thief. In fact, Thurston *starred* in the picture, and changed his name to Charles Stuart prior to the film's release. Location work was done in Blackpool, Manchester, Dartmoor, Parkhurst, and Lewes Prison. The production ended on April 9, 1947, and a trade show was held on July 28, 1948. *The Dark Road* was released on October 1 to tepid reviews. *The Kinematograph Weekly* (August 5): "Its object is apparently to prove that honesty is the best policy, but amateurish acting, uneven direction, and a dishevelled spirit prevent it from underlining the message"; and *Today's Cinema* (July 30): "Offers little that has not been seen before." Jewel thief turned actor Thurston, according to the reviewers, should have stayed with his original calling. Most of the remaining cast members were seldom heard from again, with the major exception of Michael Ripper who began an association with the company that would span its history.

Dick Barton, Special Agent

Released April, 1948 (U.K.); 70 minutes; B & W; 6242 feet; a Marylebone-Hammer Production; an Exclusive Release (U.K.); filmed at Marylebone Studios; Director: Alfred Goulding; Producer: Henry Halstead; Screenplay: Alan Stranks, Alfred Goulding, based on the BBC radio series; Director of Photography: Stanley Clinton; Art Director: James Marchant; Editor: Eta Simpson; Assistant Director: Eric Veendam; Music: John Bath; Sound: Charles Hasher; Continuity: Doreen Saunders; Casting Director: Edgar Blatt; Casting Manager: Mary Harris: USA TV Title: *Dick Barton, Detective*; U.K. Certificate: U.

Don Stannard (Dick Barton), George Ford (Snowey), Jack Shaw (Jack), Gillian Maude (Jean), Beatrice Kane (Mrs. Horrock), Ivor Danvers (Snub), Geoffrey Wincott (Dr. Caspar), Arthur Bush (Schuler), Alec Ross (Tony), Farnham Baxter (Roscoe), Morris Sweden (Regan), Ernest Borrow (Gilpin).

On special assignment to investigate smuggling, Dick Barton (Don Stannard) heads for Echo Bay with his goofy friends Snowey (George Ford) and Jack (Jack Shaw). Meanwhile, Dr. Caspar (Geoffrey Wincott) enters a fish factory on the bay, awaiting the arrival of "Johansen" and a mysterious package. He (Arthur Bush) informs Caspar that their "cover" is the study of beetles, but their real goal is unspoken.

Their first move is Dick's assassination which fails when Snub (Ivor Danvers) misses an easy shot as Dick drives past on his way to meet Jean (Gillian Maude). A delivery boy, stunned at seeing his hero, mistakenly gives Dick the package meant for Dr. Caspar, which contains stolen jewelry. After another failed attempt to kill Dick with a poisoned dart, the villains kidnap Snowey and Jack. While searching for his friends, Dick is trapped underground just as they are released by the delivery boy.

Chained to a wall, Dick reveals to Dr. Caspar that he knows that they are escaped Nazis. The doctor has a revelation of his own—to destroy Britain with plague bacillus in the water supply. Dick frees himself and alerts Sir George of the Home Office to secure the bay. With Jack's help, Dick frees Jean, who has been taken prisoner, saving both the day and Britain.

This is a terrific movie that was years ahead of its time. One of the few things close to it for the modern viewer is the 1960s' *Batman* TV series, and one can't help wondering if its creator ever caught a glimpse of Dick. It's only fitting that Hammer's first post-war hit was based on a radio series, since one of the company's best ideas was to base their films on pre-sold characters with a built-in audience. Most of Britain in 1948 tuned in to Barton following the evening news.

The Kinematograph Weekly (December 18, 1947): "Exclusive has progressed to such an extent that James Carreras claims it is the leading small producer-distributor company in the country." Although the company had actually made three post-war movies, Exclusive held the Screen Guild distribution franchise, and was holding twelve American films for release. The fourth production, *Dick Barton*, was expected to put the company on top. The second *Barton* picture was already in production, with two *more* scheduled for June and October, 1948 starts. Each feature was also planned to be released as a four episode serial.

Marylebone Studio's Henry Halstead told *Kinematograph Weekly* (October 2, 1947), "that small companies need not necessarily produce 'quota quickies,' but should make small, moderately produced pictures that are high in quality and box office appeal." He felt that two things were necessary: story selection and advance planning, and that *Dick Barton* couldn't be topped as a property due to its tremendous popularity on radio. Also making Barton a good idea for filming was the camp atmosphere with dialogue delivered in an intense, over-the-top manner, or tossed away as an aside. A great throw away visual has a boy reading a Dick Barton comic book. When Dick is to be shot on a deserted road, all we see is a rifle barrel and moving bushes with inane comments coming from behind the shrubs. Although this may not read as being especially hilarious, they *are* funny! Although comedy usually dates rapidly, the film is still funny almost fifty years later, and that's an achievement.

Who Killed Van Loon?

Released February, 1948; 48 minutes; B & W; 4500 feet; an Exclusive Films Production and Release (U.K.); Directors: Lionel Tomlinson, Gordon Kyle; Producers: Gordon Kyle, James Carreras; Screenplay: Peter Cresswell.

Raymond Lovell (John Smith/Johann Schmidt), Kay Bannerman (Anna), Robert Wyndham (Detective Inspector Oxley).

During a visit to diamond merchant Jeert Van Loon, Anna (Kay Bannerman) suffers a blackout—a legacy of her abusement in a Nazi concentration camp. When she regains consciousness, Van Loon, her father's ex-partner, is dead. Terrified, she turns to her only contact in Britain, Johann Schmidt (Raymond Lovell), a friend of her late father's. He suggests that she confess, but plead that she lost control during her "spell." She nearly believes in her own guilt, but Inspector Oxley (Robert Wyndham) is called into the case. Oxley discovers that Schmidt killed Van Loon for his collection of uncut diamonds that originally belonged to Anna's father. He finds the man—alive—in an attic above Schmidt's office. Thought to have died in a Nazi camp, he was kept prisoner due to Schmidt's belief that he was the only man capable of cutting the diamonds. When Oxley moves to arrest Schmidt, the killer dies in a fall, and Anna is reunited with her father.

Who Killed Van Loon?, at 48 minutes, barely qualified as a feature and received very little publicity. Apparently, it was filmed entirely on location with houses used in lieu of studio sets. A trade show was held on January 29, 1948, at the Hammer Theatre, 113 Wardour Street. Exclusive was the first British film company to have private trade screening facilities. The theatre was described in *Today's Cinema* (July 5, 1946) as fulfilling a "long felt need in the Street which has lacked a theatre of really generous proportions that can be hired for both trade and press shows and which, at the same time, meets the most exacting technical demands. Distributors, particularly those interested in the export market, will find Jimmy Carreras' project a valuable answer to their needs. The whole impression is one of quality."

The authors were unable to find a release date for the film, but it was reviewed on February 4, 1948. *The Kinematograph Weekly* called *Who Killed Van Loon?* "a little phoney," but felt it contained, "breathless and bloodcurdling action." *Today's Cinema* (February 4) said, "The mystery element is well enough sustained, and it is all very competently portrayed." *Who Killed Van Loon?* is one of many "lost" Hammer productions and will, unfortunately, remain a mystery for the modern viewer.

1948

Dick Barton at Bay

Released October 2, 1950 (U.K.); 68 minutes; B & W; a Hammer Film Production; an Exclusive Films Release; 6100 feet; filmed at Marylebone Studios, England; Director: Godfrey Grayson; Producer: Henry Halstead; Screenplay: Ambrose Grayson, based on the BBC Radio Series; Director of Photography: Stanley Clinton; Editor: Max Brenner; Music: Frank Spencer, Rupert Grayson; Art Director: James Marchant; Camera Operator: Stanley Clinton; Assistant Director: Eric Veendam; Makeup: Teddy Edwardes; Continuity: Prudence Sykes. Working title: *Dick Barton and the Ray of Death*. U.K. Rating: U.

Don Stannard (Dick Barton), Tamara Desni (Anna), George Ford (Snowey), Meinhart Maur (Serge Volkoff), Joyce Linden (Mary Mitchell), Percy Walsh (Professor Mitchell), Campbell Singer (Inspector Cavendish), Richard

32 Dick Barton at Bay (1948)

Hammer's first of many sequels.

George (Inspector Slade), John Arnatt (Jackson), with Beatrice Kane, George Crawford, Paddy Ryan, Ted Butterfield, Patrick Macnee, Fred Owen, Yoshihide Yanai.

Special Agent Dick Barton (Don Stannard) learns of agent Phillips and about a case involving Prof. Mitchell (Percy Walsh) before the phone line goes dead. Phillips was killed by foreign agent Volkoff (Meinhart Maur), who plans to kidnap Mitchell and his daughter Mary (Joyce Linden). Inspector Slade (Richard George) tells Barton that Mitchell has developed a ray gun and that the weapon must not fall into the wrong hands. Barton and his partner Snowey White (George Ford) find that the abduction has taken place and follow the trail to a lighthouse where Volkoff plans to test the weapon against British aircraft. Baron and Snowey break into the lighthouse and a fight ensues, during which Barton hurls Volkoff to his death from the tower. Mitchell and Mary are released and the police round up Volkoff's henchmen.

Hammer's follow-up to the highly successful *Dick Barton, Special Agent* began production on March 4, 1948, at Marylebone Studios. Marylebone was one of the smallest of England's twenty-four studios, consisting of two sound stages and twenty-three employees. Location work began on May 13, at Chichester, Eastbourne, and Beach Head lighthouse. During a sales conference held on June 18 and 19, James Carreras announced that, due to the success of the first *Barton*—with over 1,400 bookings, two more films featuring the "special agent" would be produced. An agreement was signed with Robert Lippert's Screen Guild making Exclusive that company's sole U.K. distributor.

Dick Barton at Bay was trade shown at the Rialto on September 2, 1950, two and one-half years after its production began. The company was concerned about flooding its own market, but seemed to have overdone the wait. The picture was released on October 2 to positive reviews that echoed those of the original, as in *The Kinematograph Weekly* (September 28): "There are admittedly more laughs than thrills, but most patrons will accept the whole thing in the spirit of fun." What separates *Dick Bar-*

A film recently recognized as a Hammer, 1948's *The Jack of Diamonds*.

ton at Bay from its predecessor is its combination of science fiction and "Red Menace" threat. However, the apocalyptic plot elements were still handled irreverently, since children were the target audience. Adults were invited, too.

The Jack of Diamonds

Released February 7, 1949 (U.K.); 73 minutes; B & W; 6622 feet; an Exclusive-V.S. Co-Production; an Exclusive Release (U.K.); filmed on location in France; Director: Vernon Sewell; Producers: Vernon Sewell, Walter d'Eyncourt; Director of Photography: Moray Grant; U.K. Certificate: U.

Nigel Patrick (Alan Butler), Cyril Raymond (Roger Keen), Joan Carol (Joan Keen), Dolly Bowmeester (Gisell), John Basings (Parsons), Darcy Conyers (Colin Campbell), Vernon Sewell (Engineer), Edwin Richfield (George Paxton), Guy Romano (Douanier).

Once wealthy Roger (Cyril Raymond) and Joan Keen (Joan Carol) are forced to hire out their luxury yacht. They are contacted by smooth-talking Alan Butler (Nigel Patrick), who persuades them to join him on a treasure hunt off the French coast. Seeing a chance to recoup their wealth, the Keens agree. They are joined by Giselle (Dolly Bowmeester), who confides to Roger that she is heir to the fortune and that Alan is a thief. After finding the loot, Butler sets the others adrift, but they are rescued by friends who have been searching for them. Butler is captured after a high speed chase, Giselle gets her treasure, and the Keens retrieve their yacht.

The Jack of Diamonds was an Exclusive–Vernon Sewell co-production, filmed entirely on location during the peak of the "quota-quickie" era. Sewell directed the first of his three pictures for the company, filming aboard his personal yacht, as he so often did in other movies. The film was trade shown at the Hammer Theatre on January 12, 1949, and was released on February 7. The ABC circuit teamed it with *Say It with Flowers* for a second release on May 23. *The Kinematograph Weekly* (January 13) called *The Jack of Diamonds* "A neat and thrilling story—it's certain to register with the general mien of picturegoers." The film does not seem to have survived.

Dick Barton Strikes Back

Released July 18, 1949 (U.K.); 73 minutes; B & W; 6541 feet; a Hammer Film Production; an Exclusive Films Release; filmed at Viking Studios and on location in Blackpool, Liverpool, and Pinner, England. Director: Godfrey Grayson; Screenplay: Elizabeth Baron and Ambrose Grayson, based on a story by Ambrose Grayson and the BBC Radio Series; Director of Photography: Cedric Williams; Associate Producers: Anthony Hinds, Mae Murray; Camera: Peter Newbrook; Production Manager: Don Wynne; Art Director: Ivan King; Supervising Editor: Ray Pitt; Assistant Director: Dicky Leeman; Makeup: Jack Smith; Continuity: Prudence Sykes; Supervising Electrician: Jack Curtis; Casting Director: Edgar Blatt; Casting Manager: Mary Harris; Music Score: Frank Spencer, Rupert Grayson; 2nd Assistant Director: Jimmy Sangster; Focus: Jerry Turpin; Clappers: Neil Binnie, Chief Sparks, Jack Curtis; Working Title: *Dick Barton and the Silent Plague*; U.K. Certificate: U.

Don Stannard (Dick Barton), Sebastian Cabot (Fouracada), Jean Lodge (Tina), James Raglan (Lord Armadale), Bruce Walker (Snowey White), Humphrey Kent (Colonel Gardner), Morris Sweden (Dr. Robert Creston), John Harvey (Major Henderson), Sidney Vivian (Inspector Burke), Toni Morelli (Nicholas), George Crawford (Alex), Laurie Taylor (Nick), Schulman (Flash).

Special agent Dick Barton (Don Stannard) and his sidekick Snowey White (Bruce Walker) find the body of fellow agent Creston (Morris Sweden) who has been investigating supposed arms dealer Fouracada (Sebastian Cabot). Barton and Snowey are captured by Fouracada who, before having them killed, cryptically remarks about "an experiment." The boys escape and inform the police, but Fouracada eludes them on his way to High Glen. He has developed a vibration ray which can destroy an entire city, which he proves at High Glen. Barton joins with government official Lord Armadale (James Raglan) to investigate and meets his charming secretary Tina (Jean Lodge), who soon comes under the agent's suspicion. A note she discarded reveals that she is in league with Fouracada.

Barton and Snowey follow her dog Flash to an isolated trailer where they are captured by Fouracada who again orders their deaths, but Tina has a change of heart and has Flash attack one of the thugs. Barton deduces that the Blackpool Tower will be the next site and notifies Lord Armadale who, incredibly, is the plot's mastermind with world domination his goal! He arranges for Barton and Snowey to be killed at the Blackpool Zoo, but Tina again intervenes and Dick throws Fouracada into a room of deadly snakes. Barton finds Lord Armadale in the Tower, ready to unleash the devastating vibration. During the struggle, Armadale falls to his death.

Unlike the first two Barton pictures, *Dick Barton Strikes Back* was filmed "straight," minus the expected slapstick, although there were elements of humor. The feel is so close to James Bond that one wonders if Ian Fleming had been a Barton fan. While revenues from the previous Bartons were piling up, location filming began at Blackpool, the London Zoo, and London Airport (now Heathrow) in August, 1948. Interiors were shot at Viking Studios, Kensington, from September 9 to October 28. The company planned to send a crew immediately to Kenya to shoot location footage for *Dick Barton in Darkest Africa*, but moved the picture back to summer, 1949. The change may have been due to the acquisition of Cookham Dean and the expense involved in converting the mansion into a studio. The estate, located near Marlow, had twenty-five bedrooms and a 110-by-70-foot ballroom, in 16½ acres.

Trade advertisement.

Dick Barton Strikes Back was trade shown on March 7, 1949, at the Palace, and the picture was released on July 18 to take advantage of the school vacation. On Saturday, July 9, an afternoon garden party was held at the studio to celebrate, with over two hundred guests invited. Don Stannard left with his wife Thelma and, among others, the Sebastian Cabots. *The Kinematograph Weekly* (July 14) reported that

> The vehicle was seen to swing out of the drive running down the twisted incline which links the house with the main road into Cookham Village. It got out of hand on a bend and overturned. Stannard was killed instantly, and all the passengers were taken to Maidenhead Hospital. Mrs. Stannard was unhurt, but the other passengers all suffered severe shock and lacerations.

Dick Barton Strikes Back pleased both

audiences and reviewers. *The Kinematograph Weekly* (March 10, 1949): "The film completely captures the spirit of the incredibly popular BBC feature. A good natured essay in villainy, disarming ingenuousness, good staging"; *The Daily Film Renter* (March 10): "Full of everything the fans look for"; and *Today's Cinema* (March 11): "One cannot easily envision a greater magnet for the popular public."

Stannard's death ended the plans for a fourth Barton adventure, since he had been so identified—and successful—with the role.

Dr. Morelle—The Case of the Missing Heiress

Released June 27, 1949 (U.K.); 73 minutes; B & W; 6602 feet; a Hammer Film Production; released through Exclusive; filmed at Cookham Dean; Director: Godfrey Grayson; Producer: Anthony Hinds; Screenplay: Roy Plomley, Godfrey Grayson, based on Wilfred Burr's play; Director of Photography: Cedric Williams; Camera Operator: Peter Brayan; Production Manager: Arthur Barners; Music: Frank Spencer, Rupert Grayson; Casting: Mary Harris; Makeup: Marjorie Green; Hairstyles: E. Hollis; Art Director: James Marchant; Editor: Ray Pitt; Continuity: E. Chapman; Sound Recordist: E. Vetter; Sound System: United Programmes; Assistant Director: Bob Jones; Stills: Edgar Wrather; U.K. Certificate: A.

Valentine Dyall (Dr. Morelle), Julia Lang (Miss Frayle), Jean Lodge (Cynthia Mason), Philip Leaver (Samuel Kimber), Peter Drury (Peter Lorrimer).

Miss Frayle (Julia Lang), secretary to Dr. Morelle (Valentine Dyall), a cynical investigator, is upset by the disappearance of her friend Cynthia (Jean Lodge). She goes to Cynthia's estate where her friend, heiress to a fortune, lives with her stepfather Samuel Kimber (Phillip Leaver) and obtains a position as a maid. She joins forces with the butler Bensall, and studies the activities of Kimber and Lorrimer (Peter Drury), a neighbor with whom Cynthia was in love. She finds the charred remains of a body in a brick shed, where Bensall is later murdered. Desperate for help, Miss Frayle contacts

Trade advertisement.

Morelle. He arrives at the estate and, using different disguises, observes Kimber and Lorrimer. By using his deduction methods, he unmasks Lorrimer as the murderer of Bensall and Cynthia—whose inheritance he coveted—and saves Miss Frayle from being buried alive.

Like the *Dick Barton* films, Dr. Morelle was based on a successful BBC radio character. Created on the stage by Wilfred Burr and on radio by Ernest Dudly, Morelle was a detective in the mold of Sherlock Holmes. This was the first film to be entirely financed by the Film Finance Corporation, and was budgeted at a mere $56,000. The corporation's head, James Lawrie, was pleased by his investment and said that, "James Carreras has shown pretty shrewd judgement in cashing in on such a popular BBC series."

Dr. Morelle was also the first Hammer film to be produced at Cookham Dean. Filming began there on November 15, 1948, concluded in late December, and was trade shown on May 4, 1949, at the Rialto. The picture opened to good reviews on June 27, as in *The Kinematograph Weekly* (June 30): "Ingenious story, good characterizations, well-timed thrills, popular comedy relief,

WINNER after WINNER

"Josh" Billings says—
of "The Kine"

"THE JACK OF DIAMONDS"   Nigel Patrick — Cyril Raymond

'Engaging and Exciting Piratical Yarn.
—A.B.C. Release, May 23rd

"DICK BARTON STRIKES BACK"   Don Stannard — Sebastian Cabot

'Box-Office title proposition and British at that — it should prove an industrial and provincial sitter.'
—A.B.C. Release

AND NOW

"DOCTOR MORELLE"

VALENTINE DYALL   PHILIP LEAVER
JULIA LANG   JEAN LODGE

"Miniature Super" . . .
Crisp, compact, stylishly cut Thriller . . .
Exciting Climax . . .
Box-Office Title . . .
Valentine Dyall — an ideal selection for the role.
A.B.C. Release

THEY'RE ALL "EXCLUSIVE"

Trade advertisement.

good staging, neat direction, first class camerawork, and box office title." With such praise, one wonders why *Dr. Morelle* has seemingly vanished and goes unmentioned in film guides.

Hammer's plans to produce a series of Morelle pictures ended in September, 1949, when Ernest Dudley attempted to establish his own company to film a series. The proposed Hammer series could well have been a success, based on the *Kinematograph* review of the first film and the opinion of this unidentified critic:

Dr. Morelle doesn't pretend to be a world beater—in fact it is really a second feature, but it has one essential quality about it—it is entertainment! If you can make a picture in five weeks at a cost of £14,000 as Exclusive has done, and turn out something that will please the cash customers, what more can you ask?

Trade advertisement.

The Adventures of PC 49 (The Case of the Guardian Angel)

Released July 23, 1949 (U.K.); 67 minutes; B & W; 6065 feet; a Hammer Film Production; an Exclusive Release (U.K.); filmed at Dial Close, Cookham Dean; Director: Godfrey Drayson; Producer: Anthony Hinds; Screenplay: Alan Stranks, Vernon Harris, from the BBC radio series; Director of Photography: Cedric Williams; Camera Operator: Moray Grant; Assistant Director: Leon Bijou; Production Manager: Arthur Barnes; Music: Frank Spencer; Art Director: James

Trade advertisement.

Marchant; Fasting: Mary Harris; Makeup: Phil Leakey; Hairstylist: Monica Hustler; Pre-Production: Prudence Sykes; Editor: Cliff Turner; Continuity: Renee Glynne; Sound Recordist: E. Vetter; Stills: Edgar Wrather; Electrician: Jack Curtis; Carpenter: Fred Ricketts; Post Production: Ray Pitt; U.K. Certificate: U.

Hugh Latimer (PC Archibald Berkeley Willoughby), Patricia Cutts (Joan), John Penrose (Barney), Pat Nye (Ma Brady).

Police Constable Willoughby (Hugh Latimer) bemoans the lack of excitement in his job, a lack that ends when he witnesses the theft of a truckload of whiskey and the murder of a watchman. Inspector Wilson assigns Willoughby to the case under the alias of Vince Kelly, gangster. He gains the confidence of Barney (John Penrose), second in command of the hijackers who are led by an unseen "Boss." Willoughby is recognized by Skinny Ellis and narrowly escapes with his life.

With the help of his girlfriend, Joan (Patricia Cutts), he corners the gang at Ma Brady's (Pat Nye) cafe, and reveals her as "The Boss." PC 49 then returns to his familiar beat.

Like many Hammer films, *The Adventures of PC 49* was based on a BBC production, giving it a built-in audience. One of the advantages of filming a radio show is that everyone wanted to see what sort of faces were given to familiar characters. *Spotlight* praised the

> Forty-year-old Jimmy Carreras, the man who made these radio films, who can sit back and say, "All my pictures are making money!" They are, too — about £5,000 a film, and Carreras turns out about eight a year in a country house which he rents for fifty guineas a week by the river at Bray. In the country house, the film workers can live as well as work.

Jack MacGregor, in an unidentified article, complimented Hammer's "first rate technical crew. It was a happy group, for they knew a continuous program is lined up, and that the end of *PC 49* does not mean unemployment." This was a rocky period for the film industry in general, and Hammer was one of the few small producers in the U.K. with a steady run of pictures. *The Adventures of PC 49* began on February 18, 1949, on a four-week schedule, to be followed by *Meet Simon Cherry* (April 4), *Celia* (June 20), and *The Man in Black* (August 22). Planned, but not filmed, were *Taxi*, *Inspector Hornleigh*, *Miss Dangerfield*, *The Robinson Family*, and *Armchair Detective*, which spoke well of the company's widening intentions.

The Adventures of PC 49 was trade shown on July 17, 1949, at the Rialto and was released on July 23 to reviews typical of "quota quickie." *The Kinematograph Weekly* (July 17, 1949): "Pocket thick ear, it gets away to a good start, maintains a lively pace; and although a little transparent and lacking in ringcraft, effectively interweaves conventional rough stuff with an evergreen love interest."

The film's success led to a sequel (with Brian Reece replacing Hugh Lati-mer), and helped to further establish Hammer as a producer of popular entertainment.

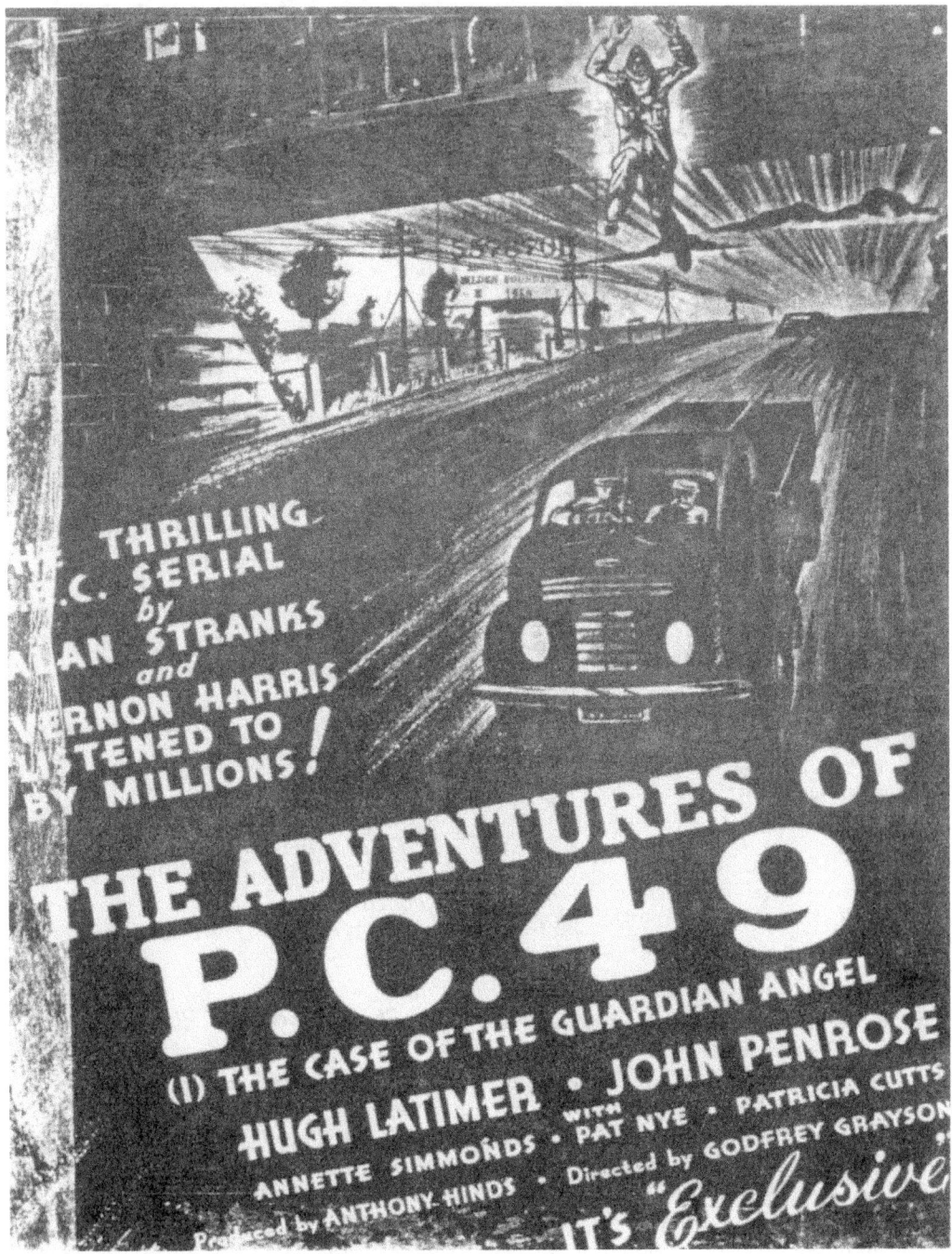

Trade advertisement.

1949

Celia—The Sinister Affair of Poor Aunt Nora

Released August 29, 1949 (U.K.); 67 minutes; B & W; 6013 feet; a Hammer Film Production; an Exclusive Films Release (U.K.); filmed at Cookham Dean, England; Director and Screenplay: Francis Searle; Producer: Anthony Hinds; Screenplay: A.R. Rawlinson, E.J. Mason, based on the BBC radio serial; Director of Photography: Cedric Williams; Music: Frank Spencer, Rupert Grayson; Camera: Peter Bryan; Production Manager: Arthur Barnes; Makeup: Phil Leakey; Editor: Cliff Turner; Art Director: Denis Wreford; Second Assistant: J. Sangster; Casting Director: Mary Harris; Pre-Planning: Prudence Sykes; Hair Styles: Monica Hustler; Continuity: Renee Glynn; Focus: Neil Binney; Clapper: Michael Read; Electricians: Percy Harms, Jack Curtis, Charles Mullett; Stills Photographer: John Jay; First Assistant Director: Leon Bijou; Sound: Edgar Vetter, Gordon Everett, Percy Britten; Construction: Fred Ricketts, Michael Lyons, Tom Money; U.K. Certificate: U.

Hy Hazell (Celia), Bruce Lester (Larry Peters), John Bailey (Lester Martin), Elsie Wagstaff (Aunt Nora), Ferdy Mayne (Antonio), Lockwood West (Doctor Cresswell), John Sharpe (Mr. Haldane), Joan Hickson (Mrs. Haldane), James Raglan (Inspector Parker), Jasmine Dee (Miss Arnold), June Elvin (Ruby), Charles Paton (Grocer), Olive Walter (Woman in shop), Grace Denbeigh-Russell (Woman in shop).

Celia (Hy Hazell), a young actress, sees a hat in a Bond Street boutique but cannot afford it. When her friend Larry (Bruce Lester), a private investigator, offers to pay her to help him on a case, Celia quickly accepts. Masquerading as a maid, Celia infiltrates the home of Aunt Nora (Elsie Wagstaff), an elderly woman who has married Lester (John Bailey), a much younger man. Larry was hired by Nora's relatives (John Sharpe, Joan Hickson) who are convinced that Lester plans to murder her. Celia discovers that Nora is being drugged by Lester's crony, Dr. Cresswell (Lockwood West), but the old lady refuses to leave the house when Celia warns her of the plot. On the night of the planned murder, Celia takes Nora's place while Larry and Inspector Parker (James Raglan) stake out the house. The plan goes awry when Lester spots Nora leaving the house, but is accidently killed by his own death-trap before any harm comes to Celia. With her well-earned fee, Celia goes back for the hat but finds, to her surprise, that Aunt Nora has beaten her to it!

Hammer's comedy-mystery *Celia* began production on April 4, 1949, at Dial Close, Cookham Dean with Francis Searle directing the first of his nine films for the company. Searle had been given rehearsal time prior to filming, but was interrupted by protests. Local residents objected to what they felt was a betrayal of the county's Planning Commission code by permitting filming at Dial Close. Letters of complaint cited that Hammer's generators caused their houses to vibrate, arc lamps that were too bright, and that the estate should not, by law, be used for commercial purposes. Hammer speeded up the production just in case the Planning Board decided with the protesters.

Jimmy Sangster recalled for the authors (August, 1993): "A dozen of us used to sleep over during the week, and Hammer employed a housekeeper to take care of us! It was during this period that I met my first wife, Monica Hustler, who was the hairdresser on all the early Hammer films."

Phil Leakey (February, 1992) told the authors,

> At the time, there was a shortage of rooms. So, for a night or so, Hy was sleeping in one of the estate's bedrooms. One morning I arrived early; and in order to get into my makeup room, I had to pass through her bedroom. I remember quite well the not-too-happy look she gave me and one of the early call artists as we banged on her door and marched through. However, she was a nice, pleasant girl and forgave us.

While Hammer's solicitors tried to hold off the angry villagers, production was completed on May 12. Due to the protests, however, Hammer was soon forced to find new accommodations and settled on Oakley Court, Bray.

Celia was released on August 29, 1949, on the ABC circuit to limited but positive

42 *Meet Simon Cherry* (1949)

Hugh Moxey (left) as the intrepid Rev. Simon Cherry.

reviews. *The Kinematograph Weekly* (August 25) called the film "A neat and tidy romantic comedy/crime melodrama. Hy Hazell contributes a good all-around performance and the support is adequate, the dialogue smooth, and the staging well up to standard." Based on a BBC radio serial, *Celia* had a built-in audience and almost certainly attracted a crowd. Hammer gave Hy Hazell a big buildup in the trade papers and was, apparently, planning for her to become a star.

Meet Simon Cherry

Released January, 1950 (U.K.); 67 minutes; B & W; 6063 feet; a Hammer Film Production; released through Exclusive (U.K.); filmed at Cookham Dean; Director: Godfrey Grayson; Producer: Anthony Hinds; Screenplay: A.R. Rawlinson, Godfrey Grayson; Original Story: Godfrey Grayson, based on the BBC radio series *Meet the Rev*; Director of Photography: Cedric Williams; Art Director: Denis Wreford; Editor: Ray Pitt; Music: Frank Spencer; U.K. Certificate: U.

Hugh Moxey (Simon Cherry, "The Rev"), Jeanette Tregarthen (Monica Harling), Anthony Forwood (Alan Colville), Ernest Butcher (Young), Zena Marshall (Lisa Colville), John Bailey (Henry Dantry), Courtney Hope (Lady Harling), Gerald Case (Doctor Smailes), Arthur Lovegrove (Charlie).

"The Rev" Simon Cherry (Hugh Moxey) is persuaded by Charlie (Arthur Lovegrove), his assistant at the Parish Boy's Club, to slow down and take a vacation. He takes off for the country in Charlie's ancient car, which breaks down, stranding Simon as a storm approaches. He finds shelter at Harling Manor where Lady Harling (Courtney Hope) asks him to spend the night, joining her daughters Monica (Jeanette Tregarthen) and Lisa (Zena Marshall), her nephew

Henry (John Bailey), and Lisa's husband, Alan (Anthony Forwood). Lisa is an invalid, and she is about to leave with Alan to recuperate in South Africa. After all retire, Young (Ernest Butcher), the butler, finds Lisa dead. Dr. Smailes (Gerald Case) is summoned, and Simon begins to investigate after Henry accuses Alan of murder.

Henry was in love with Lisa, but she rejected him in favor of Alan, who had dropped Monica in her favor. Lisa's pain was eased by sleeping pills provided by Young. Simon determines that Lisa died of a heart attack; and as he leaves, the Harlings have grown closer as a family.

A key aspect of Hammer's early success was using a presold title or character, preferably from a BBC radio production, to attract an audience. The company bought the rights to *Meet the Rev*, a BBC serial, in December, 1948, with a series of films in mind. Casting was completed by mid–December, but filming was held off until May 30, 1949. The title was changed to *Meet Simon Cherry* for the November 22 trade show at the Rialto. *The Kinematograph Weekly* (November 23) was impressed. "Hugh Moxey makes a favorable film debut. Polished mystery—melodrama illustrating an intriguing and exciting chapter from the casebook of Simon Cherry, famous fighting Padre. Competent acting and fluent direction preserve continuity and amplify the neat showmanlike climax."

The casting of the unknown Moxey indicates that he was being groomed to star in a series. Why the series never developed remains a mystery, since the film seemed to have everything in its favor. Perhaps the still running BBC program worked against the picture—why pay for entertainment that comes into your home for free?

Despite some good reviews, the Reverend-cum-sleuth Simon Cherry failed to click with moviegoers.

The Man in Black

Released January, 1950 (U.K.); 75 minutes; B & W; 6974 feet; a Hammer Film Production; an Exclusive Films Release (U.K.); filmed at Oakley Court (Bray), England; Director: Francis Searle; Producer: Anthony Hinds; Screenplay: John Gilling, based on an original story by Francis Searle and on the BBC Radio Series; Director of Photography: Cedric Williams; Editor: Ray Pitt; Art Director: Denis Wreford; Music: Frank Spencer; Sound: United Programmes; First Assistant Director: Jimmy Sangster; Second Assistant Director: Jack Cooper; Lighting Camera: Sidney James; Focus: Michael Reed; Camera: Peter Bryan; Boom Operator: Percy Britten; Stills Camera: John Jay; U.K. Certificate: U.

The Man in Black (1949)

Trade advertisement.

Betty Anne Davies (Bertha Clavering), Sheila Burrell (Janice), Sidney James (Henry Clavering/Hodson), Anthony Forwood (Victor Harrington), Hazel Penwarden (Joan), Valentine Dyall (Storyteller), Courtney Hope (Mrs. Carter), Molly Palmer (Elsie), Laurence Baskcomb (Sandford), Gerald Case (Doctor).

Wealthy Henry Clavering (Sidney James), a student of Yoga, dies suddenly—murdered by his wife Bertha (Betty Ann Davies). She and her daughter Janice (Sheila Burrell) from a previous marriage hope to inherit Oakleigh Towers, but Clavering's natural daughter Joan (Hazel Penwarden) stands in the way. They plan to have Joan declared insane, but Janice's fiancee Victor (Anthony Forwood) soon learns of the plot. He arouses Janice's jealousy by taking an interest in Joan's fortune, and threatens to reveal the conspiracy if Janice cuts him out. When the long time family servant Hodson questions Victor's motives, he is killed, and Victor hides the body in the family vault. Joan shocks the conspirators by announcing that she has communicated with Hodson.

Bertha suggests that a seance be held to contact Hodson from the other side as part of her plan to discredit Joan. Hodson suddenly appears—but it's actually Henry Clavering! His Yoga training enabled him to simulate his own death, and his information about the case enables the police to arrest Bertha, Victor, and Janice.

The Man in Black was yet another screen adaptation of a popular BBC serial and was Hammer's first production at Oakley Court. The company still owned Cookham Dean, and plans were being made to convert the studio into a prop construction facility. After moving in to Oakley Court, Hammer went to work on converting the estate into a workable studio, turning the first floor into a series of mini–sound stages, and the second into dressing, wardrobe, and makeup rooms. Phil Leakey, Hammer's resident makeup artist, recalled for the authors (February, 1992),

> The whole place was soaking wet with rain that had poured in through neglected roofs, and the floors were sagging. My first makeup room was an old bog, can, privy, toilette, W.C., or whatever you might like to refer to it as. It was halfway up a back staircase, and the 'throne' was boxed over and my store cupboard set up on it. A mirror was stuck on one wall with a few quite inadequate lights put around it. A small platform was put in the middle of the room, and a small chair was placed on that.

Leakey was not alone—stills photographer John Jay and hairdresser Monica Hustler also worked out of converted washrooms.

The Man in Black began production on August 8, 1949. Reprising his role from the radio serial as "The Storyteller" was Valentine Dyall, whose function was similar to that of "The Shadow" or "The Whistler." Sidney James made the first of his seven Hammer appearances and was described by Phil Leakey as being "great company and full of fun. He came to my room just before the day's work was finished and said, 'Let's hire a boat for the evening!' That was *some* evening! After rowing to a hotel in Bray Village, we had dinner, bought several bottles of booze, and got into the rowboat. We rowed and drifted up and down the Thames all night until it was time to report at the studio, which we did, feeling like nothing on this earth!"

Called back after directing *Celia*, Francis Searle was Hammer's most prolific director between 1949 and 1952, with nine films to his credit. Despite minor setbacks, including a noisy tractor and a constantly chiming clock, Searle brought the picture in on schedule. Reviews, following *The Man in Black*'s January, 1950, release, were sparse but positive. *The Kinematograph Weekly*: "Ingenious and thrilling, good characterization, surprise climax, elegant staging"; and *The Daily Film Renter*: "Excellent thriller and entertainment."

The Man in Black does not seem to have been released in America, which was visited by James Carreras during the film's production to begin negotiations with producer Robert L. Lippert. This proved to be an important step for the company that would pay dividends into the mid-1950s.

Room to Let

Released May 15, 1950 (U.K.); 68 minutes; B & W; 6103 feet; a Hammer Film Production; an Exclusive Films Release (U.K.); filmed at Oakley Court (Bray) and on location in London, England; Director, Screenplay: Godfrey Grayson; Producer: Anthony Hinds, based on the BBC Radio play by: Margery Allingham; Director of Photography: Cedric Williams; Editor: James Needs; Music: Frank Spencer; Camera: Peter Bryan; Cutter: Alfred Cox; Production Manager:

Arthur Barnes; Assistant Director: Jimmy Sangster; Continuity: Renee Glynn; Art Director: Denis Wreford; Sound Recordist: E. Vottor; Makeup: Phil Leakey; Hairdresser: Monica Hustler; Dress Designer: Myra Cullimore; Casting: Prudence Skyes; U.K. Certificate: A.

Jimmy Hanley (Airly Minter), Valentine Dyall (Dr. Fell), Christine Silver (Mrs. Musgrave), Merle Tottenham (Alice), Constance Smith (Molly Musgrave), Charles Hawtrey (Mike Atkinson), Aubrey Dexter (Harding), J. Anthony La Penna (JJ), Reginald Dyson (Sergeant Cranbourne), Lawrence Naismith (Editor), John Clifford (Atkinson), Stuart Saunders (Porter), Cyril Conway (Dr. Mansfield), Charles Houston (Tom), Harriet Pet-worth (Matron), Charles Mander (P.C. Smith), H. Hamilton Earle (Orderly), F.A. Williams (Butler), Archie Callum (Night Watchman).

Dr. Fell (Valentine Dyall), a tall, thin man in top hat and cloak, visits the home of Mrs. Musgrave (Christine Silver) in response to her advertisement of a "room to let." Her daughter Molly's (Constance Smith) beau, *London Gazette* reporter Curly Minter (Jimmy Hanley), visits Molly and, reading the day's paper, is irate that his story about a fire at a local mental institute has been edited and no longer mentions the fact that a patient is missing.

Dr. Fell has a Svengali-like hold on his landlady and her daughter, voicing objections to Molly's male visitors, ordering their servant about and insisting that the wheelchair-bound Mrs. Musgrave follow his medical advice. Molly hesitates to ask Fell to vacate only because she knows how badly they need the rent money.

Curly sets out to learn more about Fell, who he suspects may be the missing patient. Curly describes Fell to the local police sergeant, mentioning the hissing sound Fell sometimes emits while talking. The sergeant later remembers the only other person in his memory who had that trait—the infamous Jack the Ripper.

Convinced that Fell is the patient, Molly steals into his room and finds a map of London (with certain streets marked off) and surgical instruments. She later leaves to attend a fireworks display with another suitor, a shipping magnate (Michael Atkinson). Mrs. Musgrave finds herself alone in the house with Fell, who tells her about his maps and offers to show them to her.

A short while later, Curly and the police sergeant arrive to find Mrs. Musgrave sprawled on the floor in the hallway. Curly dashes upstairs and finds Fell's door locked. He runs to the back of the house and climbs a ladder, breaks the glass of Fell's locked window and finds Fell dead from a gunshot wound. Neither Curly nor the police can find the weapon, and the door is bolted from the inside.

Years later, Curly amuses some of his friends with the details of the story. After he leaves the party with his wife Molly, his friends speculate further and one of them realizes that the only one who could have secured the door bolt—thereby throwing off suspicion that it was Mrs. Musgrave all along—was Curly himself.

Room to Let was a preview of Hammer films to come, and, although crudely constructed, it had the Gothic flavor that would become Hammer's trademark. Jack the Ripper had been a long-time favorite screen villain. He was most notably played by Laird Cregar as *The Lodger* (1944), based on Marie Belloc Lowndes' story, which served as the basis for at least three earlier films. Hammer broke tradition by basing its picture on a television play by Margery Cellingham. Filming began at Oakley Court on October 6, 1949, with former child star Jimmy Hanley cast in a change of pace role as the hero. Valentine Dyall stole the picture as the sinister Dr. Fell. Makeup man Phil Leakey described Dyall for the authors (February, 1992). "I can still recall him chiefly for his stature and deep, impressive voice," he said, making Dyall sound like a prototype for Christopher Lee (with whom he appeared in *City of the Dead* in 1960). Constance Smith, Hanley's love interest, would again contend with the Ripper as played by Jack Palance in *Man in the Attic* (1953).

Room to Let was released on May 15, 1950, following a March 8 trade show at the Rialto, to positive reviews. *The Kinematograph Weekly* (March 9): "Theatrically effec-

Top: The authors have absolutely no idea what's going on in this photo from *The Man in Black*. *Bottom:* Musgraves (Constance Smith/Christine Silver) and Curly Minter (Jimmy Hanley) wonder if Dr. Fell (Valentine Dyall) is really the Ripper in Hammer's *Room to Let*.

Trade advertisement.

tive and faultlessly staged with a neat and tense climax. Dyall has a powerful screen presence; and *The Monthly Film Bulletin* (May): "Dyall is suitably sinister in this Victorian period piece." Told in flashback, the film's continuity seems to be unnecessarily disrupted, and Godfrey Grayson's direction is too stagy. These problems are more than offset by Grayson's and John Gilling's suspenseful screenplay, Dyall's outstanding performance, and the power of the Ripper myth. Hammer would attack the subject obliquely in the seventies in *Dr. Jekyll and Sister Hyde* and *Hands of the Ripper*.

Someone at the Door

Released June, 1950 (U.K.); 65 minutes; B & W; a Hammer Film Production; an Exclusive Films Release (U.K.); filmed at Oakley Court (Bray), England; Director: Francis Searle; Producer: Anthony Hinds; Screenplay: A.R. Rawlinson, based on a play by Major Campbell Christie and Dorothy Campbell Christie; Director of Photography: Walter Harvey; Editor: John Ferris; Music: Frank Spencer; Art Director: Denis Wreford; Production Manager: Arthur Banks; Continuity: Renee Glynn; Recordist: Edgar Vetter; Hair Stylist: Monica Hustler; Makeup: Phil Leakey; Casting: Prudence Sykes; Assistant Director: Jimmy Sangster; Camera: Peter Bryan; U.K. Certificate: U.

Yvonne Owen (Sally Martin), Michael Medwin (Ronnie Martin), Hugh Latimer (Bill Reed), Danny Green (Jim Price), Gary Marsh (Kapel), Campbell Singer (Inspector Spedding), John Kelly (P.C. O'Brien).

Sally Martin (Yvonne Owen) and her brother Ronnie (Michael Medwin) move into a shadowy manor house with a ghostly reputation. Ronnie, a newspaper reporter, is convinced that only a murder story will afford him recognition. He decides to fake a murder and set himself up as the prime suspect. Once he is arrested and convicted, his "victim" will turn up alive and well; he will then be exonerated and write his own story. When Sally inquires whom he plans to make his victim, Ronnie proclaims her the perfect candidate.

When Sally's boyfriend Bill (Hugh Latimer) visits and asks why caretaker Soames hasn't seen to the housekeeping, Sally informs him that Soames vanished. The Martins' neighbor Mr. Kapel (Gary Marsh) sent over his own gardener Price (Danny Green) to help out, but Sally confesses that she and Ronnie are intimidated by the tough-looking retainer. Ronnie lets Bill in on his proposed scheme and asks Bill, a medical student, to provide the corpse he'll need for his "crime." Bill reluctantly agrees to furnish one from the hospital morgue.

Police Chief O'Brien (John Kelly)

appears at the Martins' to investigate the disappearance of Soames. Ronnie uses the visit to plant the first seeds of suspicion in the policeman's mind, shouting at Sally and ordering the police officer off the premises. He exhibits the same sort of behavior later during a visit by neighbor Kapel who is actually a bookkeeper, and his cohort, gardener Price, has been trying to scare the Martins out of their own house via ghostly screams in the night.

On the night of Sally's "murder," Ronnie and Bill bury the morgue corpse in the greenhouse. Scotland Yard Detective Spedding (Campbell Singer) learns of Sally's "disappearance" and is instantly suspicious. Meanwhile, Sally, hiding in a secret room, finds a case containing a fortune in jewelry inside a suit of armor.

A body found in the lake turns out to be that of Soames, the double-crossing partner of Kapel and Price. Kapel and Price menace Sally, Ronnie and Bill, threatening to burn Sally's eyes with a cigar unless one of them produces the stolen jewels. In a whirlwind series of mysterious events, Kapel and Price are both shot and killed, and Ronnie deduces that it was Soames and *Detective Spedding* who pulled the jewel theft. Ronnie and Bill overpower the detective and, as Chief O'Brien takes charge of the prisoner, Ronnie calls his editor with "the story of the century."

Between November 22, 1948, and November 3, 1949, Hammer completed six features on a continuous shooting schedule at Cookham Dean and Oakley Court. Most were budgeted at £15,000 and given five-week schedules. The company was coming under the scrutiny of Britain's largest cinema chains, and Associated British Cinemas made an attractive offer. However, it was becoming obvious that to *really* succeed, Hammer needed to crack the American market, which it would soon do through its association with Robert L. Lippert. *Someone at the Door* began production on November 24, 1949. Although the company's previous six films were based on BBC radio material, it was based on a stage production. An earlier film was made in 1936 by British International.

Hammer's version of the comedy thriller contained several macabre bits—like the ghostly screams in the opening scene, and the threat to blind Sally with a lighted cigar. The energetic cast led by Michael Medwin and Yvonne Owen is enjoyable, as are the plentiful shots of Oakley Court. *Someone at the Door* was trade shown in late January, 1950, and released in June to limited reviews. *The Kinematograph Weekly* (January 27): "A humorous and exciting yarn with a well balanced cast and showmanlike treatment"; and *The Monthly Film Bulletin* (June): "Conventional." Filmed entirely on the Oakley Court grounds, the film betrays its stage origins but does so to great effect. *Someone at the Door* is a pleasant romp that leads the viewer merrily to its surprising climax. Francis Searle, Hammer's "house director" and writer, A.R. Rawlinson, found an excellent balance between thrills and comedy, making this one of the company's best early pictures.

1950

What the Butler Saw

Released September, 1950 (U.K.); 61 minutes; B & W; 5644 feet; a Hammer Film Production; an Exclusive Release (U.K.); filmed at Oakley Court; Director: Godfrey Grayson; Producer: Anthony Hinds; Screenplay: A.R. Rawlinson and E.J. Mason, based on a story by Roger and Donald Good; U.K. Certificate: U.

Edward Rigby (the Earl), Henry Mollison (Bembridge), Mercy Haystead (Lapis), Michael Ward (Gerald), Eleanor Hallam (Lady Mary), Peter Burton (Bill Fenton), Anne Valery (Elaine), Tonie MacMillan (Mrs. Thimble), Mallie Palmer (Maudie), Howard Charlton (Perks), Alfred Harris (Bishop), George Bishop (the General), Norman Pitt (Policeman).

After retiring as Governor of a tropical island, the Earl (Edward Rigby) with his butler Bembridge (Henry Mollison) returns to his ancestral home in England. While unpacking, he discovers a stowaway—Lapis (Mercy Haystead), the Island king's daugh-

50 *What the Butler Saw* (1950)

Lacking a name actor in the lead, *What the Butler Saw* soon receded into obscurity.

ter who loves Bembridge. The butler is embarrassed, and Gerald (Michael Ward), the Earl's grandson in the Foreign Office, is appalled. The government fears an incident and insists that Lapis be kept hidden, but gossip spreads through the village. However, the Earl and his broadminded granddaughter Elaine (Anne Valery) fail to see a problem. Reporter Peter Burton (Bill Fenton) is sent to investigate but falls for Elaine instead. The Earl solves the problem by having Bembridge appointed Governor and

Edward Rigby entertains his guests in *What the Butler Saw* (1950).

returns to the island with him and Lapis, serving as their butler.

What the Butler Saw was another in a string of undistinguished but competently made Hammer films that now appears to be "lost," possibly due to its lack of a star actor. Production began on January 9, 1950, with a four-week schedule. But, unlike in Hollywood, producers could not depend on the weather. A small example of this problem was addressed in *The Daily Cinema* (February 9): "Waiting for the sunshine in an English January sounds like the height of optimism, but it was justifiable for Godfrey Grayson directing the final shot of *What the Butler Saw*." In order to match the previous shot filmed a week earlier, Grayson *had* to have sunshine and waited two days for it. Despite this delay, filming ended on schedule on February 3. The picture was trade shown at the Rialto on June 22 and went into general release in September to positive reviews. *Today's Cinema* (June 23): "Unpretentious, yet lively screen farce, put over with disarming gusto by a competent cast"; and *The Kinematograph Weekly* (June 25): "Hardy light British booking. The exhuberant fooling has a touch of sex...."

What the Butler Saw was followed by another comedy, *The Lady Craved Excitement*. Neither film must have performed well, as Hammer's next comedy came twenty-four films later. The company dabbled in comedy periodically but, with few exceptions, never got it quite right.

The Lady Craved Excitement

Released September, 1950 (U.K.); 60 minutes; B & W; 6342 feet; a Hammer Film Production; an Exclusive Release (U.K.); filmed at Oakley Court; Director: Francis Searle; Producer: Anthony Hinds; Screenplay: John Gilling, Edward J. Mason, Francis Searle, from the BBC radio serial by Mason; Director of Photography:

The Lady Craved Excitement (1950)

Stoic Andrew Keir in a slapstick comedy?

Walter Harvey; Editor: John Ferris; Music: Frank Spencer; Songs: James Dyrenforth, George Melachrino; Dances: Leslie Roberts; U.K. Certificate: A.

Hy Hazell (Pat), Michael Medwin (Johnny), Sidney James (Carlo), Andrew Keir (Peterson), Thelma Grigg (Julia), Danny Green (Boris), John Longden (Inspector James), Ian Wilson (Mugsy), Barbara Hamilton, Jasmine Dee (Chorus Girls), Gordon Mulholland (Lunatic).

Pat (Hy Hazell) and Johnny (Michael Medwin) perform an act at Carlo's Club, and her penchant for excitement drives Carlo

(Sidney James) wild. While reading a newspaper, Pat learns that a mad killer, wearing a false beard, is on the loose. Naturally, she attempts to pull off the beard of Peterson (Andrew Keir), a valued club patron. Oddly, he finds Pat enchanting and asks her to pose for a painting—as Anne Boleyn, about to be beheaded!

Inspector James (John Longden), meanwhile, is investigating a series of art thefts, with Boris (Danny Green) and Mugsy (Ian Wilson), his main suspects. They kidnap Pat, following Julia's (Thelma Grigg) plan to steal an art treasure Pat discovered at Peterson's. She plans to trade a replica of the Crown Jewels for the deranged artist's priceless oil painting. Pat escapes and is "rescued" by Peterson who wants to finish his painting, but Inspector James and Johnny arrive just in time.

Following the completion of *What the Butler Saw*, Hammer rushed its second comedy in a row into production on February 28, 1950, with a location shoot. Filming moved to Oakley Court on March 6, and concluded on the 31st. *The Lady Craved Excitement* was the last of a group of five pictures produced at Oakley Court. *The Daily Cinema* (April 13, 1950) noted that after the film's conclusion, "all hands have moved to the new home at Gilston Park." This would be a short stay—after four pictures, the company would move into the new Bray Studios.

After a July 27, 1950, trade show at the Rialto, *The Lady Craved Excitement* went into general release in September. Those few who reviewed the film found it slight, but amusing. *The Kinematograph Weekly* (August 3): "Amiable nonsense, innocuous fooling"; and the British Film Institute's *Monthly Bulletin* (September): "A light crime comedy—with some impossible and quite amusing situations."

Apparently, Hammer hoped to make a star of Hy Hazell, giving her a big promotional campaign in the trade papers. After she failed to register in *The Lady Craved Excitement*, her Hammer career ended, but she continued to act regularly through the fifties. Soon after the trade show, Hammer/Exclusive entered into an agreement with Robert Lippert. "Exclusive has signed a five-year contract," *The Kinematograph Weekly* (August 3) reported, "with Lippert Productions to distribute here every film that the company makes." Their association dated back to 1948 on a picture-to-picture basis, and would last until *The Glass Cage*'s American release in 1955.

The Black Widow

Released October 22, 1951; 62 minutes; B & W; 5537 feet; a Hammer Film Production; an Exclusive Film Release (U.K.); filmed at Gilston Park, England; Director: Vernon Sewell; Producer: Anthony Hinds; Screenplay: Alan McKinnon, based on the BBC radio serial *Return to Darkness* by Lester Powell; Editor: James Needs; Director of Photography: Walter Harvey; U.K. Certificate: A.

Christine Norden (Christine), Robert Ayers (Mark Sherwin), Anthony Forwood (Paul), John Longden (Kemp), Jennifer Jayne (Sheila), John Harvey (Dr. Wallace), Reginald Dyson (Police Sergeant), Madoline Thomas (Mrs. Gladstone), Joan Carol (Manageress), Jill Hulbert (Maid), Bill Hodge (Receptionist).

While driving on an isolated road, Mark Sherwin (Robert Ayres) sees a body and stops to investigate. The "corpse" springs into life, knocks Mark unconscious, and steals his wallet. While escaping in Mark's car, the thief loses control and dies in a crash. Mark staggers to a nearby house and is taken in by Mr. Kemp (John Longden) and his daughter Sheila (Jennifer Jayne) who nurses him back to health. Having lost his memory as well as his wallet, Mark has no clue to his identity.

The chance discovery of a ticket stub leads Mark to recover his memory. But, upon returning home, he is shocked to find that his wife Christine (Christine Norden) has identified the thief's body as being his, and plans to marry her lover Paul (Anthony Forwood) after inheriting Mark's estate. After allowing the funeral to take place, the conspirators must now murder Mark. During an attempt on his life, Mark kills Paul in self-defense. When Chrsitine realizes the plot has failed, she commits suicide.

Based on the radio drama *Return to Darkness*, *The Black Widow* was Hammer's first production at Gilston Park. Production began on April 17, 1950, with Vernon Sewell directing. Former singer Christine Norden's acting career began in *Mine Own Executioner* (1947). She was given a big buildup by Hammer in the trade papers, including full page portrait shots of her in "widow weeds." Unfortunately, her career ended at age 28 after only two more films. *The Black Widow* was trade shown on June 20 and failed to impress the *Monthly Film Bulletin* (July, 1951): "The characters never seem real and act as if they wished it were over." Forty years later, *Halliwell's Film Guide* thought the movie was "a whole lot less interesting than it sounds, acting and direction being alike laborious."

Christine Norden as *The Black Widow*.

The Black Widow was a minor entry, but it was Hammer's first to feature a woman as the main villain. This was a theme that would appear with increasing regularity in the company's pictures, peaking in the early seventies with *The Vampire Lovers*, *Countess Dracula*, and *Dr. Jekyll and Sister Hyde*.

The Rossiter Case

Released January 21, 1951 (U.K.); 75 minutes; B & W; 6828 feet; a Hammer Film Production; an Exclusive Films Release (U.K.); filmed at Gilston Park, England; Director, Screenplay: Francis Searle; Producer: Anthony Hinds; Screenplay: John Hunter, based on the play *The Rossiters* by Kenneth Hyde; Director of Photography: Jimmy Harvey; Editor: John Ferris; Music: Frank Spencer. U.K. Certificate: A.

Helen Shingler (Liz Rossiter), Clement McCallin (Peter), Sheila Burrell (Honor), Frederick Leister (Sir James Ferguson), Ann Codrington (Marty), Henry Edwards (Dr. Bendix), Dorothy Batley (Nurse West), Gabrielle Blunt (Alice), Eleanore Bryan (Agnes), Ewen Solon (Inspector), Robert Percival (Sergeant), Dennis Castle (Constable), Frederic Steger (Hobson), Stanley Baker (Joe), Anthony Allen (Arthur).

Due to an automobile accident, Liz Rossiter (Helen Shingler) is confined to a wheelchair. Her marriage to Peter (Clement McCallin) is strained, and the weak-willed man is easy prey for his calculating sister-in-law Honor (Sheila Burrell). Dr. Bendix (Henry Edwards) suggests that Liz see a specialist, but her paralysis is incurable. As Peter becomes more involved with Honor, she hints that she is pregnant to force him to divorce Liz. When Liz learns of her sister's plan, she confronts Honor. They argue;

Trade advertisement.

and when Honor produces Peter's gun, Liz miraculously overcomes her disability and wrestles the weapon away. It goes off, and Honor is killed.

When the police find Honor's body and Peter's gun, he is arrested. Since he was drunk at the time of the shooting, Peter is unable to produce an alibi. Liz decides to confess and, while defending her husband, finds the power to walk. Peter realizes the folly of his actions, and he and Liz are reunited.

This little seen and long forgotten picture was based on Kenneth Hyde's stage play *The Rossiters*, which was the film's original title. It began production on May 22, 1950, and finished on June 9. A trade show was held on January 21 on the Gaumont-British circuit to limited and mixed reviews. The *Kinematograph Weekly* (January 18): "The picture makes the most of the physical disabilities and mental anguish of the luckless wife and finishes on a theatrically effective note"; and *The Monthly Film Bulletin* (February): "This melodrama, adapted from a stage play, has been almost literally transferred to the screen. The result is a film artificial in presentation and weighed down by dialogue."

Lacking major stars or a famous source, *The Rossiter Case* is not listed in any film guides and seems to have vanished.

To Have and to Hold

Released February, 1951 (U.K.); 63 minutes; B & W; 5717 feet; a Hammer Film Production; released by Exclusive; filmed at Gilston Park; Director: Godfrey Grayson; Producer: Anthony Hinds; Screenplay: Reginald Long, from Lionel Brown's play; Director of Photography: James Harvey; Editor: James Needs; Music: Frank Spencer; Song "Midsummer Day" by Frank Spencer and Reginald Long; U.K. Certificate: A.

Avis Scott (June), Patrick Barr (Brian), Robert Ayres (Max), Harry Fine (Robert), Ellen Pollock (Roberta), Richard Warner (Cyril), Eunice Gayson (Peggy), Peter Neil (Dr. Pritchard).

The marriage of June de Winter (Avis Scott) and the hard working Brian Harding (Patrick Barr) comes just in time to aid the de Winters. But, despite Brian's attempts to restore their Halston estate, his presence is resented by June's siblings Robert (Harry Fine) and Roberta (Ellen Pollock). When Robert forces Brian to ride an unmanageable horse, he is thrown and crippled. Cousin Max's (Robert Ayres) arrival from Argentina takes up the slack, and the restoration continues. He and June are attracted and, when

Brian finds out, tries to make things easier by verbally mistreating her. Roberta learns that Max has an adult daughter Peggy (Eunice Gayson) and invites her to Halston, hoping she will cause dissention and give the de Winters more control. But, due to Brian's counseling, Peggy accepts Max and June's affair. Brian is dying, and with the little time remaining, takes Peggy to Italy to study singing. He gives Max a gift of his wedding ring, inscribed "To Have and To Hold."

To Have and to Hold continued Hammer's policy of basing their films on existing works, and was the thirteenth straight picture to do so. The movie began production on June 26, 1950, at Gilston Park while *The Dark Light* was on location. Hammer's resources were stretched to the limit by the simultaneous filming, but felt it necessary to get as many films on the screen as possible. From 1950 to 1952, the company produced 22 films, and the only way to accomplish that was to double up. With this film, Hammer entered the "soap opera" genre for the first and last time, and it was a departure from the company's typical murder mystery. It's probable that the rights to Lionel Brown's play were easily (and inexpensively) obtainable. Whatever the reason for the departure, Hammer went back to its standard thriller immediately.

To Have and to Hold was trade shown on February 14, 1951, at the Rialto and was released later that month to indifferent reviews—*The Kinematograph Weekly* (no date): "The acting is a trifle uneven and much of the dialogue and sentiment is outmoded, but it hands out a pretty safe line in pulp fiction"; and the British Film Institute's *Monthly Bulletin* (February): "The situation is strained for all concerned." Continuing a tradition followed by many quota quickies, *To Have and to Hold*, with its lack of "name" actors, seems to have vanished.

The Dark Light

Released April 23, 1951 (U.K.); 66 minutes; B & W; 6025 feet; a Hammer Film Production; an Exclusive Films Release (U.K.); filmed on location in Portsmouth, England; Director and Screenplay: Vernon Sewell; Executive Producer: Anthony Hinds; Producer: Michael Carreras; U.K. Certificate: A.

Albert Lieven (Mark), David Greene (Johnny), Norman MacOwen (Rigby), Martin Benson (Luigi), Jack Stewart (Matt), Catherine Blake (Linda), Joan Carol (Joan), John Harvey (Roger), John Longden (Stephen).

The crew of the yacht *Gelert* notices that the lamp on Thimble Rock Island lighthouse is out. They search the lighthouse and find it abandoned, with a missing page from the skipper's logbook and blood dripping from the ceiling. A flashback reveals what happened the previous day.

Rigby (Norman MacOwen), the lighthouse skipper, and his assistants Matt (Jack Stewart) and Johnny (David Greene) are fogged in. When the bank lifts, they spot a motorboat drifting by. They rescue Mark (Albert Lieven), his secretary Linda (Catherine Blake) and Mark's friend Luigi (Martin Benson). Rigby learns that they are bank robbers fleeing the country when their boat failed. The criminals win over Matt and Johnny in their plan to steal the lighthouse ship, but Rigby destroys its engine. They kill him and, with Matt and Johnny, try to row away in the damaged boat. During the escape, a fight breaks out, and Matt and Mark fall overboard. Johnny has a change of heart and takes the boat to shore to give himself and the remaining gang up to the authorities.

The Dark Light was Hammer's last feature shot at Gilston Park before moving to Down Place. Written and directed by Vernon Sewell, it was primarily filmed off the coast of Portsmouth on Sewell's personal yacht and at Nab Lighthouse. Filming began on July 10, 1950, and ended on August 19, as 23-year-old Michael Carreras brought his first picture as producer in on schedule. Carreras recalled in *Little Shoppe of Horrors* 5, that after being in the Story Department, "I suppose I became a bit itchy, and they gave me my first film to do. It was to be made on a thing called Nab Lighthouse. Well, the 'Nab Tower' looked like something which the Gas Board might have thrown

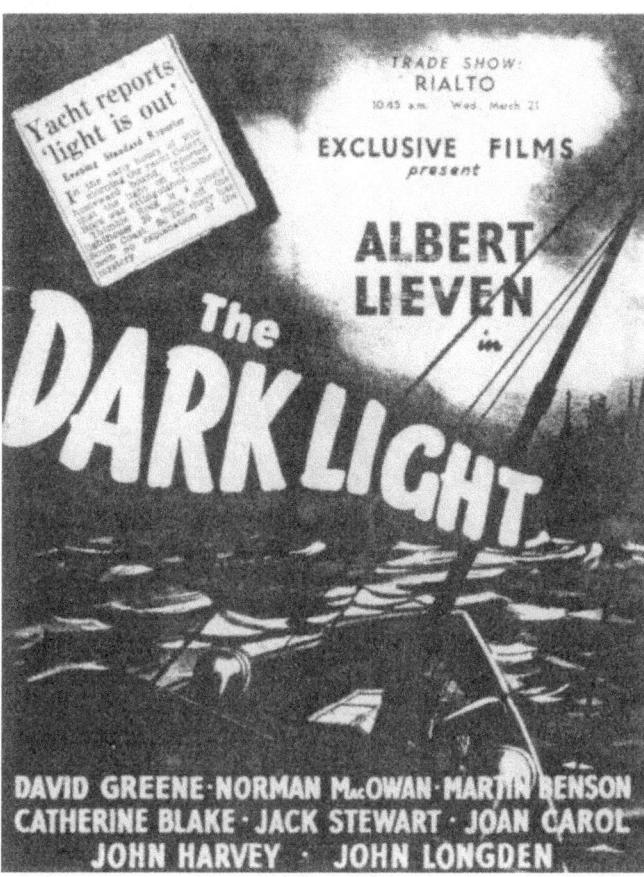

Trade advertisement.

into the sea—no shape, no style, no character—and that was my first film!" The cast of the unknowns was headed by "hero" David Greene, who was married to "villainess" Catherine Blake and later became a director (*The Shuttered Room*, 1967).

The Dark Light was released on April 23, 1951, to negative reviews. *The Kinematograph Weekly* (March 29): "A dreary, incoherent crime melodrama—completely lacks purpose and point"; and *The Monthly Film Bulletin* (May): "Incoherent plot development, clumsy handling, and generally indifferent performance." Despite these blistering reviews, Hammer was one of the few British film companies holding its own during an uncertain period. Hammer planned to make seven features, as well as thirteen shorts to be sold to American television as a series called *Yoga and You*. The sale never materialized, but three shorts were released theatrically. James Carreras also tried to negotiate a production agreement with producer Sol Lesser to co-produce nine pictures with a guaranteed American release. This too failed to materialize, and only two movies were actually made. Hammer's dream of entering the American market had to be postponed until Robert L. Lippert came into the picture.

1951

Cloudburst

Released January, 1952; 92 minutes (U.K.), 83 minutes (U.S.); B & W; 8100 feet; a Hammer Film Production; an Exclusive Release (U.K.), a Rudolph Manter Presentation, a United Artists Release (U.S.); filmed at Down Place; Director: Francis Searle; Producers: Anthony Hinds, Alexander Paal; Screenplay: Francis Searle and Leo Marks, from Marks' story; Director of Photography: Walter Harvey; Music composed by: Frank Spencer; Played by: the Royal Philharmonic; Art Director: Donald Russo; Production Manager: Arthur Barnes; Assistant Director: Jimmy Sangster; Editor: John Ferris; Sound Recordist: Edgar Wettel; Makeup: Phil Leakey; Continuity: Renee Glynn; Hairstyles: Anne Fox; Casting: Michael Carreras; Camera Operator: Peter Bryan; Production Secretary: Mary Shirtlift; U.K. Certificate: A.

Robert Preston (John Graham), Elizabeth Sellars (Carol Graham), Colin Tapley (Inspector Davis), Sheila Burrell (Lorna), Harold Lang (Mickie), Mary Germaine (Peggy), George Woodbridge (Sgt. Ritchie), Lyn Evans (Peters), Thomas Heathcote (Jackie), Edith Sharpe (Mrs. Reece), Daphne Anderson (Kate), Edward Lexy (Cardew), Noel Howlett (Johnson), James Mills (Thompson), Martin Boddey (Desk Sergeant), Robert Brown (Carter), Charles Saynor (PC Taylor), Stanley Baker (Milkman).

Cloudburst (1951)

John Graham (Robert Preston), head of the Foreign Office cypher group, and his crippled wife, Carol (Elizabeth Sellars), are expecting their first child. While looking at some land they plan to buy, Carol is run down by a speeding car driven by Mickie (Harold Lang) who, with Lorna (Sheila Burrell), is fleeing a robbery. They overpower Graham and, after reversing over Carol's body, drive off. Graham takes a leave of absence and, using his friends in the intelligence community, traces Mickie. He kills Mickie by running back and forth over him with his car. Beside himself with rage, Graham foolishly leaves behind a list of birthday presents for Carol—written in code.

The police have traced Lorna to a London suburb and are there when Graham arrives, but he escapes unnoticed. But, he is the main suspect due to the cypher and the method of Mickie's murder. Graham learns that Lorna is being transferred by van to Wordsworth Prison, and causes the van's tires to burst. He then drives over Lorna's body as she lies in the road. When questioned by Inspector Davis (Colin Tapley), Graham rashly gives himself away. Rather than face prison—and life without Carol—Graham tries to poison himself. Subdued by the police and willing to accept his fate, he calmly walks to a waiting squad car.

Early January, 1951, found James Carreras hosting a luncheon celebrating a deal with American film producer Alexander Paal, who would provide American stars for Hammer's productions and the move to Down Place. Located next to Oakley Court, Down Place would soon be known as Bray Studios. After settling in on January 8 to begin *Cloudburst*, director Francis Searle (*The Kinematograph Weekly*, January 18, 1951)

American star Robert Preston top-lined Hammer's *Cloudburst*.

said it was, "the most convenient house studio" he ever worked in. Searle enjoyed the freedom given by the house design, especially the ability to shoot through three inter-connecting rooms. Seven of the rooms were so large that sets could easily be built inside them. *The Kinematograph Weekly* (January 4) reported, "In accordance with Exclusive's current policy of securing top-line American artists, Robert Preston is being brought over from the States by Producer Alexander Paal. It is the first of seven productions lined up by Exclusive for 1951." In addition to the features, thirteen shorts—each 27 minutes long—were planned for American television.

Cloudburst wrapped up on February 15, 1951, and was trade shown at the Rialto on June 21, and released to the ABC circuit in January, 1952. One reason for the holdup

The popular policeman returned after a two-year hiatus in *A Case for P.C. 49*.

was a problem with Joseph Breen, the American Censor, who objected to Preston's character committing suicide as was done in the original version. The scene was re-shot for both American and British prints. *Cloudburst* is quite violent, and it's unnerving to see the film's "hero" commit cold-blooded revenge murders, not unlike Charles Bronson in *Death Wish*. Reviewers were not impressed: The British Film Institute's *Monthly Bulletin* (July, 1951): "A violent and implausible thriller"; *The Kinematograph Weekly* (June 21): "Bizarre, yet holding, out of the rut thick ear"; *Variety* (January 10, 1952): "This version has sufficient variations to help balance off the triteness of the basic plot."

Despite the lukewarm reviews, *Cloudburst* was a breakthrough for Hammer. It was their first Anglo-American production, and Robert Preston was their first American star. Although unmoved by the movie, the trade press was pleased with the Exclusive-Paal agreement, which was looked at as being beneficial to the whole British film industry.

A Case for P.C. 49

Released July 23, 1951 (U.K.); 81 minutes; B & W; 7250 feet; a Hammer Film Production; an Exclusive Films Release (U.K.); filmed at Down Place (Bray Studios), England; Director: Francis Searle; Producer: Anthony Hinds; Screenplay: Alan Stranks, Vernon Harris, based on the BBC radio series; Director of Photography: Walter Harvey; Music: Frank Spencer; U.K. Certificate: U.

Brian Reece (P.C. 49), Joy Shelton (Joan Carr), Christine Norden (Della Dainton), Leslie Bradley (Palantine), Gordon McLeod (Inspector Wilson), Campbell Singer (Sergeant Wright), Jack Stewart (Cutler), Michael Balfour (Chubby Price), Michael Ripper (George Steele), Joan Seton (Elsie), Edna Morris (Mrs. Bott), John Sharpe (Desk Sergeant), Frank Hawkins (Police Sergeant), John Barry (Pewter), John Warren (Coffee Dan).

Model Della Dainton (Christine Norden) and her lover Victor Palantine (Leslie Bradley) plot to murder Jimmy Pewter (John Barry), a millionaire who has named her as his sole beneficiary. She produces an old letter in which he threatened to kill her for leaving him and asks for police protection. P.C. 49 (Brian Reece) is guarding Della as Palantine kills Pewter, making it seem accidental. Joan Carr (Joy Shelton), P.C. 49's fiancée, also an officer, suspects foul play. Confident that he is not suspected, Palantine turns his attention to his disloyal employees, Cutler (Jack Stewart) and

Chubby (Michael Balfour) who are trying to enlist ex-convict George Steele (Michael Ripper) to murder their boss.

During Joan's investigation, she discovers evidence implicating Palantine in Pewter's murder, but is kidnapped before she can report it. P.C. 49 finds her in Palantine's car, and its owner knifed in his house. Steele's fingerprints are on the knife, and he is arrested but escapes. Joan finds that Della has thrown in with Cutler and Chubby. They capture her and, later, P.C. 49. The couple is freed by Steele, and he and P.C. 49 pursue Cutler and find him in his brewery hideout. During the shootout, Steele is wounded and Cutler is captured. He confesses to Palantine's murder, clearing Steele.

Hammer brought back its popular flatfoot after a two year interval, but replaced Hugh Latimer with Brian Reece, the voice of the character on the BBC. He literally began and ended his career with Hammer—his last role was in *Watch It Sailor!* The film went into production at Down Place on February 17, 1951, concluding five weeks later on March 16. *A Case for P.C. 49* was released on the ABC circuit on July 23 to mixed reviews. *The Kinematograph Weekly* (July 19, 1951): "Laughs without sacrificing essential punch"; and *The Monthly Film Bulletin* (August): "The many moments of suspense too often end in elaborate anticlimaxes and the over-complicated plot draws to an over-simplified and abrupt ending."

A Case for P.C. 49 provided Michael Ripper, who seemingly appeared in every picture the company made, with one of his most lengthy roles. A talented, versatile actor, Ripper was too often wasted by Hammer in walk-on roles beneath his ability. His quirky on-screen personality made him difficult to cast, but he always shone when given a decent role in films like *Captain Clegg* and *The Pirates of Blood River*. "I was happy to get any part I was given," he told the authors (April, 1993), "and it never bothered me to play small roles." Perhaps not, but Ripper certainly deserved better.

Death of an Angel

Released February, 1952 (U.K.); 64 minutes (U.K.); B & W; 5877 feet; a Hammer Film Production; filmed at Down Place; an Exclusive Release (U.K.); Director: Charles Saunders; Producer: Anthony Hinds; Screenplay: Reginald Long, based on an original story (*This Is Mary's Chair*) by Dr. Frank King; Director of Photography: Walter Harvey; Editor: John Ferris; Music: Frank Spencer; Makeup: Phil Leakey; Continuity: Renee Glynn; Hairstyles: Anne Box; Camera: Peter Bryan; Art Director: Donald Russo; Production Manager: Arthur Barnes; Sound Recordist: Edgar Vettel; U.K. Certificate: U.

Patrick Barr (Robert Welling), Jane Baxter (Mary Welling), Julie Somers (Judy Welling), Raymond Young (Christopher Boswell), Jean Lodge (Ann Marlow), Russell Walters (Walter Grannage), Russell Napier (Superintendent Walshaw), James Mills (Howard), Frank Tickle (Sam Oddy), Katie Johnson (Sarah Oddy), Robert Brown (Jim Pollard), John Kelly (PC James), Duggie Ascot (Taxi Driver), Hal Osmond (Railway Porter), June Bardsley (Nurse), David Stoll (Plain Clothes Man).

Christopher Boswell (Raymond Young), a young doctor, arrives at Evenbridge to replace Dr. Welling (Patrick Barr), who is ill. Boswell is accepted into village society, especially by Judy (Julie Somers), Dr. Welling's daughter. Despite the friendly atmosphere, Boswell is uneasy around the doctor. When Welling offers him a partnership, Boswell, persuaded by Judy, accepts. The next day he leaves for London with Grannage (Russell Walters), a bank manager, to collect his belongings. That night, Mrs. Mary Welling (Jane Baxter) receives a phone call from Pollard (Robert Brown), whose wife is expecting. Dr. Welling takes the case, assisted by Ann (Jean Lodge), a young dispenser. When they return home, Mary is seriously ill. Welling diagnoses appendicitis as Ann calls Boswell in London. When he arrives in Evenbridge, Mary is dead of arsenic poisoning, and the doctor is missing.

Chris and Ann find Welling hiding in a farmhouse, his nerves shattered, and using drugs. He tells them he suspected Mary of poisoning him. The night of the delivery, he switched glasses with her, assuming it would

Jean Lodge tends to her patient in *Death of an Angel*.

certainly contain a typically small dose. When Grannage arrives at the Welling home, he assumes the doctor has died. Boswell, realizing the implication, confronts Grannage who confesses that he was poisoning the doctor because he wanted Mary. He overpowers Boswell and abducts Judy, but falls to his death while pursued by the police.

Death of an Angel marked a break from Hammer's dependency on the BBC, as ten of their last sixteen films were based on BBC productions. This began a run of seven straight screenplays from other sources. Filming began on April 2, 1951, and completed its scheduled four weeks on April 27. *The Kinematograph Weekly* (April 5) said that the film "will probably be the last this year of Exclusive's solely British productions." This referred to the arrangement with Lippert who released Hammer productions in America. Hammer was becoming increasingly identified with low budget thrillers, having made five (out of six productions) in 1951. As the company's product became more interchangeable, films like *Death of an Angel* became more easily forgotten. Lacking any "name" stars or director, it melts into Hammer's other, all too similar movies.

Oddly, despite grinding out six almost identical films per year, Hammer never got much better at making them. Despite solid production values and decent casts, most of these "thrillers" failed to thrill; but due to their low cost, they invariably turned a profit and fulfilled the quota requirements. Following a January 17 trade show at the Hammer Theatre, *Death of an Angel* opened in February to lukewarm reviews, like in the British Film Institute's *Monthly Bulletin* (March): "Disjointed in development and not too well acted." Hammer would continue this restrictive exercise for the next three years with little variation.

Detective Smith (Richard Carlson) is confronted by the press in this scene from *Whispering Smith Hits London*.

Whispering Smith Hits London

Released February 3, 1952 (U.K.), March, 1952 (U.S.); 82 minutes (U.K.), 77 minutes (U.S.); B & W; 7582 feet; a Hammer Film Production; an Exclusive Films Release (U.K.), an RKO Radio Release (U.S.); filmed at Down Place (Bray) and on location in London, England; Director: Francis Searle; Producers: Anthony Hinds, Julian Lesser; Screenplay: John Gilling, Steve Fisher, based on a story by Frank H. Spearman; Director of Photography: Walter Harvey; Editor: James Needs; Music: Frank Spencer; Production Manager: Arthur Barnes; Sound Recordist: Jack Miller; Camera Operator: Peter Bryan; Assistant Director: Jimmy Sangster; Continuity: Renee Glynn; Makeup: Phil Leakey; Hair Stylist: Anne Box; Casting: Michael Carreras. Title in U.S.: *Whispering Smith Vs. Scotland Yard*; U.K. Certificate: U.

Richard Carlson (Whispering Smith), Greta Gynt (Louise), Herbert Lom (Ford), Rona Anderson (Anne), Alan Wheatley (Reith), Dora Bryan (La Fosse), Reginald Beckwith (Manson), Daniel Wherry (Dr. Taren), Michael Ward (Reception Clerk), Danny Green (Cecil Fleming), James Raglan (Supt. Meaker), Stuart Nichol (Martin), Laurence Naismith (Parker), Christine Silver (Mrs. Pearson), Vic Wise (Maxie), Middleton Woods (Station Porter), Ben Williams (Taxi Driver), Sidney Vivian (Hotel Porter), Tony Frost (Secretary), June Bardsley (Maid), Michael Hogarth (Police Constable), John Wynn (Police Sergeant), Anthony Warner (Page Boy), Ian Wilson (Small Tough), Stanley Baker, Lionel Grose (Reporters), John Singer, John Kyle (Photographers).

Vacationing in England, American detective Whispering Smith (Richard Carlson) receives a letter from Anne (Rona Anderson) who asks his help on behalf of her employer, Mr. Garde. Garde's daughter, Sylvia, supposedly committed suicide, but Garde and Anne believe she was murdered.

An attempt on Anne's life convinces him to take the case. He interviews Sylvia's attorney Hector Reith (Alan Wheatley), her fiancé Roger Ford (Herbert Lom), and Louise (Greta Gynt), Sylvia's friend. All are cooperative. Smith finds a book in Reith's safe that reveals he and Ford were blackmailing Sylvia and others. Manson (Reginald Beckwith), one of the victims, is prepared to help, but is murdered by Ford. When Smith confronts Louise, he is attacked by Reith and Ford. During the struggle, Ford accidentally kills his accomplice. Smith finds a photograph at Manson's house which implicates Louise, and rushes to protect Anne, with whom Louise is now residing. When he arrives, Louise holds him at gunpoint, and reveals that *she* is actually Sylvia and that she, Ford, and Reith murdered Louise due to a botched blackmail scheme. She hears a noise and, thinking it is the police, fires. Ford, her lover, falls into the room dead.

Boasting profits from each of their last sixteen pictures, Hammer was sought by the Lesser Organization to co-produce nine films. Announced in May, 1951, the agreement would extend into 1952 with Lesser providing the financing and Exclusive guaranteed a percentage of the profits.

However, Lesser's son Julian, of Royal Productions, became involved by the time *Whispering Smith Investigates* began production on May 14, and the original agreement was negated. Richard Carlson, fresh from *King Solomon's Mines*, was signed as Smith, the subject of four previous American pictures in which Frank Spearman's character was a railroad detective. The best known of these earlier versions was filmed by Paramount in 1948 with Alan Ladd in his first western. James Carreras bought the rights to the character and incorporated Smith into a John Gilling screenplay called *Where Is Sylvia?*

Gilling said (*Little Shoppe of Horrors*, 4) that he was upset over Spearman getting the screenplay credit, and complained to Carreras, but was brushed aside. The writer then threatened a lawsuit and "Carreras was livid, and I was told he would never use me again. But he did, many times, and I got my due rights over the screen credits."

Filming ended on June 21, 1951, and, under its new title, *Whispering Smith Hits London* was trade shown on January 17, 1952, at the Rialto and released on the ABC circuit on February 3. The picture was distributed in America by RKO as *Whispering Smith vs. Scotland Yard*. Most reviews were positive. *The Kinematograph Weekly* (January 29, 1952): "An engaging performance by Richard Carlson, good support, pleasing romance and comedy asides"; *The Monthly Film Bulletin* (March): "A fast moving and quite exciting thriller"; and *Variety* (March 12): "Lom and Wheatley do well by their dirty work."

Richard Carlson was a Hollywood "B" thriller staple of the fifties and was an excellent choice to play Smith. The versatile Herbert Lom, at home with drama, comedy, heroism, and villainy, here chose the latter and impressed both critics and audiences. By mid–January, 1953, the company was planning a sequel to be scripted by Michael Carreras, who hoped to begin production in March. It was, however, replaced on the schedule by another detective picture, *Blood Orange*.

The Last Page

Released February, 1952 (U.S.), May 19, 1952 (U.K.); 84 minutes (U.K.), 78 minutes (U.S.); B & W; 7595 feet; a Hammer Film Production; an Exclusive Films Release (U.K.), a Lippert Release (U.S.); filmed at Down Place (Bray), England; Director: Terence Fisher; Producer: Anthony Hinds; Screenplay: Frederick Knott, based on the play *The Last Page* by James Hadley Chase; Editor: Maurice Rootes; Music conducted by Frank Spencer, as played by the Royal Philharmonic Orchestra; Sound Engineer: Bill Salter; Continuity: Renee Glynn; Makeup: Phil Leakey; Wardrobe: Joy Curtis; Hair Stylist: Anne Box; Casting: Michael Carreras; Production Manager: Arthur Barnes: Assistant Director: Jimmy Sangster; Art Director: Andrew Mazzei. U.S. Title: *Man Bait*; U.K. Certificate: A.

George Brent (John Harman), Marguerite Chapman (Stella Tracy), Raymond Huntley (Clive Oliver), Peter Reynolds (Jeff Hart), Diana Dors (Ruby Bruce), Eleanor Summerfield (Vi), Meredith Edwards (Dale), Harry Fowler (Joe),

 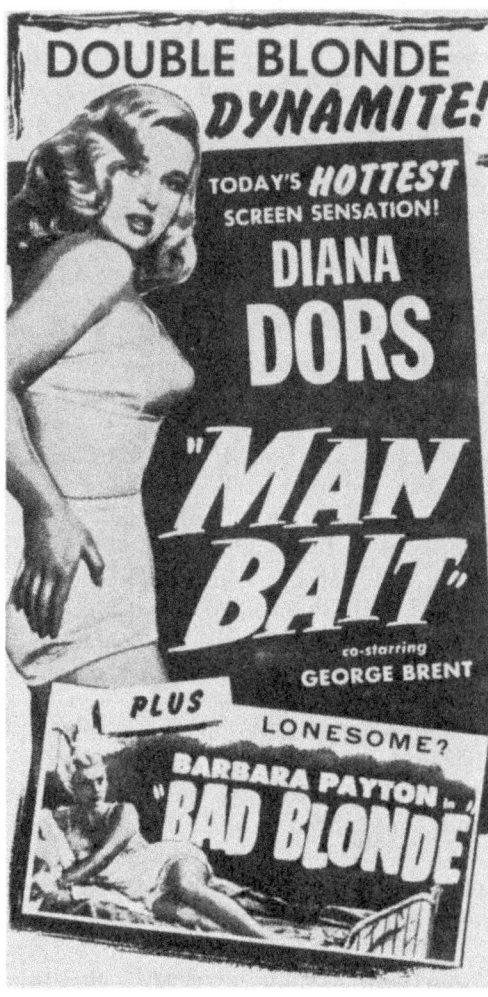

Left: Actually, he joined forces with Scotland Yard. *Right:* Retitled *Man Bait* for the U.S. market, this was the film that launched Diana Dors' American career.

Conrad Philips (Det. Todd), Lawrence Ward (Lang), Nelly Arno (Miss Rossetti), David Keir (Quince), Eleanor Bryan (Mary Lewis), Isabel Dean (May Harman), Jack Faint (Blue Club Receptionist), John Mann (Jack), Harold Goodwin (Frank), Archie Dungan (Police Constable), Sybil Saxon (Bank Clerk), Leslie Weston (Mr. Bruce), Lawrence O'Madden (1st Customer), Ian Wilson (2nd Customer).

John Harman (George Brent) is the manager of Pearson's book store, where clerk Ruby Bruce (Diana Dors) catches a customer, Jeff Hart (Peter Reynolds), attempting to steal a rare book. Instead of reporting him, she agrees to go out with him that night. At work one night, Harman kisses Ruby, then apologizes. When Ruby later meets Hart, he suggests she blackmail Harman. When Harman refuses to pay, Hart writes a letter to Harman's ailing wife May (Isabel Dean), which causes her death from a heart attack.

Dazed, Harman gives Ruby a large sum of money when she renews her demands. Hart catches her hiding part of the money and accidentally kills her, and conceals her body in a packing case. Harman later discovers the body and flees, knowing that he will be accused. Later, he phones his secretary Stella Tracy (Marguerite Chapman) and

Stella (Marguerite Chapman) stumbles upon a murderer (Peter Reynolds) in the exciting climax of *The Last Page*.

tries to get her to arrange with store clerk Clive Oliver (Raymond Huntley) to leave the store open so that he might hunt for clues. Oliver, jealous of Harman, tips off the police. Hart goes into hiding in the apartment of girl friend Vi (Eleanor Summerfield), who is apprehended when she tries to pass some of the money whose numbers have been recorded. Stella, investigating on her own, meets Hart and goes to the apartment with him. Hart renders her unconscious and sets the apartment on fire, but as he tries to leave he is met by Harman at the door. Stella awakens and screams, and Harman throws Hart aside in his haste to get her out of the blaze. The police grab Hart as Harman leads Stella to safety.

Although *The Last Page* had little to distinguish it, the film was an important one for Hammer. Introduced by Richard Gordon, James Carreras and Robert Lippert began their long association based on the American producer supplying actors to Exclusive who, in turn, released Lippert production in the U.K. Lippert reciprocated in America, releasing seventeen Hammer productions between 1952 and 1955. Filming for *The Last Page* began on July 7, 1951, and was attended by Lippert, who toured the Down Place facilities. Terence Fisher, after directing for Rank and Gainsborough, came to Hammer to begin a twenty-year relationship that would produce the company's greatest films. Unfortunately, *The Last Page*, like most of Fisher's early efforts, was not one of them. Makeup supervisor Phil Leakey recalled Fisher for the authors (February, 1992) as, "a gentle, soft-spoken man, and well thought of by all. He knew what he wanted and, in his own quiet way, got it."

George Brent was supplied by Lippert and his co-star, Diana Dors, came courtesy of Rank. Her favorable reviews led to a long term contract with Lippert that James Carreras negotiated. The two stars failed to

Hammer's first (of many) pin-up girls, Diana Dors, in the 1951 production *The Last Page* (*Man Bait* in the United States).

graph Weekly (April 24): "Competently acted and directed—a very good British programmer." On May 1, *Kine* reported that, in America, *The Last Page* had achieved "unusual success for a British film."

The Last Page was marginally better than the company's typical early fifties production, but, since it brought Lippert, Terence Fisher, and Hammer together, it was something of a landmark. The convoluted blackmail plot was well presented but, like too many early fifties Hammer "thrillers," there was a definite lack of thrills. Terence Fisher, after serving his apprenticeship, would eventually do much better. His leisurely directional style in these early films was really no style at all and gave no hint of the innovative pictures in his future.

Wings of Danger

Released May 26, 1952 (U.K.), April, 1952 (U.S.); 73 minutes; B & W; 6618 feet; a Hammer Film Production; an Exclusive Films Release (U.K.); a Lippert Release (U.S.); filmed at Hammersmith-Riverside Studios, England; Director: Terence Fisher; Producer: Anthony Hinds; Screenplay: John Gilling, based on an original story by Elliston Trevor, Peckham Webb; Director of Photography: Walter Harvey; Editor: Jim Needs; Music conducted by: Malcolm Arnold, as played by The London Philharmonic Orchestra; Assistant Director: Jimmy Sangster; Camera Operator: Peter Bryan; Sound System: RCA; Sound Supervisor: Bill Salter; Production Manager: Arthur Barnes; Casting Director: Michael Carreras; Continuity: Renee Glynn; Makeup: Phil Leakey; Hair Stylist: Bill Griffiths; Wardrobe: Ellen Trussler; Chief Electrician: Jack Curtis; Focus: Harry Oakes; Publicity: Bill Luckwell. Working Title: *Dead on Course*.

Zachary Scott (Van), Robert Beatty (Nick Talbot), Kay Kendall (Alexia), Naomi Chance (Avril), Arthur Lane (Boyd Spencer), Colin

ignite much excitement, but were able to attract an audience. Filming ended on August 16, completing a five week schedule that caused the British trades to call Carreras "Britain's fastest film-maker." Lippert, however, felt Carreras was "very good, but a bit slow." *The Last Page* was trade shown at the Rialto on April 23, 1952—eight months after its completion. The film had an American release in February, but was not released in the U.K. until May 19. Reviews were generally positive. *Variety* (January 30, 1952): "Performances are uniformly good, technical support is acceptable"; *Motion Picture Exhibitor* (February 13): "Good for a certain amount of suspense"; *The Monthly Film Bulletin* (February): "Diana Dors gives a spirited performance"; and *The Kinemato-*

Tapley (Maxwell), Diane Cilento (Jeanette), Harold Lang (Snell), Jack Allen (Truscott), Sheila Raynor (Nurse), Courtney Hope (Mrs. Clarence-Smith), June Ashley, Natasha Sokolova, June Mitchell (Blondes), James Steel, Russ Allen (Flying Officers), Darcy Conyers (Signals Officer).

While flying a special mission for his employer Boyd Spencer (Arthur Lane), Nick's (Robert Beatty) plane goes down over the Channel. His friend Van (Zachary Scott), a fellow pilot, notifies his lover—and Nick's sister—Auril (Naomi Chance). Van learns that Detective Maxwell (Colin Tapley) is investigating the airline and that Nick is suspected of having smuggled currency, so he decides to clear his friend's name. Unfortunately, Van finds out that Spencer blackmailed Nick into committing the crime and, even more surprisingly, that Nick has faked his death and is hiding with his girlfriend Jeanette (Diane Cilento).

Van uses his charm on Spencer's girl Alexia (Kay Kendall), who tells him the location of the gang's headquarters. He arrives in time to find them about to leave the country and is joined by Nick who is wounded protecting Van. They hold the gang at bay until the police arrive.

After the completion of *The Last Page*, Exclusive finalized an agreement with Lippert to jointly produce two more films—*Stolen Face* and *Wings of Danger* (which was referred to as *Dead on Course* throughout its production). Terence Fisher began location work at the seaside village of Rye on September 3, 1951. Interiors were scheduled to be shot at Bray, but an unfinished soundstage forced the production into Hammersmith-Riverside. A deal was also struck with James Brennan of Mancunian Studios to co-produce one picture (*Never Look Back*) with the option to film five more. *Wings of Danger* moved into Riverside on September 20, where Zachary Scott was interviewed by *Picture Show* on the differences between British and American studios. "In Hollywood," Scott said, "we seem to keep more to the order in which the story is written than over here. Scenes which will be put in towards the end of the picture are done before the earlier scenes have been shot; and when I come to such sequences, I must remember not to betray any sign of what I know to be the ultimate finale." Scott spent much of his Warner Bros. career playing the heavy (*Mildred Pierce*, 1945), and the opportunity to be the hero must have been a relief. Hammer often cast against type—a policy that most actors must have found attractive.

Before the film's completion in late October, Robert Lippert sent Jack Leewood, his chief supervisor, to study Hammer's production methods and to minimize the use of British idioms that confounded American audiences. *Wings of Danger* was released on May 26, 1952, on the ABC and Odeon circuits, billed over an American import (*FBI Girl*)—a first for a Hammer film. In addition, the film was one of six Hammer films in release during the month. Reviewers, though, were unimpressed. *Today's Cinema* (May 8): "Conventional in treatment and characterization but competently made"; *Motion Picture Exhibitor* (April 9): "Routine import"; and *Variety* (March 26): "Uninspired, uninteresting plot ingredients hamper this weak British entry." Despite the negative press, *Wings of Danger* did remarkably well at the box office in England. Proving that there's no accounting for taste, Exclusive re-released the film in February, 1953, and it did equally good business.

Never Look Back

Released May 26, 1952; 73 minutes; B & W; 6065 feet; a Hammer Film Production; an Exclusive Release (U.K.); filmed at Manchester Studios; Director: Francis Searle; Producer: Michael Carreras; Screenplay: John Hunter, Guy Morgan, Francis Searle; Director of Photography: Reginald Wyer; Music: Temple Abady; Editor: John Ferris; U.K. Certificate: A.

Rosamund John (Anne), Hugh Sinclair (Nigel), Guy Middleton (Guy), Henry Edwards (Whitcomb), Terence Longdon (Alan), John Warwick (Raynor), Brenda DeBanza (Molly

68 Never Look Back (1951)

Trade advertisement.

Wheeler), Arthur Howard (Vaughan), H.S. Hills (Lindsell), Bruce Beltrage (the Judge), Helen Burls (Mrs. Brock), Frances Rowe (Liz), Bill Shine (Willie), Barbara Shaw (Press Woman), David Scase (Cameraman), Norman Somers (Nigel Junior).

Anne Maitland (Rosamund John), while celebrating her appointment as a King's Counseller, tells her lover, lawyer Nigel Stewart (Hugh Sinclair), that she can't accept his proposal because of her new career. She meets Guy Ransome (Guy Middleton), her ex-fiancé, and foolishly allows him to spend the night. Guy had a fight with Peggy, his mistress, and Anne suggests that he make up with her. He returns unexpectedly later that morning after finding Peggy in her apartment—dead. When interviewed by the police, he lied about his whereabouts to protect Anne's reputation. Anne agrees to defend Guy, with Nigel as prosecutor, but she is called as a witness and must drop the case. When she provides Guy with a "too-perfect" alibi, Anne is forced to resign from the Bar. Guy is found guilty, and Anne reconsiders Nigel's proposal.

Exclusive's plans for 1952 included, in addition to releasing seven Hammer productions, the distribution of ten American-made films. Hammer's own schedule was moving so quickly that the company had to look for extra studio space to alleviate the

Trade advertisement.

back-up at Bray. As a result, *Never Look Back* was moved to the formerly dormant Manchester under a special agreement with studio head James Brennan. Michael Carreras was assigned to produce, which was another step-up for him since moving through just about every department in the company. Filming began on September 17, 1951, with Carreras pushing 3½ minutes of film "into the can" each day. He brought his first film

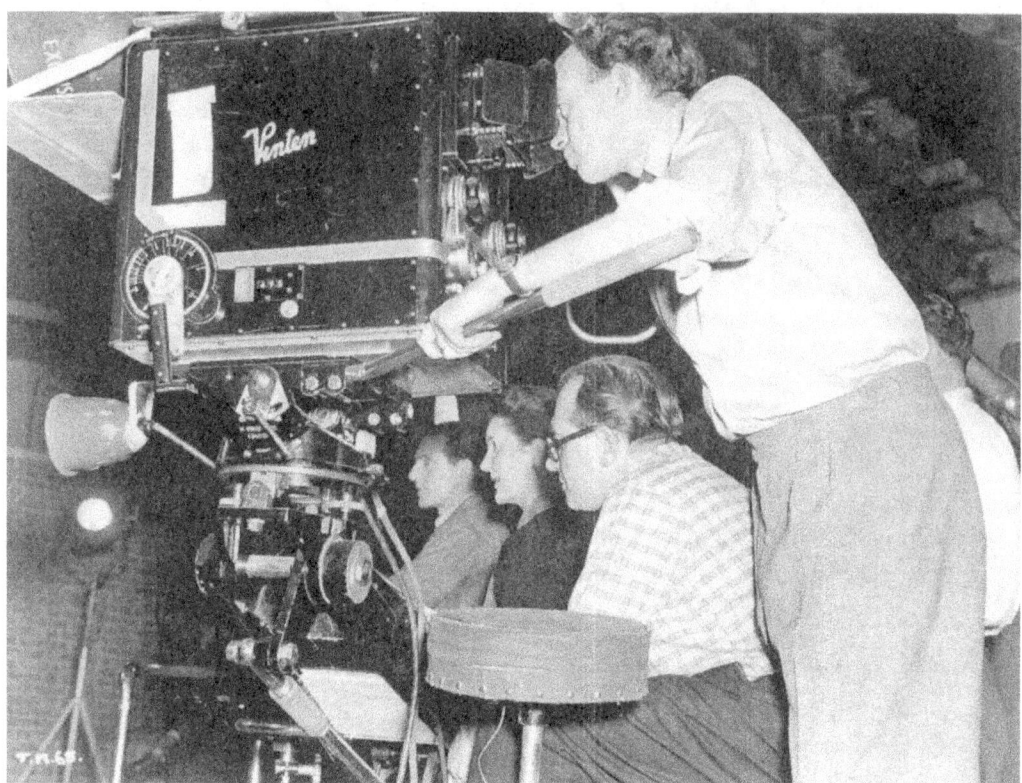

Behind the scenes on *Never Look Back*.

in on schedule, and *Never Look Back* was trade shown at the Rialto on March 19, 1952, and premiered at the Odeon on May 26, with *The Kinematograph Weekly* (March 27) dismissing the picture as "a programmer." Since it lacked recognizable performers such as Paul Henreid and Cesar Romero, who appeared in other Hammer productions of the period, *Never Look Back* was doomed from the start, despite decent reviews from other publications like the British Film Institute's *Monthly Bulletin* (May): "It has been made to seem quite plausible and improves as it progresses."

To make up the film's lack of star power, the company pushed cinema managers hard with contests—including a trip to Bray Studios for the cinema with the best display judged by Michael Carreras. The pressbook announced that, "Exclusive cannot pay travelling expenses in London or hotel expenses, although all expenses to and from the studios will be paid by Exclusive." It seems that even the company's prizes during this period were low budget. Contests aside, the main problem with *Never Look Back* was its lack of star power, which would be remedied by Robert Lippert. Hammer would make having a recognizable "name" in the lead a priority, and never looked back.

Stolen Face

Released June 23, 1952 (U.K.), June, 1952 (U.S.); 72 minutes; B & W; 6500 feet; an Exclusive Film Production; an Exclusive Films Release (U.K.), a Lippert Release (U.S.); filmed at Hammersmith-Riverside Studios, England; Director: Terence Fisher; Producer: Anthony Hinds; Screenplay: Martin Berkeley, Richard H. Landau, based on a story by Alexander Paal, Steven Vas; Director of Photography: Walter Harvey; Editor: Maurice Rootes; Music: Malcolm Arnold; Recorded by the London Philharmonic Orchestra; Piano Soloist: Bronwyn Jones; Art

Director: Wilfred Arnold; Assistant Director: Jimmy Sangster; Production Manager: Arthur Barnes; Camera: Peter Bryan; Specialty Numbers: Jack Parnell; Recordist: Bill Salter; Makeup: Phil Leakey; Hairstylist: Bill Griffiths; Casting Director: Nora Roberts; Furs by: Deanfield of London; Lizabeth Scott's Wardrobe: Edith Head; Continuity: Renee Glynn; U.K. Certificate: A.

Paul Henreid (Dr. Philip Ritter), Lizabeth Scott (Alice Brent/Lily B), Mary MacKenzie (Lily A), Andre Morell (David), John Wood (Dr. Jack Wilson), Susan Stephen (Betty), Arnold Ridley (Dr. Russell), Everley Gregg (Lady Millicent Harringay), Cyril Smith (Alf), Janet Brunell (Maggie), Grace Gawin (Nurse), Terence O'Regan (Pete Snipe), Diana Beaumont (May), Alexis France (Mrs. Emmett), John Bull (Charles Emmett), Dorothy Bramhall (Miss Simpson), Ambrosine Philpotts (Miss Patten), Russell Napier (Cutler), Hal Osmond (Photographer), William Murray (Floorwalker), Howard Doug-las (Farmer), James Valentine (Soldier), John Warren, Frank Hawkins (Commercial Travellers), Richard Wattis (Mr. Wentworth).

English plastic surgeon Dr. Philip Ritter (Paul Henreid) experiments at a women's prison, feeling that changing a criminal's face will change her personality. On vacation, he stops during a rainstorm at a country inn and there meets American concert pianist Alice Brent (Lizabeth Scott). The two fall in love, but she is already engaged to David (Andre Morell).

When Alice leaves on a concert tour, Ritter, disillusioned, transforms the horribly scarred face of Lilly (Mary MacKenzie), a convict, to that of Alice, and then marries her, hoping to change her completely. However, still a criminal, she immediately returns to theft. Meanwhile, Alice's life with David is miserable, and David announces that he's leaving her. Alice returns to Ritter, free to marry him, but Ritter explains what has happened in the interim and Alice sees the hopelessness of their situation.

Later, Ritter, Alice and Lilly all end up on the same train and there is an ugly confrontation. Lilly tries to attack Alice, but Ritter pushes Lilly away against an outside door and she fatally falls from the speeding train. Her face is horribly scarred by the fall, and an onlooker comments that she must have been beautiful.

Stolen Face, Terence Fisher's first foray into "radical surgery," is a clever combination of *Frankenstein* and *Pygmalion*. The film was a refreshing change from the bland thrillers Hammer was too often producing, and was a preview of things to come. Heading the cast were two name Hollywood stars, Paul (*Casablanca*) Henreid and Lizabeth Scott, who had recently appeared as Humphrey Bogart's love interest in *Dead Reckoning* (1947). Henreid found major American studios to be no longer interested in him after he protested the jailing of the "Hollywood Ten" for their supposed Communistic leanings. "One independent producer," he wrote in *Ladies Man*, "Robert Lippert offered me a film called *Stolen Face*. He had connections with a London outfit that paid the star's expenses and salaries, usually offering them a percentage of the film." Lizabeth Scott had understudied Tallulah Bankhead in the Broadway production of *Skin of Our Teeth*, and was a rising Paramount star of the 1940s. Her career derailed and she, like Henreid, found work in the U.K.

Production began on October 29, 1951, with thirty-two sets—the most of any Hammer film at the time. Edith Head, one of Hollywood's top costume designers, was on hand to outfit her friend Lizabeth Scott. A winner of three Oscars, Head must have been a welcome addition. Scott was doubled by Maureen Glynn, a relative of continuity girl Renee Glynn. *Stolen Face* wrapped on December 4, and was Hammer's eighth production of 1951. This was the company's biggest production year since its inception. A few days later, Anthony Hinds flew to America with a print of *Wings of Danger* and an offer to observe American studio methods. Following an April 12, 1952, trade show, *Stolen Face* premiered at the Plaza on May 2. It was the first Hammer film to open at a prestigious West End cinema. Although popular with audiences, *Stolen Face* received lukewarm reviews. *The Kinematograph Weekly* (April 24): "The co-stars gave their

Ads for *Stolen Face,* Hammer's combination of *Frankenstein* and *Pygmalion.*

best, and the staging was deluxe, but neither succeeds in bringing conviction to its extravagant plot"; and *Variety* (May 28): "The pacing is laborious."

Stolen Face was, then, a film of many firsts for Hammer. With a few horrific touches, the film could easily have fit in with the company's productions a decade later. Henreid, unfortunately, underplays his role and lacks the spark that an "obsessed surgeon" needs to be believable. Lizabeth Scott competently plays "both" roles, but Mary MacKenzie steals the film as the bitter Lilly. Andre Morell, who would become one of the company's most valued stars, makes his Hammer debut. Although Henry Higgins succeeded in making over Eliza in George Bernard Shaw's *Pygmalion,* Dr. Ritter fell far short with Lilly. This was the first of many examples in the Hammer filmography of beauty as a mask for evil.

1952

Lady in the Fog

Released October 13, 1952 (U.K.); 82 minutes (U.S.); B & W; a Hammer Film production; an Exclusive Release (U.K.), a Lippert Presentation (U.S.); filmed at Hammersmith-Riverside Studios; Director: Sam Newfield; Producer: Anthony Hinds; Screenplay: Orville H. Hampton, from the BBC racho serial by Lester Powell; Director of Photography: James Harvey; Editor: James Needs; Art Director: Wilfred Arnold; Sound: William Salter;

Production Manager: John Green; Assistant Director: Basil Keys; Dialogue Director: Patrick Jenkins; Camera: Moray Grant; Continuity: Renee Glynn; Makeup: Phil Leakey; Hairdresser: Bill Griffiths; Casting: Michael Carreras; Music: Ivor Slaney; Conducted by: Muir Mathieson; Recorded by: London Philharmonic; U.S. Title: *Scotland Yard Inspector*; U.K. Certificate: A.

Cesar Romero (Philip O'Dell), Lois Maxwell (Peggy), Bernadette O'Farrell (Heather), Geoffrey Keen (Hampden), Campbell Singer (Inspector Rigby), Alister Hunter (Sgt. Reilly), Mary Mackenzie (Marilyn), Frank Birch (Boswell), Wensley Pithey (Sid), Reed de Roven (Connors), Lloyd Lamble (Sorrowby), Peter Swanwiek (Smithers), Bill Fraser (Sales Manager), Lisa Lee (Donna), Lionel Harris (Alan), Betty Cooper (Dr. Campbell), Clair James (Miss Andrews), Katy Johnson (Mad Mary), Stuart Saunders (Policeman).

Misleading American title for *Lady in the Fog*.

Philip O'Dell (Cesar Romero), an American reporter fog-bound in London, kills time in a pub with Heather (Bernadette O'Farrell), who is waiting for her brother. A bobby enters to call for an ambulance for a hit-and-run victim—her brother, Danny (Richard Johnson). Since Danny was often in trouble, Heather suspects murder; but when O'Dell takes her to Scotland Yard, both are dismissed. O'Dell decides to investigate the matter himself and traces Danny to Peggy's Night Club and, after flirting with the owner (Lois Maxwell), gets an address from a waiter. When he enters Danny's room, O'Dell is knocked unconscious and, after waking up, finds a tape recording.

Later, Danny's girlfriend (Mary Mackenzie) takes O'Dell to film producer Chris Hampden (Geoffrey Keen), who occasionally employed Danny. O'Dell listens to the tape and gets valuable information, but stupidly erases it when he tries to play it for Heather. Following the lead, they go to Gladstone Asylum and interview Martin Sorrowby (Lloyd Lamble). Sorrowby, Hampden, and a mysterious "Margaret" were being blackmailed by Danny for murdering an inventor during the war after stealing his secret for a new carburetor. O'Dell inspects the bombed-out lab, and is attacked by Connors (Reed de Raven), Hampden's henchman, while Hampden and his wife, Margaret—Peggy—kidnap Heather. While being chased by O'Dell, Hampden falls to his death, and Margaret dies in a car crash while escaping.

"I had just completed a film in India—*The Jungle*—for Lippert," Cesar Romero told the authors (November, 1992), "and I stopped off in London on my way home. I was met at the airport by someone from Hammer who informed me that Lippert had made a deal for me while I was in the air! As a freelance actor, I've made films all over the world, so this was nothing new for me. Everyone I worked with was pleasant—especially James Carreras—a real gentleman and a nice guy. Sam Newfield was easy to work with under the conditions of a quick schedule. The details of the film are forgotten, but I sure remember the good time I had."

Lady in the Fog began production on March 24, 1952, with an American star, writer, and director, plus some concerns. *The Kinematograph Weekly* (September 11, 1952) reported that, "Doubt as to how the British technicians might adapt themselves to American methods was dispelled on the first day of shooting when, with twenty-five camera setups, no fewer than nine minutes of quality screen time was put in the can." The picture finished on schedule, despite the original misgivings, was trade shown on September 10, 1952, and released on October 13, to mixed reviews. The British Film Institute's *Monthly Bulletin* (November): "Routine mystery"; and *The Kinematograph Weekly* (September 11): "Despite some confusion, it puts plenty of variety and no little kick into its dizzy surface action."

How much one likes this film depends on one's liking for Cesar Romero. His light touch and engaging personality make many of the comedy scenes work well, especially with Katie Johnson as a lunatic at the asylum. Most of the movie, though, leaves the viewer in a fog as its many disparate parts don't add up to much.

The Gambler and the Lady

Released January 26, 1953 (U.K.), December, 1952 (U.S.); 6645 feet; 74 minutes (U.K.), 71 minutes (U.S.); B & W; a Hammer Film Production; an Exclusive Films Release (U.K.), a Lippert Release (U.S.); filmed at Bray Studios, England; Director: Pat Jenkins; Producer: Anthony Hinds; Director of Photography: Walter Harvey; Editor: Maurice Rootes; Music: Ivor Slaney; the London Philharmonic Orchestra conducted by: Marcus Dodds; Art Director: J. Elder Wills; Sound: William Salter; Production Manager: John Green; Assistant Director: Ted Holliday; Camera: Moray Grant; Makeup: Phil Leakey; Casting Director: Michael Carreras; Continuity: Renee Glynn; Hair Stylist: Pauline Trent; U.K. Certificate: U.

Dane Clark (Jim Forster), Kathleen Byron (Pat), Naomi Chance (Susan Willens), Meredith Edwards (Dave), Anthony Forwood (Peter Willens), Eric Pohlmann (Arturo Colonna), Enzo Coticchia (Angelo Colonna), Julian Somers (Lucasi), Anthony Ireland (Farning), Thomas Gallagher (Sam), Max Bacon (Maxie), Mona Washbourne (Miss Minter), Jane Griffith (Janey Greer), Richard Shaw (Louis), George Pastell (Jaco Spina), Martin Benson (Tony), Eric Boon (The Boxer), Felix Osmond (Boxing Promoter), Percy Marmont (Lord Hortland), Robert Adair (Engles), Mark Singleton (Waiter—Jack of Spades), Peter Hutton (Roger Bowen), Andre Mikhelson (El Greco), Paul Sheridan (The Croupier), Robert Brown (Waiter—Maxie's), David Keir (The Gambler), Irissa Cooper (The Tart), Laurie Taylor (Shadow), Valencia Trio (Adagio Act).

Jim Forster (Dane Clark), a recovering alcoholic and habitual gambler, arrives in Britain after serving a prison term in America for manslaughter. Living by luck and his wits, he becomes the owner of a nightclub and a race horse, both named "The Jack of Spades." Determined to better himself socially, Forster begins to associate with the "upper class," including Lady Susan Willens (Naomi Chance), daughter of Lord Hortland (Percy Marmont). He hastily ends his affair with Pat (Kathleen Byron), a dancer at his club, who does not handle the rejection well. Forster also alienates his club manager Dave (Meredith Edwards), who is unimpressed with his boss's social climbing.

Forster's luck turns bad when he refuses to sell the club to a gang led by Arturo (Eric Pohlmann) and Angelo Colonna (Enzo Coticchia), who declare war. After being swindled on a stock deal suggested by Lord Hortland, Forster sells the club to pay his

Dane Clark enjoyed working for Hammer so much he stayed on to do two more films.

debts. When Dave is murdered by the Colonnas, who blame Forster for a series of police raids, Jim seeks revenge. He is wounded in a shootout, and, as he staggers into the street, is run down by Pat in her car.

Dane Clark's successful 1940s film career began to sag in the fifties. He found work in Britain in *Highly Dangerous* (1951), which brought him to Hammer's attention, and he became the first Hollywood star to appear in three Hammer films. Anthony Hinds had originally planned to have American Sam Newfield direct *The Money*, the film's original title. He had just completed *Lady in the Fog*, and Hammer was pleased with his efficiency. However, his employment would have violated a labor quota which placed a cap on the number of foreign directors permitted on British films during any given year. The company got permission to employ a British "co-director" who would be paid the minimum and have his name in the credits. Hammer also wanted the expertise of American directors, who were, in general, less methodical than their British counterparts. With the money saved by shorter schedules, Hammer could invest more in future projects. In April, 1952, the company made an official request to the Ministry of Labor to be permitted to have an American director on their payroll on a permanent basis.

The Gambler and the Lady began production on May 19, 1952, and concluded on June 16, with location work done at Windsor Castle and the Ascot Race Course. The directional credit was given to Pat Jenkins on British prints, and Sam Newfield got co-director billing in America. Making things more confusing, *Today's Cinema* (June 16) gave Terence Fisher the credit! Oddly, *no one* received a screenplay credit. Later that year, restrictions against foreign directors were relaxed. A trade show was held on January 6, 1953, and the film went into its U.K. release on January 26—a month after premiering in America. Reviews in both countries were discouraging. *The Monthly Film Bulletin* (January, 1953): "Dane Clark deserved something rather better"; *The Motion Picture Exhibitor* (December 17, 1952): "A fair amount of action and suspense"; and *The Kinematograph Weekly* (November 13, 1952): "Lacks fire and purpose." Despite the presence of a well-cast Hollywood star, *The Gambler and the Lady* failed to please.

Mantrap

Released March 16, 1953 (U.K.); 73 minutes; B & W; 7035 feet; a Hammer Film Production; an Exclusive Release (U.K.), United Artists (U.S.); filmed at Bray Studios and on location in London; Director: Terence Fisher; Producers: Michael Carreras, Alexander Paal; Screenplay: Paul Tabori, Terence Fisher, from Elleston Trevor's *Queen in Danger*; Director of Photography: Reginald Wyer; Music: Doreen Carwithen, played by Royal Philharmonic; Conductor: Marcus Dodds; Art Director: J. Elder Wills; Sound Recordist: Jack Miller; Camera Operator: Len Harris; Production Manager: Victor Wark; Assistant Director: Bill Shore; Continuity: Renee Glynn; Makeup: D. Bonnor Morris; 2nd Assistant Director: Aida Young; 3rd Assistant Director: Vernon Nolf; Stills: John Jay; Focus: Manny Yospa; Editor: James Needs; Assistant Editor: Jimmy Groom; U.K. Certificate: A; U.S. Title: *Man in Hiding*.

Paul Henreid (Bishop), Lois Maxwell (Thelma), Kieron Moore (Speight), Hugh Sinclair (Jerrard), Lloyd Lamble (Frisnay), Anthony Forwood (Rex), Bill Travers (Victor), Mary Laura Wood (Susie), Kay Kendall (Vera), John Penrose (DuVancet), Liam Gaffney (Douval), Conrad Phillips (Barker), John Stuart (Doctor), Anna Turner (Marjorie), Christina Forrest (Joanna), Arnold Diamond (Alphonse), Jane Welsh (Laura), Geoffrey Murphy (Plainclothesman), Terry Carney (Detective), Sally Newland (Receptionist), Barbara Kowin (later Shelley) (Fashion Commere).

Having been convicted of committing a murder while insane, Speight (Kieron Moore) has escaped from prison and is on the loose in London. His wife Thelma (Lois Maxwell) is terrified. She is now the lover of Victor Tasman (Bill Travers) whose name she has taken. Publisher Maurice Jerrard (Hugh Sinclair), for whom she is an editor, is also concerned. Hugo Bishop (Paul Henreid), a private detective, attempts to find Speight before the police and stakes out the murder scene near St. Paul's Cathedral. He finds Speight, and the two form an uneasy alliance, but Bishop cannot determine the cause of the murder.

As he investigates, Bishop learns of the Speights' unhappy marriage and that the victim may have been Speight's mistress. He also learns that Speight wishes Thelma well in her new life and begins to suspect Jerrard. Bishop arranges for the principals to meet at a party—along with Inspector Frisnay (Lloyd Lamble). When Thelma spots Speight, her reaction leads to his arrest. He denounces Jerrard, who, with help from Bishop, implicates himself in front of Frisnay. Jerrard breaks free and is chased by Bishop through the streets to the original murder scene where he falls to his death. He had framed Speight, after killing the girl, so he could move in on Thelma. Speight decides to leave England, Thelma and Victor plan to marry, and Bishop *may* settle down with his secretary Vera (Kay Kendall).

Mantrap has the look of the opener to a series that never materialized. Hammer was certainly not against series characters, and this one *might* have worked, due mainly to the Nick and Nora Charles (*The Thin Man*, 1934) relationship between Hugo and Vera. Paul Henreid, not noted for his light comedy talents, is surprisingly engaging as Hugo Bishop, P.I. Henreid was on the fringe of the Hollywood "blacklist," and after he moved to England, his career never regained its momentum. Kay Kendall soon became a big star in *Genevieve* (1953), married Rex Harrison, but died at age 33 of leukemia. Kieron Moore also shines as the tormented fugitive and made the most of his limited screen time. But, despite the fine cast, *Mantrap* has too much talk, and too little action. This was one of the few films on which Terence Fisher took a writing credit, but like most directors, he usually had a hand in the script. Although his direction is fine, he must share the blame (with Paul Tabori) for the talkfest.

Mantrap was cameraman Len Harris' first Hammer film. "I had seen *The Last Page* at my local cinema," he told the authors (December, 1993),

> and I thought it was a well made little film. I had been a camera operator for years, and thought I'd like to work for this Hammer company. I went around, and the next thing I knew I was on *Mantrap*! I stayed with Hammer for the next ten years and loved every minute of it. As the camera operator, you work very closely with the director—more so than does the light-

ing cameraman. A director like Terence Fisher lets you go on with it yourself. He has his job, you have yours, and he lets you do it. Terry always, of course, had the final word, but he always listened. I was made to feel right at home at Bray. They were a wonderful group of people—when you worked for Hammer, there were no outsiders—only family. I thought *Mantrap* was a respectable picture, but seeing it now, I was confused by the plot—far too many twists!

Paul Henreid arrived in London on June 12, 1952, and filming began four days later. Reviews, following a March 1, 1953, trade show, were tepid. *The Cinema* (March 4): "The climax is effective in its contrived suspense"; *The Motion Picture Herald* (November 14): "The writers were so intent on mystifying the audience they forgot to include any cohesion in their story"; and *The Kinematograph Weekly* (March 5): "The variety of cunningly contrasted backgrounds put a healthy complexion on the crowded, slightly novelettish plot."

Mantrap was another competently made but uninspired thriller—a type of film quickly becoming a Hammer specialty.

The Four Sided Triangle

Released May 25, 1953 (U.K.), May 15, 1953 (U.S.); 81 minutes; B & W; 7332 feet; a Hammer Film Production; Released through Exclusive (U.K.), Astor Pictures (U.S.); filmed at Bray Studios; Director: Terence Fisher; Producers: Michael Carreras, Alexander Paal; Screenplay: Paul Tabori, Terence Fisher, based on William F. Temple's novel; Director of Photography: Reg Wyer; Editor: Maurice Rootes; Music: Malcolm Arnold; Played by: Royal Philharmonic, conducted by Muir Mathieson; Art Director: J. Elder Wills; Camera Operator: Len Harris; Sound Recordist: Bill Salter; Dialogue Director: Mora Roberts; Continuity: Renee Glynn; Makeup: D. Bonner-Moris; Assistant Director: Bill Shore; Hair Stylist: Nina Broe; Production Manager: Victor Wark; U.K. Rating: A.

Barbara Payton (Lena/Helen), James Hayter (Dr. Harvey), Stephen Murray (Bill), John Van Eyssen (Robin), Percy Marmont (Sir Walter), Jennifer Dearman (Young Lena), Glyn Dearman (Young Bill), Sean Barrett (Young Robin), Kynaston Reeves (Lord Grant), John Stuart (Solicitor), Edith Saville (Lady Grant).

Robin (John Van Eyssen) and Bill (Stephen Murray) have been in love with Lena (Barbara Payton) since childhood. When she returns to their village, after spending several years in America, Lena finds the pair engaged in a strange research project. The men are trying to change energy into matter and, after two years of failure, Robin's father, Sir Walter (Percy Marmont) decides to cut their funding. They are saved by their old friend, Dr. Harvey (James Hayter), who sells his practice to bail them out. Finally, they succeed in being able to duplicate any object exactly, but find themselves driven apart by Lena.

Sir Walter learns of their success and insists they turn their project over to the government, which they refuse to do. At a celebration banquet, Lena and Robin announce their engagement, crushing Bill who spends all of his time in the lab. After successfully copying a rabbit, he is ready for an insane step—duplicating Lena. Incredibly, she consents.

Bill and "Helen" leave on holiday, and all seems well until he realizes the experiment was too successful—she also prefers Robin. Distraught, Bill attempts to erase "Helen's" memory and again is too successful—she becomes a zombie. A short circuit causes a fire in the lab, destroying the unhappy couple, as Lena escapes unharmed.

This minor science fiction drama was poorly received, but was a major step toward Hammer's as yet unplanned Frankenstein film. Filmed over a five-week period during August and September, 1952, the movie's main selling point was Hollywood "bad girl" Barbara Payton. At a reception in her honor, James Carreras (*Kinematograph Weekly*, July 31, 1952) announced the company's plans for the coming year. He intended to create two separate teams that would alternate production, resulting in almost continuous film-ing. Each team would include a producer, director, production manager, and cutting staff. One was to be headed by Michael Carreras, the other by Anthony Hinds, with a maximum break of two weeks between films.

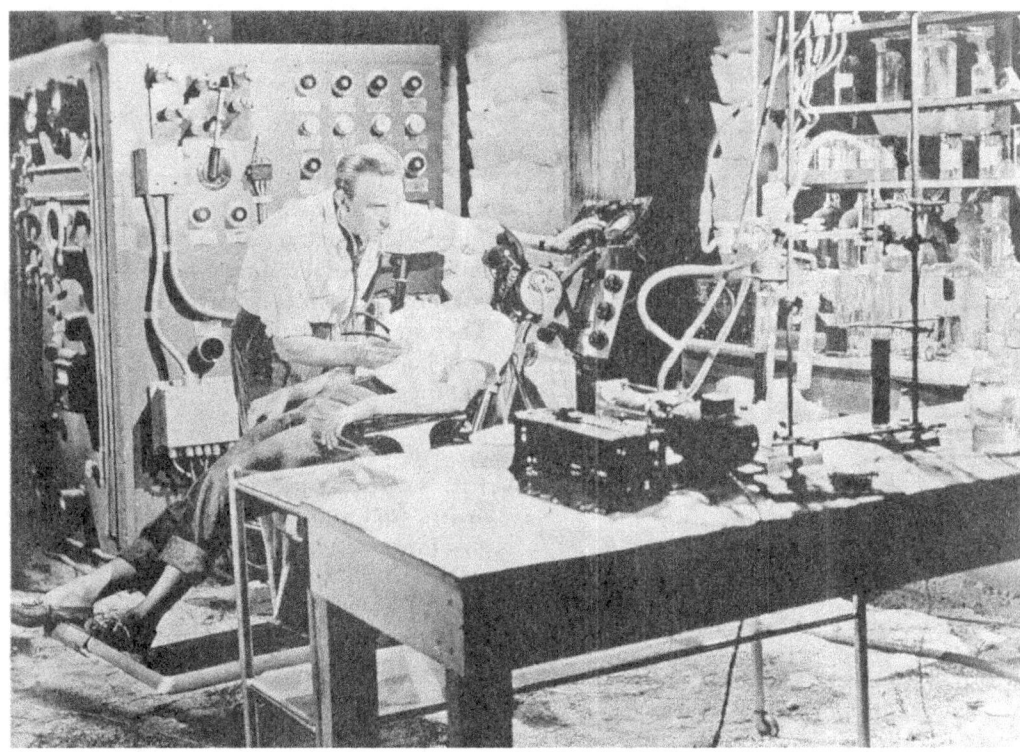

This laboratory set could have used Bernard Robinson's magic touch in this scene from Hammer's *Four Sided Triangle* (photo courtesy of Ted Okuda).

Terence Fisher, taking a rare screenplay credit, adapted (with Paul Tabori) William F. Temple's novel for his first science fiction film—a genre with which he had little success. During this period, the typical science fiction picture was concerned with space travel, giant insects, if possible, or both. *The Four Sided Triangle*, though, belonged to the "cerebral" branch of the genre, along with *Invasion of the Body Snatchers* (1956), although it wasn't in the same league as this superior film. Typically, Fisher was more interested in the effects of the duplicating experiment than in the mumbo-jumbo of its mechanics, which was at variance with the bulk of this type of film. As a result, *The Four Sided Triangle* is interesting rather than exciting. Like many Hammer films of the early fifties, it never comes to life despite often threatening to do so.

Most of the film's little excitement was related to Miss Payton, who had gained all the bad publicity one would want due to a fist fight between actors Tom Neal and Franchot Tone over her "favors." She eventually married the battered Tone—it lasted one month. *The Picture Post* (August 30, 1952) ran a provocative shot of her wearing a bathing suit, something she did better than acting. Despite her tawdry background (or due to it), she was mobbed by autograph seekers during a location shoot at Weymouth. Her performance is passable, but the film cried for a more charismatic star. The same is true of the male leads.

Reviews were condescending following the film's May, 1953, release. The British Film Institute's *Monthly Bulletin* (June, 1953): "A tedious melodrama, flatly directed, written, and played"; *The New York Times* (May 16, 1953): "An exploitation picture opening at the Rialto, and a better home for it couldn't be found." The Rialto was a notorious theatre specializing in films like,

Film noir, Hammer style: *The Flanagan Boy* was retitled *Bad Blonde* for the U.S. market.

well, *The Four Sided Triangle*. Hammer didn't give up on the genre, following this one with *Spaceways*. Sixteen films later they got it right with *The Quatermass Xperiment*.

The Flanagan Boy

Released July, 1953 (U.K.), April, 1953 (U.S.); 81 minutes; B & W; 7313 feet; a Hammer Film Production; an Exclusive Release (U.K.), a Lippert Release (U.S.); filmed at Bray Studios; Director: Reginald LeBorg; Producer: Anthony Hinds; Screenplay: Guy Elmes; Adaptation: Richard Landau, based on Max Catlos' novel; Director of Photography: Walter Harvey; Music: Ivor Slaney; Editor: James Needs; Camera: Len Harris; Production Manager: John Green; Art Director: Wilfred Arnold; Dialogue Director: Patrick Jenkins; Assistant Director: Jimmy Sangster; Continuity: Renee Glynn; Sound: Bill Salter; U.S. Title: *Bad Blonde*; U.K. Certificate: A.

Barbara Payton (Lorna), Frederick Valk (Vacchi), John Slater (Charlie), Sidney James (Sharkey), Tony Wright (Flanagan), Marie Burke (Mrs. Vecchi), Selma Vas Dias (Mrs. Corelli), George Woodbridge (Inspector), Enzo Coticchia (Mrs. Corelli), Bettina Dickson (Barmaid), Joe Quigley (Kossov), Tom Clegg (Fighter), Chris Adcock, Bob Simmonds (Booth Men), Roy Catthouse (Coloured Fighter), Ralph Moss (Kossov's Second), Laurence Naismith (Barnes).

After winning a carnival boxing match, sailor Johnny Flanagan (Tony Wright) is spotted by Sharkey (Sidney James) as having potential and is introduced to Charlie Sullivan (John Slater), a trainer. Giuseppi Vecchi (Frederick Valk), agrees to finance Johnny over the objection of his sultry wife Lorna (Barbara Payton). Johnny trains at Vecchi's estate, and he soon becomes involved with Lorna. His training goes badly, and he is ashamed of his conduct but is unable to break free. Before Johnny's big bout with Lou Koss (Joe Quigley), Sharkey confronts Lorna to no avail—Johnny is brutally beaten the next night, distracted by Lorna in the audience.

Vecchi wants to drop Johnny, but allows him to continue living on the estate. When Lorna announces her pregnancy, Vecchi is ecstatic—but Johnny knows that Giuseppi is not the father. The pregnancy pushes Johnny over the edge and, goaded by Lorna, he drowns Giuseppe. Vecchi's mother arrives from Italy and suspects the truth and forces Lorna to admit to faking the pregnancy. Johnny wants to confess to the murder, but is poisoned by Lorna who arranges his death to look like a suicide. Sharkey and Charlie are not taken in and turn her over to the police.

This is Hammer's best attempt at a Hollywood style film noir and is reminiscent of James M. Cain's classic *The Postman Always Rings Twice*, with its triangle of a belligerent young stud, wild young wife, and her unattractive husband. Barbara Payton's white bathing suit is almost a perfect match to Lana Turner's in the 1946 version, leaving little doubt of Hammer's intentions.

Filming began on September 25, 1952, and was immediately held up for several days when Tony Wright injured an ankle during a boxing scene. Wright was very convincing as a fighter, having been an amateur in the British Navy and receiving coaching from Len Harvey, a former British heavyweight. This was Wright's first film role, although he did have repertory experience in South Africa. Payton, appearing in her second Hammer film of the year, brought to *The Flanagan Boy* her main asset—a sullen sensuality that just might have been good acting. She also had a well-earned "bad girl" image that was perfect for the character. Lippert provided Hammer with Payton and almost certainly with Reginald LeBorg, who had been directing in America since the early forties (*The Mummy's Ghost*, 1944). The production closed on October 19, 1952, and *The Flanagan Boy* was trade shown on June 20, 1953, and released in July. Reviews concentrated on the film's sexual content. *The Cinema* (June 24): "It is the sex angle that dominates. Action offering for tolerant tastes"; *Variety* (April 28): "Le Borg seemingly directed Anthony Hinds' production to accent only the script's sex angles"; The British Film Institute's *Monthly Bulletin* (August): "A lurid little melodrama"; and *The Kinematograph Weekly* (June 25): "Realistic fight sequences enable it to conceal its lurid structure."

These reviews were forerunners of those that would assault many a Hammer film in the near future, as *The Flanagan Boy* was the company's first picture to be

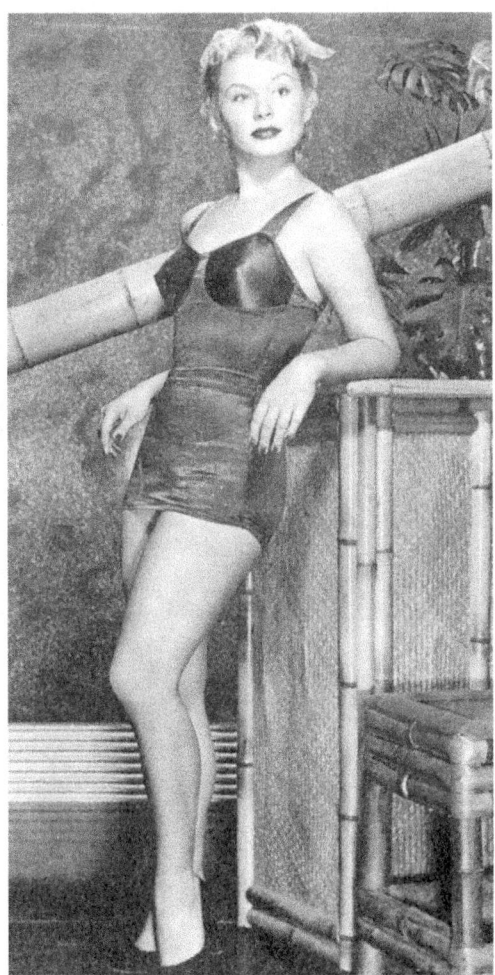

Bad girl Barbara Payton struts her stuff in *The Flanagan Boy* (photo courtesy of Ted Okuda).

attacked on "moralistic" grounds, with "lurid" an often used description. Seen today, this aspect is hardly noticeable; and what's left is a tough, entertaining melodrama with strong performances from both leads.

Spaceways

Released December 21, 1953 (U.K.), July, 1953 (U.S.); 76 minutes (U.K.), 74 minutes (U.S.); B & W; 6879 feet; a Hammer Film Production; an Exclusive Films Release (U.K.), a Lippert Release (U.S.); filmed at Bray Studios; Director: Terence Fisher; Producer: Michael

Inspector Smith (Alan Wheatley) questions his prime suspect Dr. Mitchell (Howard Duff) in Hammer's *Spaceways* (photo courtesy of Ted Okuda).

Carreras; Screenplay: Paul Tabori, Richard Landau, based on the BBC radio play by Charles Eric Maine; Director of Photography: Reginald Wyer; Editor: Maurice Rootes; Camera: Len Harris; Art Director: J. Elder Wills; Music: Ivor Slaney, played by The New Symphony Orchestra; Sound: Bill Salter; Sound System: RCA; Continuity: Renee Glynn; Makeup: D. Bonnor-Moris; Dialogue Director: Nora Roberts; Hairdresser: Polly Young; Special Effects: The Trading Post Ltd.; Process Shots: Bowie, Margutti, & Co., Ltd.; Production Manager: Victor Wark; Assistant Director: Jimmy Sangster; U.K. Certificate: U.

Howard Duff (Stephen Mitchell), Eva Bartok (Lisa Frank), Andrew Osborn (Philip Crenshaw), Anthony Ireland (General Hays), Alan Wheatley (Dr. Smith), Michael Medwin (Toby Andrews), David Horne (Minister), Cecile Chevreau (Vanessa Mitchell), Hugh Moxey (Colonel Daniels), Philip Leaver (Dr. Keppler), Jean Webster-Brough (Mrs. Daniels), Leo Phillips (Sgt. Peterson), Marianne Stone (Mrs. Rogers).

Aiding the British with their rocket experiments at the Deanfield Space Center is American scientist Stephen Mitchell (Howard Duff). His wife Vanessa (Cecile Chevreau) is bored by the strict security and lack of social life, and is having a clandestine affair with Mitchell's colleague Dr. Philip Crenshaw (Andrew Osborn), who is secretly a spy for a foreign power.

A rocket fails to return from a test at the time that Crenshaw and Vanessa inexplicably disappear from the high-security Space Center, and Mitchell is suspected of having placed his wife and her lover aboard the rocket. Mitchell and Dr. Lisa Frank (Eva Bartok), the project's chief mathematician, are in love. In order to clear himself, Mitchell offers to go up in another rocket to locate the first one, which should be floating in space. Lisa secretly replaces another scientist (Michael Medwin) who volunteered to go along with Mitchell.

Dr. Smith (Alan Wheatley), a top agent from military intelligence, succeeds in

The studio's first outer space melodrama is a dismal affair.

tracking down and arresting Crenshaw, who killed Vanessa rather than leaving her alive to testify against him. The news arrives at the Space Center too late to prevent the takeoff of the second rocket. Mitchell and Lisa are in space when they learn via radio what has transpired, but rather than abandon the mission, they opt to attempt to retrieve the stranded space capsule. The instruments freeze up and Mitchell and Lisa appear to be doomed, but Mitchell finally succeeds in freeing the emergency controls and the capsule begins to level off. Lisa radios in that they will be returning home.

Most Hammer films turned a profit, but Exclusive's release of the American made *Rocketship X-M* (1950) did far better than the company could have imagined. Mindful of its audience reactions, Hammer decided to produce their own space adventure, although *Spaceways* was more murder mystery than science fiction. Filming began on November 17, 1952. The film was to be completed on December 19, but, due to Eva Bartok's throat surgery, the schedule was extended another month. Michael Carreras (*Little Shoppe of Horrors* 4) was not in favor of making the picture. "The budget was the same as it would have been if it was about two people in bed—a domestic comedy." A factor in the film being made was the money Hammer received from the Eady Fund. Begun in September, 1950, Eady was financed by a tax on cinema tickets which was then made available to studios who wanted to increase their budgets or who needed backing after a film "flopped." Due to Eady, Hammer was able to increase its budgets by 50 percent. Even so, *Spaceways* was budgeted far less than was required and looked it. James Carreras also wanted Eady money to build two new stages at Bray, which now had sixty-eight permanent employees.

Len Harris recalled for the authors (December, 1993): "Terence Fisher wanted some quick, cheap, and easy camera effects for when the rocket was launched. The only thing I could think of was to free float the camera and let Harry Oakes shake it while I tried to get *something* on film. Elaborate effects, Hammer style! Actually, it worked pretty well and didn't cost a thing. Terry always asked for advice on matters like this. Not that it's a big thing, but many directors wouldn't 'lower' themselves. Hammer was very much a cooperative concern—no one pulled rank. Terry was always interested in other people's ideas."

Unfortunately, audiences and reviewers expect—and deserve—more than this in a science fiction movie; and, following *Spaceways*' December 21, 1953, release, neither were impressed. *The Monthly Film Bulletin* (December): "A dull and shoddy affair"; *The Kinematograph Weekly* (June 25): "Artfully colored by pseudo scientific jargon and detail"; *Motion Picture Exhibitor* (July 15): "On the slow side"; and *Variety* (July 8): "Direction is extremely methodical." Advertised as Britain's first space adventure, *Spaceways* has little to recommend it. The talk-test film betrays its radio origins and is hampered by cheap sets, stock footage, an unexciting hero, and a lack of action. Hammer would do *much* better with the *Quatermass* series.

1953

The Saint's Return

Released October 12, 1953 (U.K.), March, 1954 (U.S.); 6583 feet; 73 minutes (U.K.), 68 minutes; B & W; a Hammer Film Production; an Exclusive Films Release (U.K.), an RKO Radio Release (U.S.); filmed at Bray Studios, England, and on location in London; Director: Seymour Friedman; Producers: Anthony Hinds, Julian Lesser; Screenplay: Alan MacKinnon, based on the characters created by Leslie Charteris; Director of Photography: Walter Harvey; Editor: James Needs; Music: Ivor Slaney; Art Director: J. Elder Wills; Sound: Bill Salter; Camera Operator: Len Harris; Assistant Director: Jimmy Sangster; Production Manager: John "Pinky" Green; Continuity: Renee Glynn; Makeup: Phil Leakey; Hair Stylist: Nina Broe; Dialogue Director: Patrick Jenkins. U.S. Title: *The Saint's Girl Friday*.

Louis Hayward (Simon Templar), Sydney Tafler (Max Lennar), Naomi Chance (Lady Carol Denbeigh), Charles Victor (Chief Inspector Teal), Diana Dors (Margie), Harold Lang (Jarvis), Jane Carr (Katie French), Russell Enoch (Keith Merton), Fred Johnson (Irish Cassidy), Thomas Gallagher (Hoppy Uniatz), Ian Fleming, John Wynn, Russell Napier, George Margo.

Simon Templar (Louis Hayward), alias "The Saint," returns to London after a long absence when he receives an urgent call from an old friend, Judy Fenton. According to Fenton, her fiancé Keith (Russell Enoch), son of Lord Merton, is being blackmailed by a ruthless gang who specializes in illegal gambling dens. However, before Templar arrives, Judy is killed in a suspicious car crash.

Upon his arrival in London, Templar meets Lady Carol Denbeigh (Naomi Chance) who takes him to a floating casino moored in the upper Thames. Templar guesses correctly that this is the gang's headquarters.

With the help of several nefarious characters and his faithful henchman, Hoppy Uniatz (Thomas Gallagher), Templar sets about unmasking the guilty mobsters. However, along the way there are several attempts on his life, as well as the constant interference by Chief Inspector Teal (Charles Victor), his old rival from Scotland Yard. The Saint also has to contend with his growing attraction for Carol, who may or may not be part of the gang, and the sad news of young Keith's "suicide."

Templar unravels the mystery of Judy's and Keith's deaths and exposes the thugs responsible, including their leader, Irish Cassidy (Fred Johnson). He also uncovers Carol's connection in the case and the fact that she too had been victimized by the gangsters.

After completing five pictures in the previous twelve months, Hammer was waiting for a decision about an extension of Eady Fund support for the expansion of Bray Studios. The company's next project, a "Saint story," was announced to the trades on January 26, 1953, with Montgomery Tully scheduled to direct. Louis Hayward, who had originated the role in RKO's *The Saint in New York* (1938), was signed in mid–January. At Hayward's request, Tully was dropped in favor of Sey-

The Saint's Return: Louis Hayward is back in the role he originated in Hollywood; retitled *The Saint's Girl Friday* for the U.S. market.

mour Friedman who had directed him in *The Son of Dr. Jekyll* (1951). Friedman described *The Saint's Return* (*Today's Cinema*, February 2) as a "comedy thriller." Anthony Hinds pointed out: "Although bodies might fall out of the closets, no gore is spilt, and it will be all good, clean fun." Unlike previous *Saint* pictures—most starring George Sanders—*The Saint's Return* was not based on Leslie Charteris' stories, but on an original screenplay by Allan MacKinnon. Simon Templar's last film appearance had been a decade earlier, but the character was kept alive through comic strips and radio in addition to the 150 adventures by Charteris.

Filming began on February 2, and "guest star" Diana Dors was added to the cast a week later to play a scene draped in a bath towel. She referred to herself as "The only sex symbol Britain has produced since Lady Godiva." Always grist for the tabloid mills, Dors survived her bad press because, as she said, "I have a great sense of humor and I never believe my own publicity." Severe winter weather played havoc with the schedule, as one location shoot was halted when Hayward's canoe was capsized by a wind gust, and he had to swim 100 yards to shore. Hot water bottles were needed to keep the cameras functional, and finally, exterior filming was halted. Production ended on March 6 with final exteriors filmed at Victoria Station, Belgravia, and Stoke Pages golf course. A trade show was held at the Rialto on September 1, 1953, and *The Saint's Return* was released on October 12 to favorable reviews. *The Kinematograph Weekly* (September 3): "Adequately acted, directed, and staged"; *The Cinema* (September 2): "Hayward is amusingly suave"; and *The Reynolds News* (September 6): "Slicker, tougher, and more violent than the Yanks give us."

The Saint's Return was a fine attempt to revive the popular forties character, but his *true* return came in the form of Roger Moore in the sixties television series.

Blood Orange

Released October 10, 1953 (U.K.); 76 minutes; B & W; 6882 feet; a Hammer Film Production; an Exclusive Release (U.K.), an Astor Release (U.S.); filmed at Bray Studios; Director: Terence Fisher; Producer: Michael Carreras; Screenplay: Jan Read; Director of Photography: Jimmy Harvey; Music: Ivor Slaney: Production Designer: J. Elder Wills; Production Manager: Mickey Delamar; Editor: Maurice Rootes; Assistant Editor: Margaret Murison; Camera Operator: Don Aton; Sound Recordist: Bill Salter/RCA; Boom Operator: Percy Britten; Makeup: Phil Leakey; Wardrobe: Molly Arbuthnott; Special Gowns: Ben Pearson; Fur Models by Molho; Continuity: Renee Glynn; Hairdresser: Nina Broe; Assistant Director: Jimmy Sangster; Second Assistant: Fred Stark; Third Assistant: John Draper; Library Editor: Arthur Cox; Dialogue Director: Molly Terraine; Maintenance: J.L.V. Woodwiss; U.S. Title: *Three Stops to Murder*; U.K. Certificate: U.

Tom Conway (Tom Conway), Mila Parely (Helen), Naomi Chance (Gina), Eric Pohlmann (Mercedes), Andrew Osborn (Captain Simpson), Richard Wattis (Macleod), Margaret Halstan (Lady Marchant), Eileen Way (Fernande), Michael Ripper (Eddie), Betty Cooper (Miss Betty), Thomas Heathcote (Jessup), Alan Rolfe (Inspector), Roger Delgado (Morrow), Reed de Roven (Heath), Delphi Lawrence (Chelsea), Christina Forrest (Blonde), Ann Hanslip (Jane), Leon Davey (George), Dorothy Robson (Fitter), Leo Phillips (Harry), Robert Moore (Stevenson), Dennis Cowles (Commissionaire), John Watson (Chauffeur), Cleo Rose (Vivian).

Private eye Tom Conway (Tom Conway) and his employer Mr. Mercedes (Eric Pohlmann) arrive at Pascall's Salon to investigate a burglary during which £50,000 worth of jewelry was stolen. After conferring with Helen Pascall (Mila Parley) and Inspector Macleod (Richard Wattis), Conway learns of the convoluted relationships at the Salon. Helen loves Captain Simpson (Andrew Osborn), but he wants Gina (Naomi Chance), a model. Chelsea (Delphi Lawrence), another model, threatens to tell Helen.

A customer, Lady Marchand (Margaret Halstan), while purchasing a blood orange gown, reveals that some of the jewelry was once hers. Chelsea claims that she can find the jewels, but soon falls to her death. When he goes to question Lady Marchand, Conway finds her an apparent suicide. Mercedes decides to transfer Conway to other duties in New York, but first has him "kidnapped" to find out what he knows. Taken to Mercedes' estate, Conway escapes when Macleod arrives to interview Mercedes, who is informed that the "stolen" jewels were found in his Paris salon. Mercedes escapes and arranges to meet his "silent partner." As he waits in a car park, Mercedes is murdered by the Captain.

Conway, actually employed by an insurance company, learns that Gina and the Captain have been working with Mercedes. He follows them to Mercedes' home and finds them rifling a hidden safe. After confessing to killing Chelsea, Gina shoots the Captain, hoping to make a deal with Conway. He pushes her aside and waits for the police to arrive.

Tom Conway, George Sanders' brother, had a respectable Hollywood career basically playing himself as The Falcon. In *Blood Orange*, he *literally* did so. "It's grand to be myself," he said in *Today's Cinema* (September 24, 1953). Unfortunately, his career was practically over by this time. In all-too-common Hollywood fashion, he was found destitute in a $2 a day hotel in 1965 after earning and losing well over $1 million. He died two years later at age 63.

Filming began on March 16, 1953, including a March 30 location shoot at the Worth-Paquin Salon on Grosvenor Street. *Blood Orange* went into general release on October 10, 1953, to generally indifferent reviews:

Today's Cinema (September 24): "Conventional murder mystery"; *The Kinematograph Weekly* (September 25): "Farfetched whodunnit with highlights indifferently timed"; and *Daily Cinema* (October 10): "Entertainment for all the masses." Pictures like *Blood Orange* depend almost entirely on the star's rapport with the audience; and Conway, past his prime, has very little. He is adequate, but no more, giving Hammer what it bargained for—a "name" star on the way down.

Faded Hollywood B-star Tom Conway played himself in Hammer's *Blood Orange*.

Jimmy Harvey's photography is reminiscent of a Hollywood film noir and was singled out by *Today's Cinema* (September 24) as "the most valuable aspect" of the picture, and J. Elder Wills' art direction successfully hid the low budget. The main problem with the movie is that nothing much happens. In *Terence Fisher—The Charm of Evil*, author Wheeler Dixon confesses that he was tempted to fast forward *Blood Orange* while viewing it at the British Film Institute. He was not alone. As with too many Hammer films from this period, *Blood Orange* had a physical quality that belied its low budget, but it isn't much fun to watch.

36 Hours

Released October 25, 1954 (U.K.), December, 1954 (U.S.), 80 minutes (U.K.), 84 minutes (U.S.); B & W; 7620 feet; a Hammer Film Production; an Exclusive Release (U.K.), Lippert (U.S.); Director: Montgomery Tully; Producer: Anthony Hinds; Screenplay: Steve Fisher, based on his novel; Director of Photography: Walter Harvey; Art Director: J. Elder Wills; Editor: James Needs; Music: Ivor Slaney; Music Supervisor: John Hollingsworth; Production Manager: John Green; Sound: Bill Salter; Assistant Director: Jimmy Sangster; Wardrobe Mistress: Molly Arbuthnot; U.K. Certificate: A; U.S. Title: *Terror Street*.

Dan Duryea (Bill Rogers), Elsy Albiin (Katie), Ann Gudron (Jenny), Eric Pohlmann (Slauson), John Chandos (Hart), Kenneth Griffith (Henry), Harold Lang (Harry), Jane Carr (Sister Helen-Clair), Michael Golden (Inspector Kevin), Marianne Stone (Pam), John Wynn (Sgt. Blake), Russell Napier (Plain Clothes Detective), Jacqueline Mackenzie (Waitress), John Warren (Clerk), Stephen Verco (Ned), Robert Henderson (Pop), Gabrielle Blunt, Sheila Berry, Cleo Rose (Wrens), Christine Adrian (Mrs. Hart), Robert O'Neal (Driver), Angela Glynn (Wren), Richard Ford (Sergeant), Kenneth Brown (Cop), Lee Paterson (Joe).

36 Hours (retitled *Terror Street* for the U.S.): An American noir icon past his prime.

Bill Rogers (Dan Duryea), a U.S. Air Force pilot, is in London for a 36-hour layover, and decides to visit his estranged wife Katie (Elsy Albiin). Bill learns from a neighbor (Marianne Stone) that Katie has moved to a posh West End flat. After getting the key, Bill enters her new apartment and recalls the cause of the breakup as Katie returns home. Before they can speak, he is struck from behind by Orville (John Chandos), who then kills Katie with Bill's gun after he is unable to find a mysterious object. When Bill awakens, the police are at the door, and he hides in Jenny's (Ann Gudron) adjoining flat. She is sympathetic to his plight and agrees to help.

Bill traces Orville to his estate, but he admits to only "doing business" with Katie. He is very interested in her safe deposit box, and Jenny later poses as Katie to gain access to the box. When she enters the vault, Jenny is arrested for smuggling, a charge set up by Orville. Bill is later attacked by Henry (Kenneth Griffith) who loved Katie. After subduing him, Bill learns that he was sent by Orville, who is blackmailing Slauson (Eric Pohlmann), Henry's uncle, for smuggling diamonds. Katie was employed by Orville to ensnare smuggling suspects so that he can later blackmail them. Bill and Henry confront Slauson about the diamonds, but are followed by Orville. Bill disarms him and forces him to admit that he killed Katie over missing blackmail tapes.

Steve Fisher built up quite a reputation during the 1940s as a mystery writer through the "pulps" (*Black Mask*), novels (*I Wake Up Screaming*), and screenplays (*Lady in the Lake*, 1944). Many of his stories centered on the classic noir theme of the innocent man on the run. His screenplay for *36 Hours* rehashes many noir cliches, and could have been a passable film if not for the miscasting of another noir superstar in the lead. Despite his Ivy League background, Dan Duryea made his considerable mark in Hollywood as a whining cowardly villain (*Criss Cross*, 1949). He would have been perfect as Orville—another slimy blackmailer—but was out of his element as a hero. Also misjudged in this would-be film noir was the lack of dramatic lighting and camera work associated with the genre. The picture is photographed without any real style, and its few moments of action are poorly staged. So, despite sporting legitimate noir credentials, *36 Hours* was a half-hearted attempt.

Production began on May 4, 1953, with a location shoot mid-month at the Mayfair Bank of America which, according to *The Kinematograph Weekly* (May 21), "broke new ground." The picture kept to its four week schedule and was released on October 25, 1954, to lukewarm reviews. The British Film Institute's *Monthly Bulletin* (October): "The rather commonplace murder story loses much of its interest simply because Dan Duryea has not the look of a sympathetic character"; and *The Kinematograph Weekly* (September 9): "Adequate ... good British double bill." *Today's Cinema* (May 4, 1953) gave an interesting example of the impermanence of fame by giving its readers a pronunciation guide (Doo-re-ay) for the ten year Hollywood star's name.

The Kinematograph Weekly (September 16, 1954) reported that Peter Bryan was to direct a 3-D short for Hammer with a circus background. Nothing came of the idea, to which Hammer arrived late, since the 3-D fad was basically over by 1954.

Face the Music

Released February 22, 1954 (U.K.); 84 minutes; B & W; 7606 feet; a Hammer Film Production; an Exclusive Films Ltd. Release (U.K.), a Lippert Release (U.S.); filmed at Bray Studios, England; Director: Terence Fisher; Producer: Michael Carreras; Screenplay: Ernest Borneman, based on his original story; Director of Photography: Jimmy Harvey; Editor: Maurice Rootes; Assistant Director: Jimmy Sangster; Music conducted by: Ivor Slaney, Kenny Baker; Arrangements and Trumpet Solos by: Kenny Baker; Camera: Len Harris; Art Director: J. Elder Wills; Sound: RCA; Sound Recordists: Bill Salter, George Burgess; Continuity: Renee Glynn; Makeup: Phil Leakey; Hair Stylist: Nina Broe; Wardrobe: Molly Arbuthnot; Production Manager: Mickey Delamar; U.S. Title: *The Black Glove*.

Alex Nicol (James Bradley), Eleanor Summerfield (Barbara Quigley), John Salew (Max Margulis), Paul Carpenter (John Sutherland), Geoffrey Keen (Maurie Green), Ann Hanslip (Maxine), Fred Johnson (Inspector MacKenzie), Martin Boddey (Detective Sgt. Mulrooney), Arthur Lane (Jeff Colt), Gordon Crier (Vic Parsons), Paula Byrne (Gloria Colt), Leo Phillip (Dresser), Fred Tripp (Stage Manager), Ben Williams (Gatekeeper), Frank Birch (Trumpet Salesman), Jeremy Hawk (Recording Engineer), James Carney (Barman), Melvyn Hayes (Page Boy), Mark Singleton (Waiter), Tony Hilton (Call Boy), Robert Sansom (Doctor), Pat Jorden, Frank Pettitt (Policemen), Kenny Baker's Dozen.

James Bradley (Alex Nicol), an American trumpet star appearing at the Palladium, meets Maxine (Ann Hanslip), a blues singer performing at a jazz club in Soho. The two have dinner at Maxine's apartment, where Bradley forgetfully leaves his trumpet. When Maxine is later found murdered, the police find the horn and a pair of Scotland Yard detectives (Fred Johnson, Martin Boddey) interrogate Bradley—making it clear that he's considered one of their prime suspects. Despite Bradley's declaration of innocence, he is placed under police surveillance.

With only two clues, Bradley turns amateur sleuth. He narrows the suspects to Barbara Quigley (Eleanor Summerfield), Maxine's sister; and Gloria Colt (Paula Byrne), who once sang with Maxine and

Face the Music (1953) 89

Terence Fisher tries his hand at film noir, in *Face the Music* (*The Black Glove* in America).

Barbara; Johnny Sutherland (Paul Carpenter), pianist and former trick shot artist; and record producer Maurie Green (Geoffrey Keen).

Bradley narrowly escapes death from poison placed on the mouthpiece of his trumpet—indicating that he is on the right track. Eventually he is able to pinpoint the murder of Maxine and the poison attempt on Green, a dangerous paranoid. A gun skirmish ensues before Keen is nabbed by the police.

Alex Nicol was Hammer's American star of the moment in 1953, appearing in two movies between June and August. Nicol was a graduate of Elia Kazan's Actors Studio and, after serving in World War II, made his Broadway debut in *South Pacific*. James Carreras saw Nicol in *Champ for a Day* (1953) and offered him the lead in *Face the Music*, since the roles were similar. The production began on June 22 with location work at the London Palladium. Michael Carreras was able to indulge his love of jazz by hiring trumpeter Kenny Baker to coach Nicol. The Kenny Baker Dozen appear in this film, as does Carreras as a band member. Filming moved to Bray on June 29 and ended three weeks later. Paired with Hammer's short subject *Polo*, *Face the Music* was trade shown at the Hammer Theatre on February 2, 1954, and was released on February 22 to limited, but positive, reviews as in *Today's Cinema* (February 4): "Another of those neat, efficiently made British thrillers in which Exclusive have successfully specialized during the last few years, enlivened in this instance by some slick directorial touches." One of the "slick touches" was certainly *not* the obviously appearing/disappearing candy and flowers that Nicol holds behind his back while talking to Eleanor Summerfield—a result of the hurried schedule.

Face the Music was one of Terence Fisher's best early thrillers, helped considerably by Nicol's screen presence and the well-staged jazz milieu. Many of Fisher's movies from this period were little more than talk-fests, but he keeps Ernest Borneman's tightly written script moving. The film was Hammer's first to be filmed in a wide screen ratio, and, during its production, the shooting of a color film was first planned. Robert Louis Stevenson's *The Weir of Hermiston* was discussed, but was dropped in favor of *Men of Sherwood Forest*.

The House Across the Lake

Released May, 1954 (U.S.), June 21, 1954 (U.K.); 6158 feet; 68 minutes (U.K.), 70 minutes (U.S.); B & W; a Hammer Film Production; an Associated British–Pathe Release (U.K.), a Lippert Release (U.S.); filmed at Bray Studios; Director, Screenplay: Ken Hughes; Producer: Anthony Hinds, based on the novel *High Wray* by Ken Hughes; Director of Photography: James Harvey; Editor: James Needs; Music: Ivor Slaney; Art Director: J. Elder Wills; Sound Recordist: Bill Salter; Camera: Leonard Harris; Assistant Director: Jimmy Sangster; Production Manager: John "Pinky" Green; Continuity: Renee Glynn; Makeup: Phil Leakey; Hairdresser: Nina Broe; Stills Photographer: John Jay. U.S. Title: *Heat Wave*.

Alex Nicol (Mark Kendrick), Hillary Brooke (Carol Forrest), Susan Stephen (Andrea Forrest), Sidney James (Beverley Forrest), Alan Wheatley (Inspector MacLennon), Paul Carpenter (Vincent Gordon), Hugh Dempster (Frank), Peter Illing (Harry Stevens), John Sharpe (Mr. Hardcastle), Joan Hickson (Mrs. Hardcastle), Gordon McLeod (Doctor Emery), Monti de Lyle (Head Waiter), Cleo Rose (Abigail), Howard Lang (Inspector Edgar), Harry Brunnings (Railway Porter), Peter Evans (Butler), Angela Glynne (Maid), Christine Adrian (Receptionist).

Author Mark Kendrick (Alex Nicol) rents a cottage in the North of England and meets wealthy socialite Carol Forrest (Hillary Brooke), faithless wife of Beverley (Sidney James), who has a weak heart. Beverley is aware of his wife's infidelities and plans to cut her out of his will. Kendrick befriends him, and with Carol tagging along, the men go fishing. Their fogbound boat swerves to avoid a rock, and Beverley is knocked unconscious in a fall. Carol begs Kendrick to throw him overboard and, lured by her promises, obliges. They report the "accident" to the police, but Forrest's daughter Andrea (Susan Stephen) is suspicious, as is Inspector McLennon (Alan Wheatley). An inquest clears the couple, but McLennon does not accept the verdict.

The murderers part for appearance sake, but after not hearing from Carol for weeks, Kendrick returns to the lakeside house to find she has moved out. He meets Andrea and McLennon, who take him to Carol's new residence where she lives with her new husband Vincent (Paul Carpenter). Carol tells Kendrick that she always loved Vincent, and with nothing left to lose, he tells her that he's going to confess. Kendrick walks away, oblivious to Carol's screams.

The House Across the Lake was the prototypical "noir" concept of a basically decent man degraded by an evil woman, and eventually becoming a discarded lover and a murderer. Director Ken Hughes told the authors (February, 1992):

> When I wrote my novel *High Wray*, I 'borrowed' the style of my favorite author, Raymond Chandler. My agent sent the novel around the business, and a copy got to Hammer Film's Tony Hinds. They liked it; and when they discovered I was also 'Ken Hughes—the director'—the deal was set. So I wrote the screenplay, too. Bray was a very adaptable studio within a stone's throw of the Thames River. The studios were comfortable—if small—and emanated a kind of homey atmosphere. But, of course, it did not lend itself to major sets and had no backlot where any extensive building could take place. The stages were small, but, with a bit of ingenuity, they worked. *All* confined theatre stages and studios force you to use your imagination. The rich appearance of Hammer Films was due to the ingenuity and skill of its art directors who had to work within the confines. So, more money was available for dressing, decor, and furnishings.

The production began at Bray on August 10, 1953, following several days of location work in the Northern Lake District, and ended on September 4. Following a May 26, 1954, trade show at Studio One, *The House Across the Lake* was released on June 21 through Associated British–Pathe. This was the first time since 1947 that Exclusive did not release a Hammer Film in the U.K. *Today's Cinema* (February 1, 1954) reported, "The low production costs which quite belied the polish of the finished product must have been a factor to influence the deal." A plan to have ABP release future productions did not materialize. Reviewers were haltingly positive. *The Kinematograph Weekly* (June 3, 1954): "Neat interplay of characters"; *The Monthly Film Bulletin* (July): "well constructed and photographed"; and *The Motion Picture Exhibitor* (May 19): "An interesting yarn with adequate direction and production."

The House Across the Lake is one of Hammer's best noir thrillers. It avoids the stilted talkiness of many of the company's other attempts at the genre, and has the feel of a grade B Hollywood production, which is as authentic as noir gets. Alex Nicol was well cast as the easily duped author, following in the well-worn footsteps of many noir anti-heroes; and Hillary Brooke, with her sinister good looks, was a perfect femme fatale.

Life with the Lyons

Released May 24, 1954 (U.K.), May, 1956 (U.S.); 81 minutes (U.K.); 78 minutes (U.S.); B & W; 7326 feet; a Hammer Film Production; an Exclusive Films Release (U.K.), a Lippert Release (U.S.); filmed at Bray Studios, England; Director & Screenplay: Val Guest; Producer: Robert Dunbar; Screenplay: Robert Dunbar, based on the BBC radio series; Director of Photography: Walter Harvey; Editor: Doug Myers; Art Director: Wilfred Arnold; Music: Arthur Wilkinson; Model's Clothes by: RIMA; Sound Recordist: Bill Salter; Camera: Len Harris; Producer's Assistant: Freddie Pearson; Production Manager: Arthur Barnes; Continuity: "Splinters" Deason; Makeup: Phil Leakey; Hair Stylist: Nina Broe.

Ben Lyon, Bebe Daniels, Barbara Lyon, Richard Lyon (Themselves), Hugh Morton (Mr. Hemmingway), Horace Percival (Wimple), Molly Weir (Aggie), Doris Rogers (Florrie), Gwen Lewis (Mrs. Wimple), Arthur Hill (Slim Cassidy), Belinda Lee (Violet).

Despite the reservations of Mr. Hemmingway (Hugh Morton), a stuffy landlord, the Lyon family (Bebe, Ben, Barbara, and Richard) move into their new West End house. Hemmingway can't tolerate the chaos the exhuberant family creates, and storms out with the as yet unsigned lease. The Lyons try to redeem themselves, but every time Hemmingway returns to the house, there is a new disaster. The fear of losing their house prompts the family to maintain order long enough to finally have the lease signed, but not before Hemmingway is once more offended and storms out in a huff.

The Lyon Family, although little known in America, were as popular with the British as the Royal Family (in the days when the Royal Family *was* popular). The Lyons—Ben and Bebe Daniels—were actually Americans. Ben had been a film star (*Hell's Angels*, 1930) in Hollywood, with a career that dated back to 1919. Bebe's first film was a 1914 Selig short, and her pleasant singing voice helped her get roles in musicals like *42nd Street* (1933). They married in 1930. The Lyons settled in England, and their radio program *Hi Gang!*, which premiered in May, 1940, soon became a British institution. The show ran through the London blitz, and the Lyons endeared themselves to the British by not fleeing back to America. "During the war," noted *The Kinematograph Weekly* (no date), "the Lyons made us laugh at times when we sorely needed laughter." The program was revived in 1949 and a new show, *Life with the Lyons*, began on the BBC in 1951. The success of this show naturally attracted Hammer. "Everyone wanted to make a film with them," Val Guest told the authors (February, 1992), "and they personally came to me to ask if I'd make it—Ben and Bebe were old friends of mine. One day Ben just stopped me in the street and asked me! I had done lots of films before this one—films of all kinds, including comedies. Since we were friendly, I was a natural choice. It was my first film for Hammer."

Life with the Lyons began production on September 7, 1953. Guest combined three radio shows in the film script and used many of the original radio cast. The picture was trade shown at Studio One on January 5, 1954, and was Hammer's first film to be "sneak previewed" a week later. *Life with the Lyons* played twenty pre-release spots between January 26 and April 22, and in

Director Val Guest's first Hammer Film.

another first for the company, the stars made personal appearances. The Lyons, who did the film for half their normal salary, took a percentage of the profits. As a result of the film's success, the Lyons were given a BBC television series which debuted on April 2, 1954, and clips from the movie were shown on the first episode. *Life with the Lyons* went into general release to over two thousand theatres on the ABC circuit on May 24, 1954. It was also shown on board all Cunnard ocean liners that summer. The film was a hit with both audiences and writers. *Today's Cinema* (January 28, 1954): "Excellent enter-

Hammer's biggest moneymaker of 1954, *Life with the Lyons*, was a huge hit with audiences throughout England.

tainment for the masses"; *The Kinematograph Weekly* (January 28): "Expertly scripted, directed, and acted"; and *The Monthly Film Bulletin* (January): "A pleasant and unpretentious film." Given the company's later reputation, it's odd that this gentle family comedy would be Hammer's first hit. It grossed over £70,000 and made a lot of people happy—including Hammer.

Murder by Proxy

Released March 28, 1955 (U.K.), May 21, 1954 (U.S.); 87 minutes; B & W; length 7813 feet; a Hammer Film Production; an Exclusive Release (U.K.), a Lippert Release (U.S.); filmed at Bray Studios; Director: Terence Fisher; Producer: Michael Carreras; Screenplay: Richard Landau, based on a novel by Helen Hielsen; Director of Photography: Walter Harvey; Editor: Maurice Rootes; Camera Operator: Len Harris; Sound: Bill Salter and George Burgess; Production Manager; Mickey Delmar; Music: Ivor Slaney; Assistant Director: Jimmy Sangster; Makeup: Phil Leakey. U.K. Certificate: A.

Dane Clark (Casey Morrow), Belinda Lee (Phyllis Brunner), Betty Ann Davies (Alicia Brunner), Eleanor Summerfield (Maggie Doone), Andrew Osborn (Lance Gorden), Harold Lang (Travis), Jill Melford (Miss Nardis), Alvis Maben (Lita Huntley), Michael Golden (Inspector Johnson), Alfie Bass (Ernie).

Broke and drunk, Canadian Casey Morrow (Dane Clark) is picked up in a London club by Phyllis Brunner (Belinda Lee) who offers him £500 to marry her. Morrow passes out and awakens in a strange apartment belonging to Maggie (Eleanor Summerfield) who explains that she found him on her doorstep. He has no memory of the previous night. When he leaves, Morris is stunned to see Phyllis' picture on the front page of every newspaper. She is missing, and her wealthy father has been murdered. In Morrow's pocket is £500, and there is blood on his clothing. He finds Phyllis who says they found her father dead, and that Morrow handled the bloody murder weapon—a fire poker. He agrees to help Phyllis find the killer, but suspects a double cross. When the family lawyer (Andrew Osborn) is shot at Morrow's hotel, he becomes a suspect in two murders. Desperate, Morrow confronts Phyllis' mother (Betty Ann Davies) who

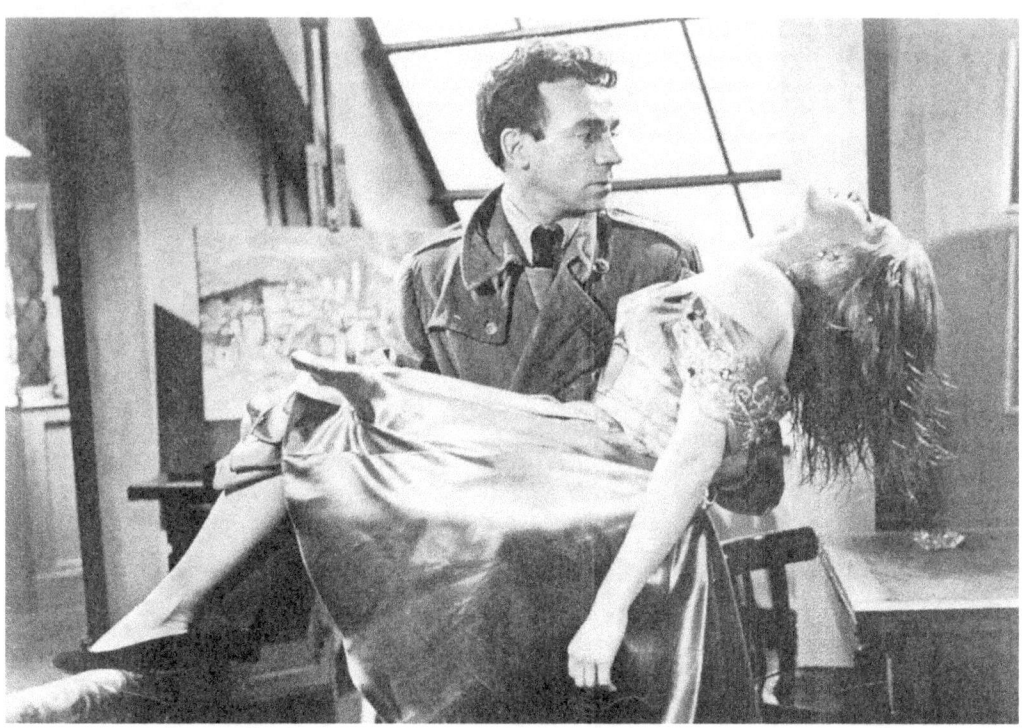

Dane Clark (holding Belinda Lee) is up to his neck in trouble in *Murder by Proxy*.

admits to both killings. She had tampered with her husband's charity funds and, when found out, committed the murders. Cleared of suspicion, Morrow must now deal with his drinking problem—and Phyllis.

Amnesia is one of the oldest—and most effective—thriller cliches, used to perfection by author Cornell Woolrich in classics like *The Black Curtain* and *Nightmare*. Hammer had its go at the subgenre in *Murder by Proxy*, which was the first of an eight picture pact with Lippert Productions. The deal was finalized at a luncheon at the Savoy on September 24, 1953, and filming began four days later. *The Kinematograph Weekly* (October 8) was on the set and described the sweeping changes at Bray. "It is no longer completely accurate to call it a country house studio, for Exclusive's inventive and ingenious craftsmen have so altered and adapted the historic mansion that it has the equivalent facilities to those of a medium size conventional studio." One wing of Down Place had three rooms converted into one, measuring 110 × 25 feet so that rooms within rooms could be constructed. A theatre for viewing rushes, along with dressing rooms and an art department office, was built on the upper floor. An out building now housed the editing department, formerly stationed in London. "The secret of Hammer's reputation for quality," enthused the *Kine* reporter, "obviously lies in teamwork."

This was Dane Clark's second film of three for Hammer, and *Murder by Proxy*'s rough scenes posed little problem for him due to a background in athletics. Due to his small size, Clark abandoned sports for a law degree, but the Depression soured his chance for a practice of his own. He started his acting career in radio, appeared on Broadway productions of *Dead End* and *Of Mice and Men*, and went to Hollywood as a junior John Garfield. Belinda Lee was a rising young star and received "introducing billing." A promising career ended when she died, at age 26, in a car crash.

Murder by Proxy was released on March 28, 1955, to indifferent reviews. *The Kine-*

A promising career that was cut short by a car crash at age 26.

matograph Weekly (March 10): "Acceptable British programmer," and the British Film Institute's Monthly Bulletin (April): "Technically, the film is competently made." Oddly, the picture was released a year earlier in the U.S. The New York Herald Tribune (May 22, 1954): "It is perhaps a bit too tricky for its own good"; The New York Times (May 22): "This ready made format is seldom compact or tingling under Terence Fisher's slack direction"; Variety (May 5): "A gabby overlong import."

Most reviewers went out of their way to denigrate Terence Fisher, who had not yet found his way. Murder by Proxy is typical of Fisher's pre–Gothic horror pictures—watchable, but not much more.

Five Days

Released June, 1954 (U.K.), August, 1954 (U.S.); 72 minutes (U.K.), 75 minutes (U.S.); 6528 feet; B & W; a Hammer Film Production; an Exclusive Films Release (U.K), a Lippert Release (U.S.); filmed at Bray Studios, England; Director: Montgomery Tully; Producer: Anthony Hinds; Screenplay: Paul Tabori; Director of Photography: James Harvey; Editor: James Needs; Music: Ivor Slaney; Art Director: J. Elder Wills; Assistant Director: Jimmy Sangster; Makeup: Phil Leakey; Production Manager: John "Pinky" Green; Assistant Director: Jimmy Sangster; Camera Operator: Len Harris; Wardrobe Mistress: Molly Arbuthnot; Hair Stylist: Nina Broe; Stills Photographer: John Jay; Sound Mixer: Bill Salter; U.S. Title: *Paid to Kill*.

Dane Clark (James Nevill), Paul Carpenter (Paul Kirby), Thea Gregory (Andrea), Cecile Chevreau (Joan), Anthony Forwood (Glanville), Howard Marion Crawford (McGowan), Avis Scott (Eileen), Peter Gawthorne (Bowman), Leslie Wright (Hunter), Hugo Schuster (Professor), Arthur Young (Hyson), Martin Lawrence (Masseur), Ross Hutchinson (Ingham), Arnold Diamond (Perkins), Charles Hawtrey (Bill), Geoffrey Sumner (Chapter).

Facing financial ruin, James Nevill (Dane Clark), head of Amalgamated Industries, takes out a large life insurance policy—naming his wife Andrea (Thea Gregory) as beneficiary—and asks his boyhood friend Paul Kirby (Paul Carpenter) to kill him within five days so that Andrea can collect. Kirby refuses to kill his friend, but is forced to go along with the plan when Nevill reveals his knowledge of an unsolved murder Kirby committed years before.

Eccentric millionaire McGowan (Howard Marion Crawford) unexpectedly agrees to back Nevill in business, doing away with the need for Kirby's services—but Nevill cannot locate Kirby. Nevill's secretary Joan (Cecile Chevreau) tries to help. Not long afterwards, Nevill narrowly escapes four separate attempts on his life. However, due to the nature and frequency of the attacks, he begins to suspect that Kirby may not be the only one trying to kill him.

Explaining the situation to Andrea, Nevill decides to go into hiding. But as he is about to leave, his business associate Glanville (Anthony Forwood) appears with a revolver pointed at him. Glanville explains that when he and Andrea learned of Nevill's deal, they kidnapped Kirby and planned to kill them both. The authorities would later be told of the plan and assume that Kirby committed suicide in remorse, leaving Glanville and Andrea free to go off together with the insurance money.

Glanville is about to pull the trigger when Joan arrives. Nevill makes a grab for the gun—Andrea is shot in the struggle, and Glanville is held for the police.

Dane Clark had been scheduled to return to Hollywood immediately following the completion of *Murder by Proxy* to star in two Technicolor westerns. However, Anthony Hinds persuaded him to remain in England by offering him the lead in *Five Days*. Filming began on November 9, 1953, under the direction of Montgomery Tully, who had previously done *36 Hours*. Both films were would-be films noir, copying an American form that had peaked in the late 1940s. The plot involving a man who hires his own murderer, then changes his mind—but not his employee's—was a noir staple. The basic plot was used in *The Whistler* series a decade earlier and would be used again, often, simply because it *is* a great plot device. Unfortunately, not even this could lift *Five Days* out of the ordinary.

A week into the production, Bray's first sound stage was completed at a cost of over £10,000. The fully equipped studio, measuring over 1200 square feet, was officially christened by Dane Clark while members of the unit and company heads looked on.

Filming ended on December 16, and several weeks later, James Carreras became Chief Barker for the Variety Club, beginning an important association for both Carreras and Hammer. *Five Days* was trade shown at the Hammer Theatre on May 12, 1954, and was released in the U.K. in June to negative reviews. *The Kinematograph Weekly* (May 20): "The picture puts a considerable strain upon the credulity of its audience"; the British Film Institute's *Monthly Bulletin* (July): "The direction is uneven, scenes are put together with little sense of movement or continuity, and the result is a thriller below average"; *The Motion Picture Exhibitor* (August 11): "The plot is of average interest."

Like too many Hammer thrillers of the period, *Five Days* failed to thrill. Although there was technically nothing wrong with the production, it lacked the bite of its American counterparts. Dane Clark managed to combine the toughness and sensitivity needed to pull off the role of a noir hero; unfortunately, Tully's direction was unable to take advantage of the plot's possibilities, and *Five Days* is just an average retelling.

1954

The Stranger Came Home

Released August 9, 1954 (U.K.), November, 1954 (U.S.); 80 minutes; B & W; 7229 feet; a Hammer Film Production; an Exclusive Release (U.K.), Lippert (U.S.); filmed at Bray Studios; Director: Terence Fisher; Producer: Michael Carreras; Screenplay: Michael Carreras, based on George Sanders'novel; Director of Photography: Jim Harvey; Editor: Bill Lenny; Production Manager: Jim Sangster; Art Director: J. Elder Wills; Camera Operator: Len Harris; Sound Camera Operator: Don Alton; Makeup: Phil Leakey; Hair Stylist: Eileen Bates; Sound Mixer: Sid Wiles; Assistant Director: Jack Causey; Continuity: Renee Glynn; Wardrobe Mistress: Molly Arbuthnot; Furs by Molino; Music: Leonard Salzedo; Music Supervisor: John Hollingsworth; U.K. Certificate: A; U.S. Title: *The Unholy Four*.

William Sylvester (Vickers), Paulette God-

Patrick Holt, Joan Merrill, and Paul Carpenter discuss William Sylvester's unwelcome return in *The Stranger Came Home*.

dard (Angie), Patrick Holt (Crandall), Paul Carpenter (Saul), Alvys Maben (Joan), Russell Napier (Treherne), David King Wood (Sessions), Pat Owen (Blonde), Kay Callard (Jenny), Jeremy Hawk (Sgt. Johnson), Jack Taylor (Brownie), Kim Mills (Roddy), Owen Evans (Redhead), Philip Lennard (Medical Examiner).

Philip Vickers (William Sylvester) returns to his country estate after being missing for three years, arriving during one of his wife Angie's (Paulette Goddard) frequent parties. Angie is off with a man, and her secretary Joan (Alvys Maben) is openly hostile. Vickers had been on holiday in Portugal with Bill Saul (Paul Carpenter), Job Crandall (Patrick Holt), and Harry Bryce. One of the trio clubbed him from behind and left him for dead, his memory gone. All three are present at the party and are interested in Angie. Bryce's body is found in the boathouse, and Inspector Treherne (Russell Napier) arrives to investigate.

Sessions (David King Wood), Vickers' accountant, and Crandall, his business manager, have been defrauding him, and during a quarrel, Sessions is killed. Crandall decides to confess to Bryce's murder also, to take the heat off Angie who is a suspect. When Trehane arrests Angie, Joan tries to protect her by implicating Vickers. When Saul arrives for a small dinner party, he murders Joan, setting up Vickers to take the blame. Vickers tells Saul that he killed Angie to get his reaction, and he is attacked. Vickers disarms Saul and beats a confession to the murder out of him—and Saul's admission to the assault in Portugal. All of the crimes were committed to get Angie for himself.

This dull, confusing film marked the end of Hollywood star Paulette Goddard's career which began in 1929. *The Stranger Came Home* was her second British picture, following *An Ideal Husband* (1948), and her return to the U.K. was treated as a major

98 *The Stranger Came Home* (1954)

Michael Carreras tries his hand at adapting a novel for the screen.

event. Production began on January 4, 1954, based on a novel by George Sanders, Hollywood's resident cad. It's too bad he wasn't *in* the film as well.

The Stranger Came Home was trade shown at the Hammer theatre on July 14, 1954, and was released on August 9 to unimpressive reviews. *The Kinematograph Weekly* (July 22, 1954): "There are no big thrills"; the British Film Institute's *Monthly Bulletin* (September): "Almost incomprehensible"; *Variety* (September 29): "Direction of Terence Fisher is plodding until a windup fight"; *The New York Times* (November 20): "A third rate British who-dunit." As so often happened during this period, Fisher—justifiably—received most of the blame. Although the premise, production values, and acting are acceptable, the film is *boring* and *slow*—and that's the director's fault. Fortunately, Hammer saw something in Terence Fisher despite his poor notices. Len Harris told the authors (December, 1993), "Terry began his career as an editor—many good directors do. He was a very dedicated man. There was no wasted film—Terry was an editor's delight. He always knew what he wanted before he shot it." Fisher himself noted (*Cinefantastique*, Vol. 4, No. 3), "My career had been attempting to find a line of direction I was good at."

There would be no second chance, though, for Paulette Goddard. She retired after completing the film and made only one film appearance since in *Time of Indifference* (1964), which would serve as a review of *The Stranger Came Home*.

Third Party Risk

Released January, 1955 (U.S.), April 4, 1955 (U.K.); 70 minutes (U.K.), 63 minutes (U.S.); B & W; a Hammer Film Production; an Exclusive Films Release (U.K.), a Lippert Release (U.S.); filmed at Bray Studios, England, and on location in Spain; Director: Daniel Birt; Producer: Robert Dunbar; Executive Producer: Michael Carreras; Screenplay: Daniel Birt, Robert Dunbar, based on a novel by Nicholas Bently; Director of Photography: James Harvey; Editor: James Needs; Music: Michael Krein; Art Director: J. Elder Wills; Sound: Sid Wiles; Production Manager: Jimmy Sangster; Assistant Director: Jack Causey; Camera: Len Harris; Continuity: Renee Glynn; Wardrobe: Molly Arbuthnot; Makeup: Phil Leakey; Hair Stylist: Eileen Bates; Sound Camera: Don Alton. U.S. Title: *Deadly Game*; U.S. Television Title: *Big Deadly Game*; U.K. Certificate: A.

Lloyd Bridges (Philip Graham), Finlay Currie (Darius), Maureen Swanson (Lolita), Simone Silva (Mitzi Molnar), Ferdy Mayne (Maxwell Carey), Peter Dyneley (Tony Roscoe), Roger Delgardo (Gonzales), George Woodbridge (Inspector Goldfinch), Leslie Wright (Sgt. Ramsey), Mary Parker (Mrs. Zeissmann), Seymour Green (Rope-Soles), Toots Pounds (Lucy), Patrick Westwood (Porter), Russell Walters (Dr. Zeissmann).

While vacationing in Spain, author Philip Graham (Lloyd Bridges) meets a wartime friend, Tony Roscoe (Peter Dyneley). He introduces Graham to Darius (Finlay Currie), a London financier, Lolita (Maureen Swanson), his niece, and Mitzi (Simone Silva) and Maxwell Carey (Ferdy Mayne). Graham is attracted to Lolita, but Tony whisks him away when he needs a ride to the airport. Graham is then asked to drive Tony's car to London and deliver an envelope. At Tony's London apartment, Graham finds Mitzi burning some letters—and, later, his friend's corpse on the floor beside a roll of microfilm. He finds more microfilm inside the envelope, and discovers that it contains a valuable chemical formula stolen from Dr. Zeissmann (Russell Walters).

After eliminating Mitzi as the killer, Graham suspects her husband who knows about the stolen microfilm. Carey sets a trap for Graham in a warehouse, but, Maxwell himself dies in a fire. When Graham goes to see Lolita, he learns that she and Darius have returned to Spain. He follows them, and with the help of the village police chief (Roger Delgado), proves that Darius masterminded the international plot.

The growing popularity of CinemaScope, Technicolor, and television was beginning to have a negative effect on small independent producers like Hammer. The company began to experiment with filming in foreign locations to ward off sagging ticket sales, but to little avail. Hammer's lucrative agreement with Robert Lippert was also about to end.

Although James Carreras made plans to produce eight more features in 1955, *Third Party Risk* was the last picture released in America through Lippert. The film began production on February 15, 1954, under the direction of Daniel Birt, who died a few months after its completion at age 48.

Len Harris recalled (August, 1993) a harrowing incident while filming the fight scene between Lloyd Bridges and Ferdy

Mayne. "We did the fire scene in an old barn which had been built for another picture. Daniel Birt, Jimmy Harvey, and I were in a gantry when the staircase was set on fire. When Birt yelled 'Cut!,' the firemen rushed in and put out the fire, but the smoke drifted up to the gantry, and we were suffocating. Usually, I would try to figure out an escape *before* I needed it, just in case. I kicked out the slats of the barn wall for some air, but the three of us were pretty sick. No one really thought of the possible danger. Because Hammer's new sound stages were unavailable, interiors for *Third Party Risk* were filmed in the Old House. We built sets within rooms, especially the big ballroom. We had put in a certain amount of sound proofing, but it was far from perfect. In the silent days, most British films were shot in old houses—it was sound that caused the problems." Recalling in-house Art Director J. Elder Wills, Harris said, "He was an 'old boy' at Hammer—and a very interesting character. During World War II, he was a colonel in the camouflage unit, put down on the Normandy beach to take soil samples to make sure that the tanks wouldn't bog down during the invasion. He was dressed like a peasant, collecting soil in a can! Anthony Hinds took his pseudonym—John Elder—from him. Wills was, I believe, a cousin of Will Hammer."

Third Party Risk was trade shown at the Hammer Theatre on March 22, 1955, but had its American release in January. The picture was released in the U.K. on April 4 to mixed reviews and slow box office. *Today's Cinema* (March 23): "The improbable adventures sweep along excitingly enough"; *The Monthly Bulletin* (May): "Unimaginative

Len Harris, James Harvey, and director Daniel Birt nearly burned to death during the making of Hammer's *Third Party Risk* (retitled *Deadly Game* for the U.S. market).

direction and routine performances"; and *The Kinematograph Weekly* (March 24): "The trimmings accentuate rather than conceal its poverty of imagination." *Third Party Risk* proved that it took more than location filming to lure audiences from their TVs.

Mask of Dust

Released December 27, 1954 (U.K.), January, 1955 (U.S.); 79 minutes (U.K.), 69 minutes (U.S.); B & W; 7114 feeet; a Hammer Film Production; Released by Exclusive (U.K.), Lippert (U.S.); filmed at Bray Studios and at various racetracks; Director: Terence Fisher; Producer:

Mask of Dust (1954) 101

Poster from *Mask of Dust* (courtesy of Fred Humphries and Colin Cowie).

Mickey Delmar; Executive Producer: Michael Carreras; Screenplay: Richard Landau, based on Jon Manchip White's novel; Director of Photography: James Harvey; Music: Leonard Salzedo; Art Director: J. Elder Wills; Editor: Bill Lenny; Camera Operator: Len Harris; Sound Mixer: Sid Wiles; Sound Camera Operator: Don Alton; Continuity: Renee Glynn; Wardrobe: Molly Arbuthnott; Makeup: Phil Leakey; Hairstyles: Monica Hustler; Production Manager: Jimmy Sangster; U.S. Title: *A Race for Life*; U.K. Certificate: U.

Richard Conte (Peter Wells), Mari Aldon (Pat Wells), George Couloris (Dallapiccola), Peter Illing (Bellario), Alex Mango (Rizett), Meredith Edwards (Lawrence), James Copeland (Johnny), Jeremy Hawk, Richard Marner, Edwin Richfield, Tom Turner, Stirling Moss, Reg Parnell, John Cooper, Geoffrey Taylor, Leslie Marr (drivers).

Since leaving the Air Force, race driver Peter Wells (Richard Conte) has been attempting to recapture his former glory. He is now the number three driver on the Italian Corsi team, and both the manager Bellario (Peter Illing) and Peter's wife Pat (Mari Aldon) want him to give it up. When fellow driver Dallapiccola (George Couloris) tries to persuade him to quit, Wells argues with his old friend. During the race, Wells learns during a pit stop that Dallapiccola has had a serious crash. He pulls out of the race—despite Bellario's warning—to see his dying friend. As a result, Wells loses his place on the team—and Pat—who leaves him when he still refuses to retire. Bellario gives him a last chance in the Italian Grand Prix by giving him an old car in poor condition. During the race, the car leaks oil, blinding Wells and making him a potential living torch. Despite Bellario's demands, Wells refuses to quit and, motivated further by Pat's presence, wins in a photo finish. After proving to everyone—and himself—that he's still a champion, Wells retires.

No matter who stars, a car racing picture is basically a bunch of cars going around in a circle with off-track cliches added to pad the length. From James Cagney's *The Crowd Roars* (1932) to Clark Gable's *To Please a Lady* (1950) to Steve McQueen's *LeMans* (1971), the story was pretty much the same. Hammer's attempt at the genre was, according to the *Kinematograph Weekly* (May 13, 1954), "The first British production written around the lives of racing drivers." Filming began on March 25, 1954, with first-time producer Mickey Delmar. Terence

Fisher had become Hammer's "house director," guiding eleven of the twenty films made since he joined the company. He was considered something of a pioneer by the cinema press after directing *Spaceways*, the first post-war British science fiction film, and, next, this racing film. Fisher took a camera unit and Richard Conte to Goodwood Track to shoot actual racing scenes during the Easter meeting. Present were top drivers Stirling Moss and John Cooper. Four stationary cameras were used to catch both the cars and the crowd reactions, plus a camera car on the track.

Richard Conte's participation caused a minor uproar in the press. "Why put a Hollywood actor in the hero's driving seat in a British film about racing cars?" whined *The Daily Cinema* (May 13, 1954). "The answer beats me. It was galling to see the camera film a closeup of Conte at the controls of a racing car and then to see British driver Geoffrey Taylor doubling for him." *Mask of Dust* was one of the first films to use racing drivers themselves. In addition to Moss and Cooper, other top drivers included Jeremy Hawk, Richard Marner, Edward Rechfield, and Reg Parnell.

Filming ended on May 8, 1954, followed by a November 23 trade show and a December 27 release. Reviews were positive, if not ecstatic. The British Film Institute's *Monthly Bulletin* (January, 1955): "Skillful use of newsreel footage in the actual racing sequences raise the routine story slightly higher than average"; *Variety* (February 7): "An OK entry for minor double billing."

Mask of Dust ended Hammer's brief fling with sports begun with *The Flanagan Boy*, and the company would return to mostly routine thrillers before hitting its stride with the *Quatermass Xperiment*.

Men of Sherwood Forest

Released December 6, 1954 (U.K.); 77 minutes; Eastman Color; 6970 feet; a Hammer Film Production; an Exclusive Release (U.K.); an Astor Release (U.S.); filmed at Bray Studios; Director: Val Guest; Producer: Michael Carreras; Screenplay: Allan Mackinnon; Director of Photography: Jimmy Harvey; Music composed by: Doreen Corwithen; Art Director: J. Elder Wills; Production Manager: Jimmy Sangster; Camera Operator: Len Harris; Continuity: Renee Glynn; Wardrobe Mistress: Molly Arbuthnot; Makeup: Phil Leakey; Sound Mixer: David Wiles; Sound Camera Operator: Don Alton; Editor: James Needs; Hair Stylist: Mary Hostler; U.K. Certificate: U.

Don Taylor (Robin Hood), Reginald Beckwith (Friar Tuck), Eileen Moore (Lady Alys), David King Wood (Sir Guy Belton), Douglas Wilmer (Sir Nigel Saltire), Harold Lang (Hubert), Ballard Berkeley (Walter), Wensley Pithy (Hugo), Leslie Linder (Little John), John Van Eyssen (Will Scarlet), Toke Townsley (Father David), Vera Pearce (Elvira), John Stuart (Moran), John Kerr (Brian of Eskdale), Raymond Rollett (Abbott); Leonard Sachs (Sheriff of Nottingham), Howard Lang (Town Crier), Jackie Lane (Mary), Tom Bowan, Bernard Bresslaw, Michael Godfrey, Dennis Wyndham, Jack McNaughton (Merry Men), and Patrick Holt (King Richard).

England, 1194. While fighting the Crusades, King Richard (Patrick Holt) is taken prisoner and his throne seized by his scheming brother, John, who is opposed only by Robin Hood (Don Taylor) and his Merry Men. When John Fitzroy is found murdered in Sherwood Forest, Robin is unjustly accused. Fitzroy was killed because he carried plans to free Richard, which did not sit well with Sir Nigel (Douglas Wilmer) and the Count of Moraine (John Stuart). Robin traces the stolen plans to Sir Guy Belton (David King Wood) and, disguised as a troubadour, enters the castle and is warmly received by the beautiful lady Alys (Eileen Moore). Sir Nigel, an agent of Prince John's, unmasks Robin and Friar Tuck (Reginald Beckwith) as spies, but they are freed by Alys. They foil the attempt to murder Richard, defeat Sir Guy's rebels, and feast with the King and Alys on stolen Royal deer in Sherwood.

Men of Sherwood Forest was Hammer's first color feature and the company's first of three stabs at the ancient legend. Like other Robin Hood pictures, it pales in comparison to the 1938 Errol Flynn classic *The Adventures of Robin Hood*, but can stand on its own

Robin Hood (Don Taylor) swings into action in Hammer's first color feature, *Men of Sherwood Forest*.

as an enjoyable little film. Val Guest (May, 1992) told the authors,

> I became involved with Robin Hood because of the success of *Life with the Lyons*. It was such a success that Hammer simply asked me to do another! They told me that *Men of Sherwood Forest* was going to be a send-up, and I thought it would be fun—and it was! I'd already done quite a few films—many of them comedies. This one wasn't much of a departure from what Hammer knew I could do. I was never under contract to Hammer at *any* time. They used to call me every now and then and ask if I was free. I always had such fun making movies for them—a wonderful company to be with—I always said yes!

Starring as Robin was Don Taylor, who made his mark as an actor in *The Naked City* (1948) and later scored as a director with *Escape from the Planet of the Apes* (1971). He recalled for the authors (May, 1992),

> I'm not really sure *how* I got involved with Hammer, to tell you the truth. I had just broken up with my wife [Phyllis Avery], and I wanted to get away, get out of the country for a while, so I went to England. The next thing I knew ... I guess with the beard and wig, I looked a bit like Errol Flynn. I had a mid-Atlantic accent so, by cheating a bit on my "a," I could blend in with the British cast. By playing with an all-British cast—a typically solid, theatrically trained cast—I never even *thought* of the film being released in the USA. As you know, Hammer was a *very* small company—shot their films out of an old house on the Thames. We ate in the same building we filmed in! We were a real family for a few weeks; and when you get that camaraderie on film, you've really got something! I remember one scene where I was on horseback, leading my Merry Men on a charge. They were all stunt men—I was the only actor who could ride! I came up fast on a fence and hoped my horse was a jumper. We didn't have time to scout the area first, and the fence was a real surprise! Val Guest was an excellent director—he knew what he wanted, and he got it. *Every* shot was outlined—except the one with the fence! I'd never worked with such a meticulous director before. I really liked working with him—especially socializing during the rushes.

104   *The Lyons in Paris* (1954)

Trade advertisement.

A *very* enjoyable time. I also enjoyed the Carreras family. Sir James—now *there* was a real businessman. He could sell a film before he even made it! I met him socially a few times, and he was a lot of fun—he set the tone for the whole company.

Men of Sherwood Forest began production in May, 1954, with location filming at Clivedon. Several actors were hospitalized for broken bones and bruises. So many swords were broken that more had to be ordered. The Eastman Color process was going well, and Michael Carreras (*The Kinematograph Weekly*, June 10, 1954) was so pleased that he planned to use it for the next scheduled production, *Break in the Circle*, and for a Cromwell era picture (which eventually was filmed as *The Scarlet Blade*). Hammer's production schedule was to finish for the year on November 1, and they were planning to rent Bray to other companies.

Men of Sherwood Forest was trade shown on October 27, 1954, at Studio One and was released on December 6. Most reviewers were impressed, including *The Kinematograph Weekly* (November 4): "Enthusiastic team, clean fun and fights, jolly to say the least"; and the British Film Institute's *Monthly Bulletin* (December): "Don Taylor makes a good-natured Robin, and the tone of the film generally is genial." The film is, within its limits, very enjoyable and not to be taken seriously. Hammer would return to contemporary subjects for its next nine features; the next "period" film would be *The Curse of Frankenstein*.

The Lyons in Paris

Released February 11, 1955 (U.K.); 81 minutes; B & W; 7618 feet; a Hammer Film Production; an Exclusive Films Release (U.K.); filmed in Southall, London, Osterley, and on location in Paris, France; Director, Screenplay: Val Guest; Producer: Robert Dunbar; based on the characters from the BBC Radio Series; Director of Photography: James Harvey; Editor: Doug Myers; Music: Bruce Campbell; Art Director: Wilfred Arnold; Production Manager: Freddie Pearson; First Assistant Director: Rene Dupont; Second Assistant Director: Roger Good; Camera Operator: Len Harris; Continuity: Renee Glynn; Wardrobe: Molly Arbuthnot; Makeup: Phil Leakey; Hair Stylist: Nina Broe; Sound Mixer: C.T. Mason; Sound Camera: John Soutar. U.S. Title: *The Lyons Abroad*; U.K. Certificate: U.

Ben Lyon, Bebe Daniels, Barbara Lyon, Richard Lyon (Themselves), Horace Percival (Mr. Wimple), Molly Weir (Aggie), Doris Rogers (Florrie), Gwen Lewis (Mrs. Wimple), Hugh Morton (Colonel Price), Reginald Beckwith (Captain Le Grand), Martine Alexis (Fifi La Pleur), Pierre Dudan (Charles), Dino Galvani (Gerrard).

The Lyon family has settled into their new home, but the usual disasters continue. Bebe (Bebe Daniels) has forgotten that she hired decorators and is afraid that Ben (Ben Lyon) has forgotten their anniversary. His perceived neglect comes to a head when their son, Richard (Richard Lyon), discovers that Ben has made a dinner date with review

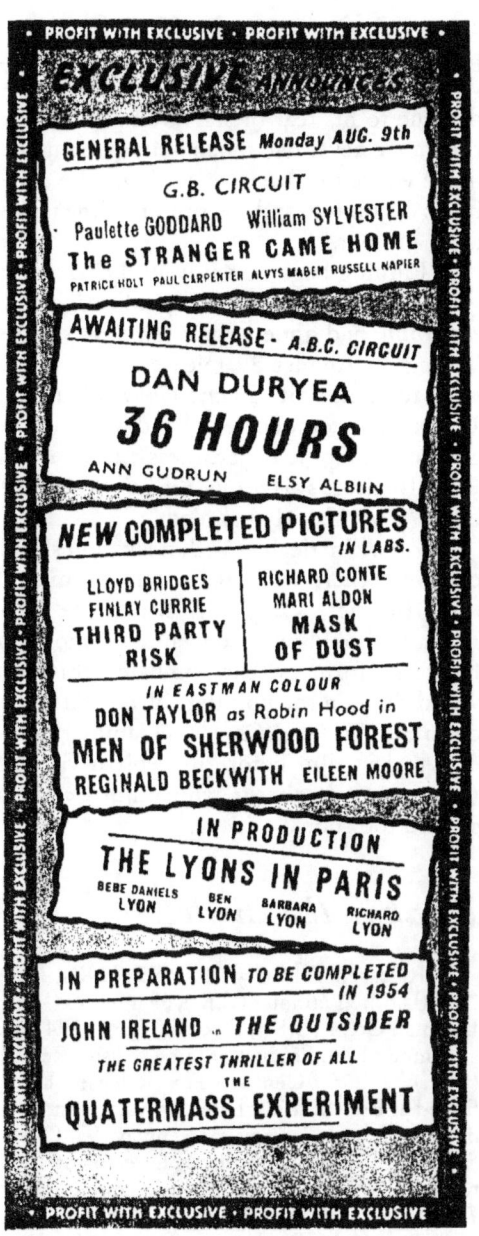

Hammer's diversity is well illustrated in this trade ad.

star Fifi La Pleur (Martine Alexis). All is forgiven when Ben reveals that he arranged to buy her Channel tickets so he could take the family to Paris to celebrate. After arriving in Paris, Ben runs into Fifi again, but their innocent meeting is misinterpreted by her jealous husband, Captain Le Grand (Reginald Beckwith). He is a champion duellist, and challenges Ben to meet him at dawn. With Fifi's help, Ben solves the predicament, and all is well for the Lyon family once again.

Hammer's faith in the Lyon family's popularity was so great that the company began production on this sequel while *Life with the Lyons* was still in release. As a cost-saving measure, Hammer arranged to film interiors for *The Lyons in Paris* at Southall Studios where the Lyons television series was produced. After completing *Men of Sherwood Forest*, Val Guest took a five-day break and was off to Paris to scout locations, and filming began on June 28, 1954. As he had done on the first film, Guest compressed three Lyons radio series episodes into one screenplay. The scheduled four week shoot ended on July 26, and included location work in Osterley, as well as Paris. *The Lyons in Paris* went into general release on February 11, 1955. Unlike its predecessor, the picture had been given a prestigious West End premiere at the Plaza on February 4. The Lyons were big business and were now treated accordingly, receiving mostly positive reviews. *The Star* (February 11): "Homey, knockout fun put over with tremendous gusto"; *The Monthly Film Bulletin* (February): "There are some amusing moments in this naive and cheerful romp"; and *The Daily Sketch* (February 11): "Guaranteed to pay off handsomely in laughs."

After two successful Lyon Family pictures, all concerned wisely decided to end the brief series. Once again, Val Guest delivered a well-made, successful picture and had become Hammer's top director.

The Glass Cage

Released August 29, 1955 (U.K.); 59 minutes; B & W; 5324 feet; a Hammer Film Production; an Exclusive Release (U.K.), a Lippert Release (U.S.); filmed at Bray Studios; Director: Montgomery Tully; Producer: Anthony Hinds; Screenplay: Richard Landau, based on A.E. Martin's novel; Director of Photography: Walter Harvey; Music composed by: Leonard Salzedo; Musical Director: John Hollingsworth; Art

Director; J. Elder Wills; Production Manager: T.S. Lyndon-Haynes; Editor: James Needs; Assembly Cutter: Henry Richardson; Camera Operator: Noel Rowland; Sound Recordist: H.C. Pearson; Makeup: H.F. Richmond; Hairdresser: Jean Bear; U.S. Title: *The Glass Tomb*; U.K. Certificate: A.

John Ireland (Pel), Honor Blackman (Jenny), Geoffrey Keen (Stanton), Eric Pohlmann (Sapolio), Sidney James (Lewis), Liam Redmond (Lindley), Sidney Tatler (Rorke), Valerie Vernon (Bella), Arnold Marle (Pop), Nora Gordon (Marie), Sam Kydd (Georgy), Ferdy Mayne (Bertie), Tonia Bern (Rena), Arthur Howard (Rutland), Stan Little (Mickelwitz), Anthony Richmond (Peter).

"Pel" Pelham (John Ireland), a devoted family man, is involved with the low end of British show business, booking sensational acts for sleazy carnivals. His latest scheme is Sapolio (Eric Pohlmann), the Fasting Man. Tony Lewis (Sidney James), Pel's friend and notorious bookmaker, is being blackmailed by Rena (Tonia Bern), an old flame, on the eve of his wedding. While a party for the carnival performers is being held at Sapolio's apartment, Rena is murdered upstairs by Harry Stanton (Geoffrey Keen), who forced her to torment Tony. He is glimpsed by Sapolio.

Enclosed in a glass cage, Sapolio begins his fast as Peel, fearing that Tony killed Rena, makes inquiries. His wife, Jenny (Honor Blackman), is kidnapped, and his son, Peter (Anthony Richmond) is threatened. When Pel calls the police, he's told Tony has been murdered. Pel's next shock is Sapolio's murder by poison. The public is told, however, that he's in a coma. Stanton, disguised as a nurse, enters the cage to finish the job and is shot by the police. Rena had threatened to expose his illegal activities, so he killed her, his blackmail victim, and the unfortunate Sapolio, who saw him in the shadows.

The Glass Cage is an absurd, poorly made film that must be seen to be believed. To start with, what could possibly be less interesting than watching a man not eat? Making this even more difficult to "swallow" is that Eric Pohlmann, the "starving man," is fifty pounds overweight! With such a ludicrous premise, even the film's few good points are easily overlooked. For example, young Peter has developed an eating disorder due to his fear of starvation. Although the movie never had much in its favor, it was made worse by extensive cutting. The editing is disjointed, and the running time is less than an hour.

Filming began on July 19, 1954, and it was trade shown a year later, indicating that *something* had gone wrong. Reviewers, following an August 29 release, didn't know what to make of it. *Today's Cinema* (July 15, 1955): "Overcomplicated plot, direction concise to the point of jerkiness"; the British Film Institute's *Monthly Bulletin* (September, 1955): "Naively handled."

For a film dealing with freaks and sleazy carnivals, there were just too many missed opportunities. Originally titled *The Outsiders*, it should have concentrated more on fringe performers that populated this odd world than on the pointless blackmail/murder plot. *The Glass Cage* was Hammer's second to last film before its rebirth via *The Quatermass Xperiment*, which didn't come a second too soon.

Break in the Circle

Released February 28, 1955 (U.K.); May, 1957 (U.S.); 91 minutes (U.K.), 69 minutes (U.S.); Eastman Color (U.K.); B & W (U.S.); 8274 feet; a Hammer Film Production; an Exclusive Release (U.K.); a 20th Century–Fox Release (U.S.); filmed at Bray Studios; Director: Val Guest; Producer: Michael Carreras; Screenplay: Val Guest, from Philip Lorraine's novel; Director of Photography: Walter Harvey; Music composed by: Doreen Carwithen; Musical Director: John Hollingsworth; Production Design: J. Elder Wills; Production Manager; Jimmy Sangster; Associate Producer: Mickey Delmar; Editor: Bill Lenny; Sound Recordist: H.C. Pearson, Ken Cameron; Camera Operator: Len Harris; Makeup: Phil Leakey; Hairdresser: Monica Hustler; Wardrobe: Molly Arbuthnot; Continuity: Connie Willis; Dubbing Editor: Dino del Campo; U.K. Certificate: U.

Forrest Tucker (Morgan), Eva Bartok (Lisa), Marius Goring (Baron Keller), Reginald Beckwith (Dusty), Eric Pohlmann (Emile), Guy Middleton (Hobart), Arnold Marle (Kudnic),

Break in the Circle (1954) 107

An early cold war thriller.

Fred Johnson (Farguarson), David King-Wood (Patchway), Guido Lorraine (Franz), Andre Mikhelson (first Russian), Stanley Zevic (second Russian), Marne Maitland (third Russian), Derek Prentice (Butler).

Adventurer Skip Morgan (Forrest Tucker) and his friend Dusty (Reginald Beckwith) earn a living delivering contraband in the *Bonaventure*, a high-powered cabin cruiser. They are hired by Baron Keller (Marius Goring), an international financier, to smuggle Kudnic (Arnold Marle), a scientist, out of Germany. Before leaving, Morgan discovers that Lisa (Eva Bartok), his neighbor, is actually an operative of British Intelligence. He assumes that she is spying on him and forces her aboard the *Bonaventure*. When they arrive in Hamburg, Morgan learns that Kudnic has been abducted. He recklessly intervenes, frees Kudnic, and takes him to England.

There, Morgan learns why he was hired—Keller wants a fuel formula Kudnic has developed that is worth millions. Morgan then raises his price to complete the deal. After being released, Lisa contacts her superiors, and the Coast Guard is present when the exchange takes place. Keller is carrying a gun, not Morgan's expected loot, and forces him to put to sea. Morgan overpowers Keller and throws him overboard to his death before surrendering to the police—and exchanging a knowing look with Lisa.

Break in the Circle was Hammer's second color film (following *Men of Sherwood Forest*). Both were directed by Val Guest, who recalled for the authors (May, 1992) Hammer's hiring policy during the mid-fifties. "Hammer had a list of actors that the American distributors would accept, and Forrest Tucker was on that list. When he came along for the lead in *Break in the Circle*, I was quite pleased—I got along very well with Tuck. No, I *didn't* request him later for *The Abominable Snowman*. He was just on the list."

With a plot centering on the cold war, *Break in the Circle* anticipated the spy dramas of the sixties, but was based in a reality far removed from Ian Fleming's James Bond. James Carreras had high hopes for the film, which *The Kinematograph Weekly* (August 19, 1954) branded as "Hammer's biggest production." Carreras had just completed his sixth film of the year and scheduled a generous six-week schedule, location work in Germany and Cornwall, plus Eastman color for *Break in the Circle*. Filming began on August 22 on location, with only two weeks spent at Bray. During the Cornwall shoot, Marius Goring nearly drowned while doing his fall from the *Bonaventure*. He was waiting for Guest to end the scene, but was too far away to hear the director shout "Cut!" The dedicated actor kept thrashing and refused to be pulled back on board.

Break in the Circle was completed on schedule, was trade shown on February 10, 1955, at Studio One, and premiered on the 28th to indifferent reviews. The British Film Institute's *Monthly Bulletin* (April): "Schoolboy adventure yarn, a rousing romp for the unsophisticated"; *The Kinematograph Weekly* (February 17): "Intriguing and exciting"; and *Variety* (May 8, 1957): "A weak entry for the American market." Despite looking good on paper, the film doesn't have much to offer. After an exciting, out of context opening of Kudnic escaping through an ominous forest, the picture quickly settles for the conventional, and may be Guest's least interesting effort for Hammer.

The Quatermass Xperiment

Released September 28, 1955 (U.K.); 82 minutes (U.K.), 78 minutes (U.S.); B & W; 7380 feet; a Hammer Film Production; an Exclusive Release (U.K.), a United Artists Release (U.S.); filmed at Bray Studios; Director: Val Guest; Producer: Anthony Hinds; Screenplay: Val Guest, Richard Landau, based on Nigel Kneale's BBC production; Director of Photography: Walter Harvey; Music composed by James Bernard; Music Supervisor: John Hollingsworth; Art Director: J. Elder Wills; Production Manager: T.S. Lyndon-Hayes; Editor: James Needs; Special Effects: Les Bowie; Sound Recordist: H.C. Pearson; Continuity: Renee Glynn; Hairstyles: Monica Hustler; Makeup: Phil Leakey; Camera Operator: Len Harris; Assistant Director: Bill Shore; U.S. Title: *The Creeping Unknown*; U.K. Certificate: X.

Brian Donlevy (Quatermass), Jack Warner (Lomax), Margia Dean (Judith), Richard Wordsworth (Caroon), David King Wood (Briscoe), Thora Hird (Rosie), Gordon Jackson (Producer), Harold Lang (Christie), Lionel Jeffries (Blake), Maurice Kauffman (Marsh), Gron Davies (Green), Stanley Van Beers (Reichenheim), Frank Phillips (BBC Announcer), Arthur Lovegrove (Sgt. Bromley), John Stirling (Major), Eric Corrie (Young Man), Margaret Anderson (Maggie), Henry Longhurst (Maggie's Father), Michael Godfrey (Fireman), Fred Johnson (Inspector), George Roderick (Policeman), Ernest Hare (Fire Chief), John Kerr (Lab Assistant), John Wynn (Best), Toke Townley (Chemist), Bartlett Mullins (Zoo Keeper), Molly Glessing (Mother at Zoo), Mayne Lynton (Zoo Official), Harry Brunsing (Night Porter), Barry Lowe (Tucker), Jane Aird (Mrs. Lomax), Sam Kydd (Station Sergeant), Arthur Gross (Floor Boy), James Drake (Sound Engineer), Edward Dane (Policeman), Basil Dignam (Sir Lionel), Betty Impry (Nurse), Marianne Stone (Nurse).

Professor Quatermass (Brian Donlevy) arrives at the scene of the crash of a rocket containing three scientists—Green (Gron Davies), Reichenheim (Stanley Van Beers), and Victor Caroon (Richard Wordsworth). Caroon stumbles out alone, with no trace of his companions, and Blake (Lionel Jeffries) demands a full investigation. Judith Caroon (Margia Dean) allows her husband to be placed under Quatermass' supervision—Victor is in an odd, zombie-like state, and his physical structure is changing. By studying film taken inside the rocket, Quatermass determines that a "disturbance" took place in space—and that the men's bodies were invaded by something alien. Judith hires Christie (Harold Lang), a private investigator, to get Victor away from Quatermass' probing, but Caroon is no longer human. It kills Christie in an elevator, its hand mutated into a cactus plant it absorbed. Judith notices "Victor's" distorted face and hand and screams.

"Victor" encounters a child at play and moves to absorb her life force, but some human remnant inside him frightens her off. Now an unrecognizable thing, it enters a zoo and absorbs the life out of several animals. The tentacled monster hides in Westminster Abbey and is discovered by a film crew. Quatermass diverts London's electrical power into the creature and destroys it, planning to start again in his space exploration.

"It was quite different from anything I'd previously done," Val Guest told the authors (May, 1992). "I was very loath to do it. I didn't think it was my cup of tea at all." Despite his misgivings, *The Quatermass Xperiment* was one of Hammer's most

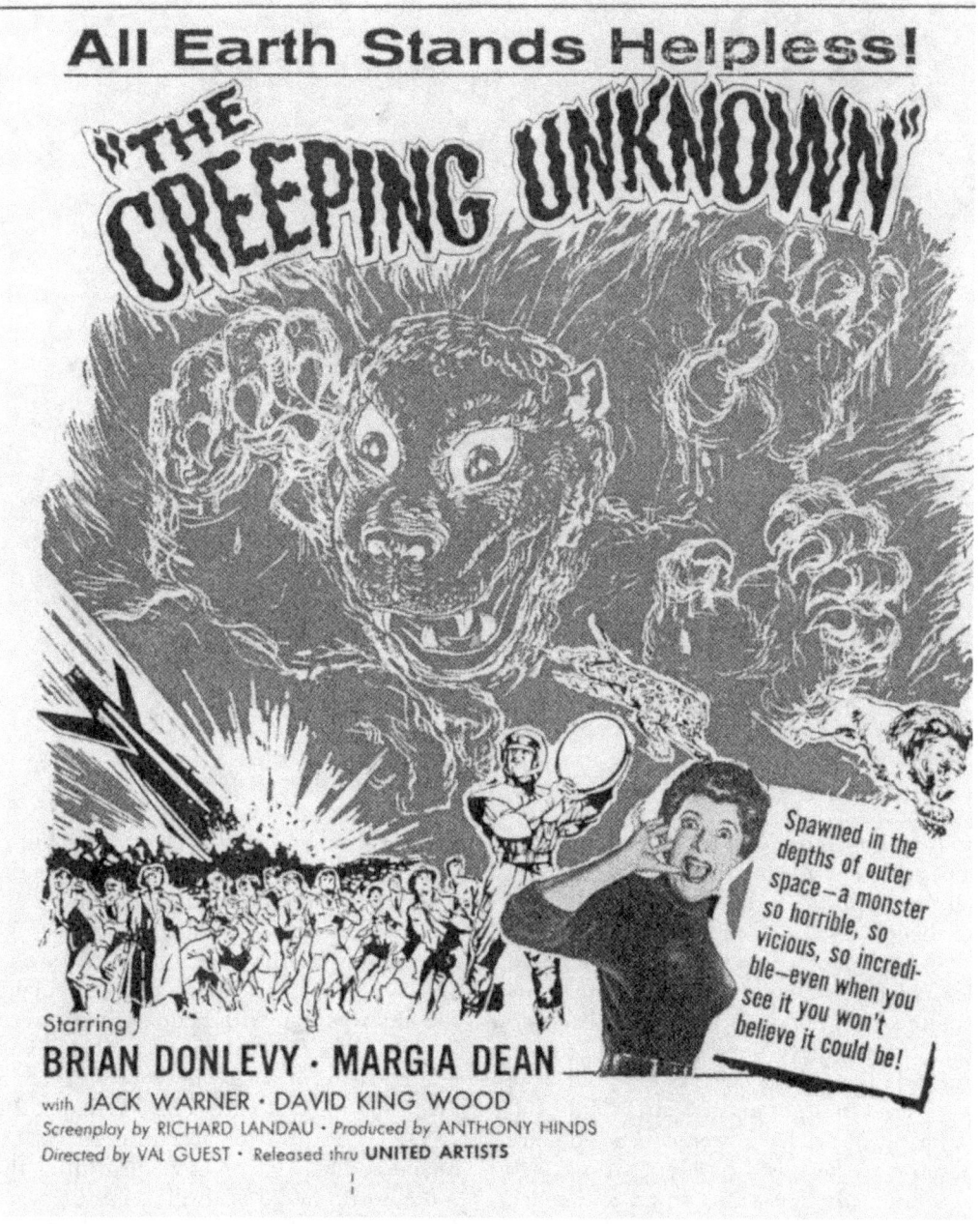

The *Quatermass Xperiment*—a science fiction classic—bore the U.S. title *The Creeping Unknown*.

important films and is among the best science fiction movies. Nigel Kneale's original story, a six-part serial broadcast on the BBC in July, 1953, ran two hundred minutes. It was incredibly popular, and Hammer was fortunate to get the film rights. A main problem was cutting over three hours of story in half to attain feature film length. Accordingly, Kneale was not pleased. "I was disappointed in the film," he said *(Starlog, February, 1989)*, "because I had very little to do with it." Val Guest was, in turn, unhappy about Kneale's reaction. "I really, honestly, am sad about the situation with Nigel," he

110 *The Quatermass Xperiment* (1954)

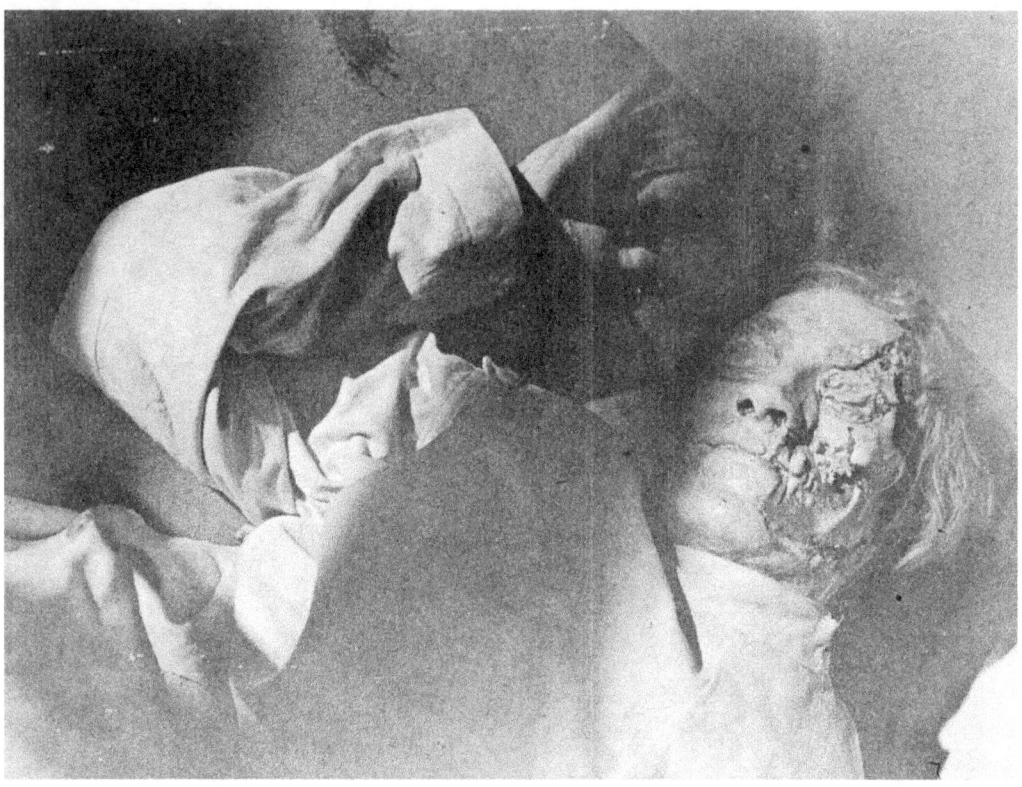

A little seen Phil Leakey makeup effect for *The Quatermass Xperiment*.

told author Tom Weaver. "He's a brilliant guy, and he's had an enormous success with all these things—and he hates every minute of them!"

A second "controversy" has centered around Brian Donlevy's performance. Although he's no one's idea of a brilliant scientist, Donlevy does bring authority to the role if nothing else. Guest told Tom Weaver, "Oh, I got on with Brian fine. But so many stories have been concocted since about how he was a paralytic drunk. It's absolute *balls*. He wasn't stone cold sober, either, but he was a pro and knew his lines." In their desire for a "name" actor—preferably an American—in the lead, Hammer was guilty of miscasting. They did much better with Andrew Keir in *Quatermass and the Pit*.

Filming began on October 18, 1954, at Bray after location work at the London Zoo on the 14th. Further location work was done in the village of Bray and near Windsor Castle. Following an August 25, 1955, trade show at Studio One, *The Quatermass Xperiment* (the "E" was dropped to emphasize the X certificate) premiered on September 28 at the Pavilion. Paired with *Rififi*, the package was chosen as the best double feature of 1955. In general release on the ABC circuit, the film went out with Hammer's featurette *The Eric Winston Show Band* and broke several house records. Reviews were generally favorable. *The London Times* (August 29, 1955): "The director certainly knows his business when it comes to providing the more horrid brand of thrills"; *The Chronicle* (August 26): "This is the best and nastiest horror film that I have seen since the war"; *The Manchester Guardian* (August 27): "A lively piece of science fiction"; *The Star*: "There can be no higher praise for a science fiction film"; *The New Statesman* (August 27): "What a surprise!"; the British Film Institute's *Monthly Bulletin* (October): "Richard Wordsworth's tortured grimace and menacing makeup suggest a pathetic as well as horrible figure"; *Variety* (September 7): "Despite its obvious horror angles, production is crammed with incident and suspense"; and *Harrison Reports* (June 23, 1956): "Adult fare."

Despite this being Val Guest's first science fiction movie, he knew exactly what he wanted. "I said I would do it, provided that I could shoot it as if some newsreel company had said, 'Go out and cover this story,'" he told the authors. "It was the first time I used a 'cinema verité technique.' I found that a fun way to do it." When asked if he would have liked the opportunity to direct *The Curse of Frankenstein*, Guest replied, "Despite the success of the horror elements in *Quatermass*, I wouldn't have been a good choice. Gothic horror has never been anything I've gone for. I don't recall if Hammer ever discussed it with me, but I wouldn't have taken it even if they had!"

Like all good movies, *The Quatermass Xperiment* was a collaborative effort. Guest's Val Lewton–like avoidance of blatant shock in favor of mood was augmented by Richard Wordsworth's stunning acting—a Karloff level performance. Phil Leakey created his first horror makeup perfectly, and James Bernard's shrieking violins added to the tension. "This was my first film score," he told the authors (July, 1994). "I thought the subject was quite stark and spare, and wrote the music accordingly. I just hoped I was right!"

The film was released in America as *The Creeping Unknown*, since the *Quatermass* name meant nothing. Supposedly, a young boy died of fright during a performance in Rockport, Illinois. That's not hard to believe—this is frightening science fiction at its best.

1955

Women Without Men

Released 1956; 73 minutes (U.K.), 71 minutes (U.S.); B & W; 6572 feet; a Hammer Film Production; an Exclusive Films Release (U.K.), an Associated Film Releasing Corp. Release (U.S.); filmed at Bray Studios; Director: Elmo Williams; Producer: Anthony Hinds; Screenplay: Val Guest, Richard Landau, based on an original story by Richard Landau; Directors of Photography: Walter Harvey, William Whitley; Editor: James Needs; Music: Leonard Salzedo; Musical Director: John Hollingsworth; Art Director: John Elphick; Camera: Jimmy Harvey; Supervising Editor: William Rivol; Assistant Directors: Herbert Glazer, Jimmy Sangster; Production Manager: Bert Sternbach; Sound: Bill Sweeney; Makeup: Phil Leakey; Wardrobe: Molly Arbuthnot; Sound Recording System: Glen Glen Sound Co. U.S Title: *Blonde Bait*; U.K. Certificate: A.

Beverly Michaels (Angie Booth), Joan Rice (Cleo Thompson), Thora Hird (Granny Rafferty), Avril Angers (Bessie), Ralph Michael (Julian Ward), April Olrich (Marguerite), Gordon Jackson (Percy), Valerie White (Prison Governor), Jim Davis (Nick Randall—American version only), Richard Travis (Kent Foster—American version only), Paul Cavanagh (Inspector Hedges—American version only), Harry Lauter (Mark—American version only), David Lodge (Patrick), Hermione Baddeley (Grace), Bill Shine ("Lindbergh"), Paul Carpenter (Nick Randall—British version only), Sheila Burrell (Bates), John Welsh (Chaplain), Maurice Kaufman (Daniels), Eugene Deckers (Pietre), Muriel Young (Helen), Olwen Brookes (Hackett), Betty Cooper (Evans), Doris Gilmore (Loveland), Fanny Carby (Brooker), Yvonne Manners (Mason), Michael Golden (Barger), Anthony Miles (Civilian), Mark Kingston (Operator), Verne Morgan (Barrowman), Charles Saynor (Man at doorway), Toots Pound, Babs Love, Vi Stevens (Scrubbers), H. Westwater, Joan Harrison, Pat Edwards, Edna Lander (Carollers), Stratford John, Sidney Brahms, Douglas Argent (Revellers), Irene Richmond (Guard), George Roderick, Thomas Glen (Policemen), Margaret Flint (Hennessey), Valerie Fraser, Mona Lillian, Anne Loxley (Inmates), John Phillips, Oscar Nation, Katherine Feliaz, Pauline Winter.

State Department investigator Kent Foster (Richard Travis) flies into Washington, D.C., from London to give a full report concerning his latest mission. At State Department headquarters, he meets with fellow agent Mark (Harry Lauter) and the details of the case are laid out.

Working with Scotland Yard, Foster was on the trail of traitor-murderer Nick Randall (Jim Davis). It was known that

Randall had been seeing American singer Angela Booth (Beverly Michaels). She had promised to marry him on New Year's Eve, though she was not to see him until then. When Angela advised her manager Julian Ward (Ralph Michael) that she was leaving the show, Ward refused to let her break her contract and slapped her when she protested. Angela grabbed a hand mirror and struck him with it when he made another threatening move. Angela was arrested and sentenced to six months in prison for the assault.

Realizing that Angela did not know Randall's real nature, Foster allowed her to escape with the aid of a fellow prisoner named "Granny" (Thora Hird). Followed by police, Angela managed to meet Randall and realized that she had been duped by him. When Foster and the police closed in, Randall was shot and killed by Foster while trying to escape.

Foster ends his story and Mark asks if Angela ever overcame her difficulties. Foster responds by showing him the front page of a recent London newspaper announcing Angela's upcoming Royal Command Performance.

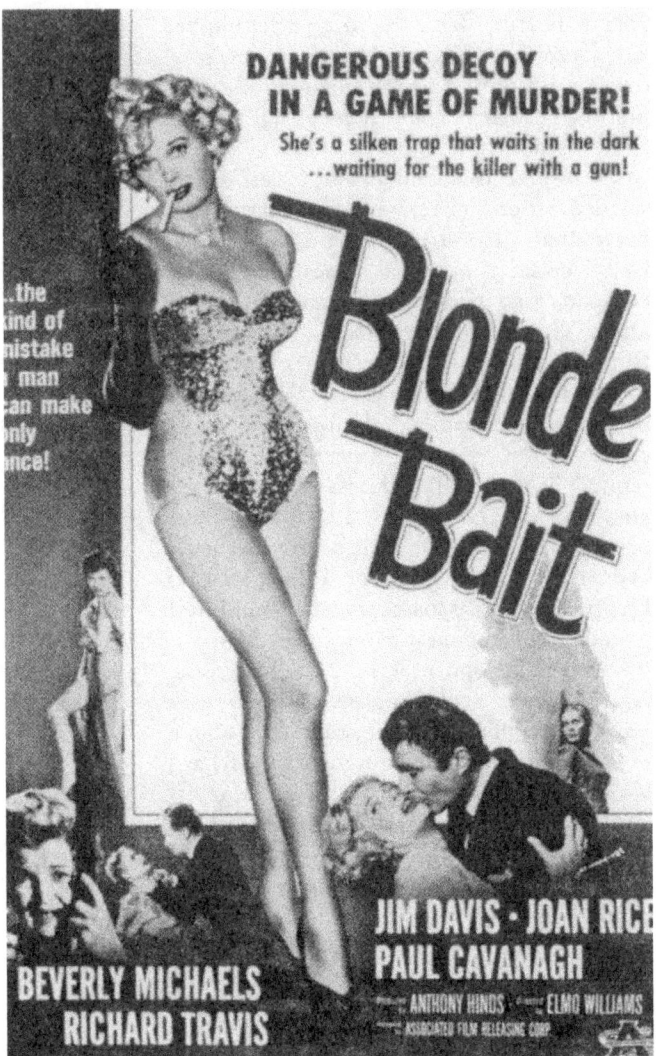

New footage and added cast made the American version of *Women Without Men* unrecognizable from the original.

Due to Hammer's newfound interest in CinemaScope shorts, the company produced only one feature length film during 1955. *Women Without Men* was planned around recent Academy Award nominee (*The High and the Mighty*, 1954) Jan Sterling, but she turned it down in favor of a Hollywood "B" film, *Women's Prison*. Anthony Hinds secured an Oscar *winner* to direct, though, when he signed Elmo Williams, who had edited *High Noon* (1952). The production began on March 28, with Beverly Michaels in the lead, and concluded on April 15. By December, *The Quatermass Xperiment* was breaking house records, and Hammer's 1956 schedule was quickly reorganized to capitalize on its success. Two science fiction horror subjects were planned: *X the Unknown* and *Quatermass 2*, with more to follow. *Women Without Men* must have seemed outdated to the company before its release. A trade show was finally held on June 14, 1956, at the Hammer theatre. The film was to be distributed in America by Associated Film Releasing (as *Blonde Bait*), but prior to that

Dr. Royston (Dean Jagger) and fellow scientist (William Lucas) puzzle over who (or what) has broken into their laboratory in Hammer's science fiction drama *X—The Unknown*.

release, several major changes were made. All of Paul Carpenter's scenes were eliminated, and new footage was shot with Jim Davis in the lead as "Nick Randall." Beverly Michaels was called back to appear with Davis and *more* new scenes were shot to tie it all together.

"Randall" was *now* a traitor and murderer who is killed by a fellow agent. "Angie's" character was also altered—she leads the assassin to Nick! Neither version was enjoyed by the critics. *The Monthly Film Bulletin* (August 1956): "Stereotyped woman's prison drama"; *The Kinematograph Weekly* (June 25): "A damp squib"; *Variety* (October 10): "For lower casing in the minor market"; and *The Motion Picture Exhibitor* (April 18): "Too much talk and too little action." These reviews probably meant little to Hammer who, after the success of *The Quatermass Xperiment*, was finally finding its way.

1956

X—The Unknown

Released November 5, 1956 (U.K.), May, 1957 (U.S.); 78 minutes; B & W; 7018 feet; a Hammer Film Production; an Exclusive Films Release (U.K.), a Warner Bros. Release (U.S.); filmed on location at Beaconsfield Gravel Pits and Gerrard's Cross, England, interiors filmed at Bray Studios; Director: Leslie Norman; Producer: Anthony Hinds; Screenplay: Jimmy Sangster; Director of Photography: Gerald Gibbs; Music: James Bernard; Musical Supervisor: John Hollingsworth; Special Effects: Jack Curtis, Bowie Margutti Ltd.; Editor: James Needs; Production Design: Bernard Robinson; Assistant Editor: Alfred Cox; Assistant Director: Chris Sutton; Makeup: Phil Leakey; Camera: Len Harris; Costumes: Molly Arbuthnot; Continuity: June Randall; Sound Mixer: Jock May; Production Manager: Jimmy Sangster; U.K. Certificate: X.

Dean Jagger (Dr. Adam Royston), Edward

Chapman (Elliot), Leo McKern (Insp. McGill), William Lucas (Peter Elliot), John Harvey (Major Cartwright), Peter Hammond (Lt. Bannerman), Michael Ripper (Sgt. Grimsdyke), Anthony Newley (Corp. Spider Webb), Ian MacNaughton (Haggis), Kenneth Cope (Pvt. Lansing), Marianne Brauns (Zena), Fraser Hines (Ian Osborne), Edwin Richfield (Old Soldier), Jameson Clark (Jack Harding), Jane Aird (Vi Harding), Michael Brook (Willie Harding), Neil Hallet (Unwin), Norman Macowan (Old Tom), Neil Wilson (Russell), John Stone (Gerry), Archie Duncan (Sgt. Yeardye), John Stirling (Police Car Driver), Shaw Taylor (Police Radio Operator), Frank Taylor (P.C. Williams), Brown Derby (Vicar), Max Brimmell (Hospital Director), Robert Bruce (Dr. Kelly), Stella Kemball (Nurse), Anthony Sager (Gateman), Phillip Levene (Security Man), Barry Steel (Soldier in Trench), Lawrence James (Guard), Brian Peck, Edward Judd (Soldiers), Stephenson Lang (Reporter).

X marks the spot for excellent science fiction.

While on maneuvers in a Scottish quarry, a small troop of soldiers under the direction of Sgt. Grimsdyke (Michael Ripper) are being tested on their aptitude with a Geiger counter. Suddenly a large fissure appears, accompanied by a tremendous rumbling sound. One soldier, Pvt. Lansing (Kenneth Cope), is mysteriously killed.

Dr. Royston (Dean Jagger), a nuclear scientist from a nearby research laboratory, is summoned to the site, where he is mystified to find that the dead private is covered with radiation burns. That night, a young boy (Michael Brook) is terrified by the sight of something he comes across in the nearby marshes. Admitted to a local hospital, he is found to be suffering from a massive dose of radiation poisoning, and later dies.

More mysterious events follow, including the death of a hospital orderly whose skin has melted away from his body. Royston speculates that the Unknown might be able to change its molecular structure and even be able to gain entry through ventilation grates and under doors. He later hypothesizes that the Unknown is a creature composed of pure energy, created at the same time the Earth was formed, and trapped under the surface since the planet's upper crust hardened. It has fed off the Earth's natural radiation for eons but now has grown in size and strength and is searching for surface sources of radiation to satiate its appetite.

Dr. Peter Elliot (William Lucas), son of the research lab's director (Edward Chapman), descends into the fissure and comes face to "face" with the Unknown before making his escape. The fissure is now cemented over but the Unknown — a glowing, pulsating blob — breaks through and makes its way across the countryside toward the nuclear installation. Royston orders the lab's cobalt be removed from the premises, prompting the Unknown to return to the fissure.

Royston, who has been developing a device to neutralize atomic bombs, hopes to use it to combat the Unknown. Using cobalt as bait, the scientists lure the Unknown out of the fissure and then bombard it with the negative energy of Royston's neutralizing device. The Unknown implodes and bursts into flames, but Royston doubts that they have seen the last of creatures from beneath the earth.

X—The Unknown was Hammer's first attempt to cash in on the success of *The Quatermass Xperiment*, with its title again informing an eager audience of the film's "X Certificate." Jimmy Sangster recalled for the authors (August, 1993):

> *The Quatermass Xperiment* had just come out and had done very, very well. Hammer said we *must* make another of these science fiction things. There was nothing on the desk or in the mail, so we were sitting around the office one day—Anthony Hinds, Michael Carreras, and myself—and somebody said, "What about a story where so and so…" and I said, "Yeah, then *this* happens," and in about thirty minutes we had a rough story. So Tony Hinds—he was the boss—said to me, "Well, you came up with the most, so you go and write it." I said, "I'm a production manager!" he said, "I'm paying you, now go write it! If we like it, we'll use it and pay you for it!" I wrote it as a treatment, they liked it, and said go do a script. I said that I knew nothing about script writing, but Tony said, "You've read a lot of scripts—you've budgeted scripts—go write it!" I wrote it, he liked it, he paid me for it. And—hey!—I was a writer! This wouldn't have happened at another company. There *weren't* any companies like Hammer!" Sangster was also production manager and was desperately miserable. A production manager runs the unit. He hires and fires the crew, runs the schedule, fixes the budget, chooses the locations, watches the cost, and gets the blame for everything. I hated that job!

X—The Unknown was an impressive start for the horror film genre's greatest writer.

The film began production in early January, 1956, with a last minute change in the director. Joe Walton (alias of Joseph Losey) was announced as the director in *The Kinematograph Weekly* on January 12. But, on January 16, the paper reported that Leslie Norman would replace "Walton" who had "fallen ill." "Leslie Norman," recalled Sangster, "didn't want to do the picture either. Losey was *supposed* to direct it, and a week before we started shooting, he—very conveniently—caught pneumonia. Not only did Norman *not* want to do it, he came into a picture that had already been cast, and for which sets had already been built, so it wasn't good for him either." Although Hammer almost always had a happy crew, few people were happy with Norman. "I didn't like him," Len Harris told the authors (August, 1993), "and I don't think *anyone* did, really. He was one of the few people that wasn't liked at Hammer, and you'll notice that, despite the film's quality, he never did another for us. He was a good technical director, but he couldn't direct people very well. Dean Jagger simply *wouldn't* be directed by him! Leslie was always complaining and could be very harsh. He didn't think much of the film, either. We all thought it would be a hit, but he had no use for it. We turned out to be right! The thing we disliked the most was his using abusive language through a loud hailer for all to hear. That simply wasn't done at Hammer! I said to Tony Hinds, 'I *never* want to work with *him* again!'" Michael Ripper (March, 1993) agreed. "When I introduced myself to Leslie Norman, he told me that he would have hired Victor Maddern in my role if he had been casting the film!"

Despite these distractions and poor weather conditions during location work, *X—The Unknown* was completed on schedule and premiered at the Pavilion on September 21, 1956. The film drew huge audiences, as it had done on its earlier release in Japan. American release of the movie had been planned by RKO, but due to corporate problems, *X—The Unknown* was picked up by Warner Bros. While on ABC circuit in Britain, the film was paired with H.G. Clouzot's classic *Diabolique*, forming one of the year's best thriller double features. Reviews were generally positive. *The Kine-*

Marsh (Bryan Forbes) and Professor Quatermass (Brian Donlevy) investigate the mysterious events taking place in the once peaceful village of Wynderden Flats in *Quatermass 2*.

matograph Weekly (August 16, 1956): "Gripping science fiction. The picture builds up big suspense and ends spectacularly"; *Films and Filming* (November): "A welcomed change from interplanetary yarns"; *The London Times* (September 24): "Vastly entertaining"; *The Daily Telegraph* (September 27): "Good, grisly fun"; and *Variety* (October 10): "A highly imaginative and fanciful meller."

As it had done previously in *The Quatermass Xperiment*, Hammer had merged science fiction and Gothic horror seamlessly. Leslie Norman, despite the complaints, did an excellent job of presenting Sangster's imaginative ideas, and he was backed up by Gerald Gibbs' moody photography and James Bernard's tense score. The success of *X—The Unknown* was another important brick in the "House of Horror."

Quatermass 2

Released June 17, 1957 (U.K.); 85 minutes; B & W; 7632 feet; a Hammer Film Production; a United Artists Release (U.S.); filmed at Elstree Studios, and on location in Essex and Sussex Downs, England; Director, Producer: Anthony Hinds; Executive Producer: Michael Carreras; Screenplay: Nigel Kneale, based on the BBC Television Series by Nigel Kneale; Director of Photography: Gerald Gibbs; Editor: James Needs; Music: James Bernard; Musical Supervisor: John Hollingsworth; Art Director: Bernard Robinson; Production Supervisor: Anthony Nelson-Keys; Assistant Director: Don Weeks; Camera: Len Harris; Makeup: Phil Leakey; Sound: Cliff Sanders; Special Effects: Bill Warrington, Henry Harris, Frank George. U.S. Title: *Enemy from Space*; U.K. Certificate: X.

Brian Donlevy (Professor Quatermass), John Longdon (Lomax), Sidney James (Jimmy Hall), Bryan Forbes (Marsh), William Franklyn (Brand), Vera Day (Sheila), Charles Lloyd Pack (Dawson), Tom Chatto (Broadhead), John Van Eyssen (The PRO), Percy Herbert (Gorman),

A worthy sequel to Hammer's *Quatermass Xperiment*.

Michael Ripper (Ernie), John Rae (McLeod), Marianne Stone (Secretary); Ronald Wilson (Young Man), Jane Aird (Mrs. McLeod), Betty Impey (Kelly), Lloyd Lamble (Inspector), John Stuart (Commissioner), Gilbert Davies (Banker), Joyce Adams (Woman MP), Edwin Richfield (Peterson), Howard Williams (Michaels), Philip Baird (Lab Assistant), John Fabin (Intern), Robert Raikes (Lab Assistant), George Merritt (Superintendent), Arthur Blake (Constable), Michael Balfour (Harry), Jan Holden (Young Girl).

Driving from London to his observatory, Professor Quatermass (Brian Donlevy) has a near-collision with a car containing a badly burned young man (Michael Balfour) who was injured while handling a hollow, meteor-like rock during a picnic at nearby Wynderden Flats. Quatermass and his assistant Marsh (Bryan Forbes) drive to the site, and to their amazement find a previously secret government/military installation that is an exact full-scale duplicate of a moon colony model city Quatermass had built. Marsh, handling one of the many meteor fragments that litter the hillside, sustains a facial burn when the rock suddenly splits open emitting a gas-like cloud. Silent armed guards from the installation take charge of Marsh and drive Quatermass away.

Quatermass learns that the mysterious installation is supposedly developing synthetic food, and that its construction was authorized by Whitehall. Delving further, he begins to suspect a conspiracy—and that alien visitors may be involved. Broadhead (Tom Chatto), a Parliament member, has been spearheading his own investigation and finally forces higher-ups to allow an inspection party to tour the facility. Broadhead tumbles into a storage dome of the "synthetic food" and is fatally burned by the deadly substance. The installation guards seize the rest of the inspection party, but Quatermass is able to make a narrow escape.

Quatermass tells Inspector Lomax (John Longdon) of Scotland Yard that aliens possess the installation personnel (dubbed Zombies by the locals) as well as the many high-ranking government officials who authorized construction of the installation, whose real purpose is to acclimatize gigantic "hive-intelligence" alien organisms to the Earth's atmosphere inside the storage dome. Scientist Brand (William Franklyn) advises Quatermass that the invaders are arriving (via the hollow meteors) from an asteroid in space.

Quatermass and Lomax turn to reporter Jimmy Hall (Sidney James) to break the news of the covert invasion, but Hall insists on a visit to the plant before he will write the story. En route, they stop at a pub in the small village whose still-human citizens have unsuspectingly helped to build the installation. The villagers shout down the strangers until one of the small meteors crashes through the roof, splits open and takes possession of a barmaid (Vera Day). Installation guards arrive, shooting and killing Hall as he attempts to phone in his story.

The villagers storm the installation and take over the control center, pumping oxygen into the storage dome in an attempt to poison the alien organism inside. Meanwhile, an alien-possessed Marsh and some Zombies arrive at Quatermass' observatory and shoot Brand, who with his dying breath launches a nuclear-powered test rocket which hurtles through space toward the asteroid.

The dome explodes and the giant blob-like creature inside is freed, but it is destroyed as the plant goes up in flames. The night sky is lit up when the nuclear rocket finds its target and destroys the asteroid. The invaders' human hosts all return to normalcy.

Hammer quickly took advantage of the success of its first Quatermass film, and by November, 1955, a script was already in progress. Over £100,000 was allotted for *Quatermass 2*—the first film sequel to be numbered. Returning were star Brian Donlevy and director Val Guest. "We shall have to put more work in on the new one," he told *The Kinematograph Weekly*, "because I don't think that the second BBC television serial was as good as the first." *Quatermass 2* was broadcast in six parts between October 22 and November 26, 1955, and was inspired by Nigel Kneale's concern about the political instability of the times. "There was much public concern about a new brand of bureaucracy," he wrote in 1979. One of the reasons that Kneale co-authored the screenplay was his dissatisfaction with how his Professor's character had been altered in the first picture.

Shortly after *Quatermass 2* began production, James Carreras gave United Artists full distribution rights in exchange for 100% financing. Due to the larger budget, Exclusive was unwilling to put that amount up front, and all future Hammer productions would be released through other distributors. Filming began with a seven day location shoot at Shell Haven on the Thames Estuary. Guest felt that the still relatively low budget could be a positive factor. "Having no money means you have to use your head, that's all," he said (interview by Tom Weaver, Mike Brunas and Rich Scrivani).

> The worst thing you can do is think, "Well, this is a low budget picture, so they can't expect too much from us." You go into the picture saying, "Nobody's going to say *this* was low budget!" and you break your skull trying to overcome it. Everybody thinks up ideas that, if you had the lazy, easy advantage of just spending more dough, nobody would have come up with.

The location work was completed with only one "major problem." While filming a windstorm powerful enough to overturn a Jeep, Brian Donlevy's toupee blew off and, according to Val Guest (*Little Shoppe of Horrors*), "All the prop men tried to catch this thing which was flying around like a bat! It was complicated by members of the public watching from a nearby hill. They must have thought we had gone mad!" Guest had nothing but praise for Donlevy. "I think he was very good—down to earth. Brian had been such a success in the first film he was the obvious choice for the second." Len Harris (August, 1993) told the authors a harrowing tale about the Irish Donlevy giving him a lift home. "We stopped for a drink at an IRA pub. The police knew all about it but no one else did. They didn't do anything to break it up—that way they knew where to find everyone. When the IRA guys saw me with Brian, they figured I was OK and never bothered me." Regarding the matte shot of the huge dome, Harris recalled, "The camera had to be anchored dead still, and a bit of set is lined up with the glass painting right on the camera. This wasn't done in the lab. If you look closely, you'll see how Brian's head *just* misses coming into the space occupied by the dome."

Quatermass 2 was trade shown at the United Artists Wardour Street theatre on March 22, 1957. The premiere at the Pa-

Leo Genn about to observe the enemy in Hammer's low-key World War II drama, *The Steel Bayonet*.

vilion at the end of May, where it ran for three weeks, broke a house record. Co-featured with *And Woman ... Was Created*, *Quatermass 2* went out on the ABC circuit on June 17 to mixed reviews. *The Kinematograph Weekly* (May 2): "Mystery and tension mount steadily as it skillfully weaves its way to its terrifying climax"; *Films and Filming* (May): "A fair to middling piece of British science fiction"; *The London Times* (May 27): "The film has an air of respect for the issues touched on"; the British Film Institute's *Monthly Bulletin* (June): "The film has lost much of the quality of the original"; and *The Daily Telegraph* (May 25), "A grisly romp."

Quatermass 2 was part of a subgenre of paranoid science fiction in which things are not quite what they seem. Included in this group are *Invasion of the Body Snatchers* (1956), *Invaders from Mars* (1953), and *It Conquered the World* (1956). And Hammer's version just might be the best.

The Steel Bayonet

Released June 3, 1957 (U.K.); 85 minutes; B & W; Hammerscope; 7652 feet; a Hammer Film Production; a United Artists Release; Director: Michael Carreras; Producer: Michael Carreras; Associate Producer: Anthony Nelson-Keys; Screenplay and Original Story: Howard Clewes; Director of Photography: Jack Asher; Music: Leonard Salzedo; Musical Director: John Hollingsworth; Editor: Bill Lenny; Art Director: Ted Marshall; Makeup: Phil Leakey; Special Effects: Sid Pearson; U.K. Certificate: A.

Leo Genn (Major Gerrard), Kieron Moore (Capt. Mead), Michael Medwin (Lt. Vernon), Robert Brown (Sgt. Gill), Michael Ripper (Pvt. Middleditch), John Paul (Lt. Col. Derry), Shay Gorman (Sgt. Gates), Tom Bowman (Sgt. Nicholls), Bernard Horsfall (Pvt. Livingstone), John Watson (Cpl. Bean), Arthur Lovegrove (Pvt. Jarvis), Percy Herbert (Pvt. Clark), Paddy Joyce (Pvt. Ames), Jack Stewart (Pvt. Wentworth), David Crowley (Pvt. Harris), Barry Lowe (Pvt. Ferguson), Michael Dear (Pvt. "Tweedle"), Ian Whittaker (Pvt. Wilson), Michael Balfour (Pvt. Thomas).

The Steel Bayonet (1956)

The Steel Bayonet was Michael Carreras' best film as a director.

Tunis, North Africa, 1943. After a series of brutal engagements with the German Afrika Corps, "C" Company is exhausted and awaiting replacements. However, Col. Derry (John Paul) reassigns them to an attack on Tunis to be led by Maj. Gerrard (Leo Genn). Their assignment is to take and hold an abandoned farmhouse no matter what. From a wind pump tower, Capt. Mead (Kieron Moore) observes the enemy while Sgt. Gill (Robert Brown) prods the men to dig in. As the tension mounts, the men begin to discuss their civilian lives, their hopes, and their current situation. Their survival depends on keeping their position a secret, and Gerrard orders the killing of a German patrol. When Mead is spotted in the tower, Gerrard prepares for an all-out attack, which he fears his outmanned troops cannot withstand.

From their slit trenches around the farmhouse, "C" Company somehow holds off the first attack and fearfully waits for the next wave. Mead directs the artillery fire as the second attack devastates the outnumbered British.

Evacuation orders are received as Lt. Vernon (Michael Medwin) leads five soldiers to take a Bren gun and turn it against its owners. The tower is consumed by a fire, killing Mead and pinning Gerrard under its debris. Gerrard radios for an all-out artillery attack on the farmhouse, destroying the Germans and himself.

The Steel Bayonet was the first and most conventional of Hammer's three World War II dramas, the others being *The Camp on Blood Island* and *Yesterday's Enemy*. It was also the first feature to be directed by Michael Carreras who had previously directed seven shorts for the company. Originally titled *Observation Post*, the film was conceived as a breakaway from the reticence shown by the typical British war movie. "The trouble with so many British pictures about the war," Carreras said in *Kinematograph Weekly* (September 26, 1956), "has been the tendency for understatement. The Americans are so much better at showing the blood and guts of war." Unlike many directors of war films, Carreras was himself a veteran. He was not alone. Most of the cast had some military experience. Screenplay author/technical advisor Howard Clewes, a veteran, explained in the same article, "One reason for this was simply that we did not want to begin training actors how to handle rifles and wear their uniforms once the picture had begun." Playing a war hero came easily to star Leo Genn since, according to the United Artists pressbook, he received the Croix de Guerre for bravery while in France with the Royal Artillery.

Because of the Suez Canal crisis, a War Office promise of tanks had to be rescinded. Four were brought from a scrap dealer and, with modifications, were used as both British and German vehicles. Standing in for Tunisia believably was the British Army Tank Training Grounds in Aldershot. The jet roar from nearby Farnbourgh Airport meant that much of the dialogue had to be post-synched. Michael Carreras tried for a documentary realism by shooting on location. An opening narration introduced the characters, and the German soldiers spoke German with English subtitles. This was quite unusual. Filming was completed on September 20, 1956, after averaging about four minutes of film per day—excellent for a location picture. (The next feature to start at Bray, on November 20, was *The Curse of Frankenstein*.)

The Steel Bayonet, probably Carreras's best directorial effort, suffers somewhat from too much talk, but this is balanced by an absence of John Wayne style heroics. Hammer succeeded with presenting a realistic, unsensational look at war. When they come, the battle scenes are rough. Trade shown in London on May 14, 1957, it went into general release on June 3. *The London Times* (May 14, 1957): "Grim, but there is something about the whole thing that does not ring quite true, although parts of it are sincere and moving." *Kinematograph Weekly* (May 16, 1957): "Women patrons will find it hard to swallow. Ticklish booking"; *Variety* (March 5, 1958): "Earnest but inept."

The Curse of Frankenstein

Premiered May 2, 1957 (U.K.), General Release May 20, 1957 (U.K.), May, 1957 (U.S.); 83 minutes; Eastman Color; 7503 feet; a Hammer Film Production; a Warner Bros. Release; filmed at Bray Studios, England; Director: Terence Fisher; Producer: Anthony Hinds; Executive Producer: Michael Carreras; Associate Producer: Anthony Nelson-Keys; Screenplay: Jimmy Sangster, based on *Frankenstein* by Mary Shelley; Music: James Bernard; Music Supervisor: John Hollingsworth; Director of Photography: Jack Asher; Production Design: Bernard Robinson; Art Director: Ted Marshall; Editor: James Needs; Production Manager: Don Weeks; Sound Recordist: Jock May; Camera Operator: Len Harris; Assistant Director: Robert Lynn; Continuity: Doreen Soan; Supervising Makeup: Phil Leakey; Hairdresser: Henry Montsash; Wardrobe: Molly Arbuthnot; 2nd Assistant Director: Derek Whitehurst; Camera Focus: Harry Oakes; Assistant Editor: Roy Norman; Stunt Work: Jock Easton; Boom Operator: Jimmy Patty; Makeup: Roy Ashton; Assistant Makeup: George Turner; U.K. Certificate: X.

Peter Cushing (Baron Victor Frankenstein), Hazel Court (Elizabeth), Robert Urquhart (Paul Krempe), Christopher Lee (the Creature), Valerie Gaunt (Justine), Noel Hood (Aunt Sophia), Melvyn Hayes (Young Victor), Sally Walsh (Young Elizabeth), Paul Hardtmuth (Prof. Bernstein), Fred Johnson (Grandfather), Claude Kingston (Small Boy), Alex Gallier (A Priest),

The Curse of Frankenstein (1956)

Patrick Troughton (Kurt), Michael Mulcaster (Warder), Hugh Dempster (Burgomaster), Anne Blake (Burgomaster's Wife), Marjorie Hume (Mother), Henry Caine (Schoolmaster), Joseph Behrman (Fritz), Raymond Rollett (Father Felix), Ernest Jay (Undertaker), J. Trevor Davis (Uncle), Bartlett Mullins (A Tramp), Eugene Leahy (Second Priest).

Baron Victor Frankenstein (Peter Cushing), awaiting execution for murder, relates his story to a disinterested priest (Alex Gallier). As a teenager, Victor (Melvyn Hayes) inherited the family wealth and hired Paul Krempe (Robert Urquhart) as his tutor. Their research led them into a study of life and death, and years later, Victor (Cushing) proposed the creation of a perfect man from parts of the dead. Their work is interrupted by the arrival of Victor's cousin Elizabeth (Hazel Court) who was promised to him in marriage when they were children. Lacking only a brain to complete the experiment, Victor pushes Prof. Bernstein (Paul Hardtmuth) to his death from a balcony and later removes his brain in the family crypt. Insensed, Paul attacks Victor and damages the brain, and refuses to continue his involvement. Victor continues alone, and during a storm, the Creature (Christopher Lee) is brought to life accidentally when a lightning bolt strikes the apparatus. It escapes from the lab and kills a blind man (Fred Johnson) and his grandson (Claude Kingston) before Victor and Paul track it down. Paul kills the Creature, but Victor later retrieves the body and restores it to life.

When Victor's mistress Justine (Valerie Gaunt) threatens to blackmail him, he uses the Creature to murder her. Before the wedding, Paul is shown the Creature and is repulsed by Victor's "perfect man." Out-

Christopher Lee catches up on the news of the day in between takes on *The Curse of Frankenstein* (photo courtesy of Tim Murphy).

raged, Paul leaves to get the authorities, and the Creature escapes. Victor sees it stalking the unsuspecting Elizabeth on the roof and, after accidentally shooting her, throws a lamp at the Creature. Ablaze, it falls through the skylight into a vat of acid.

His story finished, Victor is visited in his cell by Paul, whom he begs to verify his tale. Paul denies the Creature's existence and leaves with Elizabeth as Victor is led to the guillotine.

When *The Quatermass Xperiment* started breaking box office records in November, 1955, James Carreras set out to find why. The overwhelming response from cinema managers was the film's horrific content. "Now," he said (*ABC Film Review*) "we'll give them a classical horror picture—a real good, juicy Gothic thriller—and see what happens!" *The Curse of Frankenstein*—

Christopher Lee asks for seconds from Bray Studio canteen manager Mrs. Thompson during a lunch break on *The Curse of Frankenstein* (photo courtesy of Tim Murphy).

Hammer's most ambitious project to date—was mentioned in the trades as early as September 13, 1956, as a Hammerscope color subject. Anthony Hinds hinted in *The Kinematograph Weekly* that Hammer was working on a "new look" for their creature, quite different from the Universal-Karloff version. The company was also assuring readers that their film would employ a new level of "nastiness."

Some "twenty tall hefty brawny men" were interviewed by Hammer, who hoped to have their "monster" within two weeks. Included in the group were Bernard Bresslaw and 6'4" Christopher Lee, who said (*Lee Club Journal*) that John Redway, his agent, "knew that they needed above all somebody who was an actor and could portray a character, if necessary, without speech. I was virtually unknown, and I thought at the time that this might very well break new ground. Little did I know..." Lee had many desultory makeup tests with Phil Leakey and Roy Ashton until they hit on a design that Terence Fisher (*Films and Filming*, July, 1964) said, "fit Chris Lee's melancholy personality. We wanted a thing which looked like some wandering, forlorn mistral of monstrosity, a thing of shreds and patches." Since the Karloff look was copyrighted, an original makeup was essential, and Lee's resulting appearance was certainly that.

Peter Cushing's signing as Frankenstein was noted in *The Kinematograph Weekly* (November 8, 1956) and was quite a coup for Hammer. Cushing was Britain's top TV star and was also building a respectable film career. "We wanted him," Anthony Hinds said (*The Studio That Dripped Blood*), "and we got him." Unlike the Universal series,

Frankenstein would be the focus rather than his monster—a change for the better, as the Baron is a far more complex character. It was the best move the company ever made.

Production began on November 20, 1956, and was kicked off with a press party at Brooks Wharf at which Christopher Lee appeared in full makeup. Jimmy Sangster had just signed a three-picture contract with Hammer, and explained to *The Kinematograph Weekly* (November 29) his secrets for writing horror. "The public is more hardboiled since the Frankenstein pictures of the thirties. So many horrible things have happened since then that a film has to be really tough to get the desired reaction."

Cameraman Len Harris (August, 1993) recalled for the authors that the shoot was not without incident. "We had some near-misses. When Peter Cushing pushed the professor off the balcony, we had part of the floor padded—the part where the stunt man's head (Jock Easton) should have hit. Well ... he missed!" Easton also doubled for Lee in the climactic fire. "This was an *extremely* dangerous stunt," said Harris. "We had more men with fire extinguishers on the set than you could count! They don't pay these chaps enough!"

Originally slated for three weeks, *The Curse of Frankenstein* wrapped three weeks over schedule on January 3, 1957, at a cost of $270,000. When Fisher saw the completed cut, he said (*Cinefantastique*, Vol. 4, No. 3), "Emotionally, it had achieved more than I expected." The two Carrerases and Anthony Hinds took the print to New York and, after offering the film to several distributors, sold it to Warner Bros. The London premiere was held on May 2, 1957, at the Leicester Square Warner with the lobby

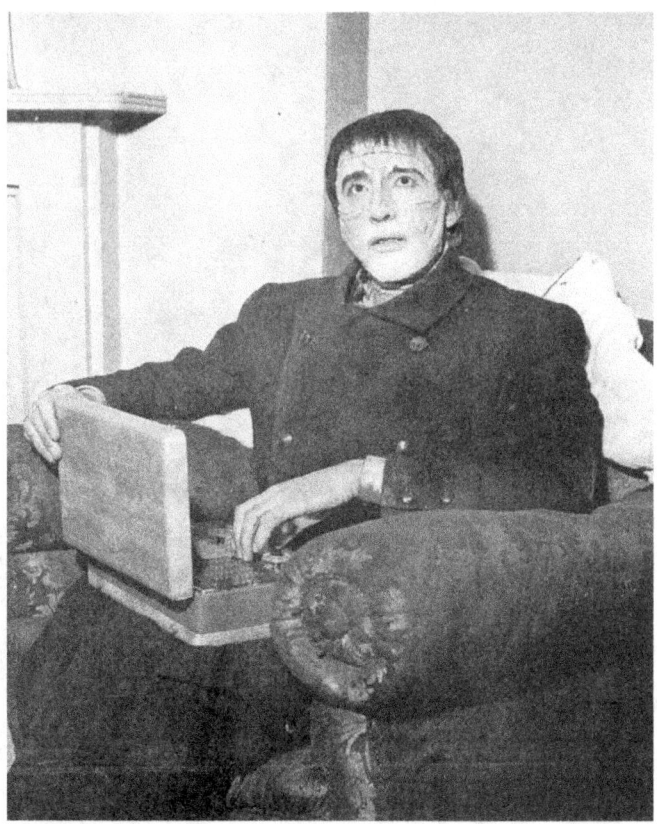

Christopher Lee listens to the Olympics during the filming of *The Curse of Frankenstein* (photo courtesy of Tim Murphy).

decorated with laboratory apparatus. Reviewers—like the public—were caught off-guard. *The Observer* (May 3): "I could not discern one moment of art or poetry"; *The Daily Worker* (no date): "Every effort is made to stress the realism and scientific detachment of Frankenstein"; *The Daily Telegraph* (no date): "For sadists only"; *The Kinematograph Weekly* (May 2): "A spine chilling story with skillful acting, direction, and realistic thrills"; and *Variety* (May 15): "Well deserves its horrific rating and praise for its handling of the macabre story." Reviewers were appalled more by what they *thought* they saw rather than what was actually on the screen. Others were offended by the story's lack of faithfulness to the novel—as if the Universal version was any closer. Most failed to recognize a new trend. When *The Curse of Frankenstein* went into general release in the U.K. on May 20, it broke records every-

Top: Hammer redefines the Gothic horror film. *Bottom:* Early trade ad while the film was still in production.

where it played. Returns from America following its May release were equally impressive.

One of the few reviewers to see the film as audiences did was Peter John Dyer in *Films and Filming* (July, 1957): "No efforts have been spared to make [the film] an improvement on the original 1931 James Whale film. Painstakingly detailed, intelligently written, beautifully photographed in Eastman color and—above all—set in period where it belongs, this must be

126 *The Curse of Frankenstein* (1956)

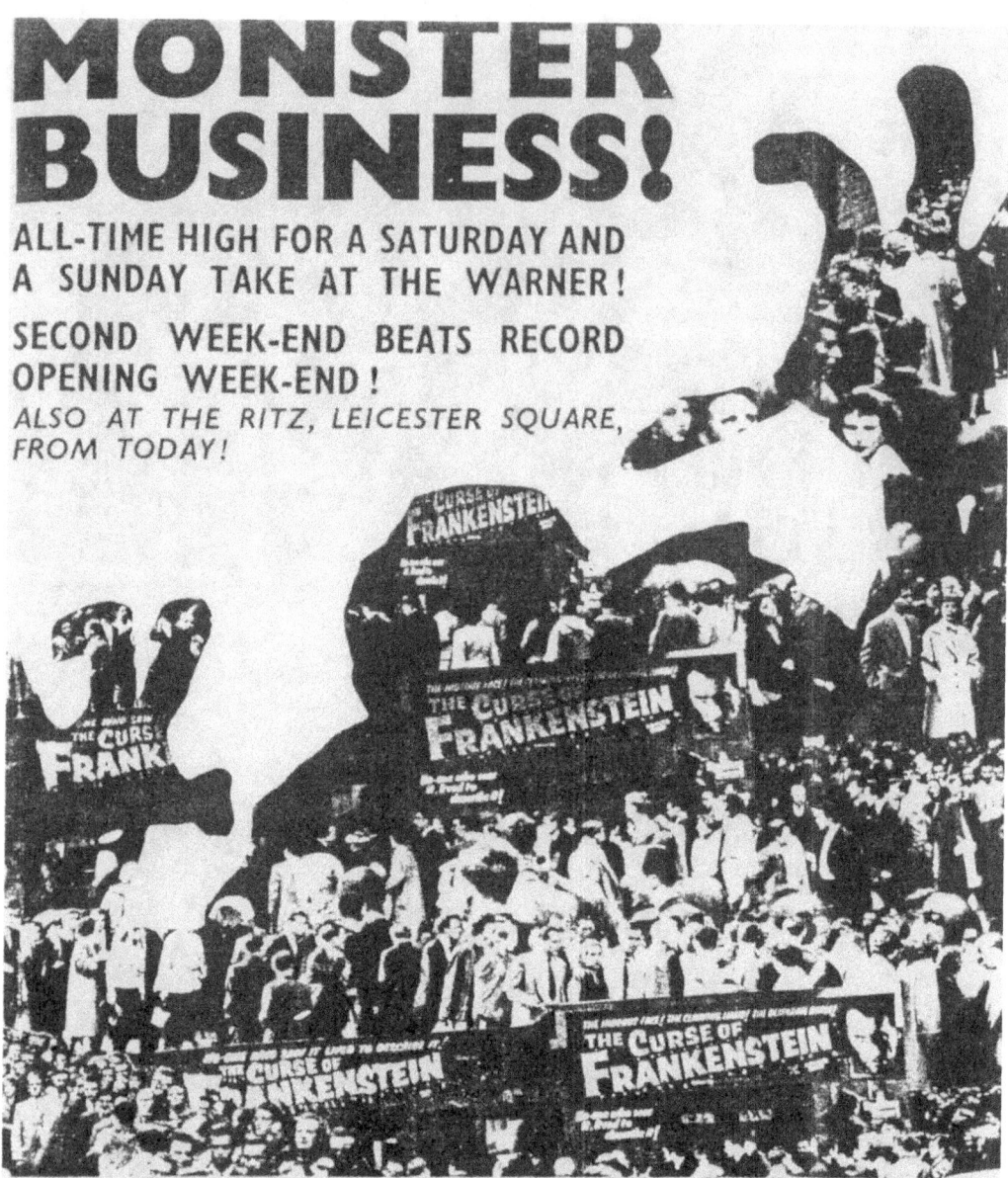

Trade advertisement.

one of the most polished horror movies ever made—a brilliant, bleak, and beastly job."

The Curse of Frankenstein grossed $8 million—almost thirty times its cost—and changed forever the public's concept of Frankenstein and of screen horror. Hammer had struck gold and was more than willing to give audiences more of what they so enthusiastically wanted.

1957

The Abominable Snowman

Released August 26, 1957 (U.K.), November, 1957 (U.S.); 83 minutes; B & W; Regal Scope; 7420 feet; a Hammer Film Production; a Warner Bros. Release (U.K.), 20th Century–Fox (U.S.); filmed at Bray and Elstree Studios and on location in France; Director: Val Guest; Producer: Aubrey Baring; Associate Producer: Anthony Nelson-Keys; Executive Producer: Michael Carreras; Screenplay and Original Story: Nigel Kneale (based on his television play *The Creature*); Music: Humphrey Searle; Music Supervisor: John Hollingsworth; Director of Photography: Arthur Grant; Production Design: Bernard Robinson; Art Director: Ted Marshall; Supervising Editor: James Needs; Editor: Bill Lenny; Production Manager: Don Weeks; Sound: Jock May; Camera: Len Harris; Assistant Director: Robert Lynn; Continuity: Doreen Soan; Dress Designer: Beatrice Dawson; Makeup: Phil Leakey; Hairdresser: Henry Montsash; Wardrobe: Molly Arbuthnot; U.S. Title: *The Abominable Snowman of the Himalayas*; U.K. Certificate: A.

Forrest Tucker (Tom Friend), Peter Cushing (Dr. John Rollason), Maureen Connell (Helen Rollason), Richard Wattis (Peter Fox), Robert Brown (Edward Shelley), Michael Brill (McNee), Wolfe Morris (Kusang), Arnold Marle (Lama), Anthony Chin (Majordomo).

Dr. John Rollason (Peter Cushing), his wife Helen (Maureen Connell), and Peter Fox (Richard Wattis) are guests of the Lama (Arnold Marle) in his remote Tibetan village where they are studying plants. But, unknown to the rest, Rollason is waiting to join adventurer Tom Friend (Forrest Tucker) on a search for the Yeti, which the doctor believes to be the "missing link." When Friend arrives with Ed Shelley (Robert Brown) and McNee (Michael Brill), Helen begs John not to go, and the Lama denies the Yeti's existence.

High in the Himalayas, Rollason discovers that "Friend" is a charlatan who plans to exhibit the "Snowman" as a sideshow freak. McNee—who has once seen a Yeti—is caught in one of Shelley's traps and injures his ankle. That night, he and the guide Kusang (Wolfe Morris) see a Yeti's hand creep under their tent. When they flee, McNee falls to his death and Kusang returns, terrified, to the village. Shelley later shoots a Snowman, and Friend places it in a cave to attract the others. Shelley is on guard—with blanks—as Friend wants one alive. When they enter the cave, Shelley dies of a heart attack.

Friend goes mad and hears Shelley calling for help, and as he fires his gun in response, he is crushed by an avalanche, leaving Rollason alone with the Yeti.

When Helen and Fox arrive, led by Kusang, they find John at the base of the cliff. When he recovers from his ordeal, he agrees with the Lama that there "is no Yeti."

Nigel Kneale's (who wrote Hammer's breakthrough film *The Quatermass Xperiment*) play, *The Creature*, was broadcast on the BBC in 1955, starring Peter Cushing and Stanley Baker. Like *Quatermass*, it attracted a huge audience—and Hammer's attention—with its quirkily unnerving story. *The Kinematograph Weekly* (December 13, 1956) reported that *The Creature* would be Hammer's first production for the new year. The company's horror image had not yet been established—*The Curse of Frankenstein* was still in post-production. Actually, the two movies couldn't be more different, and it's interesting to speculate on the company's direction if Val Guest had directed both on the strength of his helming *The Quatermass Xperiment*. He told the authors (May, 1992), "As with the *Quatermass* pictures, I did *The Abominable Snowman* on the understanding of getting that documentary feeling. And, that at no time, would I *ever* show the monster. We showed portions—eyes, arms, things like that—but at *no* time in its entirety. Quite a bit was shot in the Pyrenees under very difficult conditions. It was the first and, sadly, only picture I made with Peter Cushing. We became great pals, and we've been great pals ever since. He has the most incredible sense of humor of anyone I've ever met—a mad, darling man!"

Guest recalled for author Tom Weaver (who generously shared this interview),

> Michael Carreras was a buddy of mine and was one of the best producers I ever worked with. You could rely on the guy completely and

128 *The Abominable Snowman* (1957)

Top: The Tom Friend Expedition to find *The Abominable Snowman* (with Peter Cushing, Michael Brill, Wolfe Morris, Robert Brown, and Forrest Tucker) pause to check their bearings while searching for the legendary Yeti in Hammer's thought-provoking drama. *Bottom:* An odd combination for a double feature.

Dr. Rollason (Peter Cushing) nearly takes the secret of the Himalayas to his grave in this scene from *The Abominable Snowman*.

utterly. I was never asked to direct one of their Gothic thrillers—I don't know if I'd have been very good at Gothics—I'd have started laughing, I think! It's a strange thing about Nigel Kneale. I hear from all sorts of places that he's terribly unhappy about all his films. I don't know *why* he should be—maybe a hurt ego over the fact that some of his stuff had to be cut. He's a brilliant writer, but one who writes as though you were reading it in a book. So—you have to make it a bit more concise. It's sad that he doesn't enjoy the fruits of it all. I went out with doubles and a full unit for a couple of weeks up in the French Pyrenees. The rest was shot at Pinewood on one of their vast sound stages on which Bernard Robinson had done a complete snowscape. The Tibetan village was built on the Bray lot. Peter Cushing—he'd be in the middle of a very dramatic scene, and at the end, he'd go into a dance! Everyone would be in hysterics! And he was mad about props—we called him Props Cushing! When they showed him with the Yeti's tooth, none of us had *any* idea what was going to go on in that scene. He took a tape measure out, he scraped the tooth with a nail file, he came up with a magnifying glass—talking the whole time. It was quite hysterical!

Len Harris told the authors (December, 1993),

> Val was always *very* well prepared. You could ask him anything about the picture at any time—he had the whole film in his mind and always did his homework. He could tell you what clothing a character would be wearing in a specific scene! He did what is called a storyboard—sketches of the whole picture. Today, everybody does it, but not back then. He had all of his camera movements blocked out with arrows. *Anybody* could follow his plans. I went to the Pyrenees with Val and a small crew. It was easy to match the real mountains with the studio set due to the brilliance of Bernard Robinson's art direction. I'm sure Peter Cushing *wanted* to go, but we used doubles. He wanted everything to be right. Near the end of the production, we found we needed an insert shot of his character's hand, and Val said, "We'll do it afterwards—we'll get someone else to do it." When Peter heard this, he said, "No, I'll come in and do it." And he did—without asking to be paid! There's *no one* like Peter Cushing.

The Abominable Snowman began filming on January 28, 1957, and concluded on March 5. Publicity director Douglas Railton commented (*The Kinematograph Weekly*, May 9, 1957) that the "Horrorscope" process would, "Make fortunes, not tell them." As the film was in post-production, founder Will Hammer died on June 1 as the result of a cycling accident. A lifelong physical fitness enthusiast, he was still racing bicycles, at age 66, in 1953.

Following an August 7, 1957, trade show at Studio One, *The Abominable Snowman* went into general release on the ABC circuit on August 26. Co-featured with *Untamed Youth*, the film did not immediately click with the public or the critics, both of whom found it too tame. A few months earlier, the critics were complaining that *The Curse of Frankenstein* was too explicit! The public soon caught on, and by September 12, the film was a success. Most critics came around, too. *The Evening Standard* (August 22, 1957): "It is among the best of British science fiction thrillers"; *The Sunday Times* (August 25): "I salute *The Abominable Snowman*"; *The Christian Science Monthly*

The Camp on Blood Island (1957)

"There is no Yeti"?

(December): "A taut adventure with science fiction and character contrasts"; *Variety* (October 25): "Forrest Tucker and Peter Cushing both give substance to their roles."

There's no denying the power of Nigel Kneale's concept, and the small cast is excellent, generally under-playing their roles. It all adds up to one of Hammer's best, and should be high on anyone's list of great science fiction films.

The Camp on Blood Island

Released April 20, 1958 (U.K.), September 8, 1958 (U.S.); 82 minutes; B & W; Hammerscope; 7380 feet; a Hammer Film Production; a Columbia Release; filmed at Bray Studios; Director: Val Guest; Producer: Anthony Hinds; Executive Producer: Michael Carreras; Associate Producer: Anthony Nelson-Keys; Screenplay: Val Guest, Jon Manchip White (from his story); Director of Photography: Jack Asher; Music composed by Gerard Schurrman; Musical Director: John Hollingsworth; Production Manager: Arnold Brettell; Art Director: John Stoll; Editor: Bill Lenny; Supervising Editor: James Needs; Camera Operator: Len Harris; Sound Mixer: W.H.P. May; Sound Camera Operator: Michael Sale; Sound Camera Maintenance: Charles Bouvet; Draughtsman: Don Mingaye; Property Master: Tommy Money; Makeup: Tom Smith; Production Secretary: Cynthia Maugham; Assistant Director: Robert Lynn; Second Assistant: Tom Walls; Third Assistant: Hugh Harlow; Continuity: Doreen Dearnaley; Focus: Harry Oakes; Boom: Jim Perry; Hairstylist: Henry Montsash; Wardrobe: Molly Arbuthnot; Stills Cameraman: Tom Edwards; Publicity: Douglas Railton; Cashier: Ken Gordon; Studio Manager: A. Kelly; Construction Manager: Mick Lyons; Chief Electrician: Jack Curtis; Master Painter: Lawrence Wren; Master Plasterer: Arthur Banks; Transport Drivers: W. Epps, Wilfrid Faux; Grip: Albert Cowland; Property Buyer: Eric Hillier; U.K. Certificate: X.

Carl Mohner (Van Elst), Andre Morell (Colonel Lambert), Edward Underdown (Major Dawes), Walter Fitzgerald (Beattie), Barbara Shelley (Kate), Phil Brown (Lt. Bellamy), Michael Goodliffe (Father Anjou), Michael Gwynn (Shields), Richard Wordsworth (Dr. Keiller), Edwin Richfield (Sergeant Major), Ronald Radd (Col. Yamamitsu), Marne Maitland (Capt. Sakamura), Wolfe Morris (Interpreter), Milton Reid (Executioner), Geoffrey Bayldon (Foster), Lee Montague (Nangdon), Peter Wayn (Lt. Thornton), Michael Brill (Lt. Peters), Barry Lowe (Corporal Betts), Max Butterfield (Corporate Hallam), Jack MacNaughton, Howard Williams, Michael Dea (Prisoners), Michael Ripper (Driver), Anthony Chin (Sentry), Takai (Patrolman), S. Goh (Radio Operator), Jimmy Raphael, David Goh, Don Lee (Soldiers), Mary Merrall (Mrs. Beattie), Lillian Sottane (Mala), Grace Russell (Woman), Jan Holden (Nurse), Betty Cooper, Ann Ridler (Prisoners), Jacqueline Curtiss (Jennie).

Malaya, 1945. Japan has been defeated by the Allies, but the prisoners of war on Blood Island are still at the mercy of Colonel Yamamitsu (Ronald Radd) who, due to the failure of the camp radio, is unaware that the war is over. Only too aware of the problem is British Colonel Lambert (Andre Morell) who, along with his radio operator, Van Elst (Carl Mohner), knows the truth—and their fate when Yamamitsu finds out. In order to keep the POWs under control, Yamamitsu uses needless brutality, including the recent murder of an escapee. Still at large is another escapee, Dr. Keiller (Richard Wordsworth). Bellamy (Phil Brown), an American, parachutes near the camp and is captured along with Keiller who leaps from the Jeep as they pass the women's camp. He is machine-gunned before the horrified eyes of his wife (Barbara Shelley) and Bellamy.

After receiving a savage beating, Bellamy is dumped into the camp and, after conferring with Lambert, escapes with Van Elst. They free Mrs. Keiller who knows a route to safety, but Van Elst is killed. After Lambert explains the chilling situation, the men gather materials to use as weapons. Beattie (Walter Fitzgerald) goes mad with the tension, smuggles a grenade into Yamamitsu's office, and pulls the pin. The camp erupts as the POWs are machine-gunned from the watchtowers. Shields (Michael Gwynn) climbs one and kills the sniper, unobserved by Lambert who lofts a grenade into the tower, killing his friend. As the battle ends, the POWs have won, but at a terrible price.

The Camp on Blood Island, touted as Hammer's 50th production, was given a great deal of pre-release coverage and was thought to be a sure international success. The film *did* put Hammer's name before the public, but in a way no one could have imagined. Filming began on July 29, 1957, with Bray standing in admirably for Southeast Asia, and concluded on September 11. A trade show was held at the Columbia Theatre on April 10, 1958, and the premiere set for April 18. Held at the Pavilion, it was attended by most of the cast and crew, Columbia executive Mike Frankovich, and over two dozen former prisoners of war. After a seven week run, *The Camp on Blood Island* went into general release where it promptly broke house records recently set by *The Curse of Frankenstein*, and all was looking well.

On October 20, 1958, James Carreras and Frankovich's agreement was announced that gave Columbia 49 percent ownership of Bray Studios. *Variety* (October 28) commented that the deal "climaxes a steady rise in the international market for the British company and marks the first time that a British production firm has come under the wing of an American company." This deal officially ended Exclusive, Hammer's nominal distribution arm. Under the terms of the agreement, Hammer could release two films a year outside Columbia Pictures' control.

With *The Camp on Blood Island* racking up incredible grosses and the Columbia deal in hand, everything seemed to be going Hammer's way. "Here is a prestige picture," enthused *The Cinema* (September, 1957), "one that the trade, critics, and public will remember—and remembering, they will recall the name Hammer Films with appreciation...." Hammer was certainly remembered, as many critics made the company synonymous with gore, violence, and cheap sensationalism. The critical outrage generated by the sincere and (by today's standards) tame film are hard to fathom. A similar story would be told in *King Rat* (1965) to rave reviews. Perhaps Hammer changed the perception of Japanese conduct during the

Hammer takes to the streets to advertise their controversial World War II melodrama *The Camp on Blood Island*.

War, as well as pushing the limits of what was suitable for the screen.

The opening at the Pavilion generated mostly negative reviews. *The London Times* (April 21): "The central situation is an intensely dramatic one. The acting is workmanlike and sincere"; *The Reynold News* (April 20): "The most shameful and destructive picture of the year"; *The Evening News* (April 17): "The Frankenstein and Dracula horror film boys have now turned their attention to the box office possibilities of Japanese prison camp tortures"; *The Star* (April 17): "An orgy of atrocities"; *The Evening Standard* (April 18): "Well written and well acted, the ingredients are sadistic and substandard"; *The Daily Herald* (April 18): "Tragedy has been presented on a Frankenstein level"; *The Sunday Times* (April 20): "Sufficiently appalling"; and *The Observer* (April 20): "An abomination."

Normally, Hammer might have been amused at the attacks which had generated higher box office receipts for *The Curse of Frankenstein*. But this was serious. "Shiro Kido," reported *Variety* (September 11, 1958), "chairman of the Motion Picture Production Association of Japan, has submitted a letter to Eric Johnston (who holds a similar position in Great Britain), asking that *The Camp on Blood Island* be banned from American screens." Despite the threat, the film opened in America to positive reviews (perhaps due to Pearl Harbor?). *The New York Times* (September 18): "Directed and acted quietly to lend an air of credibility"; *The New York Herald Tribune* (September 9): "Straightforward and expert melodrama"; and *Variety* (April 23): "It will jerk out of complacency any person who now tends to regard the Japanese as not being as bad as thought." The controversy ended when *Variety* (December 31) quoted Eric Johnston,

"I don't think it was advisable to make films that bring back memories of detestable experiences of World War II." In short, Hammer was guilty of showing a truth that many wished to forget.

Val Guest told the authors (May, 1992),

The manager of the Lyric Theatre had been a POW and had kept notes that he had scribbled down on bits of lavatory paper and said that he thought it would make a good story. He gave Hammer the notes, and we thought—yes!—it's a *hell* of a story. So we all got together and got the script going. The picture was an enormous success, it broke attendance records, but we had all *sorts* of problems. I'm convinced that most of the adverse criticism leveled was because it was a Hammer production. Critics had their shots at the *Frankenstein* picture, and this was, I'm sure, a continuation of that attack. They simply had it in for the company—not just on *this* picture, either. There's *nothing* in my film that didn't really happen—and a lot of worse things *did* happen that we didn't show. You must remember, too, that this was a "forgive and forget" period. The government wanted to get things back to normal economically—then here comes Hammer with this POW picture! I think it's perfectly correct to forgive, but... We had a great cast—especially Andre Morell—and I stand by the picture.

Len Harris (December, 1993) recalled,

I had to take over for Jack Asher for a few days, and I said to Val, "We've got a problem. It's going to rain, and it won't match the previous scene that was shot in bright sunlight when we edit them. Val was never at a loss for *anything*. "We'll just put some thunder on the soundtrack," he said. He gave Michael Gwynn a new line—"I think we're going to have a storm," and that was that. Not that all of this was incredibly brilliant, but it illustrates the quick thinking that takes place on a film set that audiences are never aware of. I particularly enjoyed working with Andre Morell. Hammer was fortunate to have fine actors—and fine gentlemen—like Andre.

Although *The Camp on Blood Island* was a financial success, Hammer paid too high a price. The film made critics wary of the company, and when *Yesterday's Enemy* opened to positive reviews, the name "Hammer" was usually absent. One year after the film's proposed banning, James Carreras told *Films and Filming* (October, 1959), "We hate message films. We make entertainment."

The Snorkel

Released July 7, 1958 (U.K.), September, 1958 (U.S.); 90 minutes (U.K.), 74 minutes (U.S.); B & W; 8115 feet; a Hammer Film Production; a Columbia Release (U.S.); filmed at Bray Studios, England, and on location on the Italian Riviera; Director: Guy Green; Producer: Michael Carreras; Screenplay: Peter Myers, Jimmy Sangster, based on a story by Anthony Dawson; Director of Photography: Jack Asher; Editors: James Needs, William Lenny; Art Director: John Stoll; Associate Producer: Anthony Nelson-Keys; Assistant Directors: Tom Walls, Robert Lynn; Music: Francis Chagrin; Conducted by: John Hollingsworth; Production Manager: Don Weeks; Sound: Jock May; Makeup: Phil Leakey; Hairstyles: Henry Montsash; Wardrobe: Molly Arbuthnot; Camera: Len Harris; Re-Recording: Ken Cameron; Continuity: Doreen Dearnaley; Sound Mixer: C.L. Mounteney. U.K. Certificate: A.

Peter Van Eyck (Paul Decker), Betta St. John (Jean Edwards), Mandy Miller (Candy Brown), Gregory Aslan (The Inspector), William Franklyn (Wilson), Henry Vidon (Italian Gardener), Marie Burke (Gardener's Wife), Flush ("Toto"), Irene Prador (Frenchwoman), Robert Rietty (Station Sergeant), Armand Guinie (Waiter), David Ritch (Hotel Clerk).

In a villa on the Italian Riviera, Paul Decker (Peter Van Eyck) drugs his wealthy wife into unconsciousness, makes the bedroom airtight and allows the room to fill with gas while he hides safely in a cramped crawlspace beneath a secret trap door, breathing fresh air via snorkel. The police and Mrs. Decker's friend Wilson assume that Mrs. Decker committed suicide and that the missing Paul is on one of his frequent trips abroad. Candy (Mandy Miller), Mrs. Decker's daughter, arrives from England and tells the police she is certain that Paul (her stepfather) murdered her mother; she also believes Paul was responsible for the drowning death of her real father years before. Paul "returns" from his "trip" and is apprised of his wife's death, which an inquest rules a suicide. Candy continues to search for proof of Paul's guilt while Paul tries to plant in the mind of Candy's governess, Jean Edwards (Betta St. John), the idea that

The Snorkel (1957)

Governess Jean (Betta St. John) and Wilson (William Franklyn) refuse to believe young Candy's (Mandy Miller) claims that her stepfather has murdered her parents in *The Snorkel*.

Candy may be psychologically disturbed. After an attempt to drown the child fails, Paul lures her to the villa, drugs her and prepares the room for a second gas "suicide." But Jean and Wilson arrive unexpectedly, forcing Paul to take refuge under the floorboards. Candy, revived, insists the room be carefully searched for Paul's place of concealment, and a heavy cupboard happens to be moved atop the secret trap door. After Jean and Wilson leave, Candy hears Paul's cries for help, and gives him the impression she's leaving him to perish in his hiding place. But after riding into town with Jean and Wilson, she stops at the police station and tells the Inspector where he can find her mother's killer.

While *The Camp on Blood Island* was wrapping up at Bray, a second unit was sent to the Italian Riviera for location work on *The Snorkel*. Filming began on September 7, 1957, at a site near San Remo, which Michael Carreras and Anthony Nelson-Keys had scouted in May. Guy Green, an Academy Award–winning cinematographer (*Great Expectations*, 1946), directed his first film in 1954 and was considered to be one of Britain's most promising. He recalled for the authors (February, 1992):

> Michael Carreras was very cooperative, as well as a delightful person to be with, and very much responsible for making the film a most pleasant experience. He and I had a great time casting the smaller roles in Paris. Mandy Miller was a natural talent and a very professional girl, but a bit too mature for the part, and all our efforts failed to disguise this. Peter Van Eyck was a real pro, too. He had to do a lot of difficult swimming and, one day after spending most of the morning manfully keeping up with a motorboat from which he was being photographed, Peter said, "You never asked me if I could swim before giving me the part." It was true. I hadn't. We had to film an extra scene for the ending. Jimmy Sangster's original script had Peter left to die by Mandy under

the floor, and it was felt that her character might appear too callous.

Two weeks into the production, author Richard Matheson arrived in London to script his vampire novel, *I Am Legend*, which Hammer planned to film in the spring of 1958. However, the censor rejected the script, retitled *Night Creatures*, and the picture was never made, becoming the first Hammer horror to be cancelled. *The Snorkel* wrapped up on October 22 at a cost of £100,000, about 20 percent above average, due to location work. Warner Bros. had agreed to release the picture, but the deal fell through, and Hammer, according to *The Kinematograph Weekly* (April 25, 1957), produced *The Snorkel* without a distributor. Three days into the production, James Carreras signed a pact with Columbia, who agreed to finance 50 percent of *The Camp on Blood Island* and *The Snorkel*, and to release the then-titled *Blood of Frankenstein*.

The Snorkel had an odd premiere, shown to passengers on the *Queen Elizabeth* on its May, 1958, Atlantic crossing. The film went into general release on the ABC circuit on July 7 to encouraging reviews. *The Daily Cinema* (June 16): "A tense murder thriller"; *The Kinematograph Weekly* (June 19): "Creates considerable tension"; *Variety* (September 18): "Moments of suspense and horror"; and *The New York Herald Tribune* (September 18): "A first class specimen of its kind." With its tricky plot and psychotic killer, *The Snorkel* nicely anticipated the type of thriller Hammer would produce in the early 1960s, beginning with *Taste of Fear*. Peter Van Eyck was one of the company's best villains, and it's unfortunate *The Snorkel* was his lone Hammer performance. Jimmy Sangster's screenplay is ingenious and deserves credit for not letting down after the brilliant opening murder scene. *The Snorkel* is an underrated Hammer thriller that is inexplicably difficult to see, but worth the effort.

Up the Creek

Released June 2, 1958 (U.K.), November 10, 1958 (U.S.), 83 minutes; B & W; Hammerscope; a Hammer-Byron Production; an Exclusive Release (U.K.), a Dominant Pictures Release (U.S.); filmed at Elstree Studios, and on location on the Thames Estuary; Director: Val Guest; Producer: Henry Halstead; Screenplay: Val Guest, John Warren; Director of Photography: Arthur Grant; Production Supervisor: Fred A. Swann; Art Director: Elven Webb; Camera Operator: Moray Grant; Sound: George Adam; Makeup: Alec Garfather; Editor: Helen Wiggins Films; Music: Tony Fones, Tony Lowry; Technical Advisor: Lt. Cmdr. J.H. Pidler, R.N.; U.K. Certificate: U.

David Tomlinson (Lt. Fairweather), Peter Sellers (Bosun), Wilfrid Hyde White (Admiral Foley), Vera Day (Lilly), Liliane Sottane (Suzanne), Tom Gill (Flag Lt.), Michael Goodliffe (Nelson), Reginald Beckwith (Publican), Lionel Murton (Perkins), John Warren (Cooky), Lionel Jeffries (Steady Barker), Howard Williams (Bunts), Peter Collingwood (Chippie), Barry Lowe (Webster), Edwin Richfield (Bennett), David Lodge (Scouse), Max Butterfield (Lefty), Malcolm Ransom (Boy), Sam Kydd (Bates), Frank Pentingell (Station Master), Donald Bisset (Labourer), Leonard Fenton (Policeman), Basil Dignam (Coombes), Peter Coke (Price), Jack McNaughton (Reg. Petty Officer), Larry Noble (Chief Petty Officer), Patrick Cargill (Commander), Michael Ripper (Decorator).

Lt. Humphrey Fairweather, Royal Navy (David Tomlinson), loves building guided missiles, but they never work properly. His supervisors decide that something must be done, and put him in charge of HMS *Berkely*, an ancient destroyer. The crew is hardly an ideal one. Under the "leadership" of the Bosun (Peter Sellers), they have established a profitable business association with the villagers, and their racketeering is in jeopardy with Fairweather in command. Luckily for the crew, he knows as little about ships as he does about rockets, and is blissfully unaware of the many illegalities. Fairweather is also distracted by the sexy niece (Liliane Sottane) of the local publican (Reginald Beckwith).

By the time Fairweather tumbles to the illegalities, it is too late—the Bosun has as much "dirt" on the captain as Fairweather has on him. They are forced to join together when a surprise inspection is conducted by Admiral Foley (Wilfrid Hyde-White), who

136 *Up the Creek* (1957)

Trade advertisement.

Peter Sellers had made seven features before *Up the Creek*, performing notably in the classic black comedy *The Ladykillers* (1955). He gained national popularity on the BBC radio program *The Goon Show*, which led to theatrical shorts and to his first feature, *Penny Points to Paradise*, in 1951. By 1960, he was an international star.

Up the Creek was a co-production between Hammer and Byron Films. It has been omitted from many Hammer checklists, but there is no doubt about its being a Hammer film. *The Daily Cinema*'s (June 16, 1958) "With four box office smash hits in a row to their credit (including) *Up the Creek*..." would seem to confirm Hammer's involvement. Filming took place during November and December of 1957 at Elstree and on the Thames Estuary.

The British film industry had been in a slump due to the increasing popularity of television, but Hammer was seemingly immune. Due to the company's uncanny ability to read audiences, Hammer was never hurt by an industry-wide depression. While not all Hammer films were financial successes, it was a rare one that lost money.

Up the Creek premiered at the London Warner on May 7, 1958, and went into general release on the ABC circuit on June 2 to favorable reviews. *Films and Filming* (June, 1958): "The situation was amusing and the pace brisk"; *The Daily Cinema* (August 15, 1958): "a hit"; *The New York Times* (November 11): "diverting and spasmodically amusing"; *Variety* (May 21): "It makes up in good humor what it lacks in wit." *Variety* also mentioned that a sequel had already been started without Peter Sellers. This indicates Hammer's production speed—the reviews

accidently launches Fairweather's rocket and sinks the *Berkely*, destroying all evidence. Fairweather is back in business as a missile expert, and Bosun is just back in business.

"This one was rather interesting," Val Guest told the authors in a May, 1992, interview.

> It was a return to comedy at my request. I saw a comedian on television called Peter Sellers, and I thought he was *fabulous*. I wrote *Up the Creek* with John Warren and Len Heath as a vehicle for Peter, and took it up and down Wardour Street. *Nobody* wanted to know about it—nobody would even admit they'd ever heard of Sellers. Finally I went to Jimmy Carreras. I said that this is a knockabout comedy, and that Peter was going to be a big star. Jimmy said, "Well, we're not that big on comedy, but if you say so."

were barely in before the company had a sequel going.

Although Sellers declined to appear in the sequel due to "another engagement," *Up the Creek* gave him the final boost to stardom. The film did not do Hammer any harm, either, as it joined *Dracula* and *The Camp on Blood Island* in the West End cinemas. Despite the popularity of their horror movies, Hammer was still canny enough to be diversified.

Dracula

Released June 16, 1958 (U.K.), May 8, 1958 (U.S.); 82 minutes; Technicolor; 7332 feet; a Hammer Film Production; a Rank Release (U.K.), Universal-International (U.S.); filmed at Bray Studios; Director: Terence Fisher; Producer: Anthony Hinds; Associate Producer: Anthony Nelson-Keys; Executive Producer: Michael Carreras; Screenplay: Jimmy Sangster, based on Bram Stoker's novel; Director of Photography: Jack Asher; Music: James Bernard; Music Director: John Hollingsworth; Production Design: Bernard Robinson; Production Manager: Don Weeks; Special Effects: Syd Pearson; Supervising Editor: James Needs; Editor: Bill Lenny; Camera: Len Harris; Makeup: Phil Leakey, Roy Ashton; Hairstyles: Henry Montsash; Sound: Jock May; Costumes: Molly Arbuthnot; Assistant Director: Robert Lynn; Continuity: Doreen Dearnaley; Stills: Tom Edwards; U.S. Title: *Horror of Dracula*; U.K. Certificate: X.

Peter Cushing (Van Helsing), Christopher Lee (Count Dracula), Michael Gough (Arthur Holmwood), Melissa Stribling (Mina Holmwood), Carol Marsh (Lucy Holmwood), John Van Eyssen (Jonathan Harker), Olga Dickie (Gerda), Valerie Gaunt (Vampire Woman), Janine Faye (Tania), Barbara Archer (Inga), Charles Lloyd Pack (Dr. Seward), George Merritt (Policeman), George Woodbridge (Landlord), George Benson (Official), Miles Malleson (Marx), Geoffrey Bayldon (Porter), Paul Cole (Lad), Guy Mills (Coach Driver); deleted roles: Judith Nelmes (Woman in Coach), Stedwell Fulcher (Man in Coach), Humphrey Kent (Fat Merchant), William Sherwood (Priest).

Transylvania, 1885. Jonathan Harker (John Van Eyssen), arriving at Castle Dracula ostensibly to catalogue the Count's books, is approached by a mysterious beauty (Valerie Gaunt) who begs him to help her escape. Dracula (Christopher Lee) appears to be a courteous host, but Harker is an agent of Dr. Van Helsing who believes that the Count is the instigator of a plague of vampirism. Before Harker can act, he is attacked by the woman and the Count and is in danger of becoming one of the undead himself. The next day he drives a stake through the woman's heart but is, in turn, killed by Dracula. Van Helsing (Peter Cushing), after discovering Harker's vampiric corpse and destroying it, brings the news to the Klausenberg home of Harker's fiancée, Lucy Holmwood (Carol Marsh). He is coldly received by her brother Arthur (Michael Gough). Holmwood's wife Mina (Melissa Stribling) explains that Lucy is ill.

Lucy is worse than ill. She has been taken by Dracula, who traced her through a photograph of Harker's. She grows weaker and, despite Van Helsing's efforts, dies. After becoming a vampire, she attempts to take the child (Janine Faye) of the Holmwoods' maid (Olga Dickie). Van Helsing destroys Lucy with Arthur a horrified witness. Denied his new bride, Dracula finds another—Mina. When Van Helsing discovers Dracula's coffin in Arthur's cellar, he places a cross inside, rendering the coffin useless. The Count abducts Mina to his castle with Van Helsing and Arthur in pursuit.

After hurling Mina into an open grave, Dracula is about to disappear through a trap door when Van Helsing confronts him. As they struggle, Van Helsing breaks free and, leaping from a table, tears open the drapes. Dracula, caught in the sunlight, tries to crawl under the table but is forced back into the light by Van Helsing's crucifix and crumbles into dust, releasing Mina from his power.

Despite initial critical savaging, *Dracula* ("The blood in his veins once flowed through hers") is not only Hammer's greatest film, it is one of the finest Gothic fantasies ever made. After the initial success of *The Curse of Frankenstein*, it was

Christopher Lee in his landmark performance as Count Dracula.

only natural for Hammer to turn to Dracula, reversing the Universal approach of 1930–1931.

Lack of studio space was, as always, a problem at Bray. In the summer of 1957, construction of a new 90'×80' sound stage was under way (*Cinema Supplement*, September, 1957). It would accommodate *The Snorkel*, *Dracula*, and *Blood of Frankenstein*, among others. After reading Bram Stoker's novel, Jimmy Sangster began the script. "I didn't write it with any particular actors in mind," he said (August, 1993) to the authors. "We weren't writing them specifically for Peter Cushing and Christopher Lee yet." Realistically, Hammer could hardly have considered any other actors. The final shooting script was dated October 18, 1957, and filming was scheduled to begin on November 11.

The Cinema Supplement (September, 1957) printed a full page in black, white, and (of course) red: "Starts November 5th — A World Beater! The most famous Horror film of all time!" *The Daily Cinema* (November 12, 1957) announced: "Peter Cushing and Christopher Lee, who sent shudders around the world when they appeared in *The Curse of Frankenstein* ... are together again in a new exercise in British screen horror." "Our approach to the subject," Michael Carreras said in the same issue, "will be different from that of the old Hollywood version and should make the original look tame by comparison." This difference has split both critics and fans ever since.

Hammer's schedule was crowded. *Blood of* (later, *Revenge of*) *Frankenstein* was to have a December 30 start, with *The Phoenix* (later,

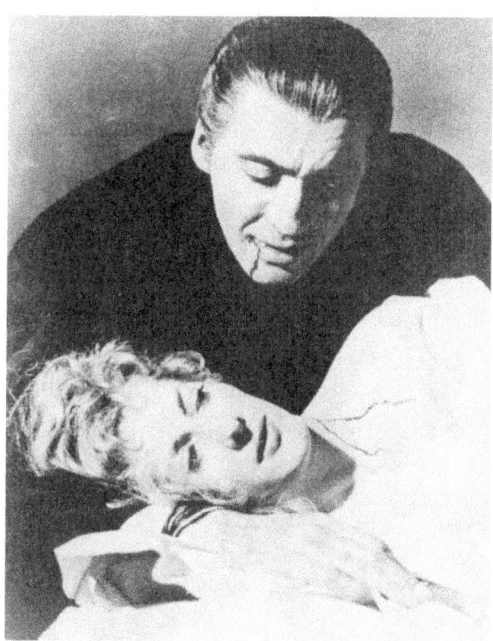

"The terrifying lover ... who died, yet lived!" Christopher Lee and Melissa Stribling in a publicity photo from *Dracula*.

Ten Seconds to Hell), *Brat Farrar*, *Build Us a Dam*, *Charter to Danger*, and *Chorus of Echoes* in "active preparation." The last three were jettisoned in the wake of Hammer's horror successes. Also never starting production was Richard Matheson's classic novel *I Am Legend*. "When I was in London in 1957," Matheson told the authors in July, 1992, "I visited Tony Hinds in his office—a very nice man. He was going to produce *I Am Legend* and Val Guest was to direct. I was sorry the project fell through. They told me it was because the film censor wouldn't pass it. I thought they were trying to spare my feelings! But then, recently, I read the same thing, so maybe it was true!"

Filming ended for *Dracula* on January 3, 1958. The film's budget has long been a matter of debate, but was probably much smaller than Hammer was willing to admit. After a May 1 trade show, *Dracula* had its U.K. premiere at the Gaumont Haymarket with a giant poster of Christopher Lee hovering over a nightgown-clad Melissa Stribling with "blood" pumped from a tube and flowing down her neck. This May 20 showing was not the world premiere. *Dracula* was, inexplicably, first shown at the Milwaukee Warner on May 4. James Carreras, Anthony Hinds, Peter Cushing, and Christopher Lee arrived for the New York premiere on May 25 at the Mayfair. Retitled *Horror of Dracula* (to avoid confusion with the Lugosi version), the picture was co-featured with the American-made *The Thing That Couldn't Die*. Hammer's four ambassadors attended a May 28 showing, with Cushing and Lee signing autographs at morning and evening shows.

Back in London, *Dracula* left the Gaumont on June 16 (having set an attendance record on June 5) to go into general release. By June 26, *The Kinematograph Weekly* judged *Dracula*'s "takings astronomical." Meanwhile, *The Camp on Blood Island*, after leaving the Pavilion, was drawing huge crowds in general release. Hammer was now riding a wave of success, at least with the public. The critics were a different matter. *The Observer*'s C.A. Lejune (May 31, 1958) led the assault, as she had done against *The Curse of Frankenstein*. "I regret to hear that it is being shown in America with emphasis laid on its British origin, and feel inclined to apologize to all decent Americans for sending them a work in such sickening bad taste." Then came Nina Hibbin in *The Daily Worker* (May 31): "I came away revolted and outraged"; *The Daily Sketch* (May 23): "Anthony Hinds and his merry men have gone far enough. *Dracula* sounds like the warning bell. One step farther and the license permitted by the censor's X certificate will be dangerously abused"; and *The Daily Telegraph* (May 31): "This British film has an X certificate. This is too good for it. There should be a new certificate—'S' for sadistic or just 'D' for disgusting. I must add that the film has been efficiently produced and is well acted." Michael Carreras said in *The Horror People*, "[Critics] are full of crap and hot air [and] rarely review horror films on the level they're aimed at." The negative reviews probably helped *Dracula*, as audiences lined up to see what the furor was about.

On the positive side were *The London Times* (May 31): "Although this is a horrific film, it is by no means an unimpressive piece of melodramatic story telling"; Paul Dehn in *The News Chronicle* (May 23): "It's fantasy for the most part rooted in the sort of realism which comes of everyone taking it and themselves quite seriously"; *The Evening Standard* (May 22): "A considerable variation on the old theme"; *The New York Daily News* (May 29): "Unlike most of Hollywood's quickies, *Horror of Dracula* has allocated time, thought, and talent, [and] some of the photography is good enough to frame"; and *Variety* (April 7): "A serious approach ... that adds up to lotsa tension and suspense."

Lee's Dracula certainly changed his life. "It has been a milestone in my career," he said in *The Films of Christopher Lee*, "and has proven to be a mixed blessing on occasions." Though he would tire of the role, audiences never tired of seeing him play it. Christopher Lee was Dracula to the "baby boomers" and always will be—yet, he is on screen for only seven minutes out of the film's 82. He has very few lines and does not speak after his first few scenes, but Lee pulls off the role with sheer presence. As for comparisons between Christopher Lee and Bela Lugosi, one need say only that each performance was right for its film, and each film was right for its time.

Peter Cushing had no ambivalence: "I don't mind at all that people may refer to me as a 'horror actor,'" he said in *L'Incroyable Cinéma*, No. 5, "because in this unpredictable profession, actors are awfully lucky. But for any actor to be associated with a form of success like Hammer's, I think it's absolutely

The standard against which all vampire films are measured (the Americans added "*Horror of*" to the title).

wonderful; and if that means being thought of as a 'horror actor,' then I think it's the most marvelous thing that could happen to me." What Cushing did is as impressive as Lee's accomplishment. He took a rather bland character (especially next to Dracula!) and created the most dynamic hero in horror films. Cushing would repeat his part, like Lee, but would not become as identified with it as he was with Frankenstein.

Terence Fisher was, as he put it, "a working director," and he modestly played

Hammer scored double gold with this 1964 U.S. reissue.

down his role in the film's success. When given the opportunity to promote himself, he invariably turned it down. "All I did was to accept the script, and the actors and actresses as they were," he said in *Cinefantastique*, Vol. 4, No. 3, "and they were very, very good. I accepted with great excitement, because I really appreciated its potential as a film subject." Lee, Cushing, and Fisher are justifiably given the bulk of the credit for *Dracula*'s success. But, as Len Harris told the authors (December, 1993), "We were a real team at Bray, and you can really see it in *Dracula*. Every aspect of the picture is first class. It has no weak spots. The music, the costumes, the photography, the props, *everything* was first rate—even the small things. We were all *very* proud of this one. It is a beautiful film." Also, one must remember the underpraised Anthony Hinds who put the entire package together.

After *Dracula*, Hammer's course was clear. Mainstream topics were postponed or, in most cases, dropped in favor of horror properties. This was not necessarily for the best. Films like *Yesterday's Enemy*, *Hell Is a City*, and *Cash on Demand* make one wish Hammer had made fewer horror movies. *Dracula* not only changed forever the genre but the entire film industry. Pictures like Ian Fleming's *Dr. No* (1962) might not have been made without Hammer's challenging what was permissible on the screen. This challenge may have led to more bad films than good, but this is not Hammer's fault.

Dracula set new standards in Japan as well. There has been the suggestion that Japanese prints of the early Hammer horrors were more violent than those seen elsewhere. *The Daily Cinema* (August 13, 1958) reported that "Jim Carreras was bursting to tell me that the Japanese version of Dracula ... has broken the all-time house record. The Japanese print of Hammer's horrifier has a much more emphatic shock content ... than its comparatively sedate British counterpart."

Hammer was planning a sequel as soon as the cash registers started ringing, but Christopher Lee was reluctant to appear. As a result, *The Brides of Dracula* was filmed without him—or Dracula. Lee, however, did appear in *Uncle Was a Vampire* (1959), a third-rate, unfunny Italian comedy. This puts some of his complaints about Hammer's plans in perspective. Coincidentally, Universal's *Dracula* sequel, *Dracula's Daughter* (1936), also failed to feature more than the Count's name. Unfortunately, Hammer's later efforts would often reduce Dracula to an afterthought.

Since Lee's initial portrayal, Frank Langella created a minor sensation in the campy 1979 version of his Broadway hit, and Francis Ford Coppola's *Bram Stoker's Dracula* gave Gary Oldman his brief moment in 1992. They joined Bela Lugosi, Lon Chaney, Jr., John Carradine, and Francis Lederer as interesting Draculas, but no one has brought to the role what Christopher Lee did.

Herman Cohen, prime mover of the fifties classics *I Was a Teenage Werewolf* and *I Was a Teenage Frankenstein*, was a friend of James Carreras. "Jimmy was a dynamic character—a tremendous man," Cohen told the authors (August, 1994).

He wasn't a picture maker as such—not a hands-on guy. His genius was in setting up a picture—he really had the pulse of the audiences. Jimmy had the final word—he said yea or nay—and he was always right. He was a real charmer, too. He made you feel like you were the most important person in the world when he was speaking to you. Jimmy was very generous—in addition to his charity work, he also helped out other filmmakers. One of the few "arguments" we had was when I made *Blood of Dracula* (1957). He felt that *he* owned the name after *his* picture. I pointed out to him that Lugosi made a Dracula film 25 years earlier and that Hammer didn't own anything! On the other hand, I *never* tried to get Peter Cushing or Christopher Lee for one of my films because I felt that they "belonged" to Hammer, that they were too closely connected with Hammer. It just wouldn't have been right to use them. I also didn't want to get Jimmy pissed off at me! Many executives think *they* made the pictures, but this wasn't true of Jimmy. He knew what he did and didn't do. When he left Hammer, his son just couldn't follow what he'd done. One of the reasons that Jimmy got out was his wife's illness. He was just devastated and wanted to devote more time to her. The majors may have looked down on Hammer, but most people knew how important Hammer was to the British film industry. During the fifites and early sixties, most films made in England were actually coproductions with American companies—*Lawrence of Arabia* (1962), for example. Independents like Hammer were among the few totally British companies making films during that period. By the way, I'd like to think I gave Hammer some good advice. I told Jimmy to make sure that his actors didn't sound "too British"—to use a mid–Atlantic speech and talk more slowly. Many actors resented this sort of thing, but it was necessary to sell a picture to the States.

Perhaps the last word on *Dracula* should be those of an ad run in the British trade press: "HAMMER—the company that's injecting fresh blood into the film industry." After *Dracula*, neither Hammer nor the horror film would be the same.

1958

The Revenge of Frankenstein

Released June, 1958 (U.S.), November 17, 1958 (U.K.); 91 minutes; Technicolor; 7982 feet; a Hammer Film Production; a Columbia Release; filmed at Bray Studios, England; Director: Terence Fisher; Producer: Anthony Hinds; Associate Producer: Anthony Nelson-Keys; Executive Producer: Michael Carreras; Screenplay: Jimmy Sangster; Additional Dialogue: Hurford Janes; Music: Leonard Salzedo; Conductor: Muir Mathieson; Musical Supervisor: John Hollingsworth; Director of Photography: Jack Asher; Production Design: Bernard Robinson; Supervising Editor: James Needs; Editor: Alfred Cox; Sound Recordist: Jock May; Production Manager: Don Weeks; Camera: Len Harris; Makeup: Phil Leakey, Hal Liesley; Hairstyles: Henry Montsash; Continuity: Doreen Dearnaley; Wardrobe: Rosemary Burrows; Chief Set Electrician: Robert Petzoldt; Assistant Director: Robert Lynn; Clapper/Loader: Tony Powell; 2nd Assistant Director: Tom Walls; Focus: Harry Oakes; Camera Grip: Albert Cowland; Working Title: *Blood of Frankenstein*; U.K. Certificate: X.

Peter Cushing (Dr. Victor Stein/Frankenstein), Francis Matthews (Dr. Hans Kleve), Eunice Gayson (Margaret), Michael Gwynn ("Karl"), John Welsh (Bergman), Lionel Jeffries (Fritz), Oscar Quitak (Karl), Richard Wordsworth (Up Patient), Charles Lloyd Pack (President), John Stuart (Inspector), Arnold Diamond (Molke), Margery Cresley (Countess Barscynska), Anna Walmsley (Vera Barscynska), George Woodbridge (Janitor), Michael Ripper (Kurt), Ian Whittaker (Boy), Avril Leslie (Girl), Michael Mulcaster (Tattoo).

Baron Frankenstein (Peter Cushing)—condemned to the guillotine to pay for his crimes—is rescued by Karl (Oscar Quitak), a crippled guard, in exchange for a new, perfect body. With a priest buried in his place, the Baron—now calling himself "Dr. Stein," establishes a thriving practice in Carlsbruck, which perturbs the city's Medical Council. One of the doctors, Hans Kleve (Francis Matthews) recognizes the Baron, but is willing to keep the secret in exchange for knowledge. The pair transplant Karl's brain into a perfect body created from the amputated limbs of Dr. Stein's charity patients. The "new" Karl (Michael Gwynn) realizes he must take care—a similar operation on an orangutan resulted in its becoming a cannibal. He is even more determined after meeting Margaret (Eunice Gayson), a volunteer at the clinic, and he revels in the thought of becoming a normal man.

After Hans foolishly tells Karl that Dr. Stein plans to put him on display, he is repelled at still being an object of curiosity, and escapes. Returning to the lab where he was "born," Karl destroys his old body, but is beaten by the janitor (George Woodbridge). Maddened, Karl strangles his attacker and is overcome by a hideous desire. His body twisting into its former shape, Karl hides in a park where he brutally attacks a young woman (Avril Leslie). Drawn to Margaret, he staggers into a party attended by Dr. Stein and Hans. He calls for Frankenstein's help, and dies at his creator's feet. When Stein's patients learn of his true activities, they attack him. Hans takes the dying Baron to the lab and, following previous instructions, transplants his mentor's brain into a previously prepared body.

At his posh London office, "Dr. Franck," his forehead scarred, greets his new patients as Hans looks on approvingly.

Hammer had accurately predicted the box office potential of *The Curse of Frankenstein* and, in March, 1957—two months before the picture was released—registered a title (*The Blood of Frankenstein*) for its sequel. When asked by *The Sunday Express* how he planned to revive the Baron, James Carreras commented, "Oh, we sew his head back on again!" He and Michael flew to New York in late October to finalize with Columbia the production of the pilot for the TV series, *Tales of Frankenstein*.

Production of the retitled *The Revenge*

Top: Karl (Michael Gwynn) crashes Margaret's (Eunice Gayson) party looking for Dr. Stein in *The Revenge of Frankenstein*. *Bottom:* Dr. Stein's (Peter Cushing) notorious past is about to catch up with him in the form of Francis Matthews.

A rare case of the sequel surpassing the original.

of Frankenstein began on January 6, 1958. Anthony Hinds (*The Daily Cinema*, January 2) assured fans that the picture "would contain all the shake, shudder, and wallop" of the original. To lower production costs, Hinds utilized several revamped sets from *Dracula*. This practice would soon bring complaints from some critics, but enabled Hammer to give its films a rich look at a discount.

When *The Kinematograph Weekly* (January 20, 1958) visited Terence Fisher on the set, he said, "It's no good having your tongue in your cheek when you are making horror films. You must be completely sincere. It is very difficult trying to stop people laughing in the wrong places. But there are also wonderful opportunities to put in intentional laughs." It was apparent that Hammer tried to make up for *Curse*'s grim premise by supplying some humor courtesy of writer George Baxt. He told the authors (June, 1992), "I 'ghosted' two scenes for *The Revenge of Frankenstein*. One was with the two grave robbers, and the other was an amputation followed by Cushing 'amputating' a roast chicken." When asked if he was the Hurford Janes who shared screen credit with Jimmy Sangster, Baxt merely laughed.

Sangster's screenplay is one of his best, and took the Hammer series in a completely different direction from its predecessor. While *Curse* at least paid lip service to the novel and earlier films, *Revenge* was pure

Hammer. "I just thought about what frightened me the most," Sangster told the authors (August, 1993). "And what frightens *me* will frighten *you*." What separates this film from the "average" horror movie is the fascinating "monster," excellently played by Michael Gwynn. Sangster created a truly sympathetic character, and Gwynn's acting makes the viewer truly uncomfortable as he goes from the elation of being "normal" to the horror of realizing that it was all for nothing. "He was a classically trained actor," Len Harris told the authors (August, 1994), "who preferred the stage and, although he was excellent in *Revenge*, he wasn't interested in pursuing a film career. He only did films occasionally but was in great demand." Harris also recalled the crowded conditions at Bray. "During the scene in which Peter Cushing was beaten, if you look closely as he is on the floor, you'll see an old blanket next to him. The blanket was thrown down as the camera moved back to cover the tracks." He also remembered a near disaster. "For some reason, the large tank that contained Michael Gwynn shattered when we were all at lunch. Thank God he wasn't in it."

Filming ended on March 4, 1958, and, two days later, the *Tales of Frankenstein* pilot starring Anton Diffring concluded in Hollywood. Michael Carreras hoped that the first of 26 further episodes would begin at Bray in June, but, as he recalled (*Little Shoppe of Horrors* 4), "Tony Hinds went to America to Screen Gems, and he ran into a lot of trouble. They didn't understand the concept, and they wanted to Americanize it. They wanted to do a series nothing like our films." As a result, the poorly made pilot was all that came of a good idea.

The Revenge of Frankenstein was released in the U.S. in June co-featured with the excellent *Curse of the Demon*, and was hailed by *Variety* (June 18) as a "high grade horror film, gory enough to give adults a squeamish second thought and a thoroughly unpleasant one." The U.K. premiere was held at midnight at the Plaza on August 27. In attendance were Valerie Hobson (Elizabeth in *Bride of Frankenstein*) and her soon-to-be disgraced husband, John Profumo. (Profumo, a member of Parliament, admitted to sharing call girl Christine Keeler with a Soviet agent.) Joining them were Peter and Helen Cushing. When asked why he enjoyed making films for Hammer, Cushing replied, "Great skill goes into their making. They demand the very best an actor can give. And it is these films, more than any others, which have done so much to establish me with world audiences." Unlike some, Cushing was always grateful to the company and never downplayed its role in his success. Reviewers were, not surprisingly, split. *The Evening Standard* (August 28): "The latest monster looks like a handsome frontrow forward recovering from a head injury"; *The News Chronicle* (August 29): "I relish shockers like [this]"; *The Observer* (August 31): "A vulgar, stupid, nasty, and intolerably tedious business"; *The Spectator* (September 5): "The lowest level to which we were obliged to crawl"; *The Daily Cinema* (August 27): "A handsome deluxe production"; and *The Kinematograph Weekly* (August 28): "Immaculately tailored, gripping and intriguing story, faultless atmosphere." The picture went into general release on November 17, generating respectable, but far less, business than *The Curse*.

The Revenge of Frankenstein set the Hammer style that would captivate audiences for years to come. "At first, people regarded color as something reserved for musicals and comedies," said photographer Jack Asher (*The Kinematograph Weekly*, January 30, 1958). "I think we proved with the first Frankenstein picture that color would heighten the dramatic effect." Audiences perceived color as the mark of a "classy" horror film, and Hammer would have the field to itself until American International's Poe series in 1960.

Ten Seconds to Hell

Released June 15, 1959 (U.K.), July, 1959 (U.S.); 93 minutes, (original running time: 131 minutes); B & W, 8448 feet; a Hammer-7 Arts Production; a United Artists Release; filmed on location in Berlin, Germany; Director, Screenplay: Robert Aldrich; Producer: Michael Carreras; Screenplay: Teddi Sherman, based on the novel *The Phoenix* by Lawrence P. Bachmann; Director of Photography: Ernest Laszlo; Editor: Henry Richardson; Supervising Editor: James Needs; Music: Richard Farrell, Kenneth V. Jones; Conductor: Muir Mathieson; Art Director: Ken Adam; Production Manager: Basil Keys; Technical Advisor: Gerhard Rabiger; Camera Operator: Len Harris; U.K. Certificate: A.

Jack Palance (Eric Koertner), Jeff Chandler (Karl Wirtz), Martine Carol (Margot Hofer), Robert Cornthwaite (Loeffler), Dave Willock (Tillig), Wes Addy (Sulke), Jimmy Goodwin (Globke), Virginia Baker (Friar Bauer), Richard Wattis (Major Haven), Nancy Lee (Ruth Sulke).

After the end of World War II, Karl Wirtz (Jeff Chandler) and Eric Koertner (Jack Palance) are released from a British POW camp and return to Berlin. Amid the ruins are thousands of unexploded bombs. Wirtz, Koertner, and their fellow POW join a demolition squad and form a unique pact. Each will contribute half of his pay to a fund which will be divided among the survivors. Wirtz and Koertner, never close, are driven farther apart by the job stress and their love for Margot Hofer (Martine Carol), a widow who runs their boarding house. One by one, the squad is decimated until only Wirtz and Koertner remain. When Wirtz finds a bomb with double fuses that requires special handling, he sees an opportunity to kill off his rival. His plan fails, and Wirtz is forced to try to dismantle the bomb alone and is killed in the attempt.

Hammer bought the rights to Lawrence P. Bachmann's novel *The Phoenix* in 1955, and James Carreras planned to film it the next year with Stanley Baker and Gregory Peck. The picture remained on Hammer's schedule through 1957, recast with Jack Palance and Peter Van Eyck. When Oscar nominee Jeff Chandler became available, Van Eyck was dropped. Michael Carreras and director Robert Aldrich flew to Berlin on January 7, 1958, to start preproduction. The film was a co-production with 7 Arts, and James Carreras enthused (*The Daily Cinema*, January 8), "We have been working on it for nearly two years. I think that when it comes to star power, the names of the three principal players carry a terrific box office wallop." While Carreras and Aldrich were in Berlin, Jack Palance, who had acted for Aldrich in *The Big Knife* (1958) and *Attack!* (1956), arrived in London. After making an enemy of Columbia boss Harry Cohn, Aldrich became expendable in Hollywood and was available for European projects.

Filming began on February 24, 1958, at Berlin's UFA Studios, but there was an immediate three day delay due to Aldrich's becoming ill. A second, more intriguing delay was caused when Gerhard Rabiger—the film's technical advisor—was called away to defuse a *real* 500 pound bomb. Len Harris recalled for the authors (August, 1994), "It was very sad going to the UFA Studio and seeing the graves of soldiers lining the road. You must remember that the war had only ended thirteen years previously and was still very real to us all. These soldiers died defending a film studio!" The West Berlin government cautioned Hammer not to demolish any sites during the production, because many walls were still strong enough to support new buildings. As a result, Hammer had to construct its own "ruins" to be demolished.

A different problem arose when Palance began to balk at the script when he considered it to be too philosophical and talky. "Palance's was the pivotal part," Aldrich recalled (*The Films and Career of Robert Aldrich*), "and when I lost control of him and he lost confidence in me, the resulting damage to the film was catastrophic." Len Harris remembered Palance as

> an odd man, but a very nice one. He was something of a 'method' actor—this was new to the old Hammer crew—and we weren't quite sure what was going on. He was trying to live the part and couldn't stand *any* interference while he was preparing himself. He'd walk around the studio, getting himself worked up, and believe me, you didn't want to get in his way. He was *definitely* unapproachable during these times.

Problems on the set continued to mount when the German technicians objected to Aldrich's directing technique. "Robert covered himself with hundreds of

Martine Carol and Jack Palance in *Ten Seconds to Hell*.

shots of the bomb," said Harris. "One from *this* side, one from *that* side, one from this angle, closeup, whatever. The German crew called the picture *Around the Bomb in Eighty Ways!*"

Ten Seconds to Hell, cut from 131 to 93 minutes by United Artists, was previewed at the Pavilion for three weeks starting in late April, 1959. Hammer's lucky streak, recently praised by the trade press, was about to end. *The Daily Mail* (April 24): "Once you've seen one such bomb dispose of its disposer, you have seen the lot"; *The London Times* (April 27): "It is a pity that Mr. Palance acts as though he is on the verge of a fit"; *The Kinematograph Weekly* (April 30): "Uninspired acting, flabby direction, and pretentious dialogue"; and *News of the World* (April 26): "This first rate idea goes very much adrift." The picture went into general release on June 15, and, by the middle of August, *The Kinematograph Weekly* (August 13) reported that *Ten Seconds to Hell* had "definitely gone down the drain." The American response was no better, and the picture became a rare late fifties failure for Hammer. Despite looking (on paper at least) like a hit, none of the movie's strong points seemed to meld properly, and what could have brought some "respectability" to Hammer brought nothing but disappointment.

Further Up the Creek

Released October 20, 1958 (U.K.); 91 minutes; B & W; HammerScope; 8166 feet; a Hammer-Byron Production; a Columbia Release; filmed at Bray Studios; Director: Val Guest; Producer: Henry Halstead; Original Story and Screenplay by Val Guest, John Warren, and Len Heath; Director of Photography: Gerry Gibbs; Music: Stanley Black; Art Director: George Provis; Camera Operator: Len Harris; Production Supervisor: Fred Swann; Production Manager: Pat Marsden; Makeup: Phil Leakey; Hairdresser: Marjorie Whittie; Wardrobe: Molly Arbuthnot; Sound: Jock May; Continuity:

Doreen Dearnaley; Technical Advisor: Commander Peter Peake; Editor: Bill Lenny; U.K. Certificate: U.

David Tomlinson (Fairweather), Frankie Howerd (Dibble), Shirley Eaton (Jane), Thora Hird (Mrs. Galloway), Lionel Jeffries (Barker), Lionel Murton (Perkins), Sam Kydd (Bates), John Warren (Cooky), David Lodge (Scouse), Harry Landis (Webster), Ian Whittaker (Lofty), Howard Williams (Bunts), Peter Collingwood (Chippy), Edwin Richfield (Bennett), Amy D'Alby (Edie), Esma Cannon (Maudie), Tom Gill (Phillippe), Jack LeWhite, Max Day (Kertoni Brothers), Mary Wilson (First Model), Katherine Byrne (Second Model), Eric Pohlmann (President), Stanley Unwin (Porter), Michael Goodliffe (Blackeney), Wolfe Morris (Algeroccan Major), John Singer (Dispatch Rider), Larry Nobel (Postman), Ballard Berkeley (Whacker), Judith Furse (Chief Wren), Michael Ripper (Ticket Collector), Joe Gibbon (Taxi Driver), Victor Brooke (Policeman), Cavan Malone (Signalman), Desmond Llewellyn (Yeoman), Basil Dignam (Flagship Commander), John Stuart (Admiral), Jess Conrad (Signalman), Patrick Holt (First Lt.), George Herbert (Officer), Charles Lloyd Pack (Ed Diablo), Walter Hudd (Consul), John Hall (Sea Scout).

The frigate *Aristotle* is sold to the Algeroccan government and its motley crew are horrified, as their illegal activities must end. As they ready the ship, the crew look to Bosun Dibble (Frankie Howerd) for "guidance." He decides to advertise the trip as a one-way luxury voyage! Lieutenant Commander Fairweather (David Tomlinson) is, as usual, unaware of Dibble's plans, and the Bosun manages to smuggle the equally unsuspecting vacationers on board. Once under sail, he explains them away as "diplomats." A quick chat with Jane (Shirley Eaton) puts Fairweather wise, and he throws Dibble in the brig. But, he releases him when the Bosun convinces Fairweather that *he* invited the passengers aboard while drunk.

When they reach Algerroca, a revolution is under way, and they are not allowed to dock. Dibble raises an Algerrocan flag causing the rebels to flee, and Fairweather is proclaimed a hero by the president (Eric Pohlmann). As Fairweather is being decorated, the British consul (Walter Hudd) announces that the Algeroccan check has bounced. The sale is off, and the crew must leave their newly found fame for Britain to enjoy.

The success of *Up the Creek* called for a sequel, and Hammer, as usual, heard the call. Unfortunately, Peter Sellers, who carried the first film, was unavailable. "By the time we got to *Further Up the Creek*," Val Guest told the authors (May, 1992), "Peter Sellers had grown too big. He was in Hollywood then—I had to take Frankie Howerd—absolutely brilliant—for the sequel." Filming began on May 19, 1958, and Howerd was announced as Sellers' replacement three days later. The picture was labeled a "Byron film for Exclusive release," but it *is* a Hammer production and was referred to as such in the trade papers. The set for the *Aristotle*'s bridge was built over 40 feet high so that trees would not be accidentally photographed when the ship was "at sea."

Val Guest was interviewed on the set (*The Kinematograph Weekly*, July 3) and commented on the danger of making a sequel. "You feel all the time that you have to do better than you did the first time, and at the back of it all is the feeling that, whatever you do, some of the critics will say it's not as good." Guest felt that Bray was an excellent place to film comedy. "Comedy needs pacing," he said, "and professionals keep pace." The production ended on July 11. "It's an absolute riot," said James Carreras (*Daily Cinema*, August 20) upon seeing the final cut. "It's bigger and better than *Up the Creek*. It ought to be. It cost a lot of money."

Further Up the Creek premiered at the Metropole Victoria on October 20, following an October 10 trade show at the Columbia. Guest's fears were justified, as reviewers were less impressed with the sequel than with the original. *The London Times* (October 16): "One of those artless British films which have a Light Programme audience in mind"; *The Monthly Bulletin* (November): "A rather assorted mixture of established gags"; and *The Kinematograph Weekly* (October 16): "The film tickles the ribs without taxing the brain." The most devastating review came

150 *I Only Arsked* (1958)

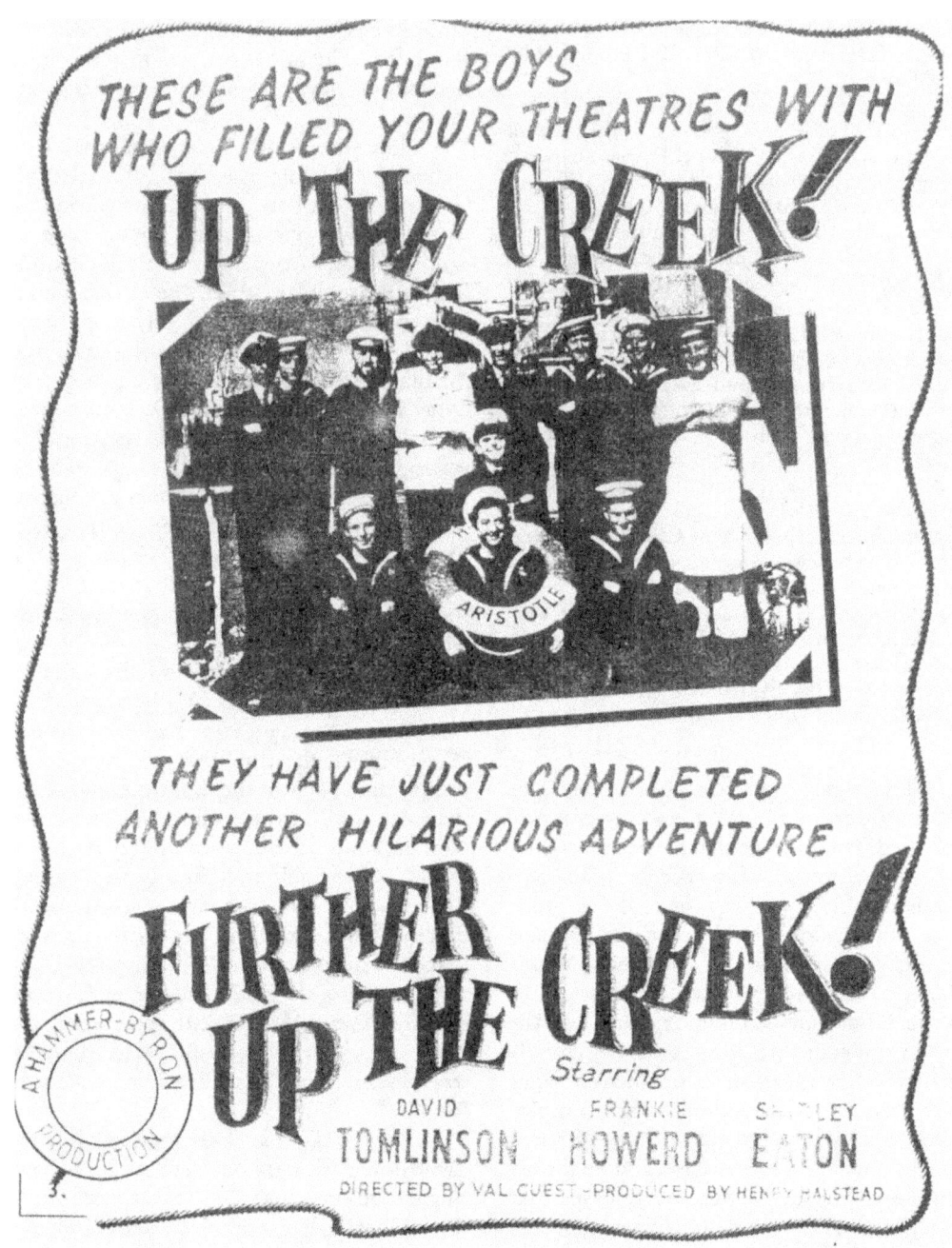

A trade ad for *Further Up the Creek*.

six years later when James Carreras (*The Sunday Times*) proclaimed *Further Up the Creek* "a disaster."

Hammer would continue its flirtation with service comedy with *I Only Arsked* and end it with *Watch It Sailor!*

I Only Arsked

Released November 8, 1959 (U.K.); 82 minutes; B & W; 7375 feet; a Hammer-Granada Production; a Columbia Release; filmed at Bray Studios; Director: Montgomery Tully; Executive

I Only Arsked (1958)

A motley crew in Hammer's service comedy, *I Only Arsked*.

Producer: Michael Carreras; Producer: Anthony Hinds; Associate Producer: Anthony Nelson-Keys; Screenplay: Sid Colin, Jack Davies, based on Granada TV's *The Army Game*; Director of Photography: Lionel Banes; Production Manager: Don Weeks; Camera Operator: Len Harris; Makeup: Phil Leakey; Supervising Editor: James Needs; Editor: Alfred Cox; Music: Benjamin Franklin; Song "Alone Together" by Walter Ridley and Sid Colin; Assistant Director: John Peverall; Special Effects: Sid Pearson; 2nd Assistant Director: Tom Walis; Sound Mixer: Jock May; Sound Camera: Peter Day; Continuity: Doreen Dearnaley; Hair Styles: Henry Montsash; Art Director: John Stoll; U.K. Certificate: U.

Bernard Bresslaw (Popeye), Michael Medwin (Cpl. Springer), Alfie Bass (Boots), Geoffrey Sumner (Maj. Upshot-Bagley), Charles Hawtrey (Professor), Norman Rossington (Cupcake), David Lodge (Potty Chambers), Arthur Howard (Sir Redvers), Marne Maitland (King Fazim), Michael Bentine (Fred), Francis Matthews (Mahmoud), Michael Ripper (Azim), Wolfe Morris (Salesman), Ewen McDuff (Ferrers), Marie Devereux, Lizabeth Page, Claire Gordon, Barbara Pinney, Pamela Chamberlain, Jean Rainer, Clarissa Roberts, Gales Sheridan, Josephine Jay, Andrea Loren, Rebecca Wilson, Anna Griffiths, Pauline Chamberlain, Jennifer Mitchell, Julie Shearing, Maureen Moore, Anne Muller, Pamela Searle (Harem Girls).

To save Britain's Middle East oil supply, Sir Redfers (Arthur Howard) requests that a "crack regiment" be sent to Darawa—where trouble is brewing. King Fazim (Marne Maitland) is about to lose his power to his shifty brother, Prince Mahmoud (Francis Matthews), and needs to strike oil—quickly. The British arrive—Popeye (Bernard Bresslaw), Major Upshot-Bagley (Geoffrey Sumner), Corporal Springer (Michael Medwin), the Professor (Charles Hawtrey), and Cupcake (Norman Rossington)—a real gang of losers. The Prince is overjoyed and plans their "removal," as the boys—already homesick—send an unauthorized message to London, indicating that they are not needed. While waiting to be recalled, they find the tunnel leading to Fazim's harem, and a reason to stay in Darawa.

The boys stage an oil strike so they can remain "on duty," but the Prince uses the diversion to seize the throne. Popeye leads Sir Redfers, the King, and the girls through the tunnel, and traps the Prince by starting an avalanche. The grateful King offers his hospitality, but the "heroes" are recalled to London.

The Army Game was a successful Granada TV series, and was fair game for the Hammer treatment. After rounding up most of the cast, Hammer began production on July 21, 1958, on *I Only Arsked*—one of Popeye's catchlines from the show. "So many people think that a box office success is merely a matter of getting a popular television team like this onto the screen," said Anthony Hinds (*The Kinematograph Weekly*, August 21). "If it were that simple, every production company in the world would be doing it." The problem, according to Hinds, was to convince people to pay for something they can see for free at home. As a result, Sid Colin's script placed *The Army Game* boys in a completely new situation, far removed from the series. Director Montgomery Tully commented that, on TV, the actors could ad-lib, but "here we have had to stick more closely to the script." A main selling point for Hammer was that the series team would not be returning intact the following season—Bernard Bresslaw was going AWOL. Highly popular on television, Bresslaw was poised to become a major film star, but never quite made it.

I Only Arsked finished production on August 22, 1958, was trade shown on November 1, and was hustled into a November 7 premiere at the Plaza. *The Kinematograph Weekly* (November 13) reported that the movie was "not breaking any records at the Plaza, but at least it's holding its own." The film gained momentum over Christmas and, outside London, outpaced *The Camp on Blood Island*, Hammer's main money winner of 1958. Following this surge in popularity, *I Only Arsked* went into general release on the ABC circuit on February 9, 1959. James Carreras told *The Daily Cinema* (January 12), "It's difficult to know what to make these days. You produce a horror film, and they eat it. Then you turn out a comedy, and they can't run into the cinema fast enough."

By late February, *I Only Arsked* was doing the box office everyone felt possible, even in London where previously cool audiences were warming up.

Reviewers, however, were cautious in their praise: *The Sunday Pictorial* (November 9, 1958): "Funny but not witty"; *The Evening News* (November 11): "Cashes in on the popularity of farces that make British soldiers look foolish"; *The New Statesman* (November 23): "Infantile plot"; and *The London Times* (November 11): "Cheerful slapstick."

At this point, Hammer could do no wrong, drawing huge crowds for films in several genres. The company would never produce as diversified a group of successful films again.

The Hound of the Baskervilles

Released May 4, 1959 (U.K.), July, 1959 (U.S.); 84 minutes; Technicolor; 7772 feet; a Hammer Film Production; a United Artists Release; filmed at Bray Studios; Director: Terence Fisher; Producer: Anthony Hinds; Executive Producer: Michael Carreras; Associate Producer: Anthony Nelson-Keys; Screenplay: Peter Bryan, based on the novel by Sir A. Conan Doyle; Music: James Bernard; Music Supervisor: John Hollingsworth; Director of Photography: Jack Asher; Editor: Alfred Cox; Supervising Editor: James Needs; Production Manager: Don Weeks; Sound Recordist: Jock May; Camera: Len Harris; Continuity: Shirley Barnes; Costumes: Molly Arbuthnot; Hairdresser: Henry Montsash; Makeup: Roy Ashton; Art Director: Don Mingaye; Production Design: Bernard Robinson; Assistant Directors: John Peverall, Tom Walls; Special Effects: Syd Pearson; U.K. Certificate: A.

Peter Cushing (Sherlock Holmes), Andre Morell (Dr. Watson), Christopher Lee (Sir Henry Baskerville), Marla Landi (Cecile), David Oxley (Sir Hugo Baskerville), Francis De Wolff (Dr. Mortimer), Ewen Solon (Stapleton), John Le Mesurier (Barrymore), Miles Malleson (Bishop Frankland), Sam Kydd (Perkins), Helen Goss (Mrs. Barrymore), Judi Moyens (Servant Girl), Dave Birks (Servant), Michael Mulcaster (Selden), Michael Hawkins (Lord Caphill), Ian Hewitson (Lord Kingsblood), Elizabeth Dott (Mrs. Goodlippe).

The Hound of the Baskervilles (1958)   153

Peter Cushing hams it up for the press while Anthony Hinds, Christopher Lee and Andre Morell look on during a pre-production visit to the Sherlock Holmes Pub in London (photo courtesy of Tim Murphy).

Sherlock Holmes (Peter Cushing) and Dr. Watson (Andre Morell) listen skeptically as Dr. Mortimer (Francis De Wolff) relates the legend of the Hound of the Baskervilles. A curse on the family was instigated by an evil ancestor, Sir Hugo (David Oxley), when he murdered a farm girl and was in turn killed by a spectral Hound. The recent mysterious death of Sir Charles has left Sir Henry Baskerville (Christopher Lee) heir to the fortune, and Mortimer fears for the baronet's safety. Holmes interviews Sir Henry at his hotel, where he is angered by a missing boot and terrified by a tarantula. Due to Holmes' heavy schedule, Watson accompanies Sir Henry to the Hall and meets the Barrymores' (John Le Mesurier, Helen Goss) long-time family servants, the odd Bishop Frankland (Miles Malleson), who collects spiders, and the surly Stapleton (Ewen Solon) and his beautiful daughter, Cecile (Marla Landi).

Watson is surprised to find Holmes on the moor where he has been since just after Watson arrived. Selden (Michael Mulcaster), an escaped convict (and Mrs. Barrymore's brother), is killed by the Hound while he is wearing a suit of Sir Henry's that she gave him. A chance remark by Watson causes Holmes to search for the Hound in a disused mine. He finds evidence of the beast, but is nearly killed by a cave-in. Sir Henry has fallen in love with Cecile, and as he walks with her across the moor, Holmes sets his trap. A portrait of Sir Hugo has revealed that Stapleton is a descendant and possible heir, and he and Cecile plan to kill Sir Henry with their savage dog. Holmes and Watson intervene; Stapleton is killed by the wounded Hound, and Cecile dies in the swamp. Back on Baker Street, Holmes reveals that the missing boot "put him on the scent."

Hammer's intention to film Sir Arthur Conan Doyle's famous story, announced in early May, 1958, generated more excitement in the British trades than any of the company's previous pictures. Naturally, there was speculation over who would play Holmes, but Hammer would not admit to any casting decisions, other than Michael Carreras' hoping that Peter Cushing would be available. He and Christopher Lee were signed on August 1 (with Lee surprisingly cast as the hero), and Terence Fisher on August 7.

The company was just beginning its most productive period. A deal with Universal-International to remake its horror library was just completed, and a dozen projects were in various stages of development, including a reworking of *The Cabinet of Dr. Caligari* (1919), which was never filmed. On September 3, Whitbread, an English brewery, hosted a party at the Sherlock Holmes Pub, located on the site of the Northumberland Hotel at which Sir Henry stayed in Conan Doyle's novel. At the reception, the recently signed "Dr. Watson," Andre Morell, was introduced to the press. "There are great hopes for this picture," Terence Fisher told *The Kinematograph Weekly* (September 11, 1958). "Sherlock Holmes is a favorite all over the world. In fact, he's so popular that half the people you speak to are not sure whether he really lived or not!" Anthony Hinds (*The Daily Cinema*, September 5) promised that Cushing would play Holmes as written—"realistically, not romantically."

The Hound of the Baskervilles began production on September 8, 1958, but Marla

Dr. Watson (Andre Morell) and Stapleton (Ewen Solon) in *The Hound of the Baskervilles*.

Landi was added to the cast three weeks later. She was discovered by Anthony Hinds, who had seen her in a special screening of *Across the Bridge*, in which Landi had a featured role. Hammer's search for the "title character" was recalled for the authors (August, 1993) by Margaret Robinson. "They had two dogs originally. One had been typecast because he once bit a barmaid! This was Colonel, who actually played the part. The other dog was owned by Barbara Wodehouse, and cost five times as much to hire. Also, Barbara wanted to double for Christopher Lee!" Robinson had been asked to design a mask for the dog, and when she measured the monster, "There was a girl sitting there all the time. I couldn't understand why she was there. She finally said, 'I'm the nurse!' I made the mask out of a rabbit fur,

The greatest screen adaptation of Sir Arthur Conan Doyle's classic.

and the dog wouldn't allow anyone else to put the mask on him. He was a lovely dog—to me, at least!"

On October 17, the main unit went on location to Frencham Ponds which stood in for the originally planned Dartmoor due to treacherous weather. "We decided it would be safer to find a location near Bray," said Anthony Hinds (*The Daily Cinema*, October 8). During the location shoot, Peter Cushing was given a first edition of the novel by the manager of a local pub. "I've based all my costumes on the original *Strand Magazine* pictures," Cushing said in *The Evening Bulletin*. "Everything is accurate right down to the old 'mouse-colored' dressing gown, which I charred with cigarettes to get the burns Holmes made during his experiments." Cushing tried to avoid cliches associated with the character. "I am avoiding the more obvious props," he said. He saw the character as "when on a case, like a dog following a scent. Holmes is not the pleasantest of characters either. He didn't suffer fools, and he must have been insufferable to live with."

Christopher Lee was eager to avoid being typecast and asked for the part of Sir Henry. "Although I was not entirely at all like the character created by the author, I felt I could create a similar personality," he said in *The Christopher Lee Club Journal* "I felt that this was the time of possible danger for me; therefore, I deliberately chose to play Sir Henry, who was not the most exciting individual." Although Lee has related a story about his terrifying encounter with the tarantula, Len Harris recalled it differently (August, 1993). "We got the spider from the London Zoo. She was twenty-five years old, and her name was Mary. Although she seemed to be harmless, we really couldn't let her walk on Christopher Lee, and you can plainly see that he and Mary are never in the same shot." Harris felt *The Hound* contained some of Jack Asher's best photography. "He used colored gels to get his special color effects, but it took *forever* to set up and light a shot. He was a painter with light."

During the final days of production, Fisher shot what was the most controversial scene, involving the Hound itself. Margaret Robinson recalled:

> They duplicated the part of the set in miniature where the dog was to leap onto Sir Henry. A small boy named Robert was dressed to duplicate Christopher Lee. The dog couldn't bear the sound of crumpled paper, and the idea was he would go straight for a propman as he crumpled it. What we didn't know is that Colonel hated small boys, too! The prop man

caught the dog in mid-air before he got to Robert.

Since the scene did not photograph properly, the idea was discarded altogether. One unexpected result of the scene was her meeting Bernard Robinson, whom she married in 1960.

The Hound of the Baskervilles was completed on October 31, and on March 31, 1959, Anthony Hinds and James and Michael Carreras flew the print to United Artists in New York and met with the American trade press. Hinds commented to *The Daily Cinema* (March 6) that everyone at Hammer was "tremendously excited. It has all the sensational box office qualities of its predecessors and is an exploiter's dream subject." The Sherlock Holmes Society of London called it "the greatest Sherlock Holmes film ever made." The trade show was held at the Hammer Theatre on March 20, and *The Hound of the Baskervilles* premiered at the Pavilion on March 28 and demolished the theatre's attendance record for a first week run. The general release was on May 4, with most reviews positive. *The Daily Express* (March 26): "A merry little romp"; *The Daily Mirror* (March 28): "Peter Cushing is a splendid Holmes"; *The Daily Mirror* (March 28): "There will be more Holmes films like this"; *The Daily Cinema* (March 23): "Beautifully made, gripping, exciting product"; *The Standard* (March 26): "Played effectively for a maximum of blood and thunder"; *The New York Herald Tribune* (July 4): "Sound version, nicely photographed and should be a pleasant introduction to the adventure"; and *Variety* (April): "It is difficult to fault the performance of Peter Cushing."

Despite the positive reviews and box office results, Hammer chose not to develop a Holmes series. The film does have its detractors, mostly harping on Peter Bryan's screenplay for not following the novel's familiar path. Peter Cushing played Holmes on the BBC a decade later, and in the 1989 television film *Masks of Death*. As Anthony Howlett of the Sherlock Holmes Society said in *The Daily Cinema* (October 17, 1958), "Peter Cushing is perfect casting."

The man responsible for the Baskerville Curse, Sir Hugo (David Oxley) in *The Hound of the Baskervilles*.

Was this the best Holmes movie? Possibly. Is Peter Cushing the best Holmes? Probably. One point rarely argued is Andre Morell's excellence as Watson. Why Hammer never followed *The Hound of the Baskervilles* with another Holmes picture remains a mystery. Although *The Hound* supposedly did not do as well as expected at the box office, its stature has grown considerably since.

The Man Who Could Cheat Death

Released November 30, 1959 (U.K.), June, 1959 (U.S.); 83 minutes; Technicolor; 7488 feet; a Hammer Film Production; released through Paramount (U.K. and U.S.); filmed at Bray Studios; Director: Terence Fisher; Executive Producer: Michael Carreras; Associate Producer: Anthony Nelson-Keys; Screenplay: Jimmy Sangster, from Barré Lyndon's play; Music: Richard Bennet; Musical Supervisor: John Hollingsworth; Director of Photography: Jack Asher; Production Design: Bernard Robinson; Supervising Editor: James Needs; Camera Operator: Len Harris; Sound Recordist: Jock May; Continuity: Shirley

The Man Who Could Cheat Death (1958)   157

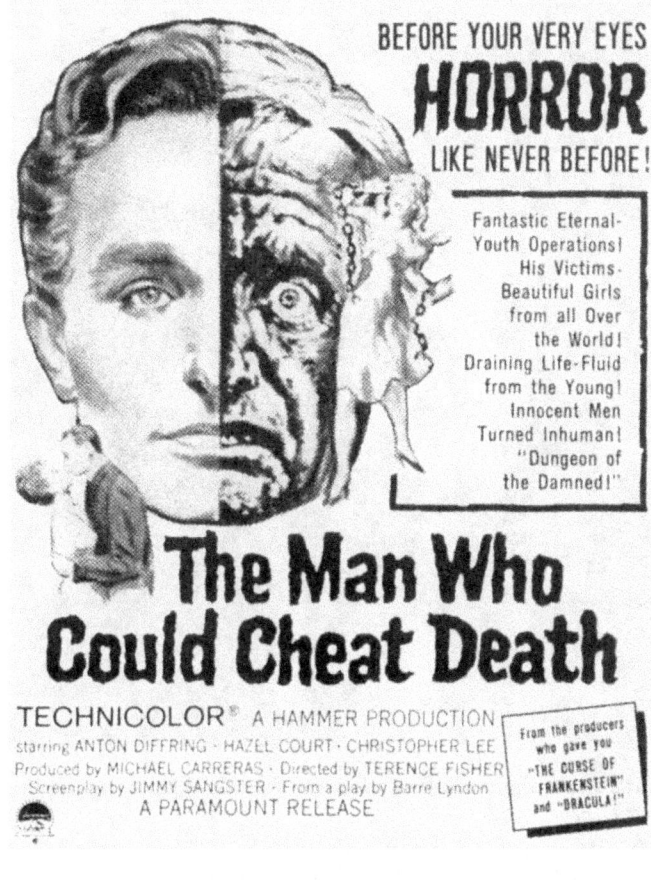

A film more subtle than its advertising.

Barnes; Editor: John Dunsford; Wardrobe: Molly Arbuthnot; Production Manager: Don Weeks; Assistant Director: John Peverall; Makeup: Roy Ashton; Hairstyles: Henry Montsash; U.K. Certificate: X.

Anton Diffring (Bonner), Hazel Court (Janine), Christopher Lee (Gerard), Arnold Marle (Dr. Weiss), Delphi Lawrence (Margo), Francis De Wolff (Legris), Gerda Larsen (Street Girl), Middleton Woods (Little Man), Michael Ripper (Morgue Attendant), Denis Shaw (Tavern Customer), Ian Hewitson (Roget), Frederick Rawlings (Footman), Marie Burke (Woman), Charles Lloyd Pack (Man at Exhibit), John Harrison (Servant), Lockwood West (First Doctor), Ronald Adam (Second Doctor), Barry Shawzin (Third Doctor).

Victorian Paris. Amateur sculptor Dr. Bonner (Anton Diffring) has a terrible secret as he unveils the bust of his model Margo (Delphi Lawrence), who is also his lover. Although he looks 35, he is 104 years old, kept young through transplants of the parathyroid. Dr. Weiss (Arnold Marle), his famous partner, has not arrived to do the surgery, and Bonner is kept alive by a green fluid. Complicating matters are the arrival of his ex-lover Janine (Hazel Court) with her escort Dr. Gerard (Christopher Lee) and Margo's petulance over the end of their love affair. After the party when she refuses to leave, Bonner, glowing greenly, sears her flesh with his hand. Weiss finally arrives. A stroke victim, he looks more than twice Bonner's age, yet is 15 years his junior. Unable to perform the operation, he suggests that Bonner find a replacement and becomes concerned that Bonner has abandoned the experiment's altruistic beginnings.

Bonner and Janine renew their affair, and, through Weiss, enlist Gerard's help. When Weiss discovers that Bonner has killed to get the gland, he destroys the fluid, and in a rage, Bonner kills him. Gerard refuses to cooperate without the "missing" Weiss, so Bonner abducts Janine to force him to perform the surgery. When Bonner arrives at the old warehouse where he has hidden Janine, he realizes that Gerard has duped him. In an instant, Bonner assumes his true age with every disease he avoided and dies, set ablaze by the imprisoned Margo.

After Warner Bros. and Columbia struck gold with Hammer Horror, Paramount was next, unearthing their 1944 *The Man in Half Moon Street* for the Hammer treatment. Based on Barré Lyndon's play, the original (starring Nils Asther) was a romantic mystery rather than a horror movie. Originally planned as Alan Ladd's first starring role, the film betrayed its stage origins, as did the Hammer remake. Although its few horror

Arnold Marle looks on as Hazel Court's rivals, Anton Diffring (second from left) and Christopher Lee, meet in *The Man Who Could Cheat Death*.

elements were well-staged, *The Man Who Could Cheat Death* is more talk than action. The fact that it is not as horrific as *Dracula* must be taken in context, since its approach is more cerebral than relying on dripping fangs.

Peter Cushing was "unavailable" for the lead, opening the door for Anton Diffring, who gave the role his usual chilly menace. He was typed as a "horror star" despite his infrequent appearances in genre films. Hazel Court played a role similar to her too trusting Elizabeth in *The Curse of Frankenstein*. She recalled for the authors (September, 1990):

> At Hammer, you had to be good on the first take, which is the way they used quality actors even in small parts. We were all a happy family at Bray, not under the pressures of a big studio. We rehearsed a lot, like for a play, which is why we could do it on one take. There was a "European version" in which I'm nude to the waist when being sculpted. Today, it doesn't mean a thing, but in those days it was something! I didn't want to do it, but I thought "I'm supposed to be modeling, so I guess it's OK." It was all kept terribly secret! Hammer really opened things up. I loved doing the film. Anton was, unlike his image, a nice, charming man. Terence Fisher was a very professional, very competent director, comfortable and happy with horror. He had a job, and he did it, never promoting himself. We gave the audience more than they expected, and they sensed our dedication. That's why the films are still popular, and I'm happy to have been a part of it. *The Man Who Could Cheat Death* was a beautiful movie.

Filming began on November 17, 1958, and concluded on December 30. To celebrate Hammer's tenth anniversary of continuous production, a party was thrown on December 12, with a luncheon held at the Hinds Head Pub in Bray Village and a print of *Dr. Morelle* run at the studio. Following a June 4, 1959, trade show, *The Man Who Could Cheat Death* was released on November 30 on the ABC circuit, teamed with *The*

Evil That Is Eve. The response from *Variety* (June 24, 1959) was prophetic. "Well made but rather mild horror item, it is well acted and intelligently conceived. But invention and embellishment in this field appear to have been exhausted. As ever greater horror is required, there is less and less that is horrible enough." This insightful review accurately predicted the genre's fate by the early seventies. Other reviewers were less insightful. The *Monthly Bulletin* (July, 1959): "Offers little in the way of entertainment beyond the sets, costumes, and props"; *The London Times* (October 4): "It is all rather too wooden and stylized"; *The Observer* (October 4): "What dreary, lifeless work the concoction of these horror pictures must be"; *The Star* (October 1): "After ... the intelligent and provocative *Yesterday's Enemy*, and the well made *The Mummy*, the horror boys at Hammer films get back to ham and ketchup"; *The Evening Standard* (October 1): "Substandard"; and *The Chronicle* (October 10): "A flop." *The Kinematograph Weekly* (June 11) stood practically alone in its praise: "A sure bet ... fascinating and thrilling."

While, admittedly, the film is not one of Hammer's *very* best, the above seems harsh. Many of the negative reviews were aimed at horror movies in general. *The Man Who Could Cheat Death* seems to have been caught in the middle, and it was attacked for being both too tame and too gruesome. The film boasts some of Hammer's most gorgeous sets and costumes, and the small cast is uniformly fine except for Christopher Lee's uninspired playing of a blandly written part. Anton Diffring made the most of his starring role, but the film just misses. Interestingly, the American advertising played up Hammer's name more than it did the cast members.

1959

Yesterday's Enemy

Released September 17, 1959; 95 minutes; B & W; 8550 feet; a Hammer Film Production; released through Columbia (U.K. and U.S.); filmed at Bray Studios/Shepperton Studios; Director: Val Guest; Executive Producer: Michael Carreras; Screenplay: Peter Newman; Director of Photography: Arthur Grant; Editors: James Needs, Alfred Cox; Camera Operator: Len Harris; Focus: Harry Oakes; Clapper/Loader: Alan McDonald; Grips: Albert Cowlard; Sound Recordist: Buster Ambler; Sound Cameraman: Jimmy Dooley; Boom: Peter Dukelaw; Sound Maintenance: Eric Vincent; Production Designer: Bernard Robinson; Assistant Director: John Peverall; Continuity: Cheryl Booth; Technical Advisor: Peter Newman; Assistant Art Director: Don Mingaye; Make-up: Roy Ashton: Wardrobe: Molly Arbuthnot; Hairdresser: Henry Montsash; Stills; Tom Edwards; Publicist: Colin Reid; Production Buyer: Eric Hillier; Special Effects: Bill Warrington, Charles Willoughby; Casting Director: Dorothy Holloway; Construction Manager: Jack Bolam; Electrical Engineer: S.F. Hillyer; Master Painter: S. Taylor; Master Plasterer: S. Rodwel; Master Carpenter: E.D. Wheatley; Property Master: Frank Burden; Floor Props: T. Frewer; Production Supervisor: T.S. Lyndon Haynes; Production Secretary: Doreen Jones; U.K. Certificate: A.

Stanley Baker (Capt. Langford), Guy Rolfe (Padre), Leo McKern (Max), Gordon Jackson (Sgt. McKenzie), David Oxley (Doctor), Richard Pasco (Lt. Hastings), Russell Waters (Brigadier), Philip Ahn (Yamazaki), Bryan Forbes (Dawson), Wolfe Morris (Informer), Edwina Carroll (Suni), David Lodge (Perkins), Percy Herbert (Wilson), Barry Lowe (Turner), Alan Keith (Bendish), Howard Williams (Davies), Timothy Bateson (Simpson), Arthur Lovegrove (Patrick), Donald Churchill (Elliott), Nicholas Brady (Orderly), Barry Steele (Brown).

Burma, World War II. A group of battered British soldiers slog through a swamp, separated from their company, and Captain Langford's (Stanley Baker) temporary command is questioned by the Padre (Guy Rolfe) and Max (Leo McKern), a war correspondent. After a fierce battle, they take control of a village and begin interrogating the Burmese. A suspected informer (Wolfe Morris) refuses to divulge information about a mysterious map, so Langford orders two innocent villagers to be shot as examples. Most of the British are horrified by Langford's brutality, and the informer's revelation of a coming Japanese attack does little to relieve their disgust. Sgt. McKenzie (Gordon Jackson) then shoots the informer.

Yesterday's Enemy (1959)

Gordon Jackson and Stanley Baker in Val Guest's controversial World War II drama, *Yesterday's Enemy*.

Langford decides to warn the company of the attack and prepares to leave the village immediately, but their escape is halted by a Japanese attack. Now prisoners themselves, the British are subjected to the same brutality they previously inflicted on the Japanese. Col. Yamazaki questions Langford, who refuses to talk, so Lt. Hastings is placed in front of a firing squad to pressure Langford. He makes a clumsy attempt to use the radio and is shot. Wearily, Yamazaki orders the remaining British to be executed.

James Carreras said in the October, 1959, *Films and Filming*, "We hate message films. We make entertainment." Since *Yesterday's Enemy* was in release at the time, and Carreras had the final word on Hammer's subjects, this was an odd statement. With the critical mauling of *The Camp on Blood Island* still fresh, one wonders why the company chose to return to World War II atrocities—and to point the finger of guilt at the British. Like many other Hammer films, *Yesterday's Enemy* was adapted from a BBC production. Peter Newman's play had caused a controversy and was a natural choice for a film. "I had many letters," he told *The Kinematograph Weekly* (January 22, 1959). "Some were congratulating me; others accused me of being anti–British. Michael Carreras saw the play and contacted Val Guest."

Guest told the authors (May, 1992),

Michael got a copy and let me have a look. I thought there was a hell of a picture in it. The film is one of my four favorites out of over ninety I've done—it was a labor of love. Stanley Baker was one of my favorites and was perfect. I did lay down one law—there would be no background music. The "score" was orchestrated with jungle noises and was, I believe, the first of its kind in England. The film was, for *many* reasons, controversial.

Yesterday's Enemy began production at Shepperton on January 12, 1959, ended there

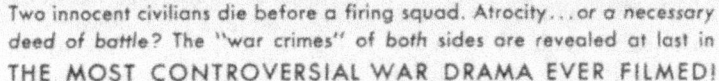

A brutal look at war crimes—committed by both sides.

on February 19, and then moved to Bray for completion. It was delivered to Columbia on May 5 as the first part of their "long-term agreement." *The Daily Cinema* (January 12) felt the film would "arouse a great storm of controversy."

The production also aroused a great storm of problems beyond the unsettling subject matter. The construction of the village set was done on a wheeled section to achieve the illusion of changing spatial areas. A tank filled with slime was built at Bray to stand in as the swamp. The biggest problem, however, was the language barrier. The

Japanese soldiers were played by employees of London's oriental restaurants and were mostly non–English speaking, so actor Philip Ahn had to interpret Val Guest's directions. Len Harris recalled (December, 1993) that when one of the Japanese "soldiers" slipped and fell into the "swamp," those in line followed, thinking they were directed to do so. Despite these and other problems (like almost blowing up a Shepperton sound stage), filming was completed on schedule.

The film had already made a great impression. *The Daily Cinema* (May 1) called it "the greatest Hammer has made." James Carreras said, "It is to World War II what *Journey's End* was to World War I." (*Journey's End* was a success on the London stage and in Hollywood [1930], directed by James Whale and starring Colin Clive who later collaborated on *Frankenstein* [1931].) Following a June 5, 1959, trade show, the film was shown to high ranking British army personnel. "I have never been so impressed or gripped by a film," Maj. Gen. H.L. Davies said in a Hammer press release. "The character portrayal is magnificent, and there is a realism and authenticity about the background which is quite frightening." Even the Japanese were moved. Lt. Col. Eich Tsuchiva, who led the assault on Burma, said, "The conflict between military discipline and humanitarianism and the cruelty of war are well expressed."

Val Guest recalled in an interview with Tom Weaver that at the September 17, 1959, premiere at the Empire, "I sat next to Lord Mountbatten, and he kept nudging me. 'I know where you shot that!' he said. He was absolutely convinced that we shot it in Burma!" The world premiere had been held a week earlier in Tokyo. Before going into general release on the ABC circuit on October 19, the film was called "every exhibitor's friend" in *The Kinematograph Weekly* (September 24). Critics were very positive, making *Yesterday's Enemy* Hammer's greatest critical success. *The London Times* (September 21, 1959): "A well-written film that stimulates argument ... something of a surprise for those who associate Hammer Films with horror"; *The Saturday Review* (October 3): "serious, if not downright philosophical"; *The New York Times* (March 4, 1960): "haunting in the right way."

Despite the excellent reviews and box office success, *Yesterday's Enemy* was one of Hammer's last "serious" productions. Its success led to an extension of the agreement with Columbia for the next five years, but inexplicably, the film has been forgotten. Leonard Maltin's *Movie and Video Guide* (1993) gives the movie 1½ stars and calls it a "mild WW2 actioner," hardly an apt description of this powerful, thought-provoking picture.

The Mummy

Released September 25, 1959 (U.K.), December, 1959 (U.S.); 88 minutes; Technicolor; 7903 feet; a Hammer Film Production; released through Rank (U.K.), Universal International (U.S.); filmed at Bray Studios; Director: Terence Fisher; Producer: Anthony Hinds; Associate Producer: Anthony Nelson-Keys; Executive Producer: Michael Carreras; Screenplay: Jimmy Sangster, Director of Photography: Jack Asher; Music Composer: Frank Reizenstein; Music Director: John Hollingsworth; Supervising Editor: James Needs; Editor: Alfred Cox; Production Design: Bernard Robinson; Makeup: Roy Ashton; Masks: Margaret Carter Robinson; Camera: Len Harris; Production Manager: Don Weeks; Sound Recordist: Jock May; Hairstyles: Henry Montsash; Costumes: Molly Arbuthnot; Egyptology Advisor: Andrew Low; Assistant Director: John Peverall; Second Assistant: Tom Walls; Third Assistant: Hugh Harlow; Continuity: Marjorie Lavelly; Focus: Harry Oakes; Clapper: Alan McDonald; Boom: Jim Perry; Sound Camera Operator: Al Thorne; Sound Maintenance: Charles Bouvet; Assistant Art Director: Don Mingaye; Stills: Tom Edwards; Publicist: Colin Reid; Casting Director: Dorothy Holloway; Assistant Director: Chris Barnes; U.K. Certificate: X.

Peter Cushing (John Banning), Christopher Lee (Kharis), Yvonne Furneaux (Isobel/Ananka), Eddie Byrne (Inspector Mulrooney), Felix Aylmer (Stephen Banning), Raymond Huntley (Uncle Joe), George Pastell (Mehemet), Michael Ripper (Poacher), John Stuart (Coroner), Harold Goodwin (Pat), Dennis Shaw (Mike), Willoughby Gray (Dr. Reilly), Stanley Meadows (Attendant), Frank Singuineau (Head Porter),

A very nervous Christopher Lee and friend in *The Mummy*.

George Woodbridge (Constable), Frank Sieman (Bill), Gerald Lawson (Irish Customer), John Harrison (Priest), James Clarke (Priest), David Browning (Sergeant).

Egypt, 1895. As archeologist John Banning (Peter Cushing) recuperates from a leg injury, his father, Stephen (Felix Aylmer), and uncle Joe (Raymond Huntley), enter the tomb of Princess Ananka despite the warning of Mehemet (George Pastell). Alone in the tomb, Stephen, while reading from the Scroll of Life, suffers a breakdown.

England, 1898. John is summoned to the Engerfield Nursing Home, where his father has spoken for the first time since being confined. He is disturbed to find Stephen babbling about a "living mummy" bent on their destruction. Nearby, Mehemet resurrects the four-thousand-year-old mummy of Kharis (Christopher Lee) from a swamp into which his coffin has sunk after a carriage accident. Kharis, Ananka's High Priest—and lover, kills Stephen. After the inquest, John and his uncle pore over the Ananka legend, discovering that Kharis was sentenced to a living death after attempting to restore her to life via the Scroll—an act of blasphemy. The mummy is now an instrument of revenge against her tomb's defilers, controlled by Mehemet who worships Karnak, Ananka's ancient god.

Kharis kills Joe and, despite being shot repeatedly by John, escapes. When told of the attack, Inspector Mulrooney (Eddie Byrne) is skeptical, and unable to protect John when he is assaulted soon afterwards. But Banning is saved by his wife Isobel's (Yvonne Furneaux) uncanny resemblance to Ananka. After confronting Mehemet at the Egyptian's home, John is attacked again. When Mehemet orders Kharis to kill Isobel, the mummy turns against his master and carries Isobel to the swamp where he is shot to pieces by Mulrooney's men, the Scroll of Life clutched in his hand.

Bernard Robinson's original designs for *The Mummy* (photo courtesy of Margaret and Peter Robinson).

After the spectacular success of *Dracula*, Universal-International gave Hammer remake rights to its library of horror classics. The first three on the list were *The Mummy*, *The Phantom of the Opera* (remade in 1962), and *The Invisible Man* (never produced). Al Daff, Universal-International President, and James Carreras had made one of the biggest deals ever between American and British film companies. Carreras described the agreement to *Kinematograph Weekly* (August 21, 1958) as "one of the greatest things that has ever happened to us."

The Mummy is often unreasonably compared to the 1932 Boris Karloff version, with which it has little in common. The movie is more sensibly compared to Universal's 1940s series with Lon Chaney, Jr. "I must, at some point, have been shown these earlier Universal films," Jimmy Sangster told the authors (August, 1993). "How else could one explain the same character names and plot elements? But I honestly don't recall doing so—it *has* been thirty-five years, you know!" As the title character, Christopher Lee combines an awesome physical presence with a great sensitivity communicated through his eyes. Kharis is one of his best horror performances, second only to Dracula (and not by much). Peter Cushing could easily have been blown off the screen by Lee's terrific performance, but he more than holds his own. The two stars have seldom been better paired, and according to *The Daily Cinema* (February 27, 1959), Universal-International considered their casting "a must."

The Mummy began filming at Bray on February 25, 1959, concluding on April 16 with two weeks thrown in at Shepperton for the swamp scenes. During the production, Terence Fisher was headlined in *The Kinematograph Weekly* (March 26) with the oddly titled "I Don't Make Horror Films." Fisher noted: "Made with care, and at Bray, we take every care, these pictures are a genuine cinema form. I have always strenuously tried to avoid being blatant in my pictures. Instead, whenever possible, I have used the camera to show things—especially nasty things—hap-

Christopher Lee makes a startling entrance in *The Mummy*.

pening by implication." This is exactly the opposite reputation both Fisher (and Hammer) had unfairly developed. He was such an expert at the above that, as Harry Ringel pointed out in *Cinefantastique*, Fisher's films often seemed more horrible than they really were.

With typical Hammer efficiency, sets from *Yesterday's Enemy* and *The Man Who Could Cheat Death* were quickly revamped. "Not only is this valuable in terms of financial outlay," Anthony Nelson-Keys proclaimed in a press release, "but it means a terrific savings in time. We can go almost immediately from one production to another." Hammer's critics have often complained about "over used sets." It is true that the company *did* cannibalize sets from one film to another, but rather than cut corners by giving audiences less, Hammer stayed on budget by this type of revision.

After an August 20, 1959, trade show at the Hammer Theatre, *The Mummy* premiered on September 25 at the London Pavilion (where the huge front-of-house display dominating Piccadilly Circus can be seen in *Gorgo* [1960], as the dinosaur is driven through London). In its first four days, *The Mummy* racked up the biggest business *ever* for a Universal-International/Rank picture at the prestigious theatre. After leaving the Pavilion on October 23, the picture went into general release on the ABC circuit, smashing records set the previous year by *Dracula*. Hammer, Universal-International, and Rank got behind the film by scheduling personal appearances by the cast and Egyptologist/technical advisor Andrew Low throughout the U.K. "I believe the real reason for Hammer's success," said publicist Philip Gerard in *The Kinematograph Weekly* (September 3, 1959), "is because Jimmy Carreras and Tony Hinds are real showmen. These men have built for Hammer an enviable reputation in American film circles by delivering a box office product which represents the best in its class."

Despite the care (courtesy of Andrew Low) given to *The Mummy*, the film was not without lapses. Margaret Robinson told the authors in August, 1993, "I pointed out to Michael Carreras that Karnak was a *place*, not a *god*. He told me, 'Don't worry. No one will know the difference.'" She had more difficulty making the Anubis mask for the burial procession. "The actor hadn't been cast yet, so I made a large mask, assuming the actor would be a big one. After the mask was completed, he came into my room—the largest Turk I ever saw! The mask was quite rigid, stiffened by piano wire; and after he struggled into it, I saw a trickle of blood run down his neck."

Reviews for *The Mummy* reflected its box office power. *The London Times* (September 28, 1959): "Hammer Films have made the most distinguished of English horror films, partly because of an imaginative use of photographic and Eastman color devices, and partly by the employment of excellent actors"; *The Observer* (September 27): "Well tried ingredients plus an Egyptological know how"; *The Evening Standard* (September 9): "Excellently mounted, well acted, highly entertaining"; *The Kinematograph Weekly* (August 13): "Spectacular. Gripping story, first rate characterization, star value"; *The Daily Cinema* (August 7): "A sure-fire box office attraction"; *The New York Herald Tribune* (December 17): "The climax is properly frantic"; and *Variety* (July 15): "Well produced."

In America, *The Mummy* was released with Universal-International's offbeat vampire western, *Curse of the Undead*, making one of the decade's best horror double features. While not Hammer's greatest horror, it is close behind *Dracula*. The two were

Hammer brings the Mummy saga back for a new generation of fans.

re-issued in the U.K. in 1964 to over 1500 bookings and broke many house records.

The Ugly Duckling

Released August 10, 1959 (U.K.); 84 minutes; B & W; 7528 feet; a Hammer Film Production; a Columbia Release; filmed at Bray Studios; Director: Lance Comfort; Associate Producer: Tommy Lyndon-Haynes; Executive Producer: Michael Carreras; Screenplay: Sid Colin, Jack Davies, based on Colin's story; Director of Photography: Michael Reed; Supervising Editor: James Needs; Editor: John Dunsford; Music: Douglas Gamley; Art Director: Bernard Robinson; Production Manager: Don Weeks; Production Secretary: Patricia Green; 1st Assistant Director: John Peverall; 2nd Assistant Director: Tom Walls; 3rd Assistant Director: Hugh Harlow; Continuity: Marjory Lavelly; Camera Operator: Len Harris; Focus: Harry Oakes; Clapper/Loader: Alan MacDonald; Sound Mixer: Jock May; Boom Operator: Jim Perry; Sound Camera Operators: Al Thorne, Michael

Poster from *The Ugly Duckling* (courtesy of Fred Humphries and Colin Cowie).

Sale; Sound Maintenance: Charles Bouvet; Sound Assistant: Maurice Smith; Assistant Art Director: Don Mingaye; Stills Cameraman: Tom Edwards; Publicist: Colin Reid; Makeup: Roy Ashton; Hairdresser: Henry Montsash; Wardrobe Mistress: Molly Arbuthnot; Wardrobe Assistant: Rosemary Burrows; Casting Director: Dorothy Holloway; Assistant Editors: Peter Todd, Alan Corder; Chief Accountant: W.H.V. Able; Cashier: Peter Lancaster; Studio Manager: A.F. Kelly; Construction Manager: Mick Lyons; Chief of Electricians: Jack Curtiss; Master Painter: Lawrence Wrenn; Master Plasterer: Arthur Banks; Property Master: Tommy Money; Production Buyer: Eric Hillier; Floor Props: Peter Allchorne; Electrical Supervisor: George Robinson Cowlard; Associate Producer's Secretary: Margot Wardle; Transport Drivers: Coco Epps, Wilfrid Faux, Sid Humphrey; U.K. Certificate: U.

Bernard Bresslaw (Jeckyll/Hyde), Reginald Beckwith (Reginald), Jon Pertwee (Victor), Maudie Edwards (Henrietta), Jean Muir (Snout), Richard Wattis (Barclay), David Lodge (Peewee), Elwyn Brook-Jones (Dandy), Michael Ripper (Fish), Harold Goodwin (Benny), Norma Marla (Angel), Keith Smith (Figures), Michael Ward (Pasco), John Harvey (Sgt. Barnes), Jess Conrad (Bimbo), Mary Wilson (Lizzie), Jeremy Phillips (Tiger), Vicky Marshall (Kitten), Alan Coleshill (Willie), Jill Carson (Yum Yum), Jean Driant (Blum), Nicholas Tanner (Commissionaire), Shelagh Dey (Miss Angers), Sheila Hammond (Receptionist), Verne Morgan (Barman), Ian Wilson (Small Man), Cyril Chamberlain (Police Sergeant), Ian Ainsley (Fraser), Reginald Marsh, Roger Avon, Richard Statman (Reporters), Robert Desmond (Dizzy), Alexander Dore (Customer).

Dandy Kingsley (Elwyn Brook-Jones) leads a gang of jewel thieves—Fish (Michael Ripper), Peewee (David Lodge), and Benny (Harold Goodwin)—and also manages the Palais, a suburban dance hall. His main attraction is Henrietta Jeckyll's (Maudie Edwards) Old Time Dancing Team. The Rockets, a teen gang led by Bimbo (Jess Conrad) and his girl Angel (Norma Marla), are regulars. Henrietta's plain brother Henry (Bernard Bresslaw), one of her dancers, is a constant butt of insults from the Rockets. During the performance, Dandy is questioned by Inspector Barclay (Richard Wattis) about a jewel heist. The next day, Snout (Jean Muir), a sympathetic Rocket, promotes Henry, unsuccessfully, for membership. When Henrietta and Victor (Jon Pertwee), another brother, leave for the Palais,

Henry is left to manage the family chemist shop—and finds the secret formula of his famous relative.

Now, as the swinging Teddy Hyde (with sideburns, a mustache, and dressed like a gangster), he goes to the Palais and moves in on Angel. When Bimbo objects, Teddy knocks him out. Dandy is impressed and offers Teddy a place in his gang, but he awakens the next morning as Henry with no memory of the previous night. He transforms again and later takes part in the robbery. Victor has discovered his secret and, with Snout's help, convinces Henry to return the jewels and turn in the gang. Henry, now wearing a Rockets jacket, becomes manager of the Palais.

Although *The Ugly Duckling* has seemingly vanished, it lives on in its basic concept of a dashing Mr. Hyde in Hammer's own *The Two Faces of Dr. Jekyll* and Jerry Lewis' *The Nutty Professor* (1963). Michael Carreras described the film (*The Kinematograph Weekly*, November 20, 1958) as "A tailor made subject for Bernard Bresslaw. We believe it will be one of the year's funniest comedies." A March 12, 1959, follow-up revealed—incredibly—that the comedy "will be followed later in the year by a 'straight' version." Initially titled *Mad Pashernate Love*, the picture began production on May 4 and concluded on June 10. During the filming, James Carreras (*The Daily Cinema*, May 11) revealed Hammer's own "secret" formula for success. "We make exploitable pictures. What we have done, others can do. There's no magic involved. It's true we did evolve a horror formula, but we have made other kinds of films as well—and they have been equally successful." He indicated that Hammer had no intention of going into television. "We're taking the best *from* television," he said. Michael Carreras addressed the wisdom of making both a comedy and straight version of the same story in *The Kinematograph Weekly* (May 28): "The two treatments are so far apart as to be practically unrecognizable. *The Ugly Duckling* will do the straight version some good. It will reacquaint people with the names Jekyll and Hyde." Director Lance Comfort noted that Bresslaw metamorphosed by the "shedding of a comedy appearance for the Hyde character. There was no tendency to laugh when he emerged." The picture's musical segments had Michael Carreras eyeing a "new style musical" that went unproduced.

Following a July 28, 1959, trade show at the Columbia Theatre, *The Ugly Duckling* went into general release on August 10 to less than admiring reviews. *The Daily Cinema* (July 29): "Little more than a peg on which to hang a series of slapstick gags"; *The Monthly Bulletin* (September): "Only intermittently and moderately amusing"; *The Daily Herald* (August 6): "The world's top horror specialist has decided to take the mickey out of the subject that made them famous." The picture was "well patronized by juveniles," but apparently by no one else. The picture itself is virtually impossible to see and goes unmentioned in most film guides. The movie would be worth seeing, if only for its role in spawning Hammer's most interesting failure later that year.

The Stranglers of Bombay

Released January 18, 1960 (U.K.), May, 1960 (U.S.); 81 minutes (U.S.); B & W; Strangloscope; 7238 feet; a Hammer Film Production in association with Kenneth Hyman; a Columbia Release (U.S.); filmed at Bray Studios; Director: Terence Fisher; Producer: Anthony Hinds; Executive Producer: Michael Carreras; Associate Producer: Anthony Nelson-Keys; Screenplay: David Z. Goodman; Director of Photography: Arthur Grant; Camera: Len Harris; Editor: Alfred Cox; Supervising Editor: James Needs; Music: James Bernard; Musical Director: John Hollingsworth; Art Director: Bernard Robinson; Assistant Art Director: Don Mingaye; Sound: Jock May; Assistant Director: John Peverall; 2nd Assistant Director: Tom Walls; Technical Advisor: Michael Edwardes; Makeup: Roy Ashton; Production Manager: Don Weeks; Hairdresser: Henry Montsash; Personnel Advisor: Jimmy Vaughn; Continuity: Tilly Day; Stills Cameraman: Tom Edwards; Wardrobe Mistress: Molly Arbuthnot; Publicist: Dennison Thornton; U.K. Certificate: X.

Guy Rolfe (Captain Harry Lewis), Allan Cuthbertson (Captain Connaught-Smith), Andrew Cruickshank (Colonel Henderson), George

Hammer's attempt at historical horror.

Pastell (High Priest), Marne Maitland (Patel Shari), Jan Holden (Mary Lewis), Paul Stassino (Lt. Silver), Tutte Lemkow (Ram Das), David Spenser (Gopali), John Harvey (Burns), Roger Delgado (Bundar), Marie Devereux (Karim), Michael Nightingale (Sidney Flood), Margaret Gordon (Dorothy Flood), Steven Scott (Walters), Jack McNaughton (Corporal Roberts), Ewen Solon (Camel Vendor), Mongoose (Toki).

In the 1820s, the British East India Company turns to the British military for help in combatting the brigands responsible for the hijacking of caravans and the disappearance of over 1,000 travelers. Captain Lewis (Guy Rolfe) volunteers to head the investigation but the assignment instead goes to an overbearing, ineffective newcomer, Captain Connaught-Smith (Allan

Cuthbertson). The terrorists belong to a fearsome religious cult—the Thuggees—worshippers of Kali who strangle and rob their victims and bury their bodies in mass graves. When the cult's high priest (George Pastell) marks Lewis for death, Lewis battles off an attacker and later resigns from the company in order to fight the cult with a freer hand. After another caravan is attacked and plundered, Lewis trails the Thuggees to their temple, where he is captured and condemned to be thrown alive onto a blazing funeral pyre. But one of the cult's new initiates (David Spenser), haunted by conscience after having killed his own brother (Lewis's former servant) at the high priest's command, cuts Lewis's bindings. Lewis and the high priest fight and the priest topples into the pyre. Their leader dead, the other cultists run off, but Lewis—restored to his former rank—knows that the army's war against the Thuggees is only beginning.

Hammer's pseudo-historical film about the Indian cult of "Thuggee" was one of the few to deal with the topic, perhaps due to the ferocity of the subject. During the cult's three-hundred-year reign of terror, over one million people were sacrificed to Kali. Originally titled *The Horror of Thuggee*, the film's production was announced on September 17, 1958, in *The Daily Cinema*. Michael Carreras called the script "the most exciting and incredible story." Author David Z. Goodman's months of research resulted in a finished script a week after the announcement. Based on W.H. Sleeman's actual attempts to destroy the cult, Goodman's script was heavily censored for its brutality—stomach slittings, corpse mutilations, and burnings—and the "overuse" of curse words. As of December, Hammer still planned to shoot the film in color, an idea later abandoned.

Anthony Nelson-Keys was appointed General Manager of Bray Studios in April, 1959. He joined Hammer in 1956, and was promoted due to the increased production caused by the Columbia pact. After a title change to *The Stranglers of Bengal*, production on *The Stranglers of Bombay* began on July 6. With Michael Carreras on vacation in Spain, Anthony Hinds supervised the filming which ended on August 27. Although the movie had no star actors, its subject matter and the Hammer name were thought to be enough. Fortunately for Hammer—but not for India—there was a renewal of cult activity after a one-hundred-twenty-year silence. When the company delivered a rough cut to Columbia, James Carreras said (*The Daily Cinema*, September 28), "In *The Stranglers of Bombay*, we have delivered the strangest and most exciting action picture we have ever made." The film premiered at the London Pavilion on December 4, and went into general release on the ABC circuit on January 18, 1960. Critics were duly horrified, as they would be in America, when the movie opened, paired with Graham Greene's *Our Man in Havana* in May. *The Evening Standard* (December 3, 1959): "Hardly my idea of a jolly entertainment theme"; *The Monthly Film Bulletin* (January, 1960): "The usual fleabitten affair relying almost entirely for its appeal on visual outrages"; *Films and Filming* (February): "It is no pleasure to record as a critic that something so unhealthy is well done, which it is"; *The Daily Worker* (December 5, 1959): "The extraordinary thing is that the background is much more authentic and intelligently handled than many a great glamour epic about the glories of the East"; and *The Kinematograph Weekly* (December 3, 1959): "Exuberant adventure melodrama."

The Stranglers of Bombay helped to solidify the reputations of both Hammer and Terence Fisher as purveyors of sadism. According to Harry Ringel (*Cinefantastique*, Vol. 4, No. 3), "The film appalled even its director when he came to see it finished." *The Stranglers of Bombay* was Hammer's most realistic horror, and Fisher showed he could jolt an audience without Technicolor, blood, or Christopher Lee. Guy Rolfe headed a fine cast, Bray stood in admirably for the "mysterious East," and James Bernard contributed an atypical but rousing score to make the film a valuable component of Hammer's most exciting period.

Don't Panic Chaps!

Released December 21, 1959 (U.K.); 85 minutes; B & W; 7612 feet; a Hammer-A.C.T. Production; a Columbia Release; filmed at Walton Studios, and on location at Chobham Common and Thurlestone; Director: George Pollock; Executive Producer: Ralph Bond; Producer: Teddy Baird; Screenplay: Jack Davies; Original Play: Michael Corston, Ronald Holroyd; Director of Photography: Arthur Graham; Art Director: Scott MacGregor; Editor: Harry Aldous; Production Manager: Clifford Parkes; Music Composed and Conducted by: Philip Green; Camera Operator: Eric Besche; Sound Camera Operator: Alan Hogben; Sound Recordist: Sid Wiles; Makeup: Peter Aramsten; First Assistant Director: Douglas Hermes; Assistant Art Director: Tom Goswell; U.K. Certificate: U.

Dennis Price (Krisling), George Cole (Finch), Thorley Walters (Brown), Harry Fowler (Ackroyd), Nadja Regin (Elsa), Nicholas Phipps (Mortimer), Percy Herbert (Bolter), George Murcell (Meister), Gerlan Klauber (Schmidt), Terence Alexander (Babbington), Thomas Foulkes (Voss).

World War II, somewhere in the Adriatic Sea. Both the Germans and British want control of an island to use as an observation post. Second Lt. Brown (Thorley Walters), Sgt. Bolter (Percy Herbert), and Pvts. Ackroyd (Harry Fowler) and Finch (George Cole) are sent to take charge, but are abandoned without supplies and forgotten. Unfortunately, four Germans, also marooned, have a camp on the other side. Capt. Von Krisling (Dennis Price), Sgt. Schmidt (Gerlan Klauber), and Pvts. Meister (George Murcell) and Voss (Thomas Foulkes) soon meet the Brits and agree to a truce.

Finch and Voss are archeologists and do some excavating, but Von Krisling and Brown become testy when Elsa (Nadja Regin) washes ashore and both sides "claim" her. Luckily, both groups are picked up by submarines.

From 1956 to 1959, Hammer made as many military pictures as horror movies. *Don't Panic Chaps* was the company's fourth service farce—a popular fifties subgenre in both Britain and America, due to the vast number of adults who had been in the War and still held a grudge against someone. It is debatable whether these films "traveled well" due to the dissimilarities between the way the military is perceived on either side of the Atlantic. Hammer and A.C.T. Films joined forces to adapt Ronald Holroyd and Michael Corston's radio play in July, 1959, on a six-week schedule with a £75,000 budget. Producer Teddy Baird said in *The Kinematograph Weekly* (August 13, 1959), "I welcome these small budget productions. I think we could be making them for even less without sacrificing quality. This is not the time for taking expensive risks." The British Film Industry (except for Hammer) had been in a minor slump, explaining Baird's reticence.

Director George Pollock pointed out that despite the temptation to deliver a message about peaceful co-existence, he was playing the film for laughs. "There is this underlying note of seriousness," he told *The Daily Cinema* (October 21, 1959), "but we're certainly not making a thing of it." James Carreras added, "It's our funniest film yet!" A trade show was held on November 24, 1959, at the Columbia, and *Don't Panic Chaps* was released on the ABC circuit on December 21 to favorable reviews. *The Daily Express* (December 19): "A good old Army comedy with never a serious moment"; *The Daily Cinema* (November 27): "A welcome, though unstressed, moral of peace among men"; *The Kinematograph Weekly* (November 26): "Wholesome, if artless humor." Interestingly, the American *Variety* panned the picture.

This was a busy time for Hammer, and in the rush, the company may have missed a major opportunity. Announced, but never filmed, was *The San Siado Killings* with Stanley Baker, to be shot in Spain. The picture sounds as though it could have been the first "spaghetti western."

Never Take Sweets from a Stranger

Released March 4, 1960 (U.K.); 81 minutes; B & W; Hammerscope; 7292 feet; a Hammer Film Production; a Columbia Release; filmed at Bray Studios; Director: Cyril Frankel; Producer:

Never Take Sweets from a Stranger (1959)

Don't Panic Chaps poster (courtesy of Fred Humphries and Colin Cowie).

Anthony Hinds; Executive Producer: Michael Carreras; Screenplay: John Hunter, based on Roger Caris' play *The Pony Cart*; Director of Photography: Freddie Francis; Music Composed by Elizabeth Lutyens; Musical Director: John Hollingsworth; Production Designer: Bernard Robinson; Art Director: Don Mingaye; Editor: Alfred Cox; Supervising Editor: James Needs; Camera Operator: Len Harris; Associate Producer: Anthony Nelson-Keys; Sound Recordist: Jock May; Production Manager: Clifford Parks; Makeup: Roy Ashton; Hairdresser: Henry Montsash; Continuity: Tilly Day; Wardrobe Mistress: Molly Arbuthnot; Assistant Director: John Peverall; Second Assistant: Ron Wall; Casting Director: Dorothy Holloway; Stills Cameraman: Tom Edwards; U.S. Title: *Never Take Candy from a Stranger*; U.K. Certificate: X.

Gwen Watford (Sally), Patrick Allen (Pete), Felix Aylmer (Olderberry Senior), Niall MacGinnis (Defense Counsel), Alison Leggatt (Martha), Bill Nagy (Olderberry Junior), Macdonald Parke (Judge), Michael Gwynn (Prosecutor), Bud Knapp (Hammond), Janine Faye (Jean), Frances Green (Lucille), James Dyrenforth (Dr. Stephens), Estelle Brody (Eunice), Robert Arden (Tom), Vera Cook (Mrs. Demarest), Cal McCord (Kalliduke), Gaylord Cavallaro (Phillips), Sheila Robins (Miss Jackson), Larry O'Connor (Sam), Helen Horton (Sylvia), Shirley Butler (Mrs. Nash), Michael Hammond (Sammy Nash), Patricia Marks (Nurse), Peter Carlisle (Usher), Mark Baker (Clerk), Sonia Fox (Receptionist), John Bloomfield (Foreman), Charles Maunsell (Janitor), Andre Daker (Chauffeur), Bill Sawyer (Taxi Driver), Jack Lynn (Dr. Montfort), William Abney (Trooper), Tom Bushby (Policeman).

Two children—Jean (Janine Faye) and Lucille (Frances Green)—are lured into his home by Mr. Olderberry (Felix Aylmer), a perverted old man. Jean's father, Pete (Patrick Allen), has just brought his family to the small Canadian town after being hired as the high school principal. That night, Jean tells him and her mother, Sally (Gwen Watford), she stepped on a nail while dancing nude for Olderberry. Rather than call the police, Pete tries to deal with Olderberry's son, Richard (Bill Nagy), but after Jean suffers a nightmare, he contacts Captain Hammond (Bud Knapp). The Captain is of little use, intimidated by Olderberry's power in the community. Worse, he hints that this is not the first such incident. When Pete confronts Richard, he threatens to remove Pete from his new position.

The case goes to court, but goes badly.

Despite the efforts of the Prosecutor (Michael Gwynn), the Defense (Niall MacGinnis), bullies Jean. The Judge (Macdonald Parke) ends the proceedings to "protect" her, releasing Olderberry. Pete resigns, and as Jean says goodbye to Lucille, they are assaulted by Olderberry. As they try to escape him in a rowboat, they find it is attached to the pier as he reels them in.

A search party finds Lucille's body in an old cabin, but Jean is found, safe, in the forest. Olderberry is taken away while Richard goes to Lucille's house to face her parents.

James Carreras' comment that "We hate message films. We make entertainment" (*Films and Filming*, October, 1959) never applied less than to this film. The movie's failure to be accepted seriously put an end to the company's fling with adult drama, and with very few exceptions, Hammer would never again attempt a higher goal than to entertain. Based on Roger Caris' play *The Pony Cart, Never Take Sweets from a Stranger* not only confronted the horror of child molestation, but its sanction by a dysfunctional community. Despite Hammer's obvious sincerity and restraint, the film might have been better accepted if made by another company, as Hammer's growing reputation for sensationalism worked against it. Also, during this period, child molestation was rarely discussed at all, and certainly not in a movie.

Filming lasted from September 14 to October 30, 1959, at Bray and Black Park. Due to the touchy subject, Carreras was relieved to get a congratulatory telegram from Columbia head Mike Frankovich, in mid–February, 1960, after a screening in New York. The trade show was held on February 26 at the Columbia, after which the film was endorsed by the National Society for the Prevention of Cruelty to Children. The Rev. Arthur Morton proclaimed it "deeply moving" (*The Daily Cinema*, February 28), and planned to tour with the film in the U.K. Release was on March 4, 1960, at the Pavilion, and the unforeseen critical attacks began. *The London Times* (March 7): "It must be condemned as a film that never should have been made"; *Films and Filming* (May): "A smart production veneer might fool people into thinking that here is a wholly adult film concerned with social and moral problems. It isn't! In years to come, film historians will no doubt be able to logically explain the success of this company dealing only with the lurid and the loathsome." Balancing these over-reactions were praise from Scotland Yard, the NSPCC ("The producers are to be congratulated on their objective presentation") and juvenile defense expert Sir Basil Enrigues ("A most enthralling film of great human interest").

A more serious problem occurred when Columbia tried to open the movie in America. *Variety* (May 15, 1960) reported, "Production Code Administration rejection of the Columbia import had been upheld by the Code's review board, finding the picture to violate the edict about the depiction of sexual perversion." Appearing for Columbia was Vice President Paul N. Lazurus, who argued that the film "is a discussion of sex in good taste and could render a meaningful public service." A month earlier, *Variety* (March 16) gave the film a positive review. "A sincere, worthy, restrained, and exceedingly well done job which should be seen by every parent and child." A year later, *Variety* (March 15, 1961) would report that the National League of Decency was in support of the picture. "This is a perennial social problem treated with moral caution and without sensationalism." But it was too late — the damage was done. Infrequent showings at metropolitan area "art houses" were the only way to see the film in America.

British reviewers remained mostly appalled. *The Sunday Express* (June 3, 1960): "The treatment is too glib, its style too melodramatic, an easy profit out of an important but nasty subject"; and *The Daily Mail* (April 3): "A workaday thriller pivoting on the activities of a sex maniac." Supporting the picture were *The New Statesman* (September 4, 1960): "A Hammer Horror on its best behavior"; *The Daily Express* (April 13): "I cannot accuse Hammer of sensationalism or indeed of any lapse of good taste"; and *The Daily Herald* (April 3): "This film could save your child's life."

Janine Faye had originally auditioned for the stage version but, because of her age (10), was rejected because it was felt the subject matter was too risqué. When Cyril Frankel interviewed over 100 children for the film, he said in *The Kinematograph Weekly* (September 12, 1960): "When I cast a child, previous acting experience is the least important requirement. If a child has acted before, I break that down and start from scratch." Faye was given a fair opportunity and won the role.

Never Take Sweets from a Stranger was the first Hammer film for Freddie Francis, who would soon become one of the company's main directors. He was one of Britain's top cinematographers, winning an Oscar for *Sons and Lovers* (1960). He told Wheeler Dixon, "It was a problem film. It wasn't designed to be a commercial success."

Even today, this is a difficult movie to find, but thanks to Dick Klemensen, the authors got to see a letterboxed video. The first thing one notices is that there is *no* attempt at sensationalism—the film could easily be shown as an afternoon television special. The only scene geared to shock involves Mr. Olderberry slowly reeling in the rowboat, and it *is* chilling. Felix Aylmer, who never speaks, is excellent, as is the rest of the cast. It is unfortunate that this film has become an obscurity. Michael Carreras (*The Horror People*) summed up the situation. "The moment the film came out the critics said, 'Oh, here we go—look at Hammer taking a social problem and capitalizing on it.' There was *never* any attempt to exploit the subject."

Hell Is a City

Released May 1, 1960 (U.K.), January 18, 1961 (U.S.); 98 minutes (U.K.), 93 minutes (U.S.); B & W; Hammerscope; 8803 feet; a Hammer Film Production; an Associated British–Warner Pathe Release (U.K.); a Columbia Release (U.S.); filmed on location in Manchester; Director: Val Guest; Producer: Michael Carreras; Screenplay: Val Guest, based on Maurice Proctor's novel; Director of Photography: Arthur Grant; Music: Stanley Black; Editors: James Needs, John Dunsford; Art Director: Robert Jones; Production Manager: Don Weeks; Sound: Leslie Hammond, Len Shutton; Camera Operator: Len Harris; Makeup: Colin Garde; Hairstyles: Pauline Trent; U.K. Certificate: A.

Stanley Baker (Martineau), John Crawford (Starling), Donald Pleasence (Hawkins), Maxine Audley (Julia Martineau), Billie Whitelaw (Chloe), Joseph Tomilty (Steele), Vanda Godsell (Lucky), Geoffrey Frederick (Constable Devery), Sarah Branch (Silver), George A. Cooper (Savage), Charles Houston (Roach), Joby Blanshard (Jakes), Charles Morgan (Lovett), Peter Madden (Darwin), Dickie Owen (Bragg), Lois Dane (Cecily), Warren Mitchell (Traveller), Alastair Williamson (Sam), Russel Napier (Superintendent).

Detective Inspector Martineau (Stanley Baker) must deal with the jailbreak of Don Starling (John Crawford) in addition to his failing marriage to Julia (Maxine Audley). Martineau had earlier arrested Starling for a jewel robbery, and the thief is out for revenge. After questioning Lucky (Vanda Godsell), Starling's former lover, Martineau is made aware that she is "available" to him whenever he wants her. Starling returns to Manchester and rejoins his old mob. The first victim is bookmaker Gus Hawkins (Donald Pleasence). They kidnap his clerk (Lois Dane), rob her of £4,000, and when she screams, kill her. Needing a hideout, Starling contacts another ex-lover, Chloe (Billie Whitelaw)—Mrs. Gus Hawkins. She allows him to stay; but after he assaults Gus, she reports him to Martineau. She also ties him into the killing due to his green fingers, stained by an exploding dye.

After raiding an illegal gambling event in which some of the dyed notes are passed, Martineau apprehends the gang. Starling breaks into Steele's (Joseph Tomilty) warehouse in which he hid the stolen jewels. Startled by Steele's handicapped granddaughter (Sarah Branch), Starling shoots her. Martineau chases Starling across the rooftops, and both are injured by gunfire.

On the day of Starling's execution, Martineau and Julia quarrel. Following a brief talk with Lucky, he walks the streets alone.

Stanley Baker (left) and Val Guest on the set of *Hell Is a City*.

"*Hell Is a City*," Val Guest told the authors (May, 1992), "is one of my favorite films. It began as a book that Michael Carreras read. He was a brilliant guy—he had foreseen all *sorts* of directions for Hammer. I read it too, at his suggestion, and thought it would make a really unusual police picture where it didn't just 'slot in' that everything went right. I specifically asked for Stanley Baker, since we worked so well together on *Yesterday's Enemy*."

Part of Carreras's "direction" included a continued diversification of product, even after the success of the horror films. Unfortunately, this ended by the mid-sixties at which time Hammer became totally identified with horror/fantasy. But that was years away, and the company was still mixing the occasional adult drama in with its more exploitative subjects.

The Daily Cinema (September 2, 1959) announced that "For the first time, Hammer is to produce a feature for release through A.B. Pathe which will be shot largely on location in Manchester." Filming began on September 21, and when *The Daily Cinema* visited the set on October 15, Stanley Baker described the half-finished film as "the psychology of a battle between two powerful individuals on the streets of a recognizable city." The original intention had been to call the city "Grantchester," but Manchester officials insisted on the actual name being used and Hammer had the complete cooperation of all city departments.

One of Hammer's concerns was to avoid an X rating due to some nasty violence and very brief nudity that Val Guest felt necessary to convey the realism he sought. This realism distinguished *Hell Is a City* from most other Hammer films. As in Guest's other pictures for the company, there is no sensationalism, and his restraint was rewarded with an A rating. Filming ended on November 5, 1959, and a trade show was held on March 11, 1960, followed by a special "northern premiere" in Ardwick on April 10. *Hell Is a City* went into general release on May 1 among the best reviews ever given to a Hammer film. Unfortunately, the name "Hammer" was seldom mentioned. *The London Times* (May 2, 1960): "Mr. Guest has directed with a powerful sense of tempo"; *The Monthly Bulletin* (May): "It has a striking outdoor appearance"; *The Daily Express* (April 29): "Crime par excellence"; *The Star* (April 28): "A cops and robbers film with a difference"; *Variety* (May 18): "One of the best British films in some time"; *The New York Times* (January 19, 1961): "A respectable job with a minimum of nonsense"; and *The New York Herald Tribune* (January 19): "Superior to what one finds in most such films."

Hell Is a City gave Stanley Baker his second excellent role for Hammer, but he quickly moved out of their price range after *Zulu* (1964). The picture's best performance is Billie Whitelaw's, who has a fleeting nude scene—Hammer's first in a *British* print. This flirtation with nudity would become, by the decade's end, a full-blown romance, but in this case it was not exploited.

Hell Is a City was Val Guest's last outstanding film for Hammer, and much of the company's success was due to his versatility. He was to Hammer what Michael Curtiz had been to Warner Bros. Guest told the authors,

> I would say it was one of the happiest periods of my life. We were one big happy family—especially down at Bray—very happy days and also, because of the lack of money and space—you had to learn your job so that you could make something look like a million when you only had ten to spend.
>
> It was a question of coming in the morning with "instant genius." We all used to say, "Have you brought your instant genius pills this morning?" They were great, great days, and we learned an awful lot—all of us—everybody there. I enjoyed working with everyone.
>
> I think the reason for Hammer's success is that they hit a happy time when people were wanting that type of film—thriller, science fiction, Gothic. I think they just happened to hit the right button at the right time. They certainly hit it right and certainly have become a milestone in the British film industry.

The Two Faces of Dr. Jekyll

Released October 24, 1960 (U.K.), May 3, 1961 (U.S.); 88 minutes; Technicolor; Megascope; 7878 feet; a Hammer Film Production; released through Columbia (U.K.), American International (U.S.); filmed at Bray and Elstree Studios; Director: Terence Fisher; Producer: Michael Carreras; Associate Producer: Anthony Nelson-Keys; Screenplay: Wolf Mankowitz, based on Robert Louis Stevenson's novelette "The Strange Case of Dr. Jekyll and Mr. Hyde"; Director of Photography: Jack Asher; Music and Songs: Monty Norman and David Hencker; Music Supervisor: John Hollingsworth; Supervising Editor: James Needs; Editor: Eric Boyd-Perkins; Production Design: Bernard Robinson; Production Manager: Clifford Parkes; Camera Operator: Len Harris; Continuity: Tilly Day; Sound: Jock May; Makeup: Roy Ashton; Hairdresser: Ivy Emmerton; Costume Designer: Mayo; Wardrobe: Molly Arbuthnot; Dances: Julie Mendez; Assistant Art Director: Don Mingaye; Casting: Dorothy Holloway; Stills: Tom Edwards; Assistant Director: John Peverall; Second Assistant: Hugh Marlow; Sound Editor: Archie Ludski; Masks: Margaret Robinson. U.S. title: *House of Fright*; U.K. Certificate: X.

Paul Massie (Jekyll/Hyde), Dawn Addams (Kitty), Christopher Lee (Paul Allen), David Kossoff (Litauer), Francis De Wolff (Inspector), Norma Marla (Maria), Joy Webster, Magda Miller (Sphinx Girls), Oliver Reed (Young Tough), William Kendall (Clubman), Pauline Shepherd (Girl in Gin Shop), Helen Goss (Nannie), Dennis Shaw (Hanger-on), Felix Felton (Gambler), Janine Faye (Jane), Percy Cartwright (Coroner), Joe Robinson (Corinthian), Joan Tyrill (Major Domo), Douglas Robinson (Boxer), Donald Tandy (Plainclothes Man), Frank Atkinson (Groom), Arthur Lovegrove (Cabby).

London, 1874. Dr. Henry Jekyll's (Paul Massie) life is in tatters. His theories about man's duality are ridiculed by his colleagues, and his wife, Kitty (Dawn Addams), is having a public affair with his "friend" Paul Allen (Christopher Lee). Ignored by his wife and ignoring warnings from his associate, Litauer (David Kossoff), Jekyll injects himself with a drug designed to free his "inner man." Released from Jekyll's moral restraints, "Mr. Hyde" (Massie) is younger, handsome, and beyond good and evil, living for his own gratification. At the Sphynx, a disorderly club, Hyde spots Kitty and Paul together, and ingratiates himself with Paul.

The Two Faces of Dr. Jekyll poster (courtesy of Fred Humphries and Colin Cowie).

Hyde pursues "his" wife sexually, but is rejected. In exchange for being introduced to London's lower depths, Hyde takes over Paul's considerable gambling debts, then gives Kitty the opportunity to "buy back" her lover.

When Kitty again refuses him, Hyde arranges a meeting between husband, wife, and lover at the Sphynx where he kills Paul with Maria's (Norma Marla) boa constrictor, which she uses in her dance act. He then rapes Kitty, who afterwards falls to her death through a skylight. Hyde takes Maria to Jekyll's home where, after "making love," he strangles her, awakening as Henry. Hyde, to continue his mastery over Jekyll, kills a laborer and burns the corpse, explaining to the Inspector (Francis De Wolff) that Jekyll died after attempting to murder him. At the inquest, Jekyll is found guilty of all the murders and declared a suicide. As a smirking Hyde leaves the courtroom, Jekyll gains mastery and returns, aged and spent. He and Litauer exult in Hyde's destruction, but both realize that Jekyll has destroyed himself.

The Two Faces of Dr. Jekyll was Hammer's biggest gamble during the company's first round of horror remakes. Why? The familiar story was completely turned on its head, and although England's greatest "monster" was in the cast, Christopher Lee did not play the monster. In fact, there *is* no monster. Earlier actors to play the dual role included John Barrymore, Fredric March, and Spencer Tracy. Hammer chose *Paul Massie*! Although the film contains little visual horror, its plot elements are morally repellent. And, earlier in 1960, Hammer's *comedy* version of the same subject, *The Ugly Duckling*, was released. With all this against the film, it remains a fascinating failure that deserves credit for at least daring to be different.

Hammer was going head-to-head with not only a literary classic, but with three Hollywood icons. Their successor was the relatively unknown Paul Massie, who was actually quite a catch for Hammer after his brilliant debut in *Orders to Kill* (1958), for which he won the British Film Academy's Most Promising Actor award. He followed this with good roles in *Sapphire* (1958) and *Libel* (1959). "I fairly jumped at the oppor-

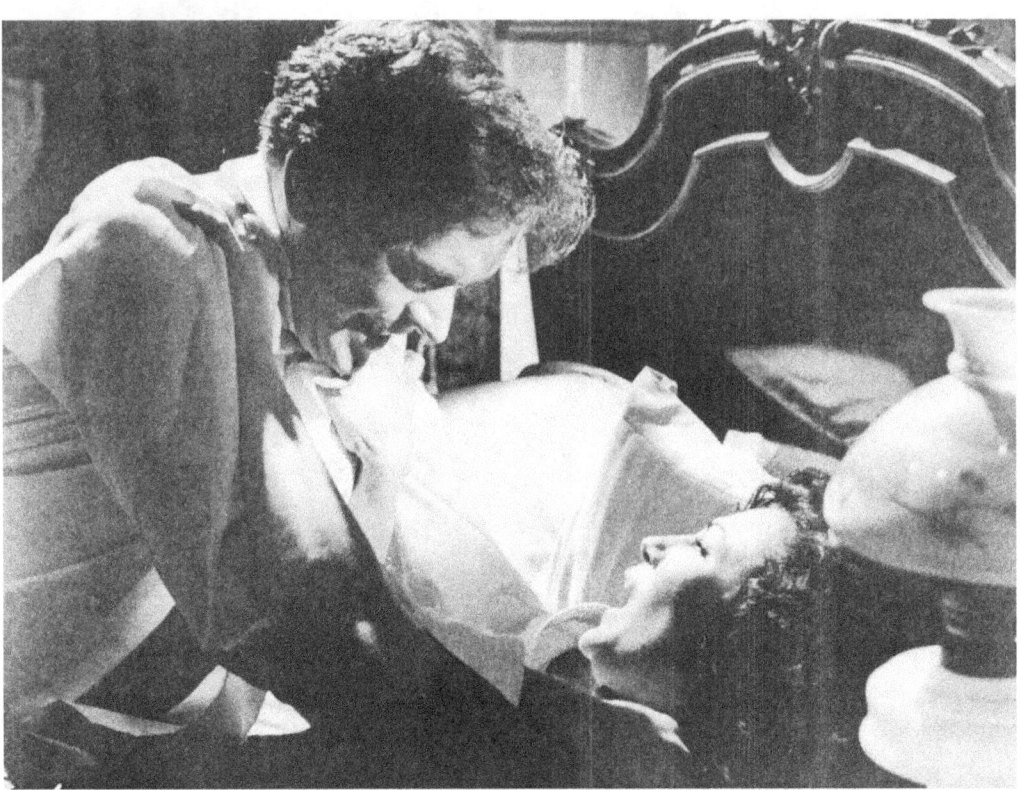

Dr. Jekyll's alter ego (Paul Massie) in *The Two Faces of Dr. Jekyll*.

tunity," he was quoted in the film's pressbook. "The role is an actor's delight and runs the emotional gamut from top to bottom." His performance has not received proper credit, perhaps due to the preconceived notion that he could not top his famous predecessors. Even the stuffy *Films and Filming* (December, 1960) allowed that "Massie's study of dualism is quite passable." Terence Fisher said in *Cinefantastique* that "Massie understood the role and felt it. There was not one redeeming character—it was an exercise, rightly or wrongly, in evil."

The movie's one brilliant (or ludicrous) concept is that instead of becoming a snarling ape, Jekyll sheds twenty years—and his beard—to become Hyde, the charming seducer. While many approved of this novel twist, the "appearing/disappearing beard" is an annoyance.

Although Massie is fine as Jekyll/Hyde, Christopher Lee steals the film with a refreshing naturalness that adroitly reveals Paul Allen's decadent charm. "The part was written for me," he said in *The Films of Christopher Lee*. "I think it was one of the best performances I've given." Making his Hammer debut was Oliver Reed, who recalled in *Reed All About Me*, "When I came out of the Army, I went to my uncle (Director Carol Reed), and he said to go into repertory if I wanted to be an actor. It was good advice, so I ignored it completely. I took my photos around, and got a bit in *Jekyll*."

The Two Faces of Dr. Jekyll was the first association between Hammer and American International, who had been friendly rivals since 1957. Sam Arkoff, AIP head, told the authors in June, 1992, "We did some business with Hammer, and we could have done more, but we had our thing going. It just never occurred to us to do a co-production until *The Vampire Lovers*. AIP had an English connection, a producer named Nat

The Two Faces... was retitled for America as *House of Fright*.

Cohen. We met Jimmy Carreras through Nat at a Variety Club benefit. Jimmy was quite a guy! He and I became great friends. We never saw each other as rivals—the market was a big one with plenty for all."

James Carreras announced his intention to remake *Dr. Jekyll and Mr. Hyde* in *The Kinematograph Weekly* (March 12, 1959), signed Paul Massie on November 19, and had the cameras turning on November 23. "The subject," Carreras said, "has been filmed before, but our script boys have come up with an astonishing new approach. This new concept is so brilliantly original, and yet so simple, that a lot of filmmakers will be kicking themselves silly that they never thought of the idea themselves." "Our problem," said Michael Carreras, "was that *Dr. Jekyll and Mr. Hyde* has already been filmed—and well-filmed, too. Wolf Mankowitz came up with a twist which virtually gives us a new story. As it is, we have a sex film rather than a horror picture."

One of the film's main characters was a python. Margaret Robinson told the authors (August, 1993) of her problems.

> The actress playing the snake charmer couldn't dance very well, so the woman who handled the snake had to dance with it in some shots, so I had to make a mask to disguise the two women. Since this was a last minute decision, I had to stay up all night. I also *made* a snake. Christopher Lee wasn't too keen on snakes, so I had to make two—one to look alive, one to look dead. I went to a lot of trouble over these snakes—they were real beauties! Afterwards, I was with Bernard, Michael, and the snake charmer, and we compared the real snake to the models. Michael picked up the real snake, thinking it was a fake! Then—after all this—they decided not to use my snakes! Michael smiled and said, "Never mind, we'll use them in another picture."

Filming ended on January 22, 1960, with two weeks at Elstree due to construction at Bray. After an August 20 trade show at the Columbia, the film premiered at the Pavilion on October 7, and was released on the ABC circuit on October 24, to mixed reviews:

The London Times (October 10): "An ingenious, though repellent variation"; *The Sunday Times* (October 9): "Paul Massie does what he can to save something from a wreck alternately risible and nauseating"; *The Observer* (October 9): "A vulgar, intentionally foolish work"; *The Spectator* (Octo-

180   *The Brides of Dracula* (1960)

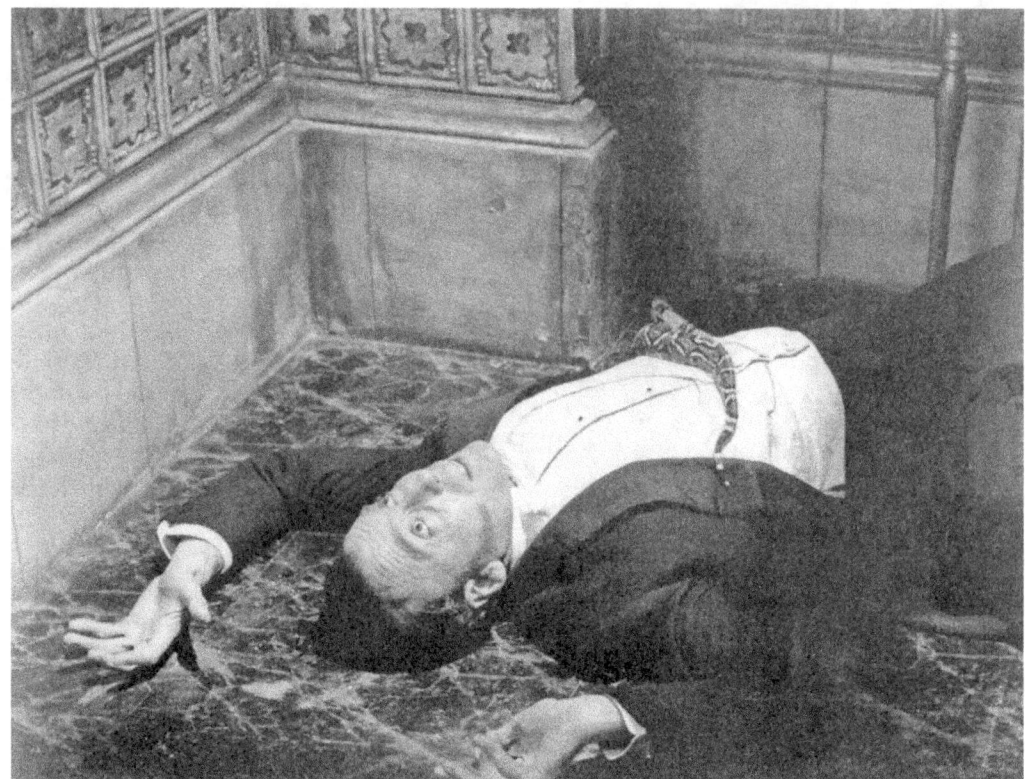

Death of a scoundrel. Christopher Lee in *The Two Faces of Dr. Jekyll*.

ber 14): "It has peculiarly horrid moral inversions"; *The News Chronicle* (October 7): "Its horrors are penny dreadful"; *The Kinematograph Weekly* (October 6): "Characterization bold, climax stern and spectacular"; *Variety* (October 19): "Terence Fisher's direction is done effectively with few holds barred. The Victorian atmosphere is well put over"; *The New York Herald Tribune* (August 24, 1961): "A colorful, ingenious remake."

The Two Faces of Dr. Jekyll was distributed in the U.S. by American International as *House of Fright* with few references to its origin in the ads. Surrounded by better horror movies like *House of Usher* and *The Brides of Dracula*, it sank without a trace, which is unfortunate.

Although it is difficult to defend many of its lapses, the picture deserves credit for finding a new way to film an old story.

1960

The Brides of Dracula

Released August 29, 1960 (U.K.), September, 1960 (U.S.); 85 minutes; Technicolor; 7674 feet; a Hammer-Hotspur Production; Released by Rank (U.K.), Universal International (U.S.); filmed at Bray Studios; Director: Terence Fisher; Producer: Anthony Hinds; Associate Producer: Anthony Nelson-Keys; Executive Producer: Michael Carreras; Screenplay: Jimmy Sangster, Peter Bryan and Edward Percy; Director of Photography: Jack Asher; Music Composed by Malcolm Williamson; Music Supervisor: John Hollingsworth; Production Design: Bernard Robinson; Art Director: Thomas Goswell; Camera Operator: Len Harris; Editors: James Needs, Alfred Cox; Special Effects: Syd Pearson; Assistant Director: John Peverall; Sound Recordist: Jock May; Sound Editor: James Groom; Makeup: Roy Ashton; Costumes: Molly Arbuthnot; Continuity: Tilly Day; Hairdresser: Frieda Steiger; U.K. Certificate: X.

Peter Cushing (Van Helsing), Martita Hunt

David Peel forces Yvonne Monlaur to join his cult in *The Brides of Dracula*.

(Baroness Meinster), Yvonne Monlaur (Marianne), Freda Jackson (Greta), David Peel (Baron Meinster), Miles Malleson (Dr. Tobler), Henry Oscar (Herr Lang), Mona Washburn (Frau Lang), Andree Melly (Gina); Victor Brooks (Hans), Fred Johnson (Priest), Michael Ripper (Driver), Norman Pierce (Innkeeper), Vera Cook (His Wife), Marie Devereux (Village Girl), Harold Scott (Severn), Michael Mulcaster (Man in Black).

Victorian Transylvania. While travelling to the Lang Academy to take a teaching position, Marianne Danielle (Yvonne Monlaur) is stranded at a small inn by her coachman (Michael Ripper), who is in league with the Baroness Meinster (Martita Hunt). She invites Marianne to spend the night at her chateau against the wishes of the innkeeper (Norman Pierce) and his wife (Vera Cook). After a meal served by Greta (Freda Jackson), Marianne discovers a handsome young man chained at the ankle. He is Baron Meinster (David Peel), a vampire who takes his mother's blood after Marianne foolishly releases him. She flees the chateau and is found unconscious by Dr. Van Helsing (Peter Cushing). He has been summoned by the local priest (Fred Johnson) to end a plague of vampirism precipitated by the Baroness' procuring of young girls for her son.

After taking Marianne to the Academy, Van Helsing destroys the vampiric Baroness. The Baron visits Marianne, and under his power, she agrees to marry him. He vampirizes Gina (Andree Melly), another teacher, and is soon traced by Van Helsing to an old windmill. Van Helsing is attacked by the now insane Greta who falls to her death, but the Baron bites the doctor's

The entrance to Oakley Court was prominently featured in *The Brides of Dracula* (photo courtesy of Tom Weaver).

throat. Van Helsing burns away the vampire's mark and, when the Baron returns with Marianne, hurls holy water in his face. As he stumbles outside, the Baron is destroyed as Van Helsing traps him in the shadow of the cross formed by the windmill blades.

Dracula's international success made Hammer the leading producer of quality horror films and led to an agreement with Universal-International to remake its library of classic thrillers. The first was *The Mummy*, but a *Dracula* sequel was high on the list and was planned as early as March, 1959. After going through several plot and title changes, a November 19, 1959, script settled on *The Brides of Dracula*. It would be credited to three authors—Jimmy Sangster, Peter Bryan, and Edward Percy. "I have no clear memory of what I wrote," Sangster told the authors in August, 1993. "Since three authors are credited, it's a certainty that *someone* was cleaning up someone else's work. I probably wrote the initial version and Hammer, for whatever reason, brought in the others. It happens all the time, and I've been on both ends."

In addition to scripting problems, the *Dracula* sequel had a more serious problem— no Dracula. Christopher Lee, saying he feared typecasting, declined to appear. Anthony Hinds had a different view. "[Lee] was either in Europe, or he was asking too much money," he said in a *Fangoria* interview. "In any case, we decided we could do without him." Enter David Peel. Peel made his first film appearance in *We Dive at Dawn* (1942), but acted primarily on the stage. Baron Meinster was his only major role, shortly after which he retired to sell real estate and, later, fine arts and antiques. Hammer never explained how Peel came to be chosen for the role with such limited experience, but it certainly was a stroke of casting genius.

Unlike Lee, Peter Cushing had no qualms about repeating his role from *Dracula*. Michael Carreras valued Cushing for more than just his acting talent. Interviewed in *Fangoria*, Carreras commented, "Cushing just wouldn't tolerate anything he thought was second best, and he used to nag me if he thought I was taking the easy way out—and

"Mother, come here!" Martita Hunt, Yvonne Monlaur and David Peel in *The Brides of Dracula*.

quite rightly." After years of struggle, Cushing was enjoying his stardom. "What I like about films," he said in a Hammer press release, "is the variety. There's the day to day excitement of watching each piece of the celluloid jigsaw being fitted together. You can also see the results of your work and improve on your performance as you go along."

The Brides of Dracula began production on January 26, 1960, and concluded on March 18, after location work in Black Park. At the premiere on July 7, at the Marble Arch Odeum, Yvonne Monlaur arrived in an opulent horse drawn carriage escorted by Peter Cushing. By all accounts, the film was a financial success after its August 27 general release. *The Kinematograph Weekly* (August 28, 1960) reported that the movie recorded several opening day records. Reviewers were slightly condescending. *The London Times* (July 7, 1960): "The cast is too good for its material"; *The Sunday Times* (July 10): "The usual concoction"; *The Kinematograph Weekly* (July 7): "Intriguing and meaty, plush presentation, rich settings"; *The Monthly Bulletin* (August): "Inappropriate color and decor, a vague pretense of period, adds little to the Dracula legend"; *The Daily Express* (July 8): "A horrible bore"; *Variety* (May 18): "A technically well made film"; and *The New York Times* (September 6): "There is nothing new or imaginative."

Reviewers are entitled to their opinions, but Bosley Crowther's *New York Times* piece is questionable. Practically *everything* was new, and it would be interesting to have had Crowther draw up a list of "similar films." *The Brides of Dracula* is one of Hammer's best horrors and is one of the great vampire movies. Terence Fisher kept his excellent cast and action highlights moving so smoothly that one does not notice several plot holes caused by the plethora of scripts and writers. The film manages to cleverly

184   *The Terror of the Tongs* (1960)

Hammer makes a hit Dracula movie—without Dracula—or Christopher Lee!

mix traditional vampire lore with some new (and slightly perverse) ideas.

The movie's original climax had Van Helsing summon the forces of darkness against the Baron. Keith Dudley in *The Horror Elite* speculated that this concept, later used in *The Kiss of the Vampire*, was jettisoned due to budgetary restrictions. The actual climax is more effective—a man to vampire confrontation seemed more appropriate.

The Terror of the Tongs

Released September 29, 1961 (U.K.), October, 1961 (U.S.); 79 minutes; Technicolor (U.K.), Eastman Color (U.S.); 6880 feet; a Hammer Film Production; a British Lion Release (U.K.), a Columbia Release (U.S.); filmed at Bray Studios; Director: Anthony Bushell; Producer: Kenneth Hyman; Associate Producer: Anthony Nelson-Keys; Executive Producer: Michael Carreras; Screenplay: Jimmy Sangster; Director of Photography: Arthur Grant; Music Composed by James Bernard; Musical Director: John Hollingsworth; Production Designer: Bernard Robinson; Production Manager: Clifford Parkes; Art Director: Thomas Goswell; Editor: Eric Boyd-Perkins; Supervising Editor: James Needs; Sound Recordists: Jock May, Alban Streeter; Camera Operator: Len Harris; Makeup: Roy Ashton; Costumes: Molly Arbuthnot; Hairstyles: Frieda Steiger; Production Secretary: Ann Skinner; Assistant Director: John Peverall; Second Assistant: Joe Levy; Third Assistant: Dominic Fulford; Continuity: Tilly Davis; Focus: Harry Oakes; Clapper: Alan MacDonald; Boom: Jim Perry; Sound Camera Operator: Michael Sale; Assistant Art Director: Don Mingaye; Wardrobe Assistant: Rosemary Burrows; Casting: Dorothy Holloway; Assistant Editor: Chris Barnes; Accountant: W.H.V. Able; Bray/Falcon Accountant: Ken Gordon; Cashier: Peter Lancaster; Studio Manager: A.F. Kelly; Construction Manager: Arthur Banks; Electrician: Jack Curtis; Master Carpenter; Charles Davis; Master Painter: Lawrence Wrenn; Master Plasterer: Stan Banks; Property Master: Tommy Money; Production Buyer: Eric Hillier; Floor Props: Peter Allchorne; Grip: Albert Cowlards; U.K. Certificate: X.

Geoffrey Toone (Jackson), Christopher Lee

(Chung King), Yvonne Monlaur (Lee), Brian Worth (Harcourt), Richard Leech (Inspector Dean), Marne Maitland (Beggar), Ewen Solon (Tang How), Burt Kwouk (Ming), Barbara Brown (Helena), Bandance Dao Gupta (Anna), Michael Hawkins (Priest), Marie Burke (Maya), Milton Reid (Guardian), Charles Lloyd Pack (Doctor), Roger Del Gado (Wang How), Eric Young (Confucius), Johnny Arlen (Executioner), Santso Wong (Sergeant), Andy Ho (Lee Chung), Arnold Lee (Spokesman).

While docking in Hong Kong on Captain Jackson's (Geoffrey Toone) ship, Mr. Ming (Burt Kwouk) discusses the power of the deadly cult of the Tong. Ming hides a list of Tong members in a book to be given to Jackson's daughter. At Tong headquarters, Chung King (Christopher Lee) sends an assassin to get the list. Ming is killed as he leaves the ship with District Superintendent Harcourt (Brian Worth), but manages to wound his murderer who is then killed by a passing "doctor" (Charles Lloyd Pack). The book is stolen from Jackson's daughter (Barbara Brown) who, along with one of Jackson's employees, is murdered.

After burning the list, Chung King turns his attention to increasing drug profits for the Central Tong, but an underground movement against him, led by a beggar (Marne Maitland) is gaining strength. Through him, Jackson is able to shake secrets from Tang How (Ewen Solon) with the help of How's slave Lee (Yvonne Monlaur). Jackson reports to Harcourt, who is a secret Tong agent, and is taken unconscious to Chung King where he is tortured by a henchman (Milton Reid). Aided by the beggar, Jackson escapes and is saved soon afterwards by Lee who kills the "doctor" with his own poisoned needle.

Chung King must now kill Jackson to save face and plots with Harcourt to lure him to the wharf. Lee intervenes and is killed by a hatchetman. Incited by the beggar, a crowd attacks Tong headquarters, and after having Harcourt murdered, Chung King orders his own death.

The Terror of the Tongs was a nasty entry in Hammer's move from Gothic horror to costume adventure. Hammer, although pulling away from Gothics, managed to include its elements into non-horror subjects. *The Terror of the Tongs* had hatchet murders, drug crazed assassins, bone scrapings, and Christopher Lee. Unfortunately, as with Lee's later Fu Manchu series, he is given nothing to do except utter philosophy and look menacing. Lee's Oriental makeup is effective, but it is disconcerting to see Charles Lloyd Pack and Ewen Solon wearing it in secondary roles. Were no Oriental actors available? Geoffrey Toone made a stalwart hero, but lacked the charisma necessary to balance Lee's moribund performance. Toone told the authors (July, 1993):

After living in Hollywood in the fifties, I returned to Britain to do stage work in the West End and some television. I interviewed for *Terror of the Tongs* and returned to L.A. to test for the lead in a TV series which was never made. While there, I got the offer from Hammer and went back to make the film. I didn't see a lot of Christopher Lee—he was sort of "King of Hammer" but didn't have a lot to do on this film. Tony Bushell, the director, had been an actor and Laurence Olivier's assistant, and was very pleasant to work with. Bray Studios had a cozy atmosphere—not a bit like working in L.A. By the way, I'm still working at age 82!

Anthony Bushell was pleased to be directing for Hammer. "The happiest thing for me was the opportunity to work at Bray," he said in *The Kinematograph Weekly* (May 5, 1960). "There's a feeling here which you don't get at many studios. Everyone, from top to bottom, seems to know exactly what's going on. The terrific enthusiasm and one-mindedness toward filmmaking here is the nearest thing to working in a French studio."

The Terror of the Tongs began production on April 18, 1960, and concluded on May 27. After a September 12, 1961, trade show at the Columbia, it premiered at the Pavilion on September 29. Drama students were invited to attend in costume, with the promise of the selected winners' appearing in *The Phantom of the Opera*. Reviews were generally negative. *The Sunday Telegram* (October 8, 1961): "No different from a hundred crime thrillers"; *The Kinematograph Weekly* (September 14): "It should whet and

186   *The Full Treatment* (1960)

Val Guest's unusual psychodrama, *The Full Treatment*.

satisfy the masses"; and *The Monthly Bulletin* (November): "Retrograde blood bath." Paired with William Castle's *Homicidal*, the duo was voted the year's best "gimmick double feature" by *The Kinematograph Weekly* (December 14, 1961) while on the ABC circuit.

Legend has it that Christopher Lee was considered for the title role in his cousin Ian Fleming's *Dr. No* (1962). Whether his performance as Chung King led to his consideration or rejection is unknown, but it is worth speculating on Hammer's history if Lee had won the part.

Despite fine individual ingredients, *The Terror of the Tongs* does not add up to much and cannot stand with similarly themed films like *The Pirates of Blood River* and *Captain Clegg*.

The Full Treatment

Released February 20, 1961 (U.K.), May 17, 1961 (U.S.); 109 minutes (U.K.), 93 minutes (U.S.); B & W; Megascope; 9852 feet; a Hilary-Falcon (Hammer) Production; a Columbia Release; filmed at Elstree Studios, England, and on location in the South of France; Director, Producer, Screenplay: Val Guest; Associate Producer: Victor Lyndon; Screenplay: Ronald Scott Thorn, based on his novel *The Full Treatment*; Assistant Director: Kips Gowans; Director of Photography: Gilbert Taylor; Art Director: Tony Masters; Costumes: Beatrice Dawson; Production Manager: Clifton Brandon; Camera: Moray Grant; Continuity: Doreen Dearnaley; Sound Recordist: Bert Ross; Editor: Bill Lenny; Makeup: Tony Sforzini; Music: Stanley Black; Hairdresser: Ivy Emmerton; Set Decorator: Scott Slimon; Assistant Art Director: Geoff Tozar; Wardrobe: Muriel Dickson. U.S. Title: *Stop Me Before I Kill!*; U.K. Certificate: A.

Claude Dauphin (Doctor David Prade), Diane Cilento (Denise Colby), Ronald Lewis (Alan Colby), Francoise Rosay (Madame Prade), Bernard Braden (Harry Stonehouse), Katya Douglas (Connie Stonehouse), Barbara Chilcott (Baroness de la Vaillon), Ann Tirard (Nicole), Edwin Styles (Doctor Roberts), George Merritt (Doctor Manfield).

Newlyweds Alan (Ronald Lewis) and Denise (Diane Cilento) Colby are involved in a car crash while on their honeymoon.

The Full Treatment (1960)   187

Stop Me Before I Kill! was the American retitle for Hammer's *The Full Treatment*.

Alan, a race car driver, suffers a head injury, blackout periods, and feelings of guilt. Even worse, when they continue their honeymoon in France, Alan develops an urge to kill Denise when they embrace. Horrified, he avoids sexual contact with her. While in the Riviera, the couple are invited to a party hosted by Dr. Prade (Claude Dauphin), an eminent psychiatrist who offers to treat Alan. He refuses, and returns to London with Denise Prade, obsessed with her, follows.

Alan finally submits to Prade's bizarre "treatments." However, instead of helping his patient, the doctor convinces Alan that he has killed Denise and carved up her body. Alan flees to the Riviera, while Prade tells Denise that her husband has been institutionalized at his clinic and offers to take her to see him. When Alan sees the two together, he confronts Prade who escapes onto a cable car. The cable snaps, sending the doctor to his death and reuniting the couple.

Val Guest bought the rights to Ronald Scott Thorn's novel *The Full Treatment* while finishing *Hell Is a City*, and told *The Kinematograph Weekly*, "I'm excited about the book. I think I've beaten Hitchcock to this one!" Guest approached Columbia who set up a co-production arrangement with Hammer. "Falcon was a 'subsidiary' of Hammer," he told the authors (July, 1994). "The boys at Hammer were always receptive to my ideas, and this was no exception. For their own reasons, the name 'Hammer' does not appear on the credits." Guest wanted Stanley Baker, his star of *Yesterday's Enemy* and *Hell Is a City*, to play the lead, but previous commitments caused Baker to be replaced by Ronald Lewis. He starred in three Hammer films, giving convincing performances but winning little acclaim.

The production began on May 2, 1960, in Cannes during the annual film festival. The unit returned to Elstree at the end of the month and filmed interiors into July. *The Full Treatment* was trade shown in early February, 1961, and went into general release on February 20. After a strong opening week at the New Victoria, it slowed to modest business for the next two. Reviews, also, were mixed. *The Observer* (February 12): "An ineptly written adventure"; *The Monthly Film Bulletin* (March, 1961): "A longwinded, lurid attempt at a psychiatry-cum-suspense mystery thriller"; and *The New York Times* (June 22): "A snug, tautly-strung little thriller." Six minutes were cut for the American release, which seemed to have helped. The leads gave good performances, but Claude Dauphin was miscast in a role requiring more charisma than he generated.

Sword of Sherwood Forest (1960)

The Sheriff of Nottingham (Peter Cushing) and Robin Hood (Richard Greene) practice in between scenes in *Sword of Sherwood Forest*.

The Full Treatment, on the surface, seems similar to the films in Hammer's psycho-thriller "series," but it lacks their plot twists, hints of the supernatural, and horrific scenes. Although competently made, *The Full Treatment* has no memorable scenes and is easily dismissed amidst the more exciting Hammer films of the early sixties.

Sword of Sherwood Forest

Released December 26, 1960 (U.K.), January, 1961 (U.S.); 80 minutes, Copyright length: 96 minutes; Technicolor; Megascope; 7185 feet; a Columbia Release; filmed at Bray Studios, England and County Wicklow, Republic of Ireland; Director: Terence Fisher; Producers: Sidney Cole, Richard Greene; Executive Producer: Michael Carreras; Screenplay: Alan Hackney; Music: Alun Hoddinott; Music Director: John Hollingsworth; Director of Photography: Ken Hodges; Supervising Editor: James Needs; Production Manager: Don Weeks (England), Ronald Liles (Ireland); Art Director: John Stoll; Camera: Richard Bayley; Makeup: Gerald Fletcher; Hairdresser: Hilda Fox; Wardrobe Supervisor: John McCorry; Continuity: Pauline Wise, Dot Foreman; Horsemaster: Ivor Collin; Construction Supervisor: John McCorry; Production Secretary: Judith Walsh; Assistant Director: Bob Porter; Editor: Lee Doig; Original Songs: Stanley Black; Sung by: Dennis Lotis; Sound: Alban Streeter, John Mitchell, Harry Tate; Wardrobe Mistress: Rachel Austin; Casting Director: Stuart Lyons; Master of Arms: Patrick Crean; Master of Archery: Jack Cooper; Main Titles: Chambers & Partners; U.K. Certificate: U.

Richard Greene (Robin Hood), Peter Cushing (Sheriff of Nottingham), Richard Pasco (Newark), Sarah Branch (Marian), Niall MacGinnis (Friar Tuck), Nigel Green (Little John), Dennis Lotis (Alan A'Dale), Jack Gwillim (Hubert Walter, Archbishop of Canterbury), Oliver Reed (Melton), Edwin Richfield (Sheriff's Lieutenant), Vanda Godsell (Prioress), Brian

Co-conspirators plot the demise of the Archbishop of Canterbury in *Sword of Sherwood Forest*.

Rawlinson (Falconer), Patrick Crean (Ollerton), Derren Nesbitt (Martin), Reginald Hearne (Man at Arms), Jack Cooper (Archer), Adam Kean (Retford), Desmond Llewellyn (Traveller), Charles Lamb (Old Bowyer), Aiden Grennell (Outlaw), James Neylin (Roger), Barry de Boulay (Officer), John Hoey (Old Jack), Andrew McMaster (Judge), John Franklin (Walter's Secretary), Maureen Halligan (Portess).

A wounded man is aided in Sherwood Forest by outlaws Robin Hood (Richard Greene) and Little John (Nigel Green), after which they discover the beautiful Marian (Sarah Branch) swimming nearby. Attracted to Robin, she instigates a meeting at the Owl Inn. Little John warns against a trap, but Robin accepts. Waiting at the Owl is the Sheriff of Nottingham (Peter Cushing), who offers Robin a pardon in exchange for the wounded man. Robin refuses, and Marian is angered by the Sheriff's attempt to capture the outlaw. At Robin's camp, the man dies after warning of danger at Bawtry. After warning Friar Tuck (Niall MacGinnis), Robin meets the Earl of Newark (Richard Pasco) who, impressed with the outlaw's archery skill, hires him as an assassin to kill a man as yet unnamed.

At Bawtry, the Sheriff attempts to claim an estate for Newark, who plans to build a fortress in defiance of the King. He is blocked by the Archbishop of Canterbury (Jack Gwillim), who is Robin's unnamed target. On the road to London, the Archbishop is joined by Marian. They are ambushed by Newark's men and take refuge in a priory. When the Sheriff learns that Newark plans to kill the holy man, he objects, and is stabbed by Melton (Oliver Reed). Newark attacks the priory and is killed by Robin, who wins Marian's hand and his freedom.

Hammer had planned a sequel to *Men of Sherwood Forest* as early as April, 1957, but

190 *Sword of Sherwood Forest* (1960)

Hammer's second stab at the legend.

the success of the company's science fiction films pushed the film off their schedule. *Sword of Sherwood Forest* finally went into production on May 23, 1960, with a cast far above its material and a star closely identified with his role. Richard Greene spent 1955 to 1958 filming *The Adventures of Robin Hood* for CBS-TV. The series was shot in England, and several episodes were directed by Terence Fisher.

Len Harris recalled for the authors (August, 1993),

> I worked the second unit at Ardmore Studios in Ireland, and nearly lost an eye on that one. We constructed a Saxon Village—all thatched roofs, you know. The Normans were to ride through and set fire to the village. It would have been no problem in England, but they had no horses trained for film work. We would just go around to farms and ask to borrow regular horses! When we waved the torches, the horses panicked. I was working a huge CinemaScope camera, and a horse knocked it on top of me—blood everywhere! It was practically the last shot, so no one was overly concerned. It was lucky it was just *me* that was damaged—we hadn't another camera!

Filming ended on July 8, and *Sword of Sherwood Forest* was trade shown in November. It was released on December 26, 1960, to positive reviews. *The Kinematograph Weekly* (November 24, 1960): "Jolly, disarmingly naive adventure comedy melodrama"; *The New York Times* (January 26, 1961): "Better than usual. This Robin Hood isn't nearly so bedraggled as the last twenty or so"; and *The New York Herald Tribune* (January 25): "There is some effort to make the dialogue sound reasonably lively." The movie's greatest asset is its cast, with Richard Greene charming and professional in the lead. Unfortunately, he was past his physical prime and was a far cry from the role's prototype, Errol Flynn. Peter Cushing, on the side of evil, must have been glad to at least have a *human* adversary for a change. The Sheriff is ruthless and cunning, but there is a limit to what he will do, and Cushing ably suggests the man's complex personality. Nottingham's murder was the film's shocking highlight, as audiences expected a traditional duel to the death between him and Robin. Unfortunately, the film dies with him. The supporting cast, especially Richard Pasco, is fine, but Oliver Reed delivers an embarrassingly awful performance.

Sword of Sherwood Forest, despite its production finesse, good acting, and location photography, fails to excite. Terence Fisher's handling of the fight scenes is so sluggish that the viewer cannot wait for them to end. For a supposed adventure movie, *Sword of Sherwood Forest* is a letdown. A Robin Hood film has *got* to have more action than talk.

Visa to Canton

Released December 26, 1960 (U.K.), February, 1961 (U.S.); 75 minutes; Technicolor (U.K.); B & W (U.S.); 6724 feet; a Hammer-Swallow Production; a Columbia Release; filmed at Bray Studios; Director: Michael Carreras; Producer: Michael Carreras; Associate Producer: Anthony Nelson-Keys; Screenplay: Gordon Wellesley; Director of Photography: Arthur Grant BSC; Music: Edwin Astley; Production Design: Bernard Robinson; Art Director: Thomas Goswell; Supervising Editor: James Needs; Editor: Alfred Cox; Continuity: Tilly Day; Sound: Jock May; Makeup: Roy Ashton; Hairdresser: Frieda Steiger; Wardrobe: Molly Arbuthnot; Assistant Director: Arthur Mann; Production Manager: Clifford Parkes; Assistant Art Director: Don Mingaye; Casting: Stuart Lyons; Stills: Tom Edwards; Second Assistant Director: Dominic Fulford; Sound: Jock May; Camera: Eric Beche; U.S. Title: *Passport to China*; U.K. Certificate: U.

Richard Basehart (Don Benton), Lisa Gastoni (Lola), Athene Seyler (Mao Tai Tai), Eric Pohlmann (Ivano), Allan Gifford (Mr. Orme), Bernard Cribbins (Pereira), Burt Kwouk (Jimmy), Hedgar Wallace (Inspector Taylor), Marne Maitland (Han Po), Milton Reid (Bodyguard), Yvonne Shima (Liang Ti), Robert Lee (Officer), Zoreem Ismail (Sweekim), Paula Lee Shiu (Croupier), Soraya Rafat (Hostess), Gerry Lee Yen (Room Boy), Ronald Ing (Sentry).

Don Benton (Richard Basehart) is an American running a Hong Kong travel agency. A former World War II pilot, he has many contacts within the Asian community, but is unwilling to take sides or spy for the U.S. government. His detachment ends when Mao Tai Tai (Athene Seyler), who sheltered him during the war, tells him her grandson, Jimmy (Burt Kwouk), is missing in Communist China. He knows Jimmy was flying a Nationalist Chinese plane, and that on the plane was Lola Sanchez (Lisa Gastoni), an American agent carrying a vital scientific formula in her memory. Through Kang (Eric Pohlmann), a Russian friend, Benton gets a visa to enter the interior.

He travels to Canton to find Lola, who is willing to sell her information. If Benton can bring her to admit to her disloyalty, he can clear Jimmy's name. Kang is interested in the formula and is killed by Lola when he tries to get it from her. Before Benton can save her, Lola is killed by Kang's bodyguard (Milton Reid). Benton returns to Hong Kong with Jimmy and, again, turns down an offer from the CIA.

Visa to Canton was planned as a pilot for a television series that never was. *The Kinematograph Weekly* (June 16, 1960) reported: "Hammer has postponed its plan to go into television production. *Visa to Canton* is now being shot at Bray as a cinema feature." It is possible that Hammer was still smarting from the failure of *Tales of Frankenstein*.

Hammer attempted to play up the movie's basis in Cold War reality. "It didn't happen," Dennison Thorton wrote in a press release, "but it could happen." The film was on the leading edge of Cold War thrillers, with the Berlin Wall and Cuban missile crisis in the not-too-distant future. The sixties would prove to be a cinematic gold mine for espionage thriller, both fanciful (Ian Fleming's *Dr. No*, 1962) and realistic (John Le Carre's *The Spy Who Came In from the Cold*, 1966). Uncharacteristically, Hammer failed to cash in on a trend they had helped to initiate.

Richard Basehart's casting indicates that Hammer had an eye on the American market. He was a recognizable name in the States through *He Walked by Night* (1948) and *Moby Dick* (1956), and his later success in the sixties series *Voyage to the Bottom of the Sea* confirms Hammer's view of him as a potential television star. Unfortunately, Basehart was unable to lift *Visa from Canton* out of the ordinary. Michael Carreras' routine direction of Gordon Wellesley's routine script resulted in a film that is not difficult to imagine as a television series. One of the few interesting touches is a faint Graham Greene flavor involving Basehart's refusal to work for the American government and his disapproval of its methods. *Visa to Canton* began production at Bray on June 9, 1960, and concluded on July 1. After a November 20 trade show, it went into release on December 26 in Technicolor, although the American print was black and white. *The Kinematograph Weekly* (November 24, 1960) was impressed: "fascinating tale, experienced and popular players, competent direction." *The Monthly Bulletin* (January 1961) disagreed: "an excess of sentimentality and melodrama." Paul V. Beckley, in *The New York Herald Tribune* (March 23) agreed: "uninspired espionage thriller."

Visa to Canton was planned as a television pilot but, with added footage, was released as a feature; the American title was *Passport to China*.

This Hammer-Swallow co-production has little of the company's "feel" and, when compared to its contemporaries, is a mediocre picture in an otherwise outstanding production year.

The Curse of the Werewolf

Released May 1, 1961 (U.K.), June 7, 1961 (U.S.); 88 minutes; Technicolor; 7920 feet; a

The Curse of the Werewolf (1960)

One of Terence Fisher's favorites—and for good reason.

Hammer-Hotspur Production; a Rank Release (U.K.), Universal-International (U.S.); filmed at Bray Studios; Director: Terence Fisher; Producer: Anthony Hinds; Associate Producer: Anthony Nelson-Keys; Executive Producer: Michael Carreras; Screenplay: John Elder, based on Guy Endore's *The Werewolf of Paris*; Director of Photography: Arthur Grant; Music: Benjamin Frankel; Production Design: Bernard Robinson; Art Director: Thomas Goswell; Assistant: Don Mingaye; Supervising Editor: James Needs; Editor: Alfred Cox; Camera: Len Harris; Sound: Jock May; Continuity: Tilly Day; Makeup: Roy Ashton; Wardrobe: Molly Arbuthnot; Hairstyles: Frieda Steiger; Special Effects: Les Bowie; Production Manager: Clifford Parkes; Casting: Stuart Lyons; Stills: Tom Edwards; Assistant Director: John Peverall; 2nd Assistant: Dominic Fulford; U.K. Certificate: X.

Clifford Evans (Professor Carrido), Oliver Reed (Leon), Yvonne Romain (Servant Girl), Catherine Feller (Christina), Anthony Dawson (Marquis), Hira Talfrey (Teresa), Richard Wordsworth (Beggar), Francis De Wolff (Landlord), Warren Mitchell (Pepe), George Woodbridge (Dominique), John Gabriel (Priest), Ewen Solon (Don Fernando), Peter Sallis (Don Enrique), Michael Ripper (Old Soaker), Sheila Brennan (Vera), Martin Matthews (Jose), David Conville (Gomez), Anne Blake (Rosa), Denis Shaw (Gaoler), Josephine Llewellyn (Marquesa), Justin Walters (Young Leon), Renny Lister (Yvonne), Joy Webster (Isabel), John Bennett (Policeman), Charles Lamb (Chief), Desmond Llewellyn (Footman), Gordon Whiting (2nd Footman), Hamlyn Benson (Landlord), Serafina DiLeo (Zumara), Kitty Attwood (Midwife), Howard Lang (Irate Farmer), Stephen W. Scott (Another Farmer), Max Butterfield (Cheeky Farmer), Ray Browne (Official), Frank Siernan

(Gardner), Michael Peake (Farmer in Cantina), Rodney Burke, Alan Page, Richard Golding (Customers), Michael Lewis (Page), Loraine Caruana (Servant Girl as a Child).

When a wandering beggar (Richard Wordsworth) insults the evil Marquis Sinestro (Anthony Dawson) at his wedding feast, the unfortunate tramp is thrown into a dungeon and forgotten by those above. The years pass, and the Marquis, now alone, makes an advance on a mute servant (Yvonne Romain) who, since childhood, has cared for the beggar. As punishment for her rebuff, she is cast into the cell with the now bestial beggar who, unable to control his lust, rapes her and dies of his exertions. After recovering from the assault, she stabs the Marquis and escapes into the forest where she is found, half-dead, by Professor Carrido (Clifford Evans) and is nursed by his housekeeper, Teresa (Hira Talfrey). After giving birth to a boy on Christmas Day, she dies.

Leon (Justin Walters), age six, exhibits signs of being a werewolf. A priest (John Gabriel) explains that due to the vile nature of his birth, Leon's soul has been invaded by a demon, and only love can save him. Due to the care of his adoptive parents, Leon (Oliver Reed) grows to manhood, free of the curse. Working at a winery, he falls in love with Christina (Catherine Feller), daughter of his disapproving employer (Ewen Solon). Frustrated, Leon goes with a co-worker (Martin Matthews) to a brothel and, under the influence of the full moon and his surroundings, murders a prostitute after a horrifying transformation. Now aware of his hidden nature, he begs to have Christina near him after being jailed. Denied her protective influence, he transforms in his cell, killing a fellow prisoner (Michael Ripper). He escapes into a belfry where he is shot dead by the Professor with a silver bullet, as Christina and Teresa embrace tearfully in the courtyard below.

Hammer had a full schedule during the summer of 1960, including *The Rape of Sabena*, which was to use the Spanish Inquisition for a background. A starting date of

Hammer's rising star Oliver Reed in *The Curse of the Werewolf* (photo courtesy of Joey O'Brien).

September 5 was announced, then, as Anthony Hinds recalled (*Fangoria* 74), "We had already built the sets when we got a tip that the Catholic Church would ban the picture. So Michael Carreras pulled out, and I was left with these sets." *The Curse of the Werewolf*, which was next in line, was moved up as a replacement. Based on Guy Endore's novel *The Werewolf of Paris*, the locale was changed to accommodate the sets. Hinds, to save money, wrote the script under the pseudonym "John Elder."

The Curse of the Werewolf was the first Hammer horror in color without the services of Peter Cushing or Christopher Lee. Hammer was banking on the exploitative title and an untried—but potentially explosive—young actor to take up the slack. Oliver Reed, only 22, had previously appeared in a half-dozen small roles, and had impressed Michael Carreras with his performance as a nightclub tough in *The Two Faces of Dr. Jekyll*. Even so, he was only one of 17 actors tested for the part. "We wanted an actor," said Terence Fisher in the Universal pressbook, "who could look really ferocious, scowl like thunder, and snarl terrifyingly." Makeup man Roy Ashton saw

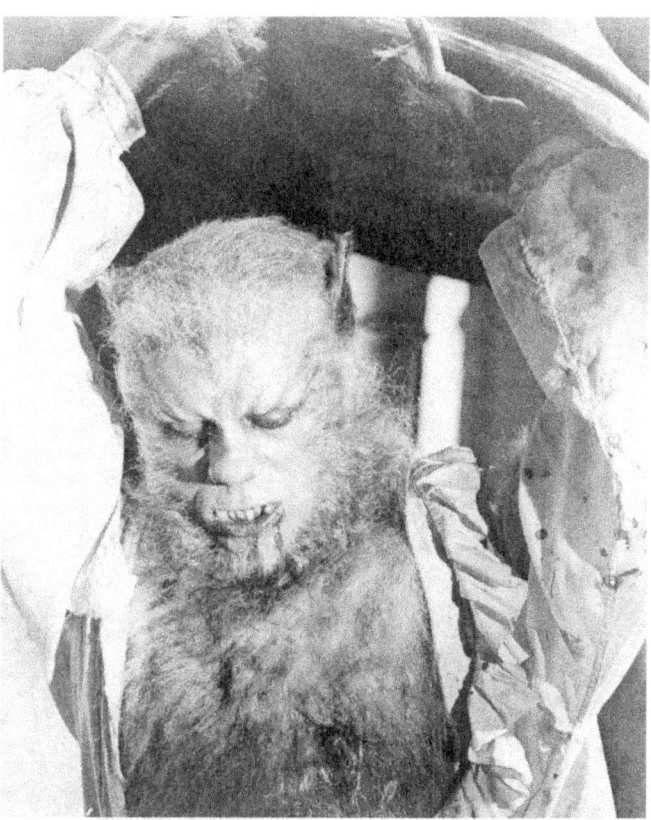

Oliver Reed in Roy Ashton's outstanding makeup from *The Curse of the Werewolf*.

those qualities in Reed. "I suggested Oliver to Tony Keys," Ashton said in *Fandom's Film Gallery*, "because he looked exactly right, especially in the structure of his bones. He already looked like half a wolf when he was getting angry anyway. He was most cooperative. He was a really professional chap and very ambitious at the time because the film offered him his big chance. Nothing was too much trouble." Len Harris recalled for the authors (December, 1993), "Oliver was an eager young man, and we all liked him. While I don't think any of us predicted international stardom, you could tell he would make it. He was interested in all that was going on, and was a real pleasure to work with." Michael Ripper (March, 1993) agreed. "Oliver was a young man on the way up. He knew what he wanted out of the business and was determined to get it—there was no holding him back. He was a real pro-

fessional and a lot of fun. I don't mind saying that he scared me in the werewolf scene we did together." Margaret Robinson (August, 1993) summed up Reed's persona: "Oliver was such a nice young man—polite, eager, but with an edge. It was the edge that made him the werewolf." Reed himself was more to the point. "They knew I looked the part already," he said in *The New York Times* (October 29, 1967), "so I got it and learned a lot."

Terence Fisher thought highly of Reed's performance. "Not since Valentino," he said (*House of Hammer 10*), "have I known such a personality produce such an instantaneous and devastating effect." Fisher was also justifiably proud of the film. "Please don't call this a horror film," he said in *Fandom's Film Gallery*, "call it an adult fairy tale with emotional, tragic, and, if you like, moral overtones." Although *The Curse of the Werewolf* is generally thought to be one of Hammer's most savage horrors, the title monster is hardly on screen at all. Fisher's skillful direction makes the film *seem* more graphic than it is. Harry Ringel pointed out (*Cinefantastique*, Vol. 4, No. 5) that the movie "spends more time preparing a sordid context for the appearance of the monster than on the creature itself."

Censor John Trevelyan must have had nightmares over the rape committed by the animalistic beggar, and one awkward cut is evident. Since the scene is crucial to the story, it had to remain. Roy Ashton (*Fandom's Film Gallery*) felt the film told "a really disgusting story," and was amused that "at the pre-production conference, the producer said, 'I think we have a jolly good picture here, but we've got to have it finished in six weeks to deliver it to America to release it for the children's holidays.'" After the film

196 *The Curse of the Werewolf* (1960)

Although Oliver Reed wanted to perform this dangerous scene he was replaced by a stuntman for insurance purposes.

was concluded on November 2, 1960, it was released on April 12, 1961, co-featured with *Shadow of the Cat* to mixed reviews. *The Kinematograph Weekly* (April 17): "The picture eschews wholesome blood and guts, and delves into murky eugenics for its thrills..."; *Variety* (May 3): "An elaborate yet meticulous production, a value characteristic of England's Hammer Films"; *The New York Times* (June 8): "A little different from the run-of-the-mill horror species"; and *The Monthly Bulletin* (June): "Even by Hammer standards, this is a singularly repellent job."

The Curse of the Werewolf, unlike Universal's excellent *The Wolf Man* (1941), spawned no sequels so it is likely that the movie did not perform up to Hammer's expectations. Due to the lack of screen time given to its monster, *The Curse of the Werewolf* is not embraced by all horror fans, either. State-of-the-art special effects, like in *The Howling* (1981), far outshine Hammer's minimal attempt at a man-to-wolf

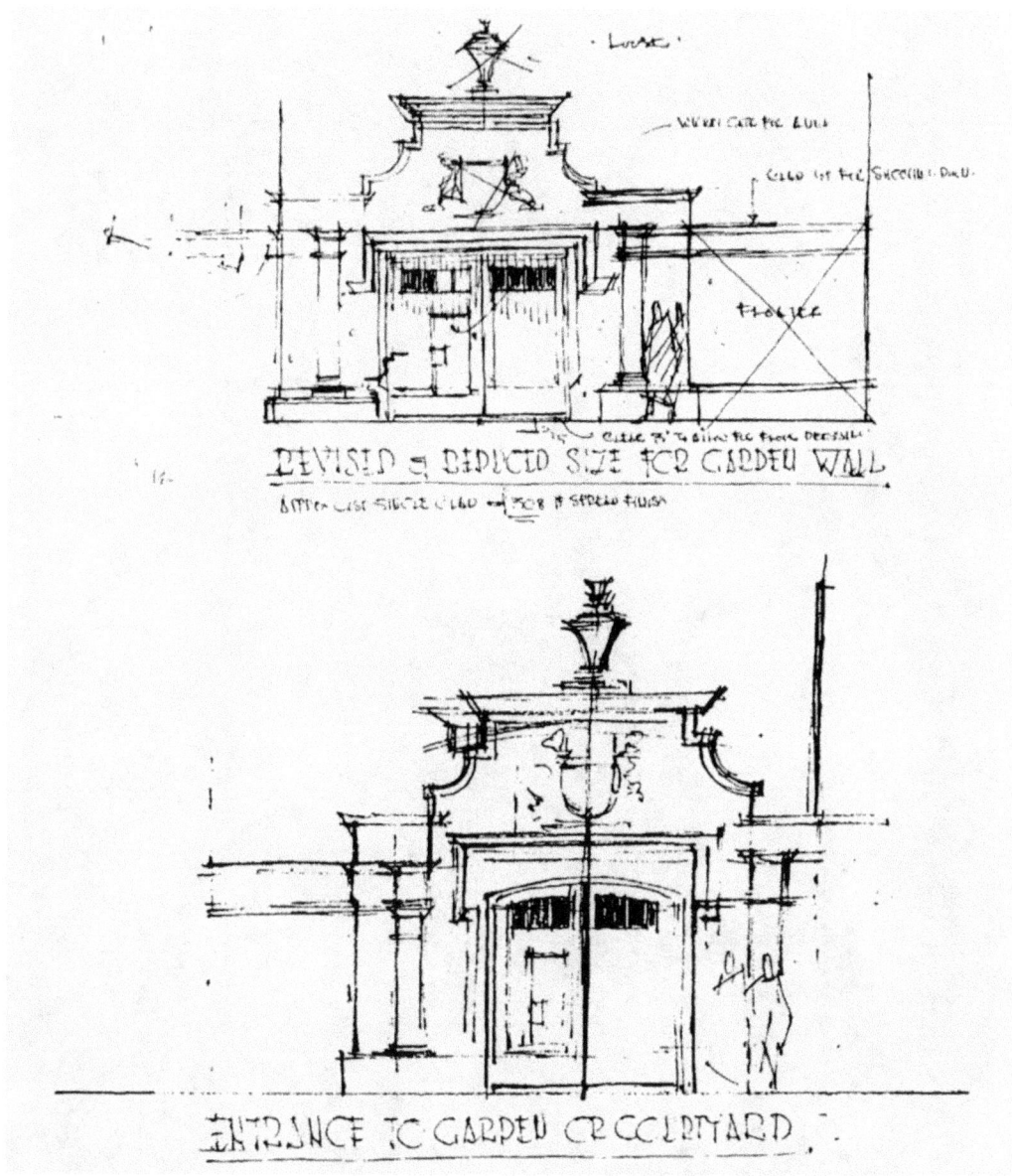

Top: Bernard Robinson's original design for the village gate in *The Curse of the Werewolf*. *Bottom:* A Bernard Robinson original design for *The Curse of the Werewolf* (both designs courtesy of Margaret and Peter Robinson).

transformation. There are no dissolves into different makeup stages, but it is unlikely that a first-time viewer will notice, due to Terence Fisher's staging and Oliver Reed's acting. Fortunately, *The Curse of the Werewolf* does not rely on effects to capture an audience. For those who give it a chance, it is a Hammer horror with a heart.

A Weekend with Lulu

Released May, 1961 (U.K.), November 1, 1961 (U.S.); 89 minutes (U.K.), 91 minutes (U.S.); B & W; 8010 feet; a Hammer Film Production; a Columbia Release; filmed at Shepperton Studios; Director: John Paddy Carstairs; Producer: Ted Lloyd; Executive Producer: Michael Car-

A Weekend with Lulu (1960)

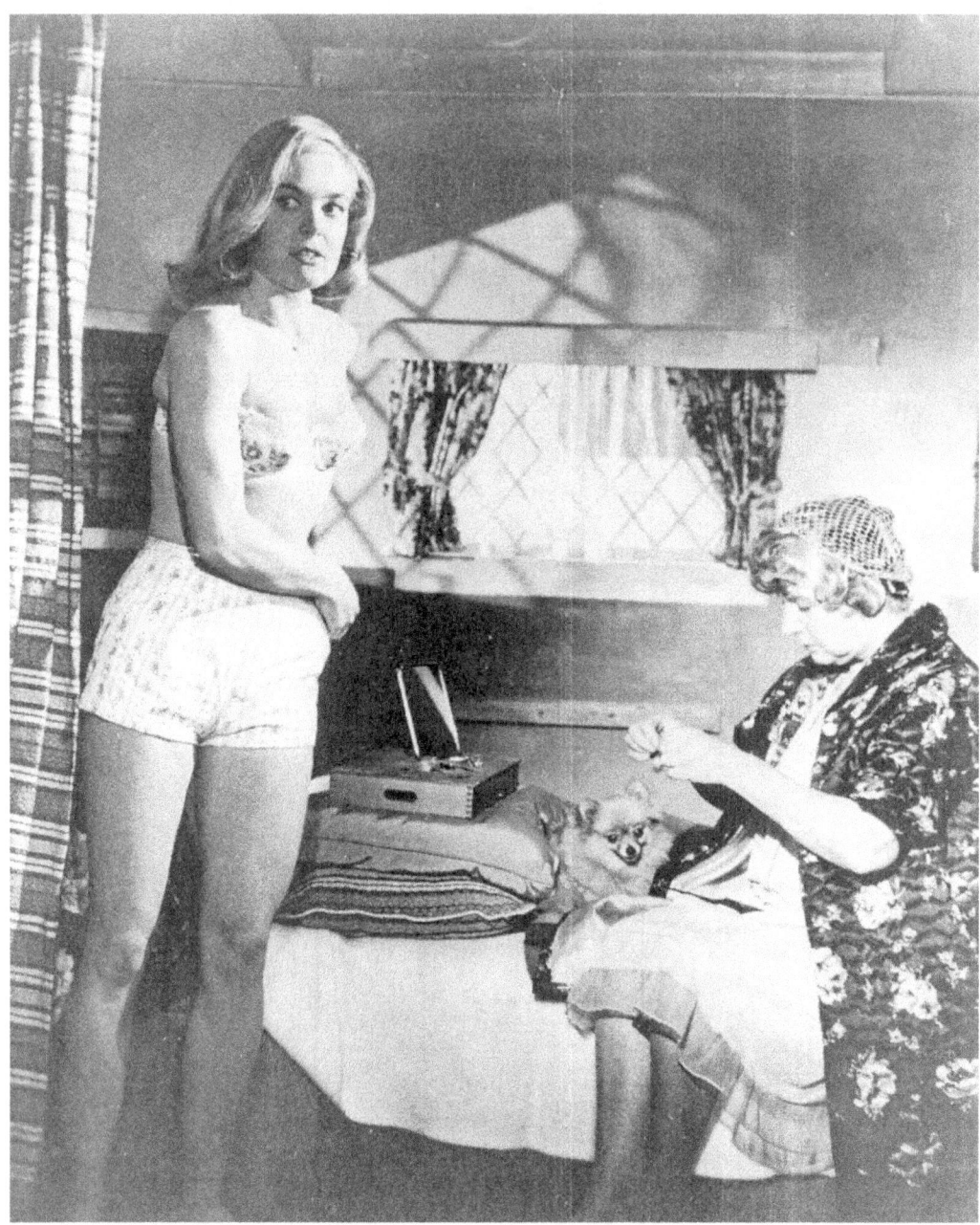

Shirley Eaton, dressed to kill, inside "Lulu" in *Weekend with Lulu*.

reras; Screenplay: Ted Lloyd; Original Story: Ted Lloyd and Val Valentine; Director of Photography: Ken Hodges; Music: Trevor H. Sanford; Conducted by: Tony Osborne; Supervising Editor: James Needs; Editor: Tom Simpson; Art Director: John Howell; Production Manager: Jacques De Lanc Lea; Camera: Brian Wert; Assistant Director: Chris Sutton: 2nd Assistant Director: Patrick Hayes; Continuity: Splinters Deason; Sound: Bill Salter; Makeup: Dick Bonner-Morris; Hairdresser: Bill Griffiths; Wardrobe Mistress: Maude Churchill; Art Department Assistant: Helen Thomas; Casting Director: Stuart Lyons; Stills Cameraman: Robert Penn; 3rd Assistant Director: Michael Klaw; Production Buyer: Charles Townsend; Boom: Tom Buchanan;

A Weekend with Lulu (1960)

Actually, "Lulu" is not wearing high heels—she's the trailer.

Publicity: Dennison Thorton; Dubbing Editor: Alan Morrison; Accountant: W. Able; Construction Manager: Jack Bolam; Grip: M. Walters; Transportation: L.C. Whenman, Peter Willetts; Clapper: Bob Stillwell; U.K. Certificate: A.

Shirley Eaton (Diedre), Leslie Phillips (Tim), Bob Monkhouse (Fred), Alfred Marks (Count de Grenable), Irene Handl (Florence), Heidi Erich, Sally Douglas, Marie Devereux, Eve Eden, Janette Rowsell (The Lulubelles).

Tim (Leslie Phillips) and Diedre (Shirley Eaton), his girlfriend, borrow Fred's (Bob Monkhouse) ice cream van named "Lulu"—and "Fred"—to take them on holiday. Unfortunately, Diedre's mother, Florence (Irene Handl), insists on joining them since she distrusts Tim and her daughter. Also unfortunately, Fred accidentally drives into a channel ferry, and the foursome are astounded to find themselves in France. Since they lack passports and money, they are immediately in trouble. Adding to their problems are a cross-section of France's leading troublemakers, including the Count de Grenable (Alfred Marks) and a crew of "working girls" (Heidi Erich, Sally Douglas, Marie Devereux, Eve Eden, and Janette Rowsell). To raise money to return home, Tim and Fred involve themselves with a swindler trying to "fix" the Tour de France bicycle race. This fails, and just when it seems they will never get home, Lulu is mistaken for an ambulance and loaded onto an air freighter.

"There just happens to be a desperate shortage of pictures," Michael Carreras said (*The Daily Cinema*, December 10, 1960). "There's no excuse for any producer being out of work today." He had every reason to gloat, as Hammer was now at the top of the British film industry. He was aware that *A Weekend with Lulu* probably would not do well in America, but so what! Hammer was so successful that it could occasionally make a film for just the domestic market. "I think there is a great place for purely domestic pictures," he said, "provided they are budgeted realistically." Carreras felt that many British filmmakers failed because they were *too* concerned with the overseas market. "They spend extra money to guarantee success abroad, then find that the extra money they spent is the difference between profit and loss."

Carreras saw Hammer soon splitting into two groups—one to continue making "exploitation" films, and one to make more "thoughtful" pictures. "During 1961," he said, "we plan to make at least three stories in this mould." He was also planning a western that would "explode the legend of the heroic western gunfighter." Actually, not much of what Hammer produced in 1961 seems terribly "thoughtful," and Carreras made the western, *The Savage Guns*, for his own Capricorn Productions. "It may well be in two or three years' time, we will form a new company with a new title to take care of our 'straighter' productions," Carreras speculated. Sadly, three years later, Hammer was making films like *The Curse of the Mummy's Tomb*.

Hammer's latest comedy was part of a five picture pact with Columbia, and began production on October 6, 1960, winding up on December 10. Due to the film's "lowbrow" appeal, it did not open in London, but in Halifax on April 10, 1961. This proved to be a wise decision, as the movie attracted huge crowds. Reviews were slightly favorable. *Variety* (May 16, 1962): "A diverting item"; *Show Business Illustrated* (November 28, 1961): "All in all, a lulu?"; *Newsday* (May 17, 1962): "It slows down enough for audiences to catch on to the obviousness of its humor and plot"; and *Film Daily* (no date): "Zestful British-made comedy."

A hard look at the cast and credits reveals few Hammer "names"—it seems as though the picture was made by another company with Hammer's name slapped on to it. Comedy travels less well than other genres, and what's funny in the U.K. is not necessarily funny in the U.S.—and vice versa. Stereotypes are different from one society to another, and topical references date quickly. As a result, *A Weekend with Lulu* does not seem terribly funny thirty years later, but it apparently did the job when it counted.

Taste of Fear

Released April, 1961 (U.K.), August, 1961 (U.S.); 90 minutes (U.K.), 81 minutes (U.S.); B & W; a Hammer Film Production; a Columbia Release (U.S.); filmed at A.B.P.C. Studios, Elstree, England; Director: Seth Holt; Producer, Screenplay: Jimmy Sangster; Executive Producer: Michael Carreras; Assistant Director: David Tomblin; Music: Clifton Parker; Musical Supervisor: John Hollingsworth; Director of Photography: Douglas Slocombe; Production Designer: Bernard Robinson; Supervising Editor: James Needs; Production Manager: Bill Hill; Editor: Eric Boyd-Perkins; Camera: Desmond Davis; Sound Recordist: Leslie Hammond; Sound: Ted Mason, Len Shilton; Continuity: Pamela Mann; Sound Editor: James Groom; Makeup: Basil Newall; Hair Stylist: Eileen Bates; Wardrobe: Dora Lloyd; Casting Director: Stuart Lyons; Art Director: Tom Goswell; Stills Photographer: George Higgins; Publicity Director: Dennison Thornton; Unit Publicist: Colin Reed; Assistant Art Director: Bill Constable; Second Assistant Director: Terry Lens; U.S. Title: *Scream of Fear*; U.K. Certificate: X.

Susan Strasberg (Penny Appleby), Ronald Lewis (Bob), Ann Todd (Jane Appleby), Christopher Lee (Dr. Gerrard), John Serret (Inspector Legrand), Leonard Sachs (Spratt), Anne Blake (Marie), Fred Johnson (Father), Bernard Brown (Gendarme), Richard Klee (Plainclothes Sergeant), Mme. Lobegue (Swiss Air Hostess).

Penny Appleby (Susan Strasberg), a cripple, has come to France at the request of her father. Meeting her at the airport is Robert (Ronald Lewis), the chauffeur, who tells her that her father is away on business. That night, Penny talks to her stepmother Jane (Ann Todd) about Maggie, her former nurse and companion, who drowned. Penny admits she nearly killed herself afterwards because they were close friends. Later, Penny sees a light in her father's summer house. Wheeling herself across the terrace, Penny enters the cottage and sees the corpse of her father (Fred Johnson) in a chair. Penny screams out and tries to wheel herself back to the main house, but the wheels of her chair hit the edge of the pool and she is thrown into the water.

Rescued by Robert, Penny tries to convince Jane and Dr. Gerrard (Christopher Lee), a family friend, that she saw the now-

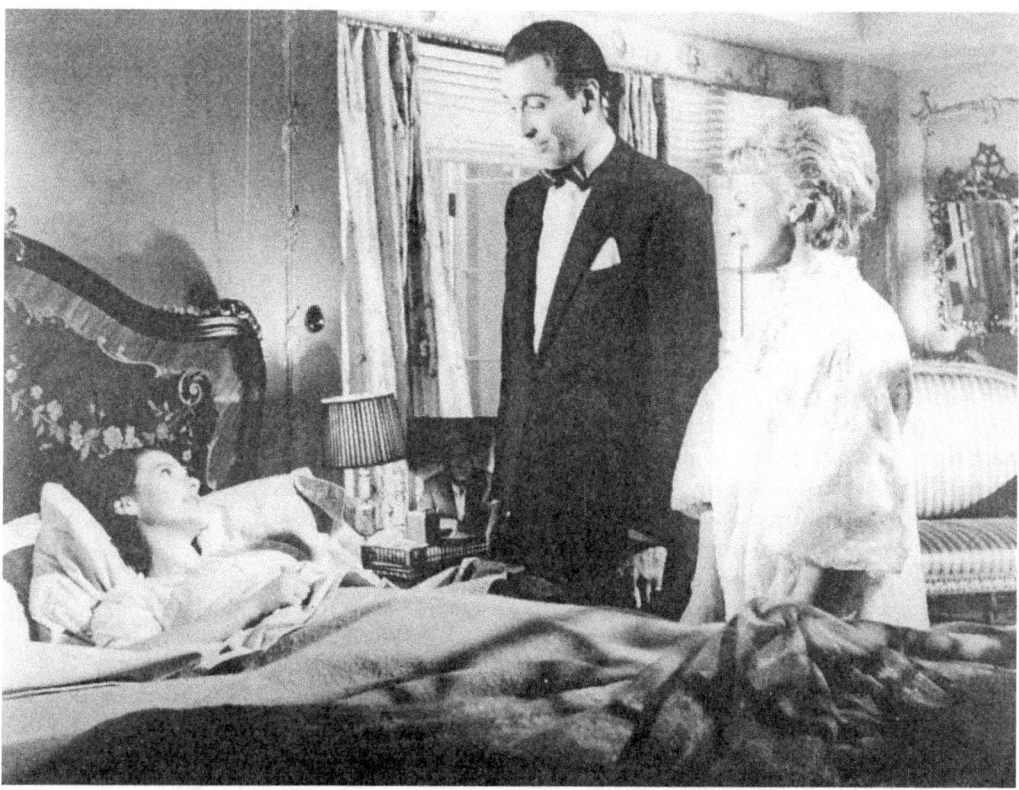

Susan Strasberg, Christopher Lee and Ann Todd in *Taste of Fear* (courtesy of Tim Murphy).

missing body. That night, Penny finds the corpse in her bedroom but once again it disappears. When Robert asks about her father's will, Penny explains that she is the primary beneficiary, but that Jane stands to inherit everything if Penny becomes incompetent or if she dies. Robert says he believes that Jane and Dr. Gerrard may have murdered her father and are trying to have Penny institutionalized before producing the body for the police to find. Robert eventually finds the body at the bottom of the pool. While driving to police headquarters, Penny and Robert see Jane standing at the side of the road. When Robert leaves the car to talk to Jane, the brakes slip and the vehicle rolls away. As the car sails off a cliff into the sea below, Penny sees her father's body lying on the floor of the front seat.

The next day, Jane tells Inspector Legrand (John Serret) that Penny was riding with her father when the accident occurred. Robert later accompanies the inspector as police frogmen dive at the accident site. Jane remains at home to discuss her husband's will with a lawyer. When she asks if there might be a delay due to the fact that father and daughter died together, the puzzled lawyer tells Jane that the woman in the car could not have been Penny because *she* committed suicide weeks before. At the same time, Inspector Legrand informs Robert that Appleby's body was the only one found in the vehicle.

The lawyer is about to leave when he asks who the young woman in the wheelchair near the cliffs is. Jane looks out and realizes that the woman who claimed to be Penny was Maggie! Maggie tells Jane that she assumed her friend's identity to expose Jane's murder plot, and that she has been working with Dr. Gerrard. Maggie walks inside as Jane drops into the wheelchair and weeps. Robert sees Jane in the chair and, believing her to be Penny, pushes it over the cliff. Dr. Gerrard and the police arrive and Robert is arrested.

Although Hammer had produced similar films, *Taste of Fear* is generally recognized as the first of the company's loosely connected "series" of psychological thrillers, and is certainly the best of the group. All five, including *Maniac*, *Paranoiac*, *Nightmare*, and *Hysteria*, were written by Jimmy Sangster and shot in black and white. "The one that I liked the best," he told the authors, "was *Taste of Fear*. I simply thought it was a good movie." Hammer nearly lost out on one of their most profitable films, as Sangster initially took his story to producer Sidney Box. Sangster recalled:

> I actually wrote it for Sidney. I was going to produce it for him, but Sidney had a heart attack. So, it was turned over to another company who didn't particularly want to make it; so I said, "I'll buy it back from you." But I added, "Give me a week—I want to make sure I can sell it to someone else!" I rushed over to see Michael Carreras, and I said I also wanted to produce it. That was my first as producer. Once the film starts, the producer's done his job. As a writer, however, I wouldn't have gone to Nice, but as a producer, well... If you've chosen your people right—director, unit manager—you shouldn't have anything to do. But you usually do. You have to make artistic decisions.

Taste of Fear was shot at Elstree and on location in France from October 24 to December 7, 1960. The picture was released during Easter week in April, 1961, to generally good reviews: *The Daily Express* (March 30): "Audiences will either be scared out of their wits or bored, like the corpse, stiff"; *The Dispatch* (April 2): "What thrills we'd

The first of Hammer's "Psycho-series," *Taste of...* became *Scream of Fear* in America.

been promised get dissipated by the nonsensical denouement"; *Cue* (August 26): "A taut, scary, well-acted little murder mystery"; *Variety* (August 9): "Contrived but expertly executed mystery shocker"; and *The New Yorker* (August 26): "I think Dad will make your flesh creep, as he did mine."

Taste of Fear also scored at the box office, becoming one of Columbia's top grossers for the year, helped by its ingenious ad campaign. The poster consisted of a screaming Susan Strasberg inside concentric circles, and was voted best of the year by the MPAA International Film Relations Committee. The film's success also solidified Hammer's relationship with Columbia, which had distributed six of the company's nine films in 1960. By associating with the Hollywood majors, Hammer availed itself to new American talent like Susan Strasberg, who is quite impressive in the lead. She made both her Broadway (*The Diary of Anne Frank*) and film (*The Cobweb*) debut in 1955. As the daughter of famed acting instructor Lee Strasberg, she was Hollywood "royalty." Ann Todd also had a "name" value that added to the film's prestige. Ronald Lewis is convincingly sympathetic—until the twist—but fourth-billed Christopher Lee could do little with his underwritten part. Director Seth Holt was considered to be a budding Hitchcock by many, but weight and alcohol problems diminished his career and contributed to a fatal heart attack in 1971.

Jimmy Sangster made his first of many trips to America on March 15, 1961, to deliver the print to Columbia's New York office. He was joined the next day by Michael Carreras, who told reporters (*The Daily Cinema*, March 20) about the "old days" at Bray. "Jimmy was the tea boy," he said, "and I looked after the petty cash."

The Shadow of the Cat

Released May 1, 1961 (U.K.), June 7, 1961 (U.S.); 79 minutes; B & W; 7110 feet; a Jon Pennington–Hammer Production, A.B.H.P. Film; a Rank Organization Release (U.K.), a Universal-International Release (U.S.); filmed at Bray Studios, England; Director: John Gilling; Producer: Jon Pennington; Screenplay: George Baxt; Director of Photography: Arthur Grant; Music Composed and Conducted by: Mikas Theodorakis; Production Design: Bernard Robinson; Art Director: Don Mingaye; Supervising Editor: James Needs; Sound: Jock May, Ken Cameron; Sound Editor: Alban Streeter; Production Manager: Don Weeks; 1st Assistant Director: Jon Peverall; Makeup: Roy Ashton; Hairstyles: Frieda Steiger; Wardrobe: Molly Arbuthnot; Special Effects: Les Bowie; Camera: Len Harris; Editor: John Pomeroy; 2nd Assistant Director: Dominic Fulford; Continuity: Tilly Day; Casting Director: Stuart Lyons; Stills Camera: Tom Edwards; Cat Trainer: John Holmes; U.K. Certificate: X.

Andre Morell (Walter Venable), Barbara Shelley (Elizabeth Venable), Freda Jackson (Clara), William Lucas (Jacob), Conrad Phillips (Michael Latimer), Alan Wheatley (Inspector Rowles), Andrew Crawford (Andrew), Catherine Lacey (Ella Venable), Vanda Godsell (Louise), Richard Warner (Edgar), Henry Kendall (Doctor), Kynaston Reeves (Grandfather), John Dearth (Constable Hamer), Fred Stone, George Doonan (Ambulance Men), Charles Stanley (Dobbins), Vera Cook (Mother), Rodney Burke (Workman), Howard Knight (Boy), Kevin Stoney (Father), Angela Crow (Daughter), Tabatha (cat).

Confined to the attic study of her ancient Victorian mansion, wealthy Ella Venable (Catherine Lacey) is forced by her domineering husband Walter (Andre Morell) to rewrite her last will, naming him her sole heir. She is later murdered by her servant Andrew (Andrew Crawford) and buried in the nearby woods by Walter, Andrew and housekeeper Clara (Freda Jackson). The police are baffled by Ella's reported "disappearance" and the three murderers' only concern is with Ella's cat Tabatha, who witnessed the killing and the burial. Walter sends for his brother Edgar (Richard Warner) and Edgar's son Jacob (William Lucas) to dispose of the cat. The crafty cat causes Andrew to topple into a bog and drown, sends Clara on a deadly tumble down a flight of stairs and frightens Walter into a fatal heart attack. Jacob searches for Ella's original will (in which her niece Elizabeth [Barbara Shelley] was named sole heir), and falls from the roof after another run-in with Tabatha. Edgar is killed by a roof cave-in while chasing the cat. Elizabeth's newsman-boyfriend Michael Latimer (Conrad Phillips) and the police inspector (Alan Wheatley) find Ella's true will and Elizabeth inherits the estate.

Although occasionally missing from Hammer filmographies, there is no doubt that *The Shadow of the Cat* was a Hammer production. "We took the idea to Hammer in the fall of 1960," writer-producer George Baxt told the authors in 1993, "and for what-

Walter Venable (Andre Morell) gets what's coming to him in *The Shadow of the Cat*.

ever reason, they turned us down. Then, in late November, they got back to us. A film that they'd already built sets for fell through, and they thought that the sets and costumes would be perfect for *Shadow of the Cat*. It *was* a Hammer Production, but the name 'Hammer' doesn't appear on the credits." The "we" Baxt spoke of were himself, - Richard Hatton, and Jon Pennington who formed BHP Productions. Hammer's current management also confirms the film as its own.

The Shadow of the Cat was filmed in just over five weeks between November 14 and December 24, 1960. The cast, especially Andre Morell, Barbara Shelley, and Freda Jackson, was far superior to the picture. Morell had last acted for Hammer as Dr. Watson in *The Hound of the Baskervilles* and deserved something better than this minor effort. He was one of the best actors that the company used regularly, in an association that ranged from *Stolen Face* to *The Vengeance of She*. The best part in *The Shadow of the Cat* went, unfortunately, to Tabatha who played the cat. Baxt recalled that director John Gilling arranged for several look-alikes to be used as doubles. "Two ran away during the scene in the swamp, and I think one was stolen. We used a mouse to get one of the cats to jump on Freda Jackson." Actually, if Baxt had gotten his way, there would have been *no* cats used. In his script, the cat "existed only in the minds of the evil doers. I was trying for a Val Lewton—*Cat People* type effect." Gilling disagreed, and the cat became the film's main character. Since the key action scenes are "seen" through the cat's eyes, cinematographer Arthur Grant used a distorting anamorphic lens and shot close to ground level.

"We could have made it as an 'A' certificate subject," said Jon Pennington, "but as it will go out with Hammer's *Curse of the Werewolf*, we are deliberately shooting for an 'X.'" This rating was questioned by *The Kinematograph Weekly* after the film's May 1, 1961, release. "A fascinating and suspenseful

"Interesting in spots, for cat lovers." *The Shadow of the Cat* was not one of Hammer's best efforts and seems even weaker for its being filmed during the company's most creative period. However, it *was* an adequate support for *The Curse of the Werewolf*, and that was all it was intended to be.

1961

Watch It, Sailor!

Released August 14, 1961 (U.K.); 89 minutes; B & W; 7289 feet; a Hammer Film Production; a Columbia/BLC Release; filmed at Bray Studios; Director: Wolf Rilla; Producer: Maurice Cowan; Associate Producer: Anthony Nelson-Keys; Executive Producer: Michael Carreras; Screenplay: Falkland Carey, Philip King, based on their stage play; Director of Photography: Arthur Grant; Music: Douglas Gamley; Music Director: John Hollingsworth; Production Design: Bernard Robinson; Supervising Editor: James Needs; Editor: Albert Cox; Production Manager: Clifford Parkes; Camera: Len Harris; Continuity: Tilly Day; Sound: Jock May; Makeup: Roy Ashton; Hairdresser: Frieda Steiger; Wardrobe Mistress: Rosemary Burrows; Casting: Stuart Lyon; Stills: Tom Edwards; Assistant Director: John Peverall; 2nd Assistant Director: Dominic Fulford; Art Director: Don Mingaye; U.K. Certificate: U.

Dennis Price (Lt. Cmdr. Hardcastle), Liz Fraser (Daphne), Irene Handl (Edie Hardcastle), Graham Stark (Bligh), Vera Day (Shirley), Marjorie Rhodes (Ma Hornett), Cyril Smith (Mr. Hornett), John Meillon (Tufnell), Frankie Howerd (Organist), Miriam Karlin (Mrs. Lack), Arthur Howard (Vicar), Renee Houston (Mrs. Mottram), Brian Reece (Solicitor), Bobby Howes (Drunk), Harry Locke (Ticket Collec-

A very satisfying early sixties double feature.

creepie, put over without recourse to cheap blood-chilling tricks." Others were less impressed. *The Monthly Film Bulletin* (June): "Fatally lacking in nuance and atmosphere"; *Variety* (May 3): "Adequate horror item"; and *The New York Herald Tribune* (June 8):

Hammer's last military comedy, *Watch It, Sailor!*

tor), William Mervyn (Captain), Marianne Stone (Woman), Diane Aubrey (Barmaid).

Seaman Albert Tufnell (John Meillon) cannot decide between the joy of marrying Shirley Hornett (Vera Day) and the horror of having Mrs. Hornett (Marjorie Rhodes) as his mother-in-law. On his way to the church with Bligh (Graham Stark), their car breaks down, and when they finally arrive, the wedding party is gone. They rush to the Hornetts' home, and after he receives a brutal tongue-lashing, a new date is set. But, this time Albert is left at the altar. It seems that he was born out of wedlock, and there is a question about his legal name, which Ma plans to use to keep Shirley single. The couple have other plans—they decide on a honeymoon first, and to marry later. They get as far as the train station when Ma catches up. The misunderstanding cleared up, they are now free to marry, but Shirley's cousin Daphne (Liz Fraser) has run off with Bligh!

Watch It, Sailor! was Hammer's fifth and last "service comedy." Filmed for the domestic market, the previous four comedies were successful within the limits Hammer placed upon them and introduced their product to those not interested in horror. One of the company's strengths was its ability to capitalize on a success in another medium. *Watch It, Sailor!*, a sequel to *Sailor Beware*, was written by Philip King and Falkland Carey, and had been a hit on the London stage. Hammer had considerable success with *Up the Creek* and its sequel, so another shot at a "service comedy" seemed right.

The production closed on March 1, 1961, completing a five week schedule, and it was released on August 14 to mostly negative reviews and little box office excitement. *The Kinematograph Weekly* (July 6): "Its humor, verbal rather than physical, produces a mere trickle of laughs"; and *The Monthly Bulletin* (July): "Slack direction and a flat-footed adaptation." The "slack direction" was by Wolf Rilla, whose career spanned three decades and produced one classic—*Village* of the Damned (1960). Since the script was written by the authors of the hit play, it seems that the film's failure was caused by Rilla's inability to punch the humor across. The box office performance of *Watch It, Sailor!* must have been terrible, since Hammer waited ten years before filming another (intentional) comedy.

Cash on Demand

Released December 20, 1961 (U.S.), December 15, 1963 (U.K.); 84 minutes (U.S.), 66 minutes (U.K.), Copyright length 77 minutes; B & W; a Hammer-Woodpecker Production; a British Lion Release (U.K.), a Columbia Release (U.S.); filmed at Bray Studios, England; Director: Quentin Lawrence; Producer: Anthony Nelson-Keys; Executive Producer: Michael Carreras; Screenplay: David T. Chantler, Lewis Greifer, based on the play *The Gold Inside* by Jacques Gillies; Music: Wilfrid Josephs; Music Supervisor: John Hollingsworth; Director of Photography: Arthur Grant; Production Design: Bernard Robinson; Art Director: Don Mingaye; Supervising Editor: James Needs; Editor: Eric Boyd-Perkins; Production Manager: Clifford Parkes; Sound Recordist: Jock May; Sound Editor: Alban Streeter; Camera Operator: Len Harris; Assistant Director: John Peverall; Continuity: Tilly Day; Makeup: Roy Ashton; Wardrobe Supervisor: Molly Arbuthnot; Wardrobe Mistress: Rosemary Burrows; Hairstyles: Frieda Steiger; Casting Director: Stuart Lyons; Assistant Director: John Peverall; U.K. Certificate: A.

Peter Cushing (Fordyce), Andre Morell (Hepburn), Richard Vernon (Pearson), Barry Lowe (Harvill), Norman Bird (Sanderson), Edith Sharpe (Miss Pringle), Charles Morgan (Collins), Kevin Stoney (Det. Mason), Alan Haywood (Kane), Lois Daine (Sally), Vera Cook (Mrs. Fordyce), Gareth Tandy (Tommy), Fred Stone (Window Cleaner).

The Christmas spirit infecting the staff of a provincial bank has eluded its prissy, petty manager, Mr. Fordyce (Peter Cushing), who is universally disliked. After giving Pearson (Richard Vernon) an unjustified reprimand, Fordyce is unsettled by the arrival of an insurance investigator, the intimidating Colonel Hepburn (Andre Morell). The staff fails to check "Hepburn's" credentials—he is actually a bank robber.

The "Colonel," through a phone call from Mrs. Fordyce, convinces her husband that unless he complies, his family will be killed. Hepburn is as interested in Fordyce's miserable personality as he is in the vault, and offers him hints on how to improve it. To atone for his misdemeanors, Pearson makes a check-up call to London, but it is delayed.

Hepburn and Fordyce descend to the vault with the "Colonel's" empty luggage and, after a few close calls, emerge with £93,000. After warning Fordyce that his family is still in danger, Hepburn—with a cheery word for all—drives off. Pearson's call is finally connected, and he learns of the "Colonel's" deception. Unaware of the consequences, Pearson calls the police, then confronts Fordyce with his suspicions. Fordyce begs him to tell the police a msitake was made, explaining that his family is in danger. Pearson and the staff support the lie, but Detective Mason (Kevin Stoney) has already apprehended Hepburn.

Unnerved by Hepburn's return, Fordyce foolishly implicates himself in the robbery, but the "Colonel"—for reasons of his own—admits he faked Mrs. Fordyce's phone call with a tape recording. Freed from suspicion, grateful for his staff's loyalty, and ashamed of his conduct, Fordyce is a changed man.

Cash on Demand was one of Hammer's best films, and an atypical sixties production that was reminiscent of the company's productions a decade earlier. Based on Jacques Gillies' play *The Gold Inside* (which aired on the London ATV network on September 24, 1960), the Hammer-Woodpecker production began on April 4, 1961. "This was an unusual picture for Hammer to have made," Len Harris told the authors (December, 1993). "It was basically a two character drama. I remember thinking as we were doing it that the picture would have worked just as well if Peter and Andre had switched roles. How many actors are that versatile? Both men were kind, considerate, and professional—always a delight to work with. Hammer got Quentin Lawrence to direct because of his television experience. He was very quick and efficient. I was actually director of photography for a few days when

Cash on Demand (1961)

Colonel Hepburn (Andre Morell) keeps up the pressure as he waits for Fordyce (Peter Cushing) to open the bank vault in *Cash on Demand*.

Arthur Grant became ill, and I stood in for him. We could do things like that in those days—the unions weren't quite so fussy! I did the robbery scene."

Peter Cushing was grateful for the break from horror movies, telling interviewer Patricia Lewis, "I was sort of carried along with the cycle. It was wonderful to work steadily on from one film to the next, but then a few weeks ago, I realized that most were X certificate." He described Fordyce as "a martinet, a man who lacks charity and warmth. In his office, as a manager of a bank, he is stern, forbidding. He derives satisfaction from holding the threat of dismissal over his staff. This, then, is the man who

Hammer's version of Charles Dickens' *A Christmas Carol*.

1961, but the British premiere came two years later. Reviews were, justifiably, positive. *The Monthly Film Bulletin* (December, 1963): "A neat and quite freshly conceived robbery thriller"; *The Kinematograph Weekly* (November 19, 1963): "Sound acting by all, especially by the two principals"; and *The New York Times* (May 17, 1962): "Neat and unpretentious." Why Hammer stopped making films like this is a mystery, as is the cause of its seeming disappearance. Not only is the film seldom shown on television, it often goes unmentioned in film guides. *Cash on Demand* is an example of the excellence the company was capable of, but seldom achieved after the fifties. With its drama, suspense, humor, and insight, *Cash on Demand* is everything one could want from a movie. It is Hammer's version of *A Christmas Carol*, and a very good one at that.

The Damned

Released May 20, 1963 (U.K.), July 7, 1965 (U.S.); 87 minutes (U.K.), 77 minutes (U.S.); B & W; Hammerscope; 7838 feet; a Hammer-Swallow Production; filmed at Bray Studios; Released by British Lion (U.K.), Columbia (U.S.); Director: Joseph Losey; Producer: Anthony Hinds; Executive Producer: Michael Carreras; Associate Producer: Anthony Nelson-Keys; Screenplay: Evan Jones, based on H.L. Lawrence's novel *The Children of Light*; Director of Photography: Arthur Grant; Production Design: Bernard Robinson; Art Director: Don Mingaye; Supervising Editor: James Needs; Editor: Reginald Mills; Music: James Bernard; Music Director: John Hollingsworth; Song "Black Leather Rock" by Evan Jones and James Bernard; Sound: Jock May; Production Assistant: Richard MacDonald; Assistant Director: John Peverall; Camera Operator:

suddenly finds himself the center of a drama that rocks him to the core and alters his life." The role was one of Cushing's best, and he is alternatingly hateful, pathetic, admirable, and funny. Andre Morell is at least his equal, and they combined to give the two best performances in any one Hammer film.

Production ended on April 16, 1961, but the film's English distribution was unaccountably delayed. Columbia released *Cash on Demand* in America on December 20,

210 *The Damned* (1961)

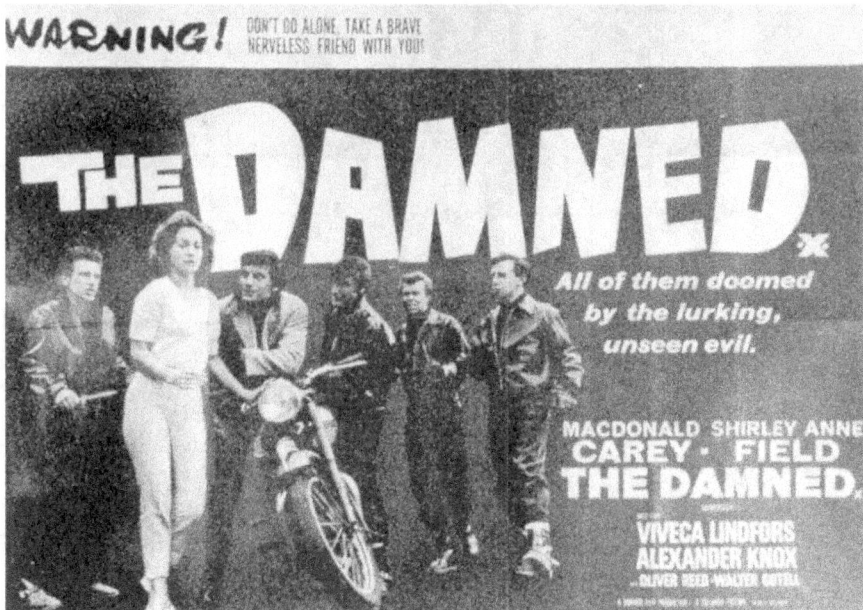

Poster from *The Damned* (courtesy of Fred Humphries and Colin Cowie).

Len Harris; Costumes: Molly Arbuthnot; Continuity: Pamela Davies; Makeup: Roy Ashton; Hairstyles: Frieda Steiger; Production Manager: Don Weeks; Casting: Stuart Lyons; Sculptures: Elizabeth Frink; U.S. Title: *These Are the Damned*; U.K. Certificate: X.

Macdonald Carey (Simon Wells), Shirley Ann Field (Joan), Viveca Lindfors (Freya), Oliver Reed (King), Alexander Knox (Bernard), Walter Gotell (Major Holland), James Villiers (Captain Gregory), Kenneth Cope (Sid), Thomas Kempinski (Ted), Brian Oulton (Mr. Dingle), Barbara Everest (Miss Lamont), Alan McClelland (Mr. Stuart), James Maxwell (Mr. Talbot), Rachel Clay (Victoria), Caroline Sheldon (Elizabeth), Rebecca Dignam (Anne), Siobhan Taylor (Mary), Nicholas Clay (Richard), Kit Williams (Henry), Christopher Witty (Wilham), David Palmer (George), John Thompson (Charles); David Gregory, Anthony Valentine, Larry Martyn, Leon Garcia, Jeremy Phillips (Teddy Boys).

Simon Wells (Macdonald Carey), a wealthy American on holiday, is picked up by Joan (Shirley Ann Field), an attractive decoy for a "teddy boy" gang led by King (Oliver Reed), her psychotic brother. Simon is beaten and robbed, and is found by security officers from a secret military installation. Taken to a hotel to recuperate, Simon meets Bernard (Alexander Knox), head of the project, and his lover, Freya (Viveca Lindfors). Later, Joan approaches Simon on his boat and tries to justify her behavior when her incestuously jealous brother arrives. She leaves with Simon, but when he makes a clumsy pass at her, asks to be put ashore. They break into Freya's cottage near the installation, make love, and leave before King arrives.

Inside the installation, Bernard addresses, via television, nine strange children who think they are being prepared for a space journey, but are part of a radiation experiment. They are immune to fallout, but can poison by their touch. The gang chases Simon and Joan into the sea where they—along with King—are rescued by Victoria (Rachel Clay) and Henry (Kit Williams), two of the children. Bernard tries to separate the children and adults, but it is too late—they are already poisoned. The adults misinterpret Bernard's actions, and try to escape with the children. King and Henry speed off in Freya's car, pursued by a helicopter. King, dying from radiation, drives off a bridge. Bernard releases Simon and Joan, who die in the boat, then shoots Freya, who knows too much.

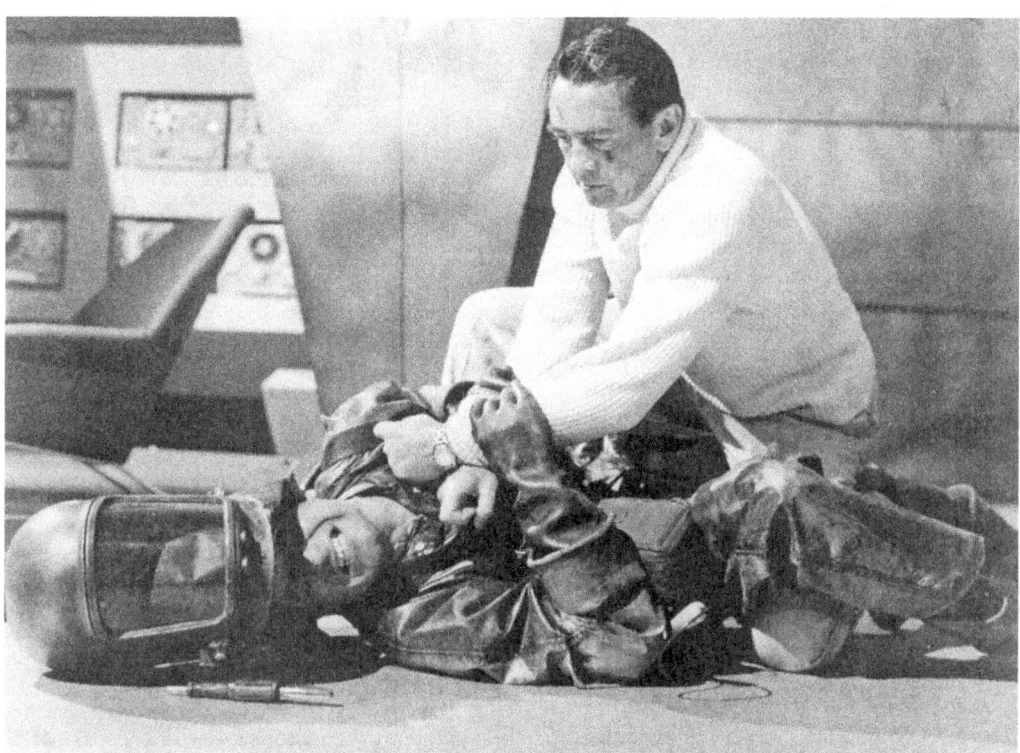

Macdonald Carey is helpless to prevent death by radiation in *The Damned*.

American director Joseph Losey, "blacklisted" during the Communist scare, relocated in England. He was given *A Man on the Beach*, a Hammer short, as one of his first assignments. Pleased with the result, Hammer offered him *The Criminal*, to star Stanley Baker, but Losey turned it down. Still keen on having Losey direct a feature, Anthony Hinds used director Carl Foreman (himself blacklisted) as a go-between. Losey, in Michael Ciment's *Conversations with Losey*, said, "When we got into trouble on the picture, Tony Hinds just disappeared and was nowhere to be found. And the man who rescued the situation for me then was Michael Carreras. I must say that Michael, ever since, has been trying to get me to do another picture with him, but he always gives me things that have so much overt violence in them I just can't consider them seriously."

Based on H.L. Lawrence's novel *The Children of Light*, *The Damned* began filming at Bray on May 8, 1961. *The Kinematograph Weekly* (June 15) visited the set and found an enthusiastic Oliver Reed about to make a record for Decca called *Lonely for a Girl*. Macdonald Carey had found success on American television, and *The Damned* was to be his British launching pad, but the rocket never took off due to the film's problem finding a release. Losey was very interested in the subject of radiation, but had reservations about two of his stars. He said in *Conversations with Losey* that he was forced to use Shirley Ann Field because she had just appeared with Laurence Olivier in *The Entertainer* (1960). Losey liked Oliver Reed personally, but felt the actor had "no training at all, and he already had a certain arrogance, so he wasn't easy." He was, however, honest enough to admit that Reed helped the movie. The production ended on June 22, 1961, and what followed was more convoluted than the film's plot. Despite an up-to-the-minute subject and a "name" director and stars, *The Damned* sat on the shelf for almost two years. When it finally premiered at the Pavilion on May 30, 1963, it was in support of *Maniac*, and would have gone unnoticed if not for its director. Since finishing *The Damned*, Losey had become a darling of the critics due to *The Servant* (1963), and his films were now the object of "serious study." Much was made of the movie's belated release caused by BLC's confusion over how to market what they thought would be a conventional "Hammer horror."

The London Times (May 30) commented, "Mr. Joseph Losey is one of the most intelligent, ambitious, and consistently exciting filmmakers now working in the country. It would be a thousand pities were his latest film, after 18 months on the shelf, to go out unremarked at the lower half of a 'double X' all horror programme." In agreement were *The Evening News* (May 23): "It carries the imprint of a master film maker"; *The Observer* (May 12): "What is Hammer-Columbia so reluctant and coy about?"; and *The Telegraph* (May 26): "Brilliant, flawed." *The Kinematograph Weekly* (March 21) singled out Oliver Reed's King as a "nasty piece of work." Yet, despite the positive reviews, *The Damned* was denied an American release. Incredibly, it won first prize at The Trieste Science Fiction Festival in July, 1964; and even more incredibly, it took another year for the film to open in New York as *These Are the Damned* on July 7, 1965. *Variety* (July 14) called it "a strange but fascinating film"; and *The New York Times* (July 8) found it "Orwellian."

The Damned paid a price for its twisted history. Due to cuts for two double features (*Genghis Khan* in the U.S.), the running time dropped from 100 to 77 minutes. If 23 minutes were removed from *Citizen Kane*, the result would be incomprehensible, too, so it is unfair to carp about vagueness and plot holes. What's left of major interest is Arthur Grant's crisp black and white photography and an outstanding job by the underappreciated Oliver Reed, who got fifth billing. There is enough left of *The Damned*, even with missing a quarter of its running time, to make it one of the decade's most interesting science fiction films.

The Pirates of Blood River

Released August 13, 1962 (U.K.), July, 1962 (U.S.); 84 minutes (U.K.), 87 minutes (U.S.); Technicolor (U.K.), Eastman Color (U.S.); 7584 feet; a Hammer Film Production; a British Lion Release (U.K.), a Columbia Release (U.S.); filmed at Bray Studios; Director: John Gilling; Producer: Anthony Nelson-Keys; Executive Producer: Michael Carreras; Screenplay: John Gilling, John Hunter, from Jimmy Sangster's story; Director of Photography: Arthur Grant; Music Composed by: Gary Hughes; Musical Director: John Hollingsworth; Production Designer: Bernard Robinson; Production Manager: Clifford Parkes; Art Director: Don Mingaye; Editor: Eric Boyd-Perkins; Supervising Editor: James Needs; Special Effects: Les Bowie; Horse Master/Master at Arms: Bob Simmons; Camera Operator: Len Harris; Assistant Director: John Peverall; Sound Recordist: Jock May; Sound Editor: Alfred Cox; Makeup: Roy Ashton; Costumes: Molly Arbuthnot; Continuity: Tilly Day; Wardrobe Mistress: Rosemary Burrows; Hair Stylist: Frieda Steiger; Casting: Stuart Lyons; U.K. Certificate: U.

Kerwin Mathews (Jonathan), Glenn Corbett (Henry), Christopher Lee (LaRoche), Marla Landi (Bess), Oliver Reed (Brocaire), Andrew Keir (Jason), Peter Arne (Hench), Michael Ripper (Mac), Jack Stewart (Mason), David Lodge (Smith), Marie Devereux (Maggie), Diane Aubrey (Margaret), Jerold Wells (Commandant), Dennis Waterman (Timothy), Lorraine Clewes (Martha), John Roden (Settler), Desmond Llewelyn (Blackthorne), Keith Pyott (Silas), Richard Bennett (Seymour), Michael Mulcaster (Martin), Denis Shaw (Silver), Michael Peake (Kemp), John Colin (Lance), Don Levy (Carlos), John Bennett (Guard), Ronald Blackman (Pugh).

Jonathan Standing (Kerwin Mathews), the son of the leader of a Caribbean Huguenot settlement, is banished to a penal colony for breaking the strict moral code established by the elders. Despite the pleas of his friend Henry (Glenn Corbett) and his sister Bess (Marla Landi), Jonathan's father Jason (Andrew Keir) remains unmoved. Jonathan escapes from the prison and is taken in by a band of pirates led by LaRoche (Christopher Lee), who rules in absolute control despite a withered arm and sightless eye. He is convinced that the colony has a cache of gold and makes a "deal" with Jonathan. If he is taken to the gold—which Jonathan denies

Kerwin Mathews (left) and Christopher Lee duel to the death in *The Pirates of Blood River*.

the existence of—LaRoche will restore democracy to the settlement.

LaRoche's true nature is revealed when he orders Hench (Peter Arne) to destroy a helpless family. Soon in charge of the settlement, LaRoche threatens to execute one person per day until the gold is procured. His men are now barely under control, as Hench kills Brocaire (Oliver Reed) in an animalistic fight over Bess. LaRoche discovers that a huge statue of the colony's founder is solid gold and takes it—with

214 *The Pirates of Blood River* (1961)

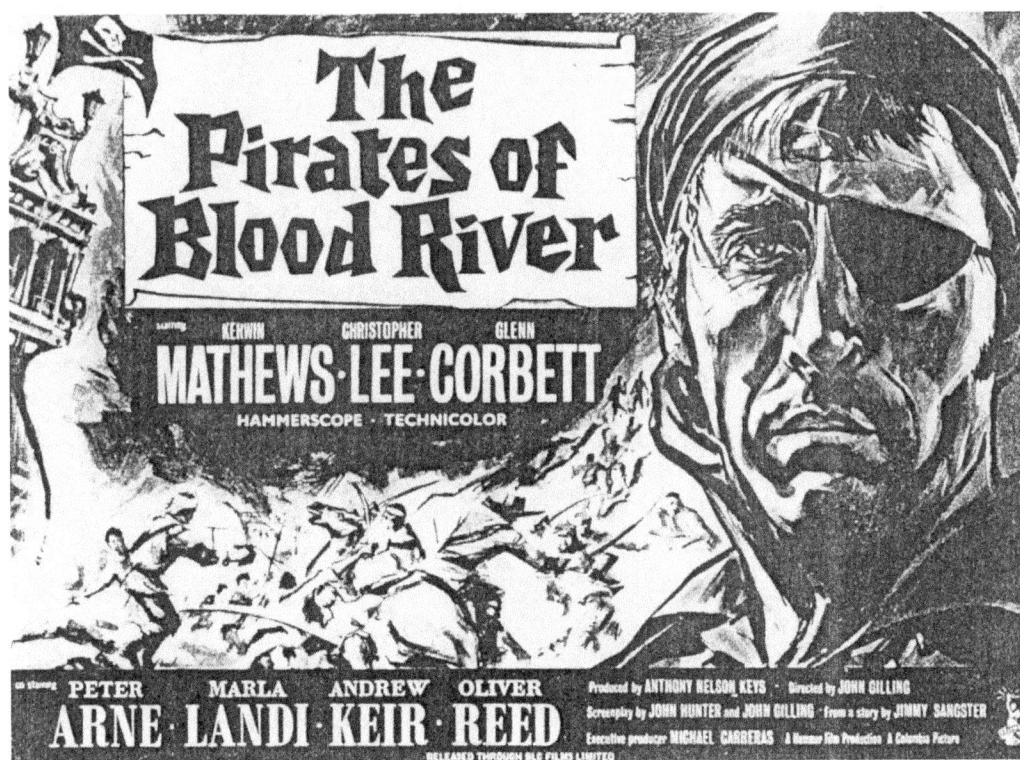

Hammer's swashbuckler was a big hit at kiddie matinees.

Jason and Jonathan as hostages—to the ship. Led by Henry, the islanders decimate the pirates through clever ambushes. Mac (Michael Ripper) leads a mutiny against LaRoche's faltering command and, with the statue lashed to a raft, attempts to reach the ship with the remaining crew. Jonathan defeats LaRoche in a duel as the sinking raft is attacked by a school of piranha, killing both the pirates and Jason Standing.

After his exhilarating performance in *The Seventh Voyage of Sinbad* (1958), Kerwin Mathews was the screen's reigning swashbuckler. He recalled for the authors (January, 1992),

I was under contract to Columbia, and they had just OK'd my living in London. I had just settled in when Hammer called. I always enjoyed working in England. The studios were first class and all the people involved were a bit more gentle than their American counterparts. John Gilling and Michael Carreras were very organized professionals and were most thoughtful of the actors and crew. Gilling had his hands full making a difficult film come in on schedule in English weather, but he was super-efficient and good for me. The film was physical and rough—it couldn't have been otherwise. One morning I had to do a scene in a swamp that had turned to quicksand. I had one of the frights of my life! I was so proud that Andrew Keir was playing my father. I thought he was such a good actor. Also, I was in awe of Oliver Reed and his famous relative, Sir Carol. [Sir Carol Reed was one of the great directors with pictures like *Odd Man Out* (1947), *The Fallen Idol* (1948), *The Third Man* (1949), and *Oliver!* (1968) to his credit.] Oliver was such a special man physically, and a fine actor. I always watched him work with envy, wishing I could be that way sometimes. He was a real pro, too. I had worked with British actors primarily in *Sinbad* and *The Three Worlds of Gulliver* (1960), so my mid–Atlantic Wisconsin college bred accent seemed to work. This was always an important consideration. Note: "Yonder lies de cassle of my faddah!" I really liked going to Bray each day and doing what I knew how to do best in a very nice place with nice people.

Originally titled *Blood River*, the film started production on July 3, 1961, and concluded on August 31 with location work at Black Park. James Carreras left for New York on January 13, 1962, to meet with Columbia executives. "It struck me," he said in *The Sunday Times*, "there was a lot of business to pick up around the kids' holiday period. Nobody had touched it except, of course, Disney, who had the field to himself." As a result, *The Pirates of Blood River* went out with the Columbia-made *Mysterious Island* and became the top earning double feature in the U.K. for 1962. Following a May 5 trade show at the Columbia Theatre, the pair premiered at the Pavilion on July 13 and went into general release a month later. Oddly, the films alternated playing "top." *The Kinematograph Weekly* (August 2, 1962) reported: "Whichever way the programme is arranged, it offers darn good value for the money. And don't forget, both films carry U certificates. What a chance for Mom to get rid of the kids!" By early September, the films were racking up record-breaking grosses on the ABC circuit, with many cinemas reporting receipts 50 percent above normal. Despite the film's popularity, many reviews were condescending. *The Monthly Bulletin* (June, 1962): "Stodgy, two-dimensional costume piece"; *Variety* (July 25): "Satisfactory adventure meller"; and *The Kinematograph Weekly* (May 10): "Thrilling story, robust characterization, hectic highlights."

The Pirates of Blood River was the first of Hammer's three unrelated pirate movies and helped to solidify the company's move away from Gothic horror in the early sixties. The cast is one of the best Hammer assembled, with the exception of Columbia throw-in Glenn Corbett. He is more than balanced by Christopher Lee's outstanding performance and by Michael Ripper in an all too rare featured role. This is one of Hammer's most satisfactory all-around films, and is an example of low budget filmmaking at its best.

Captain Clegg

Released June 25, 1962 (U.K.), June 13, 1962 (U.S.); 82 minutes; Technicolor (U.K.), Eastman Color (U.S.); 7380 feet; a Hammer-Major Production; a Rank Organization Release (U.K.), a Universal-International Release (U.S.); filmed at Bray Studios; Director: Peter Graham Scott; Producer: John Temple-Smith; Screenplay: John Elder; Director of Photography: Arthur Grant; Music composed by: Don Banks; Musical Director: Philip Martel; Production Designer: Bernard Robinson; Art Director: Don Mingaye; Editor: Eric Boyd-Perkins; Supervising Editor: James Needs; Special Effects: Les Bowie; Makeup: Roy Ashton; Assistant Director: John Pervall; Hair Stylist: Frieda Steiger; Wardrobe: Molly Arbuthnot; Additional Dialogue: Barbara S. Harper; Second Assistant Director: Peter Medak; Sound: Jock May; U.S. Title: *Night Creatures*; U.K. Certificate: A.

Peter Cushing (Dr. Blyss/Capt. Clegg), Yvonne Romain (Imogene), Patrick Allen (Capt. Collier), Oliver Reed (Harry Crabtree), Michael Ripper (Mipps), Martin Benson (Rash), David Lodge (Bosun), Derek Francis (Squire), Daphne Anderson (Mrs. Rash), Milton Reid (Mulatto), Jack MacGowran (Frightened Man), Peter Halliday (Sailor Jack Pott), Terry Scully (Sailor Dick Tate), Sydney Bromley (Tom Ketch), Rupert Osborne (Gerry), Gordon Rollings (Wurzel), Bob Head (Peg-Leg), Colin Douglas (Pirate Bosun).

1776. The High Seas. A mulatto pirate (Milton Reid) is placed on a desert island—his ears and tongue mutilated—for attacking the pregnant wife of Captain Clegg.

The years pass. Captain Collier (Patrick Allen) is investigating the smuggling of French brandy into the English village of Dymchurch—a town haunted by "Marsh Phantoms" and the grave of Captain Clegg. The vicar, Dr. Blyss (Peter Cushing), while polite, is unwilling to aid Collier's search. While dining with the Captain, the Squire (Derek Francis), and his son Harry (Oliver Reed), Blyss is attacked by Collier's "ferret"—the mulatto. Most of the town, including Rash (Martin Benson), the innkeeper, and the coffin maker Mipps (Michael Ripper) are part of the smuggling team headed by Blyss. To keep the curious off the moor, they dress like living skeletons—the marsh phantoms.

Harry and Imogene (Yvonne Romain), Rash's ward, want to marry but are stymied by their different social positions. When

Patrick Allen (left) and Peter Cushing break for tea on the set of *Captain Clegg*.

Rash drunkenly molests her, she learns that her real father was Clegg. She runs to Blyss, who confirms Rash's tale. Enraged, Harry confronts Rash who reveals him to Collier as "the scarecrow"—a lookout for the smugglers. Harry escapes, and he and Imogene are married by Blyss. Collier deduces that Blyss is actually Clegg, and exposes the "dead" pirate before the congregation. They rally behind the man who saved them from poverty, as Clegg explains that, after his botched hanging, he became a "new man." He and Mipps escape during the confusion and are attacked by the mulatto with a harpoon, and Clegg dies protecting his friend. As Clegg is buried for a second time, Collier lowers his head respectfully.

Despite Hammer's failure to mention it in the credits, *Captain Clegg* was based on Russell Thorndyke's 1915 novel *Dr. Syn*, which inspired a 1937 film starring George Arliss. After not hearing from the pirate-priest for 25 years, suddenly two films appeared in 1962 when Hammer decided, along with Walt Disney, to dust off the property. *The Kinematograph Weekly* (September 7, 1961) announced that Hammer planned to begin production of *Dr. Syn* on September 18. Meanwhile, Disney planned to shoot *Dr. Syn—Alias the Scarecrow* as an American television film to be released theatrically elsewhere. Disney had been quicker to secure the copyright than Hammer, causing the company to change the character's name (if not his intentions). No other changes were required, since Disney had only copyrighted the title.

Hammer more or less followed the plot of the 1937 film, but with two major changes—splitting the parson/scarecrow into two characters, and having the parson killed off. Production was pushed back to September 25, concluding on November 6, with location work at Black Park, Denham Village, and a deconsecrated church near Bray.

Peter Cushing (center) is coached by the Vicar of Bray while director Peter Graham Scott looks on in *Captain Clegg* (photo courtesy of Tim Murphy).

Captain Clegg provided Michael Ripper with, perhaps, his best role for Hammer, as he was given the chance to play a "real" character instead of a walk-on far beneath his ability. "I was very lucky," he told the authors (April, 1993).

I was a good stage actor and got my first job in films in quota pictures. I was "over the top" a bit due to my stage background, but in the quota pictures it didn't really matter. In one early Hammer picture, I asked the producer how I was, and he said—"terrible"—but they couldn't cut around me. I thought that would be the end of me. But, I stuck around. I learned the technique of not overacting. *Nobody* believes you when you're over the top. One of the main reasons I was in so many Hammer films was my friendship with Tony Hinds. He is a very quiet man—not at *all* like a film producer! He wrote a great many scripts, too, as John Elder, and, I suspect, he always wrote a part for me. One of my favorites was *Captain Clegg*—a great part, a great story, and a great cast. I always enjoyed Peter Cushing, of course, and Oliver Reed was a lot of fun, too. It's hard to pick my favorite Hammer film—it seems like I was in all of them!

Len Harris had, oddly, also worked on the 1937 version and recalled (December, 1993),

The last scene we shot was the attack on Dr. Syn with the harpoon. In those days, a star like George Arliss could get away with murder! He simply *refused* to work after 4:30 and would simply say, "Thank you, gentlemen," and leave. We were running late on this final shot and he just got up, bid us good day, and *left*! Strangely enough, on *Captain Clegg*, the only scene we had to be late on was—of course—the harpoon scene. Peter Cushing, however, stayed until the shot was finished!

Captain Clegg was released, paired with *The Phantom of the Opera*, on June 25, 1962, to generally favorable reviews. *The London Times* (June 28): "An almost jolly story of smugglers and king's men"; *The New York Post* (August 23): "Don't sell this thriller short"; *The New York Daily News* (August 23): "Executed as if a big spectacle was in the making"; *Variety* (May 5): "The Hammer imprimatur has come to certify solid values, and there's no mystery why these films rate audience allegiance"; *Films and Filming* (July): "A rattling good piece of comic book adventure"; *The Observer* (June 10): "Sickening makeup effects"; and *The Monthly Bulletin* (July): "The script is feeble, the acting uninspired."

Captain Clegg is the best of the company's period adventures and provided Peter Cushing with one of his greatest roles. The film solidified James Carreras' stand that Hammer had no commitment to any specific genre, and *Captain Clegg* is the type of picture Hammer should have made more of.

The Phantom of the Opera

Released June 25, 1962 (U.K.), August 15, 1962 (U.S.); 84 minutes (U.K.), 94 minutes (U.S. Television); Technicolor (U.K.), Eastman Color (U.S.); 7560 feet; a Hammer Film Production; a Rank Organization Release (U.K.), a Universal Release (U.S.); filmed at Bray Studios, England; Director: Terence Fisher; Producer: Anthony Hinds; Associate Producer: Basil Keys; Screenplay: John Elder, based on the story by Gaston Leroux; Director of Photography: Arthur Grant; Art Directors: Bernard Robinson, Don Mingaye; Supervising Editor: James Needs; Editor: Alfred Cox; Music Composed and Conducted by: Edwin Astley; Makeup: Roy Ashton; Production Manager: Clifford Parkes; Costumes: Molly Arbuthnot; Camera: Len Harris; 1st Assistant Director: John Peverall; 2nd Assistant Director: Peter Medac; Continuity: Tilly Day; Sound: Jock May; Hairdresser: Frieda Steiger; Wardrobe Mistress: Rosemary Burrows; Stills Camera: Tom Edwards; Sound Editor: James Groom; Sound Recordist: Jock May; Opera Scenes Staged by: Dennis Maunder; U.K. Certificate: A.

Herbert Lom (The Phantom/Petrie), Edward de Souza (Harry Hunter), Heather Sears (Chris-

Hammer's exciting pirate adventure *Captain Clegg* was, for American audiences, disguised as a horror movie, with the title *Night Creatures*.

tine Charles), Michael Gough (Lord Ambrose D'Arcy), Thorley Walters (Lattimer), Ian Wilson (Dwarf), Martin Miller (Rossi), John Harvey (Sgt. Vickers), Miles Malleson (Philosophical Cabby), Marne Maitland (Xavier), Michael Ripper (Long Faced Cabby), Patrick Troughton (Rat Catcher), Renee Houston (Mrs. Tucker), Sonya Cordeau (Yvonne), Liane Aukin (Maria), Leila Forde (Teresa), Geoff L'Oise (Frenchman), Miriam Karlin (Charwoman), Harold Goodwin (Bill), Keith Pyott (Weaver). Cast for U.S. Television added footage: Liam Redmond (Police Inspector), John Maddison (Police Inspector).

Lord Ambrose D'Arcy's (Michael Gough) opera, *Joan of Arc*, is plagued by vandalism and murder, causing Maria (Liane Aukin), the lead singer, to resign. Director Harry Hunter (Edward de Souza) and Lattimer (Thorley Walters), the theatre manager, audition Chris-

Herbert Lom joins Lon Chaney and Claude Rains as The Phantom.

Joan of Arc is restaged with Christine in the lead. At the premiere, Petrie confronts D'Arcy in his office, and Lord Ambrose rips off the mask. Horrified, D'Arcy runs out into the night. While Petrie weeps at Christine's beautiful singing, the dwarf is chased through the rafters by a stagehand. As he leaps onto a chandelier, the rope snaps, sending it hurling toward Christine. Tearing away his mask, Petrie leaps onto the stage and pushes Christine to safety, sacrificing his life for hers.

The Phantom of the Opera, filmed by Universal in 1925 (Lon Chaney) and 1943 (Claude Rains) was re-made by Hammer as a result of an August, 1958, agreement with Universal International. Filming began on November 21, 1961, after a false start involving—Cary Grant! Anthony Hinds recalled (*Fangoria* 74), "Cary Grant came to us and said he wanted to make a horror film. The only thing we

tine (Heather Sears), and D'Arcy, captivated by her beauty, invites her to dinner to "discuss the role." In her dressing room, a voice warns her of D'Arcy's evil intentions. That night, after Harry "rescues" her, he and Christine return to investigate the voice. After the theatre rat catcher (Patrick Troughton) is murdered by a dwarf (Ian Wilson), Christine glimpses a masked man in black—the Phantom (Herbert Lom).

Harry learns from a chance discovery of old sheet music of a Professor Petrie, a struggling composer who was swindled out of his music by D'Arcy. While attempting to destroy the stolen scores at a print shop, Petrie was severely burned but, aided by the dwarf, found refuge beneath the Opera. Christine is abducted by the dwarf and taken to Petrie's chambers, where she is soon traced by Harry. Petrie tells his sad story and begs to be allowed to instruct Christine. Moved by his sincerity, the couple agrees.

could think of was *Phantom of the Opera*. I knew he'd never make it, but he was insistent, so I wrote the thing for him." After Hinds was proven correct, Herbert Lom—rather than Peter Cushing or Christopher Lee—was signed.

"Herbert Lom was a late choice for the role," Len Harris told the authors (December, 1993), "but made the most of it. A lot of actors would have been unnerved, but he was unaffected by it all. Lom was excellent and gave something to the role that Cushing might not have. Like most Hammer stars, he was a real gentleman—and also quite a practical joker!"

Unlike Universal's 1943 version, which borrowed music from Tchaikovsky and Chopin, Hammer's Edwin Astley composed an original opera with Heather Sears convincingly dubbed by Pat Clark. Although most of the film was shot at Bray and Oakley Court, two weeks were spent at the Wimbledon Theatre. Len Harris recalled, "The theatre was much smaller than you'd think, and Terence

220 The Phantom of the Opera (1961)

Michael Gough gets the shock of his life in *The Phantom of the Opera.*

Fisher was at his wit's end to give it some size. We only used a few extras in costume to fill the seats and kept moving them around, changing hats and coats, to make it look like an army." Another problem centered around the Phantom's mask. "They had contracted a professional mask maker," said Roy Ashton (*Fangoria* 35), "who turned out many super designs—none of which they were satisfied with. My suggestion was that this chap would have picked up a discarded prop to hide his disfigurement." Hammer finally saw it his way after filming began with Lom maskless.

The Phantom of the Opera concluded on January 26, 1962, after which Bray was shut down for five months for much needed maintenance. On May 17, Rank announced that they would premiere *The Phantom of the Opera* and *Captain Clegg* at the Leicester Square on June 7—a move applauded by *The Kinematograph Weekly* as a "generous value for the money." The double feature went into general release throughout Britain on June 25. Inexplicably, the box office receipts were a major disappointment, with reviewers sharply divided. *The Kinematograph Weekly* (May 31, 1962): "The picture reinforces the emotional and musical aspect, but not at the expense of Grand Guignol thrills"; *The Observer* (June): "A very tame remake of the famous original"; *Cue* (August 25): "A pretty fair thriller"; *The New York Post* (August 23): "Eye filling"; *The New York Times* (August 23): "Ornate and pretty dull"; *Time* (August 31): "Ho-ho-horror"; and *The London Times* (June 8): "The frisson of real, genuine fear is absent."

Perhaps the most harsh criticism came from Terence Fisher. "The weakness of *The Phantom of the Opera* is that its realism isn't really justified," he said (*Cinefantastique*, Vol. 4, No. 3). "There is no complexity to the Phantom's actions; the character is never very close to us, and remains superficial." Fisher, perhaps, was being a bit hard on himself. The film's major fault is that it is not really a horror movie, and the few attempts at shock and gore seem out of place. Herbert Lom plays the Phantom for sympathy, and succeeds on a level that few Hammer "monsters" achieved. Heather Sears, who was awarded by the British Academy and the New York Film Critics for *The Story of Esther Costello* (1957), was both touching and beautiful, and rates among the best of all Hammer heroines. With the Phantom as a victim rather than a villain, there is only the sneering Michael Gough to hate, and he is more than up to the job.

Although finding financial success with *The Curse of Frankenstein* and other horrors, Hammer had yet to find "respectability"; and this remake of a Hollywood icon seemed to be the perfect vehicle. Unfortunately, despite many positives, *The Phantom of the Opera* can-with dignity, and like the Phantom, it deserves our sympathy.

Those wishing to see the film in its original form should avoid the American TV print which, like *The Kiss of the Vampire* and *The Evil of Frankenstein*, was padded with extra footage.

1962

The Old Dark House

Released July, 1966 (U.K.), October 31, 1963 (U.S.); 77 minutes (U.K.), 86 minutes (U.S.); Color; 7775 feet; a William Castle–Hammer Production; Released by BLC (U.K.), Columbia (U.S.); filmed at Bray Studios; Director: William Castle; Producer: Anthony Hinds; Screenplay: Robert Dillon, based on J.B. Priestley's novel; Director of Photography: Arthur Grant; Music: Benjamin Frankel; Production Design: Bernard Robinson; Production Manager: John Draper; Supervising Editor: James Needs; Camera: Moray Grant; Sound Recordist: Jock May; Hairstyles: Frieda Steiger; Wardrobe: Rosemary Burrows; Wardrobe Supervisor: Molly Arbuthnot; Special Effects: Les Bowie; Assistant Director: Douglas Hermes; Sound Editor: James Groom; Continuity: Pauline Wise; Makeup: Roy Ashton; Drawings: Charles Addams; Stills: Tom Edwards; 2nd Assistant Director: Dominic Fulford; Associate Producer: Basil Keys; U.K. Certificate: A.

Tom Poston (Tom Penderel), Robert Morley (Roderick Femm), Janette Scott (Cecily Femm), Joyce Grenfell (Agatha Femm), Mervyn Johns (Potiphar Femm), Fenella Fielding (Morgana Femm), Peter Bull (Casper-Jasper Femm), Danny Green (Morgan Femm), John Harvey (Receptionist), Amy Dalby (Player).

Tom Penderel (Tom Poston), a naive American, shares a London flat with Casper Femm (Peter Bull), to whom he sells a luxury car. Oddly, Casper must return to his Dartmoor estate by plane *nightly*, and asks Tom to drive the car to Femm Hall. Tom arrives during a raging storm and is taken by Potiphar Femm (Mervyn Johns) to see Casper—in his coffin—who was the "victim of a fall." Casper's lovely cousin, Cecily (Janette Scott) tells Tom that Casper was murdered and urges him to leave, but he is invited by patriarch Roderick (Robert Morley) to stay for dinner—and the night. Captivated by Cecily and the over-

A well intentioned failure.

not rate with its two more famous predecessors, and what could have been a major breakthrough for Hammer proved to be a minor disaster. The film was a turning point for the company, and could be used to mark the end of Hammer's best period. But, the movie failed

The Old Dark House (1962)

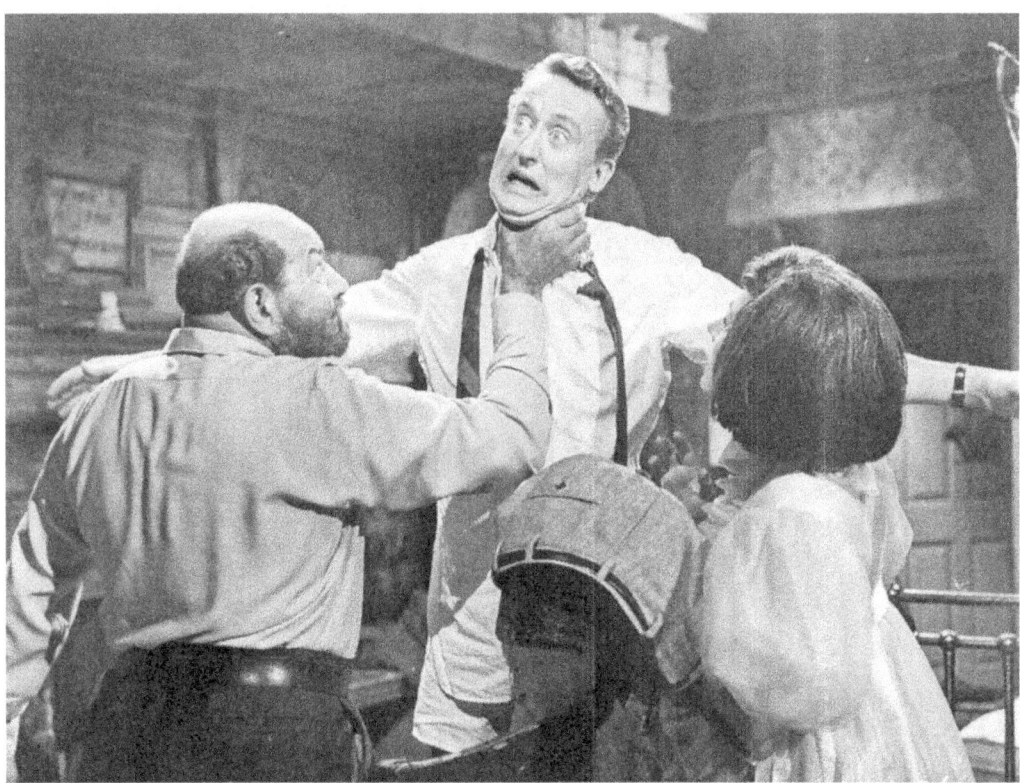

Danny Green is not amused at Tom Poston's interest in his daughter (Fenella Fielding) in the William Castle–Hammer Production of *The Old Dark House*.

whelming Morgana (Fenella Fielding), Tom agrees.

At dinner, Roderick explains that the Femms are trapped at the Hall due to a stipulation in the will of their ancestor, Morgan the Pirate. If *any* family member is absent for more than a day, their fortune is forfeited. That night, the Femms begin dying in quick succession under bizarre circumstances: Agatha (Joyce Grenfell) stabbed with knitting needles, Jasper (Peter Bull), Casper's twin, strangled by a pair of tongs, and Roderick, shot by one of his prized guns. Cecily reveals herself as the murderer when she tries to behead Morgana, and has wired the house with explosives. She is killed by one that lands at her feet. Morgana and her mad father (Danny Green) offer Tom a life at the Hall, but recent events leave him in doubt.

Novelist J.B. Priestley could hardly have been pleased by trade headlines like "Castle Buys Priestley Horror Classic." His book, *Benighted*, had been filmed earlier by James Whale as *The Old Dark House* (Universal, 1932, with Boris Karloff) as a "black comedy horror," bearing scant resemblance to the novel. Certainly schlockmaster William Castle was no serious novelist's choice as his adaptor. Although Castle's career dated back to the forties, he was just coming into his own with gimmicky shockers like *The Tingler* (1959). Due to lower production costs in the U.K., and since both Castle and Hammer released through Columbia, a deal was made to film *The Old Dark House* at Bray, despite their totally different styles.

The Kinematograph Weekly (February 8, 1962) announced that Bray would reopen after maintenance in early May for a new film. Castle arrived in London in mid–April, and got along well with his Hammer counterparts. Filming began on April 19 and concluded on June 22, with the result pleasing no one. Derek Todd (*The Kinematograph Weekly*, May 23,

The "couldn't miss" combination of Hammer and William Castle missed.

1962) reported from the set that "Those who are wondering what ghastly, ghostly gimmick will emerge from the Hammer/Castle combination will be in for a surprise. For, according to Castle, 'This picture gives equal emphasis to horror and comedy. The days of the straight shockers have just about run their course.'" James Carreras added, "It will take the mickey out of horror pictures in a most original and entertaining way."

The list of successful horror comedies is a short one, and unfortunately, *The Old Dark House* is not on it. It is not difficult to watch, being just "sick" enough to be occasionally funny, but Hammer plus Castle did not add up to much. Reviewers were restrained in their compliments. *The New York Times* (October 31, 1963): "Laboriously arch"; *The New York Herald Tribune* (October 31): "The screenplay is weak"; and *Variety* (October 23): "Succeeds only in neutralizing itself." Justifiably concerned, BLC held the film's British release back in the U.K. for three years.

The Old Dark House was a false step for both Hammer and Castle, doing no one involved any good at all. In retrospect, the whole idea was without merit, and the film seems to have been made only because of Columbia's relationship with the two producers.

Maniac

Released May 20, 1963 (U.K.), October 30, 1963 (U.S.); 87 minutes; B & W; Megascope; a Hammer Film Production; a BLC Release (U.K.), a Columbia Release (U.S.); filmed at MGM Studios, Elstree, England, and on location in France; Director: Michael Carreras; Producer, Screenplay: Jimmy Sangster; Director of Photography: Wilkie Cooper; Art Director: Teddy Carrick; Supervising Editor: James Needs; Editor: Tom Simpson; Production Design: Bernard Robinson; Music: Stanley Black; Makeup: Basil Newall; Production Manager: Bill Hill; Assistant to the Producer: Ian Lewis; Sound Editor: Roy Baker; Camera: Harry Gilliam; Sound Recordist: Cyril Swern; Hairstylist: Pat McDermott; Continuity: Kay Rawlings; Wardrobe: Molly Arbuthnot; Wardrobe Mistress: Jean Fairlie; Focus: Tommy Fletcher, Trevor Wrenn; Camera Grip: L. Kelly; Assistant Art Director: Jean Peyre; Draughtsman: Fred Carter; Scenic Artist: Felix Sergejak; Main Titles: Chambers & Partners; Boom Operator: Bill Baldwin; Sound Camera Operator: Ron Matthews; 1st Assistant Director: Ross MacKenzie; 2nd Assistant Director: Terry Lens; Production Manager: Bill Hill; Production Secretary: Marguerite Green; Prop Buyer: Margery Whittington; Still Photographer: James Swarbrick; Carpenter: Tommy Westbrook; Painter: A. Smith; Stagehand: E. Power; Rigger: V. Bailey; Electrical Supervisor: Bert Chapple; Prop Chargehand: Tommy Ibbetson; Clapper/Loader: Ray Andrew; Sound Maintenance: Peter Martingell; Assistant Makeup Artist: Stella Morris; Electrical Chargehand: Geoff Hughes; Electricians: T. Shephard, R. Stentaford, L. Scullion, A. Carroll, G. Page; Property Stand-by: M. Lord; Driver: Ron Warr; U.K. Certificate: X.

Kerwin Mathews (Geoff Farrell), Nadia Gray (Eve Beynat), Donald Houston ("Georges" Beynat), Liliane Brousse (Annette Beynat), George Pastell (Inspector Etienne), Arnold Diamond (Janiello), Norman Bird (Salon), Justine Lord (Grace), Jerold Wells (Giles), Leon Peers (Blanchard).

After 15-year-old Annette Beynat (Liliane Brousse) is raped by a neighbor, her father knocks the man unconscious, drags him to a work shed and murders him with an acetylene torch. Judged insane by the court, Beynat is committed to an asylum.

Four years later, American artist Geoffrey Farrell (Kerwin Mathews) is touring the south of France when he meets Annette and her stepmother Eve (Nadia Gray). Both women are attracted to Geoff, but he falls for Eve and they become lovers. Eve visits her husband in the asylum and returns to Geoff with the news that he will agree to a divorce but only on the condition that they provide him with a means of escape. She explains that Beynat has enlisted the aid of a male nurse to get him out and that all they need do is furnish him with transportation to the docks of Marseilles. Geoff and Eve meet Beynat at the appointed time and drive him to the Marseilles pier.

Geoff is horrorstruck when he later discovers the body of the male nurse in the car trunk. He and Eve dump the body in a canal but mysterious goings-on in and around the notorious work shed indicate that Beynat has returned to take revenge on his unfaithful wife and her lover. A series of plot twists ensues, and eventually it is revealed that Eve and the male nurse Henri (Donald Houston), lovers for two years, had hatched a plan to dispose of Beynat and Geoff in such a way that it appeared that Geoff killed Beynat. Annette, who knows the truth, is chased through an abandoned rock quarry by the murderous Henri, but he slips and falls to his death. Police arrive on the scene and arrest Eve as Geoff climbs to rescue Annette.

After writing the critically—and audience-acclaimed—*Taste of Fear*, Jimmy Sangster decided to concentrate on psychological thrillers rather than Gothic horror. Three of these scripts (*Paranoiac*, *Nightmare*, and *Maniac*) would be produced during 1962. *Maniac* began filming during the end of May in the Camargue region of southern France.

Nadia Gray finds the perfect dupe (Kerwin Mathews) for her murderous plans in Hammer's *Maniac*.

Michael Carreras, directing his second feature for Hammer, had high hopes for the picture. "It's a thriller of thrillers, so ingeniously constructed, so packed with surprises, that we defy anyone to predict correctly what's coming next or to anticipate the startling and unexpected climax." Kerwin Mathews, fresh from his starring role in *The Pirates of Blood River*, enjoyed his second Hammer film even more. He told the authors (February, 1992),

> This was my first extended stay in France, particularly in the South. I've lived there occasionally since then. I'm a blatant Francophile because of *Maniac*! Michael Carreras was just breaking through my shield of insecurities on *Maniac*, and I always wished we could have had another chance on another film as he found his way as a director and I matured as an actor. I loved working with him and also working without a sword in my hand! Because of the short schedules on Hammer films (and others I've done), I became super-organized. The quick filming didn't bother me at all. I *was* inclined to be very impatient and critical of film people, but not those at Hammer. I was *so* serious about acting as a craft I could be proud of and, acting in low budget films, hanging on to those ideals could be very often an insurmountable challenge! Believe it or not, I've never seen *Maniac*—or many of my pictures. I was usually making another one on the other side of the world when the last one came out!

Norman Bird was *not* keen on doing a Hammer horror. He told the authors (February, 1992),

> I remember that when I was offered the part, I was told it was *not* one of their usual horror films. On receiving the script, I was intrigued to see that it started with a girl pursued through the woods by her rapist who then had his head burned off by her vengeful father with an oxyacetylene blowtorch! I was, rightly, rather worried about the quality of my French accent. But, when I saw the finished film, I was surprised to hear how good it was. After a few minutes, I realized my voice had been exceptionally well dubbed! It was the only time this had ever happened, and I *must* say it improved my performance considerably!

Maniac was to move into Bray for interiors, but when *The Old Dark House* went over

226 *Paranoiac* (1962)

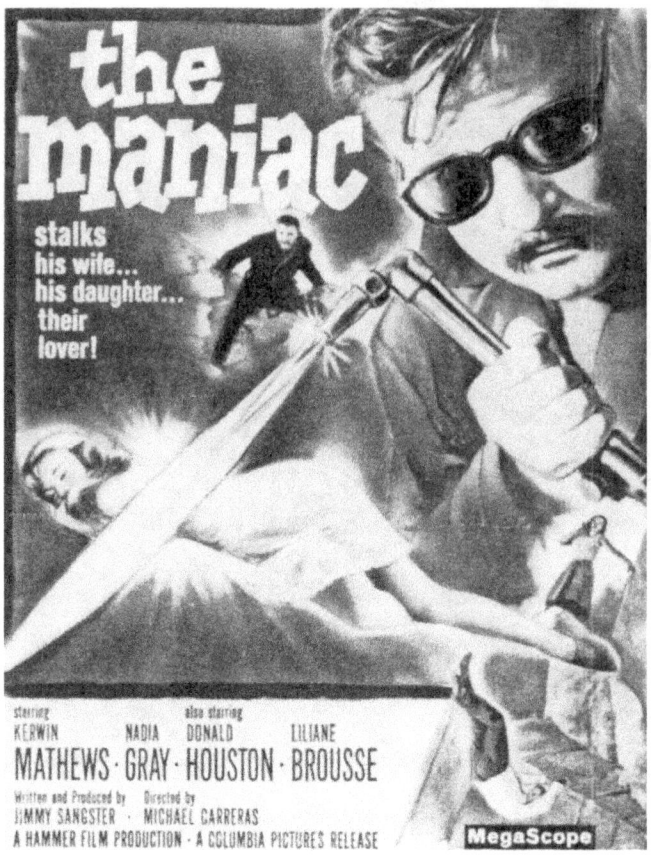

Jimmy Sangster's contrived yet effective psycho-thriller.

schedule, the scenes were shot at MGM Boreham Wood. The production ended in late July, 1962, and *Maniac* was released through British Lion on May 20, 1963, paired with *The Damned*. In America, Columbia doubled it with *The Old Dark House* in October to mixed reviews. *The New York Times* (October 31): "A plot of extraordinary cunning, not particularly well performed"; *The New York Herald Tribune* (October 31): "Well directed but the pace falters at times"; *The New York Morning Telegraph* (November 1): "Takes quite a while to figure out but by then you really don't care anymore"; and *Time* (November 15): "Good clean sadism."

It takes a while for *Maniac* to get moving, but the film's second half is as good as any of Hammer's psycho-thrillers. Kerwin Mathews makes a believable, less than perfect hero, and Donald Houston is as chilling a villain as one could wish. Jimmy Sangster's script *is* a miracle of false turns, and this is one trick picture that no one figured out half way through.

Paranoiac

Released May 15, 1963 (U.S.), January 26, 1964 (U.K.); 80 minutes; B & W; a Hammer Film Production; a Rank Organization Release (U.K.), a Universal Release (U.S.); filmed at Bray Studios, England; Director: Freddie Francis; Producer: Anthony Hinds; Associate Producer: Basil Keys; Screenplay: Jimmy Sangster; Director of Photography: Arthur Grant; Production Designer: Bernard Robinson; Art Director: Don Mingaye; Music: Elizabeth Lutyens; Musical Supervisor: John Hollingsworth; Supervising Editor: James Needs; Production Manager: John Draper; First Assistant Director: Ross MacKenzie; Continuity: Pauline Wise; Sound: Ken Rawkins; Makeup: Roy Ashton; Hairdresser: Frieda Steiger; Wardrobe Supervisor: Molly Arbuthnot; Special Effects: Les Bowie, Kit West; Wardrobe Mistress: Rosemary Burrows; Camera Operator: Moray Grant; Focus Pullers: David Osborne, Robin Higginson; Assistant Art Director: Ken Ryan; Sound Editor: James Groom; Boom Operator: Ken Nightingall; Sound Transfer Operator: H.C. Allan; Sound Camera Operator: Al Thorne; 2nd Assistant Director: Hugh Harlow; 3rd Assistant Director: Ray Corbett; Production Secretary: Maureen White; Stills Photographer: Curtis Reeks; Studio Manager: A.F. Kelly; Construction Manager: Arthur Banks; Chief Electrician: Jack Curtis; Master Carpenter: Charles Davis; Prop Master: Tommy Money; Prop Buyer: Eric Hillier; Camera Grip: Albert Cowland; Camera Maintenance: John Kerley; Clappers/Loader: Bob Jordan; Sound Maintenance: Charles Bouvet; Boom Assistant: R.A. Mingaye; Publicist: Brian Boyle; Assistant Makeup: Richard Mills; Master Painter: Lawrence Wrenn; Master Plasterer: Stan Banks; Floor Props Chargehand: W. Smith; Electrical Chargehands: George Robinson, Vic Hemmings; Transport Drivers: "Coco" Epps, Laurie Martin; U.K. Certificate: X.

Janette Scott (Eleanor Ashby), Oliver Reed

Oliver Reed needs more than a twelve-step program in Freddie Francis' *Paranoiac*.

(Simon Ashby), Liliane Brousse (Francoise), Alexander Davion (Tony Ashby/Imposter), Sheila Burrell (Aunt Harriet), Maurice Denham (John Kossett), John Bonney (Keith Kossett), John Stuart (Williams), Colin Tapley (Vicar), Harold Lang (RAF Type), Laurie Leigh, Marianne Stone (Women), Sydney Bromley (Tramp), Jack Taylor (Sailor).

Eleven years after the airplane crash that took the lives of John and Mary Ashby, the remaining members of the family attend a memorial service at the parish church. In attendance are the Ashbys' now-grown children Eleanor (Janette Scott) and Simon (Oliver Reed). The priest also recalls their brother Tony, who as a young boy left a suicide note on the high cliffs above the sea near the Ashbys' centuried estate, High Tor.

Eleanor glimpses a shadowy figure in the doorway of the church, which she believes to be her brother Tony. The event provides Simon, as well as their Aunt Harriet (Sheila Burrell), with further proof that the normally high-strung Eleanor is mentally unbalanced and therefore not entitled to her share of the family fortune. Now doubting her own sanity, Eleanor later attempts to throw herself off a cliff but she is rescued by Tony (Alexander Davion), who claims that he merely disappeared and that there was no suicide.

After convincing Kossett (Maurice Denham), the family solicitor, of his authenticity, Tony moves into the Ashby mansion where he is subjected to several violent attacks upon his life. While conducting his own investigation, Tony falls in love with Eleanor, who grows to love Tony—and to hate herself for her apparent proclivity toward incestuousness. To calm the distraught girl, Tony is forced to tell the truth: He is an imposter, hired by Kossett's son Keith (John Bonney), who (unbeknownst to his father) has been stealing money from the estate.

In due course Simon is unmasked as a paranoid who murdered the real brother and hid his body in the house's disused chapel. When the boy's corpse is discovered, the by-now hopelessly insane Simon knocks Tony unconscious and ties him to a pillar in the chapel. Aunt Harriet sets fire to it in an effort to destroy all evidence of Simon's crime. But Eleanor rescues Tony and leads him to safety. Simon, overcome with guilt, races into the burning chapel to save his "little brother" and perishes in the flames.

Paranoiac took almost ten years to get on the screen. After Hammer bought the rights to Josephine Tey's novel *Brat Farrar* in 1954, James Carreras gave the property to screenwriter Paul Dehn. Hammer put the film on their 1955 schedule, cancelled it, and tried again in 1959 with the same result. Three years later, the film surfaced as *Paranoiac*, with a new screenplay by Jimmy Sangster. "Hammer had planned to do a straight adaptation of *Brat Farrar*," he told the authors (August, 1993), "but when we did it, we just kept the basic idea and added horror elements. I admired Josephine Tey and tried to maintain as much of the framework as possible." Due to budgetary restrictions, Sangster eliminated all references to horseracing, which was a major part of the novel.

Paranoiac began production on July 23, 1962, and concluded on August 31. A trade show was held at the Hammer Theatre on September 7, 1963, and the film was released, with *Kiss of the Vampire*, on January 26, 1964. In America, *Paranoiac* went out as a single feature in May, 1963. Reviews were mixed. *The New York Times* (May 23, 1963): "Hammer Productions has now come tantalizingly close to the bullseye"; *The New York Herald Tribune* (May 23): "Idiotically entertaining, provided, of course, that you can find entertainment in blood, gore, and lunacy"; *The New York Mirror* (May 23): "Oliver Reed plays one of the worst heels ever put up on the screen ... more sadistic than Bill Sykes or Jekyll's Hyde." (Ironi-

Oliver Reed in another excellent performance for Hammer.

cally, two of Reed's future roles); *The Kinematograph Weekly* (September 12, 1963): "Rather more acting ability than is usual in this type of film"; *The Monthly Film Bulletin* (October, 1963): "Bizarre, far-fetched, and tasteless"; and *Variety* (April 10, 1963): "Reed plays with demonic skill."

Paranoiac was the first of five Hammer films directed by Freddie Francis, an Academy Award–winning cinematographer. He became the only director, other than Terence Fisher, to direct both a Hammer Frankenstein and Dracula picture. *Paranoiac* was an impressive debut and might be his best effort for the company. Although the entire cast—especially Janette Scott—is above average, this is Oliver Reed's film and he gives one of his best performances

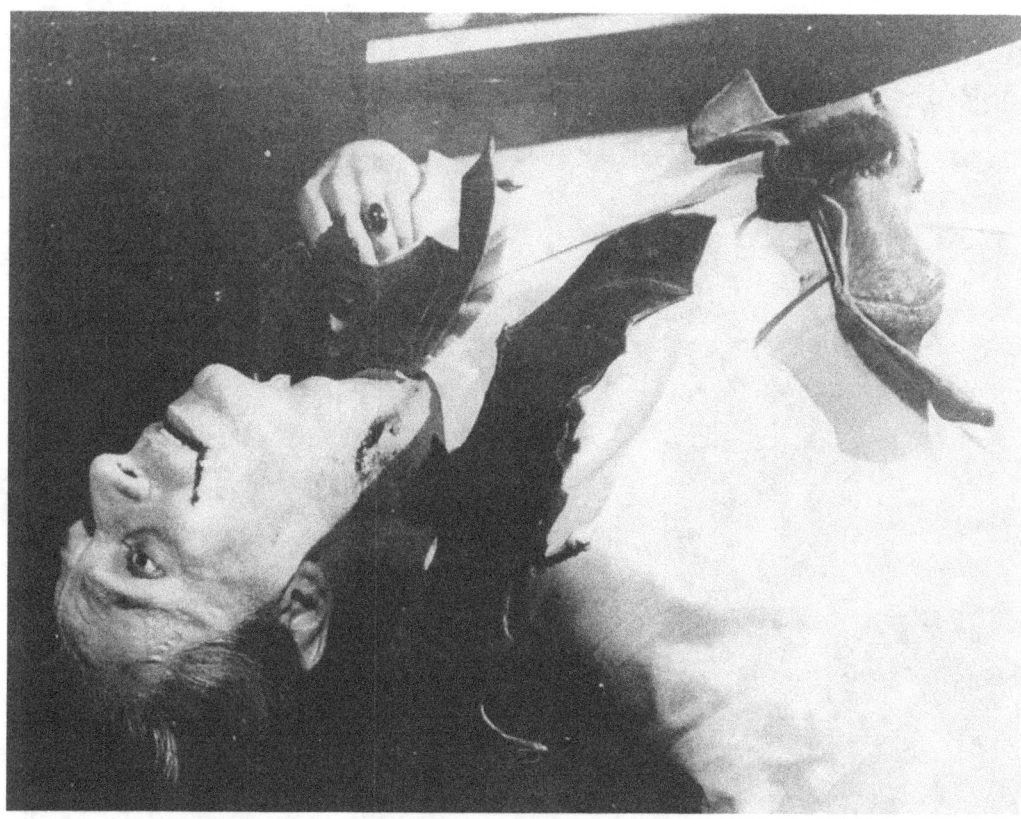

Noel Willman meets a grisly end in the thrilling climax of *Kiss of the Vampire*.

before going "mainstream." Alternatingly raving and brooding, Reed created one of the screen's most riveting madmen. Sangster and Francis added many small, deft touches that lift the picture out of the ordinary. For example, Reed's character is introduced while playing the organ at a church service while being praised by the minister. A puff of smoke envelops the instrument, followed by the smirking Reed dragging on a cigarette. Although *Paranoiac* sags at the climax, it is Hammer's most satisfactory psycho-thriller since *Taste of Fear*. Powered by Oliver Reed's excellent performance, Sangster's clever script, and Francis' crisp direction, *Paranoiac* was a near classic.

Kiss of the Vampire

Released September 11, 1963 (U.S.), January 26, 1964 (U.K.); 88 minutes; Eastman Color; a Hammer Film Production; a Rank Organization Release (U.K.), a Universal Release (U.S.); filmed at Bray Studios and Black Park, England; Director: Don Sharp; Producer: Anthony Hinds; Screenplay: John Elder; Director of Photography: Alan Hume; Production Design: Bernard Robinson; Art Director: Don Mingaye; Music: James Bernard; Musical Supervisor: John Hollingsworth; Piano Soloist: Douglas Gamley; Production Manager: Don Weeks; Supervising Editor: James Needs; Assistant Director: Douglas Hermes; Special Effects: Les Bowie; Sound Recordist: Ken Rawkins; Makeup: Roy Ashton; Camera Grip: Albert Cowland; Transport Drivers: "Coco" Epps, Laurie Martin; Prop Buyer: Eric Hillier; Wardrobe: Molly Arbuthnot; Hairdresser: Frieda Steiger; Continuity: Pauline Wise; 2nd Assistant Director: Hugh Harlow; Production Secretary: Maureen White; Camera Operator: Moray Grant; Camera Maintenance: John Kerley; Focus Puller: David Osborne; Clapper/Loader: Bob Jordan; Boom Operator: Ken Nightingall; Sound Transfer Operator: H.C. Allan; Sound Maintenance: Charles Bouvet; Sound Camera Operator: Al Thorne; Boom Assistant: R.A. Mingaye; Assistant Cut Director: Ken Ryan; Stills Cam-

Kiss of the Vampire (1962)

Jennifer Daniel and Barry Warren at the Vampire's Ball, in *Kiss of the Vampire*.

eraman: Curtis Reeks; Publicist: Brian Doyle; Assistant Makeup: Richard Mills; Wardrobe Mistress: Rosemary Burrows; Chief Accountant: W.H.V. Able; Studio Manager: A.F. Kelly; Construction Manager: Arthur Banks; Chief Electrician: Jack Curtis; Master Carpenter: Charles Davis; Master Painter: Lawrence Wren; Master Plasterer: Stan Banks; Property Master: Tommy Money; Floor Props Chargehand: Peter Day; Electrical Chargehands: George Robinson, Vic Hemmings; Casting Director: Irene Lamb; Choreographer: Leslie Edwards; U.K. Certificate: X.

Clifford Evans (Prof. Zimmer), Noel Willman (Dr. Ravna), Edward de Souza (Gerald Harcourt), Jennifer Daniel (Marianne Harcourt), Barry Warren (Karl Ravna), Jacquie Wallis (Sabena Ravna), Isobel Black (Tania), Peter Madden (Bruno), Vera Cook (Anna), Noel Howlett (Father Xavier), Stan Simmons (Hans), Brian Oulton (First Disciple), John Harvey (Police Sergeant), Olga Dickie (Woman at Graveyard), Margaret Read (1st Woman Disciple), Elizabeth Valentine (2nd Woman Disciple). Added cast for U.S. Television Broadcast: Virginia Gregg (Rosa), Sheilah Wells (Teresa), Carl Esmond (Anton).

In the Bavaria of 1910, honeymooners Gerald Harcourt (Edward de Souza) and his bride Marianne (Jennifer Daniel) run out of gasoline while touring through a forest and Gerald sets out for help. During his absence, Marianne is terrified by the appearance of a man named Professor Zimmer (Clifford Evans) who warns her that vampires inhabit an eerie chateau on the nearby mountain. After Gerald returns and they find refuge at an inn, they receive a dinner invitation from Dr. Ravna (Noel Willman), who lives at the mountaintop chateau.

Gerald and Marianne accept and Dr. Ravna introduces his son Karl (Barry Warren) and daughter Sabena (Jacquie Wallis). After dinner, Karl plays the piano which has a strange, hypnotic effect on Marianne. The next day they are invited to a masquerade ball. At the chateau, Gerald is drugged and Marianne is put into a deep trance by Ravna who prepares to sink his teeth into her neck. Ger-

Hammer's intriguing look at a vampire cult.

ald awakens but cannot find his wife and is forcibly thrown out of the castle.

Gerald goes to the police to report that his wife has been abducted by the Ravnas but the police sergeant (John Harvey) cautions Gerald about making charges against the well-respected family. As a last resort, he enlists the aid of Professor Zimmer and they return to the chateau where Gerald is attacked by a vampire, but escapes when he smears his own blood across his chest in the form of a cross. Prof. Zimmer finds Marianne and they all rush back to the inn. The evil Ravna and his cult are trapped in their castle because the Professor has sealed all exits with the sign of the cross.

Returning to his quarters, Zimmer prepares for a ceremony which, he tells Gerald, will compel the forces of evil to destroy their own. Zimmer draws the Pentacle of Solomon on the floor and invokes the power of darkness (in the form of bats) to attack the coven. Hordes of vampire bats swarm and invade the castle. Ravna, his children and all their disciples are destroyed.

Kiss of the Vampire is anything but a conventional vampire movie. Like *The Brides of Dracula*, it convincingly substituted a new character in place of the Count, and Anthony Hinds' screenplay is a departure from accepted vampire lore. Many of the vampires' mystical qualities were dropped in order to represent them as members of a perverted cult as much as being undead. Actually, the story incorporates several ideas from Universal's *The Black Cat* (1934), a satanic thriller with Karloff and Lugosi as the prototypes for Noel Willman and Clifford Evans. In place of the blatant shocks associated with Hammer horror, *Kiss of the Vampire* introduced a bit of subtlety. Director Don Sharp (*Fangoria* 31) said:

> I had actually never gone to a horror movie. Hammer sent me a script and it was good. I said, "That's fine, but I must know what it's about and how these things are treated." They decided to show me three or four of their best. I was stepping into a totally new world. I felt it might work better if, instead, we suggested the horror. I went and discussed my ideas with Tony Hinds, and I must say he was a bit aghast because I wanted to take a lot of the horror elements out.

The decision to tone down the shocks may also have been based on increasing censorship controls. Hinds said (*The Kinematograph Weekly*, October 18, 1962), "Our censors are very strict, and it's gotten particularly difficult—we invariably get back a three page letter of things they're not prepared to pass." With the censor appeased, *Kiss of the Vampire* began production on September 7, 1962. Hammer was still going through the motions of planning non-horror subjects (*Love in Smokey Regions*, *The Mercenaries*) that never saw a sound stage. "Hammer often lived hand-to-mouth," Anthony Hinds said (*Little Shoppe* of Horrors 10/11), "and occasionally there might be a 'hiccup' in the production plan—finance not forthcoming, an idea falling through—but rarely, if ever, was it a policy decision." Unfortunately, Hammer would soon abandon most other subjects in favor of horror. *Kiss of the Vampire* concluded on October 25, 1962, and, oddly, was not released in America for almost a year. Even stranger was its British premiere being pushed back to January 5, 1964. After opening at the New Victoria, it went into general release, paired with *Paranoiac* on January 26 to positive reviews. *The Kinematograph Weekly* (December 26, 1963): "Guaranteed to entertain"; *The New York Times* (October 10): "The most artistic and neatly original reprise of the Dracula theme we've seen in years"; *The Daily Cinema* (January 4, 1964): "Satisfying eerie atmosphere, some adroit horror tactics, and acting to match"; and *Films and Filming* (February, 1964): "The production standard is unusually high."

Noel Willman is a standout in a uniformly fine cast, and creates one of the screen's great vampires. The cause of his "affliction" is vaguely attributed to an "experiment that went wrong," and this deliberate withholding of information makes the vampires all the more intriguing. How did his children become undead? Why can they, within limits, walk in daylight? Barry Warren steals several scenes as the sullen Karl, most notably at the piano, hypnotically seducing the heroine to James Bernard's eerily beautiful concerto. "The effect of the music," Bernard told the authors (August, 1994), "Barry's demonic acting, and the staging all contributed to a memorable scene—one of my favorites. The piano piece is one I'm still asked to play, and I always try to keep in practice." Edward de Souza and Jennifer Daniel as the young lovers—usually a horror movie's weakest link—are among Hammer's most effective. De Souza is especially convincing when caught up in the Hitchcockian trap of being told that his wife never existed.

Bernard Robinson's lush chateau, described by Ravna as a "beautiful coffin," admirably suggests the family's perverse decadence and is beautifully captured by Alan Hume's photography. The masked ball is brilliantly staged by all concerned and would later

A less than subtle teaser for *Kiss of the Vampire*.

be parodied in Roman Polansky's *Dance of the Vampires* (1967). The only weak point in *Kiss of the Vampire* is the climactic bat attack, originally intended for *The Brides of Dracula*. Prefiguring *The Birds* (1963), the swarm of bats was beyond Hammer's effects team and, unfortunately, brings the film down a notch at its conclusion. "I think it was good for its day," recalled Don Sharp. "It was a bit different. I tried to give it a bit of style."

A censored version titled *Kiss of Evil* with extra scenes of filler added was created for American television and is best forgotten.

Nightmare

Released April 19, 1964 (U.K.); 82 minutes; B & W; Hammerscope; 7380 feet; a Hammer Film Production; a Rank Organization Release (U.K.), a Universal Release (U.S.); filmed at Bray Studios; Director: Freddie Francis; Producer: Jimmy Sangster; Screenplay: Jimmy Sangster; Director of Photography: John Wilcox; Music Composed by Don Banks; Musical Supervisor: John Hollingsworth; Production Designer: Bernard Robinson; Art Director: Don Mingaye; Editor: James Needs; Sound Recordist: Ken Rawkins; Makeup: Roy Ashton; Wardrobe Supervisor: Molly Arbuthnot; Wardrobe Mistress: Rosemary Burrows; Camera Operator: Ronnie Maasz; Production Manager: Don Weeks; Assistant Director: Douglas Hermes; Second Assistant: Hugh Harlow; Stills Cameraman: Tom Edwards; Special Effects: Les Bowie; Hairdresser: Frieda Steiger; U.K. Certificate: X.

David Knight (Henry Baxter), Moira Redmond (Grace), Brenda Bruce (Mary), Jennie Linden (Janet), George A. Cooper (John), Irene Richmond (Mrs. Gibbs), John Welsh (Doctor), Timothy Bateson (Barman), Clytie Jessop ("Woman in White"), Hedger Wallace (Sid), Julie Samuel (Maid), Elizabeth Dear (Janet as a child), Isla Cameron (Mother).

Janet (Jennie Linden) is crippled by a nightmare in which she sees her mother (Isla Cameron) sitting alone in a room which is actually a padded cell in an asylum. Mary (Brenda Bruce), her teacher, thinks that Janet needs to return home; and the pair are met at the station by John, the family chauffeur (George A. Cooper), rather than her guardian, Henry Baxter (David Knight). At the house, Janet meets Grace (Moira Redmond), who is to be her "companion."

That night, the housekeeper (Irene Richmond) reveals that the nightmare is based in reality. When she was eleven, Janet witnessed her mother kill her father. Janet now fears she, too, will go mad. After Mary returns to school, Janet suffers an even worse nightmare involving a woman wearing a shroud. Henry will not permit her to see a psychiatrist, and Janet attempts suicide. When she later meets Henry's wife (Clytie Jessop), she is identical to the woman in the nightmare. She breaks down, stabs the woman to death, and is institutionalized. Grace, wearing a mask resembling Mrs. Baxter, is revealed to be the "ghost."

Three months later, lovers Henry and Grace celebrate their success in getting rid of Mrs. Baxter. But Mary and John suspect their involvement, maneu-

Top: Jennie Linden—terrified—in *Nightmare*. *Bottom:* One of Hammer's "sleepers."

ver Grace into murdering Henry, and Janet is released.

Nightmare was the fourth in Hammer's unofficial series of psycho-thrillers written by Jimmy Sangster. Though it has been undervalued, it is more than passable entertainment. Originally titled *Here's the Knife, Dear—Now Use It*, the film went into production on December 17, 1962. "The only trouble about the title," Sangster said (*Kinematograph Weekly*, January 3, 1963), "is that it more than tells you something—it tells you everything." His formula for writing this type of movie was: "You merely put shock upon shock—and do it four times. Each shock is more terrifying than the preceding one. It's bad audience psychology to have more. Of course, the real humdinger I keep for the climax."

Filming ended on January 31, 1963, and *Nightmare* went into release on the ABC circuit on April 19 to up and down reviews. *The London Times* (April 16): "Freddie Francis can be welcomed to the short roll of British horror specialists"; *The Daily Mail* (April 18): "One long scream"; *The Sunday Times* (April 19): "Slick and smooth"; *The Observer* (April 19): "If you enjoy being frightened, see *Nightmare*"; *Films and Filming* (April): "Routine exercise"; *Kinematograph Weekly* (April 23): "Undemanding entertainment"; *Daily Cinema* (April 17): "Shocks mechanically contrived"; and *The New York Times* (June 18): "A cardboard fake."

Nightmare was Freddie Francis' fifth film as a director since leaving his Academy Award–winning position as a lighting cameraman (*Sons and Lovers*, 1960), and his second as a director for Hammer. "How do I like directing?" he asked (*Kinematograph Weekly*, January 3, 1963). "I love it. It's much easier." Despite some effective moments, *Nightmare* is fairly easily forgotten.

1963

The Scarlet Blade

Released August 12, 1963 (U.K.); 82 minutes; Technicolor (U.K.), Eastman Color (U.S.); Hammerscope; 7380 feet; an Associated British–Hammer Production; Released by Warner-Pathe (U.K.), Columbia (U.S.); filmed at Bray Studios; Director: John Gilling; Producer: Anthony Nelson-Keys; Screenplay: John Gilling; Director of Photography: Jack Asher; Music Composer: Gary Hughes; Music Supervisor: John Hollingsworth; Production Design: Bernard Robinson; Art Director: Don Mingaye; Editor: John Dunford; Supervising Editor: James Needs; Special Effects: Les Bowie; Camera Operator: C. Cooney; Makeup: Roy Ashton; Sound Recordist: Ken Rawkins; Sound Editor: James Groom; Hair Stylist: Frieda Steiger; Wardrobe Mistress: Rosemary Burrows; Production Manager: Clifford Parkes; Assistant Director: Dough Hermes; Second Assistant: Hugh Harlow; Third Assistant: Stephen Victor; Production Secretary: Pauline Wise; Camera Maintenance: John Kerley; Focus: Mike Sarafian; Clapper Loader: David Kelly; Boom: Peter Pardoe; Sound Camera Operator: Al Thorne; Stills Cameraman: Tom Edwards; Publicity: Brian Doyle; Assistant Makeup: Richard Mills; Costumes: Molly Arbuthnot; Studio Manager: A.F. Kelly; Construction Manager: Arthur Banks; Master Carpenter: Charles Davis; Master Painter: Lawrence Wren; Master Plasterer: Stan Banks; Property Master: Tommy Money; Property Buyer: Eric Hiller; Floor Props: John Goddard; Grip: Albert Cowlard; Transportation: Coco Epps; U.S. Title: *The Crimson Blade*; U.K. Certificate: U.

Lionel Jeffries (Colonel Judd), Oliver Reed (Sylvester), Jack Hedley (Edward), June Thornburn (Claire), Duncan Lamont (Major Bell), Suzan Farmer (Constance), Michael Ripper (Pablo), Charles Houston (Drury), Harold Goldblatt (Jacob), Clifford Elkin (Philip), Michael Byrne (Lt. Hawke), John Harvey (Sgt. Grey), John Stuart (Beverly), Harry Towb (Cobb), Robert Rietty (King Charles I), John H. Watson (Fitzroy), Douglas Blackwell (Blake), Leslie Glazer (Gonzalez), John Wodnutt (Lt. Wyatt), Eric Corrie (Duncannon), Denis Holmes (Chaplain).

England, 1648. Oliver Cromwell is leading a revolt against the Royalists. King Charles I (Robert Rietty) is in hiding, protected by Beverly (John Stuart) and his sons Edward (Jack Hedley) and Philip (Clifford Elkin). In pursuit are Colonel Judd (Lionel Jeffries) and Captain Sylvester (Oliver Reed). Beverly is captured and executed without a trial, and Charles is taken prisoner. Judd's daughter Clare (June Thornburn) disapproves of the revolution and, using Sylvester's desire for her, twists his "loyalty" to the crown. To avenge his father's murder, Edward adopts the name "The Scarlet Blade" and organizes the locals and a band

Hammer's version of the Cromwell era provided Lionel Jeffries with a rare starring role.

of gypsies led by Pablo (Michael Ripper) into a fighting force. Clare offers her help, and she and Edward became lovers. Sylvester, realizing he has been used, returns his "loyalty" to Judd.

While Judd is dealing with the king's imprisonment, Major Bell (Duncan Lamont) takes his command and arrests Edward's sister Constance (Suzan Farmer) to use as "bait." Edward is captured during a rescue attempt. When Judd returns, he learns of Sylvester's treachery, and after Sylvester informs on Clare, Judd shoots him. Edward and Clare escape after a brutal battle and hide in Pablo's camp. When Judd searches the camp with his troops, he recognizes them but, for reasons of his own, rides on.

Hammer excelled at making period adventures and, with the company's flair for costumes and set design, could create a period sense that rivalled the blockbusters from major studios. As in their horror films, Hammer's adventures stressed characterization over pointless action, and the focus of *The Scarlet Blade* is not Edward's swashbuckling, but the moral dilemmas of Sylvester and Judd. Also lifting the film above being a simple swashbuckler is its historical context of Cromwell's attempt to topple the throne.

Filming took place between March 1 and April 17, 1963, at Bray and nearby locations. Brian Lawrence joined the company's board shortly before the film's August 11 release to generally favorable reviews. *The Kinematograph Weekly* (June 27, 1963): "Time is taken to establish the characters"; *The Monthly Bulletin* (August): "This production is attractive with a reasonably convincing period flavour and careful detail, costumes, and settings"; and *Variety* (April 1, 1964): "Endowed with the cost of production polish that is a specialty of Hammer Films." Top-billed Lionel Jeffries gave a strong performance, but this is clearly Oliver Reed's film, and it becomes far less interesting after Sylvester's death. Jack Hedley, although a competent actor, has none of the charisma necessary for the role and prevents the picture from being a notch better. Released in London with *The Son of Captain Blood*, the pair racked up the second highest total at an ABC cinema for the year. The British Film industry was in a general slump during 1963, but Hammer—with ten films in preparation—was, as usual, immune.

Hammer would, unwisely, soon stop making movies like *The Scarlet Blade*. Of the ten films in preparation, nine were horror, science fiction, or fantasy. The company was gradually producing a less diversified group of films and was not the better for it.

Devil-Ship Pirates

Released May, 1964 (U.S.), August 9, 1964 (U.K.); 86 minutes; Technicolor; Hammerscope; 7712 feet; a Hammer Film Production; an Associated British–Warner-Pathe Release (U.K.), a Columbia Release (U.S.); filmed at Bray Studios,

Devil-Ship Pirates (1963)

Captain Robeles (Christopher Lee) informs Spain's military representative Manuel (Barry Warren) that he has his own plans for the crew of *The Diablo* in Hammer's *Devil-Ship Pirates*.

England; Director: Don Sharp; Producer: Anthony Nelson-Keys; Screenplay: Jimmy Sangster; Director of Photography: Michael Reed; Production Design: Bernard Robinson; Art Director: Don Mingaye; Supervising Editor: James Needs; Music: Gary Hughes; Production Manager: Don Weeks; Assistant Director: Bert Batt; Special Effects: Les Bowie; Musical Director: John Hollingsworth; Sound: Roy Hyde White; Sound Recordist: Ken Rawkins; Camera: Alan Hall; Continuity: Pauline Harlow; Wardrobe: Rosemary Burrows; Makeup: Roy Ashton; Hairstyles: Frieda Steiger; Fight Arranger: Peter Diamond; Sailing Master: Captain R.C.S. Garwood, C.B.E., D.S.O., R.N.; Sound System: R.C.A.; U.K. Certificate: U.

Christopher Lee (Captain Robeles), John Cairney (Harry), Barry Warren (Manuel), Ernest Clark (Sir Basil Smeeton), Natasha Pyne (Jane), Suzan Farmer (Angela), Andrew Keir (Tom), Duncan Lamont (Bosun), Michael Ripper (Pepe), Charles Houston (Antonio), Harry Locke (Bragg), Michael Newport (Smiler), Peter Howell (Vicar), Jack Rodney (Mandrake), Philip Latham (Miller), Leonard Fenton (Quintana), Barry Linehan (Gustave), Bruce Beeby (Pedro), Michael Peake (Grande), Johnny Briggs (Pablo), Joseph O'Connor (Don Jose), Annette Whiteley (Meg), June Ellis (Mrs. Blake).

The *Diablo*, a pirate ship under the command of cutthroat Captain Robeles (Christopher Lee) and commissioned to serve with the Spanish Armada, is crippled during a battle with a British ship. The ship is grounded on the Cornish coast and Manuel (Barry Warren) lies to the Squire (Ernest Clark) of the nearby village that England has been conquered by the Spanish. Captain Robeles arrives with his crew and takes over the town, but a small group of dissidents soon forms and is aided by Manuel, who has gone over to the side of the villagers. When Harry (John Cairney), son of the local blacksmith (Andrew Keir), organizes the villagers to fight the pirates, he is flogged and his father is hanged. Harry and Manuel devise a plan to sabotage the *Diablo* so that it explodes when it sets sail, but the crafty Robeles has decided to bring along hostages, including the Squire's daughter (Suzan Farmer). Harry manages to free the hostages and lights the fuse while Robeles wounds Manuel in a sword fight. Robeles is about to kill Harry when the dying Manuel shoots the pirate captain in the back. Harry leaps from

A perfect Saturday matinee double feature.

the deck of the *Diablo* as the fuse detonates the hidden store of gunpowder, destroying the ship and crew.

"At the time," Don Sharp recalled (*Little Shoppe of Horrors* 7), "in addition to the horror movies, Hammer was making one action picture that could be released at the school holidays. It had to be full of action, but it still had to get a "U" Certificate. It wasn't easy to do, what with all the floggings and everything." Like *The Pirates of Blood River*, *The Devil-Ship Pirates* was very close to the "U" limit and may not have been everyone's idea of "children's holiday entertainment." Filming began on August 19, 1963, with location work for the battles done about a mile from Bray Studios. "When we were shooting the battle scenes," Sharp added, "we had to put up a lot of smoke to cover the background because they were building the M4 motorway. The attack on the ship at the end was shot there." *The Diablo*, designed by Bernard Robinson, was 120 feet long and weighed 40 tons, and was built by Arthur Banks and his 80-man construction crew. "We based her loosely on the style of the famous *Golden Hind*," Robinson explained, "with touches of *The Mayflower* and *The Santa Maria* here and there. It was fully equipped with a small engine and took about two months to construct." After the ship was finished at a cost of £17,000, Hammer built an artificial lake by filling a gravel pit with water. Three 25-ton cranes lifted *The Diablo* into the water where it was then fitted with rigging and sails. The company had hoped to rent the ship to other filmmakers afterwards, but *The Diablo* had not been built to handle the weight of the actors and crew. Badly damaged during the production, the ship had to be destroyed after filming ended on October 4, 1963.

The Devil-Ship Pirates was released on August 9, 1964, to both good business and reviews. *The Daily Cinema* (June 3): "Sturdy swashbuckling adventure, soberly scripted and acted, but thrills ample and action well staged"; and *Variety* (March 25): "Impressively mounted adventure meller." The film performed well enough to make *The Kinematograph Weekly*'s Top Moneymakers list for 1964. Christopher Lee headed an excellent cast and added another colorful villain to his portfolio. Don Sharp (*Little Shoppe of Horrors* 7) said, "Lee is one of the most competent actors I've worked with. He's a talented man with a great screen presence." "I was cut about quite a lot in this film," Lee recalled (Christopher Lee Club, May, 1965). "At the end of the climactic battle with John Cairney, I pitched straight back into the flames, rather nearer than I intended. Besides catching my elbows an imperial crack on the deck, I also set fire to my wig!" *The Devil-Ship Pirates* shows Hammer at its best, using its production expertise to give the film a look equal to many times its cost.

Peter Cushing and Kiwi Kingston in Hammer's inferior sequel, *The Evil of Frankenstein*.

The Evil of Frankenstein

Released May 8, 1964 (U.S.), May 31, 1964 (U.K.); 84 minutes (U.K.), 86 minutes (U.S. TV); Eastman Color; a Hammer Film Production; a Rank Organization Release (U.K.), a Universal Release (U.S.); filmed at Bray Studios, England; Director: Freddie Francis; Producer: Anthony Hinds; Screenplay: John Elder; Music: Don Banks; Music Supervisor: John Hollingsworth; Director of Photography: John Wilcox; Art Director: Don Mingaye; Production Manager: Don Weeks; Supervising Editor: James Needs; Sound Recordist: Ken Rawkins; Camera: Ronnie Maasz; Assistant Director: Bill Cartlidge; Continuity: Pauline Harlow; Makeup: Roy Ashton; Hairdresser: Frieda Steiger; Special Effects: Les Bowie; Assistant Editor: Chris Barnes; Draughtman: Fred Carter; 2nd Assistant Director: Hugh Harlow; Wardrobe Mistress: Rosemary Burrows; Studio Manager: A.F. Kelly; 3rd Assistant Director: Stephan Victor; Production Secretary: Maureen White; Assistant Makeup: Richard Mills; Assistant Hairdresser: Daisy Bais; Assistant Wardrobe: Maggie Lewin; Construction Manager: Arthur Banks; Chief Electrician: Jack Curtis; Master Carpenter: Charles Davies; Master Painter: Lawrence Wrenn; Prop Master: Tommy Money; Electrical Chargehand: Vic Hemmings; Property Buyer: Eric Hiller; Electrical Supervisor: George Robinson; Camera Grip: Albert Cowland; Clapper/Loader: Tony Richardson; Boom Operator: T. Buchanan; Sound Transfer Operator: Michael Sale; Sound Maintenance: Charles Bouvet; Sound Camera Operator: A. Thorne; Boom Assistant: Ron Mingaye; Stills Cameraman: Tom Edwards; Drivers: Coco Epps, Laurie Martin; Master Plasterer: Stan Banks; Floor Props Chargehand: Danny Skundric; Focus Puller: G. Glover; U.K. Certificate: X.

Peter Cushing (Baron Frankenstein), Peter Woodthorpe (Zoltan), Sandor Eles (Hans), Duncan Lamont (Chief of Police), Katy Wild (Beggar Girl), David Hutcheson (Burgomeister), Caron Gardner (Burgomeister's Wife), Tony Arpino (Body Snatcher), James Maxwell (Priest), Alister Williamson (Landlord), Frank Forsythe (Manservant), Kenneth Cove (Cure), Michele Scott (Little Girl), Howard Goorney (Drunk), Anthony Blackshaw (Burly Constable), David Conville (Young Constable), Timothy Bateson (Hypnotized Man), Kiwi Kingston (The Creature), Derek Martin, Robert Flynn, Anthony Poole, James Garfield (Roustabouts).

Peter Cushing takes the reins in this practice run for *The Evil of Frankenstein*.

Baron Frankenstein (Peter Cushing) and his assistant Hans (Sandor Eles) are forced to flee when their experiment with a corpse is interrupted by an enraged priest (James Maxwell). They return to the Baron's abandoned chateau near Karlstadt, where Frankenstein tells Hans of the being he created years ago. The Creature (Kiwi Kingston), hunted by villagers, was shot and disappeared into a glacier.

When they arrive in Karlstadt, a carnival is underway and, in disguise, they see the Burgomeister (David Hutcheson), whom the Baron rashly accuses of stealing his ring. On the run, they find brief refuge in the carnival wagon of Zoltan (Peter Woodthorpe), a hypnotist. Joined by a mute beggar (Katy Wild), the Baron and Hans take shelter in the mountains where they find the Creature, perfectly preserved in the glacial ice. The monster is taken to Frankenstein's still functional laboratory where its body is revived, but not its mind. The Baron uses Zoltan to shock the Creature's brain, but the hypnotist is *too* successful. The monster is under his control, and Zoltan uses it to loot the village and "punish" those who drove him out. The Creature goes too far and kills the Burgomeister. Frankenstein confronts Zoltan, and they fight for control of the Creature—a battle lost by Zoltan, whom the monster kills with a spear. Frankenstein is arrested by the Chief of Police (Duncan Lamont) but escapes and returns to the chateau. In Frankenstein's absence, the Creature has become drunk on brandy and mistakenly downs a bottle of chloroform. Agonized, it sets the laboratory ablaze and the Baron, upon his return, is consumed with his creation in the inferno.

The Evil of Frankenstein is an example of what can go wrong when a film company abandons what it does best, and it shows how

The Evil of Frankenstein (1963)

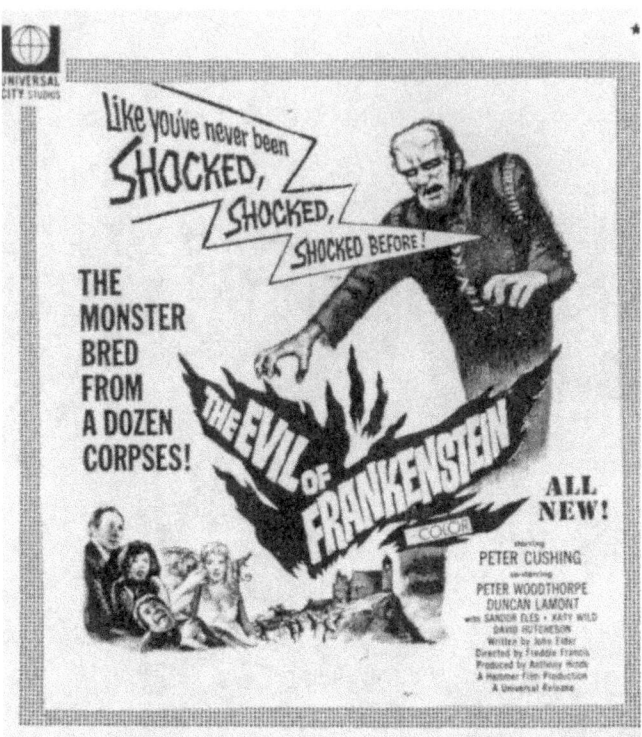

Even Peter Cushing couldn't save this one!

important Terence Fisher and Jimmy Sangster were to Hammer's success. Due to an agreement with Universal signed in 1959, Hammer had remake rights to the Universal horror library, which also included the elusive copyright to the Jack Pierce/Boris Karloff makeup. Loosely patterned on *The Son of Frankenstein*, the film has Zoltan standing in for Ygor (Bela Lugosi), controlling the monster for his own evil purposes. The picture also drew small bits from *Bride of Frankenstein* (a drunken monster) and *House of Frankenstein* (the travelling carnival). These ideas work much better than Roy Ashton's feeble makeup job, which degrades rather than copies its source. Ex-wrestler Kiwi Kingston is an easy target, but his performance—hampered by the poor makeup—is no worse than that of any Universal actor who followed Karloff as the monster. Even Peter Cushing lacks his usual spark and gives his least interesting performance as the Baron.

The film seems out of place in the Hammer saga. Anthony Hinds' screenplay offers no continuity from the ingenious finale of *The Revenge of Frankenstein*, and it explores none of the quirky themes that made Hammer's series so unique. Freddie Francis, standing in for Terence Fisher, directs competently but lacked Fisher's inspiration. Francis' idea of making a good Frankenstein movie was to concentrate on the elaborate set at the expense of the characterization and emotion that Fisher emphasized.

The Evil of Frankenstein went into production on October 14, 1963, on a closed set. This was an unusual move for Hammer, and Anthony Hinds explained that it was done to preserve the film's shocks for its future audience. Unfortunately, the audience received a different kind of shock. On November 13, James Carreras hosted a party at the Savoy Hotel to celebrate the completion of Anthony Hinds' 50th (actually 51st) production. Filming ended three days later. Carreras delivered Universal's print during a February, 1964, trip to New York, and it was released nationwide on May 8. Rank released the film (paired with *Nightmare*) on May 31 following a premiere at the New Victoria on April 19. The picture's box office returns were initially encouraging, as the Hammer, Cushing, and Frankenstein names attracted a crowd, but, once inside the theatres, most were disappointed. Reviewers were also unimpressed. *The Sunday Times* (April 19): "After seeing this Hammer production, I feel a shiver of distaste"; *The London Times* (April 16): "One or two of the actors get quite out of control"; *The Kinematograph Weekly* (April 23): "The electrical gadgets in Frankenstein's laboratory are a marvel of unscientific engineering"; and *Castle of Frankenstein* (5): "What has Hammer proven? Not much."

The Gorgon

Released October 18, 1964 (U.K.), February 17, 1965 (U.S.); 87 minutes (U.K.), 83 minutes (U.S.); Eastman Color; 7497 feet; a Hammer Film Production; a B.L.C. Release (U.K.), a Columbia Release (U.S.); filmed at Bray Studios, England; Director: Terence Fisher; Producer: Anthony Nelson-Keys; Screenplay: John Gilling, John Elder, based on a story by J. Llewellyn Devine; Music: James Bernard; Music Supervised and Conducted by: Marcus Dods; Director of Photography: Michael Reed; Supervising Editor: James Needs; Camera: Cece Cooney; Production Manager: Don Weeks; Production Design: Bernard Robinson; Art Director: Don Mingaye; Sound: Roy Hyde; Makeup: Roy Ashton; Special Effects: Syd Pearson; Wardrobe: Rosemary Burrows; Hairstyles: Frieda Steiger; Fight Arranger; Peter Diamond; Assistant Director: Bert Batt; Continuity: Pauline Harlow; Editor: Eric Boyd-Perkins; Sound Recordist: Ken Rawkins; Production Manager: Don Weeks; Stills Photographer: Tom Edwards; Wardrobe Supervisor: Molly Arbuthnot; U.K. Certificate: X.

Peter Cushing (Dr. Namaroff), Christopher Lee (Prof. Meister), Barbara Shelley (Carla), Richard Pasco (Paul), Michael Goodliffe (Prof. Heitz), Patrick Troughton (Kanof), Jack Watson (Ratoff), Jeremy Longhurst (Bruno), Sally Nesbitt (Nurse), Prudence Hyman (The Gorgon), Toni Gilpin (Sascha), Redmond Phillips (Hans), Joseph O'Connor (Coroner), Alister Williamson (Cass), Joyce Hemson (Martha), Michael Peake (Policeman).

In 1910, the Central European village of Vandorf is the scene of a series of inexplicable murders in which the victims are turned to stone. Bruno (Jeremy Longhurst), the lover of one of the female victims, hangs himself and a biased court rules murder-suicide.

Bruno's father, Professor Heitz (Michael Goodliffe), disagrees and proposes to learn the truth. His questions lead him to a hospital run by Dr. Namaroff (Peter Cushing), a brain specialist Heitz met in college. Heitz mentions his suspicions involving Megera, a Gorgon—a creature of mythology whose horrible face can turn a human to stone.

Heitz moves into his son's cottage with his old servant Hans (Redmond Phillips), but angry villagers soon set it ablaze. Fearing for his life, Heitz contacts his friend Professor Meister (Christopher Lee) who is also his son Paul's (Richard Pasco) teacher at the university. Paul takes the next train to Vandorf.

A strange sound attracts Heitz and draws him toward the notorious Castle Borski. There he sees *something*, and staggers back to the cottage. While outlining his suspicions in a letter to Paul, Heitz dies. His body has turned to stone.

When Paul arrives home and learns of his father's death, he visits Namaroff and is rudely dismissed. However, he gains the sympathy of Namaroff's nurse Carla (Barbara Shelley). Carla later visits Paul and secretly reads his father's letter which she later recites to a somber Namaroff. Namaroff reveals that Megera does exist and occasionally takes over the body of a human being. Later, Paul investigates the same sinister sound that lured his father to his death, but is saved by glimpsing the horror in a reflecting pool. He awakens five days later—aged ten years—in Namaroff's hospital.

Carla confides to Paul that while Namaroff is in love with her, she is terrified of him. Paul promises to take her with him when the mystery is solved, but Carla fears it will be too late. Paul and Professor Meister visit the chief of police (Patrick Troughton), who reveals that Carla arrived in Vandorf as an amnesiac just prior to the first murder. From stolen hospital records Meister learns that Carla only suffers from amnesia during the cycle of the full moon. He is convinced that during these episodes, Megera's spirit enters her body.

When Paul goes again to Castle Borski, Namaroff is waiting and attacks him with a sword. While they struggle, the Gorgon (Prudence Hyman) appears, turning Namaroff to stone. As the Gorgon closes in on Paul, Professor Meister steals up behind the creature and with one swift stroke of the sword beheads the monster. However, he is too late to save Paul, who dies sobbing as he watches the Gorgon's face revert to the features of his beloved Carla.

After largely drawing on English literature for its horrors, Hammer went back to Greek mythology—and an original story by J. Llewellyn Devine—for its first female monster. "The Gorgon," John Gilling said in *Little Shoppe of Horrors 4*, "was a writing assignment from Hammer that I considered one of my best screenplays." However, Gilling felt Anthony Hinds, who "re-wrote the opening and changed much of the dialogue," ruined the film in its final form.

The Gorgon (1963)

Peter Cushing, Christopher Lee, and Terence Fisher were reunited here for the first time since *The Mummy*. Although *The Gorgon* is not in the same class as the trio's fifties work, that is hardly a condemnation. Fisher had not worked for Hammer since the failure of *The Phantom of the Opera*, and he made the most of his return. "The best horror films," Fisher said (Alan Frank's *Horror Films*), "are adult fairy tales, no more, no less." The two stars had gone their separate ways and enjoyed their reunion on the set. "We're great kidders," Lee told Ron Borst, "and both of us caught the habit of making the other laugh which is, sometimes, quite disastrous." Barbara Shelley initially found Lee "rather bluff, pompous, intellectual." "But," she said (*Christopher Lee Bulletin*), "it wasn't long before I began to see another side to Chris. Without ever allowing it to interfere with his discipline or professionalism, Chris has a beautiful dry sense of humor." Shelley regretted not being allowed to play the title character. "When the Gorgon actually appeared," she said (*Little Shoppe of Horrors* 7), "it was another actress made up. If I was needed on the set as Carla, it would take two hours to switch from the Gorgon—or even longer the other way." Anthony Nelson-Keys also felt two actresses were necessary to preserve the monster's secret identity. The Gorgon's makeup—especially in the final shot—is one of the film's few weak spots.

Christopher Lee prepares to put an end to the terrible Megera (Prudence Hyman) in the climax of *The Gorgon*.

The Gorgon began production on December 9, 1963, budgeted at £150,000, and ended on January 16, 1964. It was trade shown at the Columbia Theatre on August 19, and went into release, featured with *The Curse of the Mummy's Tomb*, on October 18. The pair were a success, making *Kinematograph Weekly*'s "Top Moneymakers" list. Critics liked *The Gorgon*, too. *The Daily Cinema* (August 26): "Elegantly decked out in Hammer's best Gothic style"; *The Kinematograph Weekly* (August 27): "Sustained atmosphere of eerie foreboding and genuine suspense"; and *Variety* (August 26): "A well made, direct yarn." *The Gorgon*, while not first rank Hammer, boasts an excellent James Bernard score, some classy acting from all concerned, a clammy atmosphere courtesy of Bernard Robinson and cinematographer Michael Reed, and Terence Fisher's fine direction. It has an atypical downbeat ending for a Hammer horror that distinguishes it from the herd. Also going against type was Christopher Lee's goodhearted hero playing against Peter Cushing's cold scientist. "I played an evil man," Cushing said (in *Tales of a Monster Hunter*), "although to be fair, this character had a secret reason for behaving as he did." It all adds up to a well made, suspenseful horror package.

Hammer's first original Gothic fairy tale.

1964

Hysteria

Released June 27, 1965 (U.K.), April, 1965 (U.S.); 85 minutes; B & W; 7670 feet; a Hammer Film Production; Released by MGM; filmed at MGM/EMI Elstree Studios; Director: Freddie Francis; Producer: Jimmy Sangster; Screenplay: Jimmy Sangster; Director of Photography: John Wilcox: Production Design: Edward Carrick; Supervising Editor: James Needs; Music: Don Banks; Music Supervisor: Philip Martel; Production Manager: Don Weeks; Camera: David Harcourt; Continuity: Yvonne Axworthy; Sound Recordist: Cyril Swern; Sound Editor: Roy Hyde; Makeup: Alec Garfath; Hairstyles: Alice Holmes; Wardrobe: Maude Churchill; Assistant Director: Basil Rayburn; Titles: Chambers and Partners; U.K. Certificate: X.

Robert Webber (Mr. Smith), Anthony Newlands (Dr. Keller), Jennifer Jayne (Gina), Maurice Denham (Hemmings), Lelia Goldoni (Denise), Peter Woodthorpe (Marcus Allen), Sandra Boize (English Girl), Sue Lloyd (French Girl), and John Arnatt, Marianne Stone, Irene Richmond, Kiwi Kingston.

Dr. Keller (Anthony Newlands) is treating Mr. Smith (Robert Webber) for amnesia as a result of a car crash in which the driver who picked him up was killed. Smith is unaware of who is paying his hospital bill or is paying for his luxury flat, either. The only clue to his past is a photograph of a beautiful woman torn from a magazine. As he searches for his past, Smith hires Hemmings (Maurice Denham), a private detective, and, after moving into the flat, hears strange noises.

Smith visits photographer Marcus Allen (Peter Woodthorpe), who took the woman's photograph, and learns that she was murdered in Smith's building. Concerned about his sanity, Smith calls on Dr. Keller and is nearly run over by a car driven by a woman resembling the one in the photo. Later that night, Smith enters the next door flat and finds her there. Denise (Lelia Goldoni) claims to be the widow of the man killed in the accident and has been paying Smith's bills. When Smith finds a woman's corpse in his shower, he appears to have gone mad. But he has regained his memory, and he and Hemmings discover that the dead woman is Mrs. Keller, murdered by her husband and Denise. Smith, presumed to be an invalid, tricks the pair into admitting their guilt and their plan to frame him.

Hysteria was the last—and least—of Hammer's series of *Psycho*-clones, suffering mainly from the lack of a more charismatic star. Robert Webber is technically fine, but lacked the extra "something" necessary to pull off a hokey film like this. It was clearly time for Hammer to wrap up the "series" when they did, although they gave it another shot in the early seventies with *Straight on Till Morning* and *Fear in the Night*.

Production began on February 10, 1964, with Jimmy Sangster on the set as the producer, not the author. "If you're writing a script to sell purely as a writer," he told *The Kinematograph Weekly* (March 5), "you dress it up as you would like to see it. But if you're going to produce it as well, you often find yourself pulled in two directions. You can sometimes make a good film out of a bad story," he concluded, "but you've got to work very hard to make a bad film out of a good story." In *Hysteria*'s case, both the story and film are average. Memory loss has been a thriller cliche since Cornell Woolrich's pulp fiction, and *Hysteria* breaks no new ground.

Although *Hysteria* finished production on March 23, 1964, it was not trade shown until May 21, 1965. It went into release on June 27 to indifferent reviews. *The Daily Cinema* (May 26): "Plot too clever by half, slick horror stuff in the popular vein"; *The Kinematograph Weekly* (May 27): "The plot is just too complicated. Producer-writer Jimmy Sangster has been caught here in the web of his own cleverness"; and *The New York Times* (September): "Bland lethargy ruined a decent plot."

It does seem as if Sangster finally lost his magic touch in a genre that held surprisingly little interest for him personally. "I really don't like horror movies— really!" he told the authors (August, 1993). "I can't remember the last time I saw one on my own."

Christopher Lee on the set of *The Gorgon* (photo courtesy of Tim Murphy).

The Curse of the Mummy's Tomb

Released October 18, 1964 (U.K.), December 31, 1964 (U.S.); 80 minutes; Technicolor; TechniScope; 7210 feet; a Hammer-Swallow Production; a British Lion Release (U.K.), a Columbia Release (U.S.); filmed at MGM/EMI Elstree Studios; Director: Michael Carreras; Producer: Michael Carreras; Associate Producer: Bill Hill; Screenplay: Henry Younger (Michael Carreras); Director of Photography: Otto Heller; Production Designer: Bernard Robinson; Supervising Editor: James Needs; Editor: Eric Boyd-Perkins; Music: Carlo Martelli; Musical Supervisor: Philip Martell; Assistant Director: Bert Batt; Camera Operator: Bob Thompson; Sound Recordist: Claude Hitchcock; Sound Editor: James Groom; Continuity: Eileen Head; Makeup: Roy Ashton; Hairstylist: Tris Tilley; Wardrobe: Betty Adamson, John Briggs; Casting: David Booth; Technicolor Advisor: Andrew Low; U.K. Certificate: X.

Terence Morgan (Adam Beauchamp), Fred Clark (Alexander King), Ronald Howard (John Bray), Jeanne Roland (Annette Dubois), Bernard Rebel (Professor Dubois), George Pastell (Hashmi Bey), Jack Gwillim (Sir Giles Dalrymple), John Paul (Inspector MacKenzie), Dickie Owen (The Mummy), Michael McStay (Ra), Jill Mae Meridith (Jenny), Vernon Smythe (Jessop).

Egypt, 1900. Professor Dubois (Bernard Rebel) is murdered for daring to excavate the tomb of Pharaoh RaAntef. Alexander King (Fred Clark), a boorish American showman, is the backer of the expedition and plans to road-show the mummy at 10¢ per customer. Sir Giles Dalrymple (Jack Gwillim), the head of

The Gorgon—better than the company it kept.

the dig, is in public disgrace; and Annette (Jeanne Roland)—Dubois' daughter—and her lover John (Ronald Howard) are helpless to prevent this mockery. Hashmi Bey (George Pastell) accompanies the mummy on its voyage to England, hoping to secure it for Egypt. Sir Giles and John are attacked on the ship, but are saved by the mysterious Adam Beauchamp (Terence Morgan), who is interested in both Annette and the mummy.

King plans to present the mummy to the British press, but the coffin is empty. He, Sir Giles, and Hashmi Bey are murdered in quick succession by the living mummy, fulfilling an ancient curse upon those who tamper with the tomb. Annette is kidnapped by RaAntef who is confronted by Beauchamp—his immortal brother, cursed for murdering the pharaoh thousands of years ago. He commands the mummy to kill both him and Annette so they can be joined together through eternity. John and Inspector MacKenzie arrive to save Annette as RaAntef kills Beauchamp and then himself by collapsing the ceiling of a sewer.

The Curse of the Mummy's Tomb was another sign that Hammer was slipping. Michael Carreras, as producer, director, and (as Henry Younger) writer, was unable to repeat the spell created by Terence Fisher and Jimmy Sangster in *The Mummy*. But, it must be said that Carreras took on projects lacking name stars and with lower budgets, yet still managed to make watchable films. He had a liking for the wide screen process, and Otto Heller's photography is a strong point. "You have to be more careful in getting the setups," Carreras said, (*Midnight Marquee* 47), "particularly when we had to shoot five to six minutes a day. If you move your camera about, you can bring twenty different people into frame in the same shot."

Production began on February 24, 1964, and ended on May 8. A trade show was held on August 19, and, on October 18, *The Curse of the Mummy's Tomb* was released on the ABC circuit in support of *The Gorgon*. Reviewers felt, justifiably, that the film covered no new ground and was a poor follow-up to the company's earlier effort. *The Daily Cinema* (August 21, 1964): "Eerie but routine shocker thrills. But, hand it to Hammer, they've got this kind of scary hokum down to a grisly art."

Although the cast lacked a standout star, it was perfectly adequate, with Terence Mor-

gan particularly effective. Fred Clark is initially obnoxious, but begins to win a bit of the audience's sympathy just before his brutal murder on a foggy staircase. This is the film's most effective moment and is one of Hammer's best monster scenes. Unfortunately, it is over in a few seconds. Jeanne Roland, a supposedly French "sex kitten," was actually a Burmese that Michael Carreras met at a party. "I thought she was ornamental, he said (*Midnight Marquee*). "That's all she was meant to be, more or less." Dickie Owen's mummy is quite a letdown from Christopher Lee's streamlined monster and is closer to Lon Chaney Jr.'s Universal ragbag look.

Like too many Hammer movies of the sixties, *The Curse of the Mummy's Tomb* was more competent than inspired. It *did* fulfill its intended role as a supporting feature—perhaps too well, since it makes *The Gorgon* look so much better.

Top: This Hammer monster series entry did not quite work. *Bottom:* Michael Carreras and friend check the movie ads in this behind the scenes shot from *The Curse of the Mummy's Tomb* (photo courtesy of Ted Okuda).

The Secret of Blood Island

Released June 14, 1965 (U.K.), June, 1965 (U.S.); 84 minutes; Eastman Color (U.K.); B & W (U.S.); a Hammer Film Production; a Rank Organization Release (U.K.), a Universal Release (U.S.); filmed at Pinewood and Black Park, London, England; Director: Quentin Lawrence; Producer: Anthony Nelson-Keys; Screenplay: John Gilling; Director of Photography: Jack Asher; Production Design: Bernard Robinson; Supervising Editor: James Needs; Editor: Tom Simpson; Music: James Bernard; Camera: Harry Gillam; Music Supervisor: Marcus Dodds; Sound Recordists: Ken Rawkins, James Groom; Assistant Director: Peter Price; Production Manager: Don Weeks; Continuity: Pauline Harlow; Wardrobe: Jean Fairlie; Makeup: Roy Ashton; Hairstyles: Frieda Steiger; Special Effects: Syd Pearson; Stills Photographer: Tom Edwards; Tech-

Michael Ripper supervises a flogging.

nical Advisor: Freddy Bradshaw; U.K. Certificate: A.

Barbara Shelley (Elaine/Bill), Jack Hedley (Sgt. John Crewe), Charles Tingwell (Major Dryden), Bill Owen (George Bludgin), Michael Ripper (Lt. Tojoko), Patrick Wymark (Major Jocomo), Peter Welch (Richardson), Lee Montague (Corporal Vincent Levy), Edwin Richfield (Tom O'Reilly), Glyn Houston (Berry), David Saire (KEMPI Chief), Philip Latham (Captain Drake), Ian Whittaker (Corporal Mills), John Southworth (Leonard), Peter Craze (Red), Henry Davies (Taffy).

When her plane is shot down over Japanese-occupied Malaya, secret agent Elaine (Barbara Shelley) parachutes to earth and is discovered by Sgt. Crewe (Jack Hedley), part of a work crew from a nearby POW camp. Disguised as a man, Elaine marches with the British soldiers back to the camp, where the men try to determine how to help her get to her original destination, Kuala Lumpur. The Camp Commandant Maj. Jocomo (Patrick Wymark) tells the men that if they fail to report having seen the enemy agent within 24 hours, one man from each hut will be executed as punishment.

Elaine is taken to the hut Crewe shares with Major Dryden (Charles Tingwell), Corporal Levy (Lee Montague) and Privates Richardson (Peter Welch), Bludgin (Bill Owen) and O'Reilly (Edwin Richfield). The POWs are uneasy about her presence out of fear of reprisals, but they obey Crewe's order to keep her hidden. Crewe shows Elaine a secret compartment under the hut's floor where she can hide from guards until her escape. In private, Elaine explains to Major Dryden that her mission involves an impending invasion by Chinese troops. The daughter of a local planter, Elaine can lead the troops to bridges and communication points that must be sabotaged to insure the invasion's success.

While arrangements are being made for her breakout, it is decided that Elaine would be

The Secret of Blood Island (1964)

Hammer fails to repeat the fervor caused during the company's initial visit to "the camp" on Blood Island.

safer with the work crews during the day than if she were to remain in the camp where her hiding place might be discovered by guards. When Bludgin is caught with a cigarette that could only have come from the British spy, he is flogged to death by his Japanese captors.

A diversionary fire is set to cover Elaine's escape, but the plan fails and Elaine is soon-after detected and captured. Despite torture, she refuses to divulge any information. When the men learn that she is about to be transported out of the camp by car by the Japanese Secret Police, they prepare to fight to free her. Dryden and O'Reilly are killed intercepting the car while Crewe, mortally injured, helps her escape into the jungle. Elaine continues alone on her mission in a stolen truck.

Filmed seven years after *The Camp on Blood Island*, Hammer's follow-up was actually a "prequel" and, adding to the confusion, Barbara Shelley played different roles in both pictures. "This is a really tough, hard-hitting, blood-and-guts subject," said Anthony Nelson-Keys (*The Daily Cinema*, July 22, 1964). "It has all the ingredients—action, adventure, and agonizing suspense—which made *The Camp on Blood Island* a world box office hit." *The Secret of Blood Island* began at Pinewood on July 23 for two weeks of interiors before moving to Black Park for location work. Under Bernard Robinson's supervision, one hundred men took five weeks to build the prisoner of war camp. The twelve buildings were prefabricated at Pinewood and pieced together in Black Park. Freddie Bradshaw, a former POW in Singapore, was hired as a technical advisor. Authenticity in a POW film is not necessarily a blessing, though, as the *Blood Island* pictures are uncomfortable to watch. John Gilling's brutal script for *The Secret of Blood Island*, even though flawed, at least did not sugarcoat the truth. The second-team cast, headed by Barbara Shelley, is uniformly outstanding, but it is disconcerting to see so many Brits in oriental makeup. It also requires quite a stretch to believe that Barbara Shelley could go unnoticed disguised as a man.

One of the last scenes shot was the burning of the camp. Jack Asher recalled in *Little Shoppe of Horrors*,

Toward the end of the film, the whole camp goes up in flames. Somehow the effects men got too enthusiastic, and the whole set was in flames in a matter of seconds. My operative cameraman was dutifully completing a long and difficult tracking shot. Instead of jumping off and running away as we all did, he bravely stayed with the camera and completed the shot. We later found out that his eyebrows and hair had been singed!

The production ended on September 7; and

Three stalwart adventurers—Peter Cushing, John Richardson, and Bernard Cribbins—in *She*.

while *The Secret of Blood Island* was being edited, the company formed a new subsidiary, Hammer Television Productions. Anthony Hinds commented that this step was taken, "Just in case someone else offers us a really good TV series." *The Secret of Blood Island* was trade shown on May 13, 1965, at the Rank Theatre and went into general release on the ABC circuit, paired with *The Night Walker*, to slightly favorable reviews. *The Daily Cinema* (May 24): "The suspense is grimly punctuated with beatings, interrogations, clashes among the men"; and *Variety* (April 21): "Several facets are so good that the more discerning filmgoer will be disappointed that more care wasn't taken throughout."

The Secret of Blood Island was intended to be nothing more than a programmer and, at that level, was well done. Director Quentin Lawrence kept the action highlights moving quickly enough to hide the story's many absurdities; and the typical Hammer production values made the film look better than audiences had any right to expect.

She

Released April 18, 1965 (U.K.), September 1, 1965 (U.S.); 104 minutes; Metro Color; Cinema Scope; 9324 feet; a Hammer–7 Arts Production; an MGM Release; filmed at Elstree Studios, and on location in Israel; Director: Robert Day; Producer: Michael Carreras; Associate Producer: Aida Young; Screenplay: David T. Chantler, based on H. Rider Haggard's novel; Director of Photography: Harry Waxman BSC; Art Director: Robert Jones; Editors: James Needs, Eric Boyd-Perkins; Production Manager: Ri L.M. Davidson; Assistant to Producer: Ian Lewis; Assistant Director: Bruce Sharman; Camera Operator: Ernest Day; Music Composer: James Bernard; Music Supervisor: Philip Martel; Sound Recordist: Claude Hitchcock; Sound Editors: Jim Groom, Vernon Messenger, Roy Hyde; Continuity: Eileen Head; Makeup: John O'Gorman; Hairstylist: Eileen Warwick; Wardrobe: Jackie Cummins;

250 *She* (1964)

Assistant Art Director: Don Mingaye; Research: Andrew Low; Special Effects: George Blackwell; Special Processes: Bowie Films Ltd.; Special Effects Makeup: Roy Ashton; Construction Manager: Arthur Banks; Location Manager: Yoske Hausdorf; Choreography: Cristyne Lawson; Miss Andress' Costumes: Carl Toms; U.K. Certificate: A.

Ursula Andress (Ayesha), Peter Cushing (Major Holly), Bernard Cribbins (Job), John Richardson (Leo Vincey), Christopher Lee (Billali), Rosenda Monteros (Ustane), Andre Morell (Haumeid), John Maxim (Guard Captain), Soraya, Julie Mendez, Lisa Peake (Nightclub Dancers), Cherry Larman, Bula Coleman (Handmaidens), Oo-Bla-Da Dancers.

Palestine, 1918. Following the Great War, Major Holly (Peter Cushing), his valet Job (Bernard Cribbins), and their young friend Leo (John Richardson) are lured on a mysterious trek across the desert when Leo is led by Ustane (Rosenda Monteros) to the stunningly beautiful Ayesha (Ursula Andress). She promises Leo "all that he desires" if he joins her later in the Mountains of the Moon. While marching across the desert, the trio are attacked by Arab bandits and are saved from dehydration by Ustane, who has fallen in love with Leo. She takes them to a village ruled by her father, Haumeid (Andre Morell), who is in turn ruled by Ayesha—"She Who Must Be Obeyed."

She is thousands of years old, and believes Leo to be the reincarnation of Killikrates—a lover she murdered centuries ago. She reveals that Leo can also become immortal by bathing in a magic flame—a fact resented by her High Priest Billali (Christopher Lee). After murdering Ustane for kissing Leo, she faces a revolt led by Haumeid. During the confusion, She convinces Leo to join her in the flame, but Billali enters the chamber and demands his right to immortality. As he and Leo struggle, She leaves the flame and kills Billali. Leo and She enter the flame as Holly and Job arrive to see her aging horribly—her return has reversed the flame's power. Leo vows to wait, perhaps forever, for the flame's return to end his curse of immortal life without Ayesha.

H. Rider Haggard's classic 1887 adventure has sold over 80 million copies in almost 50 languages. It is only natural that such a successful book would be filmed, and it has been—often—most notably in a 1935 RKO production starring Helen Gahagan. It is also natural that Hammer's remake would be savaged by those fondly recalling the RKO version (not warmly received itself), which inexplicably had a polar setting. Despite its credentials, *She* is not one of Hammer's best. Like *The Phantom of the Opera*, it was a failed attempt to attract a mainstream audience. *She* deserved a Charlton Heston Epic style budget, and the resultant skimpy looking production pleased no one. On the plus side were a fine cast and crisp direction from Robert Day, who recalled his experiences for the authors (March, 1992).

I had read the novel as a boy but hadn't seen the 1935 film. My *Tarzan the Magnificent* (1960), may have had something to do with being given *She*. Producers see your shows, and you get offers—they don't always tell you *why* you were hired. Peter Cushing is a wonderful man and a pleasure to work with. I was struck by his sincerity. He puts himself completely into a role and gets away with the most melodramatic lines because he probably believes them himself. Christopher Lee is almost like the characters he so often plays—very commanding and aloof. He's got wonderful stage presence and looks good in any costume. He would often come on the set while Peter was working. They were always joking—until it was time to work. Andre Morell was another marvelous actor. Like many British actors, he was able to go back and forth between big and small films. Like Peter Cushing, he came from a "school" of acting with too few students today. When an actor of Morell's quality has seventh billing, it speaks well of any film. Ursula Andress had to do more acting in *She* than was required in *Dr. No* (1962). She's a great presence but had little experience. I really had to work with her. It wasn't easy! John Richardson was a great looking guy—and a nice one—but wasn't much of an actor. Anyway, most of his scenes were with Peter, and he didn't stand a chance! I personally cast many of the roles, including Andre and Bernard Cribbins, but not Peter and Christopher. They were part of Hammer's package, and the film was planned around them. Michael Carreras and Tony Hinds were a great team. They knew what people wanted to see. Sir James was the one who kept it all together. *She* was financed by MGM, and we spent six weeks in Israel. Political problems were there, but no more so than now. We *did* have problems with explosives and camels. Someone mislaid a charge, and it went off under Bernard and peppered his behind! One of the "experts" blew off one of his fingers, stuck it in his pocket, and yelled "Get me to the hospital!" and then apologized for his rudeness. Peter had more problems with his camel than I can recount! I enjoyed my experience with Hammer—a bunch of great people. It was nerve-wracking, but fun!

She began production on August 24, 1964, in Israel and ended at Elstree on October 17. After a March 12, 1965, trade show at Studio One, *She*—Hammer's most expensive production—went into release on the ABC circuit on April 18. Michael Carreras, in *The Kinematograph Weekly* (October 1, 1964) had hinted that *She* might signal a change for Hammer. "There's no doubt the future lies with bigger productions."

In the first week, *She* (teamed with *Pop Gear*) did £2795, which was a near record at the ABC North, following with £2555 and £2575, and £1946, making it one of the top moneymakers of 1965. The problem was that *She* cost far more than the typical Hammer film and was more difficult to make. Hammer would try the "big picture" route again with *One Million Years B.C.* and discover the future was not what Carreras had envisioned. The critics were not generous. *The New York Times* (September 2, 1965): "Ridiculously old fashioned"; *Time* (September 17): "*She* is for children"; and *The New York Daily News* (September 2): "An ageless queen plods on." On the plus side were *The Kinematograph Weekly* (March 18): "Done on a grand scale"; *The Daily Cinema* (March 17): "Ample thrills, opulent settings"; and *The New York Post* (September 2): "Handsomely produced."

Despite the justified criticisms, *She* is not hard to watch, with fine individual aspects that unfortunately do not add up to a coherent whole. If David Chantler's script had followed the novel and eliminated the endless dancing, Hammer might have produced a minor classic.

Hammer takes on a subject too big for its budget.

Fanatic

Released March 21, 1965 (U.K.); 96 minutes (U.K.), 105 minutes (U.S.); Technicolor (U.K.),

Fanatic (1964)

Tallulah Bankhead shows Stefanie Powers that she means business in *Fanatic*, which was retitled *Die! Die! My Darling!* for a U.S. market.

Eastman Color (U.S.); 8642 feet; a Hammer Film Production; a British Lion Release (U.K.), a Columbia Release (U.S.); filmed at EMI/MGM Elstree Studios; Director: Silvio Narizzano; Producer: Anthony Hinds; Executive Producer: Michael Carreras; Screenplay: Richard Matheson, based on *Nightmare* by Anne Blaisdell; Director of Photography: Arthur Ibetson; Music Composed by Wilfred Josephs; Musical Director: Philip Martell; Production Designer: Peter Proud; Production Manager: George Fowler; Editor: John Dunsford; Supervising Editor: James Needs; Camera Operator: Paul Wilson; Sound Recordist: Ken Rawkins; Sound Editor: Roy Hyde; Continuity: Renee Glynn; Makeup: Roy Ashton, Richard Mills; Hairstyles: Olga Angelinetta; Assistant Director: Claude Watson; Wardrobe: Mary Gibson; Stills Photographer: Tom Edwards; U.S. Title: *Die! Die! My Darling!*; U.K. Certificate: X.

Tallulah Bankhead (Mrs. Trefoile), Stefanie Powers (Pat), Peter Vaughan (Harry), Maurice Kauffman (Alan), Yootha Joyce (Anna), Donald Sutherland (Joseph), Gwendolyn Watts (Gloria), Robert Dorning (Ormsby), Philip Gilbert (Oscar), Diane King (Woman), Winifred Dennis (shopkeeper).

Pat (Stefanie Powers) arrives in England to meet Alan (Maurice Kauffman), her fiancé. But before they marry, she feels that she must visit the mother of her former lover, Stephen, who was killed in a car crash. Against Alan's wishes, Pat drives to the secluded estate of Mrs. Trefoile (Tallulah Bankhead). The household is made up of the maid, Anna (Yootha Joyce), her husband Harry (Peter Vaughan), and Joseph (Donald Sutherland), a retarded handyman.

A former actress, Mrs. Trefoile is now a religious fanatic to whom everything is sinful, including Pat, whom she regards as Stephen's wife. When Pat reveals that she was planning a breakup when he died, Mrs. Trefoile goes mad and imprisons her "daughter-in-law" to cleanse her soul. The entire household conspires to terrify Pat, and attempts to bribe her way out prove fruitless. When she seduces Harry to get his car keys, Mrs. Trefoile finds the pair struggling on Pat's bed and orders Harry from the house. Angered at losing his position at the estate, Harry follows Mrs. Trefoile into the basement. When he confronts her, she shoots him, point blank, in the face.

Alan tracks Pat to the house and is told that she has gone, but recognizes her brooch on a local barmaid's sweater—a gift from Harry. He returns to the house in time to save Pat, but not her captor. Anna, after finding Harry's corpse, has stabbed Mrs. Trefoile, who dies embracing her son's portrait.

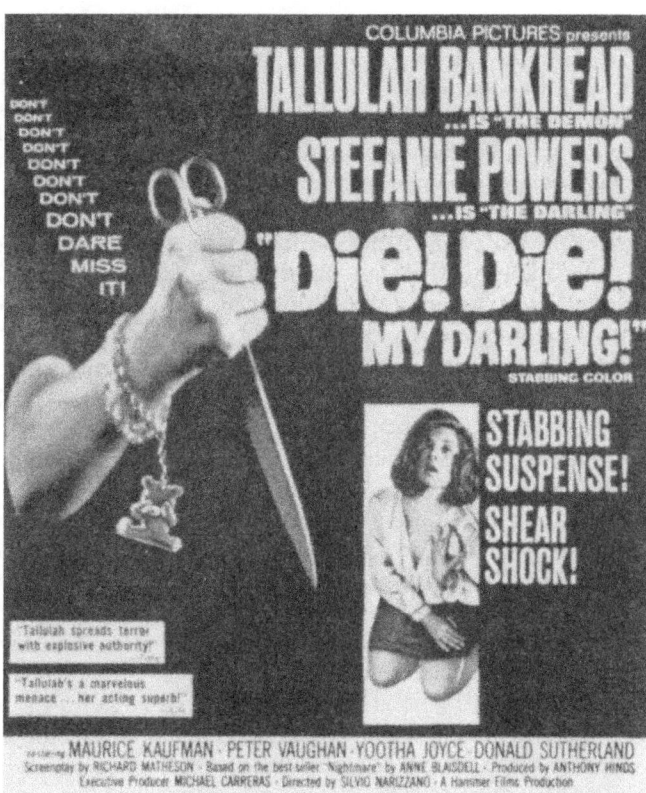

Tallulah was a terror off camera, too.

After the successful casting of aging glamour stars Bette Davis and Joan Crawford in *What Ever Happened to Baby Jane?* (1962), Hammer followed the trend by signing the legendary Tallulah Bankhead for *Fanatic*. Her "legendary" status is hard to document these days, since her greatest success was on stage. She only made seventeen movies, and her last film appearance prior to *Fanatic* was in 1953. Still, she was a "name" to many and, on the surface, quite a catch. Bankhead was in British Columbia when she received the script and was honest enough to admit (in *Miss Tallulah Bankhead*), "I needed the money, dahling."

Director Silvio Narizzano recalled in *The House of Horror* (No. 15), "The script went to Columbia who didn't know what to do with it ... so they took it down the street to Hammer. The original script had to be changed to accommodate Tallulah Bankhead." Writer Richard Matheson told the authors (May, 1992), "*Fanatic* was a production I liked a lot, except for a little scenery chewing by Tallulah and a conclusion which was a bit overly melodramatic. I thought Stefanie Powers was excellent, and the direction was first class." He explained the film's weird humor to Tom Weaver. "When something strange happens to people, if they have a sense of humor, they're going to respond. The situations were amusing to Powers—only later did it begin to dawn on her what was going on."

Tallulah Bankhead proved to be, in show business jargon, "somewhat difficult." Silvio Narizzano said in *House of Horror* (No. 15) that when production designer Peter Proud decorated the set with memorabilia from her early career (her character *was* an actress), "she threw a tantrum at first, feeling it was an impertinence. She threw occasional tantrums and walked off the set three times." Narizzano said to Dennis Bain in

Tallulah Darling, "No words can express my relief that the picture's over. She is magnificent, but impossible."

Fanatic began production at Elstree on September 7, 1964, and concluded on October 27. Three days were spent on location at Chertsey. Paired with Universal's *The Killers*, it was released on the ABC circuit on March 21, 1965. Due to the absence of Hammer "regulars" and its unfamiliar settings, *Fanatic* is hard to recognize as a Hammer film. Peter Vaughan's murder provided the one gory highlight and was a shocking scene for the mid-sixties. Naturally, reviews centered around the star. Arthur Knight (*Saturday Review*, June 6, 1965): "It is pure Grand Guignol as Tallulah ... grows progressively more fanatic and violent"; *The London Times* (March 11): "Miss Bankhead is, as one would expect, really weird and wonderful. The film is directed with flair"; *The Kinematograph Weekly* (March 11): "Bankhead pulls out all the stops."

The American title, *Die! Die! My Darling!* was a takeoff on Bette Davis' *Hush... Hush, Sweet Charlotte* (1964), but at least the line does appear in the film. Although it is not a "typical" Hammer horror, there's nothing wrong with a little variety. However, *Fanatic* is not a standout and did nothing to revive its star's career—it was her last film.

The Brigand of Kandahar

Released August 8, 1965 (U.K.); 81 minutes; Hammer Scope; Technicolor; 7319 feet; a Hammer Film Production; Released by Warner-Pathe (U.K.), Columbia (U.S.); filmed at Elstree Studios; Director: John Gilling; Director of Photography: Reg Wyer; Producer: Anthony Nelson-Keys; Screenplay: John Gilling; Music Composed by: Don Banks; Music Supervisor: Philip Martell; Production Designer: Bernard Robinson; Production Manager: Don Weeks; Editor: James Needs; Special Effects: Syd Pearson; Camera Operator: Harry Gillman; Assistant Director: Frank Nesbitts; Sound Recordist: A.W. Lumkin/RCA system; Makeup: Roy Ashton; Costumes: Rosemary Burrows; Continuity: Pauline Harlow; Hairdresser: Frieda Steiger; Fight Arranger: Peter Diamond; U.K. Certificate: U.

Ronald Lewis (Lieutenant Case), Oliver Reed (Khan), Duncan Lamont (Colonel Drewe), Yvonne Romain (Ratina); Catherine Woodville (Elsa), Glyn Houston (Marriott), Ingo Jackson (Captain Boyd), Sean Lynch (Rattu), Walter Brown (Hitala), Jeremy Burnham (Connelly), Caron Gardner (Maid), Henry Davies (Crowe), John Southworth (Barlow), Jo Powell (Color Sergeant).

India's Northwest Frontier, late 1800s. Halfcaste Lt. Robert Case (Ronald Lewis) escapes from his cell in Ft. Kandahar rather than face a court martial for cowardice. Innocent of the charge, he joins a band of Gilzhai tribesmen in revolt and forms a pact with Khan (Oliver Reed), their leader, to train them in the manner of the Bengal Lancers. Spurring him on is his desire for revenge against Col. Drewe (Duncan Lamont), who ordered the court martial. While exploring the camp, Case finds Capt. Connelly (Jeremy Burnham) a prisoner. It was his affair with Connelly's wife, Elsa (Catherine Woodville), that led to the charge against him. A London reporter, Jed Marriott (Glyn Houston), arrives to cover the fighting and, captured by the Gilzhai, is nearly executed. After saving him, Case tells Marriott about the false charges. When Case discovers that Connelly is being tortured, he mercifully kills him, but Marriott misunderstands his motives. To prove his integrity, Case allows him to escape.

Ratina (Yvonne Romain), Khan's sister, despises him and has arranged for his death during a raid on Ft. Kandahar. He returns unharmed—with Elsa as his prisoner—and accuses Case of plotting against him. After killing Khan in a duel, Case takes control of the tribe. During a battle against the Lancers, Ratina, Drewe, and Case are killed, but Marriott had learned that Case was a victim of Drew's prejudice, and plans to expose the truth.

The Brigand of Kandahar was Oliver Reed's last Hammer film, ending a nine-picture association beginning with *The Two Faces of Dr. Jekyll* in 1959. By 1964, his offbeat personality had attracted the attention of more mainstream producers, and after *Oliver!* (1968), he never looked back. Reed was one of the few actors discovered by the company to move on to bigger things, and

What's a brigand and where is Kandahar?

he recalled his Hammer days fondly in his autobiography. He was one of the company's most versatile stars, playing convincing thugs (*The Pirates of Blood River*), dashing heroes (*Captain Clegg*), and frightening psychos (*Paranoiac*), in addition to being the screen's best werewolf.

This was also a first for the company—the only time Hammer built a film around scenes from another studio's production. Columbia, with whom Hammer was associated, had action scenes cut from its 1956 *Zarak*. John Gilling, who was the film's second unit director, was hired to write a script incorporating the scenes. Even odder, *Zarak* itself contained scenes from older movies, and Roy Ashton did makeup on both *Zarak* and *The Brigand of Kandahar*.

The film is another example, like *Yesterday's Enemy*, of Hammer's sneaking a bit of social significance into its films. Although *The Brigand of Kandahar* is first an action picture and does not preach, its message of racial tolerance is there for those who want it. Filming began on October 16, 1964, and ended on November 26. After an August 8, 1965, release on the ABC circuit, it got respectable reviews, including "A good, old fashioned melodrama," from *The Kinematograph Weekly* (July 1, 1965); Oliver Reed was far less charitable, calling it (in *The World of Hammer* on the BBC), "My worst film," which is quite an indictment.

The movie, like *She*, is an example of Hammer's interest in large scope "blockbusters," but the company was just not up to competing in the Charlton Heston stakes (due more to a lack of budget than a lack of talent). Considering its less than inspired beginnings, *The Brigand of Kandahar* is a decent adventure, saved by Hammer's typical production polish and an interesting cast trying its best.

1965

The Nanny

Released October 27, 1965 (U.S.), November 7, 1965 (U.K.); 93 minutes; B & W; a Hammer–7 Arts Production; a Warner-Pathe Release (U.K.), a 20th Century–Fox Release (U.S.); filmed at MGM/EMI Studios, Elstree, England; Director: Seth Holt; Producer, Screenplay: Jimmy Sangster; Executive Producer: Anthony Hinds; Based on the novel by Evelyn Piper; Director of Photography: Harry Waxman, B.S.C.; Music: Richard Rodney Bennett; Musical Supervisor: Philip Martell; Production Design: Edward Carrick; Supervising Editor: James Needs; Production Manager: George Fowler; Editor: Tom Simpson; Assistant Director: Christopher Dryhurst; Camera: Kevin Pike; Sound Recordist: Norman Coggs; Sound Editor: Charles Crafford; Continuity: Renee Glynn; Makeup: Tom Smith; Hairstylist: A.G. Scott; Wardrobe Consultant: Rosemary Burrows; Wardrobe Mistress: Mary Gibson; Recording Supervisor: A.W. Lumkin; U.K. Certificate: A.

Bette Davis (Nanny), Wendy Craig (Virgie Fane), Jill Bennett (Penelope), James Villiers (Bill Fane), William Dix (Joey), Pamela Franklin (Bobby), Jack Watling (Dr. Medman), Maurice Denham (Dr. Beamaster), Alfred Burke (Dr. Wills), Nora Gordon (Mrs. Griggs), Sandra Power (Sarah), Harry Fowler (Milkman), Angharad Aubrey (Susy).

In their fashionable London apartment, Bill and Virgie Fane (James Villiers and Wendy Craig) are preparing for the return of their ten-year-old Joey Fane (William Dix), who was accused of drowning his own baby sister Susy and has spent the last two years in an institution for psychologically disturbed children. Virgie confides to her trusted Nanny (Bette Davis) that she is frightened of the boy and does not feel that she can cope with him after what he has done. When Bill and Nanny drive to the school to pick up Joey, Dr. Beamaster (Maurice Denham) admits that Joey may still have certain psychological problems.

At home, Joey refuses to stay in a bedroom redecorated by Nanny and to eat food prepared by her. Suffering from food poisoning, Virgie is rushed to the hospital while Nanny claims to have found a bottle of potent medicine hidden under Joey's pillow. Joey denies trying to poison his mother, and refuses to stay alone in the apartment with Nanny. Penelope (Jill Bennett), Virgie's sister, is sent for. Bobbie (Pamela Franklin), a teenage friend of Joey's, sneaks into the apartment and Joey tells her it was Nanny who poisoned Virgie and left the bottle in his bed. Penelope, who suffers from a weak heart, falls asleep in a chair and is wakened by Joey, dripping wet from his bath, who accuses Nanny of trying to drown him. The shock of Joey's accusation causes Penelope to have a mild attack, and Nanny helps her into bed. Joey goes to Bobbie's room and tells her that Susy died due to Nanny's neglect.

Penelope later catches Nanny lurking suspiciously outside Joey's door, and suffers a heart attack while struggling with the older woman. As Penelope dies, Nanny talks to her about the day Susy drowned. That was the day that Nanny got a call from a doctor concerning her own grown daughter Janet, who was given away at six months. In Janet's slum apartment, Nanny found her dead after an abortion. Returning home to the Fanes in a dazed condition, Nanny neglected Susy, who toppled into the bathtub and drowned.

The disturbed Nanny forces her way into Joey's room, knocks the boy unconscious and places him in the bathtub. Holding Joey's head under the water, Nanny suddenly sees Susy's body in the water and, in a moment of lucidity, realizes the horror of what she has done. Pulled out of the tub by Nanny, Joey wrestles out of her grasp and runs out of the room for help.

Later, Joey visits his mother in the hospital and the two are reconciled. The doctor assures Virgie that Nanny will be well cared for at the institution where she has been confined, and that she may one day fully recover.

Bette Davis was wise enough to know, and honest enough to admit, that her glamour days were over when she appeared in

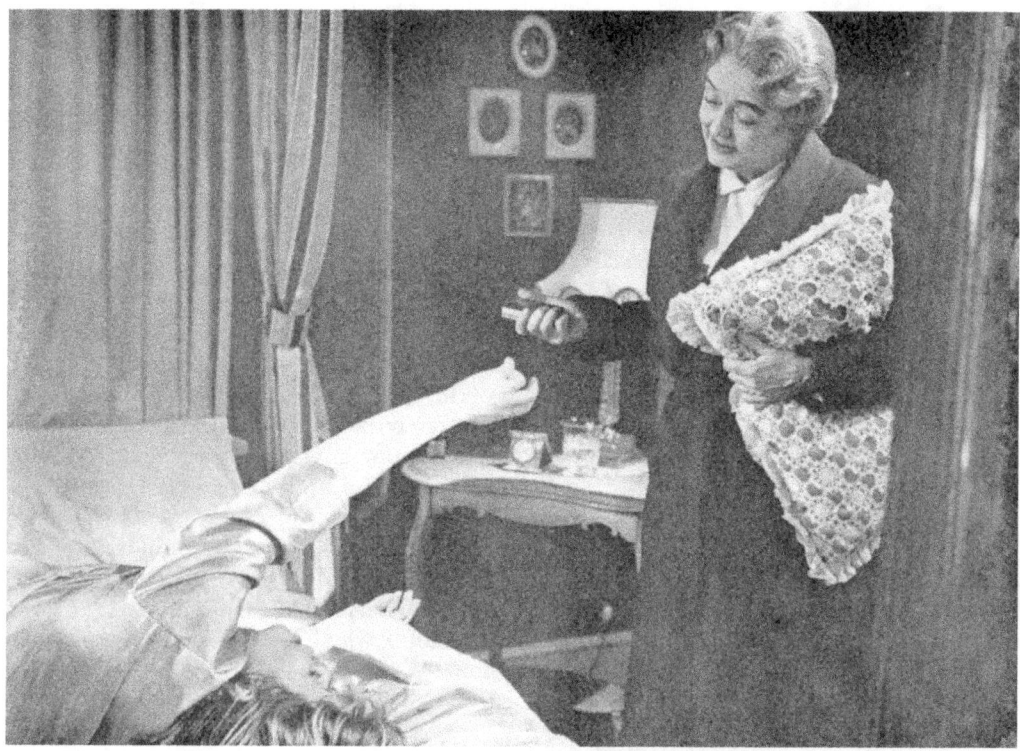

The Nanny (Bette Davis) withholds Penelope's (Jill Bennett) life-saving medicine.

What Ever Happened to Baby Jane? (1962). "I have always believed in an enormous variety of parts," Davis said on the BBC, "much more than I've been given credit for. *The Nanny*, for instance, is a complete departure from anything I've ever played." Actually, Bette Davis was not the first actress on Hammer's list. "My first choice," Jimmy Sangster told Ted Newsom, "was Greer Garson, believe it or not. I even went down to her ranch in Santa Fe to show her the script. For some reason, she didn't want to do it." With "second choice" Bette Davis on board, *The Nanny* began production at Elstree on April 5, 1965, on a seven week schedule, including ten days in London. Seth Holt, described in *Fasten Your Seatbelts* as "a kindly, bluff, outwardly charming individual, but actually a churning mass of tensions and neurosis," had the unenviable task of directing the former Hollywood queen.

Holt said,

> Davis got the flu during shooting, and sometimes she'd stay away altogether, holding up shooting while she sent in day-to-day reports on her condition. When she was on the set, still sniffling and coughing, she was drinking out of everyone's glasses and wheezing in her co-actors' faces in the best show-must-go-on manner. Oh, it was hell! She was always telling me how to direct. When I did it her way, she was scornful. When I stood up to her, she was hysterical.

Jimmy Sangster, however, saw it differently. He told the authors (August, 1993), "I thought she was the most professional actress I ever worked with." Despite the battles between *The Nanny* and her director, the production ended on schedule, was trade shown on October 1, and premiered at the Carlton on October 7. Unfortunately, young William Dix, who stole every scene he was in, could not attend due to the film's "X" certificate. Dix had to be content with being photographed with James Carreras in the lobby and with a private screening a month later. *The Nanny* was released in America on October 27, and took over $260,000 in one week in New York City alone. It went out on

Bette Davis was "the most professional actress I ever worked with," said Jimmy Sangster.

the ABC circuit on November 7 and earned £3,600 at one theatre in five days. At the year's end, *The Nanny* was named to *The Kinematograph Weekly*'s top moneymaker list after being in release for only two months. Reviewers were as pleased as the patrons. *The Daily Express* (October 8, 1965): "Adult horror, taut and tense"; *The Evening Standard* (October 8): "Nicely chilled suspense"; *The Evening News* (October 8): "Miss Davis is likely to change the universal concept of Nannydom."

While *The Nanny* was in pre-production, James Carreras approached the BBC and ITV networks with an offer to sell them a package of thirty-nine Hammer horror and science fiction movies. Both turned him down, but later purchased all of the offered pictures individually. Carreras also wanted to break into TV production and planned to film three pilots, including a Quatermass adventure. Nothing came of the idea, which seems to be a better concept than the eventually produced *Journey to the Unknown*.

Although *The Nanny* was not strictly a horror movie, it delivered as many chills as anything Hammer produced in the sixties. Bette Davis gave what is probably the best performance by an actress in a Hammer film, but at a cost—both financial and emotional. The supporting cast was excellent. William Dix was more frightening than Dracula, and Jill Bennett's heart attack, one of the film's "highlights," was almost too real to watch. *The Nanny* was sold to American television in September, 1966, for $400,000, which nearly paid for its production.

Dracula—Prince of Darkness

Released January 9, 1966 (U.K.), January 12, 1966 (U.S.); 90 minutes; Technicolor (U.K.), Deluxe Color (U.S.); Techniscope; 8100 feet; a Hammer Film Production; a Warner-Pathe Release (U.K.), a 20th Century–Fox Release (U.S.); filmed at Bray Studios, England; Director: Terence Fisher; Producer: Anthony Nelson-Keys; Executive Producer: Anthony Hinds; Screenplay: John Sansom, based on an idea by John Elder, based on the character created by Bram Stoker; Director of Photography: Michael Reed; Production Design: Bernard Robinson; Art Director: Don Mingaye; Music: James Bernard; Musical Supervisor: Philip Martell; Production Manager: Ross MacKenzie; Supervising Editor: James Needs; Special Effects: Les Bowie; Camera: Cece Cooney; Assistant Director: Bert Batt; Sound Recordist: Ken Rawkins; Editor: Chris Barnes; Makeup: Roy Ashton; Continuity: Lorna Selwyn; Wardrobe: Rosemary Burrows; Hairstyles: Frieda Steiger; Sound Editor: Roy Baker; U.K. Certificate: X.

Christopher Lee (Dracula), Barbara Shelley (Helen Kent), Andrew Keir (Father Shandor), Francis Matthews (Charles Kent), Suzan Farmer (Diana Kent), Charles Tingwell (Alan Kent), Thorley Walters (Ludwig), Philip Latham (Klove), Walter Brown (Brother Mark), George

Dracula (Christopher Lee) tries to save himself from a watery death in *Dracula—Prince of Darkness*. (Note anachronistic truck in upper left corner.)

Woodbridge (Landlord), Jack Lambert (Brother Peter), Philip Ray (Priest), Joyce Hemson (Mother), John Maxim (Coach Driver).

At a small village in the Carpathian Mountains, English tourists Charles Kent (Francis Matthews), his wife Diana (Suzan Farmer), Charles' brother Alan (Charles Tingwell) and Alan's wife Helen (Barbara Shelley) meet Father Shandor (Andrew Keir), who warns them to avoid the castle that lies near the village of Carlsbad. The next day, the Kents' hired coach driver (John Maxim) brings the carriage to a halt at the outskirts of Carlsbad, telling the travelers that he will not enter the village after dark. When Charles and Alan protest, the frightened driver orders them off at knife-point.

A driverless coach soon appears and, after the vacationers have climbed aboard, heads directly for the forbidden castle. There Klove (Philip Latham), an eerie-looking servant, explains that his late master Count Dracula left him instructions to see to the needs of travelers stranded in the area. When Alan explores the castle late that night, Klove knifes him and, suspending his corpse with a rope above a coffin filled with human ashes, cuts his throat. Alan's blood pours into the coffin and the ashes take on the form of Count Dracula (Christopher Lee). Klove next lures Helen to the scene and she becomes Dracula's first new victim. Stalked the next night by Dracula and the now-undead Helen, Charles and Diana ward off the vampires with crosses and escape in Klove's carriage.

Shandor finds the terrorized tourists and takes them to his Kleinberg monastery. But Dracula has traced them to the holy retreat and gains admittance by taking telepathic control of the weak-minded bookbinder Ludwig (Thorley Walters). Dracula and Helen gain access to Diana's room, but

Christopher Lee in *Dracula—Prince of Darkness*.

she is saved by the timely arrival of Charles and Shandor. Helen is later captured by other monks, and as Charles looks on in horror, she is staked through the heart by Shandor.

Meanwhile, Dracula abducts Diana and places her body in a coffin in a wagon which is driven back to the vampire's castle by Klove. Charles and Shandor pursue them on horseback, shooting Klove. Dracula's coffin (with the Count inside) falls from the wagon, down an embankment and across the frozen surface of the castle moat. Bursting out, the vampire fights with Charles on the ice as Shandor—remembering that running water is fatal to the undead—directs his riflefire at the ice. Dracula drops through a hole in the ice and descends to his doom in the icy water.

After an eight year wait, Hammer finally filmed its second Dracula picture. Christopher Lee (either fearing typecasting or asking for too much money) was not included in the misleadingly titled semi-sequel, *The Brides of Dracula*. Since his first appearance as Dracula, Lee had become Hammer's resident character star, playing a mummy, pirates, a drunken cad, an oriental, and even a romantic hero. He had also developed a career on the Continent due to his fluency in several languages and, no doubt, felt it safe to play Dracula again.

Terence Fisher and Jimmy Sangster are rightfully given credit for creating the style of the Hammer Dracula series, yet this was only their second—and last—association with the character. After *Dracula—Prince of Darkness*, the series would become less interesting productions guided by lesser hands. Sangster was, apparently, not satisfied with the finished picture and appears in the credits as "John Sansom." Despite having almost a decade to plan the Count's return, the results are disappointing. Setting the tone for the rest of the series, Dracula seems to be an afterthought and not the film's central

Despite the juvenile advertising gimmicks, an excellent double feature.

character. Still, no Hammer Dracula that followed would be an improvement, given Terence Fisher's understanding of vampire lore and of the sexual nature of the monster. Fisher told interviewers Sue and Colin Cowie:

> He's basically sexual. He has the powers of evil to prey on the victims' sexual feelings so that they believe at the moment he bites it is the culmination of a sexual experience. This is because he is the personification of evil and will always prey on the weakness of every victim, no matter whether its greed or sexuality. His is the personification of temptation.

Dracula appears on screen for the first time without dialogue. Hammer stated that the character was an "embodiment of evil," and Lee claimed that he refused to speak the lines given him, so use your own judgment. Actually, he had little to say in the first film, and not much worth hearing in later pictures. Also gone from the mix was Peter Cushing's Van Helsing, replaced by a new—and very different—character, Father Shandor.

After the completion of *The Gorgon*, Bray Studios was shut down for almost a year for repairs. James Carreras had a novel plan for the reopened studio. "We shall make four horror pictures," he said (*The Daily Cinema*, January, 1965). "The titles have not yet been decided, but the pictures will be made back-to-back, in pairs, and released as two of the greatest all-horror programs seen in years!" Filming began on *Dracula—Prince of Darkness* on May 31, 1965, and concluded on July 4. Almost immediately, *Rasputin—The Mad Monk* was begun, using much of the same cast, crew, and sets. The third film in the package, *The Plague of the Zombies*, began on July 28, 1965, followed by *The Reptile* (September 13). *Dracula* was paired with *Zombie*, and the duo was released on January 9, 1966, on the ABC circuit following a December 17 trade show. They took £10,190 on opening day, double the normal amount, and even most reviews were positive. *The London Times* (January 9, 1966): "The latest Dracula is the best of those they have made up to now"; *The Kinematograph Weekly* (December 30, 1965): "This is an extremely well-made example of its classic ghoulish horror"; *Films and Filming* (March, 1966): "Christopher Lee, bloodshot and speechless, makes a powerful figure out of Dracula"; and *Variety* (January 9, 1966): "Terence Fisher has directed it with his usual know-how."

The cast was one of Hammer's strongest for a Dracula film, with Barbara Shelley a standout. "Terry pointed out that when one becomes a vampire," she told Al Taylor (*Little Shoppe of Horrors* 7), "one's sexual proclivities are no longer heterosexual. I did, in fact, do a lot of preparation for this particular role because I wondered how one could play a vampire as the epitome of evil and decadence. So, I went back to my old days when I used to study the old Greek dramas and studied the use of that sort of feeling the Furies." Christopher Lee saw his character (*Films and Filming*) as, "A man of great power, presence, physical impact. I see him as an abhuman who is controlled by a force that is beyond his own powers of control." Andrew Keir's priest was one of the screen's few lusty holy men, warming his bottom in front of an entire tavern-full of people, guzzling wine, and carrying a rifle slung across his shoulder. Francis Matthews, Suzan Farmer, and Charles Tingwell managed to give their stock characters more realism than similar roles would receive in future Hammer Draculas.

The script created more than the usual problems with the censor, who rejected it three times because of its "violent content." Considering the graphic throat-slitting given to Charles Tingwell that appears in the film, one shudders at what must have been excised. Another problem was caused by Suzan Farmer's forced drinking of Dracula's blood in one of the few scenes in the film actually taken from Bram Stoker. As usual, James Bernard contributed an excellent score, and Bernard Robinson's sets were up to his high standard. "I've tried to give the decor and the rooms a feeling of uncertainty," he said, "everything a little off-center, just enough to disturb the eye but looking ostensibly normal." It all added up to a superior horror package that was one of Britain's top ten money winners that year.

Rasputin—The Mad Monk

Released March 6, 1966 (U.K.), April 6, 1966 (U.S.); 92 minutes; Technicolor (U.K.); DeLuxe Color (U.S.); Cinemascope; 8196 feet; a Hammer–7 Arts Production; Released by Warner-Pathe (U.K.), 20th Century–Fox (U.S.); filmed at Bray Studios; Director: Don Sharp; Producer: Anthony Nelson-Keys; Screenplay: John Elder; Director of Photography: Michael Reed; Production Design: Bernard Robinson; Supervising Editor: James Needs; Editor: Roy Hyde; Production Manager: Ross Mackenzie; Camera: Cece Cooney; Art Director: Don Mingaye; Sound Recordist: Ken Rawkins; Sound Editor: Roy Baker; Continuity: Lorna Selwyn; Makeup: Roy Ashton; Hair Styles: Frieda Steiger; Wardrobe: Rosemary Burrows; Music: Don Banks; Music Supervisor: Philip Martell; Assistant Director: Bert Batt; Dance Director: Alan Beall; U.K. Certificate: X.

Christopher Lee (Rasputin), Barbara Shelley (Sonia), Richard Pasco (Dr. Zargo), Francis Matthews (Ivan), Suzan Farmer (Vanessa), Dinsdale Landen (Peter), Renee Asherton (Tsarina), Derek Francis (Innkeeper), Alan Tilvern (Patron), Joss Ackland (Bishop), John Welsh (Abbott), Robert Duncan (Tsarvitch), John Bailey (Court Physician).

Czarist Russia. Rasputin (Christopher Lee), a debauched peasant monk, has mysterious healing powers which he demonstrates by saving a woman's life. Forced to flee due to his violent behavior, he sets off for the capital in St. Petersburg. After winning a drinking contest against the alcoholic Dr. Zargo (Richard Pasco), he offends the Czarina's Lady in Waiting, Sonia (Barbara Shelley). She is "slumming" with Vanessa (Suzan Farmer), her brother Ivan (Francis Matthews), and her own brother Peter (Dinsdale Landen). Sonia inexplicably falls under Rasputin's power and, at Dr. Zargo's apartment where he has taken up residence, becomes the monk's "lover."

Sonia and Vanessa are responsible for the Royal Child (Robert Duncan), and Rasputin orders Sonia to injure the boy so that he can heal him and gain the Czarina's favor. After healing the child, Rasputin is accepted at Court, and installs Dr. Zargo as Court Physician. Tired of his "relationship" with Sonia, he causes her to commit suicide. Dr. Zargo, fearing Rasputin's power, enlists Ivan and Peter as allies. After mutilating Peter, Rasputin is lured to Ivan's home with the promise of "meeting" Vanessa. There, after being poisoned and stabbed, he is

Christopher Lee in one of his favorite roles as *Rasputin—The Mad Monk*.

thrown out a window to his death by Ivan, but Dr. Zargo has died in the struggle.

Rasputin was one of Christopher Lee's favorite roles—"Certainly one of the best parts I ever had," he said (*The Films of Christopher Lee*). "One of the best performances I've given." Lee *is* quite good and is the main reason to watch the film, which looks uncharacteristically cheap despite B.R. sets. One never gets the feeling of being anywhere but on the film set, and certainly not in Czarist Russia. Although Rasputin was a real historical character, the film has little to do with history, since director Don Sharp was aware of possible legal difficulties. "It was more historically accurate in the first draft," he said (*Fangoria*, No. 31). "But Count Youssaupoff was still alive; there was the threat of a lawsuit, so we had to change everything." He candidly told *The Kinematograph Weekly* (July 15, 1965), "Let's be quite honest that this is a Hammer film, and is not by any means a historical biography." Rasputin is a fascinating character, and Hammer was not the first or last to film his story. Others to play the role include Lionel Barrymore (*Rasputin and the Empress*, 1932), Edmund Purdom (*The Night They Killed Rasputin*, 1962), Gert Frobe (*Rasputin*, 1967), and Tom Baker *Nicholas and Alexandra*, 1971). Boris Karloff even had a go on television in *Suspense* (1953).

Rasputin—The Mad Monk was, like *She*, a subject too big for Hammer to realistically take on. A film like this needs a much larger budget and location shooting to be believable. Viewers could easily be tricked into accepting Bray as a fantasy Transylvania, but not a realistic Russia. Filming was done under hurried conditions, and it shows. Francis Matthews explained when interviewed by Sue and Colin Cowie, "On the day we finished *Dracula—Prince of Darkness*, we started on *Rasputin*. We used the same sets revamped. We did the exteriors on the ice, while the palace set was redressed. I had a marvelous fight with Christopher Lee that wasn't seen in the finished film. I don't know why they cut it—usually they keep all the action and cut the dialogue scenes!" Also returning from the *Dracula* picture were the female leads. Barbara Shelley was outstanding in both, creating two memorable characters for a company that generally played down female roles.

The film began production on June 8, 1965, and was completed on July 20. Paired with *The Reptile*, it was trade shown at Studio One on February 14, 1966, and the pair was released on the ABC circuit on March 7. Reviewers were unimpressed. *The Kinematograph Weekly* (February 24, 1966): "A curiously unconvincing atmosphere"; *The Daily Cin-*

Christopher Lee is the life of the party in *Rasputin—The Mad Monk*.

ema (February 16): "Garbled version with conventional Hammer shocks and historical inaccuracies." Despite Christopher Lee's attempts to elevate the film above his other work for Hammer, this is "just" a horror movie—and a fairly entertaining one—but no more. It is similar to Universal's 1939 *Tower of London* with Basil Rathbone, Boris Karloff, and Vincent Price: Despite the historical trappings, it is a horror movie at heart.

The Plague of the Zombies

Released January 9, 1966 (U.K.), January 12, 1966 (U.S.); 90 minutes; Technicolor (U.K.), DeLuxe Color (U.S.); a Hammer–7 Arts Film Production; an Associated British–Warner-Pathe Release (U.K.), a 20th Century–Fox Release (U.S.); filmed at Bray Studios, England; Director: John Gilling; Producer: Anthony Nelson-Keys; Executive Producer: Anthony Hinds; Screenplay: John Elder, Peter Bryan, based on an original story by Peter Bryan; Director of Photography: Arthur Grant; Production Designer: Bernard Robinson; Supervising Editor: James Needs; Production Manager: George Fowler; Editor: Chris Barnes; Assistant Directors: Bert Batt, Martyn Green; Camera: Moray Grant; Art Director: Don Mingaye; Sound Recordist: Ken Rawkins; Sound Editor: Roy Baker; Continuity: Lorna Selwyn; Makeup: Roy Ashton; Hairstylist: Frieda Steiger; Wardrobe: Rosemary Burrows; Special Effects: Bowie Films Ltd.; Music: James Bernard; Musical Supervisor: Philip Martell; U.K. Certificate: X.

Andre Morell (Sir James Forbes), Diane Clare (Sylvia Forbes), Brook Williams (Dr. Peter Thompson), Jacqueline Pearce (Alice Thompson), John Carson (Squire Clive Hamilton), Alex Davion (Harry Denver), Michael Ripper (Sergeant Swift), Marcus Hammond (Martinus), Dennis Chinnery (Constable Christian), Louis Mahoney (Coloured Servant), Roy Royston (Vicar), Ben Aris, Tim Condron (John Martinus/Zombie), Bernard Egan, Norman Mann, Francis Willey (The Young Bloods), Jerry Verno (Landlord), Jolyan Booth (Coachman), Del Watson, Peter Diamond (Zombies).

Sir James Forbes (Andre Morell) receives a letter from former student Peter Thompson (Brook Williams) asking for his mentor's advice concerning a strange disease reaching epidemic proportions in the Cornish village where Thompson practices. Forbes' daughter Sylvia (Diane Clare) suggests they pay the Thompsons a visit since Thompson's wife Alice (Jacqueline Pearce) was her best friend at school.

Sir James and Thompson open the grave of one of the plague victims to perform a post mortem, but they find the coffin empty. Police Sgt. Swift (Michael Ripper) catches them in the act but Sir James convinces the police officer to work with them to find the answers to all the mysterious events taking place in the town.

Walking corpses are seen near an abandoned mine on the estate of Hamilton (John Carson), the local squire. After Alice is killed, Sir James determines that someone in the village has been practicing voodoo. He believes that Alice has been victimized and states that he intends to watch over her grave. Against Sir James' wishes, Peter goes with him. That night, they witness the rebirth of Alice as a zombie. Thompson, frozen with fear, watches as Alice moves toward him threateningly. Sir James grabs a sexton's shovel and decapitates the corpse.

Sir James confronts Squire Hamilton and accuses him of practicing voodoo rites (Hamilton learned voodoo in Haiti and created the zombies to work the still-profitable mine). When Hamilton denies the charges, Sir James leaves, but then sneaks back in and watches while hiding as Hamilton recites the voodoo rites that will mentally link him with Sylvia. Sylvia "hears" the summons and, in a hypnotic trance, makes her way to the mines. Thompson follows her out into the night.

In a battle with a masked man in ceremonial robes in Hamilton's study, a lamp is overturned and the room is set ablaze. Sir James escapes and makes his way to the mines, where Alice is about to be sacrificed. But the fire in Hamilton's home ignites a number of clay figures representing Hamilton's victims. The zombies, magically linked to these figures, begin to smolder and then turn on their master. Thompson and Sylvia take advantage of the diversion to get away, making it out of the mine before it is enveloped in flames.

Hammer's third film in their twin double feature package started production on July 28, 1965—just over a week after the completion of *Rasputin—The Mad Monk*. Two days earlier, Anthony Hinds left for New York to join James Carreras and meet with 7 Arts to discuss the upcoming *One Million Years B.C. The Plague of the Zombies* combined shooting at Bray with location work at Black Park, Oakley Court, and Cobham under John Gilling's direction. He had previously directed three costume adventures for Hammer, and this was his first horror movie for the company. "*The Plague of the Zombies* and *The Reptile*," he said (*Little Shoppe of Horrors* 7), "were offered to me on a back-to-back basis. They each contained a good idea which attracted me. I agreed to undertake the job on the condition that I had full control of the scripts, which I re-wrote more or less as I went along." Chief villain John Carson recalled that Gilling "had a reputation of being a bit of an SOB. I found John to be a man of humor, discipline, energy, kindness with schmaltz, imagination, and passion. He loved the business, but it wasn't the be all and end all. John had just the right mixture of knowing when to cool you down and when to kick your backside."

Andre Morell, in his seventh Hammer film, delivered his typically excellent performance. Morell had the ability to get roles in both big (*Ben Hur*, 1959) and small pictures, and Hammer was fortunate to get his services as often as they did. He was on vacation when his agent contacted him. "My agent rang me," he told David Soren, "and said, 'Come back and do this Hammer film for good money.' 'What is it?' I asked. He stammered out that this was … a-uh-costume drama. I asked him what it was called, and he said *The Plague of the Zombies*. I said I didn't believe it and had to ask him what it was about. I absolutely loved it. We had great fun. To make a film like this, of course, one doesn't believe in zombies, but one says this is it and does it seriously." Morell

Top: Brook Williams and Tim Condron rehearse on the set of *The Plague of the Zombies*. *Bottom:* Brook Williams, Diane Clare and Andre Morell find Jacqueline Pearce's body in *The Plague of the Zombies*.

"Cornwall" via Bray Studios. Sound stages peek out from behind the tin mine set in this scene from *The Plague of the Zombies*.

added a touch of sly humor to his authoritarian role, resulting in one of Hammer's best heroes.

The fifteen "zombies" made their first appearance on the set on August 20. No one zombie had any real impact, and all took a back seat to John Carson, similar to the situation in *White Zombie* (1932) with zombie master Bela Lugosi. Filming ended on September 6, and by mid–October, Hammer had decided to pair *The Plague of the Zombies* and *Dracula—Prince of Darkness*, forming the decade's best horror package. "People have to remember," enthused Anthony Nelson-Keys (*The Daily Cinema*, August 10, 1965), "that these are morality tales, not unlike Greek heroes crusading against evil. Surely it's far better to make costumed horror films, rather than those modern sadistic and neurotic films where there are definite everyday associations and messages." Unfortunately, this is the type of picture Hammer would soon be making. A trade show was held at Studio One on December 20, 1965, and the double feature went into general release on January 9, 1966, to mostly good reviews. *The Daily Cinema* (December 29, 1965): "John Gilling has contrived some truly terrifying effects." *The Kinematograph Weekly* (December 30): "Like nearly all Hammer films, this is very well staged, and one or two of the action scenes are as good as anything in the way of cinematic excitement"; and *The New York Post* (May 5, 1966): "So predictable that its standard scare tactics are merely tedious." *The Plague of the Zombies* has, over the years, attracted more than one pretentious critique. When the British Film Institute ran a Hammer tribute in the fall of 1971, the program guide pointed out, "The conflagration at the end of the film is an apt metaphor for suggesting the burning anger

268 *The Reptile* (1965)

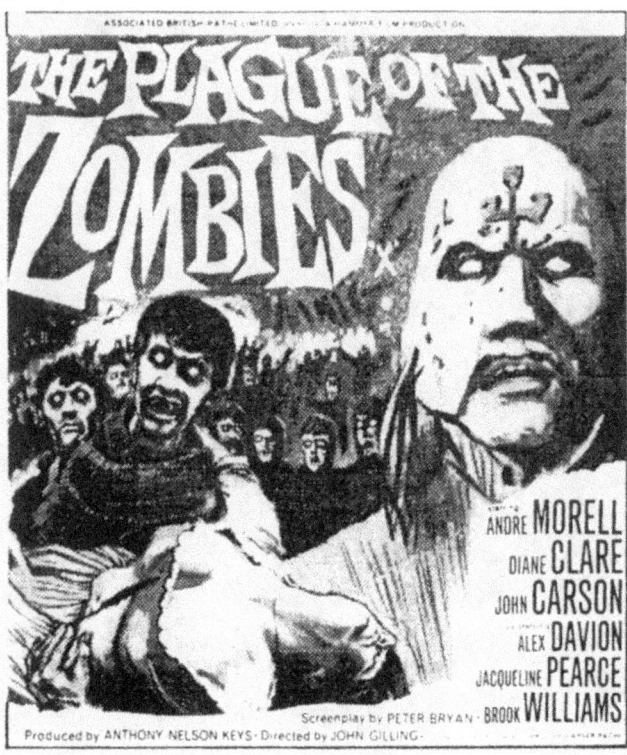

The first of John Gilling's Cornwall classics was unappreciated in its day, but time has since proved otherwise.

and fiery rebellion of the exploited who turn on their oppressors."

This aside, *The Plague of the Zombies* did deliver more than simply routine shocks. Andre Morell and Diane Clare were a charming father-daughter team, balanced by John Carson and Alex Davion as the arrogant villains. The "Young Bloods" are reminiscent of Sir Hugo's pack of degenerates in *The Hound of the Baskervilles*, which is not surprising, since Peter Bryan wrote both scripts. Bernard Robinson's sets convincingly set a place and time despite the more rushed than usual conditions, and James Bernard's outstanding score added the right touch to one of Hammer's best sixties horrors.

The Reptile

Released March 6, 1966 (U.K.), April 6, 1966 (U.S.); 91 minutes; 8140 feet; Technicolor (U.K.), DeLuxe Color (U.S.); a Hammer-7 Arts Production; a Warner-Pathe Release (U.K.), a 20th Century–Fox Release (U.S.); filmed at Bray Studios, England; Director: John Gilling; Producer: Anthony Nelson-Keys; Screenplay: John Elder; Music: Don Banks; Musical Supervisor: Philip Martell; Executive Producer: Anthony Hinds; Director of Photography: Arthur Grant; Production Manager: George Fowler; Editor: Roy Hyde; Assistant Director: Bill Cartlidge; Camera: Moray Grant; Art Director: Don Mingaye; Sound Recordist: Bill Buckley; Sound Editor: Roy Baker; Makeup: Roy Ashton; Hairstylist: Frieda Steiger; Wardrobe: Rosemary Burrows; Special Effects; Les Bowie; Continuity: Lorna Selwyn; Supervising Editor: James Needs; Production Design: Bernard Robinson; U.K. Certificate: X.

Noel Willman (Dr. Franklyn), Jennifer Daniel (Valerie Spalding), Ray Barrett (Harry Spalding), Jacqueline Pearce (Anna), Michael Ripper (Tom Bailey), John Laurie (Mad Peter), Marne Maitland (Malay), David Baron (Charles Spalding), Charles Lloyd Pack (Vicar), Harold Goldblatt (Solicitor), George Woodbridge (Old Garnsey).

Returning home late one evening to his cottage on the Cornwall heath, Charles Spalding (David Baron) finds a note asking him to come to Dr. Franklyn's manor. When his knock goes unanswered, Charles enters the house and is attacked by a shadowy figure that bites his throat. Charles topples down a flight of stairs to his death. Franklyn (Noel Willman) and his servant Malay (Marne Maitland) converge on the body, whose face is grotesquely mottled and blackened. Under cover of darkness, Malay dumps the body in the nearby churchyard.

Charles' brother Harry (Ray Barrett) inherits Charles' cottage and moves in along with his wife Valerie (Jennifer Daniel). Harry suspects that Charles did *not* die of heart failure and enlists the aid of Mad Peter (John Laurie), a local eccentric, to help unravel the

Jacqueline Pearce attacks in *The Reptile*.

mystery. But Mad Peter is also killed in the same manner as Charles.

Franklyn's daughter Anna (Jacqueline Pearce) invites the Spaldings to dinner. In the over-heated house, Anna plays a tune on a sitar which causes her father to react violently and smash the instrument.

Harry and one of the locals, pub proprietor Tom Bailey (Michael Ripper), disinter the bodies of Charles and Mad Peter and find on their throats the bite mark of a king cobra. Later, Harry finds a note from Anna asking for help. He goes to Franklyn's manor where he, too, is attacked by the nightmare creature—part-woman, part-reptile. Harry makes it back home and Valerie cuts into the wound and draws out the venom.

As Harry rests, Valerie finds the note from Anna and visits the Franklyn home, secretly following Franklyn as he descends into his cellar armed with a sword. In the cellar is a sulfur pit and a female figure covered by a blanket. When Franklyn raises his sword to strike, he is attacked by Malay. Franklyn tosses Malay into the sulfur pit.

Upstairs, Franklyn tells Valerie that he is responsible for Anna's horrible condition. Years before, he and Anna lived in Borneo where Franklyn antagonized a cult of snake worshippers who subsequently abducted Anna and, through a series of secret rituals, transformed her into the Reptile. The Franklyns managed to escape the country but were found by one of the cult's members, Malay, who continued to perform the ritual that transforms Anna into the monster.

A fire which started during Franklyn's fight with Malay spreads through the manor. The Reptile attacks and kills Franklyn and then chases Anna, who is rescued by Harry and Tom. The three escape as the house and the Reptile are completely engulfed in flames.

Although *The Reptile* is the least appreciated of Hammer's twin double features of

1965, it is one of the company's most underrated fantasies. It was a rare attempt by Hammer to create a "new" monster—and a female one at that—but the creature's roots could actually be traced to Universal's *Cult of the Cobra* (1955). Jacqueline Pearce was the only Hammer actress to play two monsters (a zombie and a snake creature), and she headed a spirited, if "second team," cast. Noel Willman and Jennifer Daniel returned to Hammer for the first time since *The Kiss of the Vampire*, but it was Michael Ripper who was finally singled out for some praise. *The Daily Cinema* (February 18, 1966) felt that, "Ripper's portrayal of the dullest character in all these horror movies, the helpful friend, is a most sensitive job of acting. It's time they started giving awards for the most distinguished roles, rather than for the best performances in the best roles: then the artists who are truly the backbone of the industry would get the credit that's due to them." Ripper commented (*Photon*), "I think that you can get away with a lot more when it's in period, because people will accept a possibility that they just wouldn't accept in modern life. The more outlandish your story, the more necessary it probably becomes to put it in a remote time."

The Reptile began filming on September 13, 1965, and concluded on October 22. The Cornish village on the Bray lot was the same as in *The Plague of the Zombies*, and John Gilling made every effort to disguise that fact by using different camera angles. Nearby Oakley Court stood in for the exterior of the Franklyns' manor house. A trade show was held at Studio One on February 16, 1966, and *The Reptile* went into release, with *Rasputin—The Mad Monk*, on March 6, to positive reviews. *The Kinematograph Weekly* (February 24): "Directed with intelligence—an excellent shocker"; and *The Daily Cinema* (February 18): "Gilling and scriptwriter Elder have gone to great pains to promote suspense through characterization and inter-relationship."

This was the last Hammer film for which Roy Ashton was solely responsible for the makeup, and the result was credible except when in closeup. Fortunately, Gilling confined

Hammer's attempt to create a new monster almost worked.

the creature to shadows for most of the film, "Lewton style," giving only fleeting glimpses of the monster. *The Reptile* is about as good as a supporting feature horror movie gets. It may have been a "B" movie, but all concerned deserve an "A" as Hammer, once again, put all of its investment in the picture on the screen.

One Million Years B.C.

Released December 30, 1966 (U.K.), February 21, 1967 (U.S.); 100 minutes (U.K.), 91 minutes (U.S.); Technicolor (U.K.), Deluxe Color (U.S.); filmed in Panamation; 9031 feet; a Hammer–7 Arts Production; a Warner-Pathe Release (U.K.), a 20th Century–Fox Release (U.S.); filmed at Associated British/EMI Studios, Elstree, England, and on location in the Canary Islands; Director: Don Chaffey; Producer, Screenplay: Michael Carreras; Associate

One Million Years B.C. (1965)

John Richardson and Raquel Welch seek a well-hidden refuge in *One Million Years B.C.*

Producer: Aida Young; Adapted from an original screenplay by Michael Novak, George Baker, Joseph Frickett; Special Animated Effects: Ray Harryhausen; Music and Special Music Effects: Mario Nascimbene; Musical Supervisor: Philip Martell; Art Director: Robert Jones; Supervising Editor: James Needs; Costume Design: Carl Toms; Director of Photography: Wilkie Cooper; Editor: Tom Simpson; Assistant Director: Denis Bertera; Camera: David Harcourt; Continuity: Gladys Goldsmith, Marjorie Lavelly; 2nd Unit Camera: Jack Mills; Assistant Art Director: Kenneth McCallum Tait; Mechanical Special Effects: George Blackwell; Sound Editors: Roy Baker, Alfred Cox; Sound Mixer: Bill Rowe; Sound Dubbing: Len Shilton; Makeup: Wally Schneiderman; Hairdresser: Olga Angelinetta; Wardrobe Mistress: Ivy Baker; Prologue Designed by: Les Bowie; Production Manager: John Wilcox; Publicity Directors: Alan Thompson, Robert Webb; Stills Cameraman: Ronnie Pilgrim; 1st Camera Assistant: Geoffrey Glover; Camera Assistant: E. Deason; 2nd Camera Operator: Kenneth Nicholson; Draughtsman: Colin Monk; Scenic Artist: Bill Beavis; 1st Assistant Editor: Robert Dearberg; Assistant Editors: Antony Sloman, Chris Barnes; 2nd Assistant Director: Colin Lord; 3rd Assistant Director: Ray Atchelor; Production Secretary: Eileen Mathews; Animal Sculptures: Arthur Hayward; Executive Producer: Anthony Hinds; U.K. Certificate: A.

Raquel Welch (Loana), John Richardson (Tumak), Percy Herbert (Sakana), Robert Brown (Akhoba), Martine Beswick (Nupondi), Jean Wladon (Ahot), Lisa Thomas (Sura), Malya Nappil (Tohana), Richard James (Young Rock Man), William Lyon Brown (Payto), Frank Hayden (1st Rock Man), Terence Maidment (1st Shell Man), Micky DeRauch (1st Shell Girl), Yvonne Horner (Ullah).

When caveman Tumak (John Richardson) fights with his father, Akhoba (Robert Brown), chief of the Rock Tribe, Tumak is defeated and sent into exile. His mate Nupondi (Martine Beswick) is claimed by Tumak's brother Sakana (Percy Herbert). Tumak

272 *One Million Years B.C.* (1965)

wanders through the rugged terrain for days until he reaches the ocean where he collapses. A group of women appears and one of them, Loana (Raquel Welch), is tending to him when a giant turtle approaches menacingly. Loana blows into a large conch shell, attracting warriors who attack the giant beast with their spears.

While Tumak regains his strength under the care of Loana and other members of her Shell Tribe, his father, Akhoba, is badly wounded when he is pushed off a cliff by Sakana. Sakana proclaims himself chief of the Rock Tribe.

Tumak is adjusting to life among the gentle Shell People, learning how to use a spear from warrior Ahot (Jean Wladon) and how to spear-fish from Loana. When an Allosaurus attacks one of the tribe children, Tumak kills the monster. But he soon clashes with Ahot and is caught stealing. The chief of the Shell People banishes him and Loana follows.

Tumak and Loana return to the Rock Tribe's territory. On the journey, the couple narrowly escape being captured by ape-like cave dwellers and witness a battle between a Ceratosaurus and a Triceratops. When Loana is captured by Sakana and his warriors, Tumak fights and defeats his brother.

Loana and Tumak return to the Rock Tribe dwelling. Loana is attacked by Nupondi, who wants to reclaim Tumak as her mate, but Loana wins the battle. Tumak becomes leader of the tribe while she teaches them the ways of her people. She is teaching them to swim when she is seized and carried away by a Pterodactyl. Loana gets away when the giant bird battles with another of its species.

The Shell People find her and she convinces Ahot and others to take her back to Tumak, who is overjoyed to find his mate alive.

This was the way it wasn't!

Ahot and his warriors are about to return to the sea when Sakana and his followers attack Tumak. Ahot joins forces with Tumak to fight the dissenters, and during the fight, Tumak kills Sakana.

Peace for the Rock Tribe finally seems at hand when nature intervenes in the form of a violent volcanic eruption. Many of the tribe are killed by falling rocks, others are swallowed up by the heaving earth. Afterwards, only a handful of the two tribes survive the tumult. Tumak and Loana band together with the survivors to find a new home and a bright future together.

One Million Years B.C. was Hammer's biggest financial gamble, boasting a budget in excess of £2.5 million. James Carreras (*The*

Daily Cinema, January, 1965) called the project "A fantastic, fascinating, and spectacular subject." It was a remake of Hal Roach's *One Million B.C.* (1940), using Ray Harryhausen–animated monsters, rather than magnified iguanas, as the original had done. Lacking dialogue—at least that anyone could understand—the film would depend on its visuals for success. Two of the "visuals," in addition to Harryhausen's creatures, were Raquel Welch and John Richardson, reprising the roles played by Carole Landis and Victor Mature. Harryhausen began preliminary work at Elstree on May 27, 1965. He recalled (*Little Shoppe of Horrors* 6), "Hammer had seen a number of my films, and then they got the rights to *One Million B.C.* It was on-and-off and on-and-off for quite a while before it actually got started." He began collecting photographs from the Museum of Natural History in New York and based his model armatures on the skeletons in the British Natural History Museum. Eight models were eventually built. "Accuracy and detail are especially important this time," Harryhausen said (*The Daily Cinema*, December 17, 1965), "because we're dealing with animals that actually once existed."

Harryhausen worked on his sketches for four months. "I made three or four big drawings," he told *Little Shoppe*, "and then I made a lot of storyboard sketches at EMI. I had a year to finish the effects." After the sketches were approved, he began to construct the models. "Each animal is built with intricate mechanisms inside; some will breathe. The framework is constructed in America, the rest I do myself." Harryhausen spent six weeks on location, choreographing the actors who would eventually interact with the creatures on film. "I'd have a story conference with Don Chaffey before the scene was done. Naturally, reactions must always be gauged in terms of the limitations of the special effects stage."

Ray Harryhausen averaged twelve hour workdays at Elstree. "Sometimes," he said (*Daily Cinema*, December 17, 1965), "it's difficult to leave an awkward shot overnight without losing the rhythm of a scene. Also, everything is critical with temperature, which might cause a slight but crucial movement in one of the models. You have to try to finish a shot at a moment when you can cut." Actress Martine Beswick, interviewed by Steve Swires (*Fangoria*, 55), recalled Harryhausen as "A lovely man, but sort of a 'mad scientist' who was very quiet, and deep and totally committed to what he was doing. For the dinosaur attacks, he rode in the back of a truck mounted with a camera and told us actors where to look and move." He and director Don Chaffey had worked together previously on *Jason and the Argonauts* (1963) and had a good relationship. Michael Carreras also admired Chaffey. "Don is an extraordinary man in terms of telling a story with no dialogue."

Two months before shooting began, Anthony Hinds and James Carreras flew to America to plan publicity strategies with 7 Arts. One used in Britain involved a competition to find a girl to appear in the film. The winner was Yvonne Horner, a secretary from Surrey who appeared as "Ullah." Principal photography began on October 18, 1965, in the Canary Islands. The picture was launched as Hammer's 100th, but due to the company's odd history, it is more likely that *One Million Years B.C.* was their 116th. By November 20, the unit had returned to film interiors at Elstree, and filming continued until January 7, 1966. *Slave Girls* would soon begin production on the same sets. Ray Harryhausen completed the special effects by spring; due to his workload, the film's pre-credit sequence was designed by Les Bowie, who claimed that he created the earth in six days for £1100 and made his "lava flows" with porridge.

One Million Years B.C. was trade shown on October 25, 1966, at the Warner, and the film went into general release on the ABC circuit on December 30. Although many critics dismissed the movie as juvenile, audiences knew entertainment when they saw it. *The New York World Journal Tribune* (February 22, 1967): "This idiot tale won't even amuse the kiddies"; *The New York Morning Telegraph* (February 22): "The film might be best described as *Bikini Beach* with dinosaurs"; *Films in Review* (March): "The monsters are realistically constructed and manipulated and, technically, their involvement with humans in the same scenes is beyond reproach"; *Variety* (December 28, 1966): "It is the trick photography

The infamous white rhino from *Slave Girls*.

that does the trick"; and *Sight and Sound* (Winter 1966): "The film is a huge success." It certainly was, and by the end of January, 1967, the trades were reporting "mammoth business." *The Daily Cinema* (January 6) felt that "The spectacular picture looks set to become one of the biggest grossing productions of the year." In fact, D.J. Goodlatte, president of ABC Theatres, reported that *One Million Years B.C.* had broken the circuit's all-time record. All told, the film made the Top Ten Box Office Winners for 1967, earned $9 million, and launched Raquel Welch on a long and successful career.

1966

Slave Girls

Released July 7, 1968 (U.K.), January, 1967 (U.S.); 74 minutes (U.K.), 95 minutes (U.S.); Technicolor (U.K.), DeLuxe Color (U.S.), Cinema Scope; 6658 feet; a Hammer/7 Arts Production; filmed at MGM/EMI Elstree Studios; a Warner-Pathe Release (U.K.), 20th Century–Fox (U.S.); Director: Michael Carreras; Producer: Michael Carreras; Screenplay: Henry Younger (Michael Carreras); Director of Photography: Michael Reed; Music: Carlo Martelli; Music Supervisor: Philip Martell; Choreography: Denys Palmer; Art Director: Robert Jones; Supervising Editor: James Needs; Editor: Roy Hyde; Costumes: Carl Toms; Production Manager: Ross MacKenzie; Assistant Director: David Tringham; Associate Producer: Aida Young; Camera: Robert Thomson; Continuity: Eileen Head; Dubbing Editor: Charles Crafford; Sound Mixer: Sash Fisher, Len Shilton; Makeup: Wally Schneiderman; Hairdresser: Olga Angelinetta; Sound Editor: A.W. Lumkin; U.K. Certificate: A; U.S. Title: *Prehistoric Women*.

Martine Beswick (Kari), Edina Ronay (Saria), Michael Latimer (David), Stephanie Randall (Amyak), Carol White (Gido), Alexandra Stevenson (Luri), Yvonne Horner (First Amazon), Sydney Bromley (Ulio), Frank Hayden (Arja), Robert Raglan (Colonel Hammond), Mary Hignett (Mrs. Hammond), Louis Mahoney (Head Boy), Bari Johnson (High Priest), Danny Daniels (Jakara), Steven Berkoff (John).

While on a safari in Africa, David Marchant (Michael Latimer) pursues a wounded leopard into the bush. After spotting the image of a rhinoceros carved on a tree, his frightened guides desert him. Marchant is soon captured by a hostile tribe and taken to a temple guarded by a statue of a white rhino. When a lightning bolt splits the temple wall, Marchant runs through and enters a prehistoric world where he meets the striking blonde Saria (Edina Ronay) who violently rebuffs him. He is held captive again by a tribe of brunette Amazons led by Kari (Martine Beswick) who has enslaved the fair-haired ones. Kari is supported by males to whom she gives the blonde women as rewards. When Marchant spurns her advances, he is thrown into a cell where he again meets Saria. She begs him to give in to Kari for the sake of them all. A riot breaks out, pitting blonde against brunette, and as the battle thickens, Kari is killed by a charging white rhino. Marchant awakens from a "dream-state" at the rhino statue. Later, he finds a rhino talisman given to him by Saria—who closely resembles a young woman in the newly formed safari.

Slave Girls is a terrible movie, and it is embarrassing to include it in a book about one's favorite film company. Even worse, it is not endearingly bad like *Plan 9 from Outer Space* (1959). It is just plain *bad*, and the less said about it, the better. The picture was announced in *The Kinematograph Weekly* (December 16, 1965) as a "large scale subject in the vein of the current *One Million Years B.C.*" The reality was different. The movie was filmed entirely at Elstree between January 5 and February 18, 1966, with no location work, and the closest thing to an animated monster was the white rhino, and that's not nearly close enough. Seven Arts must have realized that the finished product was a disaster and decided to delay its release, as if it would improve while sitting on the shelf. It was released in the U.K. on July 7, 1968, two years after its completion at only 74 minutes, compared to 95 in America. Both versions are unwatchable, since Hammer's typically excellent production values serve only to point out how terrible everything else is.

Taking the blame for this is Michael Car-

They can't *all* be classics! *Slave Girls* was retitled *Prehistoric Women* for the Americans.

reras who wrote (as Henry Younger), produced, and directed, and excelled at none of them. There is more style in one minute of *The Steel Bayonet* than in all 74 (or 95) minutes of *Slave Girls*, and one wonders if he made it for laughs. If so, it is not evident, since no one, including the audience, has much fun with it. In fact, the film is anything *but* "good clean fun"—it has a very nasty edge. Criticism was, by necessity, unkind. *The Kinematograph Weekly* (July 13, 1968): "This is really an absurd mixture of silly make-believe"; *Films and Filming* (August): "One of the feeblest Hammer films to date"; *Variety* (January 1, 1967): "In questionable taste, openly perverse"; *The New York Herald Tribune* (March 16): "A really terrible movie."

Basically, *Slave Girls* was an excuse to

parade Martine Beswick, Edina Ronay, and a host of other attractive women across the screen in skimpy clothing. One leaves this one feeling cheated, which is a rarity for a Hammer film, but at least there was no sequel. Martine Beswicke (an "e" has since been added) showed a great deal of class and good humor when she cheerfully accepted "The Worst Hammer Film" award at FANEX in Baltimore in July, 1994. "We used to argue about who was in the worst one," she laughed. "Now I've got the proof!"

The Witches

Released December 9, 1966 (U.K.), March 15, 1967 (U.S.); 8156 feet; a Hammer Film Production; Released by Warner-Pathe (U.K.), 20th Century–Fox (U.S.); filmed at MGM/EMI Elstree Studios; Director: Cyril Frankel; Producer: Anthony Nelson-Keys; Screenplay: Nigel Kneale, based on Peter Curtis' novel *The Devil's Own*; Director of Photography: Arthur Grant BSC; Music: Richard Rodney Bennett; Music Director: Philip Martell; Choreographer: Denys Palmer; Production Design: Bernard Robinson; Supervising Editor: James Needs; Editor: Chris Barnes; Production Manager: Charles Permane; Sound: Ken Rawkins; Sound Editor: Roy Hyde; Makeup: George Partleton; Camera: Ceece Cooney; Hairstyles: Frieda Steiger; Wardrobe Supervisor: Molly Arbuthnot; Wardrobe Master: Harry Haynes; Assistant Director: David Tringham; Continuity: Anne Deeley; U.S. Title: *The Devil's Own*; U.K. Certificate: X.

Joan Fontaine (Gwen Mayfield), Kay Walsh (Stephanie Bax), Alec McCowen (Alan Bax), Ann Bell (Sally), Ingrid Brett (Linda), John Collin (Dowsett), Michele Dotrice (Valerie), Gwen F. Ffrangcon-Davies (Granny), Duncan Lamont (Bob Curd), Leonard Rossiter (Dr. Wallis), Martin Stephens (Ronnie), Carmel McSharry (Mrs. Dowsett), Viola Keats (Mrs. Curd), Shelagh Fraser (Mrs. Creek), Bryan Marshall (Tom).

Gwen Mayfield (Joan Fontaine) secures a teaching position at the Haddaby School after suffering a breakdown in Africa caused by a brush with voodoo. Haddaby is run by Alan Bax (Alec McCowen) and his sister Stephanie (Kay Walsh). Alan dresses like a cleric despite failing to qualify because it makes him "feel secure." Gwen initially revels in the peacefulness of Haddaby, but senses "undercurrents." A harmless relationship between Ronnie (Martin Stephens) and Linda (Ingrid Brett) leads to disaster—Ronnie is struck down by witchcraft.

Gwen confides in Stephanie who admits that witchcraft is rampant in the area and suggests that they investigate. Gwen's major suspect is Mrs. Rigg (Gwen Ffrangcon-Davies) who exerts a strange power. Ronnie's father (John Collin) confronts her and is found the next morning—drowned. Gwen has a nightmare and awakens—an amnesiac—under the care of Dr. Wallis (Leonard Rossiter) in a rest home. When her memory returns, she realizes that Haddaby is in great danger, and escapes. Back in Haddaby, Gwen learns the horrible truth. Stephanie is a witch who plans to sacrifice Linda—a virgin—to the voodoo gods. Forced to participate in the orgy, Gwen contaminates Stephanie's pure garment with blood, and the witch dies screaming. Released from the witches' control, Haddaby—and Alan—return to a normal life with Gwen at its center.

The Witches brought director Cyril Frankel back to Hammer for the first time since his outstanding—and controversial—*Never Take Sweets from a Stranger*. Frankel's feature film output was limited in the interim and he was, presumably, brought back for *The Witches* due to his experience in directing young actors. Unfortunately, *The Witches* fell far short of his previous Hammer outing despite some impressive "names" being involved.

The Daily Cinema (April 18, 1966) announced that "Academy Award winning actress, Joan Fontaine, has arrived in London to star in the Hammer-7 Arts production. Anthony Hinds greeted Miss Fontaine who will spend six months in England." She brought more than just her acting talent, having brought Peter Curtis' novel *The Devil's Own* to Hammer's attention. Her last film role had been four years earlier (*Tender Is the Night*), and, like other legendary Hollywood actresses, Fontaine found herself in a horror movie. And, like others in the same position, she qualified her appearance in it by calling the film "a detective story rather than straight horror." Frankel was quite impressed with his star, saying (*The Daily Cinema*, April 29, 1966), "She brings a good deal of intelligent prepara-

Kay Walsh and Duncan Lamont in Hammer's disappointing voodoo thriller, *The Witches*.

tion to a highly emotional role. Her sense of dramatic imagination is very strong indeed." His star returned the compliment by saying, "He directs me with relaxed authority."

Screenwriter Nigel Kneale was one of the most important figures in British science fiction/horror after writing the teleplay for George Orwell's *1984* (1954), which made Peter Cushing a star. He was best known for his *Quatermass* trio on the BBC in the fifties, all eventually filmed by Hammer. He made a second career in the eighties by complaining about Hammer's versions of the first two pictures, and Peter Curtis could well have done the same of Kneale's treatment of his novel. The screenplay is dull and generates no suspense or surprises. Considering Kneale's brilliance, this one is an embarrassment.

The Witches began production on April 18 with extensive location work in Hambleden village and on the estate of Lord Hambleden, owner of the huge W.H. Smith bookstore chain. Filming ended on schedule and without incident on June 10, as Joan Fontaine rose above others in her position by not demanding special treatment.

Following a November 14, 1966, trade show at Studio One, the film premiered at the Pavilion (November 21), and went into general release on December 9 to good reviews. *Kine Weekly* (November 19): "Quite pleasing atmosphere of village life"; *The Daily Cinema* (November 16): "Quality horror"; *Films and Filming* (January, 1967): "Very enjoyable thriller"; and *The New York Times* (March 16, 1967): "The best occult teaser since *Burn Witch Burn*." These reviews are hard to take seriously after one sits through the film. One of the movie's few high points *is* the lovely village, but this is supposed to be Hammer horror, not a travelogue.

The Viking Queen

Released March 26, 1967 (U.K.), August 16, 1967 (U.S.); 91 minutes; Technicolor (U.K.),

The Viking Queen (1966)

DeLuxe (U.S.); a Hammer–Seven Arts Production; a Warner-Pathe Release (U.K.), a 20th Century–Fox Release (U.S.); filmed at Ardmore Studios, and on location in the Wicklow Mountains, Ireland; Director: Don Chaffey; Producer: John Temple-Smith; Screenplay: Clarke Reynolds, based on an original story by John Temple-Smith; Music: Gary Hughes; Musical Supervisor: Philip Martell; Director of Photography: Stephen Dade; Production Designer: George Provis; Supervising Editor: James Needs; Production Manager: Rene Dupont; Second Unit Director: Jack Causey; Second Unit Camera: John Harris; Assistant Director: Dennis Bertera; Makeup: Charles Parker; Costume Designer: John Furness; Hairstylist: Bobbie Smith; Editor: Peter Boita; Special Effects: Allan Bryce; Camera: David Harcourt; Sound Editor: Stan Smith; Sound Mixers: H.L. Bird, Bob Jones; Master of Horse: Frank Hayden; Production Liaison: William O'Kelly; Continuity: Ann Skinner; Wardrobe Supervisor: Hilda Geerdts; Wardrobe Master: Jack Gallagher; U.K. Certificate: A.

Don Murray (Justinian), Carita (Salina), Donald Houston (Maelgan), Andrew Keir (Octavian), Adrienne Corri (Beatrice), Niall MacGinnis (Tiberion), Wilfrid Lawson (King Priam), Nicola Pagett (Talia), Percy Herbert (Catus), Patrick Troughton (Tristram), Sean Caffrey (Fergus), Denis Shaw (Osiris), Philip O'Flynn (Merchant), Brendan Mathews (Nigel), Gerry Alexander (Fabian), Patrick Gardiner (Benedict), Paul Murphy (Dalan—Maelgan's Son), Arthur O'Sullivan (Old Man at Tax Inquiry), Cecil Sheridan (Shopkeeper at Protest Gathering), Anna Mannahan (Shopkeeper's Wife), Nita Lorraine (Nubian Girl Slave), Bryan Marshall (Dominic), Jack Rodney (Boniface).

Carita rehearses her death scene in *The Viking Queen* (photo courtesy of Tim Murphy).

As Priam (Wilfrid Lawson), an astute tribal king of ancient Britain, dies, he places the mantel of responsibility on his daughter Salina (Carita), knowing she will further his policy of peaceful existence under Roman domination. Salina soon shows that she combines her father's wisdom with the energetic spirit of her deceased mother, a Viking queen. She manages to hold in check the rebellious intent of the Druid high priest Maelgan (Donald Houston).

Salina is strongly attracted to Justinian (Don Murray), the humane Roman Governor General, who treats the subject Britons with tolerance despite the urgings to harsher measures by his second-in-command Octavian (Andrew Keir). When an unruly tribal element attacks some of Justinian's men, the commander withdraws his permission for Salina to accord a Druid ritual cremation to the dead Priam. She orders the ceremony to go ahead in private, but Osiris (Denis Shaw), a merchant, betrays her, hoping to win favor, and Octavian takes it into his own hands to punish the queen. Fortunately, Justinian arrives on the scene before any bloodshed occurs.

Salina's coronation ceremonies and celebrations help to ease the tension, and on a wild boar hunt together, she and Justinian passionately realize their love for each other. The Druids refuse to permit a marriage between them, but Justinian wins favor with the tribe when he deals with fairness and generosity in the matter of Roman taxes.

The conspiring Osiris bribes the Druids to stir up a distant rebellion so that Justinian will be kept busy suppressing it. Left with the field clear, the tyrannical Octavian starts up a terror campaign of extortion and cruelty. One of his first victims is Salina, whom he has publicly whipped. The atrocity incites the tribe to bloody revolt. Although unarmed, they quickly break free of their Roman oppressors.

Salina is finally resolved on full-scale revolution when the young Talia is raped by Octavian. At the reins of a knife-hubbed chariot, a fiery Viking goddess of war, she leads the men

Once again, Hammer rewrites history.

and women of her tribe in a sweeping attack on Octavian's column. The troops are mowed down, and Salina turns to face her lover, Justinian, returned from his campaign with a strong force.

They meet under flag of truce, and Salina proclaims that she must continue the war as her people cannot be held back when so close to regaining their freedom. With a breaking heart, she returns to her army and leads the deadly chariots against Justinian's ranks. This time, the Romans outmaneuver her and the tide turns against the Britons. A tremendous battle ensues, culminating with the death of Salina in her lover's arms.

"The pictures we make are tailor made to popular market requirements," said James Carreras (*Kinematograph Weekly*, May 30, 1963). "The production of a highly promotional product is our concern. The big epics are beyond our means." Carreras would soon change his belief with pictures like *She, One Million Years B.C.*, and unwisely, *The Viking Queen*. The production began on June 15, 1966, at Ardmore Studios in Ireland, a change from the planned May start at Elstree. A press reception was held to link Carita with Ursula Andress and Raquel Welch via life-size cardboard cutouts, which, unfortunately, her performance matched. Christopher Lee had been offered the role of Justinian, but Don Murray, who had had an impressive Hollywood career in the 1950s, won the part. After an auspicious start (*Bus Stop*, 1956), Murray began rejecting scripts on moral grounds. Perhaps the role of a benevolent general appealed to the former Korean conflict conscientious objector. It is unfortunate that he did not object this time as well. The weak script was loosely based on an historical incident in which Queen Boadicea led her people in a revolt against the Roman oppressors. Hammer was in over its head from the beginning, and director Don Chaffey correctly handled the material in comic book style.

One of the film's few strong points was the location shooting at Powerscourt Waterfall, Loch Tay, Wicklow Gap, Sally Gap, and Kilruddery Estate, which took up half of the eight-week schedule. During the last week of July, production designer George Provis recreated an entire village for the final three weeks of filming. One thousand Irish soldiers were used as extras, playing both Romans and Britons. The production ended on August 18, and a trade show was held on March 6, 1967, at Studio One. *The Viking Queen* was released on the ABC circuit on March 26, to dismissive reviews. *The Daily Cinema* (March 8): "For unsophisticated audiences"; *The Kinematograph Weekly* (March 11): "Simple, uncomplicated escapism"; and *The Monthly Film Bulletin* (April): "A scrappy and often startlingly anachronistic script."

While *The Viking Queen* was in production, Pan Books announced their paperback *The Hammer Horror Omnibus*, which contained adapted versions of *The Curse of Frankenstein*, *The Revenge of Frankenstein*, *The Gorgon*, and *The Curse of the Mummy's Tomb*. These were the films that audiences wanted from Hammer, and while there is certainly nothing wrong with variety, the company was going in the wrong direction with pictures like *The Viking Queen*. Only a strong, fact-based script and a huge budget could have done justice to Queen Boadicea's story, and *The Viking Queen* offered neither. An accomplished actress in the lead would have been nice, too.

Frankenstein Created Woman

Released March, 1967 (U.S.), June 18, 1967 (U.K.); 92 minutes; Technicolor (U.K.), DeLuxe Color (U.S.); 7758 feet; a Hammer–7 Arts Film Production; a Warner-Pathe Release (U.K.), a 20th Century–Fox Release (U.S.); filmed at Bray Studios, England; Director: Terence Fisher; Producer: Anthony Nelson-Keys; Screenplay: John Elder; Music: James Bernard; Music Supervisor: Philip Martell; Director of Photography: Arthur Grant; Supervising Editor: James Needs; Camera: Moray Grant; Production Design: Bernard Robinson; Art Director: Don Mingaye; Production Manager: Ian Lewis; Wardrobe: Rosemary Burrows, Larry Stewart; Hairstyles: Frieda Steiger; Special Effects: Les Bowie; Assistant Director: Douglas Hermes; Editor: Spencer Reeve; Sound Editor: Roy Hyde; Sound Recordist: Ken Rawkins; Continuity: Eileen Head; Makeup: George Parleton; Casting Director: Irene Lamb; U.K. Certificate: X.

Peter Cushing (Baron Frankenstein), Susan Denberg (Christina), Thorley Walters (Dr. Hertz), Robert Morris (Hans), Peter Blythe (Anton), Barry Warren (Karl), Derek Fowlds (Johann), Alan MacNaughton (Kleve), Peter Madden (Chief of Police), Kevin Flood (Gaoler), Philip Ray (Mayor), Ivan Beavis (Landlord), Colin Jeavons (Priest), Bartlett Mullins (Bystander), Alec Mango (Spokesman), Duncan Lamont (Hans' Father), Stuart Middleton (Hans as a Boy), John Maxim (Police Sergeant).

In a 19th century Balkan village, Baron Frankenstein (Peter Cushing) and Dr. Hertz (Thorley Walters) are endeavoring to transfer the souls of the dead into other bodies. Their assistant Hans (Robert Morris) is a local boy ostracized by the villagers because his father was guillotined for murder years before. One night Hans visits his girlfriend Christina (Susan Denberg), a cripple with a birthmark on her otherwise pretty face, at the cafe of her father Kleve (Alan MacNaughton). Kleve disapproves of their relationship because of Hans' father and treats his daughter's beau with contempt.

Kleve is murdered by Anton (Peter Blythe), Karl (Barry Warren) and Johann (Derek Fowlds), three young dandies from wealthy local families. Hans is later arrested because his coat was found at the scene, and the local prosecutor proposes that the accused has "inherited" his sire's evil traits. Hans is found guilty, sentenced to death and guillotined at dawn. The Baron sends Dr. Hertz to claim Hans' body and traps the young man's soul in a specially designed apparatus in his laboratory. Christina, meanwhile, is overcome by despair after the execution of Hans and drowns herself in a river.

Frankenstein and Dr. Hertz succeed in bringing Christina back to life with no sign of either her lameness or her facial blemish—and with Hans' soul housed in her. As a result,

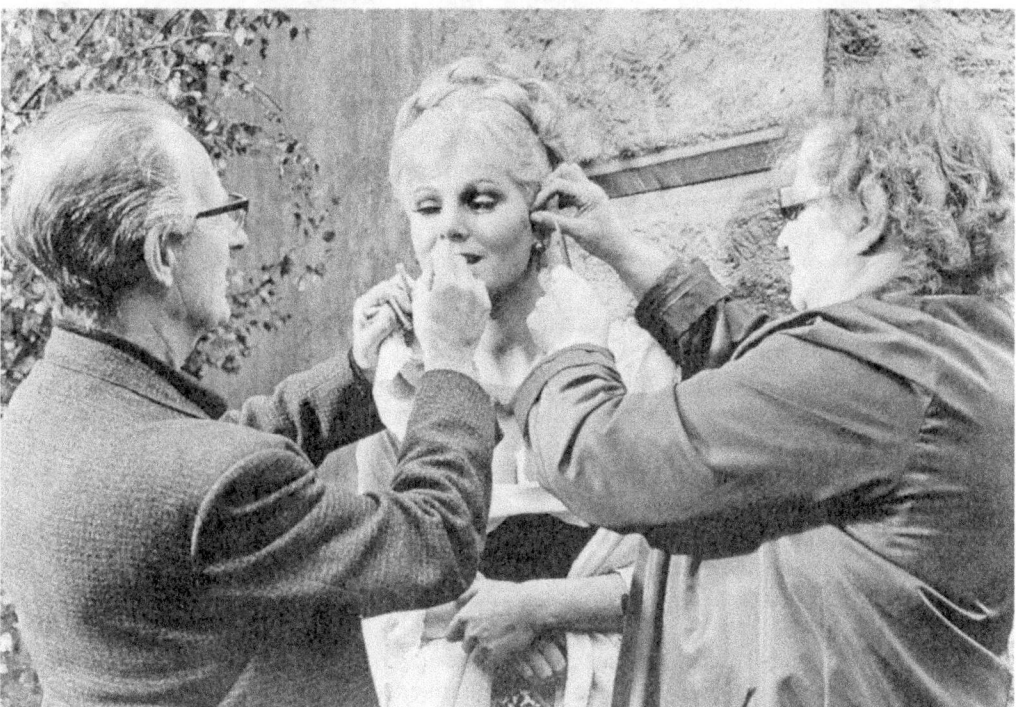

Top: Peter Cushing goes over the next scene with director Terence Fisher on the set of *Frankenstein Created Woman* (photo courtesy of Tim Murphy). *Bottom:* Susan Denberg has her makeup touched up in between takes on the set of *Frankenstein Created Woman* (photo courtesy of Tim Murphy).

Frankenstein Created Woman (1966)

Peter Blythe, tormented by his earlier victim, Susan Denberg, in *Frankenstein Created Woman*.

Christina is consumed with Hans' passion for revenge. One night she slips out of the house and goes to the village where she seduces and then murders Anton. The next evening, she does the same to Karl.

Frankenstein discovers that Christina is behind the murders and reasons that Hans' spirit is directing her. He races after her but is too late to save Johann. Despite his pleas, she then commits suicide as she had once before, throwing herself into the river and drowning in the churning surf.

In 1958, Anthony Hinds wrote a screenplay called *And Frankenstein Created Woman*, a parody of the title of the then-popular Brigitte Bardot film, *And God Created Woman*. Hammer dusted it off eight years later and began production at Bray on July 5, 1966. Back for the fourth time as the Baron was Peter Cushing who, in addition to his acting talent, helped set a standard of behavior at Bray. "What I remember most about the film," Peter Blythe told the authors (February, 1991), "is that on the first morning on the set, Peter Cushing made a point of introducing himself and welcoming one to the film with such sincerity and warmth that he not only endeared himself to me, but immediately created an atmosphere of goodwill and calmness that proved to be (in the extremely tight six-week shooting schedule that Hammer demanded) invaluable." Filming, which included location work at Chobham Commons, ended on August 12, 1966.

Despite having a female "monster," *Frankenstein Created Woman* has nothing in common with *Bride of Frankenstein* (1935). Although certainly inferior to the Universal classic, it still has much to recommend it. Frankenstein did not actually "create" a woman, but he *did* perform some remarkable plastic surgery. Peter Cushing, as usual, carried the picture with his expected fine performance, making up for a less than satisfying effort in

The Evil of Frankenstein. The difference may well have been Terence Fisher's return to the series. Fisher took Frankenstein, but not himself, seriously, and told Harry Ringel (*Cinefantastique*, Vol. 4, No. 3) that the Baron "is consecrated to one thing and one thing only, and that is to perfect the human body and human mind. He is singleminded and completely ruthless in what he does. But he is governed by idealism. He is not trying to achieve evil. He is not out to do anything but perfect what he considers God has not done." Frankenstein's search for perfection resulted in the Austrian actress Susan Denberg in her first starring role. She had previously been a Playboy "Playmate" (August, 1966), and only turned 22 during the production. A party was held at the London Playboy Club, and among the lucky celebrants were Peter Cushing, James Carreras, and Anthony Nelson-Keys. Despite her engaging performance and beauty, Denberg's career stalled, and like Christina, she died a suicide. Oddly, the provocative shots of her bikini bandaged body used to promote the film were not seen in the release print.

Also adding to the film's interest were Thorley Walters, whose Dr. Hertz had a Dr. Watson-like relationship with Frankenstein, and James Bernard's hauntingly beautiful score.

Following a May 2, 1967, trade show, *Frankenstein Created Woman* premiered at the New Victoria on May 19, and was released on the ABC circuit (paired with *The Mummy's Shroud*) on June 18. Reviews were generally positive. *The London Times* (May 18): "A nice sense of the balance between horror and absurdity"; *The Daily Cinema* (May 5): "A novel variation on the Frankenstein theme"; and *Variety* (March 15): "This latest variation on the Frankenstein theme has the excellent technical assets which have come to be expected of the Hammer film people." Special mention was made of Duncan Lamont's brief appearance in a pretitle sequence. He is only on screen for two minutes, but makes quite an impression.

Despite a plot that is ridiculous even for a Frankenstein movie, it does raise some intelligent points. The implications of the Baron's soul-transference theories are interesting, as is his desire to provide his "creation" with a conscience. This time, Frankenstein has done his job too well and Christina, overcome by remorse, kills herself—freeing both herself and her lover's soul. Although the film is not Hammer's best in the series, it is the most poignant.

The Mummy's Shroud

Released June 18, 1967 (U.K.); 84 minutes (U.K.), 90 minutes (U.S.); Technicolor (U.K.), DeLuxe Color (U.S.); 7591 feet; a Hammer–7 Arts Production released through Warner-Pathe (U.K.), 20th Century–Fox (U.S.); filmed at Bray Studios; Director: John Gilling; Producer: Anthony Nelson-Keys; Screenplay: John Gilling, based on a story by John Elder; Director of Photography: Arthur Grant; Production Design: Bernard Robinson; Art Director: Don Mingaye; Supervising Editor: James Needs; Editor: Chris Barnes; Music: Don Banks; Musical Supervisor: Philip Martell; Production Manager: Ed Harper; Special Effects: Les Bowie; Sound Editor: Roy Hyde; Sound Recordist: Ken Rawkins; Camera Operator: Moray Grant; Continuity: Eileen Head; Makeup: George Partleton; Mummy Costume: Rosemary Burrows; Hairstylist: Frieda Steiger; Assistant Director: Bluey Hill; Wardrobe Mistress: Molly Arbuthnot; Wardrobe Master: Larry Steward; Casting: Irene Lamb; U.K. Certificate: X.

John Phillips (Stanley Preston), Andre Morell (Sir Basil Walden), David Buck (Paul Preston), Elizabeth Sellars (Barbara Preston), Maggie Kimberly (Claire), Michael Ripper (Longbarrow), Tim Barrett (Harry), Roger Delgado (Hasmid), Catherine Lacey (Haiti), Eddie Powell (The Mummy), Dickie Owen (Prem), Richard Warner (Inspector Barrani), Bruno Barnabe (Pharaoh), Toni Gilpin (Pharaoh's Wife), Toolsie Persaud (Kah-to-Bey), Andrea Malandrinos (Curator).

Egypt, 1920. An archeological team headed by Sir Basil Walden (Andre Morell) and consisting of Claire deSangre (Maggie Kimberly), Harry Newton (Tim Barrett), and Paul Preston (David Buck) become lost while searching for the tomb of Kah-to-Bey. They are rescued by the team's financier, Paul's father Stanley (John Phillips), just as they discover the tomb. Hasmid Ali (Roger Delgado), the guardian, warns of a curse which is disregarded. Kah-to-Bey is taken to Cairo and placed next to the mummy of Prem, his protector. Kah-to-Bey is wrapped in a hieroglyphic-covered shroud that terrifies Claire.

284 *The Mummy's Shroud* (1966)

A fine actor (Andre Morell) was wasted in this indifferent movie.

Stanley has Sir Basil institutionalized so he alone can reap the glory as Ali restores Prem to life by reading from Kah-to-Bey's shroud. Sir Basil escapes from the asylum and becomes Prem's (Eddie Powell) first victim. The mummy then kills Harry and Longbarrow (Michael Ripper), Stanley's aide. Stanley attempts to flee Egypt but is also killed. Claire and Paul, the only survivors, are trapped in the museum by Prem and Ali, but she intones the shroud's Words of Death, causing Prem to crumble to dust.

The Mummy's Shroud was the last Hammer film to be shot at Bray, ending a sixteen-year association. It would be impossible to overstate the contribution of the studio to Hammer's success, and it was a sad day when that association ended. Hammer had become too "big" for the studio, which was now too small for the company's plans. But very few films produced by Hammer after their departure from Bray had any real merit.

Although *The Mummy* was one of Hammer's best, the company had no luck with its follow-ups. This was also true for Universal—there is just so much one can do with a mummy. *The Mummy's Shroud* was filmed between September 12 and October 21, 1966. Following a trade show at Studio One on May 3, 1967, it premiered at the New Victoria and went into general release on the ABC circuit on June 18. The film united critics everywhere—they all disliked it. Even genre publications like *Castle of Frankenstein* (12) were appalled: "Hopeless, grade B British mummy item that drags out again all the trite and tired nonsense." Mainstream viewers were also unimpressed. *The Evening News* (May 18, 1967): "Hammer are going a little soft at the centre"; *The Daily Telegraph* (May 19): "It takes up, somewhat crudely, the old theme of the curse of the tomb"; *The London Times* (May 18): "Static and stodgy"; *The Kinematograph Weekly* (May 13): "There is absolutely nothing new"; *Films and Filming* (June): "Stilted rehash"; *The Daily Cinema* (May 5): "Heavy going"; and *Variety* (March 29): "Routine chiller."

The Mummy's Shroud was an ill-advised

1967

Quatermass and the Pit

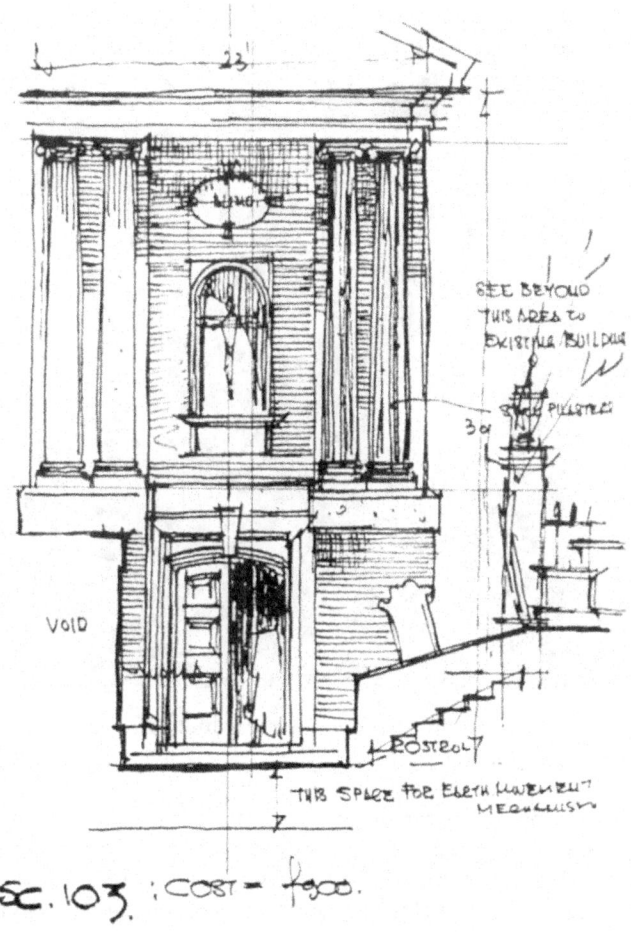

A Bernard Robinson design for *Quatermass and the Pit* (courtesy of Margaret and Peter Robinson).

Released November 19, 1967 (U.K.), March, 1968 (U.S.); 100 minutes (U.K.), 98 minutes (U.S.); Technicolor (U.K.), DeLuxe Color (U.S.); a Hammer–7 Arts Film Production; a Warner-Pathe Release (U.K.), a 20th Century–Fox Release (U.S.); filmed at MGM/EMI Studios, Elstree, England; Director: Roy Ward Baker; Producer: Anthony Nelson-Keys; Screenplay & Story by: Nigel Kneale; Director of Photography: Arthur Grant; Music: Tristram Cary; Musical Supervisor: Philip Martell; Production Design: Bernard Robinson; Art Director: Ken Ryan; Supervising Editor: James Needs; Editor: Spencer Reeve; Special Effects: Bowie Films Ltd.; Sound Recordist: Sash Fisher; Sound Editor: Roy Hyde; Makeup: Michael Morris; Wardrobe: Rosemary Burrows; Hairstyles: Pearl Tipaldi; Production Manager: Ian Lewis; Assistant Director: Bert Batt; Casting: Irene Lamb; Camera: Moray Grant; Continuity: Doreen Dearnaley; U.S. Title: *Five Million Years to Earth*; U.K. Certificate: X.

James Donald (Doctor Roney), Andrew Keir (Professor Quatermass), Barbara Shelley (Barbara Judd), Julian Glover (Colonel Breen), Duncan Lamont (Sladden), Bryan Marshall (Captain Potter), Peter Copley (Howell), Edwin Richfield (Minister of Defense), Grant Taylor (Police Sergeant Ellis), Maurice Good (Sergeant Cleghorn), Robert Morris (Jerry Watson), Sheila Steafel (Journalist), Hugh Futcher (Sapper West), Hugh Morton (Elderly Journalist), Thomas Heathcote (Vicar), Noel Howlett (Abbey Librarian), Hugh Manning (Pub Customer), June Ellis (Blonde), Keith Marsh (Johnson), James Culliford (Corporal Gibson), Bee Duffell (Miss Dobson), Roger Avon (Electrician), Brian Peck (Technical Officer), John Graham (Inspector), Charles Lamb (News Vendor).

While building an extension to the London subway system, workmen at the Hobbs

vehicle from the start, and not even Hammer's production quality could save it. But it must be said that, unlike most bad horror movies, the film does not invite derisive laughter. No Hammer horror has ever sunk to the depths of, say, *The Ape Man* (1943) to become a darling of the "so bad it's good" crowd. Made to support *Frankenstein Created Woman*, *The Mummy's Shroud* does its job well—it makes its partner look 100 percent better than it would have on its own. Perhaps its greatest sin was in killing off Andre Morell, the film's main asset, far too early. But this is a minor point, as nothing in the film (except Michael Ripper's amusing performance) is in any way memorable, and *The Mummy's Shroud* was a big step on the road to Hammer's decline.

Quatermass and the Pit (1967)

Barbara Shelley, James Donald and Andrew Keir stumble upon the missing link in *Quatermass and the Pit* (photo courtesy of Ted Okuda).

End station discover skulls and skeletons of what appear to be subhuman creatures. Further investigation by Dr. Roney (James Donald) and his assistant Barbara Judd (Barbara Shelley) of the National Historical Research Institute reveals a strange missile, thought at first to be an unknown Nazi V-weapon of World War II.

As work continues on the missile, rocket research expert Professor Quatermass (Andrew Keir) studies the history of the area and learns that it has always been associated with demons, dating as far back as the Roman occupation of England. When the door to the missile is finally opened, the scientists are horrified to discover the bodies of locust-like creatures, which Quatermass maintains are dead Martians. Quatermass believed that these beings have influenced the evolution of man and that their power survives.

Quatermass' theory becomes manifest when a monstrous insect-like horned creature hundreds of feet high materializes above the excavation pit, causing panic in the streets of London. Quatermass learns that whenever a human comes near the creature, which contains all the concentrated forces of evil, that person's mind is controlled and redirected by the Devil. Quatermass is also reminded of one of the ancient remedies used to battle the devil and the one thing it was purported to fear — iron. With the future of mankind threatened, Dr. Roney drives a large overhead crane into the center of the creature, causing it to dissolve. In so doing, however, he sacrifices his own life.

Hammer bought the rights to the BBC serial *Quatermass and the Pit* shortly after its initial episode was telecast on December 22, 1958. The six-part program starred Andre Morell and, like the first two serials, was a hit. The film version was to start in November, 1961, but was moved back to 1963. Explaining the delay, James Carreras said (*New York World Telegraph*, October 19, 1963), "Hammer Films steers clear of science fiction. Science fiction films are not easy to make. They call for lots of trick photography which sends the budget soaring and the faking has got to be good. Teenagers are quick to spot the inaccuracies."

Professor Quatermass and Dr. Roney meet one of their ancestors in *Quatermass and the Pit*.

The company was finally ready in 1967, and production began on February 27. Filming was moved from Elstree, due to overcrowding, to MGM Borehamwood. The planned director (Val Guest) and star (Peter Cushing) both had to be replaced due to schedule conflicts.

Producer Anthony Nelson-Keys (*Little Shoppe of Horrors* 7) recalled, "I wanted a director who had a great deal of technical know-how." He turned to Roy Ward Baker, who sank the *Titanic* in *A Night to Remember* (1958). "I was looking for a film after five years in television," said Baker. "Once I read the script, I thought, 'This is it!' It was the most wonderful, bogus, believable clap-trap I'd read in my life!" Andrew Keir stepped in for Cushing and was the best Professor Quatermass in the Hammer series. James Donald traded in his usual military attire for a tweed jacket for his edgy performance as the odd Dr. Roney, but Barbara Shelley stole the film with her intense performance.

Author Nigel Kneale had become well aware of the importance of visuals over words in movies. "More and more scripts," he said (*Daily Cinema*), "are going back to the silent era, letting the pictures tell the story and putting the dialogue in a subordinate position." Roy Ward Baker added (*Starlog* 180), "We went through the script together and discussed it. Kneale visited the set and saw a bit of the shooting. He was very happy with the picture when it was done." This was praise indeed, considering Kneale's dissatisfaction with aspects of the first two pictures. Baker's reading of James Carreras and Anthony Nelson-Keys was, "They weren't interested in art. In fact, I was quite anxious *not* to discuss the underlying overtones with them." These overtones were quite disturbing, raising many unsavory questions about the origin of man, making *Quatermass and the Pit* the most intellectually challenging of the series. Like its predecessors, the movie fails only in its special effects.

Filming ended at the end of April, and *Quatermass and the Pit* was trade shown at the Leicester Square Warner on September 27, 1967. The premiere was held on November 7, and the picture went into general release on November 19. As with the previous films, the *Quatermass* name was dropped in America, and the title changed to *Five Million Years to Earth*. Unfortunately, its release coincided with that of Stanley Kubrick's spectacular *2001*. Reviews, on both sides of the Atlantic, were mostly positive. *The Sunday Telegraph* (November 5, 1967): "The third of an honorable trilogy"; *The Morning Star* (November 4): "Kneale's creepy legend was given a new lease on life on the big screen"; *The Monthly Film Bulletin* (November): "A pity that the most interesting of Kneale's *Quatermass* parables proves the least satisfactory as a film"; *The Kinematograph Weekly* (September 30): "An ingenious and inventive plot"; and *The New*

288　*A Challenge for Robin Hood* (1967)

Hammer's thought provoking finale to the series, *Quatermass and the Pit*, was retitled for the American audience.

York Free Press (June 13): "Makes *2001* look like a nursery story." To really see the story, one should watch the BBC serial with Andre Morell's excellent acting, and the benefit of a longer running time. However, Hammer's version is a fine one; an example of thought provoking science fiction at its best.

A Challenge for Robin Hood

Released December 24, 1967 (U.K.), June, 1968 (U.S.); 96 minutes (U.K.), 85 minutes (U.S.); Technicolor (U.K.), DeLuxe Color (U.S.); a Hammer–7 Arts Film Production; a Warner-Pathe Release (U.K.), a 20th Century–Fox Release (U.S.); filmed at Pinewood Studios, England; Director: C.M. Pennington-Richards; Producer: Clifford Parkes; Executive Producer: Michael Carreras; Screenplay: Peter Bryan; Director of Photography: Arthur Grant; Supervising Editor: James Needs; Editor: Chris Barnes; Art Director: Maurice Carter; Music: Gary Hughes; Musical Supervisor: Philip Martell; Sound Editors: George Stephenson, Laurie Barnett, Jack T. Knight; Special Effects: Bowie Films; Fights Arranged by: Peter Diamond; Makeup: Michael Morris; Hairstyles: Bill Griffiths; Production Manager: Bryan Coates; Assistant Director: Ray Corbett; Camera: Moray Grant; Continuity: Elizabeth Wilcox; Wardrobe: Dulcie Midwinter; Casting Director: Irene Lamb; U.K. Certificate: U; MPAA Rating: G.

Barrie Ingham (Robin Hood), James Hayter (Friar Tuck), Leon Greene (Little John), Gay Hamilton (Maid Marian Fitzwarren/Mary), Peter Blythe (Roger de Courtenay), Jenny Till ("Lady Marian"), John Arnatt (Sheriff of Nottingham), Eric Flynn (Alan-a-Dale), Alfie Bass (Pie Merchant), John Gugolka (Stephen Fitzwarren), Reg Lye (Much), William Squire (Sir John de Courtenay), Donald Pickering (Sir Jamyl de Penitone), Eric Woofe (Henry de Courtenay), John Harvey (Wallace), Douglas Mitchell (Will Scarlet), John Graham (Justin), Arthur Hewlett (Edwin), Norman Mitchell (Dray Driver).

In 12th century England, Robin de Courtenay (Barrie Ingham) vows revenge when young Stephen Fitzwarren's (John Gugolka) father is murdered by Norman overlords led by Robin's evil cousin Roger (Peter Blythe). When Roger's father, Sir John (William Squire), learns that King Richard has been captured while returning from the Crusades, he suffers a heart attack and, before dying, includes Robin in his will. Roger tries to enlist his brother Henry (Eric Woofe) to kill Robin, and when he refuses, Roger kills him. Roger orders Robin's arrest for the murder, but Friar Tuck (James Hayter) knows the truth and helps Robin escape into Sherwood Forest. They are attacked by the Sheriff of Nottingham's (John Arnatt) men, but the poor forest dwellers rescue them. After Robin shows his prowess with bow and quarterstaff, he becomes their leader. The Sheriff and Roger plan to lure Robin from the forest by executing his friend Will Scarlet (Douglas Mitchell). Robin and his band infiltrate the castle, but he is captured and ordered to hang with Will. With the help of Little John (Leon Greene) and a pie fight orchestrated by Tuck, he escapes.

Robin learns that a woman he met at Sir John's castle disguised as a handmaiden is ac-

Robin Hood (Barrie Ingham, right) falls into the clutches of his evil cousin Roger de Courtenay, in *A Challenge for Robin Hood*.

tually "Lady Marian" Fitzwarren (Gay Hamilton), daughter of the murdered man. She thanks him for helping Stephen, with whom she has been reunited. When the sister and brother are taken prisoner by Roger, he offers himself in exchange. Led by Little John, the men of Sherwood storm Roger's castle and free their leader. Roger is killed in the battle, and Robin and Marian plan to marry.

Hammer returned to the Robin Hood legend for the third time to fulfill its commitment to produce at least one picture a year for general audiences. Despite a meager budget, an unknown star, and a fledgling director, *A Challenge for Robin Hood* was an impressive effort. Barrie Ingham, a former member of the Old Vic, had only four films to his credit and, while a far cry from the typical Hollywood leading man, was a worthy successor to the role. Peter Bryan, who scripted some of Hammer's best movies, contributed his last for the company. His version is more violent than one would expect for a children's film but, then, this *was* a Hammer production. Former cameraman C. Pennington-Richard's directorial debut began on May 1, 1967, at Pinewood, with location shooting done at Bodiam Castle in East Sussex. First time producer Clifford Parkes insisted that his actors play their roles straight. Two members of his supporting cast were reprising their roles from previous productions—James Hayter (Friar Tuck in *The Story of Robin Hood and His Merrie Men*, 1952) and John Arnatt (the Sheriff in Richard Greene's television series). Chief villain Peter Blythe recalled for the authors (February, 1992):

> Not all of the actors were veterans. The first day of shooting included a young New Zealand actor that was new to the business. The first day went smoothly enough. We were about halfway into the first scene the next morning when he suddenly burst onto the set, sweating profusely, out of breath. Almost in tears, he cried out to the director, to the cast, to *anyone*, "I'm sorry! My alarm didn't go off!" Someone—perhaps me—asked, "What time was your call?" "Call?" he responded. It was then gently explained that you only come to the studio when called.

The production ended on May 1, 1967, and *A Challenge for Robin Hood* was trade shown on November 28 at Studio One taking advantage of the Christmas school break, the film was released on the ABC circuit on December 24, to positive reviews. *The Kinematograph Weekly* (December 2): "Barrie Ingham has a fine presence as Robin Hood"; *The Monthly Film Bulletin* (January, 1968): "Lively rendering of the familiar legend"; and *The New York Times* (January 18, 1968): "Excellent. The picture moves with such intelligent speed, in fact, that the fairly modest budget seldom shows." The film is a lighthearted romp with no pretentions or subplots. Its characters are clearly defined, and Pennington-Richards gave his actors a free hand. Comedy, thrills, and romances are evenly distributed in Hammer's best Robin Hood.

The Anniversary

Released February 18, 1968 (U.K.), February 7, 1968 (U.S.); 95 minutes; 8505 feet; Technicolor (U.K.), DeLuxe Color (U.S.); a Hammer–7 Arts Film Production; a Warner-Pathe Release (U.K.), a 20th Century–Fox Release (U.S.); filmed at MGM/EMI Studios, Elstree, England; Director: Roy Ward Baker (replaced Alvin Rakoff); Producer & Screenplay: Jimmy Sangster, based on a play by Bill MacIlwraith; Director of Photography: Harry Waxman; Art Director: Reece Pemberton; Supervising Editor: James Needs; Editor: Peter Weatherly; Musical Supervisor: Philip Martell; Title Music: The New Vaudeville Band; Production Manager: Victor Peck; Assistant Director: Bert Batt; Camera: Gerry Anstiss; Sound Recordist: Les Hammond; Sound Editor: Charles Crafford; Continuity: June Randall; Makeup: George Partleton; Hairdresser: A.G. Scott; Wardrobe: Mary Gibson; Recording Supervisor: A.W. Lumkin; U.K. Certificate: A.

Bette Davis (Mrs. Taggart), Sheila Hancock (Karen Taggart), Jack Hedley (Terry Taggart), James Cossins (Henry Taggart), Elaine Taylor (Shirley Blair), Christian Roberts (Tom Taggart), Timothy Bateson (Mr. Bird), Arnold Diamond (Head Waiter), Albert Shepherd, Ralph Watson (Construction Workers), Sally Jane Spencer (Florist).

Mrs. Taggart (Bette Davis), a domineering matriarch, is celebrating the tenth anniversary of the death of her unloved husband. The eyepatch-sporting Mrs. Taggart has maintained a cruel hold over her grown sons, executives in the Taggart Home Construction company, by learning their weaknesses and using that knowledge to keep them in line. She emotionally blackmails her oldest son, Henry (James Cossins), a transvestite, by threatening him with the law. Terry (Jack Hedley) is determined to emigrate to Canada with his wife Karen (Sheila Hancock) in order to get away. Youngest son Tom (Christian Roberts) shows up with a new fiancée each year and announces his intention to marry his latest, Shirley (Elaine Taylor), who is pregnant.

Mrs. Taggart venomously battles with her sons' women in order to keep iron control. To remind Terry that it was his carelessness with an air rifle that cost her her eye, she leaves her glass eye between the covers of a bed to shock Shirley.

The sons and their lovers all stand up to the insidious Mrs. Taggart, but in the end she

Bette Davis celebrates in Hammer's black comedy *The Anniversary*.

plays her final cards, binding her sons and their women even closer to her: She telephones her attorney and authorizes him to begin legal proceedings to collect money from Karen. She then authorizes the solicitor to terminate the service agreement Taggart Home Construction holds with Tom. Admitting that Shirley reminds her of herself, Mrs. Taggart also tells the attorney to authorize a check for £5000 in the bride's name and speculates how long their marriage will last with Shirley holding the pursestrings.

Before retiring for the night, Mrs. Taggart locks up her deceased husband's study and remarks that it has been a lovely anniversary after all.

James Carreras bought the rights to Bill MacIlwraith's black comedy about the ultimate dysfunctional family shortly after its West End opening on April 20, 1966. While the stage version starred Mona Washbourne, Carreras hoped to get Bette Davis for the lead, and producer Jimmy Sangster's screenplay was sent to her. Jack Hedley, Sheila Hancock, and James Cossins were signed to repeat their stage roles. Filming began on May 1, 1967, with Alvin Rakoff directing—for a week—before Davis demanded that he be replaced. "Rakoff didn't have the first fundamental knowledge of making a motion picture," she said in *Mother Goddam*, "let alone what an actor is all about." Roy Ward Baker, Davis' neighbor years before in Malibu, was Rakoff's "lucky" replacement. "The change," he said in *Starlog*, "was all done over one weekend. I didn't even bother to see any of Rakoff's footage. I threw it away, and we started fresh Monday morning." Davis' next move was to demand that the script be changed, and Baker agreed. "As a play," he recalled, "it was a kind of slapstick comedy in which the mother set up the jokes for the other characters to crack." Bette told Jimmy Sangster, "I must be the pivotal figure, and they have to set up the jokes for me to crack. Otherwise, they don't want *me*!" The supporting cast were, naturally, concerned that their roles would be sacrificed to appease the star.

Originally set for eight weeks, *The Anniversary* wrapped on July 22, two weeks over schedule. The premiere was held at the Rialto on January 11, 1968, where the film earned £8000 in its two-week run. The film also did well in general release, which began in February, and made *The Kinematograph Weekly*'s Top Money Winner's list. Reviews were mixed, as one would expect for a black comedy. *The Sun* (January 11): "A frequently funny black comedy"; *The Sunday Express* (January 11): "Unnerving, yet wickedly funny"; *The Daily Telegraph* (January 11): "Sloppy and uninvolving"; *The New York Post* (February): "So exaggerated that it shatters the credibility needed to be effective satire"; and *Variety* (January 24): "A vehicle for the extravagant tantrums of Bette Davis."

Sadly, her tantrums were not confined to the screen. Sheila Hancock recalled in Charles Higham's *Bette*, "I wasn't prepared for Miss Davis' great entourage and for the fawning attitude it had towards her. I was shocked when the producer gave us a lecture saying that Miss Davis liked to be treated with great adulation."

This was a far cry from Peter Cushing's queuing behind an electrician in the Bray lunch line, and the fawning was hardly worth the trouble.

292 The Vengeance of She (1967)

As annoying off camera as on?

The Vengeance of She

Released April 14, 1968 (U.K.), May 1, 1968 (U.S.); 101 minutes; Technicolor (U.K.), DeLuxe Color (U.S.); a Hammer–7 Arts Production; a Warner-Pathe Release (U.K.), a 20th Century–Fox Release (U.S.); filmed at MGM/EMI Studios, England, and on location in Monte Carlo and Southern Spain; Director: Cliff Owen; Producer: Aida Young; Screenplay: Peter O'Donnell, based on the characters created by H. Rider Haggard; Music and Special Musical Effects: Mario Nascimbene; Musical Supervisor: Philip Martell; Saxophone Solo: Tubby Hayes; Director of Photography: Wolf Suschitzky; Supervising Editor: James Needs; Production Designer: Lionel Couch; Costume Designer: Carl Tomo; Production Manager: Dennis Bertera; Editor: Raymond Poulton; Assistant Director: Terence Clegg; Camera: Ray Sturgess; Sound Recordist: Bill Rowe; Sound Editors: Roy Hyde, Jack Knight; Continuity: Phyllis Townshend; Makeup: Michael Morris; Hair Stylist: Mervyn Medalie; Wardrobe: Rosemary Burrows; Special Effects: Bob Cuff; Ritual Sequences Designer: Andrew Low; Recording Director: A.W. Lumkin; U.K. Certificate: A; MPAA Rating: G.

John Richardson (Killikrates), Olinka Berova (Carol), Edward Judd (Dr. Philip Smith), Colin Blakely (George Carter), Jill Melford (Sheila Carter), George Sewell (Captain Harry), Andre Morell (Kassim), Noel Willman (Za-Tor), Derek Godfrey (Men-Hari), Daniele Noel (Sharna), Gerald Lawson (The Seer), Derrick Sherwin (No. 1), William Lyon Brown (Magus), Charles O'Rourke (Servant), Zohra Segal (Putri), Christine Pockett (Dancer), Dervis Ward (Lorry Driver).

While dazedly wandering on the coast of Southern France, a young woman named Carol (Olinka Berova) is plagued by hallucinatory voices calling her "Ayesha." A truck overtakes her and the driver (Dervis Ward) offers her a lift. When the driver tries to attack her, Carol flees. The driver pursues her through the woods but is run over by his own truck when it mysteriously slips into gear and careens toward the struggling pair. Carol seems unaffected by what has happened.

Carol arrives at Monte Carlo and stows aboard a yacht bound for North Africa. On board she meets Dr. Philip Smith (Edward Judd), a psychiatrist who senses that some compelling force is pulling the tormented girl toward the East. Upon reaching Haifa, Carol flees into the desert and falls into the clutches of a pair of Arabs. Philip, who has followed, rescues her and decides to accompany Carol to her unknown destination.

When they eventually reach the lost city of Kuma, Carol is greeted as the reincarnation of Queen Ayesha (She), the beloved of King Killikrates (John Richardson). After Philip has been imprisoned in one of the palace chambers, he is visited by Za-Tor (Noel Willman), the leader of a secret sect, who reveals that Killikrates has promised his High Priest, Men-Hari (Derek Godfrey), the secret of immortality if he can bring back Ayesha. Hypnotized by Men-Hari into believing that she is the lost queen, Carol prepares to enter the sacred flames that will render her immortal.

Philip, released by Za-Tor, persuades Killikrates that he had been betrayed and the king kills the villainous Men-Hari. Then, longing to

Top: Men-Hari (Derek Godfrey) and fellow citizens of the city of Kuma await the arrival of their reincarnated queen in *The Vengeance of She*. *Bottom:* Killikrates (John Richardson) believes he has found his immortal Ayesha (Olinka Berova) in *The Vengeance of She*.

294 *The Vengeance of She* (1967)

A totally unnecessary sequel.

Hammer's plans. A new title, *Vengeance of She*, appeared in June, 1967, with, supposedly, Susan Denberg slated to star. She was dropped in favor of Andress look-alike Olinka Berova, who had eleven movies to her credit in Czechoslovakia. Filming began in Monte Carlo on June 26, 1967, with Hammer newcomer Cliff Owen directing. Aida Young, an associate producer on three previous Hammer films, took full production responsibilities, as she would for five future pictures for the company. Six weeks of interiors followed at Elstree, and on August 19, the unit left for more location work at Almeria, Spain. The production ended on September 16, and while the film was being edited, Hammer and 20th Century–Fox began negotiations for the co-production of a television series. Fox was to assume 75 percent of the financing for the tentatively titled *Tales of the Unknown*.

Vengeance of She was trade shown on March 21, 1968, at the Warner-Pathe. It went into

join Ayesha, Killikrates walks into the flames. Carol and Philip watch in horror as Killikrates ages before their eyes and crumbles to dust.

Moments after Carol and Philip make their way safely out of Kuma, the dying Za-Tor invokes the gods of light to destroy the city. There is a gigantic explosion and all that is left of Kuma is rubble and ashes.

Hammer had planned a sequel to *She* within three months of its completion, but there was no further word until July, 1965. It was then announced that Ursula Andress had been signed to star in *Ayesha—Daughter of She*, but the picture was not on Hammer's 1965 schedule. In January, 1966, a brief mention appeared in the trades about *The Return of She*, but Andress' contract had expired, and so did

general release on April 14, disappointing audiences and critics alike. *The Sun* (April 5): "A remarkably dull load of hokum"; *The Morning Star* (April 6): "A cheap and gaudy piece of mumbo-jumbo"; *The Kinematograph Weekly* (March 20): "The plot is a load of melodramatic rubbish"; and *The Monthly Film Bulletin* (May): "The dialogue is literally unspeakable." The film fared no better in America, and it sank without a trace. The film seemed to exist solely to parade Olinka Berova across the screen and completely wastes it main assets—Andre Morell and Noel Willman. It is hard to believe that a picture with *those* actors could be *this* bad. Strangely enough, neither actor worked for Hammer again.

The Devil Rides Out

Released July 20, 1968 (U.K.), December, 1968 (U.S.); 95 minutes; Technicolor (U.K.), DeLuxe Color (U.S.); 8584 feet; a Hammer–7 Arts Production; a Warner-Pathe Release (U.K.), a 20th Century–Fox Release (U.S.); filmed at MGM/EMI Elstree Studios; Director: Terence Fisher; Producer: Anthony Nelson-Keys; Screenplay: Richard Matheson, based on Dennis Wheatley's novel; Director of Photography: Arthur Grant; Music: James Bernard; Musical Supervisor: Philip Martell; Supervising Art Director: Bernard Robinson; Supervising Editor: Spencer Reeve; Camera Operator: Moray Grant; Sound: A.W. Lumkin; Sound Recordist: Ken Rawkins; Sound Editor: Arthur Cox; Continuity: June Randall; Makeup: Eddie Knight; Hairstyles: Pat McDermott; Wardrobe Supervisor: Rosemary Burrows; Wardrobe: Janet Lucas; Casting: Irene Lamb; Special Effects: Michael Stainer-Hutchins; Choreographer: David Togure; U.K. Certificate: X; MPAA Rating: G; U.S. Title: *The Devil's Bride*.

Christopher Lee (Duc de Richleau), Charles Gray (Mocata), Nike Arrighi (Tanith), Leon Greene (dubbed by Patrick Allen) (Rex Van Ryn), Patrick Moyer (Simon), Gwen Ffrangcon-Davies (The Countess), Sarah Lawson (Marie), Paul Eddington (Richard), Rosalyn Landor (Peggy), Russell Waters (Malin).

England, 1920s. The Duc de Richleau (Christopher Lee) and Rex Van Ryn (Leon Greene) are rebuffed when they visit their friend Simon Aron (Patrick Moyer) by his group of new "friends"—a devil cult headed by Mocata (Charles Gray). After discovering the truth about Mocata's so-called "astrological society," the Duc and Rex spirit Simon to de Richleau's home, but Mocata's power is too great and he regains control of his minion. When they return to Simon's house, the Duc and Rex are greeted by a demon. Rex persuades Tanith (Nike Arrighi), a cult member, to go with him to the home of his friends Richard (Paul Eddington) and Marie (Sarah Lawson) Eaton, but Mocata lures her away. Rex follows her to a demonic ceremony in the forest—the conjuring of Satan. Joined by the Duc, he frees Simon and Tanith, and they return to the Eaton's home.

While the men are away, Mocata arrives and places Marie under a hypnotic spell, broken by the entrance of her child Peggy (Rosalyn Landor). Later, to protect the others from Mocata's power, Rex takes Tanith from the house. The Duc realizes that Mocata will stop at nothing to return Simon and Tanith to his fold and prepares for the worst by drawing a holy circle on the floor. He, Simon, and the Eatons are attacked by Mocata's induced horrors—a huge spider and the Angel of Death, which kills Tanith. During the confusion, Peggy is abducted and taken to Mocata's home. By using a potent ritual, the Duc and Marie destroy the coven and the friends return, unarmed, back at the Eatons' home—including Tanith. Due to the ritual's magic, time had been reversed, and Mocata was taken in her place.

Dennis Wheatley was—and still is—Britain's leading writer of the occult, churning out over fifty best sellers, including *The Devil Rides Out* (1935). Wheatley took Black Magic quite seriously and warned his readers against even a casual involvement. *The Devil Rides Out* was the first filming of a Wheatley novel, and he was on the set at Elstree on September 15, 1967. Both he and his wife were impressed after meeting the cast and crew. Oddly, his *Lost Continent* was being shot by Hammer at the same time. *The Kinematograph Weekly* (September 23) felt that Wheatley had been "untapped by filmmakers until now because of the vast scope of the adventure stories and the supernatural content of the black magic books." Hammer was, as usual, on the leading edge—not only with Wheatley but with filming Satanic subjects. Both *The Devil Rides Out* and *The Witches* were in production before *Rosemary's Baby*, which is usually given "credit" for recreating interest in the occult. Actually, Hammer planned to film *The Devil Rides Out* as early as 1964.

The production began at Elstree on August 7, 1963, and was completed on September 29. After a May 17, 1968, trade show at the Warner-Pathe, the picture premiered at the New Victoria on July 20, and was released on the ABC circuit on July 20. It was well received by the critics—a rare event for Hammer in the sixties. *The Daily Express* (June 7, 1968): "The manner and period are faithfully reproduced"; *The Daily Mirror* (June 7): "As

296 *The Devil Rides Out* (1967)

Top: On the set of *The Devil Rides Out* (note column braces and mop on left side of the stage). *Bottom:* Christopher Lee, Nike Arrighi, Leon Greene, and Patrick Moyer encounter the ultimate evil in this adaptation of Dennis Wheatley's exciting novel *The Devil Rides Out*.

The screen's first adaptation of a Dennis Wheatley work, *The Devil Rides Out* was presented in the United States as *The Devil's Bride*.

flesh crawling stuff it's not bad"; *The Kinematograph Weekly* (May 25): "It has moments of chilling appeal"; *The Daily Cinema* (May 22): "Gripping excitement"; *Variety* (June 12): "Suspenseful"; and *Films and Filming* (August, 1968): "Hammer has returned to its original standard."

Hammer would produce over thirty more films after this, but only *Frankenstein Must Be Destroyed* equalled its quality. Christopher Lee was perfectly cast, although purists may have felt he was too young. His stern demeanor usually does not lend itself to heroic roles, but in this case it worked. It is unfortunate that Hammer did not start a de Richleau series—there were certainly enough books, and Lee may have preferred the role to Dracula. This would be his last non–Dracula part for Hammer until Wheatley's *To the Devil—A Daughter* (1976). As good as Lee is, the film is "stolen" by Charles Gray's excellent job as Mocata. His appearances are brief and well-timed—not unlike Lee's Dracula. The re-mainder of the cast is fine with former model Nike Arrighi a standout, but Leon Greene is disconcertingly dubbed by Patrick Allen.

Although the film is considered one of Terence Fisher's best, he had some doubts. "The love angle," he told Harry Ringel, "was very superficial. I don't know why, probably my fault. The relationship between Nike Arrighi and Leon Greene never develops as it should have. The film would have been much stronger if it had." Wheeler Dixon mentions in his study of Fisher that the director was moved by a telegram from Dennis Wheatley. "Saw film yesterday. Heartiest congratulations. Grateful thanks for splendid direction." Fisher might have felt better about the film if it had not indirectly led to the end of his career. He was hit by a car while crossing a road after a post production session. His broken right leg kept him from directing *Dracula as Risen from the Grave* (taken over by Freddie Francis), and he would only direct two more films before his retirement in 1972.

The film has only one major flaw—the ordinary special effects. Richard Matheson (May, 1992) told the authors that during an earlier published interview he "spoke out of turn about the direction. There was nothing wrong with Fisher's directing. I found a few of the actors subpar, Lee and Charles Gray certainly not among them. Some of the effects were a little chintzy, but all in all, it was quite well done." Most of Hammer's best films did not rely on special effects, but this one did, and the movie is badly let down. It is hard to take Mocata seriously through his conjuring—it is Gray's performance that carries across the menace. Bernard Robinson's sets beautifully recreated England in the 1920s, the antique cars are as good as anyone could see in a museum, and James Bernard's score adds immeasurably to the tension.

Although the film has its weak spots, mostly caused by the budget, it manages to rise above them and is one of Hammer's last great horrors.

The Lost Continent

Released July 27, 1968 (U.K.), June 19, 1968 (U.S.); 98 minutes (U.K.), 83 minutes (U.S.); Technicolor (U.K.), Color by DeLuxe (U.S.); 8830 feet; a Hammer–7 Arts Production; a Warner-Pathe Release (U.K.), 20th Century–Fox (U.S.); filmed at MGM/EMI Elstree Studios; Director: Michael Carreras; Producer: Michael Carreras; Associate Producer: Peter Manley; Screenplay: Michael Nash, based on Dennis Wheatley's novel *Uncharted Seas*; Director of Photography: Paul Beeson; Music: Gerard Schurmann; Music Supervisor: Philip Martell; Songs by: Roy Philips; Sung by: The Pedlars; Production Design: Arthur Lawson; Special Effects: Robert Mattey, Cliff Richardson; Consultant: Arthur Haynaid; Modeller: Arthur Fehr; Editor: Chris Barnes; Camera: Russell Thomson; Supervising Editor: James Needs; Costume Design: Carl Toms; Assistant Director: Dominic Fulford; Continuity: Doreen Scan; Assistant Art Director: Don Picton; Casting: Irene Lamb; Makeup: George Partleton; Hairdresser: Elsie Alder; Wardrobe: Mary Gibson; Sound Editor: Roy Baker; Sound Mixer: Dennis Whitlock; Sound Recordist: A.W. Lumkin; U.K. Certificate: X; MPAA Rating: G.

Eric Porter (Lansen), Hildegard Knef (Eva), Suzanna Leigh (Unity), Tony Beckley (Harry), Nigel Stock (Webster), Neil McCallum (Hemmings), Benito Carruthers (Ricaldi), Jimmy Hanley (Pat), James Cossins (Chief), Dana Gillespie (Sarah), Victor Maddern (Mate), Reg Lye (Helmsman), Norman Eshley (Jonathon), Michael Ripper (Sea Lawyer), Donald Sumpter (Sparks), Alf Joint (Jason), Charles Houston (Braemar), Shivendra Sinha (Hurri Curri), Darryl Read (El Diablo), Eddie Powell (Inquisitor), Frank Hayden (Sergeant), Mark Heath, Horace James (Men).

On uncharted seas, Captain Lansen (Eric Porter) is transporting illegal explosives and a motley collection of passengers: Harry (Tony Beckley), a drunken pianist; Dr. Webster (Nigel Stock), who is being sued for malpractice; Unity (Suzanna Leigh), his oversexed daughter; Eva (Hildegard Knef), former mistress of a South American dictator; and Ricaldi (Benito Carruthers), a security agent on her trail. A hurricane is coming, but Lansen ignores First Officer Hemming's (Neil McCallum) warning. The crew mutinies, and the ship is abandoned. As their lifeboat drifts aimlessly, Webster is eaten by a shark and Ricaldi by an octopus before they miraculously are returned to the ship, now engulfed by intelligent—and hungry—seaweed.

After boarding the ship, they drift into a mysterious sea where countless survivors of previous disasters have gone, finding a land ruled by El Diablo (Darryl Read). With the

A "realistic" set from the indescribable *The Lost Continent*.

help of Sarah (Dana Gillespie), Lansen sets the seaweed ablaze, and they escape their captors as the lost continent is destroyed by a volcanic eruption.

This was Hammer's second Dennis Wheatley story, but the company was without a map as it adapted his *Uncharted Seas*. The film is a stylistic mess, totally absurd, but entertaining in a *Plan 9 from Outer Space* sort of way. The film was announced in *The Kinematograph Weekly* (June 17, 1967) as a "large scale action-adventure subject ... to be made in the tradition of *She* and *One Million Years B.C.*, and will take a full year to complete." Hammer (supposedly) sent a team to London's Natural History Museum to "consult marine biologists" to ensure accuracy. A month later, *The Lost Continent* was *still* being described as a large scale production, and Hammer was *still* engaged in "research." The major roles were cast by September 3, 1967, and the only holdup was waiting for *The Devil Rides Out* to finish at Elstree. The "authentic" monsters were finished in time for an October start.

The Lost Continent ended Hammer's three-year, seventeen-picture association with 20th Century–Fox. James Carreras told *The Kinematograph Weekly* (February 24, 1968), "No hard feelings. Hammer ought to get back to its former policy of playing the field." He expressed his pride in Hammer's continued independence, finding all of its pre-production costs from their own resources. Under consideration were a quick reunion with Fox, and the re-opening of Bray, for a proposed television series that became *Journey to the Unknown* for ABC-TV.

When *The Lost Continent* was released on the ABC circuit on July 27, 1968, audiences were not exactly treated to a "large scale subject" planned the previous year. But even the

Just about everybody was lost on this one!

most negative reviewers grudgingly admitted to being entertained. *Films and Filming* (August, 1968): "This is one of the most ludicrously enjoyable bad films"; *The New York Times* (June 20): "Marvelously absurd"; *Variety* (July 3): "The result is quite a stew." It's –difficult to defend something like *The Lost Continent*—its special effects are not especially special, and they were planned as a major drawing point. But, it *is* fun.

1968

Dracula Has Risen from the Grave

Released November 24, 1968 (U.K.), February 6, 1969 (U.S.); 92 minutes; Technicolor; 8283 feet; a Hammer Film Production; a Warner-Pathe Release (U.K.), a Warner Brothers–7 Arts Release (U.S.); filmed at Pinewood Studios, England; Director: Freddie Francis; Producer: Aida Young; Screenplay: John Elder (Anthony Hinds), based on the character created by Bram Stoker; Director of Photography: Arthur Grant, B.S.C.; Supervising Art Director: Bernard Robinson; Music: James Bernard; Musical Supervisor: Philip Martell; Supervising Editor: James Needs; Production Manager: Christopher Sutton; Editor: Spencer Reeve; Special Effects: Frank George; Construction Manager: Arthur Banks; Matte Artist: Peter Melrose; Assistant Director: Dennis Robertson; Sound Recordist: Ken Rawkins; Sound Editor: Wilfred Thompson; Camera: Moray Grant; Continuity: Doris Martin; Makeup: Rosemary McDonald-Peattie, Heather Nurse; Hair Stylist: Wanda Kelley; Wardrobe Mistress: Jill Thompson; U.K. Certificate: X; MPAA Rating: G.

Christopher Lee (Dracula), Rupert Davies (Monsignor Ernst Muller), Veronica Carlson (Maria Muller), Barry Andrews (Paul), Barbara Ewing (Zena), Ewan Hooper (The Priest), Marion Mathie (Anna Muller), Michael Ripper (Max), George A. Cooper (The Landlord), John D. Collins (Student), Chris Cunningham (Farmer), Norman Bacon (Boy), Carrie Baker (Girl Hanging in Church Bell).

The shadow of Dracula's hilltop castle continues to hang ominously over the nearby village, whose locals have given up on the church. To prove that the castle is empty, the newly arrived Monsignor (Rupert Davies) orders the village priest (Ewan Hooper) to accompany him there. When the Monsignor performs the service of exorcism outside the castle gates, thunder and lightning rise and the priest, running in fright, topples down an incline toward a frozen stream. Blood from his cuts trickles down onto the lips of Count Dracula (Christopher Lee), encased in the ice, resuscitating him. The priest, now Dracula's slave, tells him that it was the Monsignor who barred the castle entrance with an altar cross.

Dracula (Christopher Lee) rehearses his scene with director Freddie Francis and Maria (Veronica Carlson) on the set of *Dracula Has Risen from the Grave*.

The Monsignor returns to Keinenburg, rejoining his brother's wife Anna (Marion Mathie) and her daughter Maria (Veronica Carlson). At Maria's birthday party, her boyfriend Paul (Barry Andrews) admits that he is an atheist, precipitating a row with the Monsignor.

Zena (Barbara Ewing), a serving girl at the local cafe, falls victim to Dracula, who commands her to lure Maria to his cellar lair. Zena complies but Maria is able to escape. Furious, Dracula kills Zena.

Maria becomes Dracula's next victim, but the Monsignor recognizes the mysterious symptoms. When Dracula returns the next night, the Monsignor appears out of the shadows of the room and drives Dracula off with a crucifix.

The Monsignor, felled by the priest, instructs Paul on how to fight Dracula. Paul sees the priest on the street and brings him along to Maria's home. At the sight of the priest, the Monsignor cries out and dies.

With the aid of the crucifix, the priest is able to escape from the vampire's powers and, together with Paul, sets out after Dracula. Paul drives a stake into Dracula's body, but because Paul refuses to say a Latin prayer, the vampire escapes. Dracula abducts Maria and takes her to his castle, where she removes the altar cross and drops it into the valley below. In a fight with Paul, Dracula is tripped over the edge of the mountain wall and is impaled on the cross. The priest arrives and says the required prayer, sealing Dracula's doom. With a terrifying cry, he disappears into the mist.

On April 21, 1968—four days before *Dracula Has Risen from the Grave* started filming—Hammer was selected as a recipient of the Queen's Award to Industry for Export Achievement. Although 84 others were awarded, Hammer was the first film company

Yet another magnificent Bernard Robinson set in Hammer's *Dracula Has Risen from the Grave*.

to be honored. Within a three-year period, Hammer had generated over five million pounds for Britain and now deserved a measure of respect. "After all these years of denigration and sneers from the industry," said Christopher Lee (*Illustrated London News*, April 27, 1968), "we have shown beyond a doubt that our films are as popular as any made all over the world." The award was presented to James Carreras and Anthony Hinds at Pinewood on May 29.

Dracula Has Risen from the Grave was the third in the company's series and the first not to be directed by Terence Fisher. He was replaced, as in *The Evil of Frankenstein*, by Freddie Francis who was technically competent but lacked Fisher's intuitive feel for the subject. "This was my second sort of monster-horror film," he said (*Little Shoppe of Horrors*), "and, quite honestly, I don't like doing them." He also told John Brosnan (*The Horror People*), "I was more interested in the love affair between the boy and the girl than with Dracula. He was just a fly in the ointment." Christopher Lee was also back under protest. "I got a call at home from Jimmy Carreras," he said (*Starlog 6*), "saying, 'You must do this film, on my knees, I beg you. Do you know how many people you will keep from working at Hammer if you don't agree to do this film!' It really was a form of emotional blackmail."

At least Veronica Carlson was happy to be there in her first starring role. "Jimmy Carreras spotted me in a photo layout," she explained (*Scarlet Street* 4). "I had done a shoot on a beach, and Jimmy Carreras saw it in a newspaper. He contacted my agent and asked me to come down and test for the role. I never thought I'd get the part." She told the authors (July, 1992), "It was doubly exciting to get the role because I had always been a fan of those films. My friends and I used to skip school to see them. Freddie was patient and supportive. Of course, I was inexperienced on that film and needed that support." She was also quite taken by Bernard Robinson's rooftop sets.

Freddie Francis proves that he's no Terence Fisher!

"They were so beautifully designed and lighted. It was like walking into a painting." However, meeting Christopher Lee in person was like walking into a nightmare. "I looked up and there he was," she said (*Fangoria* 28), "staring down at me with those red eyes of his. I felt as though I were looking at the real Dracula!"

Barry Andrews had a different impression of Lee. He told the authors (February, 1991),

> On the day we filmed the staking scene, it happened to be his birthday and, as he wrestled to pull the stake from his heart, the lights went out and suddenly two beautiful maidens appeared bearing a cake with many candles on it. *Happy Birthday* was sung by everyone on the set and, slowly, Mr. Lee began to rise from his coffin, "blood" dripping from his hands and chest, and he sank the stake into the center of the cake! He hissed, his fangs glinting in the light of the candles. "Suck off"! Everyone roared before breaking into uncontrollable laughter.

Filming ended on July 6, 1968, and the trade show was held at the Warner-Pathe on November 4. It premiered the following day at the New Victoria and broke an opening day record at the theatre by taking in £12,000. *Dracula Has Risen from the Grave* went into general release on November 24, and on February 6, 1969, in America to generally condescending reviews. *The Los Angeles Times* (February 7, 1969): "Tepid bore"; *Variety* (November 20, 1968): "It's a jaded charade with even the technical credits showing lack of imagination"; and *The New York Times*: "Judging by this junky British film, he can descend again." Despite the negative reviews, the picture was Hammer's highest grossing in the series and had enough novel twists to be very entertaining. However, *Dracula Has Risen from the Grave* was a definite step downhill from the Fisher films and was a hint of worse things to come.

When Dinosaurs Ruled the Earth

Released October 25, 1970 (U.K.), March, 1971 (U.S.); 100 minutes (U.K.), 96 minutes (U.S.); Technicolor; a Hammer–7 Arts Production; a Warner-Pathe Release (U.K.), a Warner Bros. Release (U.S.); filmed at Shepperton Studios, and on location in the Canary Islands; Director, Screenplay: Val Guest; Producer: Aida Young, based on an idea by J.G. Ballard; Director of Photography: Dick Bush; Art Director: John Blezard; Editor: Peter Curran; Music: Mario Nascimbene; Musical Supervisor: Philip Martell; Sound Recordist: Kevin Sutton; Special Effects: Jim Danforth; Mechanical Effects: Allan Bryce, Roger Dicken, David Allen, Brian Johncock; Production Manager: Chris Sutton; Costume Design: Carl Toms; 2nd Unit Camera: John Cabrera; 2nd Unit Continuity: Susana Merry; Makeup: Richard Mills; Hairdresser: Joyce James; Wardrobe Master: Brian Owen-Smith; Assistant Director: John Stoneman; Sound: Frank Golding, Ted Karnon; U.K. Certificate: A; MPAA Rating: G.

Victoria Vetri (Sanna), Robin Hawdon (Tara), Patrick Allen (Kingsor), Drewe Henley (Khaku), Sean Caffrey (Kane), Magda Konopka (Ulido), Imogen Hassall (Ayak), Patrick Holt (Ammon), Jan Rossini (Rock Girl), Carol-Anne Hawkins (Yani), Maria O'Brien (Omah), Connie Tilton (Sand Mother), Maggie Lynton (Rock Mother), Jimmy Lodge (Fisherman), Billy Cornelius (Hunter), Ray Ford (Hunter).

When Dinosaurs Ruled the Earth (1968)

Ayak and Kane comfort Khuku's mate, Ulido, in *When Dinosaurs Ruled the Earth*.

Kingsor (Patrick Allen), chief of the combined Rock and Shell Tribes, believes that the sun is the giver of all life and chooses for human sacrifice several young women, among them Sanna (Victoria Vetri). During an eclipse Sanna escapes, diving from a cliff into the sea. She is rescued by a group of fishermen led by Tara (Robin Hawdon), members of the Sand Tribe. Kane (Sean Caffrey), one of Kingsor's men, sees Sanna being rescued and tells Kingsor, who sets out with his men to bring her back.

Sanna is welcomed by the chief of the Sand Tribe (Patrick Holt), but Tara's mate, Ayak (Imogen Hassall), resents the newcomer. When a Plesiosaur captured by the tribesmen breaks free, Tara cuts open hides containing animal fat and sets fire to it, burning the monster to death.

After Tara and the fishermen leave one day, Kingsor arrives to reclaim his sacrifice. Sanna escapes again. Thinking that she has taken refuge in a cave, Kane's men surround it. Without warning, they are attacked by the cave's occupant, a Triceratops. All but Kane are killed by the animal.

When Tara returns and finds Sanna gone, he and his men search the jungles. The Triceratops attacks them, mortally wounding Tara's friend Khaku (Drewe Henley). Tara leads the beast to the edge of a cliff and it tumbles to its death.

Kingsor turns the Sand People against Sanna, and Tara, who knows they will kill her if she is found, sets out alone to find her. But mistakenly thinking that she has been devoured by a carnivorous plant, he returns to his people. Meanwhile, Sanna has been mistaken by a mother dinosaur as her own offspring. She adapts well to her new "family" and spends time training the baby dinosaur to come to her when summoned.

Tara is stalked and carried off by a Pterodactyl, but manages to free himself and kill the beast. Making his way back through the rugged terrain, he is stunned to see Sanna

Top: One of Jim Danforth's Oscar-nominated effects for *When Dinosaurs Ruled the Earth*. *Bottom:* Tara (Robin Hawdon) defends his village against a rampaging Plesiosaur in Hammer's prehistoric fairy tale.

being followed by the mother dinosaur. Certain the beast will kill her, he rushes to her side only to discover that the monster obeys her commands.

Sanna is soon hunted again by Kingsor and his warriors, but she is saved by the sudden arrival of the mother dinosaur. Tara is brought back to the village and is about to be executed when a phenomenon in the sky creates a massive wave which threatens to engulf the Sand People's village. Tara is rescued by Sanna, and together with Kane and his bride Ulido (Magda Konopka), they climb aboard Tara's raft and ride out the devastating tidal wave. Coming to rest in an unexplored region, the quartet looks up into the night sky and witnesses the world's first full moon.

The success of *One Million Years B.C.* called for a follow-up, and Hammer naturally answered the call. Ray Harryhausen, whose animated dinosaurs highlighted the first picture, was working on *The Valley of Gwangi* and was replaced by young Jim Danforth. He was only eighteen when he began his career as an animator, and *The Time Machine* (1960), his first feature, won an Oscar for special effects. Twenty-five years after making *When Dinosaurs Ruled the Earth*, Danforth still has mixed emotions about his experience with Hammer, which he shared with the authors in July, 1993.

> I received an early inquiry from Hammer saying that they would not commission the screenplay unless I was available. After I gave the commitment, I was "out of the loop" in that I was not asked to give any input. I was told by Aida Young, "Just tell us what you need, and I'll get it for you." This would have been a workable procedure if Hammer had stood behind it. But eventually I apparently passed their secret budget figure, and the Hammer management began to get hostile. The locations had all been chosen before I started on the production, and I didn't see them until I arrived in the Canary Islands to begin shooting. Given Aida's generous nature, I feel certain that she would have included me in the location scouting and early planning phase of the picture if she could have. I was totally unable to alter some of the misguided planning which had occurred before I arrived. This cost Hammer a great amount of money and time because it necessitated many matte paintings (some of which were done twice) to enhance studio sets which had been built too small to contain the dinosaur action. The basic problems of producing visual effects films stem from the fact that producers and directors who, on a normal film are entirely competent, are in over their heads. Since they don't realize this, they are reluctant to relinquish to the visual effects designer that portion of control he needs to do the job for which he was hired. Hammer was initially more friendly and considerate than most companies. Unfortunately, I wasn't asked to help in some vital areas, and I was unable to figure out a way to control those areas from which I was excluded. The result was that Hammer was extremely annoyed with me because of the excessive time and money required, and I became angry with them when I was blamed for conditions which I believed were not of my making. If I had simply said, "I'm just an animator, this is somebody else's problem," I probably would not have been held responsible. Many of the very exciting and elaborate scenes which Val had originally written had to be cut out at my insistence because they would have taken an enormous amount of time to do. There was a much greater sense of the elemental forces of nature in Val's original screenplay, but these are precisely the most expensive scenes to do. I could never figure out what kind of a film they were trying to make. Although I think many of Val's live action scenes are extremely well-directed, I think the film is badly conceived. I thought that it is a misguided film. It is neither realistic enough to be taken seriously, nor is it flamboyant enough to be a grand adventure. Although I remain extremely grateful for the opportunity, I really had no high expectations.

Val Guest told Tom Weaver,

> Aida Young called me at my holiday pad in Malta and asked if she could come over, so she flew over and said, "Jimmy Carreras wants to do another dinosaur film." She brought a few sheets of paper with ideas that matched up with the poster Carreras had sent to Hollywood. I thought it might be fun. I'd never done anything like that, so I said, "Why not?"

The budget was set at £2.5 million, and the production began on October 12, 1968, when two charter planes left for the Canary Islands. Danforth returned to Shepperton on November 18 to complete work on full-size props, and interiors were to be shot there on a five-week schedule. On March 8, 1969, *The Kinematograph Weekly* reported that "Jim Danforth is now adding complicated scenes of the world's evolution, including tidal waves and a celestial view of the moon breaking away from the sun." Originally contracted for one year, Danforth would need seventeen months to complete the

Animator Jim Danforth received an Academy Award nomination for his magnificent special effects.

effects which were finally completed in February, 1970. *When Dinosaurs Ruled the Earth* was trade shown on September 29 at Studio One and premiered at the New Victoria later that week. The first week's take was an excellent £3500. By November 6, the picture had taken over £51,000 during its northern release on the ABC circuit. By the end of 1970, it made *The Kinematograph Weekly*'s Top Money Maker List, despite only being in release for three months, and reviews were mostly positive. *Variety* (October 14, 1970): "The special effects, excellently contrived, steal the show"; *The Los Angeles Times*: "It has plenty of of panache, supplied by respected writer-director Val Guest who never condescends to the genre and tells his story well"; *Cue* (March 27, 1971): "The special effects are fun, the cast attractive"; and *The Kinematograph Weekly* (October 3, 1970): "The monsters are routine, showing familiar shortcomings in animation and matching."

It is pointless to discuss acting in a film like this, and former "Playmate of the Year" (1968) Victoria Vetri (the former Angela Dorian) delivered what she was hired for. So did Jim Danforth, who received Hammer's first and last Oscar nomination. Not surprisingly, he lost to Disney's *Bedknobs and Broomsticks*.

1969

Frankenstein Must Be Destroyed

Released June 8, 1969 (U.K.), February 11, 1970 (U.S.); 97 minutes; Technicolor; 8771 feet; a Hammer Film Production; a Warner-Pathe Release (U.K.), a Warner Bros.–7 Arts Release (U.S.); filmed at MGM/EMI Elstree Studios, England; Director: Terence Fisher; Producer: Anthony Nelson-Keys; Screenplay: Anthony Nelson-Keys, Bert Batt; Music: James Bernard; Music Supervisor: Philip Martell; Director of Photography: Arthur Grant; Camera: Neil Binney; Editor: Gordon Hales; Production Design: Bernard Robinson; Production Manager: Christopher Neame; Makeup: Eddie Knight; Hairdresser: Pat McDermott; Continuity: Doreen Dearnaley; Sound Supervisor: Tony Lumkin; Assistant Director: Bert Batt; Supervising Editor: James Needs; Sound Recordist: Ken Rawkins; Sound Editor: Don Ranasingher; Construction Manager: Arthur Banks; Wardrobe Mistress: Lotte Slattery; Wardrobe Supervisor: Rosemary Burrows; Publicist: Bob Webb; Special Effects: Studio Locations, Ltd.; U.K. Certificate: X; MPAA Rating: PG.

Peter Cushing (Baron Frankenstein), Veronica Carlson (Anna), Freddie Jones (Prof. Richter), Simon Ward (Karl), Thorley Walters (Inspector Frisch), Maxine Audley (Ella Brandt), George Pravda (Brandt), Geoffrey Bayldon (Police Doctor), Colette O'Neil (Mad Woman), Harold Goodwin (Burglar), George Belbin, Norman Shelley, Frank Middlemass, Michael Gover (Guests), Jim Collier (Dr. Heidecke), Alan Surtees, Timothy Davies (Policemen), Peter Copley (Principal).

Frankenstein Must Be Destroyed (1969)

The Baron (Peter Cushing, right) and his unwilling assistant, Karl (Simon Ward), in *Frankenstein Must Be Destroyed*.

After his secret laboratory is discovered by Inspector Frisch (Thorley Walters), Baron Frankenstein (Peter Cushing) is on the run. Calling himself Fenner, he takes a room at Anna Spengler's (Veronica Carlson) boarding house. Overhearing a conversation between other lodgers, he learns that his colleague, Dr. Brandt (George Pravda), is incarcerated in a nearby asylum. Brandt developed a new transplant technique before going mad, and Frankenstein is determined to get it from him. Anna's lover Karl (Simon Ward) is a doctor at the asylum and steals drugs to sell to pay Anna's mother's medical expenses. Frankenstein blackmails the couple into helping him kidnap Brandt. During their escape, Brandt suffers a heart attack and is near death. The Baron then abducts Dr. Richter (Freddie Jones), another asylum doctor, and plans to transplant Brandt's brain into his healthy body. With the police—and Mrs. Ella Brandt (Maxine Audley)—in pursuit, Frankenstein and his victims hide in an abandoned house as Brandt/Richter heals.

After "he" regains consciousness, the terrified Anna misinterprets his actions and stabs him. After "he" staggers away, Frankenstein kills Anna and tracks the creature to Brandt's house with Karl not far behind. Ella is horrified and rejects the pathetic creature's plea for understanding. After she leaves, he prepares a trap for Frankenstein with his notes, hidden in a kerosene-soaked room, as bait. As Frankenstein enters the inferno, Karl arrives and the creature shoots him. Clutching the notes, Frankenstein runs from the house but is tackled by the dying Karl. The creature lifts Frankenstein to his shoulders and carries him back into the blazing house.

Frankenstein Must Be Destroyed was the last Hammer film to combine the talents of Peter Cushing, Terence Fisher, James Bernard,

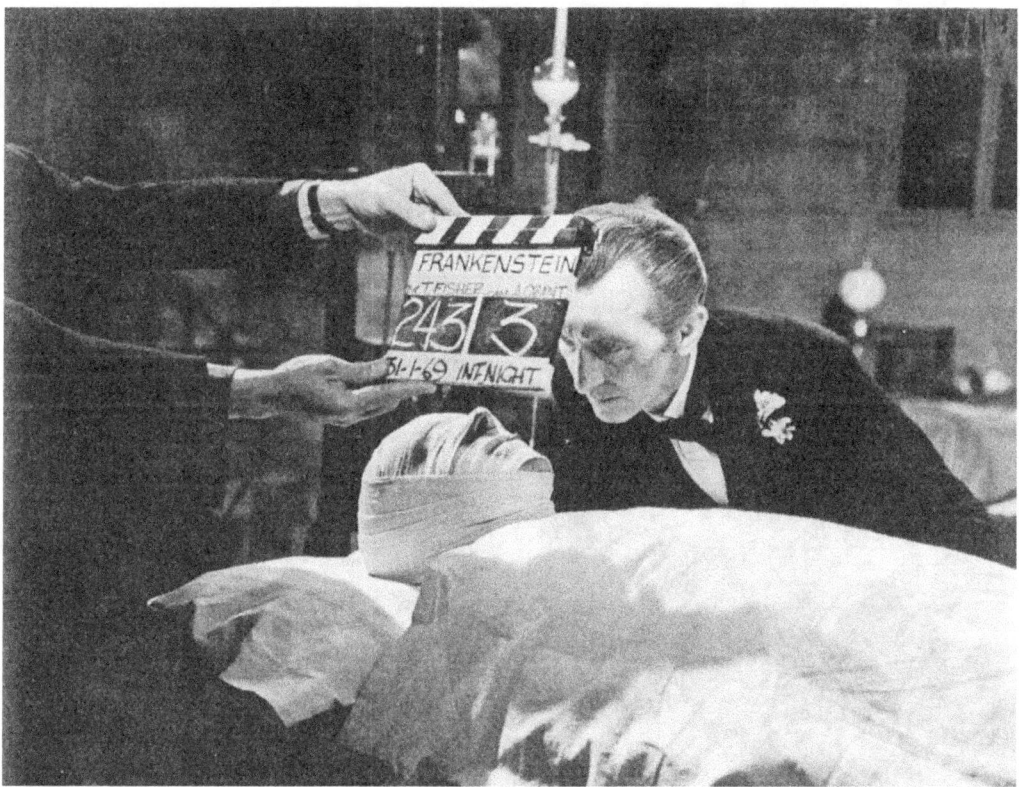

Terence Fisher is about to shout "Action!" in this third take from *Frankenstein Must Be Destroyed* (photo courtesy of Tim Murphy).

and Bernard Robinson. It was also the only Hammer Frankenstein not written by either Jimmy Sangster or Anthony Hinds. Anthony Nelson-Keys was working on *Lock Up Your Daughters* when Hinds asked if he would like to produce another Frankenstein. "But this time," Keys recalled in *Little Shoppe of Horrors*, "Hinds said, 'You have to write the story.'" Also working on *Daughters* was Bert Batt, who, in addition to being an assistant director, had done some writing which Keys thought was "extraordinarily good." Together they worked out an outline which Batt turned into a screenplay unlike anything Hammer had previously produced. In the past, the villain always got his due and the hero triumphed, but in *Frankenstein Must Be Destroyed*, there were no heroes—only villains and victims. Even the pathetic Brandt/Richter creature does "the right thing" only for revenge, and not from any sense of duty. The times were changing, and Hammer was changing with them.

Filming began on January 13, 1969, on the company's best film of the decade. Terence Fisher specifically asked for Freddie Jones as the film's nominal "monster." Like Michael Gwynn's Karl in *The Revenge of Frankenstein*, Brandt is far more wronged than wrong. "To lend verisimilitude to a character who awakens to find himself in another body makes a powerful demand upon the actor," Jones told the authors (March, 1992).

> Incredibly, I recall the logical sequence I followed: fearful headache, therefore a desire to touch and perhaps discover some things. On its way up to the head, the hand naturally came into view. *Shock!*—as the hand was instantly unfamiliar! More spontaneous perfunctory investigation and then, I notice the shiny surface of a kidney-shaped bowl—a mirror! And the truth. I don't recall any role making a greater demand.

Young Simon Ward had just left the Royal Academy of Dramatic Arts, and this was his first film. "I just didn't know what was going on," he confessed in *Screen International*

310 *Frankenstein Must Be Destroyed* (1969)

Hammer brings a new look to an old theme.

German ad for *Frankenstein Must Be Destroyed*.

(June 4, 1977). "Peter Cushing was absolutely marvellous, and I don't know what I would have done without him." Equally in need of his help was Veronica Carlson who, against almost everyone's wishes, was pushed by James Carreras into performing a rape scene with Cushing. Carreras felt the film needed more sex, and Carlson told the authors (August, 1991) that "I couldn't refuse to do it. Peter was disgusted with the scene, and he didn't want to do it. Terence Fisher was very understanding, but it was totally embarrassing and humiliating." It was also an afterthought and does not fit with the previously shot scenes which it renders false. "It gives my character no credence," Carlson rightly complained. Fortunately, the scene was cut from American prints. Recently re-inserted by Turner Broadcasting, the scene does little for the film, although it *was* well acted and directed.

During the picture's production, Hammer was the subject of BBC's *Made in Britain*, which acknowledged the company's receiving the Queen's Award to Industry. "We give the customers what they want," he said, "and they want to be frightened out of their wits!" *Frankenstein Must Be Destroyed* wrapped on February 26. Not even a heavy snowfall interfered with additional outside filming as an army of workmen swept the street set so the continuity would not be compromised. The trade show was held at the Warner on May 20, and premiered at the same theatre on the 22nd. After a two-week run (during which it took £4208 and £3175), the movie went into general release on the ABC circuit on June 8. Despite the film's pessimism and graphic horror, reviews were surprisingly positive. The

British Film Institute's *Monthly Film Bulletin* (June): "The most spirited Hammer horror in some time"; *The Kinematograph Weekly* (May 24): "The period atmosphere and lowering settings keep the excitement at a fine active simmer"; *Variety* (June 11): "There's nothing tongue in cheek about Fisher's directing"; and *The London Times* (May 22): "As nasty as anything I have seen in the cinema for a very long time."

Frankenstein Must Be Destroyed was Hammer's last outstanding film, with all concerned at the top of their form. Although set in period, the story caught the negativity of the Vietnam era, and wove in expertly the topicality of drug abuse. It is practically flawless and stands next to *Dracula* as Hammer's greatest horror film, but is a difficult film to enjoy. Terence Fisher (*Cinefantastique*, Vol. 4, No. 3) called it "The one which nobody else seems to care for." Peter Cushing was never better in a horror movie, and at the 1994 FANEX Hammer Convention in Baltimore, his performance was voted as the best given in a Hammer film.

Moon Zero Two

Released October 26, 1969 (U.K.), March, 1970 (U.S.); 100 minutes; Technicolor; 8999 feet; a Hammer/Warner Bros./7 Arts Production; a Warner-Pathe Release (U.K.), Warner Bros./7 Arts (U.S.); filmed at MGM/EMI Elstree Studios; Director: Roy Ward Baker; Producer: Michael Carreras; Screenplay: Michael Carreras, from a story by Frank Hardman, Gavin Lyall, and Martin Davidson; Director of Photography: Paul Beeson; Art Director: Scott MacGregor; Music: Don Ellis; Musical Supervisor: Philip Martell; Editor: Spencer Reeve; Sound: Roy Hyde; Sound Recordist: Claude Hitchcock; Special Effects: Les Bowie; Production Manager: Hugh Harlow; Choreography: Jo Cook; Assistant Director: Jack Martin; Costumes: Carl Toms; Special Photography: Kit West, Nick Allder; U.K. Certificate: U; MPAA Rating: G.

James Olson (Bill Kemp), Catherina Von Schell (Clementine Taplin), Warren Mitchell (J.J. Hubbard), Adrienne Corri (Liz Murphy), Ori Levy (Karminski), Dudley Foster (Whitsun), Bernard Bresslaw (Harry), Neal McCallum (Space Captain), Michael Ripper, Robert Tayman (Card Players), Sam Kydd (Barman), Keith Bonnard (Junior Customs Officer), Leo Britt (Senior Customs Officer), Carol Cleveland (Hostess), Roy Evans (Workman), Tom Kempinski (Officer), Lew Luton (Immigration Officer), Claire Shenstone (Hotel Clerk), Chrissie Shrimpton (Botigue Attendant), Amber Dean Smith, Simorie Silvera (Hubbard's Girls).

The year 2021. After decades of space exploration, the glamour is gone for many space heroes, including Bill Kemp (James Olson), who with his sidekick Karminski (Ori Levy) is piloting a rundown ferry ship, the *Moon Zero Two*. In order to keep flying—against the wishes of Liz Murphy (Adrienne Corri), an antagonistic police chief—Kemp agrees to corral a sapphire asteroid. This will put him closer to J.J. Hubbard (Warren Mitchell), who runs things on the moon. But first, Kemp plans to help Clementine Taplin (Catherina Von Schell) to find her missing brother Wally, who turns up dead. Kemp and Clementine are attacked by Hubbard's hired guns—he wants the Taplins' claim as a landing site for the asteroid. Hubbard's gunslinger Harry (Bernard Bresslaw) kills Liz and forces Kemp and Clementine to land the asteroid. They do—on top of Hubbard's gang. Clementine now owns the sapphire and Kemp has reclaimed his former status as a hero.

Moon Zero Two is another example of Hammer over-reaching itself. Beginning with *She*, Hammer became involved in projects that required more money than the company was used to spending. There is nothing wrong with this film that a bigger budget would not have cured. *Moon Zero Two* was described as a "space western," meaning that Western clichés were updated to the future—an idea that worked much better in Sean Connery's *Outland* (1981). Production began with special effects work on March 8, 1969, and live action shooting started on March 31. Hammer launched the picture with a barrage of publicity and press luncheons, at which James Carreras (*Kinematograph Weekly*, April 15, 1969) enthused, "Nineteen sixty nine is the year of the moon—everyone's going there. This lunch is to celebrate Hammer's and Great Britain's occupation of the moon." The production wrapped on June 10, and the company made every effort to link their movie with the American moonshot scheduled for July—the best

312 *Moon Zero Two* (1969)

Top: Hammer's ill-advised "space western," *Moon Zero Two*. *Bottom:* A good idea done badly—and upstaged by NASA.

free advertising available! Unfortunately, the public was *far* more interested in the real thing.

A special screening was held during the first week of October, followed by an October 8 trade show at the Warner and an October 26 release on the ABC circuit. Carreras predicted in *The Kinematograph Weekly* (April 5) that *Moon Zero Two* would be Hammer's "biggest box office picture ever" and was even planning a sequel, *Disaster in Space*. Unfortunately, *Moon Zero Two* was enough of a disaster, as *The Kinematograph Weekly* (November 8) reported. It was "disappointingly below average in all situations." The film might have succeeded a few years earlier, but it could not compete with an actual moon landing. Unlike *2001—A Space Odyssey* (1968), *Moon Zero Two* was rooted in a semi-plausible reality which paled before the awesome truth. In short, James Olson was no match for Neil Armstrong.

Roy Ward Baker (*Starlog* 21), said, "*Moon Zero Two* was a bad picture. It was hopeless and never got off the ground." Concerning Michael Carreras, Baker commented, "He's a delightful man, but he was inclined to take on tasks that were much better left to other people. But, he took on a bit too much. Then, he took on the running of Hammer itself, and he *really* overstretched himself." Critics generally agreed with Baker. *The London Times* (October 16, 1969): "The special effects are none too special"; *The Observer* (October 19): "As silly a piece of pseudo-science fiction as you could loathe to find"; and *The Guardian* (October 17): "It's dreadfully made from start to finish."

Moon Zero Two was definitely one small step for Hammer.

Crescendo

Released June 7, 1970 (U.K.), November, 1972 (U.S.); 95 minutes (U.K.), 83 minutes (U.S.); Technicolor (U.K.); a Hammer/Warner Bros./7 Arts Production; a Warner-Pathe Release (U.K.), a Warner Bros./7 Arts Release (U.S.); filmed at MGM/EMI Studios, Elstree, England, and on location in France; Director: Alan Gibson; Producer: Michael Carreras; Screenplay: Jimmy Sangster, Alfred Shaughnessy; Director of Photography: Paul Beeson; Art Director: Scott MacGregor; Editor: Chris Barnes; Music: Malcolm Williamson; Music

Is it Georges or Jacques? Stefanie Powers fights for her life in *Crescendo*.

Performed by: The London Symphony Orchestra; Piano Soloist: Clive Lithgoe; Saxophone Soloist: Tubby Hayes; Production Manager: Hugh Harlow; Assistant Art Director: Don Picton; Assistant Director: Jack Martin; Camera: John Wilbolt; Continuity: Lillian Lee; Construction Manager: Arthur Banks; Makeup: Stella Morris; Hairdresser: Ivy Emmerton; Wardrobe: Jackie Breed; Property Buyer: Ron Baker; Set Dresser: Freda Pearson; Sound Mixer: Claude Hitchcock; Dubbing Mixer: Len Abbott; Sound Editor: Ron Hyde; Recording Supervisor: A.W. Lumkin; Sound: RCA Sound System; U.K. Certificate: X; MPAA Rating: PG.

Stefanie Powers (Susan Roberts), James Olson (Georges/Jacques), Margaretta Scott (Danielle Ryman), Jane Lapotaire (Lillianne), Joss Ackland (Carter), Kirsten Betts (Catherine).

Susan Roberts (Stefanie Powers), an American music teacher, comes to France to write a biography on the life of composer Henry Ryman. She has been invited to stay at the home of Ryman's widow (Margaretta Scott), who lives in a country manor house with her wheelchair-bound son Georges (James Olson). Georges is addicted to painkilling heroin which is administered by Lillianne (Jane Lapotaire), the maid, who seduces Georges behind closed doors, using the needed

Crescendo (1969)

Hammer strikes a discordant note.

injection as a bribe to force his cooperation. As the painkiller takes effect, Georges slips into a deep sleep and relives once again a terrifying nightmare.

Susan comes across a photo of a young woman who looks like herself. Mrs. Ryman explains that her name was Catherine and that her son was in love with her. However, after his accident, she left him. Susan later realizes that Mrs. Ryman may be trying to make her into another "Catherine" to torment Georges.

Mysterious happenings ensue, like piano music in the night and the murder of Lillianne, who is stabbed to death in the swimming pool by an unseen assassin. Georges suffers a painful attack, and this time Susan administers the heroin he needs. Mrs. Ryman tells Susan that in France, not only is the drug addict subject to imprisonment, but also anyone administering the drug. Mrs. Ryman agrees not to press the issue if Susan marries her son.

Susan finds that Georges has a mad twin brother, Jacques (also James Olson), who is responsible for killing Lillianne and who thinks Susan is Catherine. Jacques stalks her throughout the estate and is about to shoot her when Mrs. Ryman appears and saves her, shooting Jacques in the back. Slipping out through the front gate, Susan runs for her life, leaving behind Georges and his mother, who had hatched an insane plot to carry on the Ryman musical legacy through the birth of Jacques' child with Susan.

Crescendo was Hammer's first psycho-thriller since *The Nanny* four years earlier, but the picture was not worth the wait. Filming began on July 14, 1969, turning one of Elstree's largest sound stages into a French Provincial estate, complete with swimming pool and gardens. Directing was former actor Alan Gibson, who was given his first feature after his involvement with several BBC series. As he would further prove with *Dracula A.D. 1972*, Gibson had little understanding of what Hammer films were all about. After wrapping at Elstree on August 23, the production moved to the Camargue for location work. *Crescendo* was trade shown at Studio One on May 7, 1970, and premiered the same day at the New Victoria supporting *Taste the Blood of Dracula*. The pair went into general release on June 7, and the package was voted onto *Kinematograph Weekly*'s Top Moneywinner's list. This was totally on the strength of the *Dracula* picture, as *Crescendo* had practically nothing to offer. Critics were united in their condemnation of this thrilless thriller. *Today's Cinema* (May 22, 1970): "A run-of-the-mill suspense story"; *New York* (December 4, 1972): "It's all clunking nonsense"; *Newsday*: "Witless—a reject from the ABC Movie of the Week"; and *The New York Daily News*: "Disintegrates under the direction of Alan Gibson."

Not much could have improved *Crescendo*, which was critically injured from its inception. It had all been done before, and

Lord Courtley (Ralph Bates) calls upon the powers of darkness to resurrect Count Dracula in *Taste the Blood of Dracula*.

better. Stefanie Powers and James Olson give their expected professional performances, but they are not nearly enough. Powers remarked (Warner Bros. press release), "There is no Dracula or Frankenstein in the cast." Maybe there should have been.

Taste the Blood of Dracula

Released June, 1970 (U.K.), September 16, 1970 (U.S.); 95 minutes; Technicolor; a Hammer Film Production; a Warner-Pathe Release (U.K.), a Warner Bros. Release (U.S.); filmed at MGM/EMI Studios, Elstree, and on location in Hertfordshire, and Highgate Cemetery, London; Director: Peter Sasdy; Producer: Aida Young; Screenplay: John Elder, based on the character created by Bram Stoker; Director of Photography: Arthur Grant; Art Director: Scott MacGregor; Music: James Bernard; Musical Supervisor: Philip Martell; Special Effects: Brian Johncock; Production Manager: Christopher Sutton; Assistant Director: Derek Whitehurst; Editor: Chris Barnes; Sound Recordist: Ron Barron; Sound Editor: Roy Hyde; Construction Manager: Arthur Banks; Makeup Supervisor: Gerry Fletcher; Continuity: Geraldine Lawton; Wardrobe: Brian Owen-Smith; Dubbing Mixer: Dennis Whitlock; Hairdressing Supervisor: Mary Bredin; Recording Supervisor: Tony Lumkin; U.K. Certificate: X; MPAA Rating: GP.

Christopher Lee (Dracula), Geoffrey Keen (William Hargood), Gwen Watford (Martha Hargood), Linda Hayden (Alice Hargood), Peter Sallis (Samuel Paxton), Isla Blair (Lucy Paxton), John Carson (Jonathan Secker), Martin Jarvis (Jeremy Secker), Anthony Corlan (Paul Paxton), Ralph Bates (Lord Courtley), Roy Kinnear (Weller), Shirley Jaffee (Betty, Hargood's Maid), Michael Ripper (Cobb), Russell Hunter (Felix), Reginald Barrett (Vicar), Keith Marsh (Father), Peter May (Son), Madeline Smith (Dolly), Lai Ling (Chinese Girl), Malaika Martin (Snake Girl).

Stranded near Castle Dracula, Weller (Roy Kinnear), an antiques dealer, witnesses Dracula's death by impalement on a crucifix and retrieves the Count's ring, cloak, and a vial of blood.

Taste the Blood of Dracula (1969)

Christopher Lee and the Goat of Mendes from *Taste the Blood of Dracula*.

Outside London, Hargood (Geoffrey Keen), Secker (John Carson), and Paxton (Peter Sallis) live outwardly as family men, but indulge themselves in monthly visits to a brothel. One night they meet Lord Courtley (Ralph Bates), a decadent who challenges them to sell their souls in exchange for "ultimate pleasure." He takes them to Weller's shop where they purchase Dracula's remains. They meet in an abandoned chapel where Courtley mixes Dracula's blood with his own, but the men refuse to drink it. Courtley takes his own dare and is convulsed in agony. As Courtley lies dying, Hargood returns home to his wife (Gwen Watford) and daughter Alice (Linda Hayden). Meanwhile, Courtley's corpse metamorphoses into Dracula (Christopher Lee), who swears to avenge his servant's death.

Hargood, who is hypocritically protective of Alice, forbids her relationship with Paxton's son Paul (Anthony Corlan). His abusive behavior leads her to an encounter with Dracula, who uses her to destroy the three families, as she kills her father with a shovel and lures Paul's sister Lucy (Isla Blair) into vampirism. When Paxton and Secker return to the chapel, they find Lucy's vampiric corpse, but Paxton wounds Secker before he can stake her. He realizes his error too late—she kills her own father, as does Jeremy Secker (Martin Jarvis), under her vampiric spell.

Paul learns that Dracula is the cause of the deaths and sets out to save Alice. He traps Dracula in the chapel where he has substituted Christian symbols for the blasphemous ones on the altar. Dracula tries to escape through a window, but is overcome by the symbols of righteousness and falls to his death, releasing Alice from his power.

Due to the success of *Dracula Has Risen from the Grave*, Hammer planned to produce a sequel per year as long as the market demanded it. However, Anthony "John Elder" Hinds was now under pressure to come up with the new variations on a threadbare theme. Following the previous pattern, Hinds dropped Dracula into a situation that did not really warrant his inclusion and treated the Count as an afterthought. Assigned to direct *Taste the Blood of Dracula* was Peter Sasdy, a veteran of over 100 television shows. Sasdy had taught drama and journalism at Budapest University, but left Hungary during the 1956 revolution. He continued to teach in Britain before breaking into television. "One of the most pleasing things about this particular Dracula subject," he said (*Kinematograph Weekly*, December 13, 1969), "is that for the first time (in a Hammer film), the setting is in London. This means the characters are

The beginning of the end of a great series.

not strange people in a foreign land—they are the sort of people whom audiences in Britain and America are going to recognize more readily." One must certainly question Sasdy's opinion about the "normality" of the Hargood family.

Filming began on October 27, 1969, and due to Sasdy's television experience, he averaged six minutes of screen time per day, finishing on December 5. "The basic advantage which television gives you," he said, "is the ability to work at speed." A trade show was held on May 6, 1970, at Studio One, and the film premiered at the New Victoria. *Taste the Blood of Dracula* went into general release in the U.K. on June 7 and in American on September 16, to mixed reviews. The *London Times* (May 10): "A surprise—well played and directed"; *The Monthly Bulletin* (May): "Absolutely routine"; *Today's Cinema* (May 15): "Not as eerie as previous episodes"; *New York Magazine* (November 2): "Honors the tradition and kind of adds to it"; and the *New York Post* (October 29): "Directed and acted with the usual stylishness of Hammer Films."

Christopher Lee, again, seemed to do a Dracula picture under protest. He said in his fan club journal, "On November 3, I start what I hope will positively be my last film for Hammer. As usual, words fail me as indeed they will also do in the film." Lee later changed his mind, telling interviewer Bill Kelley, "I liked certain elements of the storyline; and apart from the absence of Peter Cushing, we had the best cast of any of the Dracula films."

Ralph Bates, fresh from the BBC's *Caligula*, made his splashy film debut as Lord Courtley in the first of his five Hammer films. The company was looking for young actors to assume the roles that would eventually be vacated by Cushing and Lee, and Bates seemed to be a perfect choice. But Hammer's demise came faster than anyone could have imagined, and replacing the two stars never became an issue.

Hammer's fifth Dracula was a huge financial success, making *The Kinematograph Weekly*'s "Top Moneymakers" list and was the last film in the series to have any merit. Despite demoting Dracula to a minor character, the film has much to recommend it, especially James Bernard's outstanding score. The cast is above average, and Peter Sasdy managed to get across the perversion without resorting to the excesses that would soon become Hammer's hallmark. Using Dracula, the ultimate in decadence, as the agent to destroy Victorian hypocrisy was one of the last clever ideas in the series.

1970

The Vampire Lovers

Released October 4, 1970 (U.K.); 91 minutes (U.K.), 89 minutes (U.S.); Technicolor; 8188 feet; a Hammer Film Production; Released through MGM/EMI (U.K.), American International (U.S.); filmed at MGM/EMI Elstree Studios; Director: Roy Ward Baker; Producers: Harry Fine, Michael Style; Screenplay: Tudor Gates, based on J. Sheridan Le Fanu's novel *Carmilla*; Director of Photography: Moray Grant; Music: Harry Robinson; Music Supervisor: Philip Martell; Editor: James Needs; Art Director: Scott MacGregor: Production Manager: Tom Sachs; Sound: Roy Hyde; Costumes: Brian Box; Recording Supervisor: Tony Lumkin; Continuity: Betty Harley; Makeup: Tom Smith; Hairdresser: Pearl Tipaldi; Wardrobe: Laura Nightingale; Construction Manager: Bill Greene; Dubbing Mixer: Dennis Whitlock; Camera: Neil Binney; Sound Recordist: Claude Hitchcock; Assistant Director: Derek Whitehurst; U.K. Rating: X, MPAA Rating: R.

Ingrid Pitt (Mircalla/Marcilla/Carmilla), Pippa Steele (Laura), Madeline Smith (Emma), Peter Cushing (General Von Spielsdorf), Dawn Addams (The Countess), Kate O'Mara (Madam Perrodot), Douglas Wilmer (Baron Hartog), Jon Finch (Carl Ebbhart), Kirsten Betts (First Vampire), John Forbes-Robinson (Man in Black), Harvey Hall (Renton), Ferdy Mayne (Doctor), George Cole (Roger), Janey Key (Gretchen), Charles Farrell (Kurt).

Baron Hartog (Douglas Wilmer) attempts to destroy the vampiric Karnstein family after they take his sister, but one of them escapes. Later, General Spielsdorf (Peter Cushing), while hosting a lavish party, greets the Countess (Dawn Addams), and her daughter, Marcilla (Ingrid Pitt). The Countess leaves unexpectedly, and the General offers to shelter Marcilla. She and Laura (Pippa Steele), the General's niece, become friendly—and more. After coming between Laura and Carl (Jon Finch), her fiancé, Marcilla seduces her and takes her blood, eventually killing her.

Now calling herself Carmilla, Marcilla reappears at Roger Morton's (George Cole) estate and, as she has done so often before, "befriends" a beautiful young girl. Emma Morton (Madeline Smith) soon falls under Carmilla's spell, as does Madam Perrodot (Kate O'Mara). Renton (Harvey Hall), a servant, suspects the worst and contacts his traveling master, who joins forces with Baron Hartog and the General. The vampire hunters, now aware that Carmilla is a Karnstein, track her to her castle where the General drives stake through her heart and cuts off her head.

The Karnsteins are now thought to be destroyed, but a mysterious Man in Black (John Forbes-Robinson) has been watching.

By 1970, with films like the *Horror of Frankenstein* and *Scars of Dracula*, Hammer had stooped to the level that critics had long claimed the company wallowed—gratuitous sex and violence. Times had changed, and audiences needed more and more of the above to get the same charge they received from *The Curse of Frankenstein* and *Dracula*. This was a pivotal period for Hammer, and the change would be for the worse. After *The Vampire Lovers*, Hammer would produce almost thirty pictures, and none would begin to approach the quality productions the company turned out in the late fifties.

The Vampire Lovers was based on J. Sheridan Le Fanu's 1871 *Carmilla*, which served as the basis for *Vampyr* (1931), *Blood and Roses* (1960), and *Terror in the Crypt* (1963), among others. Film censorship and the public's taste had changed so much by 1970 that the lesbianism hinted at in earlier versions could be shown with little reticence. Harry Fine told author Bruce Hallenbeck (*Little Shoppe of Horrors* 4): "With great difficulty, I managed to find a copy of LeFanu's original story after finding stills from a stage adaptation of *Carmilla*." He approached Tudor Gates to write a treatment which was sent to James Carreras, who was entranced by the title. "*The Vampire Lovers*!," he said. "I think I can set it up right away." Fine and

Behind-the-scenes on *The Vampire Lovers*—Ingrid Pitt primps as Peter Cushing looks on (photo courtesy of Ted Okuda).

ended on March 4, with a September 3 trade show at Metro House followed by an October 4 premiere at the New Victoria. Paired with *Angels from Hell* on the ABC circuit, the package broke several attendance records and made *The Kinematograph Weekly*'s Top Moneymaker list for 1970. One might wonder if the crowds were attracted by the film's horror or lesbian sex. "The permissiveness of the sixties," Harry Fine said (*Little Shoppe of Horrors* 4), "finally caught up with Hammer at the end of the decade." As so often happened in these early days of film nudity, those involved found it necessary to justify their involvement. "If the film requires nudity," Ingrid Pitt told Al Taylor (*Filmfax* 15), "I'm not against it. The nudity was there to make a point." She told the authors (July, 1994), "Sex and nudity are very natural for human beings and nothing to be ashamed of." Pitt enjoyed her scenes with Peter Cushing, despite his cutting off her head! "It was a bit unnerving," she said, "to have my family see stills of Peter holding my severed head." Unlike Pitt's casual attitude towards the nudity, Madeline Smith (*Bizarre* 6) felt differently. "I hated doing it. I would never do it now." Oddly, Valerie Gaunt (in *Dracula*) managed to be far more sensuous while wearing far more clothing. *The Vampire Lovers* is a bit obvious and far too earnest in its attempt to titillate.

Michael Style finalized an agreement with Hammer on November 25, 1969, and a month later, Carreras secured financing through American International Pictures. Former AIP head Samuel Z. Arkoff told the authors (May, 1992),

> We went to England in 1964 to do the second half of our Poe series, and Roger Corman got tired of it all. We stayed in England because of lower production costs, and *might* have approached Hammer, but we didn't. We had always done them ourselves. We finally joined together with *The Vampire Lovers*—which Jimmy sold to us over a meal! Hammer always had a great style for their horror films. They were fundamentally adult, not geared toward teenagers. Jimmy *never* gave ground to teenagers!

The Vampire Lovers began production on January 19, 1970, at Elstree, with location work at the Moor Park golf course. Filming

Reviews were kinder than Hammer may have expected: *The Sunday Times* (September 6, 1970): "The days of aesthetic horror seem remote"; *The Kinematograph Weekly* (September 5): "This spooky nonsense is really very good fun on its own level of entertainment"; and *The New York Times* (February 4, 1971): "A departure from a hackneyed bloody norm."

Peter Cushing double-checks his diction in this behind-the-scenes shot from *The Vampire Lovers* (photo courtesy of Tim Murphy).

Although *The Vampire Lovers* is one of Hammer's best seventies films, it cannot stand with the company's initial horror efforts, proving that it takes more than nudity and blood to grab an audience. Despite a good cast and crisp direction from Roy Ward Baker, production values were down, and Hammer continued to move farther away from the days of *The Hound of the Baskervilles*.

Horror of Frankenstein

Released November 8, 1970 (U.K.); 95 minutes; Technicolor (U.K.), DeLuxe Color (U.S.); 8589 feet; a Hammer Film Production; an Anglo-EMI Release (U.K.), a Continental Release (U.S.); filmed at MGM/EMI Elstree Studios; Director: Jimmy Sangster; Producer: Jimmy Sangster; Screenplay: Jimmy Sangster, Jeremy Burnham; Director of Photography: Moray Grant; Music: Malcolm Williamson; Musical Supervisor: Philip Martell; Art Director: Scott MacGregor; Production Manager: Tom Sachs; Editor: Chris Barnes; Assistant Director: Derek Whitehurst; Sound Recordist: Claude Hitchcock; Sound Editor: Terry Poulton; Camera Operator: Neil Binney; Continuity: Betty Harley;

Ingrid Pitt dominates this retelling of the *Carmilla* story.

Makeup: Tom Smith; Hairdresser: Pearl Tipaldi; Wardrobe: Laura Nightingale; Construction Manager: Arthur Banks; Recording Director: Tony Lumkin; Dubbing Mixer: Bill Powe; U.K. Rating: X, MPAA Rating: R.

Ralph Bates (Victor Frankenstein), Kate O'Mara (Alys), Veronica Carlson (Elizabeth), Dennis Price (Bodysnatcher), Joan Rice (His Wife), Graham James (Wilhelm), Bernard Archard (Professor), Jon Finch (Officer), Dave Prowse (Monster).

Young, handsome, intelligent, and amoral, Victor Frankenstein (Ralph Bates) murders his father and inherits his title, wealth, and mistress Alys (Kate O'Mara). After a brief stay at Vienna University, he returns home with Wilhelm (Graham James), bent on creating a being from the dead. With parts supplied by the local bodysnatcher (Dennis Price) and his wife (Joan Rice), he proceeds, but Wilhelm has misgivings and is conveniently electrocuted.

Victor murders a neighboring professor (Bernard Archard) for his brain, but his "code of conduct as a gentleman" forces him to shelter his victim's daughter Elizabeth (Veronica Carlson), who has loved him since childhood. As he transplants the brain into his man-made man, the bodysnatcher—whoops!—drops it, but Victor pushes on

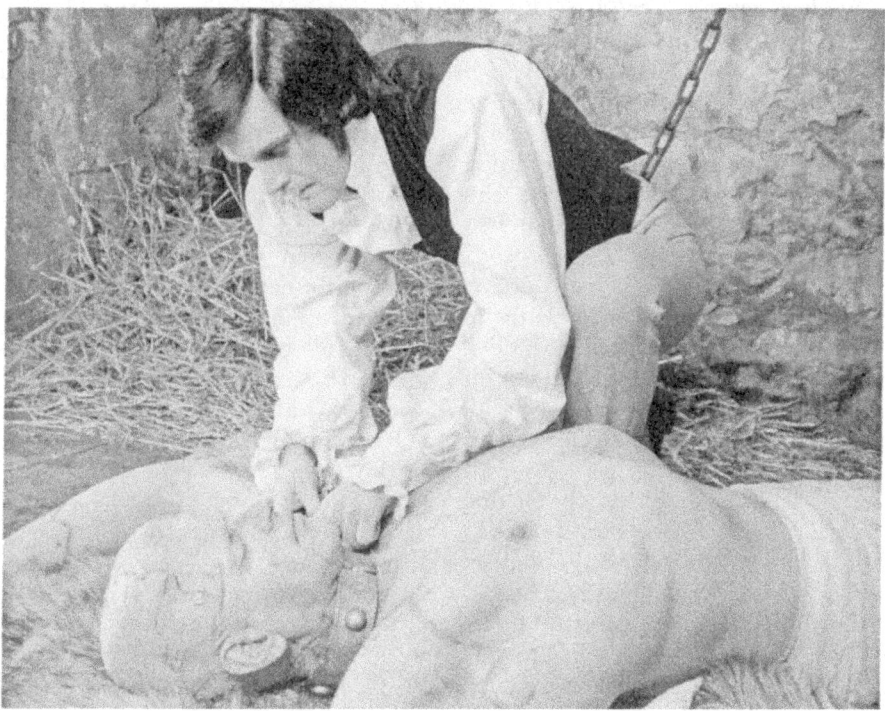

Top: Ralph Bates (left) and Graham James in Jimmy Sangster's tongue-in-cheek *Horror of Frankenstein*. *Bottom:* Frankenstein (Ralph Bates) secures the restraints on his uncooperative creation (Dave Prowse) in *Horror of Frankenstein*.

Horror of Frankenstein (1970)

A long way from *The Curse of Frankenstein*.

Jimmy Sangster said (*Fangoria* 10), "Hammer first told me that they were going to remake *The Curse of Frankenstein* and wanted me to write the script, but I turned the assignment down. Then they offered to let me produce, but again I said no. When I told them I might be interested if they would let me direct as well, Hammer said that I could. Hammer wanted to do a straight remake, but I thought it would work better as a satire. That idea was ultimately a mistake." Befitting Sangster's approach, Peter Cushing was never considered to star. Chosen as his replacement was Ralph Bates, who had recently scored in *Taste the Blood of Dracula*. "Purists" seldom include Bates or the film in discussions of Hammer's Frankenstein series, and the film is an entertaining "one—off" and nothing more.

Since Hammer never concentrated on the monster character, there was never a problem in replacing any actor in the role. Their five previous Frankenstein movies had five different monsters played by five different performers. Dave Prowse's casting disturbed no one because, except for Freddie Jones, all of the previous monsters were played by "unknowns." Prowse, 6'7" and 260 pounds, was a former British weightlifting champion (1962–64). He told the authors (May, 1993),

> It was a lot less formal working for Hammer than for other companies. They had their own stable of actors and crews, and one got to know everyone. I'd seen earlier Hammer movies and, after getting involved in the acting scene, I went to their Wardour Street office. "Would you be interested in me doing one of your Frankensteins?" I asked. Well! I got thrown out of the office! They asked me to leave! The next time I went back was four to five years later—when they signed me for the monster. I've done all sorts of movies—worked with

after disposing of the blunderer in an acid tank. A chance bolt of lightning brings the creature (Dave Prowse) to life after which he escapes into the forest. After capturing his creation, Victor silences the jealous Alys and the nosy wife of the body snatcher, courtesy of the monster.

The police (led by Jon Finch) arrive, bringing with them a child who claims to have seen a monster. The Baron has hidden his creature in an empty acid vat, but not for long; the child accidentally releases the acid, destroying the monster and freeing Victor of any charges against him.

Jimmy Sangster described the picture to the authors as "The one nobody liked." While it is difficult to defend the film on any level, it *does* qualify as a "guilty pleasure" and, if seen in the right mood, is quite amusing. After establishing itself as a "horror" specialist by remaking the Universal classics, Hammer's next logical step was to make sequels to its own movies. But, by 1970, this was beginning to wear thin, and Hammer found itself remaking its own remake!

Stanley Kubrick, comedies, James Bond, *Star Wars*—but I don't think I've ever had so much fun or worked in such a pleasant atmosphere as I did with Hammer.

Since Jimmy Sangster was fulfilling three roles, he found himself in an unusual situation. "Writers are *never* welcome on the set," he told the authors. "Anywhere. In my case, I was also the producer and the director. I *still* was not welcome on the set!"

Ralph Bates had no illusions about the role or about replacing its originator. "It's nice to be asked to play such a famous role," Bates said in the EMI pressbook, "although people are already asking me if I shall play it in subsequent films and am I afraid of being typecast. I just don't know. Peter Cushing played the role five times, and I do not consider him typecast. Peter is a very comforting example to me."

Veronica Carlson, after two excellent roles opposite Peter Cushing and Christopher Lee, was not enthralled with the film but enjoyed working with the people. She told the authors (July, 1992):

> Peter took it very seriously. Christopher Lee took it seriously, too, and you have to respect that. Neither Ralph nor Jimmy took it seriously. They had a jolly good laugh! Some of the lines, well, you couldn't take them seriously, could you? If I had my choice, I'd prefer the serious. But, either way, I was working with great people. I think Hammer wanted to see if a "young Frankenstein" could work. If they could reintroduce the character and get more mileage out of him. Maybe they realized it wasn't as successful as the traditional ones that everybody loved. As for my character, she certainly wasn't as substantial as Anna in my previous Frankenstein film! I did quite a bit to help publicize the film—radio, TV, public appearances. The crew in this—and all the Hammer films—was wonderful. It was just like family. There was no tension, no aggravation. It was just happy! Everyone did their job well, got on with each other very well. They all made me feel very special. You couldn't hope for a nicer group of people to work for!

Horror of Frankenstein went into production on March 16, 1970, concluding on April 29. Reviews, following the October 15 trade show at Metro House, were more positive than one would expect. *The Express* (October 30): "Synthetic blood and tongue in cheek horror"; *The New York Times* (May 18, 1971): "The first hour is not only painless, but also fun. The screenplay is as bright as could be"; *Variety* (October 21, 1970): "Lighthearted."

The picture certainly did not do Hammer or Frankenstein much good, but what can one say about a movie in which a severed hand gives the finger when charged with electricity?

Scars of Dracula

Released November 8, 1970 (U.K.), December 23, 1970 (U.S.); 94 minutes, Original Running Time: 96 minutes; Technicolor; a Hammer Film Production; an Anglo-EMI Release (U.K.), an American Continental (Levitt-Pickman) Release (U.S.); filmed at MGM/EMI Elstree Studios, England; Director: Roy Ward Baker; Producer: Aida Young; Screenplay: John Elder, based on *Dracula* by: Bram Stoker; Director of Photography: Moray Grant; Art Director: Scott MacGregor; Music: James Bernard; Musical Supervisor: Philip Martell; Special Effects: Roger Dickens, Brian Johncock; Assistant Director: Derek Whitehurst; Editor: James Needs; Construction Manager: Arthur Banks; Makeup: Wally Schneidermann; Makeup Assistant: Heather Nurse; Sound Editor: Roy Hyde; Dubbing Mixer: Dennis Whitlock; Sound Recordist: Ron Barron; Recording Supervisor: Tony Lumkim; Production Manager: Tom Sachs; Continuity: Betty Harley; U.K. Certificate: X; MPAA Rating: R.

Christopher Lee (Dracula), Jenny Hanley (Sarah Framsen), Dennis Waterman (Simon Carlson), Patrick Troughton (Klove), Christopher Matthews (Paul Carlson), Anoushka Hempel (Tania), Wendy Hamilton (Julie), Michael Gwynn (Priest), Delia Lindsay (Alice), Bobb Todd (Burgomeister), Michael Ripper (Landlord), Toke Townley (Elderly Wagonmaster), David Lealand, Richard Durden (Officers), Morris Bush (Farmer), Margot Boht (Landlord's Wife).

Dracula (Christopher Lee), revived once again, renews his reign of terror, killing a village girl. A mob of townsmen led by the local innkeeper (Michael Ripper) storms the castle, manhandling servant Klove (Patrick Troughton) and setting fire to the structure. But during the men's absence from town,

Scars of Dracula (1970)

Christopher Lee in *Scars of Dracula*.

Dracula's army of bats attacks and kills their wives and children.

In nearby Klinenburg, Sarah Framsen's (Jenny Hanley) birthday is celebrated by Simon (Dennis Waterman) and his brother Paul (Christopher Matthews). The Burgomeister's servants arrive in search of Paul, who compromised the officials' daughter. Paul escapes, and after an involved series of events, he finds himself a guest of the Count at Castle Dracula. Paul beds Tania (Anoushka Hempel), one of Dracula's vampire brides, but just as she is about to sink her fangs into his throat, Dracula appears and stabs the girl to death. Paul is made a prisoner.

Simon and Sarah follow Paul's trail to the Castle and Dracula invites them to spend the night. As Sarah sleeps she is approached by Dracula, but is saved by the cross around her neck. Dracula orders Klove to remove it, but the lovestruck Klove refuses to obey.

The next morning, Klove warns Simon about Dracula and urges him to take Sarah away. Simon and Sarah make it back to the village where Simon tries to enlist the aid of the villagers to find Paul. They refuse, but the priest (Michael Gwynn) offers his assistance. En route to Castle Dracula, the priest loses his resolve and Simon continues alone. He finds Dracula in his coffin and positions his wooden stake but the vampire's powers, even in sleep, stay Simon's hand.

Back in town, the doors of the chapel suddenly swing open and Sarah and the priest are attacked by a bat who swoops down on the priest, killing him. As Sarah rushes toward the Castle, Simon finds Paul's body impaled on a metal hook.

Dracula tries to place Sarah under his hypnotic spell but Klove warns her in time

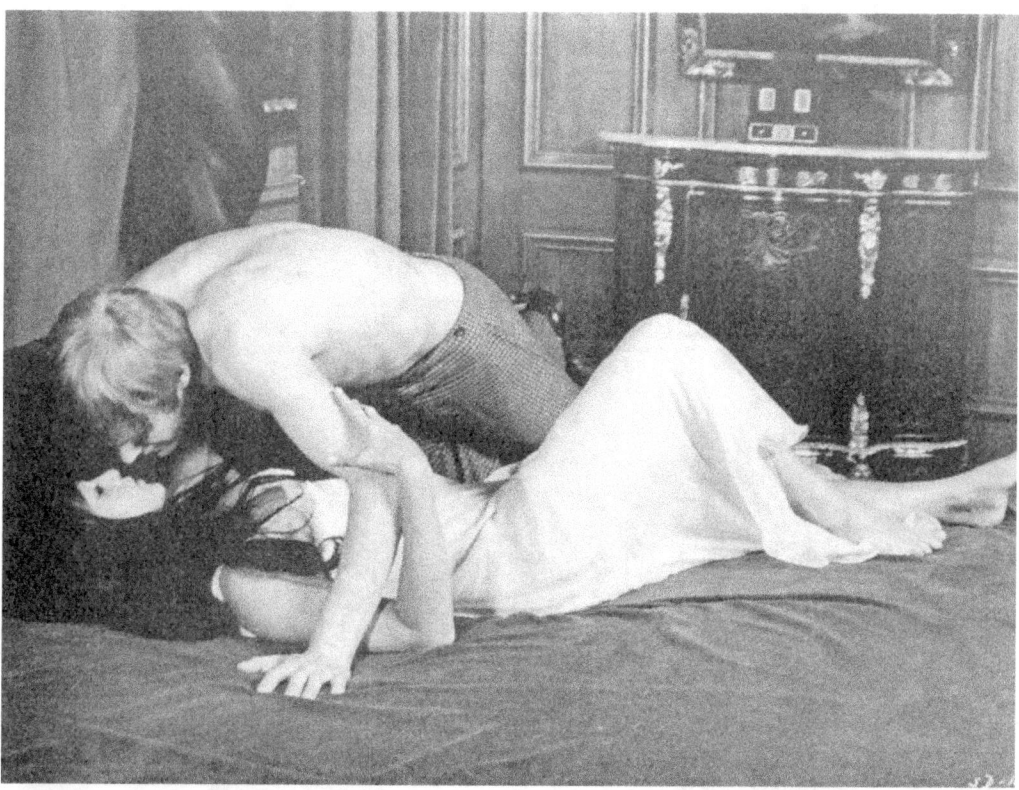

Paul (Christopher Matthews) romances Tania (Anoushka Hempel) and is about to realize his mistake in *Scars of Dracula*.

and she holds off the vampire with her cross. The vampire flings Klove off a cliff. Simon impales Dracula with a metal spike, but it misses his heart. Dracula pulls out the spike and is leveling it at Simon when a bolt of lightning strikes it, setting fire to Dracula's cloak. Simon and Sarah watch as fire consumes Dracula and he topples from the precipice.

By the time *Scars of Dracula* began production on May 7, 1970, the series was showing hints of burnout that this picture would confirm. Although audiences were still attracted, they were growing weary of the rehashed themes and Christopher Lee's limited screen time. So was Lee, who said (*The Films of Christopher Lee*), "*Scars of Dracula* was the weakest and most unconvincing of the Dracula stories. Instead of writing a story around the character, they wrote a story and fit the character into it. A really bad film in my opinion." He added (*Photoplay*, March, 1973), "What I really object to is the gratuitous violence packaged into films as a deliberate policy to appeal to the sadistic in people."

Roy Ward Baker was wisely hesitant to direct, but not wise enough to resist. "I'd been asked to do *Dracula* or *Frankenstein* before, but I always declined, saying politely that I didn't think I knew anything about horror pictures," he told *Little Shoppe of Horrors*. "Violence is, I think, a question of taste and a question of style," he added.

"When I made *Scars*, films were becoming increasingly violent, so it was expected by the audience, and Hammer was trying to keep up to date." One of the few things Baker found to be proud of about the film was a scene out of Stoker's novel shot for the first time. "I realized," Baker said (*Fangoria* 36), "when I re-read *Dracula*, that there was that gripping description of Dracula climbing down the tower wall, crawling down face

326 *Scars of Dracula* (1970)

The beginning of the end.

first. That to me is the magic of Dracula, part of his fatal fascination. So I filmed that."

Scars of Dracula and co-feature *Horror of Frankenstein* were part of a multi-picture deal with Associated British Picture Corporation. James Carreras and Bernard Delfont's agreement marked the first time in over a decade that a Hammer film was totally financed in Britain. "With one hundred percent British finance," Carreras said (*Today's Cinema*, March 17, 1970), "the world receipts will come direct to Britain." Each film was budgeted at under £200,000, and both were shot at Elstree. *Scars of Dracula* ended production on June 23, 1970, and was trade shown on October 23 at Metro House. Oddly, the film premiered on the same day

A film best forgotten! The abysmal prehistoric drama *Creatures the World Forgot*.

at the New Victoria. The pair did respectable business following a November 8 release on the ABC circuit, but reviewers were unimpressed. *Today's Cinema* (October 23, 1970): "I fear the Count must have been drinking blood of the wrong group; otherwise, he would never stoop so low as to stab a woman to death or burn a disobedient servant with a red hot sword"; and *The New York Times* (June 18): "It's garish, gory junk."

Other than James Bernard's typically outstanding score, *Scars of Dracula* has little to recommend it. The sets look cheap, the photography is muddy, the young leads are miscast, and Christopher Lee looks more uninterested than ever before. The "plot"— which drops Dracula into the middle of *another* story in which he does not belong— is awash in unappetizing sex and violence. The film is totally lacking in artistry, and any comparison to the company's 1957 classic would be unkind. Combined with its Frankenstein co-feature, *Scars of Dracula* was a sad indication of the direction Hammer was taking in the seventies.

Creatures the World Forgot

Released April 18, 1971 (U.K.), September, 1971 (U.S.); 95 minutes; Technicolor; a Hammer Film Production; a Columbia Release; filmed on location in Southwest Africa in the Namib Desert; Director: Don Chaffey; Producer & Screenplay: Michael Carreras; Director of Photography: Vincent Cox; Production Designer: John Stoll; Editor: Chris Barnes; Music: Mario Nascimbene; Musical Supervisor: Philip Martell; Art Directors: Roy Taylor, Josie MacAvin; Makeup: Bill Lodge; Special Effects: Syd Pearson; Stunts Arranged by: Frank Hayden: Sound Editors: Roy Hyde, Terry Poulton, John Streeter, Ken Barker; Wardrobe: Rosemary Burrows, Roy Ponting; Makeup: Bill Lodge; Hairstyles: Jeanette Freeman; Production Manager: Jack Martin; Assistant Director: Ferdinand Fairfax: Second Unit Photography: Ray Sturgess; Lighting: Mole Richardson; Second Assistant Director: Simon Peterson; Continuity: Lolly Walder; Assistant Art Directors: Josie McAlvin, Roy Taylor; Location Management: Sun Safaris; Technical Advisor: Adrien Boshner; Stills Cameraman: Albert Clarke; Casting Director: James Liggat; Special Effects: Sid Person; Animals: Uwe D. Schulz; U.K. Certificate: A; MPAA Rating: GP.

Julie Ege (Nala), Brian O'Shaughnessy

(Mak), Tony Bonner (Toomak), Robert John (Rool), Sue Wilson (Noo), Rosalie Crutchley (Old Crone), Marcia Fox (Mute Girl), Gerard Bonthuys (Young Toomak), Josje Kiesouw (Young Mute Girl), Don Leonard (Old Leader), Beverly Blake, Doon Baide (Young Lovers), Frank Hayden (Murderer), Rosita Moulan (Dancer), Fred Scott (Marauder Leader), Ken Hare (Fair Tribe Leader), Derek Ward (Hunter), Hans Kiesouw (Young Rool), Leo Payne (Old Tribal Artist), Tamsin Millard, Christine Hudson (Rock Women), Heinke Thater, Cheryl Stewardson, Trudy Inns, Samantha Bates, Debbie Aubrey-Smith (Rock Girls), Joan Boshier (Rock Widow), Audrey Allen (Rock Mother), Vera P. Crosdale, Mildred Johnston, Lilian M. Nowag (Old Rock Women), Jose Rozendo, Jose Manuel, Mark Russell, Dick Swain, Alwyn Van Der Merwe, Manuel Neto, Mike Dickman (Rock Men).

In prehistoric times, a volcanic eruption destroys the encampment of the Rock People. The chief (Don Leonard), trapped under a fallen boulder, is killed by his own son (Frank Hayden), who smashes his head with a rock. He later challenges his own brother Mak (Brian O'Shaughnessy) for the right to rule the tribe. The two men fight, and Mak kills his brother with a spear.

Now the Rock Tribe's chief, Mak leads his people across the desert, seeking a new land. Along the way they encounter the Fair Tribe. Mak and the chief of the Fair Tribe (Ken Hare) are prepared to fight until they see their own children playing peacefully together.

Mak is offered, Noo (Sue Wilson), one of the young women of the Fair Tribe, by the leader. Mak, Noo and the Rock People continue on the search and find a fertile valley where they make their new home.

Noo dies giving birth to twin sons. Years later, Toomak (Tony Bonner) is good and his brother Rool (Robert John) is evil, and the two compete for a mute cave girl (Marcia Fox). When Rool tries to rape the girl, she flees and is captured by the leader (Fred Scott) of another tribe. Toomak and his warriors follow the abductors to their camp and defeat them in a pitched battle. Toomak claims the dead chief's daughter Nala (Julie Ege) as his mate.

Mak is attacked by a wildebeest and, dying, names Toomak his heir. Rool challenges his brother's right to rule but is crippled and bested by Toomak in battle. Toomak, Nala and some of his warriors abandon the tribe and set off to find a new colony. Knowing that he will never have the respect of his people while Toomak lives, Rool and his followers track Toomak to his camp and carry off Nala. Toomak follows his brother alone.

Unknown to either man, the mute girl follows Toomak and arrives to find the brothers once again locked in combat. As Rool raises his knife to kill Toomak, she stabs Rool, who falls from a precipice.

This, the last film in Hammer's "prehistoric trilogy," is best left forgotten itself. Spurred on by the success of *One Million Years B.C.* and *When Dinosaurs Ruled the Earth,* Hammer apparently forgot that dinosaurs had been the lure of the first two pictures. Producer/writer Michael Carreras left London in March, 1970, to scout locations in South West Africa and covered nearly 12,000 square miles until concentrating on the Namib Desert. He then checked on hotel accommodations, got government permission to film in the desert, hired a safari company to provide on-site facilities, and consulted with the curator of the Museum of Man and Science. It is sad that all this effort produced such a mediocre picture. While Carreras was toiling in Africa, his father busied himself with a more enjoyable job—finding the "sex symbol of the seventies" in a contest sponsored by Hammer and Columbia. From over 3,000 candi-dates, the winner was Julie Ege, a beautiful Norwegian non-actress. "The moment Julie Ege walked through my door," Carreras said (Columbia press release), "we knew our search was ended. She had the same utterly feminine, earthy, sexy quality as Raquel Welch." The only thing missing was talent, as director Don Chaffey soon found out.

Filmed entirely on location, *Creatures the World Forgot* began production on July 1, 1970, with an eight week schedule that

The film audiences would like to forget!

dragged on until October. A trade show was held on March 19, 1971, and it premiered at the New Victoria on March 28, where it took an excellent £2,959 in the first week. Carried by audience expectations and great advertising, *Creatures the World Forgot* packed in crowds after its general release on April 18, but word-of-mouth soon caught up. Offering semi-nude women in lieu of dinosaurs, action, and suspense, this is one of Hammer's worst pictures, as duly noted by the critics. *The Daily Express* (March 3, 1971): "What we get here is a lot of hairy chaps dressed in bits of fur rushing about bashing each other over the head with rocks, and numerous ladies without even rudimentary brassieres"; and *The Monthly Film Bulletin* (May): "A feeble excuse for arbitrary sadism and brutality." The movie is absolute torture to sit through, and is made even worse by its being completely lacking in humor—unless one finds mediocrity funny.

Lust for a Vampire

Released January 17, 1971 (U.K.), September, 1971 (U.S.); 95 minutes; Technicolor; 8574 feet; a Hammer Film Production; an Associated British Picture Corp. Release (U.K.), an American Continental Films (Levitt-Pickman) Release (U.S.); filmed at MGM/EMI Studios, Elstree, England; Director: Jimmy Sangster; Producers: Harry Fine, Michael Style; Screenplay: Tudor Gates, based on the characters created by: J. Sheridan Le Fanu; Director of Photography: David Muir; Art Director: Don Mingaye; Musical Supervisor: Philip Martell; Assistant Director: David Bracknell; Editor: Spencer Reeve; Costumes: Laura Nightingale; Production Manager: Tom Sachs; Camera: Chic Antiss; Continuity: Betty Harley; Sound: Ron Barron; Hairdresser: Pearl Tipaldi; Makeup: George Blackler; Music: Harry Robinson; Song: "Strange Love," sung by Tracy, lyrics by Frank Godwin; Boom Operator: John Hall; Construction Manager: Bill Green; Recording Director: Tony Lumkin; Dubbing Mixer: Len Abbott; Choreographer: Bobbie McMannis; U.K. Certificate: X; MPAA Rating: R.

Ralph Bates (Giles Barton), Barbara Jefford (Countess Karnstein/Heritzen), Suzanna Leigh (Janet Playfair), Michael Johnson (Richard LeStrange), Yutte Stensgaard (Mircalla/Carmilla), Mike Raven (Count Karnstein/Dr. Froheim), Helen Christie (Miss Simpson), David Healy (Raymond Pelley), Michael Brennan (Landlord), Pippa Steele (Susan Pelley), Luan Peters (Trudi), Christopher Cunningham (Coachman), Judy Matheson (Amanda McBride), Eric Chitty (Prof. Hertz), Christopher Neame (Hans), Harvey Hall (Inspector Heinrich), Caryl Little (Isabel Courtney), Jack Melford (The Bishop), Erica Beale, Jackie Leapman, Melita Clarke, Patricia Warner, Christine Smith, Vivienne Chandler, Sue Longhurst, Melinda Churcher (School Girls).

Every 40 years the vampiric Karnstein family returns to terrorize the village sitting in the shadow of Karnstein castle. Richard LeStrange (Michael Johnson), a writer of horror stories, arrives to research a book on the Karnsteins and visits the Castle where he meets Giles Barton (Ralph Bates), schoolmaster of a nearby girls' school. At the school, LeStrange meets the principal, Miss Simpson (Helen Christie), and gym instructor Janet Playfair (Suzanna Leigh). LeStrange is attracted to a new student, Mircalla (Yutte Stensgaard), who arrives with her aunt Countess Heritzen (Barbara Jefford). That night at the local inn, after a serving girl dies suddenly (with puncture wounds on her throat), LeStrange runs into Biggs, the school's incoming English Literature teacher, an unpublished writer who admires LeStrange's work. In order to take Biggs' place at the school (and be close to Mircalla), LeStrange suggests they collaborate on a novel and pays his expenses for a research trip. Lying to Miss Simpson that Biggs is laid up with a broken leg, LeStrange gets the job.

Unusual goings-on ensue as LeStrange realizes that Barton is obsessed with the Karnsteins and Barton finds the body of murdered student Susan (Pippa Steele) and hides it in an abandoned well. Barton knows that Mircalla is actually the vampiress Carmilla, restored to life and youth with the blood of another recently murdered girl. Barton meets her in the castle ruins and begs her to make him her undead slave. When his blood-drained body is later found, the Countess' personal physician Dr. Froheim (Mike Raven)—actually Count Karnstein—lies that he died of a heart attack.

LeStrange realizes that Mircalla is actually Carmilla but makes love to her anyway. Meanwhile, Police Inspector Heinrich (Harvey Hall) has learned of Susan's disappearance and, discovering the well, lowers himself by rope into its depths. He discovers her body but as he climbs up, the rope is cut and he falls to his death. Janet, who is in love with LeStrange, tries to enlist his help, but LeStrange, who loves Mircalla, ignores her pleas. Mircalla later attempts to attack Janet, but the teacher is saved by the crucifix around her neck.

Susan's father, Mr. Pelley (David Healy), arrives with Professor Hertz (Eric Chitty) to look into his daughter's death. The Countess tries to convince them that Susan died a suicide but Pelley and Hertz soon hear the locals rumbling about vampires at large. They later join a mob of villagers in a march on Karnstein Castle. When the mob sets fire to the edifice, LeStrange rushes inside to try to save Mircalla. Count Karnstein orders her to destroy him, and under his power, she closes in menacingly, but a fiery beam drops from the ceiling and impales her. Pelley rushes in and saves LeStrange just before the ceiling crashes down upon the vampires.

Lust for a Vampire is one of the few Hammer horrors to have nothing to recommend it. The film was a low point for the company and is embarrassing—or should be—for all concerned, including the audience. Part of the trilogy of Karnstein pictures, it glorified the worst excesses of its predecessor, *The Vampire Lovers*, while lacking any of that film's positives. Although Peter Cushing was scheduled to star and withdrew due to his wife's illness, it is doubtful that even he could have elevated the movie to an acceptable level. Screenwriter Tudor Gates told Randy Palmer (*Fangoria* 40), "Peter is an actor of great stature, and I think this was one thing that caused *Lust for a Vampire* not to be the picture it could have

Teachers Giles Barton (Ralph Bates, left) and Richard LeStrange (Michael Johnson) are both in love with the same student in Hammer's disastrous *Lust for a Vampire*.

been. Of course, when Peter Cushing canceled, I re-tailored that part of the script to suit Ralph Bates who was hired to replace him." Poor Bates came in at the last minute to rescue the film due to his good nature. "I did it," he said (*Bizarre* 3), "as a favor to Peter and Jimmy Sangster. I thought it was a tasteless film, and I regret having anything to do with it. But again, Jim is a close, close friend, and so is Peter, so as a friend, I was happy to get them out of a very unhappy situation."

Sangster also had his regrets. "Terry Fisher was supposed to direct *Lust for a Vampire*," he said (*Fangoria* 10). "Suddenly, Terry broke a leg, and Hammer was right up the proverbial creek. I was on the lot, and they asked me if I'd like to do it. Feeling rather flush having just finished directing my first picture, I said, 'Yes, sure.'" He had only one week to prepare before the film's start on July 6, 1970. Saddled with a supporting cast of non-actors (Yutte Stensgaard, Mike Raven), the tongue-in-cheek approach taken was the only way out. The production ended on August 18, and, on the same day, James Carreras signed an agreement with Associated British to make nine movies over the next three years. Associated British would finance the films and provide space at Elstree, with Anglo EMI to handle the domestic releases. It was up to Hammer to find overseas distributors or, in some cases, not. Due to this and other arrangements, Bray became expendable, mainly since Hammer had not used it since 1966. James Carreras estimated its value to be £250,000, but the company would have to split any profits from a sale with Columbia and EMI.

Lust for a Vampire was trade shown on December 8, 1970, at Metro House, and was released on January 17, 1971, on the ABC circuit. Reviewers were justifiably dismissive. *The Kinematograph Weekly* (December 19, 1970): "Fairly routine vampire stuff, using the well-worn props"; and *Variety* (September 15): "Tepid horror film of interest to the

332 Countess Dracula (1970)

Garbage!

least discriminating of audiences." The film's combination of nudity, lesbianism, gore, bad acting, and a ludicrous theme song added up to something no one needed to see.

Countess Dracula

Released February 14, 1971 (U.K.), October, 1972 (U.S.); 93 minutes; Eastman Color (U.K.), DeLuxe Color (U.S.); a Hammer Film Production; a Rank Organization Release (U.K.), a 20th Century–Fox Release (U.S.); filmed at Pinewood Studios, England; Director: Peter Sasdy; Producer: Alexander Paal; Screenplay: Jeremy Paul, based on a story by: Alexander Paal, Peter Sasdy, and an idea by Gabriel Ronay; Director of Photography: Ken Talbot; Art Director: Philip Harrison; Music: Harry Robinson; Music Supervisor: Philip Martell; Production Manager: Christopher Sutton; Assistant Director: Ariel Levy; Camera: Ken Withers; Costumes: Raymond Hughes; Editor: Henry Richardson; Makeup: Tom Smith; Sound Mixer: Kevin Sutton; Special Effects: Bert Luxford; Sound: Al Streeter, Ken Barker; Choreography: Mia Nardi; U.K. Certificate: X; MPAA Rating: R.

Ingrid Pitt (Countess Elizabeth Bathory), Nigel Green (Captain Dobi), Sandor Eles (Imre Toth), Maurice Denham (Master Fabio), Patience Collier (Julie), Lesley Anne Down (Ilona), Peter Jeffrey (Captain Balogh), Jessie Evans (Rosa), Andrea Lawrence (Ziza), Leon Lissek (Bailiff Sergeant), Susan Brodrick (Teri), Ian Trigger (Clown), Nike Arrighi (Gypsy Girl), Peter May (Janco), John Moore (Priest), Joan Haythorne (Cook), Marianne Stone (Kitchen Maid), Charles Farrell (The Seller), Sally Adcock (Bertha), Anne Stallybrass (Pregnant Woman), Paddy Ryan (Man), Michael Cadman (Young Man), Hulya Babus (Belly Dancer), Leslie Anderson, Biddy Hearne, Diana Sawday (Gypsy Dancers), Gary Rich, Andrew Burleigh (Boys), Ismed Hassan, Albert Wilkinson (Midgets).

At the funeral of Count Nadasdy, his elderly widow, Elizabeth Bathory (Ingrid Pitt), is attracted to handsome young Imre Toth (Sandor Eles), son of the Count's best friend. Elizabeth later attends the reading of the will and is outraged to learn that she is to share her inheritance with her daughter Ilona (Lesley Anne Down).

That night, one of Elizabeth's serving girls is cut by a blow from the cruel Countess, and blood spatters across Elizabeth's face. As the girl flees, Elizabeth makes a startling discovery: In the places where blood touched her, her face glows with youthful freshness. Elizabeth orders her maid Julie (Patience Collier) to bring back the girl. Not long afterward, Captain Dobi (Nigel Green), Elizabeth's steward and longtime lover, stares incredulously as Elizabeth, young again, confronts him. Elizabeth arranges to have her own daughter Ilona abducted and plans to assume her identity.

The now-youthful Countess pursues Imre, who believes her to be Ilona. When–

Widow Elizabeth Bathory (Ingrid Pitt) and Captain Dobi (Nigel Green) attend the reading of Count Nadasdy's will in *Countess Dracula*.

ever her youthful appearance begins to fade, her maid finds another victim. When Elizabeth announces her engagement to Imre, Dobi is overcome by jealousy. He reminds the Countess that each time she loses her beauty, she grows more hideous.

After a night of revelry, Dobi and Imre return to the castle with a serving wench. Elizabeth has confined herself to her room, once again aged. Dobi taunts the Countess and brings her to Imre's room where she sees him in bed with the serving girl. Furious, Elizabeth murders the girl, but bathing in her blood has no effect. Dobi and the Countess go to the library to consult an occult volume. Fabio (Maurice Denham), the castle librarian, confronts them, holding the book they were seeking and reads a passage pertaining to the magical properties of virgin blood. The serving wench was not a virgin, and therefore her blood failed to produce the desired effect. The Countess offers to reward Fabio in exchange for his silence. Fabio appears willing but later is overheard by Dobi trying to warn Imre. Imre soon finds Fabio's body, and accuses Dobi of the murder. Dobi takes Imre to the Countess's rooms, where the young man witnesses the Countess bathing in the blood of another victim. Elizabeth assures him that she and "Ilona" are one and the same, and threatens to have him falsely accused of Fabio's murder if he exposes the truth.

Investigating Fabio's death, Police Captain Balogh (Peter Jeffrey) orders a search of the castle and uncovers the bodies of several missing girls. Balogh orders everyone but "Ilona" and the Countess placed under house arrest. Without access to victims, the Countess begs Dobi to find someone for her. On the day of Elizabeth's wedding, the real Ilona is brought to the castle by Dobi to be the next victim. Julie, who raised Ilona since birth, brings Imre to her and pleads with

Imre to save the girl. Imre tells Julie to bring the girl to the stables during the wedding; he will arrange safe passage for her. Ilona pleads with him to leave with her, but Imre knows that he has implicated himself and that he will never be able to escape.

During the wedding ceremony, Elizabeth loses her beauty as all in attendance witness the horrible transformation. Elizabeth, now insane, sees Ilona and tries to stab her, and Imre is killed in a struggle. Later, as the Countess awaits the hangman, the villagers whisper the new name they have given her: Countess Dracula.

Hammer's version of the "Blood Countess" is far more tame than the real Elizabeth Bathory!

Hammer proclaimed its latest picture as "The first Horror film to be based *completely* on a true story." Actually, Elizabeth Bathory—the "Blood Countess"—had lived a life of such depravity that not even Hammer dared to tell her story. Composer Harry Robinson told *Little Shoppe of Horrors'* Bruce Hallenbeck that, originally, director Peter Sasdy was not interested in making a horror picture. "They were making a historical drama. The only thing was, I think they just got lost. Somebody from the front office said, 'This is supposed to be a horror movie, so they put something in. It would have been more horrific if they'd actually stuck to what Elizabeth Bathory did." Ingrid Pitt told Sam Irvin Jr. (*Bizarre*) that the film was "absolutely butchered by various people. It wasn't really much of a horror film. I didn't think it was cruel enough, horrifying enough. It needed more cruelty, throat slashing, blood hounds, blood! She ripped girls apart with her blood hounds; she froze them in the snow. She did incredible atrocities." The Countess was accused of having killed over six hundred fifty people and is listed in *The Guinness Book of World Records.*

Production began on *Countess Dracula* on July 27, 1970. The screenplay was a combination of ideas from Sasdy, producer Alexander Paal, and Gabriel Ronay who later published *The Truth About Dracula* based on his research. The picture was Hammer's first of three to be co-produced with Rank, although 20th Century–Fox handled the overseas distribution. *Countess Dracula* wrapped on September 4. While it was being edited, Peter Sasdy described to *The Kinematograph Weekly* how he perceived the "Hammer audience" by splitting it into three groups. "One: the large number of people who go to the films to be frightened; Two: those who go for a certain kind of laugh; and Three: the type of audience that goes for sexual thrills."

Countess Dracula was trade shown on February 3, 1971, at the Rank Theatre and premiered on a double bill with *Hell's Belles* on February 6 at the New Victoria. The package took £3,718 the first week, but business tailed off quickly. Michael Carreras later admitted that the company lost money, and the reviewers were more impressed than the audiences. *The Kinematograph Weekly* (February 6, 1971): "Ingrid Pitt manages to give her two ages notably different personalities"; *The Monthly Film Bulletin* (March): "At its best the film employs the kind of

Andrew Keir gets his from the villainous James Villiers in *Blood from the Mummy's Tomb*.

romantic imagery one associates with Keats"; *The New York Daily News* (October 7, 1972): "A pleasant surprise in the horror film genre"; and *The New York Times* (October 12): "Better than most in a sea of trashy competition."

Although *Countess Dracula* does have its merits, it was another step down and miles away from "real" Hammer movies like *The Brides of Dracula*. Sadly, this was Nigel Green's last film. He committed suicide on May 15, 1972.

1971

Blood from the Mummy's Tomb

Released October 14, 1971 (U.K.), May, 1972 (U.S.); 94 minutes; Technicolor: 8,460 feet; a Hammer/EMI Production; an Anglo EMI Release (U.K.), American International (U.S.); Director: Seth Holt (completed by Michael Carreras); Producer: Howard Brandy; Screenplay: Christopher Wicking, based on Bram Stoker's *Jewel of the Seven Stars*; Director of Photography: Arthur Grant; Production Design: Scott MacGregor; Music: Tristam Cary; Musical Supervisor: Philip Martell; Editor: Peter Weatherley; Sound Editor: Roy Hyde; Continuity: Betty Harley; Makeup: Eddie Knight; Wardrobe: Rosemary Burrows; Wardrobe Mistress: Diane Jones; Assistant Director: Derek Whitehurst; Hairdresser: Ivy Emmerton; Special Effects: Michael Collins; Sound Recordist: Tony Lumkin; Sound Camera: Tony Dawe, Dennis Whitlock; Production Supervisor: Roy Skeggs; Production Manager: Christopher Neame; U.K. Certificate: X; MPAA Rating: PG.

Andrew Keir (Fuchs), Valerie Leon (Margaret/Tera), James Villiers (Corbeck), Hugh Burden (Dandridge), George Coulouris (Berigan), Mark Edwards (Tod Browning), Rosalie Crutchley (Helen Dickerson), Aubrey Morris (Dr. Putnam), James Cossins (Older Male Nurse), David Jackson (Younger Male Nurse), David Markkham (Dr. Burgess), Joan Young (Mrs. Caporal), David Jackson (Young Man), Penelope Holt,

Angela Ginders (Nurses), Tex Fuller (Patient), Madina Luis, Omar Amoodi, Abdul Kader, Ahmed Osman, Oscar Charles, Soltan Lalani, Saad Ghazi (Priests).

Ancient Egypt. The beautiful Queen Tera (Valerie Leon) is feared by her high priests due to her supernatural powers. After severing her right hand, on which she wears a magic ruby, they entomb her—they think—forever.

In modern times, Professor Fuchs (Andrew Keir), heading a British team, enters her tomb and finds her still beautiful body. Her severed hand, still bleeding, rests on her stomach. At that moment, Fuch's wife dies in England giving birth to a baby girl. Twenty years later, Margaret Fuchs (Leon) is a beautiful young woman. After being given Tera's ring as a gift, she begins to resemble the Queen physically and spiritually, exhibiting the same sensual cruelty. Margaret breaks off with her fiancé, Tod (Mark Edwards), and takes up with Corbeck (James Villiers), a team member bent on reincarnating Tera. He has split with Fuchs and is attempting to procure tomb relics to help restore Tera to life.

Using Tera's magic, Margaret kills three team members and takes their relics. When Tod intervenes, Margaret causes his death in a car crash. Now in possession of the Scroll of Life, Corbeck is ready. Professor Fuchs, now aware of the plot, is injured in an attack by Tera's hand, but is able to kill Corbeck as he tries to resurrect Tera. Supernatural powers are unleashed, reducing the building to rubble.

The only survivor, taken to a hospital, is a woman wrapped in bandages like a mummy.

Based on *Dracula* author Bram Stoker's *Jewel of the Seven Stars* (1903), the film is

James Villiers (left), Valerie Leon, and Mark Edwards gaze at Tera in *Blood from the Mummy's Tomb*.

usually discussed as either "the one where the director, Seth Holt, died before its completion," or "the one from which Peter Cushing withdrew due to his wife's illness." Neither is a fair assessment of this above-average horror movie which, unfortunately, has little identity of its own. Filming began on January 3, 1971. "Early in January," Cushing said in his autobiography, "I started a film at Elstree. At the end of the first day, Joyce (Broughton, his long-time secretary), rang to say that Helen (Mrs. Cushing) had been taken to Canterbury Hospital for a check up." She had been ill for years, and when her condition dramatically worsened, Cushing requested her release so he could care for her at home. She died on January 14, shortly after Cushing had withdrawn from the Fuchs role. He was replaced by Andrew Keir, and production resumed after a short delay.

Seth Holt had scored for Hammer a decade earlier with *Taste of Fear*, but had never established himself as a "genre director." Several of Holt's earlier films did involve violence, and he felt that in a horror film "the terror should gradually build up to one really traumatic shock," as he said in *Kinematograph Weekly* (January 30, 1971). First-time producer Howard Brandy, a former film publicist, had acquired the rights to Stoker's novel and gave a script to Sir James Carreras. Brandy admired Holt's work and was delighted to sign him. Unfortunately, Holt's physical condition was not delightful. Alcoholic and overweight, he died of a heart attack on February 14 at age 47. Holt was described in *Kinematograph Weekly* (February 20, 1971) as "one of those directors who can stamp their own distinctive gifts on the most unlikely and unpretentious material." He was replaced by Michael Carreras for the sixth and final week.

Obviously, when a film loses both its star and director, it is in trouble. Thanks to Andrew Keir and Carreras, *Blood from the Mummy's Tomb* overcame its real-life tragedies to become one of Hammer's few good seventies horrors. Filming ended on February 20, and a trade show was held at Metro House on October 7. It was also shown on the same day at the National Film Institute's tribute to Hammer, which ran until November 14 and featured the films of Terence Fisher. Following the Queen's Award in 1968, this was the second major vindication of Hammer which, a decade earlier, was the subject of public vilification. Reviews, following the October 14, 1971, release, were generally positive. *Today's Cinema* (October 15): "This is the real thing. It could well turn out to be a cult rave for more sophisticated devotees"; *The New York Times* (May 22, 1972): "Tremendous fun, skillful, and wonderfully energetic"; *Variety* (October 27, 1971): "Polished and well acted."

Blood from the Mummy's Tomb is not one of Hammer's very best, but it deserves credit for doing something different, as well as surviving its tragedies. A second adaptation of Stoker's novel was released in 1980 as *The Awakening*, starring Charlton Heston, to much less effect.

Hands of the Ripper

Released October 17, 1971 (U.K.), July, 1972 (U.S.); 85 minutes; 7,650 feet; Technicolor; a Hammer Film Production; a Rank Organization Release (U.K.), a Universal Release (U.S.); filmed at Pinewood Studios, England; Director: Peter Sasdy; Producer: Aida Young; Screenplay: L.W. Davidson, based on an original story by Edward Spencer Shew; Director of Photography: Kenneth Talbot, B.S.C.; Production Manager: Christopher Sutton; Art Director: Roy Stannard; Editor: Chris Barnes; Assistant Director: Ariel Levy; Sound: Kevin Sutton; Makeup Supervisor: Bunty Phillips; Hairdressing Supervisor: Pat McDermott; Wardrobe Supervisor: Rosemary Burrows; Music: Christopher Gunning; Musical Supervisor: Philip Martell; Special Effects: Cliff Culley; Sound Re-Recording: Ken Barker; Sound Editing: Frank Goulding; Sound Recording: Kevin Sutton; U.K. Certificate: X; MPAA Rating: R.

Eric Porter (Dr. John Pritchard), Angharad Rees (Anna), Jane Merrow (Laura), Keith Bell (Michael), Derek Godfrey (Dysart), Dora Bryan (Mrs. Golding), Marjorie Rhodes (Mrs. Bryant), Norman Bird (Police Inspector), Katya Wyeth (1st Pub Prostitute), Margaret Rawlings (Madame Bullard), Elizabeth MacLennan (Mrs. Wilson), A.J. Brown (Reverend Anderson), April Wilding (Catherine), Anne Clune, Vicki Woolf, Beulah Hughes, Tallulah Miller (Prostitutes), Peter Munt (Peasants), Philip Ryan (Police Constable), Molly Weir (Maid), Charles Lamb (Guard), Marjie Lawrence (Dolly), Barry Lowe (Mr. Wilson), Lynda Baron (Long Liz), Ann Way (Seamstress). U.S. television footage only: Severn Darden.

Jack the Ripper, returning home after committing one of his brutal murders, murders his own wife when she finally realizes that he is the fiendish killer. Their tiny daughter Anna witnesses the gruesome scene and then stares at her mother's body and at the leaping flames within the fireplace.

Fifteen years later, Anna (Angharad Rees) is a sweet and innocent young woman in the employ of fake medium Mrs. Golding (Dora Bryan). John Pritchard (Eric Porter), a doctor and admirer of Sigmund

Hands of the Ripper (1971)

THE HANDS OF JACK THE RIPPER LIVE AGAIN...
as his fiendish daughter kills again... and again... and again!

"HANDS OF THE RIPPER" starring Eric Porter · Jane Merrow
guest star Dora Bryan · also starring Angharad Rees · Derek Godfrey
Screenplay by L. W. DAVIDSON • From an original story by EDWARD SPENCER SHEW
Produced by AIDA YOUNG • Directed by PETER SASDY
A HAMMER PRODUCTION
A UNIVERSAL RELEASE in COLOR

The Ripper legend takes an odd turn.

Freud, attends one of Mrs. Golding's séances and, after a grieving couple has left, searches and finds Anna's hiding place (she provides the ghost voices). After Pritchard leaves, another guest, Dysart (Derek Godfrey), offers Mrs. Golding money for a night with Anna. Mrs. Golding is found murdered minutes later impaled on a door with a fireplace poker. Dysart is suspected but not charged. Pritchard feels that Anna has severe psychological problems and offers to act as her guardian, bringing her into his home.

Dysart warns Pritchard that Anna killed Mrs. Golding, but Pritchard is unconvinced until he returns home one night to find Anna covered with blood and the maid, her throat slit, dead in the bathtub. Pritchard covers up the crime but Anna later escapes and, in another spell of madness, kills a streetwalker. The Royal Medium Madame Bullard (Margaret Rawlings) "sees" into Anna's past and reveals to Pritchard that Anna's father was the Ripper—and that Anna is possessed by his evil spirit. Anna, falling into the deadly trance, stabs the medium before Pritchard can stop her.

Pritchard realizes that the sight of glimmering objects (a la the fireplace flames) sets Anna off. Anna later stabs Pritchard with a sword and escapes once again, but Pritchard and his son Michael (Keith Bell) track her to St. Paul's Cathedral, where she has gone with Laura (Jane Merrow), Michael's blind fiancée. Anna chokes Laura, but the madness passes before she can kill her. Realizing she will never be free of her murderous heritage, the tormented Anna flings herself from a high gallery to her death. Pritchard succumbs to his wounds and crumples to the floor near Anna's broken body.

Jack the Ripper was a natural subject for Hammer to film, and two decades after *Room to Let*, the company returned to the character. But instead of offering yet another variation on *The Lodger*, Hammer continued its "series" of female monsters by concentrating on the Ripper's daughter. As a gauge of our troubled times, it is worth remembering that the real Ripper killed "only" five people. This is certainly small time in today's world of serial killers and mass murderers, yet the Ripper was by far the most famous criminal of his era. *Hands of the Ripper* managed to incorporate a few factual references, including the character of "Long Liz" Stride and Whitechapel locations like Berner Street.

In early January, 1971, Rank's managing director Frank Poole ordered two features to follow *Countess Dracula*—*Hands of the Ripper* and *Twins of Evil*. "We, at Rank Film Distributors," he said (*The Kinematograph Weekly*, January 9), "are very enthusiastic and pleased to be further associated with Hammer—the acknowledged masters in this field." The typical Hammer period picture was being filmed for £200,000, which was easily recouped in the U.K. alone. The rest of the world's receipts were pure profit. "Before we tell a writer to complete a full script," Michael Carreras said (*Cinefantastique*, Vol. 1, No. 3), "we plan our advertising campaign, decide if the story is exploitable and saleable, and then we ask if it can be made for $480,000. An added bonus for Hammer are production distribution agreements with major U.S. studios, under which Hammer need put up no production front money yet partakes of half the profits." Unfortunately, those types of deals were less plentiful in the early seventies.

Hands of the Ripper began on January 25, 1971, with Aida Young producing her last Hammer film. The cast, although lacking a "name" star, was uniformly excellent with Eric Porter a standout. His character, Dr. John Pritchard, was named after, oddly enough, a real-life convicted murderer. Angharad Rees also shone in the difficult role of the Ripper's daughter, creating one of the company's most interesting—and most dangerous—female characters. After wrapping in mid–March, *Hands of the Ripper* was trade shown on September 17, 1971, at the Rank. The picture premiered at the New Victoria a week later and took in £11,000 during its two week run. Paired with *Twins of Evil*, it was released on October 17, to poor reviews. *The London Times* (October 15): "Has its moments of fog bound atmosphere"; *The Monthly Film Bulletin* (October): "Disappointingly routine Hammer with the usual virtues of good performances and period authenticity but all the faults as well—a basic appeal to sadism rather than imagination in the horror sequences"; *Today's Cinema* (October 5): "The flimsiest of plots"; and *Variety* (October 13): "It could be a sleeper." The plot's central idea is vaguely similar to that of *Cat People* (1942), in which Simone Simon turned into a killer leopard when her passions were aroused, notably by her psychiatrist (Tom Conway). *Hands of the Ripper*, clearly the "second feature" in the package, more than fulfilled that role, but it is unfortunate that Hammer did not use its still-potent resources to film a more realistic investigation of the unsolved murders. When *Hands of the Ripper* was sold to ABC-TV, severe cuts and even an alteration of the plot were necessary due to the film's extreme violence.

However, Michael Carreras told Colin Cowie (*Little Shoppe of Horrors* 4) that ABC paid the highest price ever offered to televise a Hammer film.

Dr. Jekyll and Sister Hyde

Released November 7, 1971 (U.K.), April, 1972 (U.S.); 97 minutes (U.K.), 95 minutes (U.S.); Technicolor; a Hammer-EMI Film Production; an Anglo-EMI Release (U.K.), an American International Pictures Release (U.S.); filmed at MGM/EMI Studios, England; Director: Roy Ward Baker; Producers: Albert Fennell, Brian Clemens; Screenplay: Brian Clemens, based on the characters created by Robert Louis Stevenson; Music: David Whitaker; Musical Supervisor: Philip Martell; Song: "He'll Be There"; Words and Music: Brian Clemens; Editor: James Needs; Sound Editors: Charles Crafford, Bill Rowe; Production Design: Robert Jones; Wardrobe Supervisor: Rosemary Burrows; Wardrobe Mistress: Kathleen Moore; Director of Photography: Norman Warwick; Makeup Supervisor: John Wilcox; Hairdressing Supervisor: Bernie Ibbetson; Continuity: Sally Ball; Casting Director: Jimmy Liggat; Production Supervisor: Roy Skeggs; Production Manager: Don Weeks; Assistant Director: Bert Batt; Camera: Godfrey Godar; Art Director: Robert Jones; Makeup: Trevor Crole-Rees; Publicity: Hugh Samson; U.K. Certificate: X; MPAA Rating: PG.

Ralph Bates (Dr. Jekyll), Martine Beswick (Sister Hyde), Gerald Sim (Professor Robertson), Lewis Fiander (Howard), Susan Brodrick (Susan), Dorothy Alison (Mrs. Spencer), Ivor Dean (Burke), Paul Whitsun-Jones (Sgt. Danvers), Philip Madoc (Byker), Tony Calvin (Hare), Dan Meaden (Town Crier), Virginia Wetherall (Betsy), Julia Wright (Street Singer), Geoffrey Kenion (1st Policeman), Irene Bradshaw (Yvonne), Anna Brett (Julie); Jackie Poole (Margie), Rosemary Lord (Marie), Petula Portell (Petra), Pat Brackenbury (Helen), Liz Romanoff (Emma), Will Stampe (Mine Host), Roy Evans (Knife Grinder), Derek Steen, John Lyons (Sailors), Jeanette Wild (Jill), Bobby Parr (Young Apprentice), Neil Wilson (Older Policeman).

Dr. Jekyll and Sister Hyde (1971)

In the late 1800s, Dr. Henry Jekyll (Ralph Bates) is on the trail of an elixir of youth. Using female hormones obtained from corpses, he prolongs the lifespan of a fruit fly from a few hours to over three days. He hires body snatchers Burke (Ivor Dean) and Hare (Tony Calvin) to supply him with bodies, then tries the formula on himself, collapsing to the floor in pain. He regains consciousness and, to his amazement, discovers that he has been transformed into a beautiful young woman (Martine Beswick). The transformation only lasts a few hours, but Jekyll is fascinated by the turn his research has taken.

When Burke and Hare are captured, Jekyll is forced to kill to further his experiments. He begins to hunt prostitutes in Whitechapel. The area's residents are convinced that Jack the Ripper is responsible for the new murders. Professor Robertson (Gerald Sim), a confidant of Jekyll's, becomes suspicious when he examines the body of a murder victim. Discovering that the woman's sex glands have been removed, Robertson suggests that Jekyll's apartment be placed under surveillance. But "Sister" Hyde, free to come and go, leaves and murders another woman.

Dr. Jekyll (Ralph Bates) hunts for victims to satisfy his alter ego, Sister Hyde, in *Dr. Jekyll and Sister Hyde*.

Jekyll realizes that Hyde is growing stronger with each transformation. When Hyde murders Robertson and later tries to kill Jekyll's neighbor Susan Spenser (Susan Brodrick), Jekyll decides to rid himself of Hyde forever. But he is betrayed by Hare and forced to flee from the police, climbing to the roof. Jekyll attempts to work his way across the face of a building, but as he passes a window he is shocked to see that Hyde is attempting to work her way out of him. Before she can succeed in a full transformation, Jekyll allows himself to fatally fall from the roof to the pavement far below.

Hammer's third adaptation of Robert Louis Stevenson's famous story was brought to the company by producer Brian Clemens. "The idea came to me quite suddenly," he said (EMI pressbook). "I jotted it down on the back of an old envelope and took it to Sir James Carreras." Along with Albert Fennell, Clemens had produced *The Avengers*, one of Britain's most successful television shows, and the pair were given the go-ahead. Clemens wrote the screenplay and Roy Ward Baker, another *Avengers* alumnus, was signed to direct. "I aim never to make the same film twice," Baker said (EMI pressbook). "I am only as good as my last production."

By the nature of the male/female transformation, tradition was broken in that Jekyll and his alter ego had to be played by two different performers. Ralph Bates, Hammer's heir apparent to Cushing and Lee, was an easy choice for Dr. Jekyll. However, Sister Hyde was a different matter. "The part of Sister Hyde is going to make whoever plays it the personality of 1971," enthused an "open letter" to the trade papers. "The guidelines are quite simple. We want the most beautiful girl in the world." Oddly enough, she was right under Hammer's nose all along. Martine Beswick had appeared in *One Million Years B.C.* and *Slave Girls* for the company, but had relocated to Hollywood. She had just returned to Britain as the search began, and when Clemens and Fennell learned she was back, their search was over. "Nobody realized," Roy Ward Baker said (*Fangoria* 36), "how much Ralph and Martine looked alike until they arrived on the set. It certainly helped to externalize Jekyll's narcissism." This left Ralph Bates with what was, in his mind, only half a role. "Actually, I wished I had played *both* parts," he said (*Fangoria* 55). "It could have been the original *Tootsie*." Beswick, however, was taking it all very seriously. "The picture," she said (*Filmfax* 34), "had a very interesting premise—the male and female in each of us. I was going for it totally. I was serious about what I was doing."

Filming began on February 15, 1971, and was not without its problems, which centered around Baker's insistence that Beswick *completely* disrobe during the first transformation. "I totally agreed to what was in the script," she recalled (*Fangoria* 55), "which was bare breasts but *not* full frontal nudity. Then I got on the set and Roy Ward Baker said, 'I don't want to have to shoot around your panties, so I would prefer you not have anything on in this scene.' I wanted a closed set, but Roy pulled another trick on me. There were *dozens* of people hanging from the rafters, but I did the scene anyway." After all of the problems the shot caused, it was eventually cut down to a brief view of her breasts. This is an all too obvious example of the direction in which both Hammer

Hammer's gender-bender version of Stevenson's classic novella.

and the film industry in general were heading, as nudity was becoming the main thing that too many movies had to offer. The trend *did* save Hammer some money, though. Costumer Monty Berman (*Today's Cinema*, October 1, 1971) estimated that the average cost of Hammer's last six pictures was down two percent.

The production ended on March 30, 1971, and was trade shown at the Metro on October 6. The next week, excerpts were shown at the National Film Theatre's tribute to Hammer. Paired with *Blood from the*

Dr. Jekyll and Sister Hyde was emblematic of the new trends in the film industry.

Mummy's Tomb, the picture premiered at the New Victoria in mid–October, taking £2,376 in its first week. However, a week after its release on the ABC circuit, *Dr. Jekyll and Sister Hyde* slumped to £1,248, and favorable reviewers were more numerous than its patrons. *The London Times* (October 15, 1971): "Quite a nicely kinky idea"; *Today's Cinema* (October 15): "Basic idea very ingenious"; *The Monthly Film Bulletin* (November): "A welcome reminder that Hammer can still be highly enterprising myth-makers. Baker, although pleased with the film, pointed out (*Little Shoppe of Horrors* 4), "There was one great flaw. They've only got one body between the two of them, so you never see the two of them together." Oddly, while *Dr. Jekyll and Sister Hyde* was being cast, Amicus had started filming *I, Monster*, another Jekyll/Hyde version, with Christopher Lee and Peter Cushing. Perhaps *that* was the movie Hammer should have made instead.

On the Buses

Released August 8, 1971 (U.K.); 88 minutes; Technicolor; 7867 feet; a Hammer Film Production; Released through MGM/EMI (U.K.); filmed at EMI Elstree Studios; Director: Harry Booth; Producers: Ronald Wolfe and Ronald Chesney, based on the BBC TV series; Director of Photography: Mark McDonald; Music: Max Harris; Music Director: Philip Martell; Songs by Geoff Unwin, Roger Ferris; Performed by Quinceharmon; Camera: Neil Binney; Editor: Archie Ludski; Sound: John Purchese; Sound Editor: Peter Keen; Continuity: Doreen Dearnaley; Makeup: Eddie Knight; Wardrobe: Rosemary Burrows; Wardrobe Mistress: June Kirby; Hairdresser: Ivy Emmerton; Production Manager: Christopher Neame; Production Design: Scott MacGregor; Assistant Director: Derek Whitehurst; Assistant Director: Ron Benton; Construction Manager: Bill Greene; Recording Director: Tony Lumkin; Dubbing Mixer: Bill Rowe; U.K. Certificate: A.

Reg Varney (Stan Butler), Doris Hare (Stan's Mum), Michael Robbins (Arthur); Anna Karen (Olive), Stephen Lewis (Blake), Bob Grant (Jack), Andrea Lawrence (Betty), Pat Ashton (Sally), Brian Oulton (Manager), Pamela Cundell (Ruby), Pat Coombs (Vera), Wendy Richards (Housewife), Peter Madden (Mr. Brooks), David Lodge (Busman), Brenda Gogan (Bridget), Caroline Dowdeswell (Sandra), Eunice Black (Ada), Claire Davenport (Peggy), Maggie McGrath (Mavis), Jeanne Varney (Mavis), Nosher Powell (Betty's Husband), Tex Fuller (Harry), Terry Duggan (Nobby), Anna Michaels (Eileen), Norman Mitchell (Official), Ivor Salter, George Roderick (Policemen), Gavin Campbell

(Motorcycle Cop), David Rowlands (Parson), Hilda Barry (Old Woman), Jeanette Wild (Suzy), Moira Foot (Katy), Reginald Peters (Orderly).

When the Town and District Bus Company finds itself short of drivers, Inspector Blake (Stephen Lewis) angers veterans Stan (Reg Varney) and Jack (Bob Grant) by hiring women. The pair begin a reign of terror to rid themselves of the women, and no trickery is beneath them. They are not against women in general, however, and attempt to prove it nightly, with Jack usually the more successful.

Olive (Anna Karen), Stan's sister, discovers to her surprise that she is pregnant. When her time comes unexpectedly, Olive uses Stan's bus as an ambulance. Her mum (Doris Hare) is delighted at the birth of her 13-pound grandson. Meanwhile, Stan and Jack's dirty tricks have been, up to a point, successful. Most of the women have stopped driving since being promoted to Bus Inspectors.

On the Buses was a huge hit on the London television network, usually placing in the top five and seen by over eight million viewers weekly. This was enough for Hammer, who started their feature version on March 8, 1971, at Elstree, featuring most of the series regulars. It was a daring venture. Making a cinema version of a television show that could be watched at home for free is not normally a sound business move. But, as usual, Hammer knew what audiences wanted. This was the company's first comedy since *Watch It, Sailor!*, and they correctly felt the time was right.

Filming ended on April 7, 1971, and *On the Buses* was found in theatres on August 8. From starting date to general release in five months was quite an effort, even for Hammer. The gamble paid off, as the film did tremendous business, racking up a weekly gross of £1758 and £5201 for the month at one London cinema. In its first week of release, *On the Buses* did £400,000 in the U.K.—an incredible figure for a low budget film. Eighty-eight all-time house records were broken by mid–August. All told, the movie smashed 142 house records in the U.K., and did equally well in, of all places, the Netherlands, where it was playing to twice the average daily rate.

Part of *On the Buses'* success was due to a huge advertising campaign pushed by MGM/EMI. Despite the popularity of the series, the distributor was taking no chances. Posters were placed on London buses and were seen by countless people every hour. The main title theme by Quinceharmon was released by Columbia Records, and music stores were stocked with film stills.

Cinema TV Today was so impressed with *On the Buses* that it ran a breakdown of the film's box office takings as of March, 1973: U.K. (£1,500,000), and overseas (£1,000,000). Hammer's profit was £532,000, with MGM/ EMI taking slightly less, and the Eady levy was £200,000. The pound was worth, at that time, $2.50. Considering that the film had no American release, everyone did very well on what was certainly a small investment. *On the Buses* was such a hit that lukewarm reviews meant little. *The Kinematograph Weekly* (July 10, 1971): "Simple, crude, farcical comedy"; and *Today's Cinema* (July 3): "Crude and spiteful tomfoolery." As with the Hammer horrors, negative reviews helped to feed the frenzy. A sequel was mentioned as early as August, 1971, indicating that Hammer was becoming serious about comedy. "Since the success of *On the Buses*," Michael Carreras said in *Today's Cinema* (August 8, 1971), "three comedy projects have been brought to us which we may do."

He was now in charge of the company which he had taken over from his father six months previously, during which time five films were completed at a total cost of £1 million. Carreras hoped to "Modify Hammer to fit the realities of the early seventies film world. That doesn't mean that we shall get away from the basic philosophy of my father." He also wanted to push Hammer into a higher echelon. "Lindsay Anderson will do a film for us, and I can attract the new talent on British films today." Variety was also high on Carreras' mind—a return to the more diversified period of the late fifties. "There will still be horror films in our pro-

Hammer's lovely Collinson sisters in *Twins of Evil*.

gram," he said, "but I also want to attract writers and directors of better quality."

What Carreras wanted to do was to reform the company, envisioning more "mainstream" movies, higher budgets, and big name talent. Unfortunately, little of this happened. After *On the Buses*, Hammer would make less than two dozen films—mostly graphic horror and low brow comedy.

Twins of Evil

Released October 17, 1971 (U.K.), June 1972 (U.S.); 87 minutes; Eastman Color; 7830 feet; a Hammer Film Production; a Rank Release (U.K.), Universal (U.S.); filmed at Pinewood Studios; Director: John Hough; Producers: Harry Fine and Michael Style; Screenplay: Tudor Gates, based on characters created by J. Sheridan Le Fanu; Director of Photography: Dick Bush; Music: Harry Robinson; Music Supervisor: Philip Martell; Editor: Spencer Reeve; Production Manager: Tom Sachs; Camera: Dudley Lovell; Sound: Stan Samworth; Art Director: Roy Stannard; Wardrobe: Rosemary Burrows; Makeup: George Blackler; Hairdresser: Pearl Tipaldi, Casting: Jimmy Liggat; Sound Mixer: Ron Barron; Assistant Director: Patrick Clayton; Special Effects: Bert Luxford; Second Unit Photography: Jack Mills; Assistant Makeup: John Webber; U.K. Certificate: X; MPAA Rating: R.

Madeline Collinson (Frieda Gellhorn), Mary Collinson (Maria Gellhorn), Peter Cushing (Gustav Weil), Kathleen Byron (Katy Weil), Dennis Price (Dietrich), Harvey Hall (Franz), Isobel Black (Ingrid Hoffer), Damien Thomas (Count Karnstein); David Warbeck (Anton Hoffer), Alex Scott (Hermann), Katya Wyeth (Countess Mircalla), Roy Stewart (Joachim), Maggie Wright (Aleta), Luan Peters (Gerta), Ingio Jackson (Woodman), Judy Matheson (Woodman's Daughter), Sheelah Wilcox (Lady in Coach), Kirsten Lindholm (Young Girl), Peter Thompson (Jailer).

Frieda (Madeline Collinson) and Maria (Mary Collinson) Gellhorn are beautiful twins, recently orphaned and placed in the care of their kindly Aunt Katy (Kathleen Byron) and her stern husband, Gustav Weil (Peter Cushing). Gustav is the leader of the Brotherhood, a fanatical Puritan cult dedicated to ending the plague of evil infesting their village. Count Karnstein (Damien Thomas) makes a mockery of all that is decent with the help of Dietrich (Dennis Price), a loathsome procurer who obtains village girls for the Count's "pleasure." The body of a young girl (Maggie Wright) is used to reincarnate the Count's vampire ancestor, Mircalla (Katya Wyeth), who initiates the Count into the Undead.

Angered by Gustav's harsh discipline, Frieda rebels and comes under the Count's influence, dining with him at the castle where she becomes a vampire when he takes her blood. The plague spreads, claiming

Ingrid (Isobel Black), sister of the choirmaster, Anton (David Warbeck), who loves Maria. When Frieda is found with blood on her lips, Gustav jails her, but the Count replaces her with Maria. When Anton visits "Maria" in her room, she attacks him, but he wards her off with a crucifix. He halts "Frieda's" execution, and, led by Gustav, a mob storms the castle.

As Frieda tries to escape, Gustav beheads her, but the Count abducts Maria. Gustav confronts him but is killed with an axe. Anton then impales the Count with a lance, reducing him to a skeleton.

Twins of Evil was the last, and best, of the "Karnstein Trilogy," which included *The Vampire Lovers* and *Lust for a Vampire*. The trio, in addition to chronicling the Karnstein saga, had their share of fairly graphic scenes of sex and violence. Originally titled *Vampire Virgins*, *Twins of Dracula*, and *The Gemini Twins*, the film went into production on March 24, 1971, with, as in the previous two films, Harry Fine and Michael Style as prime movers. Although Peter Cushing heads the cast and gives the best performance, the main source of interest was the Collinson twins. They were *Playboy* magazine's first twin centerfold subjects, and were so alike that no one on the set could tell them apart—including makeup man George Blackler. He told *Today's Cinema* (March 30, 1971), "Sit them together, and I will defy anyone to tell the difference." Madeline offered, "The situation will be solved as soon as I get my fangs!" Born in Malta, the twins' English was not fluent enough, so both their voices were dubbed. Hammer came through with a third "discovery," Damien Thomas, who makes one wish Hammer had used him instead of Christopher Lee in the later Dracula films in which Lee's disenchantment with the role is all too obvious.

Filming ended on May 8, 1971, and *Twins of Evil* was trade shown at the Rank Theatre on September 29, 1971, prior to its October 17 release on the ABC circuit. Cofeatured with Hammer's *Hands of the Ripper*, the two had a successful premier engagement at the New Victoria with lines stretching for several hundred yards. Despite the

A worthy follow-up to *The Vampire Lovers*.

movie's extreme violence and sexual content, *Twins of Evil* received surprisingly positive reviews. The *Monthly Bulletin* (November, 1971): "It is easily the best of Hammer's vampire films in some time." *The Los Angeles Times* (August 25, 1972): "Among the most sophisticated horror pictures ever produced by Hammer Films, distinguished by an exceptionally well wrought script, richly detailed period atmosphere, and graceful camera movement"; *Variety* (October 20, 1971): "An above-average horror entry"; *Today's Cinema* (October 1, 1971): "This is a more plausibly constructed story than most of its kind"; and *The New York Times* (July 14, 1972): "Credit the Hammer movie team with providing variations on standard horror themes."

As *Twins of Evil* was Hammer's last outstanding vampire film, a prophetic review for *The Man Who Could Cheat Death* twelve years previously bears recall: "As even greater horror is required, there is less and less that is horrible enough." Where does one go after decapitation, nudity, and lesbian sex? Any pushing of these limits could have well resulted in pornography, which many already felt these films to be. The public realized this all too well; and before long, both this type of movie—and Hammer—were on their way out.

This aside, *Twins of Evil* is among Hammer's best horrors. Led by Peter Cushing in an atypically unsympathetic role, the cast is uniformly excellent, and John Hough (with an assist from Irving Moore for the American television print) nicely prevents the story from being overshadowed by the sex and violence. While not in the same league as the company's fifties' classics, it is as good as almost anything Hammer made afterwards.

Vampire Circus

Released April 30, 1972 (U.K.), October, 1972 (U.S.); 87 minutes (U.K.), 84 minutes (U.S.); Deluxe Color; a Hammer Film Production; a Rank Organization Release (U.K.), a 20th Century–Fox Release (U.S.); filmed at Pinewood Studios, England; Director: Robert Young; Producer: Wilbur Stark; Screenplay: Judson Kinberg: Based on a story by George Baxt, Wilbur Stark; Music: David Whitaker; Conductor: Philip Martell; Director of Photography: Moray Grant; Editor: Peter Musgrave; Special Effects: Les Bowie; Art Director: Scott MacGregor; Makeup: Jill Carpenter; Sound: Claude Hitchcock; Production Supervisor: Roy Skeggs; Production Manager: Tom Sachs; Assistant Director: Derek Whitehurst; Publicity: Frank Law; Sound Camera: Laurie Reed; Camera: Walter Byatt; Continuity: June Randall; Wardrobe: Brian Owen-Smith; Hairdresser: Ann McFayden; Technical Advisor: Mary Chipperfield; Executive Producer: Michael Carreras; Casting Director: James Liggat; Publicity: Frank Law; U.K. Certificate: X; MPAA Rating: PG.

Adrienne Corri (Gypsy Woman), Thorley Walters (Burgermeister), Robert Tayman (Count Mitterhouse), Anthony Corlan (Emil), John Moulder-Brown (Anton Kersh), Laurence Payne (Professor Mueller), Richard Owens (Dr. Kersh), Lynne Frederick (Dora Mueller), Elizabeth Seal (Gerta Hauser), Domini Blythe (Anna Mueller), Robin Hunter (Hauser), Mary Wimbush (Elvira), Lalla Ward (Helga), Robin Sachs (Heinrich), Roderick Shaw (Jon Hauser), Barnaby Shaw (Gustav Hauser), Christina Paul (Rosa), Dave Prowse (Strongman), Jane Darby (Jenny Schilt), Skip Martin (Michael), Milovan & Serena (The Webbers), John Brown (Schilt), Sibylla Kay (Mrs. Schilt), Dorothy Frere (Grandma Schilt), Jason James (Foreman), Arnold Locke (Old Villager), Sean Hewitt (First Soldier), Giles Phibbs (Sexton), Bradford & Amoro (Helga & Heinrich's Doubles).

In the forest near the Middle European village of Schtettel, Professor Mueller (Laurence Payne) sees his wife Anna (Domini Blythe) leading one of the village children into the castle of the vampire Count Mitterhouse (Robert Tayman). Mueller rushes back to the village to gather enough brave men to free the child. The townspeople storm the chateau only to find the child dead and Anna in the Count's embrace. The villagers attack the Count and the vampire is impaled on a stake. Mitterhouse curses the village and its people.

As the years pass, plague and other hardships befall the villagers. The Emperor orders the village quarantined and soldiers are dispatched to establish a blockade. Dr. Kersh (Richard Owens) offers to journey through the blockade and bring back medical supplies. As Kersh prepares to leave, a troupe of circus performers enters the village, apparently having slipped past the blockade. That night they put on their show. The Burgermeister (Thorley Walters) notices that his daughter Rosa (Christina Paul) is singled out by Emil (Anthony Corlan), one of the performers, who is actually Mitterhouse's vampire cousin. Emil seduces Rosa and turns her into his slave.

After the next evening's performance, the troupe invites the Burgermeister to enter a special tent and gaze upon the "Mirrors of Life." Reflected in one glass is Count Mitterhouse holding the Burgermeister's lifeless body. Before passing out, the Burgermeister warns his family and others that the Count has returned. One family attempting to flee through the forest is attacked and killed by the circus panther (Emil in animal form). When the Hauser brothers are later killed, their father and the Burgermeister kill the circus animals. However, when the Burger-

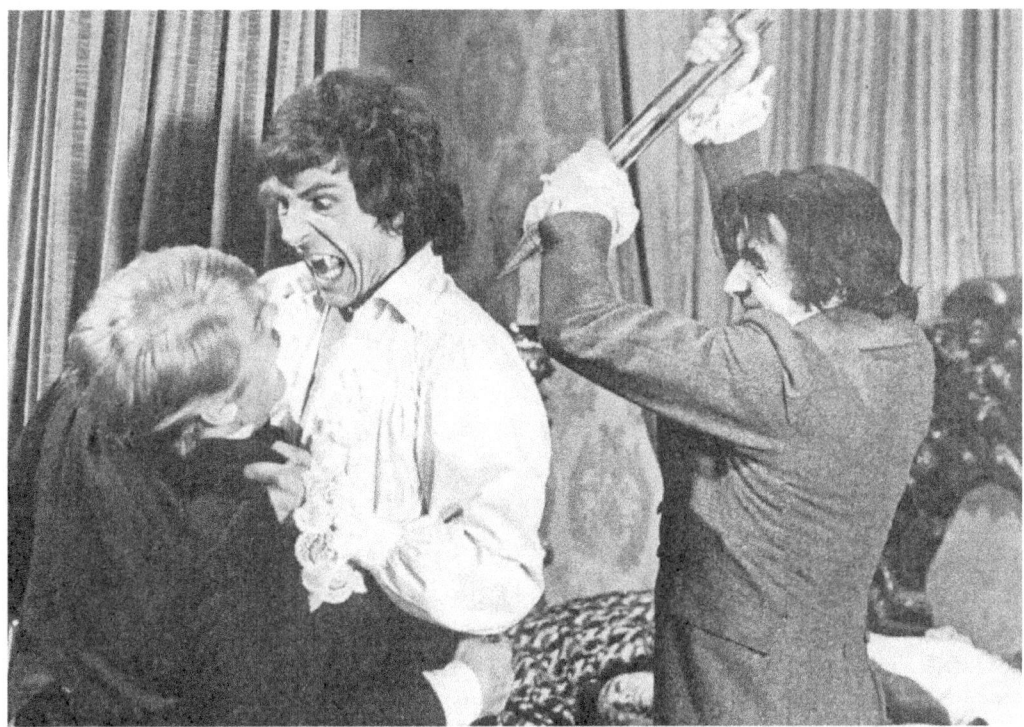

The Burgermeister (Thorley Walters, left) is attacked by the vampire Count Mitterhouse (Robert Tayman), but the schoolmaster Mueller (Laurence Payne) intervenes, in *Vampire Circus*.

meister takes aim at the panther, it transforms into Emil. The Burgermeister's heart fails and he falls dead. His daughter Rosa later follows Emil to the crypts below Castle Mitterhouse where Emil attacks and kills her. The next night, Dora Mueller (Lynne Frederick) is lured by twin acrobats Helga and Heinrich (Lalla Ward and Robin Sachs) into the "Mirrors of Life" tent. Heinrich tries to bite Dora but her crucifix saves her.

Kersh learns that Emil is a kinsman of the Count and that the troupe are responsible for all the deaths. Kersh's son Anton (John Moulder-Brown) tries to protect Dora but the vampires manage to lure him away. The two acrobats follow Dora into a church where a falling cross impales Helga. Her twin also suffers the effects and is likewise destroyed. Later, Dora is abducted by the circus strongman (Dave Prowse) and taken to the castle caves.

The village elders set fire to the circus and kill the strongman. In the caves, Emil stalks Dora, but one of the circus performers, a gypsy woman (Adrienne Corri), pushes her daughter to safety and Emil kills her instead. The villagers, headed by Mueller, Anton and Kersh, enter the crypt. Mueller is savagely injured, but the dying man manages to pull the stake from Count Mitterhouse's body and impales Emil. When the Count rises, Anton grabs a crossbow, traps the vampire's head in the weapon's bow string and fires an arrow which severs the Count's head from his body.

Although Hammer's greatest profits came from the *Dracula* pictures, some of the company's most innovative vampire concepts were in films outside the series. In *Vampire Circus*, the undead defy gravity and metamorphose into sensuous cats. There are hints of bestiality and incest, as well as characters who are human/vampire hybrids. The film began production on August 9, with Robert Young, a Hammer newcomer, as director. Young had been hired to direct *Neither the Sea nor the Sand*, but Hammer's rights expired, and Michael Carreras offered him *Vampire Circus* instead. Young was influenced by European filmmaking techniques and wanted to achieve the same effects. "They've taken horror films a stage further," he told Sue and Colin Cowie, "and I love to see the way in which the stories grow from an apparently ordinary event." During six weeks of pre-production, Young was able to give the script a more surrealistic texture than Judson Kinberg had originally included. He also insisted on real animals interacting with his cast. "I wanted to have a real bat in the film," Young told the Cowies. "I wanted to get it close to reality as opposed to cardboard cutouts." Kinberg enjoyed the creative freedom Hammer offered. "I loved the idea that if you were doing a circus horror picture you were free from all the restraints in terms of what you could do and not do." Production ended on September 21, prompting Dave Prowse to tell the authors (February, 1993), "The trouble with Hammer was that you had to get it done in six weeks, and if you hadn't finished it, you had to cut it according to what you filmed. When time ran out, there were still scenes that hadn't been shot, so Robert had to cut around the missing footage to finish it."

Vampire Circus was trade shown at the Rank Theatre on April 13, 1972, premiered at the New Victoria on April 20, and went into general release on April 30. Reviewers seemed to be confounded. *The Guardian* April 23): "Very, very weird"; *Cinema TV Today* (May 6): "The story is a jumble of bits and pieces, and suspense fails to build because it is spread too thinly over too many incidents and characters"; *The Monthly Film Bulletin* (June): "Hammer refurbishes their themes with remarkable ingenuity." In America, *Vampire Circus* was released in some areas paired with *Countess Dracula*.

Although *Vampire Circus* did add some new touches and had an energetic cast and

Hammer creates yet another variation on the legend.

director, it lacked the elegance of Hammer's best vampire movies.

Demons of the Mind

Released November 5, 1972 (U.K.); 89 minutes (U.K.); Technicolor (U.K.); 7965 feet; a Hammer–Frank Godwin Production; an MGM/EMI Release (U.K.), an International Co-Productions Release (U.S.); filmed at MGM/EMI Elstree Studios; Director: Peter Sykes; Producer: Frank Godwin; Screenplay: Christopher Wicking, based on a story by Christopher Wicking and Frank Godwin; Director of Photography: Arthur Grant; Production Design: Michael Streinger; Editor: Chris Barnes; Music: Harry Robinson; Musical Supervisor: Philip Martell; Assistant Director: Ted Morley; Continuity: Gladys Goldsmith; Sound Editor: Terry Poulton; Wardrobe: Eileen Sullivan; Makeup: Trevor Crole-Rees; Hairdresser: Maud Onslow; U.K. Certificate: X; MPAA Rating: R.

Paul Jones (Carl), Patrick Magee (Falkenberg), Yvonne Mitchell (Hilda), Robert Hardy (Zorn), Gillian Hills (Elizabeth), Michael Hordern (Priest), Kenneth J. Warren (Klaus), Shane Briant (Emil), Virginia Wetherell (Inge).

Bavaria, 1830. Elizabeth Zorn (Gillian Hills) has escaped from an institution where her father, the Baron (Robert Hardy), has placed her under Dr. Falkenberg's (Patrick Magee) care to cure the "evil in her blood." Shortly after meeting Carl (Paul Jones), she is abducted by Klaus (Kenneth Warren), her father's henchman. The Baron fears that she and her brother, Emil (Shane Briant), are cursed due to generations of inbreeding.

The village is plagued by a series of brutal murders of young girls, whose corpses are covered with rose petals. A raving priest (Michael Hordern) startles a carriage shared by Carl and Dr. Falkenberg, who are en route to Zorn's castle. When the doctor later uses his mesmeristic devices on the Baron's children, Zorn relates his family's grotesque history. Emil has an unnatural affection for his sister, and the two are kept apart. When Carl is taken to Elizabeth, she is in a coma. The Baron and Falkenberg have an obscene plan to cure Emil by procuring a prostitute (Virginia Wetherell) and disguising her as Elizabeth. Frightened by Emil, she runs off, but he kills her and showers her corpse with roses.

Falkenberg feels that Emil's actions are being willed by the Baron. After Emil escapes with Elizabeth, Zorn kills the doctor and shoots Emil. The priest impales him with a burning cross as Elizabeth and Carl watch in horror.

Demons of the Mind is not for all tastes, but it is one of Hammer's most interesting seventies' productions. It is a trip down a very different road compared to the tired Dracula sequels and low brow comedies. The characters are a bizarre lot, and it is difficult to choose the most outré, but Shane Briant, making his film debut as Emil, is high on the list. Along with Ralph Bates, Briant was being groomed to replace Peter Cushing and Christopher Lee. He began acting with the Dublin University Players in *Hamlet* in 1969, but despite his talent and odd screen personality, Briant's career never developed. Close behind Briant on anyone's tally of weird characters must be Patrick Magee, whose voice could make any line menacing. Baron Zorn, as played by Robert Hardy, is easily the sickest character to ever appear in a Hammer film.

Director Peter Sykes had lived a lifetime in his thirty-two years, having been a ballet choreographer, an opal miner, television director, and African rhino herder. He brought a kinky sense of style to *Demons of the Mind*, but his career as a director for Hammer (or anyone) never came to much. His film was part of Hammer's "second phase" of production, as described in *Today's Cinema* (August 17, 1971). This involved a £1 million package for five films to be made between summer and Christmas, including a two picture program called *Women in Fear* (*Straight On Till Morning* and *Fear in the Night*). The British film industry was in a slump, but as usual, Hammer was immune. "The major companies have to have product," Michael Carreras said, "and we are considered safe." Although its subject matter was anything but safe, *Demons of the Mind* (originally called *Blood Will Have Blood*), began production on August 16, 1971, at Elstree in association with Frank Godwin Productions. Its six week schedule called for location work in Bavaria where production designer Michael Stringer adapted a mansion built in 1770 to stand in as Castle Zorn.

Demons of the Mind was trade shown on October 7, 1972, at Metro House and released on November 13. *Cinema TV Today* (October 21, 1972) spotted the film's strength and weakness. "Although it has a number of original touches, it is likely to prove too confusingly disoriented for the average addict of the macabre." Like too many Hammer films of the seventies, it suffered from poor American distribution. Many fans are now seeing it for the first time, on video, twenty years after its release. Although *Demons of the Mind* is confusing and a bit hysterical, at least it is different; and in the copy-cat world of horror movies, that is worth something.

Dracula A.D. 1972

Released September 27, 1972 (U.K.), November, 1972 (U.S.); 95 minutes; Eastman Color, 8429 feet; a Hammer Film Production; a Columbia-Warner release (U.K.), Warner Bros. (U.S.); filmed at MGM/EMI Elstree Studios; Director: Alan Gibson; Producer: Josephine Douglas;

Dracula A.D. 1972 (1971)

Having no stakes at hand against Dracula (Christopher Lee, bottom), Van Helsing (Peter Cushing) improvises in *Dracula A.D. 1972.*

Screenplay: Don Houghton; Director of Photography: Dick Bush; Art Director: Don Mingaye; Editor: James Needs; Continuity: Doreen Dearnaley; Sound Editor: Roy Baker; Recording Director: A.W. Lumkin; Dubbing Mixer: Bill Rowe; Casting: James Liggatt; Music Composer: Michael Vickers; Music Supervisor: Philip Martell; Songs: "Alligator Man" by Sid Valentino, and "You Better Come Through" by Tim Barnes; Production Supervisor: Roy Skeggs; Production Manager: Ron Jackson; Special Effects: Les Bowie; Makeup: Jill Carpenter; Hairdresser: Barbara Ritchie; Wardrobe Supervisor: Rosemary Burrows; Assistant Director: Robert Lynn; U.K. Certificate: X; MPAA Rating: PG.

Christopher Lee (Count Dracula), Peter Cushing (Lorrimer and Lawrence Van Helsing), Stephanie Beacham (Jessica), Christopher Neame (Alucard), Michael Coles (Inspector), William Ellis (Mitchum), Marsha Hunt (Gaynor), Janet Key (Anna), Philip Miller (Bob), Michael Kitchen (Greg), David Andrews (Detective Sergeant), Caroline Munro (Laura), Lally Bowers (Matron), Stoneground (Band).

London, 1872. Van Helsing (Peter Cushing) and Count Dracula (Christopher Lee) die when a fight atop a coach ends with a violent crash. Dracula's remains are buried by a disciple (Christopher Neame) outside the small cemetery in which Van Helsing was placed.

London, 1972. Johnny Alucard (Neame), the disciple's descendant, plans to restore Dracula to life with the assistance of a group of bored teenagers. Among them is Jessica Van Helsing (Stephanie Beacham), who lives with her grandfather Lawrence (Cushing). Most are frightened off by the satanic ceremony, but Laura (Caroline Munro) stays behind and is attacked by the rejuvenated Count (Lee). Scotland Yard Inspector Murray (Michael Coles) questions Jessica, but unwisely ignores Van Helsing's warnings. Like his ancestor, Lawrence is an expert on the occult.

Dracula hides in a desanctified church, and Alucard, under his power, brings members of the group to him for his blood supply. Jessica's boyfriend Bob (Philip Miller) is now vampirized, and Dracula orders him to bring Jessica to him. Van Helsing counters by destroying Alucard. He then lures the Count into the churchyard where he hurls holy water into the vampire's face. Blinded, Dracula falls into a grave Van Helsing has lined with stakes and is reduced to dust.

Although both Peter Cushing and Christopher Lee had repeated their roles from *Dracula*, they had not done so in the same film. *Dracula A.D. 1972* was the first time in fourteen years that Van Helsing and Dracula came face to face. Unfortunately, Hammer had long since run out of ideas for Dracula films. But, since the movies made a profit, Hammer continued to plan new ones, and Lee, despite his complaints, continued to play the role.

The basic idea of updating the characters was not necessarily a bad one. Universal's *Dracula*, (1931), placed the Count in contemporary London, and no one seemed to mind. However, Hammer had established the precedent of keeping *its* Dracula in the Victorian era. The solution was to bring the Count to present day London, but to limit his activities to a Victorian church. Although Hammer deserves credit for trying something new, the concept was poorly executed and stripped Dracula of his menace, since the viewer always knows where the vampire is. Unlike a period film that never really ages, *Dracula A.D. 1972* was dated by 1973. One cannot help laughing at the over-age "teenagers" in their "hip" clothing mouthing their "groovy" dialogue.

Can a Hammer film with Peter Cushing and Christopher Lee be all bad?

Originally titled *Dracula Chelsea '72*, then *Dracula Today*, the film went into production in October, 1971. Interviewed by *Cinefantastique* (Summer, 1972), an optimistic Peter Cushing felt the public would accept the updating and feel that it "was just one of the many battles that Van Helsing and Dracula have had over many years." When asked about a sequel, Cushing candidly replied, "As long as these pictures make money I will always do them if I'm asked." Christopher Lee was having a more difficult time dealing with the role that made his career, becoming outspoken about his desire not to be typecast and of his disenchantment with the character. "I never saw the film," he admitted in *The Films of Christopher Lee*. "At first I had misgivings, but the film wasn't a bad idea." In a Warner Bros. press release he said, "It's been a considerable disadvantage to me in the past because some people think Dracula is the only role I play. People love to stick labels on you."

James Carreras commented in *Bizarre* (No. 3), "He has been saying this for years about Dracula, but he keeps on playing Dracula. If he said every time the press interviewed him, 'I love Dracula, I'm going to play Dracula forever,' the press would stop interviewing him."

Dracula A.D. 1972 went into general

release on September 27, 1972. Most reviewers were unimpressed. The *Chicago Sun Times* (December 13, 1972): "There seems to be a general decay at Hammer films"; *The New York Daily News* (November 30): "If you can't laugh at the stilted talk, you'll be bored stiff instead of scared stiff"; and *Films and Filming* (December, 1972): "Nothing new here." Genre publications seemed to be personally offended, as *Photon* 23 railed, "It is impossible to review *Dracula A.D. 1972* without making it as the definitive example of the depths of decadence to which Hammer films have fallen."

Dracula A.D. 1972 was a mistake made by a company that seemed to be losing its way. The return to slapstick comedy with *On the Buses* indicated that Hammer saw the coming demise of their type of horror film. Peter Cushing noted in a Warner Bros. press release, "You can't flood the market with this kind of picture unless it is something pretty good, because if people see two or three bad ones, they'll stop going to see them."

Hammer planned a sequel before *Dracula A.D. 1972*'s disappointing reviews and receipts came in, but found that Warner Bros. was not enthusiastic about repeating the lame results. *The Satanic Rites of Dracula*, although slightly better, would not find an American release until six years after its completion.

Straight On Till Morning

Released July 9, 1972 (U.K.); 96 minutes; Technicolor (U.K.); 8738 feet; a Hammer Film Production; an MGM/EMI Release (U.K.), an International Co-Productions Release (U.S.); filmed at MGM/EMI Studios, Elstree, England; Director: Peter Collinson; Producer: Roy Skeggs; Executive Producer: Michael Carreras; Screenplay: John Peacock; Director of Photography: Brian Probyn; Production Manager: Tom Sachs; Camera: Roy Ford; Assistant Director: Clive Reed; Continuity: Betty Harley; Sound Mixer: John Purchase; Art Director: Scott MacGregor; Editor: Alan Pattillo; Casting Director: James Liggat; Publicist: Jean Garioch; Wardrobe Supervisor: Laura Nightingale; Stills Cameraman: Ronnie Pilgrim; Hairdresser: Pearl Tipaldi; Makeup: George Blackler; Music: Roland Shaw; Musical Supervisor: Philip Martell; Song "Straight On Till Morning," Music & Sung by Annie Ross, Lyrics by John Peacock and Annie Ross; 2nd Camera: Keith Jones; Assistant Art Director: Richard Rambaut; Construction Manager: Bill Greene; Dubbing Recordist: Dennis Whitlock; Recording Director: Tony Lumkin; Sound Editor: Alan Bell; U.K. Certificate: X; MPAA Rating: R. Video Releases: *Till Dawn Do Us Part* (Neon Video), *Dressed for Death* (Academy Video).

Rita Tushingham (Brenda Thompson), Shane Briant (Peter), Tom Bell (Jimmy Lindsay), Annie Ross (Lisa), Katya Wyeth (Caroline), James Bolam (Joey), Claire Kelly (Margo), Harold Berens (Mr. Harris), Tommy Godfrey (Mr. Godfrey), Mavis Villiers (Indian Princess), Lola Willard (Customer), John Clive (Newsagent), Tinker (Dog).

Brenda (Rita Tushingham), unattractive and unloved, lives in a fantasy world of Camelot and Prince Charming. She leaves her mother for London, hoping to find a man to father her child, but is quickly swallowed up by the city. Brenda finds a job at a boutique and is befriended by the beautiful Caroline (Katya Wyeth), a co-worker, who offers her a room in her apartment. Out walking one night, Brenda scoops up a mongrel dog belonging to a handsome young man. She washes it, fits it with a pink ribbon, and returns it to Peter (Shane Briant)—her Prince. He is kind and attentive, and Brenda confesses her plot. Peter agrees to impregnate Brenda in exchange for her keeping house. She collects her belongings, leaves a note for Caroline that she has gone home, and moves in.

After settling in, she fails to notice some disconcerting aspects of Peter's life—the dog, Tinker, has vanished, and although obsessed with his own beauty, he is repelled by it in others. Brenda—now called "Wendy"—foolishly plans to attract Peter by making herself pretty, and goes to a beautician. Caroline, who has traced Brenda through Tinker's collar, arrives and allows Peter to seduce her. After turning on a tape recorder, he kills her, recording her screams. Displeased with "Wendy's" new look, he smears her makeup.

Concerned about a police search for the

women, Peter confines "Wendy" to the house. When she rebels, he plays his tapes of Caroline and Tinker, only two of his many victims. Later, Peter sits alone, listening to a tape of "Wendy" screaming.

Conceived, along with *Fear in the Night*, as a package called "Women in Fear," *Straight On Till Morning* was part of Hammer's "new direction" away from Gothic horror. The film went into production on November 1, 1971, at Elstree and concluded on December 17, with extensive location shooting in London. The pair went into release on the ABC circuit on July 9, 1972, but barely surfaced in America. The few British critics who reviewed the double feature were appalled by *Straight On Till Morning*. *Cinema TV Today* (July 15): "Singularly nasty. How Rita Tushingham could lend her considerable talent is a mystery"; and *The Monthly Film Bulletin* (August): "The film limps along like some nightmarish crossbreeding of *A Taste of Honey* and *The Penthouse*. Practically nothing in the plot can be taken seriously."

"The main character is called Peter," said scriptwriter John Peacock (EMI pressbook). "He is a man whose childhood has left a fantastic impression on him, and he is a Peter Pan insofar as he has never grown up sufficiently to cope with life." Parallels with Peter Pan are scattered throughout—Peter's dog is named "Tinker," and he hopes to one day find his "Wendy." Shane Briant had made his film debut seven months earlier in Hammer's *Demons of the Mind*, and does as well as anyone could in such a thankless role. Briant's slightly off-center good looks were perfect, but his character was given little motivation to explain his behavior.

Rita Tushingham was a catch for the company. She was a high ranking star for a decade, but was not able to do much in a role clearly subservient to Briant's. Peter Collinson, a "new breed" director who started on television, said (EMI pressbook), "I think movies should entertain. I don't set out to moralize. I just don't think I can change the world." Unfortunately, there is little entertainment in this well-made but morbidly downbeat movie, other than Shane Briant's fine acting.

A fine Shane Briant performance wasted.

Fear in the Night

Released July 9, 1972 (U.K.), limited 1972 U.S. release; 96 minutes/94 minutes/86 minutes; Technicolor; 8434 feet; a Hammer Film Production; Released through Anglo/EMI (U.K.), International Co-productions/Pisces (U.S.); filmed at MGM/EMI Elstree Studios; Director: Jimmy Sangster; Producers: Jimmy Sangster, Michael Syson; Director of Photography: Arthur Grant; Editor: Peter Weatherley; Production Manager: Christopher Neame; Music: Don McCabe; Musical Director: Philip Martell; Camera Operator: Neil Binney; Sound: Claude Hitchcock; Wardrobe: Rosemary Burrows; Production

Fear in the Night (1971)

Red herring Peter Cushing in *Fear in the Night*.

Design: Don Picton; Stills Cameraman: G. Whitear; Makeup: Bill Partleton; Production Accountant: Ken Gordon; First Assistant Director: Ted Morley; Focus Puller: R. Jordan; Clapper/Loader: R. Barron; Casting: James Liggatt; Sound Editor: Ron Hyde; Production Secretary: C. Langley; Unit Runner: P. Campbell; Draughtsman: R. Benton; Hairdresser: Helen Lennox; Set Dresser: Penny Struthers; U.K. Certificate: X; MPAA Rating: R.

Judy Geeson (Peggy Heller), Joan Collins (Molly Carmichael), Ralph Bates (Robert Heller), Peter Cushing (Michael Carmichael), Gillian Lind (Mrs. Beamish), James Cossins (Doctor), John Brown, Brian Grellis (Policemen).

Peggy (Judy Geeson) and Robert (Ralph Bates) are planning to spend their honeymoon at the boarding school where he teaches. Recently recovered from a breakdown, Peggy claims to have been attacked in her room by a one-armed man, but Robert is skeptical. When they arrive, the school is empty due to a "term break." Peggy meets Michael (Peter Cushing), the headmaster. A sophisticated middle-aged man, his artificial arm is hidden by his academic gown.

When Robert goes to London, Peggy is attacked again, but he is unwilling to call the police when he returns. Later, while walking through the woods, Peggy meets Michael's sullen wife, Molly (Joan Collins). Robert is again sent to London and leaves a shotgun with Peggy, which she uses on Michael when she sees his prosthesis. When Robert returns, Peggy is nearly catatonic and is unable to tell him what happened. Frustrated, he goes to Molly—his lover. The two have primed Peggy to kill the unwanted Michael. Robert tells her he has been Michael's nurse since a fire destroyed the school, Michael's arm, and reason.

Peggy remains silent, so the lovers plan to force the truth from her, and then fake her suicide by hanging. But—Michael is alive! Suspecting a plot, he had put blanks in the shotgun. During a scuffle, Robert accidentally kills Molly. When the police arrive, Robert's body sways from a noose and Peggy is led away.

Fear in the Night was yet another variation on Henri George Clouzot's *Diabolique* (1954), the ultimate "tricky plan to drive someone mad" movie. Although falling far short of the original, the film is no worse than *Diabolique*'s many other clones. At almost 100 minutes, though, it is too long and might have worked better as an hour-long television play—which it was originally intended to be. Michael Carreras was planning to enter the American television market, and *Fear in the Night* was to be a prototype. But, like many of Hammer's seventies plans, nothing came of this good idea.

After forsaking Gothic horror following *The Brides of Dracula*, Jimmy Sangster concentrated on *Diabolique*-like thrillers with mixed results, ranging from the teriffic (*Taste of Fear*) to the ho-hum (*Hysteria*). He took on *Fear in the Night* because of the opportunity to write, produce, and direct. "I used to think it was a bad combination," Sangster told *Cinema TV Today* (September, 1971). "Now, I think it's marvelous—you haven't got anyone to argue with except the actors! I'm the first to say I'm not writing deathless prose. If the actors want to change anything, let them, as long as it doesn't alter the story." He told the authors (August, 1993), "I'm just a regular guy. I figure if something scares me, it will scare you."

Originally titled *The Claw*, the picture began on November 15, 1971, with location work at Piggot's Manor (13 days), Aldenham Estates, Toddington Motorway Cafe, and Haberdasher's Playing Field (two days each). This accounted for one hour of script time, with the remainder filmed at Elstree

Jimmy Sangster's farewell to Hammer.

between December 6 and 17. Dick Klemensen supplied the following salary breakdown: Jimmy Sangster (£10000), Michael Carreras (£3000), Judy Geeson (£5000), Ralph Bates (£4000), Peter Cushing (£1000 for four days), and Joan Collins (£2100 for seven). The remainder of the small cast totaled £250. The total budget was £141,000, including editing the lab work (£9065), studio rental (£6908), and sets (£6400). Since the figures are over two decades old, their only value is in their relation to one another. For a dollar equivalent, multiply by 2.5.

Fear in the Night was Jimmy Sangster's last Hammer film, and his role in the company's success cannot be overstated. He wrote 23 screenplays, produced eight times, and directed three pictures. He revamped both the Frankenstein and Dracula legends, and dabbled in psycho-thrillers, costume adventure, and science fiction. Sangster's best horror writing is as good as it gets, despite his not being a fan. "I'm not really crazy about horror movies," he told the authors. "I know this sounds odd, but I *never* go to see them. Like Hammer, I got into horror by accident, and we both had a good run." Unfortunately, *Fear in the Night*, although adequate, was not one of his best.

As was too often true, Peter Cushing is much better than his material, and gives one of his creepiest performances. His scenes with Judy Geeson are genuinely unnerving. Ralph Bates was being groomed as the company's new horror star, but after gaining a following (especially in *Dr. Jekyll and Sister Hyde*), this was his last film for Hammer. His ambition was to run an old-style stock company, and he remained active in all aspects of performing until his untimely death, at age 51, in 1991.

Fear in the Night was released with *Straight On Till Morning* as a package titled "Women in Fear" on July 9, 1972, to few theatres and indifferent reviews: "An acceptably exciting second feature for uncritical audiences," (*Cinema TV Today*, July, 1972), and "The central idea has sufficient power," (*Films and Filming*, August, 1972). The film was barely released at all in America before finding its natural home on television.

1972

Mutiny on the Buses

Released July 30, 1972 (U.K.); 88 minutes; Technicolor; 7920 feet; a Hammer Film Production; an Anglo-EMI Release (U.K.); filmed at Elstree Studios, England; Director: Harry Booth; Producers, Screenplay: Ronald Wolfe, Ronald Chesney; Based on the television series; Director of Photography: Mark McDonald; Art Director: Scott MacGregor; Editor: Archie Ludski; Music: Ron Grainer; Production Supervisor: Roy Skeggs; Production Manager: Christopher Neame; Camera Operator: Neil Binney; 1st Assistant Director: Ken Baker; Continuity: Doreen Dearnaley; Sound Mixer: John Purchese; Wardrobe Mistress: Dulcie Midwinter; Makeup: Eddie Knight; Hairdresser: Ivy Emmerton; Casting Director: James Liggat; Publicist: Jean Garioch; U.K. Certificate: A.

Reg Varney (Stan Butler), Doris Hare (Mrs. Butler), Anna Karen (Olive), Michael Robbins (Arthur), Bob Grant (Jack), Stephen Lewis (Inspector Blake), Pat Ashton (Norah), Janet Mahoney (Susy), Caroline Dowdeswell (Sandra), Kevin Brennan (Mr. Jenkins).

Stan Butler (Reg Varney), bus driver and local terror, announces his engagement to Susy (Janet Mahoney). His mother (Doris Hare), her son-in-law Arthur (Michael Robbins), and her daughter Olive (Anna Karen), who sponge off Stan, are horrified. They ask Stan to postpone the wedding, but—with fellow driver Jack (Bob Grant)—contrive to get Arthur a driving position. Stan teaches Arthur to drive a bus, disrupting the company's timetable. Labor relations are made worse by the arrival of Mr. Jenkins (Kevin Brennan), a new depot manager. Somehow, Arthur gets the job, but due to a raise in his rent, Stan still cannot marry. He tries to get a transfer to a better route, and blackmails the flirting Jenkins into arranging it. Unfortunately, the route is to Windsor Safari Park, and Stan's unlocked bus attracts several lions and monkeys on a trial run. Adding to Stan's misery, Jack is transferred, and Inspector Blake (Stephen Lewis), who accompanied him on the safari run, has been demoted. He is now a conductor on Stan's bus.

Hammer celebrated its 25th anniversary in November, 1972, but the company's productions that year gave little artistically to celebrate. *On the Buses* had been a major hit the previous year, earning back seven times its cost. Hammer got the sequel going by offering £1000 for the best title in a contest run in *The Sun*. Production began on February 21, 1972, with many of the original's cast and crew returning. On the same day, the company opened its new office, Little Hammer House, at Elstree. Filming ended on April 1, and *Mutiny on the Buses* was released on the ABC circuit on July 30 with *The Cowboys*. At the Edgeware Road Cinema, the pair brought in a healthy £1868. *Cinema TV Today* (August 5) called the film "very big," but U.S. distributors showed no interest in a sequel to a film based on a British television series. Reviews were

Mutiny on the Buses poster (courtesy of Fred Humphries and Colin Cowie).

uncomplimentary, but failed to deter anyone, as *Mutiny on the Buses* earned sizable profits. Typical was *Cinema TV Today*'s (July 1): "More tightly written and plotted than its predecessor, but the jokes are too obvious, and performances too exaggerated."

Although films like this *did* earn a profit, they did little to enhance the company's reputation.

Kronos

Released 1973 (U.K.), June, 1974 (U.S.); 91 minutes; Movie Lab Color (U.S.); a Hammer Film Production; an Avco-Embassy Release (U.K.), a Paramount Release (U.S.); filmed at MGM/EMI Elstree Studios, England; Director, Producer, Screenplay: Brian Clemens; Producer: Albert Fennell; Director of Photography: Ian Wilson; Production Supervisor: Roy Skeggs; Music: Laurie Johnson; Musical Supervisor: Philip Martell; Editor: James Needs; Production Design: Robert Jones; Production Manager: Richard Dalton; Assistant Director: David Tringham; Continuity: June Randall; Casting Director: James Liggat; Fight Arranger: William Hobbs; Camera: Godfrey Godar; Makeup: Jim Evans; Hairdresser: Barbara Ritchie; Assistant Art Director: Kenneth McCallum Tart; Wardrobe Supervisor: Dulcie Midwinter; Sound Recordist: Jim Willis; Dubbing Mixer: Bill Rowe; Sound Editor: Peter Lennard; Recording Director: A.W. Lumkin; Sound System: RCA; Film Processing: Humphries Labs; Publicity: Jean Garioch; U.K. Certificate: X; MPAA Rating: R. U.S. Title: *Captain Kronos—Vampire Hunter*.

Horst Janson (Kronos), John Carson (Dr. Marcus), Shane Briant (Paul Durward), Caroline Munro (Carla), John Cater (Prof. Grost), Lois Daine (Sara Durward), Ian Hendry (Kerro), Wanda Ventham (Lady Durward), William Hobbs (Hagen), Brian Tully (George Sorell), Robert James (Pointer), Perry Soblosky (Barlow), Paul Greenwood (Giles), Lisa Collings (Vanda Sorell), John Hollis (Barman), Susanna East (Isabella Sorell), Stafford Gordon (Barton Sorell), Elizabeth Dear (Ann Sorell), Joanna Ross (Myra), Neil Seiler (Priest), Olga Anthony (Lilian), Gigi Gurpinar (Blind Girl), Peter Davidson (Big Man), Terence Sewards (Tom), Trevor Lawrence (Deke), Jacqui Cook (Barmaid), Penny Price (Prostitute).

The tiny village of Durward has seen several of its local girls mysteriously drained of youth. Dr. Marcus (John Carson) sends for his friend Captain Kronos (Horst Janson), who arrives with his hunchbacked partner, the brilliant Professor Grost (John Cater), and Carla (Caroline Munro), a young woman they befriended on their way to the village. Kronos, a professional vampire hunter, tells Marcus that vampires come in many different varieties yet all drain the life from their victims in one way or another.

Grost and Carla set to work burying toads in small caskets along the roads outside the village. According to folklore, if a vampire passes near a dead toad, the animal will return to life. The vampire hunters return later and, unearthing the boxes, find a living toad. Kronos finds a set of fresh carriage tracks nearby, and he and the others follow the trail. Marcus notices that they are near the estate of the Durward family. He excuses himself and pays Paul Durward (Shane Briant) a call, hoping to find clues.

Dr. Marcus (John Carson, left) confers with the vampire hunters (Horst Janson, with boots, and John Cater) in *Kronos*.

Both Paul and his elderly mother (Wanda Ventham) hold Marcus responsible for the death of Paul's father, Lord Hagen, during a plague years before. Later, Marcus is attacked by a mysterious hooded figure.

Marcus, now young-looking, realizes that he has been made a victim of the vampire and begs Kronos to kill him. Kronos and Professor Grost try every known method, but none is successful. In a fit of rage, Marcus lunges toward the men and then dies, the doctor's steel crucifix having been embedded in his chest during the struggle.

Kronos' investigation leads him to suspect the Durwards. Carla infiltrates the mansion and is offered lodging by Paul and his sister Sara (Lois Daine). Later that night, Carla is visited by Lady Durward. Hearing Carla's screams, Paul and Sara arrive and are astonished to see their mother no longer aged, but young and beautiful. Lady Durward explains that she was born a Karnstein—one of the infamous family of vampires. She also tells them that their father did not die of the plague, but was given a new existence as one of the undead. While Paul and Sara look on, Lord Hagen (William Hobbs) enters. It was he who preyed on the women of the village. Kronos intervenes in time to save Carla, engaging Lord Hagen in a swordfight and running him through with a steel blade. Lady Durward throws herself at Kronos and is also fatally impaled.

Having accomplished their mission, Kronos and Professor Grost depart, continuing their quest to rid the world of evil.

Kronos was a departure from Hammer's standard vampire tale, much as *The Kiss of the Vampire* had been a decade earlier. The vampires are not of the usual blood drinking variety—they drain their victims of youth. Time honored methods of vampire extermination were discarded in favor of the magical properties of steel. Gone were detection

Poor promotion ended a potentially fine series of vampire hunter adventures; note amplified American release title for *Kronos*.

by mirrors and crosses. They were replaced by the laying of dead toads in the suspected vampire's path. If the suspect *is* undead, the toads are returned to life.

The film was Brian Clemens' first as a director, and he had a definite plan. "The basic concept behind *Kronos*," he told *The Monster Times*, "is a very deep one: to liberate horror pictures." He asked to see other Hammer films to get a feel for the subject. "What I found," he said, "was that by the time I got to the third Dracula, I couldn't distinguish it from the first one." Clemens had accurately pointed out Hammer's problem—repetition—and sought to cure it. Concluding that Dracula had inadvertently been made a hero, Clemens said (*Starburst* 30), "You're rooting for a villain, even though you know he's going to end up staked through the heart. I thought it would be good to change the emphasis and have a proper hero." Looking ahead, Clemens planned using Kronos (which is Greek for time) in a series of films in which he would move through the centuries. Unfortunately, although Horst Janson looked the part, he lacked the conviction (or the talent) to be totally believable. John Cater's Professor Grost was an ideal sidekick, with his physical deformity a direct contrast to Kronos' physical perfection. The supporting actors were well-cast, especially Shane Briant in another excellently played off-beat role.

Despite the film's fresh approach, Michael Carreras was unimpressed. "The 'Clemens team' didn't have the proper expertise with this type of material," he said (*Fangoria* 63). "During the shooting, I discovered they weren't making *Kronos* with the same reverence as the experienced Hammer team. It may be totally my own failing, but I wasn't in tune with their approach." Unfortunately, Carreras—who was seeking a new look for the company—failed to see that he'd found it.

After spending three weeks preparing the script, Clemens began filming on April 10, 1972, with a £160,000 budget and a seven week schedule, wrapping on May 27. The film was distributed in the U.K. by Avco Embassy, and Paramount released it in America in October in support of *Frankenstein and the Monster from Hell*.

Kronos suffered poor distribution in both Britain and America and received few reviews, but most were vaguely positive. *Cinema TV Today* (March 25, 1974): "An ingeniously different variation." *The New York Times* (October 31): "Foolish, though elaborately produced"; and *Variety* (June 26): "Clemens keeps his plot going for 91 minutes with a sincerity which almost makes it work." The film, even with its flaws, was one of the company's most entertaining seventies productions. Janson might have grown into the part if a series had developed, but it was not to be.

That's Your Funeral

Released 1973 (U.K.); 81 minutes; Eastman Color; 7315 feet; a Hammer Film Production; a Fox-Rank Release (U.K.); filmed at Pinewood Studios, England, and on location; Director: John Robins; Producer: Michael Carreras; Screenplay: Peter Lewis, based on the television series; Director of Photography: David Holmes; Editor: Archie Ludski; Art Director: Scott MacGregor; Production Supervisor: Roy Skeggs; Production Manager: Ron Jackson; Camera Operator: Chick Antiss; 1st Assistant Director: Bill Cartlidge; Continuity: Leonora Hail; Sound Mixer: Les Hammond; Wardrobe Supervisor: Rosemary Burrows; Makeup: Eddie Knight; Hairdresser: Jeannette Freeman; Casting Director: James Liggat; Publicist: Jean Garioch; Music: David Whitaker; U.K. Certificate: A.

Bill Fraser (Basil Bulstrode), Raymond Huntley (Emanuel Holroyd), David Battley (Percy), John Ronane (Mr. Smallbody), Dennis Price (Mr. Soul), Sue Lloyd (Miss Peach), Richard Wattis (Simmonds), Roy Kinnear (Mr. Purvis), Eric Barker (Pusher), Hugh Paddick (Window Dresser), John Sharp (Mayor), Michael Ripper (Arthur), Frank Thornton (Town Clerk), Geoffrey Sumner (Lord Lieutenant), Dudley Foster (Mr. Grimthorpe), Bob Todd (Funeral Director), Peter Copley (1st Funeral Director), Michael Robbins (2nd Funeral Director), Harry Brunning (Invalid), Geraldine Burnett (Petrol Pump Attendant), Stacy Davies (Grimthorpe's Driver), Michael Knowles (Man with Car), Verne Morgan (Pensioner), Carol Catkin (Model in Window), Ken Parry (Porter), Clifford Mollison (Whiterspoon), Michael Sharvell-Martin (Policeman), John J. Carney (2nd Policeman).

After burying Mr. Grimthorpe (Dudley Foster), their longtime rival, the partners of the Holroyd Funeral Home—Emanuel (Raymond Huntley), Percy (David Battley), and Basil (Bill Fraser)—celebrate at the Undertakers' Ball. Their joy, however, is short lived when a new competitor—The Haven of Rest—fills the vacuum. Eager for business, Emanuel jumps at the chance to bury Mr. Taylor, an important official. He runs into Mr. Smallwood, the Haven's owner, at the train station when he goes to collect the body. Smallwood, actually a drug dealer, is waiting for a coffin filled with marijuana, and naturally, each takes the wrong coffin. Emanuel is now forced to "borrow" a wax effigy of Taylor for the viewing.

The two begin a grotesque battle over the coffin, and, totally confused, Percy and Basil take the wrong coffin to the crematorium. When they realize their error, they hand out the drugs to the mourners. Smallwood's gang is arrested, and the ceremony is judged to be a great success. When Mr. Purvis (Roy Kinnear), the waxworks proprietor, comes to claim his effigy for bronzing, he ends up with Mr. Taylor's corpse. The body is duly dipped and set in cement in the town square.

After spending many years terrifying audiences with corpses, Hammer decided to use one for laughs. Based on a popular television series, *That's Your Funeral* was filmed between June 12 and July 7 at Pinewood by first-time Hammer director John Robins. Not surprisingly, this "lowbrow" effort was panned by the critics after its spotty release. *Cinema TV Today* (January 19, 1974): "A minuscule plot stretched too thin to conceal its weakness. The comic capers are repetitive and predictable, and the pace slows to a crawl at the end while all the loose bits of plot are gathered up into a bundle"; and *The Monthly Film Bulletin* (July): "Another nail in the British film industry's coffin."

The film's premise *was* a bit thin, but Robins, a veteran of the *Benny Hill* series, was a perfect choice to get the most out of the script's double entendres and bad puns. The veteran cast was a plus, as was an unexpected surprise for those "in the know." Appearing under the opening credits as mourners were Robins, Roy Skeggs, and Michael Carreras, as well as members of the crew. The company's love affair with spinoffs of low life television series is hard to fathom, and Hammer would have been wise to view the title of this one as a warning.

Nearest and Dearest

Released June, 1973 (U.K.); 86 minutes; Color; 7686 feet; a Hammer Granada Production; an Anglo EMI Presentation; an MGM/EMI Release (U.K.); filmed at Elstree Studios; Director: John Robins; Producer: Michael Carreras; Associate Producer: Roy Skeggs; Screenplay: Tom Brennard, Roy Bottomley, based on the television series by Vince Powell and Harry Driver; Director of Photography: David Helms; Production Manager: Ron Jackson; Art Director: Scott MacGregor; Editor: Chris Barnes; Assistant Director: Bill Cartlidge; Sound Recordist: Les Hammond; Sound Editor: Frank Goulding; Camera Operator: Chick Antiss; Continuity: Lorley Farley; Makeup: Eddie Knight; Wardrobe Supervisor: Rosemary Burrows; Hairdresser: Jeanette Freeman; Assistant Art Director: Don Picton; Construction Manager: Arthur Banks; Dubbing Mixer: Gordon McCallum; Casting Director: James Liggatt; Music Composer: Derek Hilton; Music Supervisor: Philip Martell; Song "Nearest and Dearest" by Hylda Baker and Derek Hylton; Sung by Hylda Baker; U.K. Certificate: A.

Hylda Baker (Nellie Pledge), Jimmy Jewel (Eli Pledge), Eddie Malin (Walter), Madge Hindle (Lilly), Joe Gladwin (Stran), Norman Mitchell (Vernon), Pat Ashton (Freda), Bert Palmer (Bert), Peter Madden (Bailiff), Norman Chappell (Man on Bus), Yootha Joyce (Mrs. Rowbottom), John Barrett (Joshua Pledge), Adele Warren (Stripper), Carmel Cryan (Hostess), Sue Hammer (Scarlet O'Hara), Janie Collinge (Vinegar Vera), Donald Bisset (Vicar), Kerry Jewell (Claude), Nosher Powell (Bouncer).

Joshua Pledge (John Barrett), founder of Pledge's Purer Pickles, is dying and wants to see Eli (Jimmy Jewel), his long lost son, one final time. His daughter, Nellie (Hylda Baker), traces Eli through a newspaper ad, and he returns home just in time to see his father die—and pop out his false teeth. Eli and Nellie now own the company, but Eli would rather have received money. He decides to modernize the plant despite Nellie's objections.

When the plant closes for summer holiday, they go to a Blackpool boarding house run by the Widow Rowbottom (Yootha Joyce). She falls for Eli, who has eyes for only Freda (Pat Ashton). He plans to marry Nellie off to Vernon Smallpiece (Norman Mitchell) and have the business to himself. Vernon is shy, but urged on by Eli, makes his move. Complicating matters, Cousin Lilly (Madge Hindle) and her husband, Walter (Eddie Malin), soon arrive.

When the holiday ends, the plant reopens, and Vernon pops the question to the sadly ignorant Nellie, who is coached in "the facts of life" by Eli. When "The Day" arrives, the pickle people assemble as Eli walks Nellie down the aisle. Vernon is still undecided, but has his mind made up when he is arrested for his many unpaid bills.

Nearest and Dearest was yet another example of Michael Carreras' attempt to remake Hammer. Although the company continued to make horror movies, it was relying more and more on comedies. A new type of advertising began to appear in the British trade papers, casting Hammer as a producer of "fun films" rather than trading off its Frankenstein/Dracula image. Like so many Hammer films before it, *Nearest and Dearest* had its beginning on television.

The film went into production on July 2, 1972, on a four week schedule, produced by Michael Carreras—only his fifth in this capacity in the seventies. The production was ignored by the trade papers, who were perhaps tired of the company's television spinoffs. It is difficult to understand Hammer's direction at this time. Although the comedies made money, they were unreleasable in America, and the once profitable horror movies were dying at the box office. Despite Carreras' intentions, Hammer had *not* gone upscale. Instead of being associated with horror, the image of the company was now of a "low-life" producer of comedies.

Following an April 26, 1973, trade show at Metro House, *Nearest and Dearest* was released in June on the ABC circuit to indifferent reviews like *Cinema TV Today*'s (April 28, 1973): "Should prove popular whenever traditional variety shows are produced. Love it or loathe it." A sequel, *Nearer and Dearer*, was planned, but like many seventies projects, it was cancelled along with a soccer comedy, *Just for Kicks*. A filmed-in-Australia thriller, *A Gathering of Vultures*, suffered the same fate.

Sadly, some projects that were cancelled seem more interesting than those actually filmed, as Hammer was laughing its way out of business.

Frankenstein and the Monster from Hell

Released May, 1974 (U.K.), October, 1974 (U.S.); 99 minutes (U.K.), 93 minutes (U.S.); Technicolor; 8921 feet; a Hammer Film Production; an Avco Embassy Release (U.K.), a Paramount Release (U.S.); filmed at MGM/EMI Elstree Studios, England; Director: Terence Fisher; Producer: Roy Skeggs; Screenplay: John Elder; Music: James Bernard; Music Supervisor: Philip Martell; Violin Soloist: Hugh Bean; Director of Photography: Brian Probyn, BSC; Art Director: Scott MacGregor; Editor: James Needs; Sound Recordist: Les Hammond; Production Manager: Christopher Neame; Camera: Chick Antiss; Makeup: Eddie Knight; Continuity: Kay Rawlings: Wardrobe Supervisor: Dulcie Midwinter; Hairdresser: Maud Onslow; Assistant Director: Derek Whitehurst; Sound Editor: Roy Hyde; Dubbing Mixer: Maurice Askew; Construction Manager: Arthur Banks; Casting Director: James Liggat; Assistant Art Director: Don Picton; Processed by: Studio Film Labs. Ltd.; Sound Recording: RCA; U.K. Certificate: X; MPAA Rating: R.

Peter Cushing (Baron Frankenstein), Shane Briant (Dr. Simon Helder), Madeline Smith (Sarah), David Prowse (The Monster), John Stratton (Asylum Director), Michael Ward (Transvest), Elsie Wagstaff (Wild One), Norman Mitchell (Sergeant), Clifford Mollison (Judge), Patrick Troughton (Body Snatcher), Philip Voss (Ernst), Chris Cunningham (Hans), Charles Lloyd Pack (Prof. Durendel), Lucy Griffiths (Old Hag), Bernard Lee (Tarmut), Sydney Bromley (Muller), Andrea Lawrence (Brassy Girl), Jerold Wells (Landlord), Sheila Dunion (Gerda), Mischa De La Motte (Twitch), Norman Atkyns (Smiler), Victor Woolf (Letch), Peter Madden (Coach Driver), Janet Hargreaves (Chatter), Winfred Sobine (Mouse), Tony Harris (Inmate).

Dr. Simon Helder (Shane Briant) is arrested for accepting delivery of a stolen corpse and sentenced to the Carlsbad Asylum. An admirer of Baron Frankenstein, Helder is looking forward to meeting his mentor there. However, when he tricks his way into the asylum director's (John Stratton) office, the supervisor informs him that although the Baron was a former "resident," he is now dead.

Two brutal warders drag Helder off and are hosing him down with a high-pressure water hose when the asylum director, Dr. Victor (Peter Cushing), appears. Helder recognizes him as the Baron. "Victor" orders that Helder be brought to his clinic where his mute assistant, Sarah (Madeline Smith), tends his wounds. Frankenstein offers Helder a position as his assistant.

Frankenstein later introduces Helder to his "special" patients Tarmut (Bernard Lee), a sculptor, and Durendel (Charles Lloyd Pack), a former mathematics professor. That night, Helder witnesses the burial of Tarmut and notices that the inmate's hands are missing.

Helder finds Frankenstein's secret lab where an incredible creature (David Prowse) is confined in a cage. More Neolithic than human, the creature is eyeless and has the hands of Tarmut. Frankenstein discovers Helder in his lab and explains that the creature was once an inmate who was committed for slashing people with broken glass. When the inmate attempted to commit suicide, Frankenstein kept him alive as a framework for a new creation, and has replaced his hands in hopes of eliminating his murderous traits.

After Durendel hangs himself, Frankenstein and Helder transplant his brain into the body of the creature. But Helder's mounting suspicions concerning his mentor's sanity are confirmed when the Baron confides his plan to mate Sarah with the monster. When the Baron leaves the asylum to purchase equipment, the creature escapes and kills the director. Surrounded by screaming inmates, the creature panics. Sarah, shocked back into speech, rushes to protect it but the inmates, fearing that the creature will harm her, attack the monster and tear it to pieces.

When the Baron returns, he quiets the patients and returns to his lab. While Helder stares in disbelief, Frankenstein says that he now knows where he went wrong and is ready to begin once again.

Frankenstein and the Monster from Hell ended a great deal of Hammer history. It was the last of Peter Cushing's six appearances as the Baron and was the last Hammer film for both director Terence Fisher and

Top: Terence Fisher smiles as Peter Cushing and Shane Briant look on (photo courtesy of Ted Okuda).
Bottom: The Baron has sinister plans for his assistant, Sarah (Madeline Smith) and his creature (Dave Prowse) in *Frankenstein and the Monster from Hell* (photo courtesy of Ted Okuda).

writer Anthony (John Elder) Hinds. Although far from the best, it was an appropriate end to the sixteen-year-old series. The picture began production on September 18, 1972, and wrapped up on October 27. Back for a second—and much better—outing as the monster was 6'7" Dave Prowse, hidden under a Neolithic mask and hairy body suit designed by Eddie Knight and Les Bowie. Prowse painted a grim picture for the *ABC Film Review*. "I could only wear the costume for short periods. It was warm and thirsty work. The costume got terribly hot after a time working under all those studio lights, and, for part of the day, I couldn't see where I was going as the mask covered my eyes."

Fisher was opposed to this excessive makeup, and told interviewer Sam Irvin, "I disagreed with them from the start and tried my best to limit the makeup. However, they had sold Paramount on the idea that the monster would be this grotesque hairy beast, so I could not make him human, but I reduced him as far as I could without ruining what they had sold it on." Prowse thought highly of his director and told the authors (February, 1993), "Terry was a wonderful person to work with—sort of the doyen of the horror film. He was really a wonderful guy and gave me a lot of help and direction—unlike many who give you nothing at all except to have you just get on with it. This film probably gave me more satisfaction than any other I've done—including *Star Wars* (1977). For example, Peter and I did a stunt; when we were finished, everyone on the set just stood up and applauded. It was the first time I'd ever seen anything like that! It was just great!" Fisher's ability to install sympathy for his Frankenstein monsters is one of his enduring qualities as a director. "It is really a very sad story," he said (Hammer press release). "He is a sad, pathetic creature."

Frankenstein and the Monster from Hell is the most symbolic in the series. The Baron has found refuge in the only place that truly fits him—a mental institution—for he is now truly insane. Gone is his goal to create "the perfect man," as Prowse's monster

Peter Cushing and Terence Fisher's farewell to the Frankenstein series.

obviously illustrates. Each of the patients who "contribute" to its creation embodies a facet of Frankenstein's own character: the delusion of being God, a brilliant intellect, the refusal to give up, and the ability to compensate for a physical infirmity. As in *The Revenge of Frankenstein*, the Baron again uses his patients for body parts, but this time there is no hint of concern for the afflicted.

The picture was released on May 12, 1974, in the U.K., following premier engagements at the Astoria and the New Victoria, during which it took £1774 and £1308 in the first week. These modest figures reflected the public's waning interest in the characters, and it was, apparently, time to put the series to rest. Critics were, however, split. *The*

London Times (May 5, 1974): "Efficiently horrible"; *The Daily Express* (May 3): "Dr. Helder should learn a trade"; *Cinema TV Today* (May 11): "Peter Cushing's Baron throws a cloak of elegance over the gruesome malarkey"; *Variety* (June 26): "An economy of filmmaking that is missed in more ambitious efforts"; and *The New York Times* (October 31): "Chock full of the old horror film values we don't see much of anymore."

Although the film has an open ending, there was really nowhere for the series to go. Unlike the Dracula series, Frankenstein went out with a bit of dignity. The series was never updated, and if one discounts *Horror of Frankenstein* (which really *wasn't* a series entry), the Frankenstein pictures were all quality productions. The Hammer Frankenstein series went out as it came in, led by Peter Cushing's typically fine performance and Terence Fisher's sound direction.

The Satanic Rites of Dracula

Released January 13, 1974 (U.K.), November, 1978 (U.S.); 87 minutes; Color; 7830 feet; a Hammer Film Production; a Columbia–Warner Bros. Release (U.K.), Dynamite Entertainment (U.S.); filmed at MGM/EMI Elstree Studios; Director: Alan Gibson; Producer: Roy Skeggs; Associate Producer: Don Houghton; Screenplay: Don Houghton; Director of Photography: Brian Probyn; Camera Operator: Chick Antiss; Music: John Cacavas; Assistant Director: Derek Whitehurst; Continuity: Elizabeth Wilcox; Sound Mixer: Claude Hitchcock; Art Director: Lionel Couch; Wardrobe Supervisor: Rebecca Breed; Makeup: George Blackler; Hairdresser: Maud Onslow; Casting: James Liggat; Stills Cameraman: Ronnie Pilgrim; Editor: Chris Barnes; Production Secretary: Sally Pardo; Dubbing Mixer: Dennis Whitlock; Production Manager: Ron Jackson; Music Supervisor: Philip Martell; Special Effects: Les Bowie; U.S. Title: *Count Dracula and His Vampire Bride*; U.K. Certificate: X; MPAA Rating: R.

Christopher Lee (Count Dracula), Peter Cushing (Van Helsing), William Franklyn (Torrence), Michael Coles (Inspector Murray), Joanna Lumley (Jessica), Freddie Jones (Prof. Keeley), Barbara Yu Ling (Chin Yang), Valerie Ost (Jane), Richard Vernon (Col. Mathews), Maurice O'Connell (Hanson), Patrick Barr (Lord Carradine), Lockwood West (Gen. Freeborne), Peter Adair (Doctor), Richard Mathews (Porter), Maggie Fitzgerald, Mia Martin, Finnula O'Shannon, Pauline Peart (Vampires), Marc Zuber (Mod C), Graham Reese (Guard), Ian Dewar (Guard), and John Harvey, Paul Weston.

London, 1972. A secret branch of British Intelligence has five important officials under surveillance at Pelham House. The agent assigned to the case has gone mad, raving of Black Magic. Inspector Murray (Michael Coles) calls on Professor Van Helsing (Peter Cushing) for help. Murray and Jessica (Joanna Lumley), Van Helsing's granddaughter, unwisely go to Pelham House and are taken prisoner. Van Helsing later recognizes an old friend—Professor Keeley (Freddie Jones)—in a surveillance photo. When he encounters Keeley, the man is raving, and confesses that he has been forced to develop a new strain of plague—with no antidote.

Van Helsing learns that the project is being funded by D.D. Denham, a reclusive billionaire never seen in daylight. After Keeley is murdered before his eyes, Van Helsing discovers that Denham is actually Count Dracula (Christopher Lee). Bored with his immortality, Dracula plans to destroy all life on earth, ending his blood supply. But first, to avenge himself against the Van Helsings, he plans to take Jessica as his "bride." Taken to Pelham House by Dracula, Van Helsing finds that the officials are all under the Count's power. When Porter (Richard Mathews) accidently drops a phial of the bacillus, Murray escapes in the confusion and sets the house ablaze, destroying the virus. After Murray frees Jessica, they are pursued into the forest by Dracula who dies when he becomes entangled in a hawthorn bush.

Compared to Hammer's original *Dracula*, Lee's final appearance as the Count was a disgrace, and one can easily sympathize with his decision not to play the part again. Dracula had simply been done to death. The updating idea had failed, and that was that. No series character can go on forever, and Dracula had a long run; but the race was over before *The Satanic Rites of Dracula* got to the

Trapped in a hawthorn bush, Count Dracula (Christopher Lee) awaits his inevitable demise in *The Satanic Rites of Dracula*.

starting line. "Every Dracula film beginning with *Has Risen*," said Don Glut (*Monsters of the Movies* 2), "has not really been the Count's story. Hammer's writers design a tale about some secondary characters, then search their brains for some way in which to insert Dracula." Lee told Glut, "I'm doing this one under protest. I don't think people appreciate it either, because people who go to see a character like this go to see him seriously." Hammer also seemed to be rudderless, announcing *fifteen* upcoming productions, *none* of which was made.

The Satanic Rites of Dracula began filming on November 13, 1972, with location work in and around London. The working title—*Dracula Is Dead and Well and Living in London* was kept, incredibly, throughout the editing stage—as late as February 17, 1973. By this time, Lee had become disenchanted with horror movies in general. He told *Cinema TV Today*, "I have no desire to make any more horror films that are not good ones." He clearly indicated the one just completed. Lee was not alone in his lack of enthusiasm for the film. After its completion on January 3, 1973, *The Satanic Rites of Dracula* could not find a distributor. A few years earlier, a Hammer Dracula with Peter Cushing and Christopher Lee would have had distributors standing in line. But, as Ron Borst pointed out (*Photon* 21), "These days of blind faith and confidence seem to be quickly disappearing." A few things had happened since the picture was planned. *Dracula A.D. 1972* had been a disappointment, and *The Exorcist* (1973) took the horror movie into another dimension. Suddenly, a new Dracula movie did not look like much.

The film finally opened at the London Rialto on January 13, 1974, earning a decent £4211 the first week. But as word of mouth spread the bad news, the tickets stopped selling, reaching a low point of £847 at the Columbia Warner. The scheduled spring opening in America was dropped, as was one planned for Halloween. The film eventually surfaced as *Count Dracula and His Vampire Bride* in 1978, released through Dynamite. Critics were not amused. *Cinema TV Today* (January 26, 1974): "A hodgepodge of incidents and bare-breasted girl vampires"; *The Sunday Times* (January 20): "It offers no great novelty"; *The Los Angeles Times* (November 24, 1978): "Routine Hammer horror fare"; and *Variety* (November 24): "Silly and dull."

This was a sad way to end both Christopher Lee's Dracula performances and his Hammer association with Peter Cushing, who found this one beyond even *his* powers to save.

1973

Love Thy Neighbor

Released August 26, 1973 (U.K.); 85 minutes; Technicolor; 7612 feet; a Hammer Film Production; an EMI-MGM Release (U.K.); filmed at Elstree Studios, England; Director: John Robins; Producer: Roy Skeggs; Screenplay: Vince Powell, Harry Driver, based on the television series; Director of Photography: Moray Grant; Art Director: Lionel Couch; Editor: James Needs; Music Composed by: Albert Elms; Production Manager: Ron Jackson; Musical Supervisor: Philip Martell; Assistant Director: Ken Baker; Sound Recordist: Claude Hitchcock; Sound Editor: Roy Hyde; Camera Operator: Chick Antiss; Continuity: Sally Ball; Makeup: George Blackler; Wardrobe Supervisor: Laura Nightingale; Hairdresser: Maud Onslow; Assistant Art Director: Don Picton; Construction Manager: Ken Softley; Dubbing Mixer: Dennis Whitlock; Casting Director: James Liggat; Publicity: Jean Garioch; U.K. Certificate: A.

Jack Smethurst (Eddie Booth), Rudolph Walker (Bill), Nina Baden-Semper (Barbie), Kate Williams (Joan Booth), Bill Fraser (Mr. Granger), Charles Hyatt (Joe), Keith Marsh (Jacko), Patricia Hayes (Annie), Arthur English (Carter), Tommy Godfrey (Arthur), Melvyn Hayes (Terry), Azad Ali (Winston), Clifford Mollison (Registrar), Lincoln Webb (Charlie), Andrea Lawrence (Norma), Norman Chappell (Indian Conductor), Dan Jackson (Black Groom), Anna Dawson (Betty), John Binden (White Groom), Lesley Goldie (White Bride), Bill Pertwee (Postman), George Tovey (Airport Porter), Berry Cornish (Airport Clerk), Pamela Cundell (Dolly), Annie Leake (Lil), Patrick Durkin (Van Driver), Horace James (Colored Driver), Damaris Hayman (Woman on Bus), George Roderick (Man at Bus Stop), Nosher Powell (Bus Driver), Isobel Hurll (Clippie), Princess Tamara (Susie), Siobhan Quinlan (Carol), James Beck (Cyril), Michael Sharvell-Martin (Police Constable), Kubi Chaza (1st Black Girl), Venicia Day (2nd Black Girl), Corinne Skinner (Black Bride), Fred Griffiths (Taxi Driver).

Eddie (Jack Smethurst) and Joan (Kate Williams) Booth live in a neat rowhouse next to Jamaicans Bill (Rudolph Walker) and Barbie (Nina Baden-Semper) Reynolds. Eddie, an avowed racist, constantly abuses the affable Bill, but their wives are close friends. The boys' private war extends to their jobs at a local factory, where Bill refuses to pay his union dues. Eddie organizes the white members to strike, and Bill retaliates by forming a new, all-black union. Eddie is pushed to new limits when his mother, Annie (Patricia Hayes), becomes friendly with Bill's father, Joe (Charles Hyatt), a recent arrival from Trinidad. They fail to return after a night of sightseeing, and phone the next morning to say they are at the Registry Office. Eddie and Bill fear that their parents are getting married and, finally united, rush to the Office. In their relief that their parents were only attending a friend's wedding, they temporarily reconcile their differences.

Joan and Barbie have won a cruise in a contest—"Love Thy Neighbor"—sponsored by a local newspaper, and the foursome go off together. Aboard ship, Joan runs into her brother Cyril (James Beck) who has married Carol (Siobhan Quinlan)—Barbie's sister. Eddie is dumbstruck that he and Bill are now related!

In 1972, *Love Thy Neighbor* was Britain's fifth rated television series with over 8 million viewers. Hammer's 1973 schedule reflected the country's interest in comedy and growing disenchantment with horror—only *Legend of the Seven Golden Vampires* with a proposed fall start looked like a "real" Hammer picture. "The situation comedy type of television spin-off seemed just about right at the time," said Michael Carreras (*Little Shoppe of Horrors*, 4). "Even if the film wasn't what could be considered a masterpiece, it took in a fortune at the box office. Hammer is a commercial operation, and therefore, you have got to follow a successful formula with other films that are likely to repeat that success." With that thought in mind, *Love Thy Neighbor* began production on January 1, 1973, with most of the television cast repeating their roles. As did *Till Death Do Us Part* (the basis for *All in the Family*), the storyline jabbed at serious racial and political issues under the guise of low brow humor. *Love Thy Neighbor* wrapped on February 2, and was trade shown at Metro House on July 4. The picture was an immediate hit following its August 26 release on the ABC circuit. It placed fifteenth on *Cinema TV Today*'s list of Box Office Winners, despite being trashed by the magazine's reviewer (July 21): "Perhaps I should have found it funnier without the gimmickry of the opening title which shows a black man attacking his white neighbor's front door with an axe, and another chucking a brick through a window." *The Monthly Film Bulletin* (August) found the picture "asinine and charmless." Recently unable to produce worthwhile films, Michael Carreras began plans to diversify Hammer's interests with television movies, books, a memorabilia museum, and even a restaurant chain! One of the few projects to be completed was *Hammer Presents: Dracula*, a long playing record narrated by Christopher Lee backed by James Bernard's music.

Man at the Top

Released September 16, 1973 (U.K.), November 10, 1973 (U.S.); 87 minutes; Technicolor, CinemaScope; 7836 feet; a Hammer/Dufton Production; Released through MGM/EMI; Director: Mike Vardy; Producers: Peter Charlesworth, Jack Jacobsen; Executive Producer: Roy Skeggs; Production Supervisor: Roy Skeggs; Screenplay: Hugh Whitemore, based on characters created by John Braine; Additional Material: John Junkin; Director of Photography: Brian Probyn; Editor: Chris Barnes; Art Director: Don Picton; Music: Roy Budd; Musical Supervisor: Philip Martell; Sound Editor: Terry Poulton; Sound Recordist: Claude Hitchcock; Production Manager: Ron Jackson; Assistant Director: Ken Baker; Camera Operator: Chic Antiss; Continuity: Sally Ball; Makeup: George Blackler; Wardrobe: Laura Nightingale; Hairdresser: Elaine Bowerbank; Construction Manager: Arthur Banks; Casting Director: James Liggat; U.K. Certificate: X.

Kenneth Haigh (Joe Lampton), Nanette Newman (Alex), Harry Andrews (Lord Ackerman), John Quentin (Digby), Mary Maude (Robin), Danny Sewell (Weston), Paul Williamson (Tarrant), Margaret Heald (Eileen), Angela Bruce (Joyce), Charlie Williams (George), Anne Cunningham (Mrs. Harvey), William Lucas (Marshall), John Collin (Wisbech), Norma West (Sarah Tarrant), Tim Brinton (Newsmaker), Clive Swift (Massey), Jaron Yalton (Taranath), John Conten (Black Boxer), Patrick McCann (White Boxer), Nell Brennan (Waitress).

Lord Ackerman (Harry Andrews), head of a large drug company, hires the aggressive Joe Lampton (Kenneth Haigh), who promptly seduces his boss's wife (Nanette Newman) at a house party. Lampton's predecessor Taranath (Jaron Yalton) has committed suicide over the company's failure to test a new drug properly. A hasty meeting is called, but Lampton is not invited. Undaunted, he gathers all of Taranath's files and arrives at Ackerman's estate, confronting the executives with his knowledge. The next day, during a hunt, Lampton has sex with Robin (Mary Maude), Ackerman's daughter, who rides off afterwards on Joe's horse.

While slogging through the underbrush, Lampton realizes he is being followed. Surrounded by the Ackerman family, Joe's employer threatens him into keeping silent. Lampton later calls Wisbech (John Collin), a sleazy journalist, and maneuvers Ackerman into buying their silence with high paying jobs. When Massey (Clive Swift), Joe's successor, criticizes his amorality, Lampton smiles.

Part of the "angry young man" syndrome, Joe Lampton made his debut (played by Laurence Harvey) in *Room at the Top*

(1959). Critics were enthralled by the film's frankness and all-around quality, and bestowed upon it many awards, including the British Film Academy's Movie of the Year. A lesser but still interesting sequel followed in 1965, in which Joe discovers that *Life at the Top* is not all he had hoped for. Naturally, a British television series followed.

By 1973, Hammer was in sad shape artistically, and Michael Carreras was looking for new directions. *Man at the Top*, to be based on the successful series, seemed to be an answer, both artistically and commercially since it had a huge built-in audience. The series was also involved in a controversy. Jackie Davis, the producer, was pilloried by angry female viewers for "having created a classic example of the male chauvinist pig." Davis did not care much for Joe herself, telling *Cinema TV Today* (November 17, 1973), "Joe Lampton's awful, but that was the character I was given, and it was no good trying to change it." The series had problems with the censor, too. "It's a matter of how far you can go," she said. "The writers and Kenneth Haigh would want to go as far as they felt they could get away with." A film version seemed like a natural for Hammer.

Man at the Top, with series star Haigh, went into production at Elstree on March 3, 1973, and ended on April 7. It was rushed into a Metro House trade show on August 21. Hammer had every reason to believe the film would be a hit, since the series peaked at number 2, and was seen in 7 million homes. With the series star, Technicolor, and CinemaScope, how could the movie go wrong? Following its September 16 release on the ABC circuit, *Man at the Top* started well, taking £2847 at the Edgeware Road in the following week. At the ABC New Street, it did £3246. Unfortunately, the film lacked "legs" and sank to the bottom. Part of the problem (other than enduring Joe for 87 minutes) was that the series was on television for free. Perhaps Hammer's timing was wrong. Another problem was that many of the company's early seventies films had little appeal for American audiences. Almost ten years had passed since *Life at the Top*, and the series did not run on American television, so Joe Lampton had no "name" value.

Reviewers were unimpressed. *Cinema TV Today* (September 1, 1973): "Soup made from boiled bones and turnip tops for the disgruntled poor"; and *Variety* (November 28): "No blockbuster, but professionally crafted."

Man at the Top plays very much like a television program, which may have been the main problem. Although watchable, it does little to remind one of the film that started it all in 1959.

Holiday on the Buses

Released December 26, 1973 (U.K.); 85 minutes; Technicolor; 7650 feet; a Hammer Film Production; an MGM/EMI Release; filmed at Elstree Studios; Director: Bryan Izzard; Producers: Ronald Wolfe, Ronald Chesney; Screenplay: Ronald Wolfe, based on the London Weekend television series; Director of Photography: Brian Probyn; Editor: James Needs; Art Director: Don Picton; Production Supervisor: Roy Skeggs; Production Manager: Ron Jackson; Music: Denis King; Musical Supervisor: Philip Martell; Choreography: Malcolm Clare; Sound Editor: Roy Hyde; Sound Recordist: Claude Hitchcock; Assistant Director: Ken Baker; U.K. Certificate: A.

Reg Varney (Stan), Stephen Lewis (Inspector Blake), Doris Hare (Mrs. Butler), Michael Robbins (Arthur), Anna Karen (Olive), Bob Grant (Jack), Wilfred Brambell (Bert), Kate Williams (Joan), Arthur Mullard (Wally), Queenie Watts (Lil Briggs), Henry McGee (Mr. Coombs), Adam Rhodes (Little Arthur), Michael Sheard (Depot Manager), Hal Dyer (Mrs. Coombs), Franco Derosa (Luigi), Gigi Gatti (Marla), Eunice Black (Mrs. Hudson), Maureen Sweeney (Mavis), Sandra Bryant (Sandra), Carolae Donoghue (Doreen), Tara Lynn (Joyce), Alex Munro (Patient).

After an accident at the station, Stan (Reg Varney), Inspector Blake (Stephen Lewis), and Jack (Bob Grant) are dismissed. Stan and Jack find work at a Welsh holiday camp where Blake is employed as head of security. Stan invites Mum (Doris Hare), Arthur (Michael Robbins), and Little Arthur (Adam Rhodes) for a holiday. While Stan works on Mavis (Maureen Sweeney),

Jack steals Blake's girl Joan (Kate Williams). While supposedly baby-sitting Little Arthur, Stan is attracted to Sandra (Sandra Bryant), and the child spray paints the camp chalet.

Stan and Jack quickly "redecorate," but it is for nothing when Arthur accidentally blows up the camp sewer system. After equally destroying the camp dance, the family leaves. Out for revenge, Blake gets Stan in trouble with tough guy Luigi (Franco Derosa), but succeeds only in getting himself fired. The boys themselves are soon fired for driving the camp bus into the sea. At the employment office, they find Blake in charge.

By 1973, Hammer looked more like a television network than a film company, with five of eight pictures based on television shows. *Holiday on the Buses* was the last of three *On the Buses* spin-offs, and beginning with that 1971 release, Hammer produced seven comedies and eleven horror movies.

The company was never committed to filming anything but what audiences wanted, and in the early seventies, they obviously wanted to laugh. *Holiday on the Buses* began production on May 10, 1973, with a five week schedule. The film was trade shown on November 28 at Metro House, and was released on the ABC circuit on December 26.

Carried over from the first two films were the stars and the critics' upturned noses. *Cinema TV Today* (December 8): "Much as before"; and *The Monthly Bulletin* (December): "Dire third spinoff. The cast emit dirty sniggers every time a piece of skirt comes into view." But films like this are beyond criticism; every cheap shot taken by the critics is true, but who cares? Despite the repetition of crude jokes (or because of them), *Holiday on the Buses* packed U.K. cinemas in a way that the contemporary Hammer horrors found to be elusive. But, like too many of the company's seventies films, it had no American release.

One must question Hammer's judgment in shutting off the huge U.S. market, since only five more films lay in the company's future.

The Legend of the Seven Golden Vampires

Released October 6, 1974 (U.K.), 110 minutes, cut to 89 minutes (U.K.), 83 minutes (U.S.); Color; Panavision; a Hammer-Shaw Production; filmed in Hong Kong; a Columbia-Warner Bros. Release (U.K.); Dynamite Entertainment (U.S.); Director: Roy Ward Baker; Producers: Don Houghton, Vee King Shaw; Screenplay: Don Houghton; Directors of Photography: John Wilcox, Roy Ford; Editor: Chris Barnes; Assistant Editor: Larry Richardson; Camera Operator: Roy Ford; Sound Recordist: Les Hammond; Continuity: Renee Glynn; Production Secretary: Jean Walter; Boom Operator: Tommy Staples; Assistant to the Producer: Christopher Carreras; Production Manager: Chau Lam; Art Director: Johnson Tsau; Makeup: Wu Hsu Ching; Costumes: Lui Chi-Yu; Music: James Bernard; Musical Supervisor: Philip Martell; Sound Editor: Frank Golding; Production Manager: Chua Lam; Assistant Director: Erh Feng; Hairdresser: Peng Yeh Lien; Props Master: Li Wu; Floor Manager: Peng Chang; U.S. title: *The Seven Brothers Meet Dracula*; Presented by Michael Carreras and Run Run Shaw; U.K. Certificate: X; MPAA Rating: R.

Peter Cushing (Van Helsing), David Chiang (Hsi Ching), Julie Ege (Vanessa Beren), Robin Stewart (Leyland), Shih Szu (Mai Kwei), John Forbes-Robinson (Dracula), Robert Hanna (British Council), Chan Sen (Kah), James Ma (Hsi Ta), Lui Chia Yung (Hsi Kwei), Feng Ko An (Hsi Sung), Chen Tein Loong (Hsi San), Wong Han Chan (Leung Hon).

Transylvania, 1804. Count Dracula (John Forbes-Robinson) takes on the form of Kah (Chan Sen), an Oriental disciple of the occult. A century later, Professor Van Helsing (Peter Cushing) lectures a group of Chinese students on the Seven Golden Vampires of Ping Kuei village. Only Hsi Ching (David Chiang) shows any interest and offers to guide Van Helsing and his son, Leyland (Robin Stewart), to the village and free it from the curse. They are joined by Vanessa Beren (Julie Ege), a wealthy young widow, and Hsi Ching's sister, Mai Kwei (Shih Szu), who, like her brother, is adept at the martial arts.

On the journey to Ping Kuei, the party is attacked—first by an unwanted suitor of

Vanessa's, then by the vampires. Vanessa's blood is taken by one of the horde, and she is destroyed by her lover, Hsi Ching, who then commits suicide. Mai Kwei is carried off to a derelict temple by the vampires, pursued by the Van Helsings. They destroy the Golden Vampires (so named due to their grotesque golden masks), but one monster remains— Dracula, who has been guiding the attacks. After the Count assumes his true form, he and Van Helsing begin a battle-to-the-death, won by the Professor when he impales Dracula with a lance.

"The best review I've read in years," said Michael Carreras (*The Horror People*), "was in *Melody Maker* magazine. I mean, the guy tore it to shreds. He put his finger on everything absolutely rightly, and then at the end he says, 'Don't let me indicate that I'm trying to put you off seeing this film, because I'm going to see it again tomorrow!'" The film in question was *The Legend of the Seven Golden Vampires*, and it *is* easily torn to shreds. It is a poorly made picture, not even a standout as Hammer was winding down, but it is not without interest. The film has the novelty, of course, of being a martial-arts horror movie, it has Peter Cushing, and it has James Bernard's final score for Hammer.

James Bernard's contributions to Hammer have been, perhaps, under-appreciated. While he was not as important to the company's success as Terence Fisher, Jimmy Sangster, or Christopher Lee, he is not far behind. If you think of your half-dozen favorite Hammer films, Bernard probably scored three or four of them. He also made more than a few mediocre pictures—like this one—more watchable (listenable?). The composer shared his thoughts on Hammer— and music—with the authors (July, 1993).

A film (retitled *The 7 Brothers Meet Dracula* for its U.S. release) only marginally better than its advertising.

I started improvising nonsense at the piano from about the age of six, and fortunately, my two boarding schools encouraged one's musical interests—especially Wellington College, from which I departed to go straight into the Air Force. On my mother's side, I have a distinguished musical ancestor, Dr. Thomas Arne (1710–1778), who, amongst other things, wrote theatrical incidental music, as well as *Rule Britannia*.

After leaving the Air Force, Bernard joined the BBC, composing mostly for radio. Through his friend and screenwriter, Paul Dehn, he met others in the industry, and Bernard soon began doing television—and films. He continued,

I was not familiar with Hammer films before *The Quatermass Xperiment*. It was to have been scored by John Hotchkiss, who was taken ill. Anthony Hinds needed a quick replacement, and John Hollingsworth, with whom I was friendly, suggested me—beginning a long association for us all. I'm very glad that they found my music original. There are bound to be many influences at work, but I think that any originality is simply a gift, unconscious and coming from within. I'm so glad when people don't find me repetitious. Of course, with Dracula, I have been purposely repetitious, but I have consciously tried to avoid unintended repetitions—not always successfully! I think, perhaps, my "sound" comes from my somewhat idiosyncratic harmonic style. I always found textbook harmony quite a struggle, not something that came naturally. Big budget movies often use entire established orchestras, but Hammer—with their smaller budgets—picked and chose according to what was required for each film. Hence, no credit for particular orchestras.

A film's musical director is in charge of all the music for the film, whether it is specially composed or music already written. It is his responsibility to plan it (naturally, with the composer, the editor, and director, if he's interested), to arrange the orchestra, organize the copying of parts, and to conduct the orchestra and see that the music all fits. Some composers like to conduct their own scores—but I simply *cannot* conduct, and in any case, I think it's important for the composer to be in the control room with the recording engineer to try to make sure that the balance is correct and that the music fits exactly as intended. Incidentally, for each section of music, the relevant section of film is projected on a large screen behind the orchestra with the timings superimposed—so everyone (except, of course, the players) can see how things are fitting. I also put timings on my scores all the way through, particularly marking for the conductor, all important synchronization points ("Cut from Lucy, restless in bed, to C/U of Dracula at the window").

Visiting the set during production is not much use musically, but it can be helpful to see some rough cuts—just to start to get the feel of the film, and perhaps some musical ideas. The really important moment is the music breakdown session. This is when one sits in a little viewing theatre with the music director, editor, assistant editor, and the film director and producer (if they are interested), and watches the final cut of the film reel-by-reel, stopping after each reel to discuss and plan exactly where the music is needed, where it should start and stop. One foot of film takes two-thirds of a second so everything can be worked out mathematically. One most important thing is to know when dialogue starts and stops. During dialogue, if there has to be music, I like to keep it slow-moving, sometimes static, and at a different pitch from the timbre of the voices. The main thing about Hammer was, I think, the sort of cozy, unassuming family atmosphere they created, using the same teams over and over. Perhaps one could say they were the "Merchant-Ivory" of Gothic horror in those days. Michael Balcon's comedy team was another such entity—in the right place at the right time. My personal regret is that the composer comes too late onto the scene and I never get to know the Hammer actors as well as I would have liked.

Just when it seemed that Christopher Lee would *never* turn down a Dracula role, he did it at the right time. The role is poorly conceived and is acted even more poorly by "would-be Lee" John Forbes-Robinson. Peter Cushing, however, plays Van Helsing with the same suave surety he exhibited in the original *Dracula*. Fortunately, he is in almost every scene. Filming began in Hong Kong on October 22, 1973, and the picture premiered at London's Warner Rendezvous on August 29, 1974. It went into general release on October 6, doing fantastic business in both the U.K. and the Far East. Unfortunately, after a sneak preview at the *Famous Monsters of Filmland* Convention in New York in November, 1975 (attended by Peter Cushing and Michael Carreras), the film failed to find an American distributor. It re-surfaced—as *The Seven Brothers Meet Dracula* in 1979—minus seventeen minutes.

Critics were restrained in their praise. *Cinema TV Today* (August 31, 1974): "It is a pity that this blend of two popular genres could not have been more carefully thought out"; *The Sunday Times* (August 25): "It would be tedious if it were not for the distinguished presence of Peter Cushing." Director Roy Ward Baker kept things moving, but not much more, helping to make *The Legend of the Seven Golden Vampires* a sad way to end one of the great horror series.

Shatter

Released 1974 (U.K.), January, 1976 (U.S.); 90 minutes; Color; a Hammer–Shaw Brothers Production; an Avco Embassy Release; filmed in Hong Kong; Director: Michael Carreras;

Shatter (1973) 373

Top: Chinese martial arts superstar Ti Lung fights off thugs in *Shatter*. *Bottom:* Shatter (Stuart Whitman, right) wants a cool $1 million from Leber (Anton Diffring) in exchange for his list of drug processing labs in *Shatter*.

Shatter (1973)

Producers: Michael Carreras, Vee King Shaw; Screenplay: Don Houghton; Directors of Photography: Brian Probyn, BSC, John Wilcox, BSC, Roy Ford; Sound: Les Hammond; Continuity: Renee Glynn; Production Manager: Chua Lam; Production Secretary: Jean Walter; Art Director: Johnson Tsau; Dubbing Editor: Dennis Whitlock; Assistant to Producer: Christopher Carreras; Music: David Lindup; Editor: Eric Boyd-Perkins; Special Effects: Les Bowie; Assistant Director: Geoffrey Ho; Title in U.S.: *Call Him Mr. Shatter*; U.K. Certificate: A; MPAA Rating: R.

Stuart Whitman (Shatter), Ti Lung (Tai Phah), Lily Li (Mai Mee), Peter Cushing (Rattwood), Anton Diffring (Leber), Yemi Ajibade (M'Goya), Liu Ka Yong, Huang Pei Chi (Bodyguards), Liu Ya Ying (Leber's Girl), Lo Wei (Howe), James Ma (Thai Boxer), Chiang Han (Korean Boxer), Kao Husing (Japanese Boxer).

Shatter (Stuart Whitman), an international "hit" man, murders Badawain President M'Goya (Yemi Ajibade), steals his document case, and flies to Hong Kong to collect his fee. After an attempt on Shatter's life, he learns from British agent Rattwood (Peter Cushing) that the U.S. government did not order the "hit" as he had believed. When Shatter refuses to leave Hong Kong, Rattwood has him brutally beaten. Shatter is nursed back to health by Tai Phah (Ti Lung), a martial arts instructor, and Mai Mee (Lily Li), who becomes his lover. He hires Tai Phah as his bodyguard and, after a confrontation with Rattwood, learns that the Badawai are governed by Leber's (Anton Diffring) drug syndicate. M'Goya was "hit" so that Leber could replace him with his more cooperative twin, Dabula (Yemi Ajibade). Shatter is now a marked man because of the drug information in the document case, but he refuses Rattwood's offer of $25,000. Instead, he sets up a deal with Leber, but the exchange—for $1 million—is botched and Mai Mee is killed.

Outraged, Shatter traces Leber to a Macao casino and, with Tai Phah, confronts the kingpin. After being overpowered, Shatter is told he will be taken to Badawai—minus his vocal cords—to stand trial for M'Goya's murder. In an ensuing fight, Leber and Dabula are killed. Shatter gives the document case to Rattwood and glares disdainfully at his "reward."

For a company that started so many trends, Hammer, surprisingly, came to the martial arts after the craze was over. Kung Fu superstar Bruce Lee's death in 1973 halted the popular genre after the market had been flooded for several years with martial arts pictures. *Shatter* was the second—and last—co-production between Hammer and the Hong Kong–based Shaw Brothers, and their combined expertise might have produced a hit a year earlier.

Roger Corman protégé Monte Hellman began directing *Shatter* on location on December 17, 1973, but left the film "by mutual agreement" after several weeks. He was replaced by the always game Michael Carreras who did a creditable job, given the circumstances. The production returned to Elstree on June 15, 1974, for editing with Hammer thinking it had a major hit on its hands. Carreras was planning a television series to star Stuart Whitman and Peter Cushing, but that was quashed when Avco Embassy failed to put the picture into release. The picture opened very quietly in America in January, 1976, and then quickly vanished as it had done earlier in Britain. *Variety* (January 9, 1976) was one of the few to review the picture, calling it a "thrown together mishmash. Pic is dull and sloppy."

Technically, *Shatter* was a mess, with shoddy camerawork, sets, and dubbing. Don Houghton's script presented a worn-out theme that offered no surprises, and Ti Lung's lack of screen presence ruled him out as a Bruce Lee successor. Stuart Whitman gives a good performance as Shatter, but the character is hardly one that the audience can identify with. It is nice to have Peter Cushing and Anton Diffring along for the ride, but neither has much to do. Some of the action scenes are thrilling, but not enough of them to balance *Shatter*'s many deficiencies.

It is truly unfortunate that such an indifferent movie was Peter Cushing's last one for Hammer.

1974
Man About the House

Released: December 22, 1974 (U.K.); 90 minutes; Color; 8139 feet; a Hammer Film Production; an EMI Release (U.K.); filmed at Elstree Studios; Director: John Robins; Producer: Roy Skeggs; Screenplay: Johnnie Mortimer, Brian Cooke; Music Composed by: Christopher Gunning; Title Song: "Man About the House," Music: Christopher Gunning, Lyrics: Annie Farrow; Director of Photography: Jimmy Allen, B.S.C.; Editor: Archie Ludski, G.B.F.E.; Art Director: Don Picton; Assistant Director: Derek Whitehurst; Sound Editor: Roy Hyde; Makeup Supervisor: Eddie Knight; Hairdressing Supervisor: Betty Sherriff; Production Manager: Dennis Hall; Camera: Chick Antiss; Continuity: Renee Glynn; Sound: Claude Hitchcock; Wardrobe: Laura Nightingale; Stills Photographer: Albert Clarke; U.K. Certificate: A.

Richard O'Sullivan (Robin Tripp), Paula Wilcox (Chrissy), Sally Thronsett (Jo), Brian Murphy (Mr. Roper), Yootha Joyce (Mrs. Roper), Doug Fisher (Larry Simmonds), Peter Cellier (Morris Pluthero), Patrick Newell (Sir Edmund Weir), Aimi McDonald (Hazel Lovett), Jack Smethurst (Himself), Rudolph Walker (Himself), Spike Milligan (Himself), Melvyn Hayes (Nigel), Michael Ward (Mr. Gideon), Bill Grundy (Interviewer), Berry Cornish (P.A.), Norman Mitchell (Doorman), Michael Robbins (Second Doorman), Johnnie Briggs (Milkman), Bill Pertwee (Postman), Bill Sawyer (Chauffeur), Aubrey Morris (Lecturer), Arthur Lowe (Spiros), Andria Lawrence (Miss Bird), Julian Orchard (Producer), Damaris Hayman (Old Lady), Robert Dorning (Colonel Manners), Mark Rogers (Boy Scout), Bill Maynard (Chef), Pauline Pearl (Secretary), Arthur Hewlett (Elderly Man), Annie Leake (Tweedy Lady), Corinne Skinner (Housewife).

Robin Tripp (Richard O'Sullivan) shares an apartment with two young women, Chrissy (Paula Wilcox) and Jo (Sally Thronsett). The threesome get along well, except when Robin's hormones get the best of him.

Their landlords, the Ropers (Brian Murphy, Yootha Joyce), are friendly enough, especially Mrs. Roper, who spends more time in Robin's apartment than in her own. When the Ropers learn that Mr. Pluthero (Peter Cellier), a real estate developer, wants to buy their building, Mrs. Roper refuses and the roommates circulate a petition to protest the entire development. Sir Edmund (Patrick Newell), a member of Parliament, is interested in the petition because he keeps his mistress, Miss Bird (Aimi McDonald), in the building.

Pluthero learns of Sir Edmund's indiscretion and blackmails the MP into pushing the sale, but the company head is afraid of negative publicity. He orders Pluthero to make a conciliatory television appearance explaining the sale has been cancelled due to the company's commitment to the environment. But Mr. Roper, who *wants* to sell, is unaware of the policy change. When Mrs. Roper and the tenants discover his duplicity, they storm the television station. After the dust settles, all concerned realize that their building is safe.

Man About the House was the last Hammer film to be adapted from a television series. This early seventies trend resulted in a group of cheaply made films that nevertheless generated a very creditable amount of business.

The basic concept of *Man About the House* was adapted for American television as *Three's Company*, and thereupon became an even bigger hit than its cross-the-Atlantic cousin.

Hammer's version began production in March, 1974, under the direction of sitcom conversion specialist John Robins with most of the series' cast members. Filming ended on April 12, and *Man About the House* was released on December 22, 1974, on the ABC circuit. During the film's first week at the ABC Edgewater, it took £2,000, and by January 11, 1975, the total of the London releases netted almost £90,000. *Cinema TV Today* (December 7, 1974) found that the film "provides acceptable excuses for a profusion of set piece comedy scenes that are always amusing and sometimes exceedingly funny."

Like Hammer's other comedies of the early seventies, *Man About the House* had no American release. This was unfortunate, since the television show *Three's Company* became a huge success in which Hammer was unable to participate.

To the Devil ... A Daughter (1975)

Two big stars could not save this feeble Dennis Wheatley adaptation.

1975

To the Devil ... A Daughter

Released March 4, 1976 (U.K.), July, 1976 (U.S.); 92 minutes; Technicolor; a Hammer-Terra-Anglo Production; an EMI Release (U.K.), a Cine Artists Release (U.S.); filmed at MGM/EMI Studios, Elstree, England, and on location in Berlin and West Germany; Director: Peter Sykes; Producer: Roy Skeggs; Screenplay: Chris Wicking, based on the novel by Dennis Wheatley; Adaptation by: John Peacock; Director of Photography: David Watkin; Camera: Ron Robson; Continuity: Sally Jones; Production Manager: Ron Jackson; Production Assistant: Jean Clarkson; Assistant Director: Barry Langley; 2nd Assistant Director: Mike Higgins; 3rd Assistant Director: Roy Stevens; Art Director: Don Picton; Special Effects: Les Bowie; Hairdresser: Jeannette Freeman; Makeup: Eric Allwright, George Blackler; Music: Paul Glass; Musical Supervisor: Philip Martell; Sound Recordist: Dennis Whitlock; Costumes: Laura Nightingale; Wardrobe: Eddie Boyce; Editor: John Trumper; Casting: Irene Lamb; Stills Photographer: Ray Hearne; Publicity: Mike Russell; Sound Editor: Mike Le Mare, G.B.F.C.; Recording Director: Tony Lumkin; Dubbing Mixer: Bill Rowe; Construction Manager: Wag Hammerton; Gaffer: Ted Hallows; Production Accountant: Ken Gordon; U.K. Certificate: X; MPAA Rating: R.

Richard Widmark (John Verney), Christopher Lee (Father Michael), Nastassja Kinski (Catherine), Honor Blackman (Anna Fountain), Michael Goodliffe (George), Denholm Elliott (Henry Beddows), Eva Marie Meinke (Eveline de Grasse), Anthony Valentine (David), Petra Peters (Sister Helle), Derek Francis (The Bishop), Isabella Telezynska (Margaret), Constantin de Guguel (Kolde), Anna Bentinck (Isabel), Frances de la Tour (Salvation Army Major), Irene Prador (German Matron), Brian Wilde (Attendant), William Rideoutt (Porter at Airport), Howard Goorney (Critic), Zoe Hendry (First Girl), Mindy Benson (Second Girl), Jo Peters (Third Girl), Bobby Sparrow (Fourth Girl).

Excommunicated priest "Father" Michael (Christopher Lee) engineers his godchild Catherine's (Nastassja Kinski) return from Bavaria to England to celebrate her eighteenth birthday on All-Hallows Eve. In London, occult expert John Verney (Richard Widmark) is begged by her father, Henry Beddows (Denholm Elliott), to free her from a satanic cult. After her arrival, Verney takes Catherine to his apartment where she has a horrific dream about the birth of a demonic child. Verney asks his friends Anna (Honor Blackman) and David (Anthony Valentine) to help protect her. Michael, with Eveline (Eva Marie Meinke) and George de Grasse (Michael Goodliffe), principals of Catherine's Bavarian "convent," establish an occult contact with her. Verney learns from the Bishop (Derek Francis) that twenty years ago, Michael attempted to bring the demon Astaroth into the world through a human host, and had been excommunicated. He plans to do so again, using Catherine.

Under Michael's influence, Catherine kills Anna and escapes from the apartment. After confronting Beddows, Verney and David go to an abandoned church where they find the symbol of the demon—a necklace that incinerates David. Beddows tells Verney that Catherine is to be baptized in the blood of Astaroth's demon child, which

Christopher Lee and Nastassja Kinski star in Hammer's final horror film, *To the Devil ... A Daughter* (photo courtesy of Tim Murphy).

will transform her into the devil himself. Verney challenges Michael in the abandoned cemetery, and turns Astaroth's power against him, saving both himself and Catherine.

To the Devil ... A Daughter, Hammer's last horror, was too little, too late. By the time this film of Dennis Wheatley's novel was released in the spring of 1976, blockbusters like *The Exorcist* (1973) and *The Omen* (1976), covering similar territory, had claimed the market. Instead of being on the leading edge, Hammer was uncharacteristically cashing in. Since Hammer had had the rights to Wheatley's book since February, 1964, the company could have beaten them all. However, when Anthony Nelson-Keys left Hammer and, with Christopher Lee, formed Charlemagne Productions, they took with them the rights to *To the Devil ... A Daughter*.

After failing to get backing, Lee and Keys went back to Hammer. "The script at that time," said Peter Sykes (*Bizarre*), "was by Brian Hayles. Hammer was going to make it as a co-production with Charlemagne. When it came time for Charlemagne to produce some money, they couldn't, and Charlemagne went out of business. Lee and Keys sold the rights to Hammer, but they had Lee on contract to star in the film."

Roy Skeggs' production was scheduled for June, 1974, then postponed to January, 1975, and finally began on September 3. Peter Sykes was not impressed with the Hayles script and called in Chris Wicking. The film was to be released in Britain by EMI, who arranged for co-financing through Terra Filmkunst, a German company. The deal hinged on Hammer's casting a German in a leading role. Meanwhile, problems continued with the script, centering on its unsatisfying climax.

The search for an American actor for the lead added to Hammer's problems, with Richard Chamberlain, Kris Kristofferson, Cliff Robertson, and Richard Dreyfuss suggested. Finally, Richard Widmark, who had just completed *Murder on the Orient Express*, was signed. Nastassja Kinski satisfied the German backers' requirement on the pivotal female role. The teenagers' nude scenes gave the film some much needed publicity, but added little to it.

During the film's eight week schedule, location work was done in the Rhineland and the Dashwood Mausoleum. *To the Devil ... A Daughter* went into general release on the ABC circuit on March 4, 1976. American International had shown some interest in the picture, but Cine/Artists picked it up for a limited U.S. release in July. Reviewers in both Britain and America were unimpressed. *The Financial Times* (March 5, 1976): "The film spends a mountain of time constructing its molehill of a plot"; *The Evening Standard* (March 4): "It reduces Dennis Wheatley's Satanist novel to an obsession with gynecological deliveries, bloodstained wombs, and sacrificed babies"; *The Daily Express* (March 5): "If we are going to have horror films, they should at least be constructed with some sense of logic within their own terms"; *Films and Filming* (April): "About as artistic as picking one's nose in public"; and *Variety* (March 10): "Lack lustre occult melodrama." Other than Denholm Elliott's performance, the film has little to recommend it. Hammer's last horror was a sad affair, and a clear indication that the company had lost its way.

1978

The Lady Vanishes

Released May 9, 1979 (U.K.), limited U.S. release; 97 minutes; Eastman Color; Panavision; 8730 feet; a Hammer Film Production; a Rank Release (U.K.), Group One (U.S.); filmed at Pinewood Studios; Director: Anthony Page; Producer: Tom Sachs; Executive Producers: Michael Carreras, Arlene Williams, Alex Winitsky; Screenplay: George Axelrod, based on the novel *The Wheel Spins* by Ethel Lina White; Director of Photography: Douglas Slocombe; Editor: Russell Lloyd; Music: Richard Hartley; Musical Director: Philip Martell; Production Design: Wilfred Shingleton; Art Directors: Bill Alexander, George Von Kierseritzky; Costume Design: Emma Porteous; Production Managers: Nicholas Gillott, Albert Schwinges; Location Managers: Dusty Symonds, Christian Jungbluth; Assistant Directors: Michael Dryhurst, Michael Mertineit; Camera Operators: Chic Waterson, John Harris; Sound Mixer: Peter Handford; Dubbing Editor: Alfrex Cox; Dubbing Mixer: Ken Barker; Background Process: Don Hansard; Special Effects: Martin Gutteridge; Wardrobe: Jackie Cummins; Makeup: Neville Smallwood; Hairdresser: Stephanie Kaye; Casting: Allan Foenander, Irene Lamb; Continuity: Kay Rawlings; Production Accountant: Duncan Stewart; Construction Manager: Tony Graysmark; Electrician: Bert Bosher; Theme Song: Les Reed; Lyrics: Peter Callander; Unit Publicist: Chris Nixon; Stills Cameraman: Keith Hamshere; Railroad Facilities: Austrian Federal; U.K. Certificate: A.

Elliott Gould (Robert Condon), Cybill Shepherd (Amanda Kelly), Angela Lansbury (Miss Froy), Herbert Lom (Dr. Hartz), Arthur Lowe (Charters), Ian Carmichael (Caldicott), Gerald Harper (Mr. Todhunter), Jean Anderson (Baroness Kisling), Jenny Runacke (Mrs. Todhunter), Vladek Sheybel (Trainmaster), Madlena Nedeva (Jenny), Wolf Kahler (Helmut), Madge Ryan (Miss Rose Flood-Porter), Rosalind Knight (Evelyn), Jonathan Hackett (Waiter), Barbara Markham (Frau Kummer).

Charters (Arthur Lowe) and Caldicott (Ian Carmichael), two Britons abroad, complain about the cancellation of their train out of Germany due to Nazi military maneuvers. Also inconvenienced are Miss Froy (Angela Lansbury), Robert Condon (Elliott Gould), Dr. Hartz (Herbert Lom), and a wild American heiress, Amanda Kelly (Cybill Shepherd). She angers the Nazis with a crude imitation of Hitler and is fortunate not to be arrested. As the train finally leaves, it is boarded by Gestapo agents. Miss Froy and Amanda share a compartment and a brief conversation. When Amanda awakens after a nap, Miss Froy is gone—and no one can recall even seeing her in the first place. Only Robert shows any inclination to believe that Miss Froy was ever on the train.

As Amanda and Robert search the train, it makes an unscheduled stop so that Dr. Hartz can take on board an accident victim in heavy bandages and a nun, Sister Jenny (Madlena Nedeva), who is caring for her. Robert drifts in and out of belief, but is finally convinced that something is wrong when he and Amanda notice that Sister Jenny is wearing high heels. They confront Dr. Hartz with their suspicion that Miss Froy is now hidden under the bandages—switched with the "accident victim." Sister Jenny—actually Mrs. Hartz—tires of the plot and frees Miss Froy, who is in possession of a coded message that is harmful to the Nazis, given to her by her German employer who opposes Hitler. After a shoot-out with the Gestapo, Miss Froy escapes and finds her way to London where she is joined by Amanda and Robert, the message safely in the hands of British Intelligence and her mission completed.

Alfred Hitchcock's 1938 version was one of his most popular comedy-thrillers, and its success led him to Hollywood. The picture was set to be directed by Roy William Neill (who found fame with the Basil Rathbone *Sherlock Holmes* series), but Hitchcock replaced him and became a superstar. The original film's reputation indicates the direction Michael Carreras had planned for Hammer when he chose to refilm Ethel L. White's novel. It took Carreras almost three years to put the package together, first planning it as a film for American television. This fell through, and Rank—who held the remake rights—lost interest, so Carreras went to Columbia for financing. Columbia withdrew and Rank, finally, agreed to 100 percent backing.

Anthony Page was hired six weeks before filming began and was, understandably, concerned about comparisons with Alfred Hitchcock. "We're not competing with Hitchcock," he said (*Screen International*, December 9, 1978), "but with people's memories of the film." Michael Carreras was quick to point out that the picture was "not a remake, but a remold."

The Lady Vanishes began location shooting in Klangentort, Austria, on December 11, 1978, with a £2 million budget. On board were slumping American stars Elliott Gould and Cybill Shepherd, well supported by Angela Lansbury and Herbert Lom, making his first Hammer appearance since *The Phantom of the Opera*. After a month in Austria, the production moved to Pinewood and location work in London, finishing on December 7. A "World Charity Premiere" was held on May 5, 1979, to aid Birthright and the Voluntary Research Fund, followed by a party at the Royal Lancaster Hotel. *The Lady Vanishes* then opened on May 9 at the Leicester Square Odeon to generally good reviews: *The New Statesman* (May 11): "A pretty skillful, appealing, and courageous job"; *The Observer* (May 13): "An amiable entertainment"; *The Daily Mirror* (May 12): "Even if you know the plot you will be entertained and intrigued"; *The Guardian* (May 12): "A faster pace than Hitchcock"; *The Sun* (May 12): "Good, rollicking stuff"; and *News of the World* (May 12): "A delightful film."

Although the film passed the "Hitchcock comparison test" with many critics, it left audiences cold and was barely released in America. Despite excellent production quality and beautiful location photography, the lack of chemistry between the leads (plus their poor performances) sinks the picture. The seventies also had a surfeit of similar—and better—movies like *Murder on the Orient Express* (1974) and Rank's own remake of *The 39 Steps* (1978). The failure of *The Lady Vanishes* ended not only Hammer's production but Hammer itself, and it remains the company's last feature film. Even though Michael Carreras was unable to save his company, his final picture was a sincerely made one.

SHORT SUBJECTS

In the early days of film production, short subjects were, along with cartoons and newsreels, an important part of "going to the movies." The company produced over seventy-five of these featurettes from 1935 to 1961 in both black and white and in color. A variety of subjects were covered, including musicals, instructionals, travelogues, and even fiction. Some of the following entries are covered at length because of their subject matter or participants. This listing may be incomplete.

1935 *Polly's Two Fathers* (DIR: George Mozart)
1936 *Musical Merrytone No. 1* (DIR: Will Hammer)
1945 *Old Father Thames* (DIR: Hal Wilson, Ben R. Hart)
        The Peke Speaks
1946 *Pekes Sold a Pop*
        Bred to Stay (DIR: A.A. Housset)
        Candy's Calendar (DIR: Horace Shepherd)
        Cornish Holiday (DIR: Horace Shepherd)
        Crime Reporter (DIR: Ben R. Hart)
        An Englishman's Home (DIR: John Miller)
        It's a Dog's Life (DIR: Eric Leslie)
        Perchance to Sail (DIR: J. Blake Dalrymple)

Hammer's scenic cruise through the war-ravaged countries of Eastern Europe.

        Skiffy Goes to Sea (DIR: Harry May)
        Tiny Wings
        We Do Believe in Ghosts (DIR: Walter West)
1947 *Birthplace of Fame*
        Life Is Nothing Without Music (DIR: Horace Shepherd)

Material Evidence (DIR: Darrell Catling)
Paddy's Milestone (DIR: J. Blake Dalrymple)
What the Stars Foretell (DIR: Tommy Tomlinson)

1948 *The End of the Bridge* (DIR: Richard Fisher)
Highland Story
Emerald Isle
Tale of a City (DIR: Richard Fisher)

1950 *Queer Fish*
Monkey Manners

1951 *Village of Bray*

1952 *Call of the Land* (DIR: Richard Fisher/Color)
Giselle (DIR: Henry Caldwell)
Made for Laughs (Extracts from silent comedies)
River Ships (DIR: Peter Bryan)

1953 *A Day in the Country* (Filmed in 3-D)
Between Two Frontiers
Cathedral City
Sky Traders (DIR: Peter Bryan)
Valley of Peace
The World's Smallest Country

1954 *Denis Compton*
Holiday on Skis
The Mirror and Markheim (DIR: John Lamont)
Polo

1955 *Archery*
A Body Like Mine
Cyril Stapleton and the Show Band (DIR: Michael Carreras/Color/Scope)
Dick Turpin—Highwayman (DIR: David Paltenghi)
Eric Winstone's Stagecoach (DIR: Michael Carreras/Color/Scope)
Just for You (DIR: Michael Carreras/Color/Scope)
A Man on the Beach (DIR: Joseph Losey/Color)
Parade of the Bands (DIR: Michael Carreras/Color)
The Right Person (DIR: Peter Coles/Color/Scope)
Setting the Pace

1956 *Belles on Her Toes*
Copenhagen (DIR: Michael Carreras/Color/Scope)
History Repeats Itself
The Magic Carpet (DIR: Patrick Young)
Pleasure Hunt (DIR: Patrick Young/Color)

1957 *Danger List* (DIR: Leslie Arliss)
Dangerous Drugs
Sunshine Holiday
Yoga and You
Keeping Fit with Yoga
Yoga and the Average Man

An import and two Hammer shorts.

Italian Holiday
Seven Wonders of the World
Day of Grace (DIR: Francis Searle)
The Edmundo Ros Half-Hour (DIR: Michael Carreras/Color/Scope)
Enchanted Island
Man with a Dog (DIR: Leslie Arliss)

1958 *Blue Highway* (DIR: Patrick Young)
Cathay Pacific (DIR: Patrick Young)
Clean Sweep (DIR: Maclean Rogers)
Riviera Express (DIR: Patrick Young)

1959 *Ticket to Happiness*

Operation Universe (DIR: Peter Bryan/Color/Scope)
1961 O Hara's Holiday (DIR: Peter Bryan/ Color)
Highway Holiday
Land of the Leprechauns
Modern Ireland
National Sporting Club

Polly's Two Fathers (1935)

Released January, 1936 (U.K.); 23 minutes; 2200 feet; B & W; a W.H. Films Production; an Exclusive Film Release (U.K.); Director/Screenplay: George Mozart; Producer: Will Hammer.

George Mozart (Jack), Will Hammer (Bill), Apri Vivian (Polly), Pat Aherne (Fred), Ian Wilson (Lord Stockridge).

Jack (George Mozart) and Bill (Will Hammer) are two down on their luck fishermen. About to be evicted, they are saved by Polly through her meager savings. She also saves Lord Stockridge (Ian Wilson) from drowning and is amply rewarded by his parents.

Polly's Two Fathers was trade shown at the Gaumont Theater on January 10, 1936. *Today's Cinema* (January 13) felt that it "provides an adequate background to the stagy treatment."

Crime Reporter (1946)

35 minutes; 3243 feet; B & W; a Knightsbridge-Hammer Production; an Exclusive Release (U.K.); Director: Ben R. Hart; Producer: Hal Wilson; Screenplay: James Corbett.

John Blythe (Reporter), George Dewhurst (Inspector), Stan Paskin (Taxi Driver), Jackie Brent (Girl), Van Boolen (Crook), Agnes Brantford (Landlady).

A "sincerely made" Hammer short.

A reporter (John Blythe) investigates the murder of a taxi driver and brings a gang of black-marketeers to justice.

The story was based on an actual incident that happened in the early 1940s. *Crime Reporter* was previewed with *Skiffy Goes to Sea* on January 23. *The Kinematograph Weekly* (January 24) found the picture "unpretentious, but by no means unexciting"; and *Today's Cinema* (January 24) felt it had a "sincerity of purpose and clarity in design that emphasized the story values."

We Do Believe in Ghosts (1946)

36 minutes; 3205 feet; B & W; a W.W. British–Exclusive Film Production; an Exclusive Release (U.K.); Director, Producer: Walter West.

John Latham (Gray), Arthur Dibbs (Henry VIII), Valerie Carlish (Anne Boleyn). With: Stephen Philpott, G.W. Shelton.

This short was comprised of a trio of ghost stories followed by a discussion on their possible existence. It was filmed entirely on location at Hampton Court, Woodcraft Manor, and the Tower of London. A trade show was held at the Hammer Theater on March 6, 1947, and *Today's Cinema* (March 11) found it to be a "crude recitation of three historic ghost stories. Poor direction, wooden portrayals, fair photography."

Material Evidence (1947)

35 minutes; B & W; 3100 feet.; a G.B. Instructional–Exclusive Film Production; an Exclusive Release (U.K.); Director: Darrell Catling.

Ingrid Forrest, Constance Smith, Gordon McLeod.

Two dress designers (Ingrid Forrest, Constance Smith) vie for fame and fortune in the clothing business, but after finding success, abandon their careers for marriage.

Material Evidence was trade shown in January, 1948, and *The Kinematograph Weekly* (April 8) found it "A documentary with a story, it'll easily blend with most programs."

Tale of a City (1948)

36 minutes; 3306 feet; B & W; an Exclusive Film Production; an Exclusive Release (U.K.); Director, Screenplay: Richard Fisher.

Joyce Cummings (Irene Benentt), Michael Hawley (John Boulton).

In Birmingham, a reporter (Irene Bennett) saves a bus conductor (John Boulton) from crooks. *The Kinematograph Weekly* (December 23, 1948) called it "A silly crime story, badly acted and indifferently directed."

The Mirror and Markheim (1954)

25 minutes; 2512 feet; a Motley–Exclusive Film Production; an Exclusive Release (U.K.); Director, Screenplay: John Lamont; Producer: Norman Williams.

Phillip Saville (Markheim), Arthur Lowe (Arthur Henry), Ruth Sheil (Maid), Lloyd Lamble (Kelly), Christopher Lee (Visitant), Marius Goring (Narrator).

Markheim (Phillip Saville), an immoral young man, plans to rob and kill a shopkeeper. However, after a "mirror figure" (Christopher Lee) shows him his fate if he commits the crime, Markheim changes his mind.

Based on Robert Louis Stevenson's short story, this picture was Christopher Lee's first association with Hammer/Exclusive, and *may* have played some part in his being cast in *The Curse of Frankenstein*. A trade show was held on January 14, 1955, and *The Kinematograph Weekly* (January 20) felt "The acting is true to the stiff late nineties' period, the detail is convincing, and the twist ending effective."

A Body Like Mine (1955)

1192 feet; B & W; an Exclusive Film Production; an Exclusive Film Release (U.K.).

An underdeveloped young man is left by his girlfriend for a muscleman. He takes a body building course, but gives it up after winning a fortune. His girl returns, more attracted to money than muscle. The short was trade shown on January 28, 1955, and *Today's Cinema* (February 2) found it "very good and amusing."

Dick Turpin— Highwayman (1955)

22 minutes; 2377 feet; Eastman Color; Hammerscope; a Hammer Film Production; an Exclusive Release (U.K.); filmed at Bray Studios; Director: David Paltenghi; Producer: Michael Carreras; Screenplay: Joel Murcott; Director of Photography: Stephen Dade; Editor: James Needs: Art Director: Ted Marshall; Production Manager: Jimmy Sangster.

Philip Friend (Dick Turpin/Palmer), Diane

Hart (Liz), Alan Cuthbertson (Jonathan Redgrove), Gabrielle May (Genevieve), Hal Osmond (Mac), Raymond Rollett (Hawkins), Norman Mitchell (Rooks), John McDonald (Stableboy), George Mossman (Coachman), Barry DuBoulay, Ivor Collins (Ruffians), D. Thomas (Lord Wembley), Terry Yorke (Double for Turpin), Tom Yeardye (Double for Rooks).

Jonathan Redgrave (Alan Cuthbertson), after collecting his bride's dowry, is robbed by Dick Turpin (Philip Friend), a notorious highwayman. When Redgrave later refuses to marry Genevieve (Gabrielle May) due to the lost gold, Turpin determines that he was only interested in the loot. The bandit, for reasons of his own, foils Redgrave's plan by forcing him to marry the girl and abandon his band of gold thieves.

Hammer's fictionalization of the real-life robber (1706–1739) was trade shown in late December, 1956. *The Kinematograph Weekly* (January 3, 1957) enjoyed Philip Friend's "appropriate swagger," and felt that the chases were "expertly timed."

Dick Turpin Rides Again!

A Man on the Beach (1955)

29 minutes; 2606 feet; Eastman Color; a Hammer Film Production; an Exclusive Release (U.K.); Director: Joseph Losey; Producer: Anthony Hinds; Screenplay: Jimmy Sangster, based on the story "Chance at the Wheel" by Victor Canning; Director of Photography: Wilkie Cooper; Editor: Henry Richardson; Art Director: Edward Marshall; Music: John Hotchkis.

Michael Medwin (Max), Donald Wolfit (Dr. Carter), Michael Ripper (Chauffeur), Edward Forsyth (Clement), Alex de Gallier (Casino Manager).

"Lady M," apparently a member of British high society, surprises a casino manager (Alex de Gallier) by knocking him out with a pistol and robbing him. Later, in a chauffeur (Michael Ripper) driven Rolls Royce, "she" removes "her" wig and makeup to reveal Max (Michael Medwin). Max plans to keep all of the money and, after a fierce struggle, stuffs the chauffeur's body in the Rolls' trunk and pushes it over a cliff. Suffering from a shoulder wound, Max passes out from the loss of blood. When he wakes up, he finds footprints leading away from where he lay, and follows them to a cottage on the beach. Carter (Donald Wolfit), the owner, is an odd man who is seemingly unconcerned by the pistol Max is constantly waving. After cleaning his wound with alcohol, Max faints again and, when he awakens, his shoulder is professionally bandaged. Max confesses his crime to Carter, who he now realizes is a doctor. When

The Right Person (1955)

The Right Person, but the wrong approach.

Released January 9, 1956; 30 minutes; 2726 feet; CinemaScope; Eastman Color; a Hammer Film Production; an Exclusive Release (U.K.); Director: Peter Coles; Producer: Michael Carreras; Associate Producer: Mickey Delamar; Screenplay: Philip Mackie, based on his story; Music: Eric Winstone; Conducted by: John Hollingsworth; Director of Photography: Walter Harvey, B.S.C.; Editor: Spencer Reeve; Sound: RCA; Sound Recordists: Bill Sweeney, York Scarlet.

Margo Loren (Martha Jorgensen), Douglas Wilmer, David Markham.

While honeymooning in Copenhagen, Martha Jorgensen (Margo Loren) is visited by Mr. Rasmussen while her husband is out. He claims that he and Jorgensen were the only survivors of a Resistance group betrayed to the Nazis by a traitor with the code name "Toralf." Martha gradually realizes that Rasmussen suspects her husband of being "Toralf," and has come to murder him. When Jorgensen arrives at the hotel, Rasmussen studies him closely and decides he is *not* the traitor who caused a dozen deaths and made off with one hundred thousand kroner.

Jorgensen and Martha decide to celebrate, and he spends a large amount of money which, he claims, he inherited. The estate is worth £5,000—equal to one hundred thousand kroner.

The Kinematograph Weekly (December 8, 1955) was not impressed. "Although the players meet all demands, no attempt is made to break up the talk. Wordy and inconclusive, it's more suited to TV than the silver screen."

Sgt. Clement (Edward Forsyth) arrives later to take Carter fishing, Max tries to shoot him through the window, but the doctor disarms him. As Clement enters the home, Max is stunned to learn that Carter is blind.

Jimmy Sangster recalled in *Little Shoppe of Horrors* that he "just sort of fell into writing it. I remember sitting around the office one day, and Mike (Carreras) came up with a story idea and someone said, 'why don't *you* write it!'" Blacklisted Joseph Losey, who would later direct *The Damned* for the company, was in need of work and accepted a short after years of making acclaimed feature films. He said in *Conversations with Losey* that he was "amused with a transvestite disguise escape" and with the opportunity to experiment with color. *The Kinematograph Weekly* (April 19, 1956) called *A Man on the Beach* "an absorbing and entertaining oracle."

Copenhagen (1956)

16 minutes; 1428 feet; Eastman Color; CinemaScope; a Hammer Film Production; an Exclusive Film Release (U.K.); Director/Producer: Michael Carreras; Director of Photography: Len Harris; Editor: Bill Lenny; Music: Eric Winstone.

Tom Conway (Narrator).

Michael Carreras not only produced and directed this travelogue, but appeared in it with his son Christopher. Len Harris recalled for the authors (December, 1993),

This was filmed on so low a budget that you wouldn't believe it! We went to Copenhagen originally to film some backgrounds for a short called *The Right Person*. Michael Carreras, Harry Oakes, and me. Before we came home, Michael said, "Let's make a documentary while we're here." We used the short ends of unused film from *The Right Person*. I actually directed most of it, not that much was required for a film like this. Michael was always off checking locations and getting permits. We had no script—just guidebooks. When we finally got to the city's famous statue of the mermaid, it was all boarded up! It was being cleaned. We were only there a few days— there'd be no coming back tomorrow. I thought we might have been able to shoot a poster of it at Bray and use it as an insert, but it didn't work out. So our film lacked the city's most obvious monument. Everyone who saw the picture that knew me was "kind" enough to point that out! We were so low on film that every shot was held for a shorter duration than it warranted. Back at Bray, we extended each shot in the lab by repeating the last frame. This gave Tom Conway enough time to talk! All things considered, it's an entertaining little film.

Kinematograph Weekly (August 16, 1956) called *Copenhagen* "entertaining and informative."

Danger List (1957)

22 minutes; 2037 feet; B & W; a Hammer Film Production; an Exclusive Film Release (U.K.); Director: Leslie Arliss; Producer: Anthony Hinds; Associate Producer: Anthony Nelson-Keys; Executive Producer: Michael Carreras; Director of Photography: Arthur Grant; Screenplay: J.D. Scott; Sound Recordist: W.H.P May; Art Director: Ted Marshall; Supervising Editor: James Needs; Editor: A.E. Cox.

Philip Friend (Dr. Jim Bennett), Honor Blackman (Gillian Freeman), Mervyn Johns (Mr. Ellis), Constance Fraser (Mrs. Ellis), Alexander Field (Mr. Carlton), Muriel Zillah (Mrs. Coombe), Amanda Coxell (Laura Coombe), Evelyn Gregg (Neighbor), Pauline Olsen (Young Nurse), Jeremy Longhurst (Mobile Policeman), Patricia Cree (Audrey), David Browning (Policeman), George Hirste (Postman).

During a routine check of her patients, Nurse Gillian Freeman (Honor Blackman) discovers that her assistant (Pauline Olsen) may have given one of three outpatients— Mr. Carlton (Alexander Field), Mrs. Ellis (Constance Fraser), and young Laura Coombe (Amanda Coxell)—a fatal drug instead of their medication. She contacts Dr. Bennett (Philip Friend) who alerts the police. Mr. Carlton is stopped moments before taking his pills, and Laura was prevented from taking hers due to a faulty water tap. Bennett and Freeman arrive at the Ellis home and find that Mr. Ellis (Mervyn Johns) has already given his wife the deadly pills. After her death, he admits that he took the remainder himself.

Day of Grace (1957)

Released June, 1957; 26 minutes; 2430 feet; Eastman Color; Hammerscope; a Hammer Film Production; an Exclusive Release (U.K.); Director/Producer: Francis Searle; Screenplay: John Manchip White, Francis Searle; Director of Photography: Denny Densham; Editors: Bill Lenny, Stanley Smith; Art Director: Bernard Robinson; Production Manager: Tom Connochie; Assistant Director: Stanley Goulder; Sound Recordist: Cliff Sandell.

Vincent Winter (Ian), John Lawrie (Uncle Henry), Grace Arnold (Aunt Helen), George Woodbridge (Mr. Kemp), Nora Gordon (Mrs. Kemp), David Grahame (Poacher), Jeanne of Bothkennar (Dan).

Young Ian's (Vincent Winter) only friend is Dan, his aging sheepdog. But after Dan causes an accident that nearly kills Ian, the boy's Uncle Henry (John Lawrie) determines to destroy the animal. He hires a poacher (David Grahame) to kill Dan, but Ian and the dog run off. They are found in his barn by Kemp (George Woodbridge), who suggests a plan to save Dan. He will pay Ian to help him on his farm, but the money will go to Henry to pay for Dan's keep. Ashamed of his harsh behavior, Henry agrees.

The Kinematograph Weekly (June 13, 1957) was impressed, calling it "admirably suited to child audiences." The story was praised as being "handled with sympathy," and Vincent Winter's performance was hailed as having "unusual merit."

Man with a Dog (1957)

20 minutes; 1865 feet; a Hammer Film Production; an Exclusive Release (U.K.); Director: Leslie Arliss; Producer: Anthony Hinds; Executive Producer: Michael Carreras; Associate Producer: Anthony Nelson-Keys; Director of Photography: Arthur Grant; Editors: James Needs, A.E. Cox; Art Director: Ted Marshall; Production Manager: Don Weeks; Sound Recordist: W.H.P. May.

Clifford Evans (Dr. Bennett), Maurice Denham (Mr. Keeble), Sarah Lawson (Vicky Alexandra), John Van Eyssen (Dr. Langham), Marianne Stone (Mrs. Stephens), Jan Holden (Nurse), Margaret Boyd (Mrs. Tidmarsh), Malcolm Knight (Bert), Anthony Ford (Alf), Andrew Mott-Harrison (Giles), Clive Marshall (Jim).

Mr. Keeble (Maurice Denham), an aging war veteran with a painful leg ailment, is told by Dr. Bennett (Clifford Evans) that he must have an immediate operation. Keeble refuses because he does not want to be parted from his dog Lancelot and his fish—the lonely man's only companions. Vicky (Sarah Lawson), a hospital volunteer, persuades Keeble that if he agrees to the surgery, she will see to it that his pets are well cared for. As he is being wheeled into the operating room, he meets the children who will feed the dog and run his newspaper stand. The biggest surprise is that the unsentimental Dr. Bennett has volunteered to care for the fish.

Man with a Dog was filmed at Bray from March 25 to 29, 1957. *The Kinematograph Weekly* found the short "reminiscent of the TV *Emergency Ward 10* series, quite well acted and staged."

Clean Sweep (1958)

Released May 26, 1958; 2581 feet; 29 minutes; a Hammer Film Production; Director: Maclean Rogers; Producer: Anthony Hinds; Associate Producer: Anthony Nelson-Keys; Executive Producer: Michael Carreras; Director of Photography: Arthur Grant; Production Manager: Don Weeks; Sound Recordist: W.H.P. May; Art Director: Ted Marshall; Supervising Editor: James Needs; Editor: A.E. Cox.

Eric Barker (George Watson), Thora Hird (Vera Watson), Vera Day (Beryl Watson), Ian Whittaker (Dick Watson), Wallas Eaton (Ted), Bill Fraser (Bookmaker).

George Watson's (Eric Barker) idyllic family life is shattered when his wife Vera (Thora Hird) discovers that he has begun to gamble again. She banishes him to the spare room and refuses to cook for him. They communicate through messages carried by their children (who also smuggle meals to him). When George wins a small fortune on the sweepstakes, he and Vera are united. Their joy is short-lived, however—his ticket is disputed by the judges. They relent, and with his winnings, George buys a partnership in a bookmaking business.

Hammer on Television

Hammer's interest in home entertainment dates back to the beginning of the company. As has already been, perhaps, overstated, most of Hammer's late forties/early fifties productions were based on BBC radio plays. Since radio was, in a sense, the television of that period, it shows that the company was keenly aware of the potential power of both mediums. *The Quatermass Xperiment*, Hammer's first big international success, was based on a popular BBC-TV serial and it was this film that really launched the company. Also, Peter Cushing, Hammer's greatest star, had his first big success on the BBC network, and it was his television stardom that attracted the company.

Hammer's first television project was *Tales of Frankenstein*, filmed in Hollywood as a co-production with Columbia. Planned as a pilot for a series, it generated little excitement and nothing further developed. *Visa to Canton* was also planned as a pilot but was released, instead, as a feature. Because of Hammer's success at the box office, there was really no need until the late sixties for the company to become seriously involved in television. However, Hammer's success in the theatres began to wane a bit, and the company's association with 20th Century–Fox led to the production of a television series, *Journey to the Unknown*. After the completion of *A Challenge for Robin Hood*, the series went into production at Elstree Studios and lasted through most of 1968. In all, seventeen stories were filmed by producer Joan Harrison, who had made her mark on *Alfred Hitchcock Presents* a decade earlier. The episodes featured performers who were recognizable to American audiences and premiered on the ABC network on September 26, 1968. The series ran until January 30, 1969, but made little impact in America.

Hammer made an attempt to return to television in 1973, with Michael Carreras now running the company. *Cinema TV Today* (June 9) announced, "Michael Carreras, new boss of the company, follows the American majors into TV production and wishes he'd done it sooner." With Hammer's box office clout slipping, an all-out assault on television was a good move to make. Carreras was canny enough to plan a different direction for these films. "Everyone is going to say, 'Oh, more Draculas, Frankensteins, werewolves, and mummies,'" he said. "But they'll be wrong—there won't be one in sight." Due to the constant showing of Hammer horror classics on television, Carreras wisely chose not to compete with himself.

He also planned to release these 90 minute thrillers theatrically in the U.K., with *Fear in the Night* and *Straight On Till Morning* as examples. Other ideas included *The Sword of Robin Hood* (in half hour segments), *Raffles—Gentleman Crook* ("one hour of Victorian Skullduggery"), and *Tower of London* ("a series of two hour star name excursions"). Why Hammer chose to jettison these great ideas in favor of television spin-offs like *Love Thy Neighbor* remains a mystery. The company would make no more noises about television while Michael Carreras was in charge.

When Roy Skeggs acquired Hammer, rather than leap into feature production, he wisely chose to re-establish the company through television. In association with Sir Lew Grade's Associated Communication Corporation, Skeggs produced thirteen one-hour episodes directed by such recognizable "Hammer names" as Peter Sasdy, Robert Young, Alan Gibson, and Don Sharp. Best of all, starring in *The Silent Scream* was Peter Cushing.

The "new" Hammer's new production base was Hampden House. "This is a house of many industrial styles," said Skeggs, "from Medieval to Victorian Gothic. The Studios will be situated in the main house, and the beautiful wooded grounds are ideally suited for all types of locations." Titled *The Hammer House of Horror*, the series was a success in both the U.K. and America on late night television during 1980-1981.

Roy Skeggs followed up this success with *The Hammer House of Mystery and Suspense* with backing from 20th Century–Fox. Consisting again of thirteen episodes, the series generally featured a name American star to insure acceptance in the States. Former Hammer directors were again engaged—Val Guest, Peter Sasdy, John Hough, and Cyril Frankel. The first episode premiered in the U.K. on September 5, 1984, and the series ended on May 9, 1986.

Although Hammer's involvement with television was far overshadowed by its feature films, the company did produce three series totaling 43 individual episodes. While these efforts were certainly less brilliant than *The Twilight Zone* or *Alfred Hitchcock Presents*, several individual episodes can more than hold their own.

The following were produced by Joan Harrison

Date	Film	Cast	Director
1968	Eve	Carol Lynley Dennis Waterman	James Hill
	The New People	Robert Reed Mike O'Shea	Peter Sasdy
	Jane Brown's Body	Stefanie Powers David Buch	Alan Gibson
	Indian Spirit Guide	Julie Harris Tom Adams	Roy Ward Baker
	Miss Belle	George Maharis Barbara Jefford	Peter Sasdy
	Do Me a Favour, Kill Me	Joseph Cotten Kenneth Haigh	Gerry O'Hara
	Paper Dolls	Michael Tolan Nanette Newman	James Hill
	Girl of My Dreams	Michael Callan Justine Lord	Peter Sasdy
	Matahitas Is Coming	Vera Miles Guy Hamilton	Michael L. Hogg

Date	Film	Cast	Director
	Somewhere in a Crowd	David Hedison Jane Asher	Alan Gibson
	Poor Butterfly	Chad Everett Edward Fox	Alan Gibson
	Beckoning Fair One	Robert Lansing John Fraser	Don Chaffey
	Stranger in the Family	John Rule Peter Brown	Peter Duffell
	Last Visitor	Peter Duke Kay Walsh	Don Chaffey
	Killing Bottle	Barry Evans Roddy McDowall	John Gibson
	Madison Equation	Jack Hedley Barbara Bel Geddes	Rex Fisher

The following were produced by Roy Skeggs

Date	Film	Cast	Director
1980	Thirteenth Reunion	Julia Foster Dinah Sheridan	Peter Sasdy
	Witching Time	John Finch Prunella Gee	Don Leaver
	Rude Awakening	Denholm Elliott Pat Heywood	Peter Sasdy
	Growing Pains	Gary Bond Barbara Kellerman	Francis Megahy
	Charlie Boy	Angela Bruce Leigh Lawson	Robert Young
	The House That Bled to Death	Nicholas Ball Rachel Davies	Tom Clegg
1981	Carpathian Eagle	Anthony Valentine Suzanne Danielle	Francis Megahy
	Guardian of the Abyss	Roy Lonnen Rosalyn Landor	Don Sharp
	Silent Scream	Peter Cushing Brian Cox	Francis Essex
	Mark of Satan	Peter McEnery Georgina Hale	Don Leaver
	Children of the Full Moon	Diana Dors Christopher Cazenove	Tom Clegg
	Two Faces of Evil	Gary Raymond Anna Calder Marshall	Alan Gibson
	A Visitor from the Grave	Simon McCorkindale Kathryn Leigh Scott	Peter Sasdy
1983	Czech Mate	Susan George Patrick Mower	John Hough
	Sweet Scent of Death	Dean Stockwell Shirley Knight	Peter Sasdy

Date	Film	Cast	Director
	A Distant Scream	David Carradine Stephanie Beacham	John Hough
	The Late Nancy Irving	Christina Raines Simon Williams	Peter Sasdy
1984	In Possession	Carol Lynley Christopher Cazenove	Val Guest
	Black Carrion	Season Hubley Lehigh Lawson	John Hough
	Last Video and Testament	Deborah Raffin David Langton	Peter Sasdy
	Mark of the Devil	Dirk Benedict Jenny Seagrove	Val Guest
	The Corvini Inheritance	David McCallum Jan Francis	Gabrielle Beaumont
	Paint Me a Murder	Michelle Phillips James Laurensen	Alan Cooke
	Child's Play	Mary Cosby Nicholas Clay	Val Guest
	And the Walls Came Tumbling Down	Barbi Benton Brian Deacon	Paul Annett
	Tennis Court	Peter Graves Hannah Gordon	Cyril Frankel

Afterword

1994—and I can hardly believe that it is almost forty years since, in a delirium of excitement and panic, I embarked on composing my first film score, *The Quatermass Xperiment* (alias *The Creeping Unknown*). Little did I guess, as I sat before my empty manuscript paper, that I was to become a small twig of a whole great tree which would soon spread its branches round the world. The entire Hammer team of those early days, with their down-to-earth unpretentious approach, would, I am sure, have been equally surprised by the future.

So now, as a lively twig, I express my great admiration and gratitude to Deborah Del Vecchio and Tom Johnson for this comprehensive and expert history, and affectionate critique, of the Hammer tree.

James Bernard

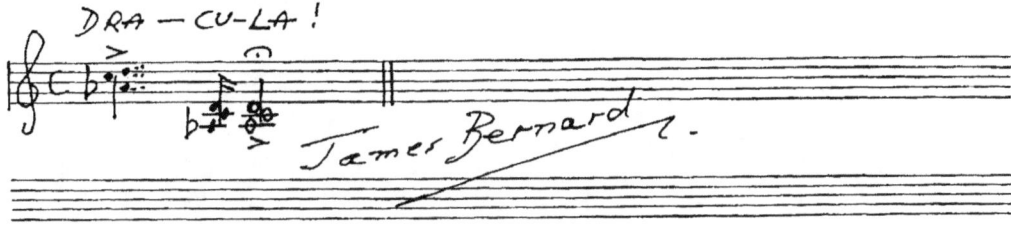

Epilogue

After seemingly coming to an end in 1979, Hammer—just like its monsters—refused to stay dead. Richelle Wilder (March, 1993) explains. "In 1979, a well-known industrial company's pension fund which had been a major investor moved in, claiming negatives, residuals, and the home. The misfortune that befell the company in the late 1970s was dramatically reversed with the implementation of a new corporate structure in 1980. Roy Skeggs and Brian Lawrence were well-versed in company affairs, having worked for Hammer during its heyday and were well aware of its capabilities and potential. Adept financial management and seasoned judgment allowed the company to buy the pension funds loan and all the shareholding within two years, and the deficit they inherited was turned into a healthy profit. Roy Skeggs gained full equity in the company in 1986. Since this time, the Hammer library has been rejuvenated and successfully exploited throughout the media markets of the world with substantial revenues being accrued. With a full production program established, the 1990s will see the company complementing the list of the top film companies worldwide, introducing a new generation of cinemagoers to the quality of entertainment which is synonymous with Hammer."

Based at Elstree during the 1980s, the company was directed by Roy Skeggs, Sir John Terry, Timothy Kirby, Arthur Buck, and Andrew Mitchell, BME, and produced films for television in the Hammer Horror tradition. Hammer recently negotiating with American studios concerning a Quatermass remake. If this venture is successful, Hammer will have come full circle. Remember what the first one started?

SELECTED BIBLIOGRAPHY

Books

Brooks, Tim, and Earle Marsh. *The Complete Directory to Prime Time Network TV Shows*. New York: Ballantine, 1979.
Brosnan, John. *The Horror People*. New York: St. Martin's, 1976.
Buberman, Martin B. *Paul Robeson*. New York: Knopf, 1988.
Ciment, Michael. *Conversations with Losey*. London: Methuen, 1989.
Cushing, Peter. *Peter Cushing, An Autobiography*. London: Weidenfeld and Nicholson, 1986.
———. *Past Forgetting—Memoirs of the Hammer Years*. London: Weidenfeld and Nicholson, 1988.
Dixon, Wheeler. *The Films of Freddie Francis*. Metuchen, N.J.: Scarecrow, 1990.
———. *Terence Fisher—The Charm of Evil*. Metuchen, N.J.: Scarecrow, 1991.
Eyles, Allen, Robert Adkinson, and Nicholas Fry. *The House of Horror—The Story of Hammer Films*. London: Lorrimer, 1973.
Fry, Ron, and Pamela Fourzon. *The Saga of Special Effects*. Englewood Cliffs, N.J.: Prentice-Hall Inc., 1977.
Gifford, Denis. *The British Film Catalogue 1895–1985*. New York: Facts on File, 1986.
Graham, Shirley. *Paul Robeson—Citizen of the World*. New York: Messner, 1946.
Haining, Peter. *The Frankenstein File*. London: New English Library, 1977.
Harryhausen, Ray. *Film Fantasy Scrapbook*. Cranbury, N.J.: A.S. Barnes & Co., Inc., 1972.
Hoyt, Edward. *Paul Robeson, American Othello*. Cleveland: World, 1967.
Hutchings, Peter. *Hammer and Beyond—The British Horror Film*. New York: St. Martin's, 1993.
Israel, Lee. *Miss Tallulah Bankhead*. New York: Putnam, 1972.
Katz, Ephraim. *The Film Encyclopedia*. New York: Crowell, 1979.
Lloyd, Ann, and Graham Fuller. *The Illustrated Who's Who of the Cinema*. New York: Portland House, 1987.
Palmer, Scott. *British Film Actors' Credits, 1895–1987*. Jefferson, N.C.: McFarland, 1988.
Pirie, David. *Hammer—A Critical Case Study*. London: BFI, 1992.
———. *A Heritage of Horror: The English Gothic Cinema, 1946–1972*. New York: Avon Books, 1973.
Pohle, Robert W., Jr. and Douglas C. Hart. *The Films of Christopher Lee*. Metuchen, N.J.: Scarecrow, 1983.
Quinlan, David. *The Illustrated Encyclopedia of Movie Character Actors*. New York: Harmony Books, 1985.
Rovin, Jeff. *From the Land Beyond, Beyond*. New York: Berkley-Windhover, 1977.

Silver, Alain, and James Ursini. *The Vampire Film.* South Brunswick, N.J.: A.S. Barnes, 1975.
Skal, David. *Hollywood Gothic.* New York: Norton, 1990.
Stoker, John. *The Illustrated Frankenstein.* New York: Sterling Publishing, 1980.
Weaver, Tom. *Science Fiction Stars and Horror Heroes.* Jefferson, N.C.: McFarland, 1991.
_____. *Attack of the Monster Movie Makers.* Jefferson, N.C.: McFarland, 1994.
Willis, Donald C. *Horror and Science Fiction Films.* Metuchen, N.J.: Scarecrow, 1972.

Periodicals

Bizarre. Pit Company, Asheville, N.C. Editor and publisher, Sam L. Irvin.
Cinefantastique. Oak Park, Ill. Editor and publisher, Fred S. Clarke.
The Daily Cinema. London, England. Editors, C.H.B. Williamson and John Ware.
Fangoria. Starlog Communications International, New York. Publisher, Norman Jacobs; Editor, Anthony Timpone.
Films and Filming. London, England.
The Halls of Horror. London, England. Top Sellers Ltd. Editor, Dez Skinn.
Horror Elite. London, England. Editors, Sue Cowie and Colin Cowie.
The House of Hammer. London, England. Top Sellers Ltd. Editor, Dez Skinn.
Kinematograph Weekly. London, England. Editor, William G. Altria.
L'Incroyable Cinéma. Editors, Harry Nadler and Marie Nadler.
Little Shoppe of Horrors. Des Moines, Ia. Editor and publisher, Dick Klemensen.
Midnight Marquee. Baltimore, Md. Editors, Sue Svehla and Gary Svehla.
The Monster Times. New York. Publishers, Larry Brill and Les Waldstein; Editor, Allan Asherman.
Starburst. London, England. Editor, Alan McKenzie.
Starlog. New York. Publisher, Norman Jacobs; Editor, David McDonnell.

INDEX

The Abominable Snowman (1957) 107, 127–29
Addams, Dawn 176, 177, 179, 318, 320
The Adventures of P.C. 49 (1949) 38–40
Ahn, Philip 162
Ajibade, Yemi 374
Albiin, Elsy 87
Aldon, Marie 101
Aldrich, Robert 147
Alexis, Martine 105
Allen, Patrick 172, 215, 216, 218, 297, 304
Andress, Ursula 250, 251, 252, 279, 294
Andrews, Barry xi, 301, 303
Andrews, Harry 368
The Anniversary (1967) 290–92
The Ape Man (1943) 285
Arkoff, Samuel Z. xi, 178, 179, 319
Arliss, George 216, 217
The Army Game (TV) 152
Arnatt, John 288, 290
Arne, Peter 213
Arrighi, Nike 295, 296, 298
Asher, Jack 18, 133, 146, 155, 248
Ashton, Pat 361
Ashton, Roy 123, 194, 195, 220, 240, 255, 270
Attack! (1956) 147
Audley, Maxine 174, 308, 310
The Awakening (1980) 337
Aylmer, Felix 163, 172, 174
Ayres, Robert 53, 55

Bad Blonde see *The Flanagan Boy*
Baker, Hylda 361
Baker, Roy Ward 287, 288, 291, 292, 312, 325, 326, 340, 341, 372
Baker, Stanley 147, 159, 160, 161, 171, 174, 175, 176, 187, 211
Baker, Tom 263
The Bank Messenger Mystery (1936) 26–27
Bankhead, Tallulah 71, 252, 253, 254

Baron, David 268
Barr, Patrick 55, 60
Barrett, John 361
Barrett, Ray 268, 270
Barrett, Tim 283
Barrymore, John 177
Barrymore, Lionel 263
Bartok, Eva 81, 82
Basehart, Richard 191, 192
Bates, Ralph 316, 317, 320, 321, 322, 323, 330, 331, 332, 340, 341, 349, 354, 355, 356
Batt, Bert 309, 311
Baxt, George xi, 145, 204
Bayldon, Geoffrey xi, 15
Beacham, Stephanie 350, 351
Beatty, Robert 67, 68
Beck, James 367
Beckley, Tony 298, 300
Beckwith, Reginald 63, 102, 104, 105, 107, 135
Beery, Wallace 24
Bennett, Jill 256, 258
Benson, Martin 215
Beren, Vanessa 370
Berman, Monty 341
Bern, Tonia 106
Bernard, James xi, 19, 111, 170, 232, 242, 262, 283, 297, 308, 317, 327, 368, 371, 372, 393
Berova, Olinka 292, 294
Beswick, Martine xi, 271, 273, 275, 276, 340, 341
The Big Knife (1955) 147
Bird, Norman xi, 225
Birt, Daniel 99
Black, Isobel 345
The Black Cat (1934) 231
The Black Glove see *Face the Music*
The Black Widow (1950) 53–54
Blackman, Honor 106, 387
Blackout see *Murder by Proxy*
Blonde Bait see *Women Without Men*
Blood and Roses (1960) 318

399

Blood from the Mummy's Tomb (1971) 335–37, 341–42
Blood Orange (1953) 63, 85–86
Blythe, Domini 346
Blythe, Peter xi, 280, 282, 289
A Body Like Mine (1955) 384
Bogart, Humphrey 71
Bonner, Tony 227
Bonney, John 227
Borst, Ron 242, 366
Bowie, Les 364
Box, Sidney 202
Bram Stoker's Dracula (1992) 142
Branch, Sarah 174, 189, 190
Break in the Circle (1954) 104, 106–08
Brent, George 63, 65
Bresslaw, Bernard 151, 152, 167, 168, 311
Briant, Shane 349, 352, 353, 357, 362, 363, 364
Bride of Frankenstein (1935) 146, 240, 282
The Brides of Dracula (1960) xi, 13, 16, 142, 180–84, 231, 260, 335, 355
Bridges, Lloyd 99, 100
The Brigand of Kandahar (1964) 254–56
Broderick, Susan 340
Bromley, Sidney 216
Brooke, Hillary 90, 91
Brosnan, John 302
Broughton, Joyce 336
Brousse, Liliane 224, 226, 228
Brown, Barbara 185
Brown, Robert 60, 120, 127, 128, 271
Brunas, Michael 118
Bryan, Dora 337
Bryan, Peter 88, 182, 184, 268, 290
Buck, Arthur 395
Buck, David 283, 284
Bull, Peter 221, 222
Burnham, Jeremy 254
Burrell, Sheila 44, 45, 54, 227, 228
Bushell, Anthony 185
Byrne, Eddie 163
Byron, Kathleen 344

Cabot, Sebastian 34, 35
Caffrey, Sean 304
Cairney, John 236, 237
Call Him Mr. Shatter see *Shatter*
Calvin, Tony 340
The Camp on Blood Island (1957) 130–33, 134, 135, 137, 139, 152, 248
Captain Clegg (1961) 215–18, 220
Captain Kronos, Vampire Hunter (1972) see *Kronos*
Carey, Falkland 206
Carey, Macdonald 210, 211
Caris, Roger 173
Carita 278, 279

Carlson, Richard 63
Carlson, Veronica xi, 301, 302, 303, 308, 309, 310, 311, 320
Carmichael, Ian 378
Carol, Martine 147, 148
Carpenter, Paul 89, 90, 95, 97, 98, 113
Carreras, Christopher 386
Carreras, Enrique 7, 8, 14, 21, 29
Carreras, Sir James 1, 8, 11, 14, 15, 17, 30, 31, 32, 36, 39, 45, 57, 58, 63, 66, 74, 89, 99, 104, 107, 118, 122, 131, 135, 139, 142, 143, 147, 152, 160, 164, 165, 168, 170, 173, 178, 179, 215, 218, 223, 228, 240, 256, 266, 272, 273, 279, 283, 286, 287, 291, 299, 302, 306, 310, 311, 318, 326, 328, 331, 337, 340, 351
Carreras, Michael 3, 4, 5, 8, 15, 17, 19, 56, 63, 69, 70, 77, 82, 86, 89, 98, 104, 115, 120, 121, 134, 138, 179, 182, 184, 192, 193, 194, 199, 200, 203, 211, 225, 226, 245, 246, 251, 252, 272, 275, 276, 300, 311, 328, 329, 337, 339, 342, 347, 348, 349, 353, 354, 359, 360, 361, 367, 368, 371, 374, 379, 386, 389, 390
Carson, John 265, 267, 316, 357, 358
A Case for P.C. 49 (1951) 59–60
Cash on Demand (1961) 142, 207–09
Castle, William 222, 223, 224
Cat People (1942) 339
Cater, John 357, 358
Celia (1949) 41–42
Chaffey, Don 272, 273, 328, 329
Chamberlain, Richard 377
Chance, Naomi 67, 68, 74, 83, 84, 85, 86
Chandler, Jeff 147
Chandos, John 87
Chaney, Lon, Jr. 142, 164, 246
Chaney, Lon, Sr. 219
Chantler, David 251
Chapman, Marguerite 64, 65
Cloudburst (1951) 57–59
Clouzot, Henri-George 355
Cohen, Herman xi, 142
Cohen, Nat 178
Cohn, Harry 147
Cole, George 171, 318
Coles, Michael 350, 351, 365
Colin, Sid 152
Collins, Joan 354, 355
Collinson, Madeline 344, 345
Collinson, Mary 344, 345
Collinson, Peter 383
Comfort, Lance 168
Conan Doyle, Sir A. 154, 156
Connell, Maureen 127
Connery, Sean 311
Conte, Richard 101, 102
Conway, Tom 85, 86, 339, 386
Cook, Vera 181
Cooper, George A. 233
Copenhagen (1956) 387

Corbett, Glenn 212, 214, 215
Corlan, Anthony 316, 346, 348
Corman, Roger 374
Corri, Adrienne 311, 313
Corridors of Blood (1958) 8
Corston, Michael 171
Count Dracula and His Vampire Bride see *The Satanic Rites of Dracula*
Countess Dracula (1970) 54, 332–35, 339, 348
Court, Hazel xi, 13, 122, 125, 126, 157, 158
Cowie, Sue xi, 261, 263, 348
Cowin, Colin xi, 25, 101, 167, 172, 177, 210, 261, 263, 339, 348, 357
Craig, Wendy 256, 258
Crawford, Joan 252
Crawford, John 174
Creatures the World Forgot (1970) 327–29
The Creeping Unknown see *The Quatermass Xperiment*
Cregar, Laird 46
Crescendo (1969) 312–14
Crime Reporter (1946) 383
The Crimson Blade see *The Scarlet Blade*
Crowther, Bosley 183
Cult of the Cobra (1955) 269
Currie, Finlay 99, 100
The Curse of Frankenstein (1956) xi, 1, 8, 13, 104, 111, 121–26, 137, 139, 143, 220, 280
Curse of the Demon (1958) 146
The Curse of the Mummy's Tomb (1964) 200, 242, 244–46
Curse of the Undead (1959) 166
The Curse of the Werewolf (1960) 16, 192–97, 204, 205
Curtis, Peter 276, 277
Cushing, Helen 146, 336
Cushing, Peter xi, 1, 13, 14, 15, 16, 19, 22, 122, 123, 124, 125, 126, 127, 128, 129, 130, 131, 138, 139, 140, 141, 143, 144, 145, 146, 153, 154, 155, 156, 158, 163, 164, 166, 181, 182, 183, 184, 188, 190, 191, 194, 207, 208, 209, 215, 216, 217, 218, 238, 240, 241, 242, 243, 249, 250, 251, 252, 261, 277, 280, 281, 283, 287, 291, 308, 309, 311, 316, 317, 318, 319, 320, 322, 323, 330, 331, 336, 341, 344, 345, 346, 349, 350, 354, 355, 356, 362, 363, 364, 365, 366, 367, 370, 371, 372, 374, 389, 390
Cuthbertson, Allan 170, 385
Cutts, Patricia 39

Daff, Al 164
The Damned (1961) 209–12
Dance of the Vampires (1967) 232
Danforth, Jim xi, 305, 306, 307
Danger List (1957) 387
Daniel, Jennifer 230, 231, 232, 268, 270
Daniels, Bebe 91, 92, 104
Danvers, Ivor 30
The Dark Light (1950) 56–57
The Dark Road (1947) 29
Dauphin, Claude 186, 187
Davies, Betty Ann 44, 45, 94
Davies, George 9
Davies, Gron 108
Davies, H.L., Gen. 9
Davies, Rupert 300, 301
Davion, Alexander 227, 268
Davis, Bette 252, 254, 256, 257, 258, 290, 291, 292
Davis, Jackie 369
Davis, Jim 111
Dawson, Anthony 194
Day, Robert xi, 250, 252
Day of Grace (1957) 387
Deadly Game see *Third Party Risk*
Dean, Isobel 64
Dean, Ivor 340
Dean, Lorna 28
Dean, Margia 108, 109
Death in High Heels (1947) 27–28
Death of an Angel (1951) 60–61
Death Wish (1974) 59
Dehn, Paul 228, 371
Del Vecchio, Ann xi
Del Vecchio, Carl xi
Delfont, Bernard 326
Delgado, Roger 99, 283
Delmar, Mickey 101
Demons of the Mind (1971) 348–49
Denberg, Susan 280, 281, 282, 283, 294
Denham, Maurice 227, 243, 256, 333, 388
de Souza, Edward 218, 230, 232
Devereaux, Marie 199
The Devil Rides Out (1967) 295–98, 299
Devil-Ship Pirates (1963) 235–37
The Devil's Bride see *The Devil Rides Out*
The Devil's Own see *The Witches*
Devine, J. Llewellyn 241, 243
De Wolff, Francis 153, 157, 177, 193
Les Diaboliques (1955) 115, 355
Dick Barton at Bay (1948) 31–33
Dick Barton Strikes Back (1948) 34–36
Dick Barton—Special Agent (1947) 4, 30–32
Dick Turpin, Highwayman (1955) 384
Dickens, Roger 303, 323
Dickie, Olga 137
Die! Die! My Darling! see *Fanatic*
Diffring, Anton 146, 157, 158, 159, 373, 374
Dix, William 256, 257, 258
Dixon, Wheeler 86, 174, 298
Dr. Jekyll and Mr. Hyde (1932) 178
Dr. Jekyll and Mr. Hyde (1941) 178
Dr. Jekyll and Sister Hyde (1971) 339–42, 356
Dr. Morelle—The Case of the Missing Heiress (1948) 36–37, 158
Dr. No (1962) 142, 192

Dr. Syn (1937) 216
Donald, James 286, 287, 288
Donlevy, Brian 108, 109, 110, 111, 116, 117, 118
Don't Panic Chaps! (1959) 171
Dorian, Angela *see* Vetri, Victoria
Dors, Diana 65, 66, 67, 85
Down, Lesley Ann 332
Dracula (1931) 139, 140
Dracula (1957) xi, 13, 137–43, 164, 165, 182, 311, 319
Dracula (1979) 143
Dracula A.D. 1972 (1971) 314, 349–52
Dracula Has Risen from the Grave (1968) 298, 300–03, 316
Dracula—Prince of Darkness (1965) 258–62, 267
Dracula's Daughter (1936) 142
Drury, Peter 36
Dudley, Ernest 36, 37
Dudley, Keith 184
Duff, Howard 81
Dyall, Valentine 36, 45, 46, 48
Dyneley, Peter 99

Easton, Jock 124
Eaton, Shirley 149, 150, 198, 199
Edwards, Mark 336
Edwards, Maudie 167
Ege, Julie 328, 329, 370
Elder, John *see* Hinds, Anthony
Eles, Sandor 239, 332, 334
Elliott, Denholm 376, 378
Endore, Guy 194
Enemy from Space see Quatermass 2
Enoch, Russell 83
Evans, Clifford 193, 194, 230, 231, 232, 388
The Evil of Frankenstein (1963) 221, 238–39, 241, 283
Ewing, Barbara 301
The Exorcist (1973) 377

Face the Music (1953) 88–90
The Fall of the House of Usher see House of Usher
Fanatic (1964) 251–54
Farmer, Suzan 235, 236, 259, 262, 263
Faye, Janine 172, 174
Fear in the Night (1971) 243, 349, 353–56, 389
Feller, Catherine 193, 194
Fennell, Albert 340
Ffrangcon-Davies, Gwen 276
Field, Shirley Ann 210, 211
Fielding, Fenella 222, 223
Finch, Jon 318, 323
Fine, Harry 55, 318, 345
Fisher, Steve 88

Fisher, Terence 2, 3, 13, 18, 19, 22, 65, 66, 67, 71, 72, 75, 76, 77, 78, 83, 86, 89, 95, 99, 102, 123, 125, 140, 141, 154, 155, 164, 170, 178, 179, 183, 185, 190, 193, 194, 197, 219–20, 240, 242, 260, 261, 262, 281, 283, 298, 302, 308, 309, 311, 331, 362, 363, 364, 365
Fitzgerald, Walter 131
Five Days (1953) 95–96
Five Million Years to Earth see Quatermass and the Pit
The Flanagan Boy (1952) 79–80, 82
Floyd, Sir Henry 17
Flynn, Errol 102, 103, 191
Fontaine, Joan 276, 277
Forbes, Bryan 116, 117
Forbes-Robinson, John 318, 370, 371, 372
Ford, George 30, 32
Forwood, Anthony 43, 45, 53, 96
Foster, Dudley 360
Four Sided Triangle (1952) 77–78
Fowlds, Derek 280
Fraiser, Liz 206
Francis, Derek 215, 376
Francis, Freddie 174, 228, 229, 234, 240, 241, 298, 301, 302
Frank, Alan 242
Frankel, Cyril 174, 276, 390
Frankenstein (1931) 1, 125
Frankenstein and the Monster from Hell (1972) 359, 362–65
Frankenstein Created Woman (1966) 280–83
Frankenstein Must Be Destroyed (1969) 297, 307–10
Frankiss, Betty 21
Franklin, Pamela 256
Franklyn, William 117, 134
Frankovich, Mike 131, 173
Fraser, Bill 360
Frederick, Lynne 346, 347
Friedman, Seymour 84
Friend, Philip 385, 387
Frobe, Gert 263
The Full Treatment (1960) 186–88
Furneaux, Yvonne 162, 163
Further Up the Creek (1958) 148–50

Gahagan, Helen 250
Gallagher, Thomas 84
Gambler and the Lady (1952) 74–76
Garson, Greer 257
Gates, Tudor 318, 330, 332
Gaunt, Valerie 122, 137, 319
Gayson, Eunice 143, 144
Geeson, Judy 354, 355, 356
Genn, Leo 119, 120
Gibbs, Gerald 116
Gibson, Alan 314
Gillies, Jacques 208

Gilling, John 48, 63, 204, 234, 241, 248, 255, 265, 267, 268, 270
The Glass Cage (1954) 53, 105–06
The Glass Tomb see *The Glass Cage*
Glut, Don 366
Glynn, Maureen 71
Glynn, Rene 71
Goddard, Paulette 99
Godfrey, Derek 292, 293
Goldoni, Lelia 243
Goodliffe, Michael 241, 243, 376
Goodwin, Frank 349
Goodwin, Harold 167
Gordon, Richard xi, 8, 9, 24, 29, 65
Gorgo (1960) 165
The Gorgon (1963) 241–43, 245, 261, 280
Goring, Marius 107, 108
Goss, Helen 153
Gough, Michael 137, 218, 220
Gould, Elliott 378, 379
Grant, Arthur 204, 208
Grant, Bob 343, 356, 369
Gray, Charles 295, 297, 298
Gray, Nadia 224, 225, 226
Grayson, Godfrey 48, 51
Green, Danny 52, 53, 222, 223
Green, Francis 172
Green, Guy xi, 134
Green, Nigel 189, 332, 333, 335
Greene, David 56
Greene, Leon 288, 295, 298
Greene, Richard 188, 189
Gregory, Thea 95
Grenfell, Joyce 222, 224
Greth, Linda xi
Grey, Shirley 22, 25
Griffith, Kenneth 87
Guest, Val xi, 19, 91, 92, 103, 105, 107, 108, 109, 111, 118, 127, 130, 133, 139, 149, 150, 160, 161, 162, 174, 175, 176, 186, 187, 287, 306, 307, 390
Gwillim, Jack 189, 190, 244, 246
Gwynn, Michael 130, 133, 143, 144, 145, 146, 173, 309, 324
Gynt, Greta 63

Haggard, H. Rider 250
Hahn, Elaine xi
Hahn, Tammy xi
Haigh, Kenneth 368, 369
Hall, Harvey 318, 330
Hallenbeck, Bruce 318, 334
Halstead, Henry 28, 29, 30
Hamilton, Gay 289
Hammer, Will *see* Hinds, Will
Hancock, Sheila 290, 291
Hands of the Ripper (1971) 48, 337–39
Hanley, Jimmy 324

Hardtmuth, Paul 122
Hardy, Robert 348, 349
Hare, Doris 343, 356, 359
Harris, Len xi, 5, 10, 14, 19, 76, 81, 99, 100, 115, 118, 124, 129, 133, 141, 146, 147, 155, 190, 195, 207, 217, 219, 386
Harrison, Joan 389
Harryhausen, Ray 272, 273, 306
Hart, Debbie xi
Harvey, Jimmy 86, 100
Harvey, John 232
Harvey, Laurence 368
Harvey, Len 80
Hawdon, Robin 304, 305
Hawk, Jeremy 102
Hayden, Frank 328
Hayden, Linda 316
Hayes, Melvyn 122
Hayles, Brian 377
Haysted, Mercy 49
Hayter, James 77, 288
Hayward, Louis 83, 84
Hazell, Hy 41, 42, 52
Head, Edith 71
Heat Wave see *The House Across the Lake*
Hedley, Jack 234, 235, 247, 290, 291, 292
Hell Is a City (1959) 16, 142, 174–76, 187
Heller, Otto 245
Hellman, Monte 374
Hemple, Anoushka 324, 325
Henreid, Paul 71, 72, 76, 77
Henry, Leonard 21
Herbert, Percy 171, 271
Heston, Charlton 337
Hickson, Joan 41
Hills, Gillian 348
Hindle, Madge 361
Hinds, Anthony (a.k.a. John Elder) 7, 71, 72, 74, 77, 80, 84, 90, 96, 99, 109, 115, 123, 124, 125, 139, 142, 145, 146, 152, 154, 165, 182, 184, 193, 194, 224, 231, 240, 241, 249, 250, 254, 273, 282, 302, 316, 364, 371
Hinds, Will (a.k.a. Will Hammer) 4, 7, 8, 14, 21, 24, 49, 129
Hird, Thora 112, 388
Hitchcock, Alfred 17, 19, 203, 379
Hobbs, William 358
Hobson, Valerie 146
Hoey, Dennis 23
Holiday on the Buses (1973) 369–70
Hollingsworth, John 371
Holroyd, Ronald 171
Holt, Patrick 97, 98, 102, 304
Hooper, Ewan 300
Hordern, Michael 349
Horror of Dracula see *Dracula* (1957)
Horror of Frankenstein (1970) 318, 320–23, 365
Hough, John 346, 390
Houghton, Don 374

The Hound of the Baskervilles (1958) 153–56, 204
The House Across the Lake (1953) 90–91
House of Frankenstein (1944) 240
House of Fright see *The Two Faces of Dr. Jekyll*
House of Usher (1960) 180
Houston, Donald 224, 226
Howard, Arthur 151
Howard, Ronald 245
Howerd, Frankie 149, 150
The Howling (1981) 196
Hughes, Ken xi, 90
Hume, Alan 237
Humphries, Fred xi, 101, 167, 172, 177, 210, 357
Hunt, Martita 181
Huntley, Raymond 65, 163, 360
Hush...Hush, Sweet Charlotte (1964) 213, 254
Hustler, Monica 41, 45
Hutcheson, David 239
Hyatt, Charles 367
Hyde-White, Wilfrid 135, 137
Hyman, Prudence 241, 242
Hysteria (1964) 202, 243–44

I, Monster (1971) 342
I Only Arsked (1959) 150
I Was a Teenage Frankenstein (1957) 142
I Was a Teenage Werewolf (1957) 142
Illing, Peter 101
Ingham, Barrie 288, 289, 290
Invasion of the Body Snatchers (1956) 78, 119
Ireland, John 105, 106
Irvin, Sam, Jr. 334, 364

Jack of Diamonds (1948) 34
Jackson, Freda 181, 184, 203, 204
Jackson, Gordon 159, 161
Jagger, Dean 113, 115
James, Graham 320
James, Sidney 45, 53, 79, 90, 106, 117
Janson, Horst 357, 358, 359
Jayne, Jennifer 53
Jeffrey, Peter 333
Jeffries, Lionel 108, 234, 235
Jenkins, Pat 75
Jessop, Clytie 233
John, Rosamund 68
Johns, Mervyn 221
Johnson, Fred 84, 88, 122, 184, 200
Johnson, Katie 74
Johnson, Michael 73
Johnston, Eric 132
Jones, Freddie xi, 308, 309, 310, 311, 322, 365
Jones, Paul 349
Journey to the Unknown (TV) 258, 299, 389
Journey's End (1930) 162
Joyce, Yootha 252, 254, 361

Karloff, Boris 1, 25, 110, 123, 222, 231, 240, 264
Kauffman, Doug xi
Kauffman, Maurice 252, 254
Keen, Geoffrey 73, 89, 106, 316, 317
Keir, Andrew 52, 53, 110, 212, 214, 236, 259, 262, 278, 279, 286, 287, 288, 335, 336, 337
Kelley, Bill 317
Kendall, Kay 67, 76
Kimberly, Maggie 283, 284
King, Philip 206
Kingston, Kiwi 238, 239, 240
Kinnear, Roy 315, 360
Kinski, Nastajassia 376, 377
Kirby, Timothy 395
Kiss of Evil see *Kiss of the Vampire*
Kiss of the Vampire (1962) 184, 221, 229–32, 270, 358
Klemensen, Dick xi, 174, 355
Knapp, Bud 172
Kneale, Nigel 109, 118, 127, 129, 130, 277, 287, 288
Knef, Hildegard *see* Neff, Hildegard
Knight, David 233, 234
Knight, Eddie 364
Knox, Alexander 210
Korda, Alexander 16
Kristofferson, Kris 377
Kronos see *Captain Kronos, Vampire Hunter*
Kubrick, Stanley 287
Kwouk, Burt 185, 191

Lacey, Catherine 203
Ladd, Alan 63
The Lady Craved Excitement (1950) 9, 51–53
Lady in the Fog (1952) 72–74, 75
The Lady Vanishes (1938) 378
The Lady Vanishes (1978) 377–79
Lamont, Duncan 235, 239, 254, 277
Landau, Richard 109
Landen, Dinsdale 262
Landi, Marla 153, 154, 212
Landis, Carole 273
Landor, Rosalyn 294, 295
Lang, Harold 58, 68, 108
Lansbury, Angela 378, 379
Lapostaire, James 312
The Last Page (1951) 63–66
Latham, Philip 259
Latimer, Hugh 39, 48, 60
Latimer, Michael 275
Laughton, Charles 21
Lauter, Harry 111
Lawrence, Brian 235, 395
Lawrence, Delphi 85, 157
Lawrence, H.L. 211
Lawrence, Quentin 249

Lawrie, James 36
Lawson, Sarah 295, 298
Lawson, Wilfred 278
Lazurus, Paul N. 173
Leakey, Phil xi, 2, 9, 10, 41, 45, 49, 65, 111, 123
LeBorg, Reginald 80
Lederer, Francis 142
Lee, Belinda 93, 94
Lee, Bernard 362
Lee, Bruce 313, 374
Lee, Christopher 1, 2, 8, 10, 13, 15, 17, 19, 22, 122, 123, 124, 125, 126, 137, 138, 139, 140, 141, 153, 154, 155, 157, 158, 159, 163, 164, 166, 170, 176, 177, 178, 179, 180, 182, 184, 185, 186, 194, 200, 201, 203, 212, 213, 214, 215, 236, 237, 241, 242, 243, 244, 246, 250, 259, 260, 261, 262, 263, 264, 295, 296, 297, 298, 300, 301, 302, 303, 316, 317, 318, 323, 324, 325, 326, 327, 341, 349, 350, 351, 365, 366, 367, 368, 371, 372, 376, 377, 384
Le Fanu, J. Sheridan 317, 318, 329, 344
The Legend of the Seven Golden Vampires (1973) 367, 370–72
Leigh, Suzanna 298, 300
LeMesurier, John 153
Leon, Valerie 336, 337
Lesser, Julian 63
Lesser, Sol 63
Lewis, Jerry 168
Lewis, Ronald 186, 187, 200, 203, 254
Lewis, Stephen 343, 369
Lewton, Val 111, 129, 204, 270
Li, Lilly 374
Libel (1958) 177
Lieven, Albert 56
Life at the Top (1965) 369
Life with the Lyons (1953) 91–93
Lilley, Jessie xi
Lillibridge, Gloria xi
Linden, Jennie 233, 234
Linden, Joyce 29, 32
Lindfors, Viveca 210
Lippert, Robert L. 9, 11, 45, 49, 53, 65, 66, 67, 70, 71, 73, 80, 89, 99
Lodge, Jean 35, 36, 60, 61
The Lodger (1944) 46
Lom, Herbert 63, 219, 220, 221, 378, 379
Longden, John 53, 117
Losey, Joseph 115, 211, 212, 386
The Lost Continent (1968) 295, 298–300
Love Thy Neighbor (1973) 367–68
Low, Andrew 165, 166
Lowe, Arthur 378
Lowndes, Marie Belloc 46
Lucas, William 113, 203
Lugosi, Bela 8, 23, 24, 25, 139, 140, 142, 213, 240, 267
Lumley, Joanna 365

Lung, Ti 373, 374
Lupino, Ida 27
Lupino, Stanley 27
Lust for a Vampire (1970) 329–32, 345
Lyndon, Barre 157
Lyon, Barbara 91, 92
Lyon, Ben 91, 92, 104
Lyon, Richard 91, 92, 104
The Lyons in Paris (1954) 104–05

McCallum, Neil 298
McCowan, Alan 276
MacGinnis, Niall 189, 190
MacKenzie, Mary 70, 72, 73
McKern, Leo 159, 161
MacNaughton, Alan 280
Madden, Peter 230
Maddern, Victor 115
Magee, Patrick 349
Mahoney, Janet 356
Maitland, Marne 151, 185, 268
Malleson, Miles 153
Maltin, Leonard 162
Man About the House (1974) 375
Man at the Top (1973) 368–69
Man Bait see *The Last Page*
The Man in Black (1949) 43–44
The Man in Half Moon Street (1944) 157
Man in Hiding see *Mantrap*
Man in the Attic (1953) 46
Man on the Beach (1955) 385
The Man Who Could Cheat Death (1958) 156–59, 165, 345
Man with a Dog (1957) 388
Maniac (1962) 202, 212, 224–26
Mank, Greg xi
Mankowitz, Wolf 179
Mantrap (1952) 76–77
March, Fredric 177
Marla, Norma 167, 177
Marle, Arnold 107, 127, 157
Marmont, Percy 74, 77
Marsh, Carol 137
Marshall, Zena 42
Mask of Dust (1954) 100–02
Massie, Paul 176, 177, 178, 179
Material Evidence (1947) 384
Matheson, Richard xi, 135, 139, 252, 254, 298
Mathews, Kerwin xi, 212, 213, 214, 224, 225, 226
Mathie, Marion 301
Matthews, Christopher 324, 325
Matthews, Francis xi, 15, 19, 143, 144, 145, 151, 259, 262, 263
Mature, Victor 373
Maude, Mary 368
Maxwell, James 239
Maxwell, Lois 73, 76

406 *Index*

Mayne, Ferdy 99, 100
Medwin, Michael 48, 49, 52, 81, 120, 151, 385
Meet Simon Cherry (1949) 42–43
Meillon, John 206
Melly, Andree 181
Men of Sherwood Forest (1954) 102–04
Merrow, Jane 339
Michaels, Beverly 112, 113
Middleton, Guy 68
Miller, Mandy 133, 134
Miller, Mark xi
The Mirror and Markheim (1954) 384
Mitchell, Anthony M.B.E. 395
Mohner, Carl 131
Mollison, Henry 49
Monkhouse, Bob 199
Monlaur, Yvonne 181, 183
Monteros, Rosenda 250, 251, 252
Moon Zero Two (1969) 311–12
Moore, Eileen 102
Moore, Roger 85
Morell, Andre 70, 72, 131, 133, 153, 154, 156, 203, 204, 205, 207, 208, 209, 250, 265, 266, 267, 268, 283, 284, 285, 286, 288, 294
Morgan, Terence 245, 246
Morley, Robert 221, 224
Morris, Robert 281
Morris, Wolfe 127, 128, 159
Morton, Hugh 91
Moss, Stirling 102
Moxey, Hugh 42, 43
Moyer, Patrick 295, 296
Mozart, George 21, 23, 26
Muir, Jean 167
Mulcaster, Michael 153
The Mummy (1932) 164
The Mummy (1959) 3, 13, 159, 162–66, 182, 284
The Mummy's Ghost (1944) 80
The Mummy's Shroud (1967) 283–85
Munro, Caroline 350, 357
Murcell, George 171
Murder by Proxy (1953) 93–95
Murder on the Orient Express (1974) 379
Murphy, Brian 375
Murphy, Tim xi, 13, 16, 153, 201, 217, 244, 281
Murray, Don 278, 279
Murray, Stephen 77
Mutiny on the Buses (1972) 356–57
Mysterious Island (1961) 215
Mystery of the Mary Celeste (1935) 8, 22–25

Nagy, Bill 172
The Nanny (1965) 256–58, 314
Narizzano, Silvio 253, 254
Neal, Tom 78
Neame, Christopher 250

Nearest and Dearest (1972) 360–61
Needs, Jim 3
Neff, Hildegard 298
Neill, Roy William 379
Nelson-Keys, Anthony 12, 134, 165, 170, 195, 235, 242, 248, 249, 267, 270, 283, 287, 309, 314, 377
Never Look Back (1951) 68–70, 71
Never Take Candy from a Stranger see *Never Take Sweets from a Stranger*
Never Take Sweets from a Stranger (1959) 171–74, 276
Newell, Patrick 375
Newfield, Sam 74, 75
Newlands, Anthony 243
Newman, Nanette 368
Newman, Peter 160
Newsom, Ted 257
Nicol, Alex 88, 89, 90, 91
Night Creatures see *Captain Clegg*
Nightmare (1962) 202, 224, 232–33
Norden, Christine 53, 54, 59
Norman, Leslie 115, 116
Nye, Pat 39

O'Brien, Joey xi, 194
O'Farrell, Bernadette 73
Okuda, Ted xi, 11, 24, 80, 247, 286, 319, 363
The Old Dark House (1932) 222
The Old Dark House (1962) 221–22, 225
Oldman, Gary 142
Oliver! (1968) 254
Olson, James 311, 312, 313, 314, 315
O'Mara, Kate 320, 322
The Omen (1976) 377
On the Buses (1971) 342–43, 352, 356
One Million B.C. (1940) 273
One Million Years B.C. (1965) 251, 265, 270–74, 275, 279, 299
Orders to Kill (1958) 177
Osborn, Andrew 81, 85, 86, 93
Oscar, Henry 181
O'Shaughnessy, Brian 328
O'Sullivan, Richard 375
Our Man in Havana (1960) 170
Outland (1981) 311
Owen, Cliff 294
Owen, Dickie 246
Owens, Yvonne 48, 49
Oxley, David 153, 156

Paal, Alexander 58, 334
Pack, Charles Lloyd 185, 362
Page, Anthony 379
Paid to Kill see *Five Days*
Palance, Jack 46, 147, 148
Palmer, Randy 330

Paranoiac (1962) 202, 224, 226–29, 255
Parley, Mila 85, 86
Parnell, Reg 102
Pasco, Richard 189, 190, 191, 241, 243, 262, 263
Passmore, H. Fraser 21, 25
Passport to China see *Visa to Canton*
Pastell, George 163, 170, 245, 246
Patch, Wally 28
Paul, Christine 346
Paul, Louis xi
Payne, Laurence 346, 347, 348
Payton, Barbara 77, 78, 79
Peacock, John 353
Pearce, Jacqueline 265, 266, 268, 269, 270
Peck, Gregory 147
Peel, David 181, 182, 183
Peel, Edna 27
Pennington, Jon 204
Pennington-Richards, C. 290
Penrose, John 39
Percy, Edward 180, 182
Percy, Esme 26
Pertwee, Jon 167
The Phantom of the Opera (1925) 164, 219
Phantom of the Opera (1943) 219
The Phantom of the Opera (1962) 185, 218–21, 250
Phantom Ship see *Mystery of the Mary Celeste*
Phillips, John 283, 284
Phillips, Leslie 199
Pierce, Jack 240
Pierce, Norman 181
The Pirates of Blood River (1961) 212–15, 237, 255
Pitt, Ingrid xi, 318, 319, 320, 332, 333, 334
Pizor, William 9, 11
Plague of the Zombies (1965) 261, 264–68, 270
Plan 9 from Outer Space (1959) 275, 299
Pleasence, Donald 174
Pohlmann, Eric 74, 85, 86, 87, 106, 149, 191
Pollock, Ellen 55
Pollock, George 171
Polly's Two Fathers (1935) 383
Poole, Frank 338
Porter, Eric 298, 300, 337, 338, 339
Poston, Tom 221, 224
Powell, Eddie 284
Powers, Stefanie 252, 254, 312, 315
Pravda, George 305
Prehistoric Women see *Slave Girls*
Preston, Robert 58, 59
Price, Dennis 171, 320, 344
Price, Ernie xi
Price, Vincent 264
Priestley, J. B. 222
Provis, George 280
Prowse, David xi, 321, 322, 323, 324, 348, 362, 363, 364
The Public Life of Henry the Ninth (1935) 7, 21–22

Quatermass and the Pit (1967) 285–88
The Quatermass Xperiment (1954) 80, 108–10, 371, 381
Quatermass 2 (1956) 116–19
Quigley, Joe 79
Quitak, Oscar 143

A Race for Life see *Mask of Dust*
Radd, Ronald 131
Raglan, James 34, 41
Rains, Claude 219
Rakoff, Alvin 291
Rasputin—The Mad Monk (1965) 261, 262–63, 265, 270
Rathbone, Basil 264
Raven, Mike 330, 331
The Raven (1935) 25
Rawlinson, A.R. 49
Raymond, Cyril 34
Rebel, Bernard 244
Rechfield, Edward 102
Redmond, Moira 233, 234
Reed, Michael 242
Reed, Oliver 189, 191, 193, 194, 195, 197, 210, 211, 212, 213, 214, 215, 217, 218, 227, 228, 229, 234, 235, 254, 255
Reed, Sir Carol 214
Rees, Angharad 337, 338, 339
Regin, Nadja 171
Reid, Milton 185, 191, 215
The Reptile (1965) 268–70
The Revenge of Frankenstein (1957) 3, 13, 135, 143–46, 240, 280, 309, 364
Reynolds, Peter 64, 65
Rice, Joan 320
Richardson, John 249, 250, 251, 252, 271, 272, 273, 292
Richmond, Anthony 106
Richmond, Irene 233
Rietty, Robert 234
Rigby, Edward 49
The Right Person (1955) 386
Rilla, Wolf 206
Ringel, Harry 165, 170, 195, 283, 297
Ripper, Michael xi, 19, 30, 60, 114, 115, 167, 181, 194, 195, 214, 215, 217, 235, 248, 265, 268, 269, 270, 284, 285, 323, 385
River Patrol (1947) 28–29
Roach, Hal 273
Robbins, Michael 356
Roberts, Christian 290
Robertson, Cliff 377
Robeson, Paul 26
Robins, John 360, 375
Robinson, Bernard 17, 18, 78, 129, 156, 164, 179, 197, 232, 237, 242, 248, 262, 263, 285, 298, 302, 309
Robinson, Harry 334

Robinson, Margaret xi, 18, 154, 155, 164, 166, 179, 195, 197, 285
Robinson, Peter xi, 164, 197, 285
Rocketship X-M (1950) 83
Roland, Jeanne 245, 246
Rolfe, Guy 159, 160, 169, 170
Romain, Yvonne 193, 194, 215, 218, 254
Romero, Cesar xi, 70, 73, 74
Ronay, Edina 275, 276
Ronay, Gabriel 334
Room at the Top (1959) 368
Room to Let (1949) 45–48
Rosemary's Baby (1968) 295
Rossington, Norma 151
Rossiter, Leonard 276
The Rossiter Case (1950) 54–55

St. John, Betta 133
The Saint's Girl Friday see *The Saint's Return*
The Saint's Return (1953) 83–85
Sallis, Peter 316
Sanders, George 84, 86, 97
Sanders of the River (1935) 26
Sangster, Jimmy xi, 3, 4, 19, 41, 115, 116, 124, 125, 134, 145, 146, 182, 184, 203, 224, 226, 234, 240, 243, 244, 245, 257, 258, 260, 291, 292, 309, 321, 322, 323, 324, 337, 355, 356, 386
Sansom, John *see* Sangster, Jimmy
Sapphire (1959) 177
Sasdy, Peter 316, 317, 318, 334, 338, 390
The Satanic Rites of Dracula (1972) 352, 365–67
The Savage Guns (1961) 200
The Scarlet Blade (1963) 104, 234–35
Scars of Dracula (1970) 318, 323–27
Scorsese, Martin 7
Scotland Yard Inspector see *Lady in the Fog*
Scott, Avis 55
Scott, Janette 221, 224, 227, 228
Scott, Margaretta 312
Scott, Peter Graham 217, 218
Scott, Pippa 330
Scott, Zachary 67
Scream of Fear see *Taste of Fear*
Searle, Francis 41, 45, 49, 58
Sears, Heather 219, 220
The Secret of Blood Island (1964) 246–48
Sellars, Elizabeth 58
Sellers, Peter 135, 136, 137
Serret, John 201
The Seven Brothers Meet Dracula see *Legend of the Seven Golden Vampires*
The Seventh Voyage of Sinbad (1958) 214
Sewell, Vernon 54, 56
Seyler, Athene 191
The Shadow of the Cat (1960) 196, 203–05
Sharp, Don 230, 231, 232, 237, 263, 390

Shatter (1973) 372–73
Shaw, Denis 278
Shaw, Jack 30
She (1935) 249
She (1964) 17, 249–51, 279, 299, 311
Shelley, Barbara 12, 131, 203, 204, 241, 242, 243, 247, 248, 249, 259, 262, 263, 286, 288
Shepherd, Cybill 378, 379
Shingler, Helen 54
The Shuttered Room (1967) 57
Silent Scream (TV) 390
Silva, Simone 99, 100
Sim, Gerald 340
Sinclair, Hugh 68, 76
Singer, Campbell 49
Skeggs, Roy xi, 360, 377, 390, 395
Slave Girls (1966) 16, 273, 275
Smethurst, Jack 367
Smith, Constance 46
Smith, Cornelia 26
Smith, Madeline 318, 319, 362
The Snorkel (1957) 133–35, 138
Solon, Ewen 153, 154, 185, 194
Someone at the Door (1949) 48–49
Somers, Julie 60
Sommerland, Ume xi
Son of Frankenstein (1939) 240
Song of Freedom (1935) 25–26
Soren, David 265
Sottane, Liliane 135, 137
Spaceways (1952) 80–81
Sporting Love (1936) 27
Stannard, Don 28, 30, 32, 34, 35
Star Wars (1977) 364
Stark, Graham 206
The Steel Bayonet (1956) 119–21, 275
Steele, Pippa 317, 318, 330
Stensgaard, Yutte 330, 331, 332
Stephens, Martin 275
Stevenson, Robert Louis 179, 340, 384
Stewart, Robin 370
Stock, Nigel 298
Stoker, Bram 140, 262, 326
Stolen Face (1951) 67, 70–72, 204
Stoner, Kevin 207
Stop Me Before I Kill see *The Full Treatment*
Straight On Till Morning (1971) 243, 349, 352–53, 356, 389
The Stranger Came Home (1954) 96–99
The Stranglers of Bombay (1959) 168–71
Strasberg, Susan 200, 201, 203
Stratton, John 362
Stribling, Melissa 139
Stringer, Michael 349
Stuart, Charles 29
Stuart, John 102, 234
Style, Michael 319
Summerfield, Eleanor 65, 88, 89, 93
Sutherland, Donald 252

Svehla, Gary xi
Svehla, Sue xi
Swires, Steve 273
Sword of Sherwood Forest (1960) 188–91
Sykes, Peter 349, 377
Sylvester, William 97, 98
Szu, Shih 370

Tabori, Paul 76
Tales of a City (1948) 384
Tales of Frankenstein (TV) 146, 191
Tapley, Colin 58, 66
Tarzan the Magnificent (1960) 249
Taste of Fear (1960) 200–02, 224, 229, 337
Taste the Blood of Dracula (1969) 315–18, 323
Taylor, Al 262
Taylor, Don xi, 102, 103, 104
Taylor, Geoffrey 102
Taylor, Robert 24
Tayman, Robert 346, 347, 348
Teenage Frankenstein see *I Was a Teenage Frankenstein*
Ten Seconds to Hell (1958) 139, 146–48
Terror in the Crypt (1963) 318
Terror of the Tongs (1960) 184–86
Terror Street see *36 Hours*
Terry, Sir John 395
Tey, Josephine 328
That's Your Funeral (1972) 360
These Are the Damned see *The Damned*
The Thing That Couldn't Die (1958) 139
Third Party Risk (1954) 99–100
36 Hours (1953) 87–88, 96
Thomas, Damian 344, 345
Thornburn, June 234
Thorndyke, Russell 216
Three Stops to Murder see *Blood Orange*
Three Worlds of Gulliver (1960) 213
The Time Machine (1960) 306
Timpone, Anthony xi
The Tingler (1959) 222
Tingwell, Charles 247, 248, 249, 259, 262
To Have and to Hold (1950) 55–56
To the Devil—A Daughter (1976) 297, 376–77
Todd, Ann 200, 201, 202, 203
Tomlinson, David 135, 137, 149, 150
Tone, Franchot 78
Toone, Geoffrey xi, 185
Tower of London (1939) 264
Tracy, Spencer 177
Travers, Bill 76
Trevelyan, John 195
Troughton, Patrick 219, 241, 323
Tucker, Forrest 107, 127, 128, 129, 130
Tully, Montgomery 84, 96, 152
Turner, Lana 80
Tushingham, Rita 352, 353
Twins of Evil (1971) 338, 344–46

The Two Faces of Dr. Jekyll (1959) 168, 176–80, 194, 254
2001—A Space Odyssey (1968) 287, 312

The Ugly Duckling (1959) 166–68, 177
Uncle Was a Vampire (1959) 142
The Unholy Four see *The Stranger Came Home*
Up the Creek (1958) 134–36, 206
Urquhart, Robert 122, 124, 125

Valentine, Anthony 376
Valk, Frederick 79
Valley, Richard xi
The Valley of Gwangi (1968) 306
Vampire Circus (1971) 346–48
The Vampire Lovers (1970) 178, 318–20, 345
Vampyr (1931) 318
Van Beers, Stanley 108
Van Eyck, Peter 133, 134, 147
Van Eyssen, John 77, 137
Varney, Reg 343, 369
Vaughan, Peter 252, 254
The Vengeance of She (1967) 204, 292–94
Ventham, Wanda 358
Vernon, Richard 207
Vest, Randy xi
Vetri, Victoria 304, 307
Victor, Charles 84
The Viking Queen (1966) 277–80
Village of the Damned (1960) 207
Villiers, James 256, 335, 336
Visa to Canton (1960) 191–92, 389
Von Schell, Catherine 311
Voyage to the Bottom of the Sea (TV) 192

Walker, Bruce 34
Walker, Rudolph 367
Wallis, Jacquie 230
Walsh, Kay 276, 277
Walters, Russell 60, 99
Walters, Thorley 171, 218, 259, 280, 281, 283, 308, 310, 346, 347, 348
Warbeck, David 345
Ward, Michael 50
Ward, Simon 308, 309, 310, 311
Warren, Barry 230, 231, 232, 236, 280
Warrington, Ken 28
Washbourne, Mona 181
Watch It, Sailor! (1961) 150, 205–07, 343
Waterman, Dennis 324
Watford, Gwen 172, 316
Wattis, Richard 85, 127, 167
We Do Believe in Ghosts (1946) 383
Weaver, Tom xi, 9, 110, 118, 127, 162, 182, 252, 306
Webber, Robert 243

A Weekend with Lulu (1960) 197–200
Welch, Elisabeth 26
Welch, Raquel 272, 273, 274, 279
Wellesley, Gordon 192
Werner, Carol xi
Werner, Steve xi
Wetherell, Virginia 348, 349
Whale, James 1, 125, 162, 222
What Ever Happened to Baby Jane? (1962) 252
What the Butler Saw (1950) 49–51, 53
Wheatley, Alan 63, 81, 90
Wheatley, Dennis 62, 63, 295, 296, 298, 299, 300, 376, 378
When Dinosaurs Ruled the Earth (1968) 303–07, 328
Whispering Smith Hits London (1951) 62–63
Whispering Smith vs. Scotland Yard see *Whispering Smith Hits London*
White, Ethel 379
White, Jon Manchip 130
White Zombie (1932) 267
Whitelaw, Billie 174, 176
Whitman, Stuart 373, 374
Who Killed Van Loon? (1947) 31
Wicking, Christopher 377
Widmark, Richard 376, 377
Wilcox, Paula 375
Wild, Jeanette 339, 342
Wild, Katy 239
Wilder, Richelle xi, 13, 395
Williams, Arthur 26
Williams, Brook 265, 266
Williams, Kate 370
Williams, Kit 210
Willman, Noel 229, 230, 231, 232, 268, 270, 292, 294
Wills, John Elder 21, 86, 99
Wilmer, Douglas 318, 320, 387

Wilson, Ian 52, 53, 219
Wincott, Geoffrey 30
Wings of Danger (1951) 66–67, 71
The Witches (1966) 276–77, 295
Wodehouse, Barbara 154
The Wolf Man (1941) 196
Wolfit, Sir Donald 385
Women Without Men (1955) 111–13
Wood, David King 97, 102, 109
Woodbridge, George 143
Woodthorpe, Peter 239, 243
Woodville, Catherine 254
Woolrich, Cornell 94, 244
Wordsworth, Richard 108, 110, 131, 194
Worley, Brent xi
Worley, Rebecca xi
Worth, Brian 185
Wright, Maggie 344
Wright, Tony 79
Wyeth, Katia 352
Wymark, Patrick 247, 249
Wyndham, Robert 31

X—The Unknown (1956) 4, 113–16

Yesterday's Enemy (1959) 142, 159–62, 165, 175, 187, 255
Young, Aida 294, 306, 318, 338, 339
Young, Raymond 60
Young, Robert 347, 348

Zarak (1956) 255

www.ingramcontent.com/pod-product-compliance
Lightning Source LLC
Chambersburg PA
CBHW081533300426
44116CB00015B/2610